开发性金融治理与发展创新

全球开发性金融发展报告（2016）

中国开发性金融促进会　编著

GOVERNANCE AND DEVELOPMENT INNOVATION OF DEVELOPMENT FINANCING

GLOBAL DEVELOPMENT FINANCING REPORT (2016)

中信出版集团 · 北京

图书在版编目（CIP）数据

开发性金融治理与发展创新：全球开发性金融发展
报告：2016 / 中国开发性金融促进会编著 .-- 北京：
中信出版社，2017.8
　ISBN 978-7-5086-7695-1

　I.① 开…　II.① 中…　III.①国际金融－研究报告
IV.① F831

中国版本图书馆 CIP 数据核字〔2017〕第 120367 号

开发性金融治理与发展创新：全球开发性金融发展报告（2016）

编　　著：中国开发性金融促进会
出版发行：中信出版集团股份有限公司
　　　　　（北京市朝阳区惠新东街甲 4 号富盛大厦 2 座　邮编　100029）
承 印 者：北京鹏润伟业印刷有限公司

开　　本：787mm×1092mm　1/16　　印　张：31.75　　字　数：600 千字
版　　次：2017 年 8 月第 1 版　　　　印　次：2017 年 8 月第 1 次印刷
广告经营许可证：京朝工商广字第 8087 号
书　　号：ISBN 978-7-5086-7695-1
定　　价：78.00 元

编　委　会

目 录
CONTENTS

序

　　这是一份具有开创性和前瞻性的报告，对增进各界了解开发性金融的现状以及发展趋势有重要意义。开发性金融历史悠久，发源于两百年前的欧洲，并在第二次世界大战后蓬勃发展，为推动各国经济增长、可持续发展、维护经济金融安全做出了卓越贡献。据粗略统计，世界开发性金融机构联盟、各区域开发银行协会的成员累计达 328 家，是国际金融体系举足轻重的力量。当前，全球发展对开发性金融提出了新的要求，但是人们对开发性金融的认识还不全面，对开发性金融运作原理和主要功能的理解还有待深入，这份报告及时地呈现了开发性金融机构的总体面貌和发展趋势，是开发性金融领域的一项重要报告。

　　同时，该报告也为开发性金融机构之间相互交流与学习提供了契机。开发性金融的主要特征是服务政府发展目标，以中长期投融资为手段，依托政府信用支持，通过市场化运作缓解经济社会发展的瓶颈制约，维护经济金融稳定。由于各国的政治制度、法律体系、经济政策和优先发展任务等不同，因此各开发性金融机构结合本地实际，形成了各自的运作模式、实践经验和专业优势。开发性金融发展的差异化和多样化是国际开发性金融创新发展的源泉，各开发性金融机构只有相互借鉴、取长补短，才能共同促进全球开发性金融的健康发展，该报告对全球主要开发性金融机构的持续关注恰恰体现了互鉴互学的精神。

　　随着各国相互联系日益紧密、相互依存日益加深，区域和跨区域合作蓬勃兴起，互联互通建设加速推进，加强开发性金融机构的互信与合作变得越来越重要，这既是维护地区金融稳定和金融安全的重要保障，也是增强经济中长期发展动力的重要支撑，更是亚洲各经济体良性互动、协调发展，共建亚洲命运共同体的重要推动力。过去 20 年，以国家开发银行为代表的中国开发性金融把国际经验与中国国情和发展的阶段性特征相结合，为国际金融的创新发展贡献了中国经验和中国智慧；展望未来，随着政府对开发性金融的重视以及市场对开发性金融的需求，开发性金融将有更大的发展空间。同时，由于各国市场规则不统一，市场体系不完善，因此需要各国开发性金融机构加强合作，共同建设市场，共同应对风险与挑战，携手开创未来，这正是本报告所追求的目标，也是本报告将持续开展下去的根本动力。

衷心希望各开发性金融机构为推动全球可持续发展、增进人类福祉做出新的贡献。

第十二届全国政协副主席
中国开发性金融促进会会长

第一篇　完善金融治理

第一章　开发性金融机构概述

开发性金融机构的职责定位是一个基础性的问题，只有明确了这一点，我们才能进一步回答其他问题。比如，开发性金融机构的业务范围是什么？如何对开发性金融机构的经营业绩进行考核？如何构建与其职责定位、业务范围相适应的内部风险控制机制和外部监管体系？

从全球范围来看，发达国家大多制定了专门适用于开发性金融机构的法律，并详细规定了开发性金融机构的基本定位、权利义务、业务范围等。对于中国的开发性金融机构，不仅需要回答上述问题，而且还要思考更多现实的、甚至动态的约束条件，比如，中国是一个发展中大国，各地区发展相对不平衡，很多领域存在突出的结构性问题，财政和金融体系的改革也在不断推进。但是在加入这些具体的约束之前，我们还是要从一般性的角度，对开发性金融机构的职责定位、业务范围、业绩考核、监管体系进行梳理。

开发性金融机构的职责

开发性金融机构是指以主权信用为依托，利用市场机制开展活动，通过融资推动制度建设和市场建设，以实现某国、某地区或某几个国家的公共政策或战略性目标为宗旨的金融机构。不同于政策性金融机构和商业性金融机构，开发性金融机构带有政策性和市场性双重性质，其业务可以简单地理解为前两者的交叉部分。开发性金融机构成立的初衷就是为国家经济发展提供中长期发展资金，以满足国家或地区的战略性资金需求，在提供资金的过程中发挥政策性功能、引导性功能以及补充性功能。

政策性功能

政策性是开发性金融机构最基本的特征，即开发性金融机构是服务于国家政策的工具，其宗旨是实现国家特定的战略性目标，而不是像商业性金融机构那样追求盈利。因此，开发性金融机构不可避免地带有较强的政治色彩。也正因如此，它才能依靠国家信用在资本市场上开展融资业务。开发性金融机构政策性功能的发挥主要体现在以下几个方面：

第一，提供公共产品。公共产品因具有较强的外部性和非排他性，存在"搭便车"问题，因而追求利益最大化的私营部门不愿意投资相关领域，最明显的就是大型基础设施，以及医疗卫生、教育等。

事实上，以提供公共产品为目标的不只有开发性金融机构，还有政策性金融机构。帕尼萨（Panizza）将后者定义为：专门向具有积极外部性，但商业信贷难以满足的项目提供长期融资的金融机构[1]。因此，国家或政府部门就自然成为公共产品的提供者，此时政策性金融机构将成为最主要的资金供给者。然而，政策性金融机构最突出的特征就是完全的"政治性"，即完全依赖政府财政拨款和补贴运作，没有任何的盈利业务，而这远远无法满足公共产品供给所需的巨额资金；更重要的是，一旦财政资金不足或者国家财政收支状况恶化，这些政策性金融机构便会失去资金供应，无法继续满足公共产品的融资需求。

正因如此，推进政策性金融机构逐步向开发性金融机构改革，尤其是鼓励其开展市场化运作，成为政策性金融机构改革的重点内容。开发性金融机构自身的特性决定了其有意愿和能力参与国家的公共产品供给。一方面，开发性金融机构的"政策性"特征决定了其在开展业务时以国家关切的重要领域为导向，而不是单纯地追求机构的利益，因此它们会将资金投入到公共产品供应部门；另一方面，开发性金融机构"市场化"或"商业化"的运作机制（如发行债券）确保其能够在资本市场上获取足够的资金，满足公共产品的资金投入。

第二，支持新兴产业或弱势产业发展。对于一些战略性新兴产业，在发展初期，由于其发展存在较大的不确定性，因此私营部门不愿投资，商业性金融机构的贷款意愿也不强烈，此时就需要开发性金融机构向其提供早期

---

① Panizza U., Eduardo L., Alejandro M., "Should the Government be in the Banking Business? The Role of State-owned and Development Banks", Inter-American Development Bank Working Paper, 2004, P. 15.

扶持。

开发性金融机构可以采取"国家规划——开发性金融机构投资——私营部门和商业性金融机构介入"的流程推进新兴产业的发展。具体而言，首先，国家或政府部门对想要发展的战略性新兴产业制定相关的发展规划；其次，开发性金融机构根据国家规划，对指定的新兴产业项目开展可行性研究，对适合的项目给予资金支持和培育相应的市场机制；最后，具备一定的条件后，开发性金融机构逐步退出，由私营部门独立经营这些战略性新兴产业，并由商业性金融机构提供信贷支持。

可见，开发性金融机构对战略性新兴产业的扶持最明显地体现了其"开发"性质，且这一"开发"作用不仅仅是提供资金支持，还包括开发和完善产业发展所需的市场机制、制度环境等。为了平衡各个产业之间的发展，对于一些弱势产业（如农业），开发性金融机构也会通过类似的机制给予支持。因此，开发性金融机构通过对一些产业提供支持，发挥着提高资源配置效率、优化产业结构和经济结构的政策性功能。

第三，缓和经济周期波动。开发性金融机构的核心业务是中长期投融资，因此它可以根据经济的运行状况调整投融资的规模、结构等，以影响经济中的投资活动，从而缓和经济周期波动带来的冲击。例如，当经济过热时，开发性金融机构可以收缩投资规模，减小对产业的扶持力度，同时增加债券发行，以起到回笼市场资金的作用，最终降低经济热度；反之，当经济萧条时，开发性金融机构则可以扩大投资规模，加大对相关产业的投资和扶持力度，并减少债券发行和资本市场操作，起到逆周期的作用。

引导性功能

开发性金融机构的引导性作用是指它可以间接地吸引社会资本流向特定的产业或领域。特别是，它可以吸引私营部门和商业性金融机构进入符合国家或地区政策意图或长远发展目标的产业。

众所周知，开发性金融机构是以国家信用为依托开展投融资活动的，其宗旨是实现国家的战略性发展目标，这无形中给私营部门和商业性金融机构一种暗示，即开发性金融机构所支持和进入的产业是国家鼓励未来发展的产业，国家信用无疑是对产业不确定性风险的一种担保，从而提升私营部门的投资意愿以及商业性金融机构的放贷意愿。

与此同时，开发性金融机构的先期投入已经为产业或项目发展奠定了一定的基础，这会引导私营部门和商业性金融机构紧随其后，争相"搭便车"。因此，当国家希望优先发展某些产业时，如重工业或者环境友好型产业等，就可以要求开发性金融机构增加对这些产业的信贷和投资，从而吸引私营部门和商业性金融机构随后跟进，达到引导经济发展方向的目的。

补充性功能

开发性金融机构、政策性金融机构、商业性金融机构之间是相互补充的关系，而不是替代和竞争的关系。有人认为，开发性金融机构的基本功能是解决市场失灵，从这个角度而言，开发性金融机构是为了弥补商业性金融机构的不足，为商业性金融机构不愿进入的领域或产业提供优惠的中长期贷款。不过，解决市场失灵首先应该是政府部门的责任，直接的解决方式是要求政策性金融机构代表国家进行市场干预，而市场失灵也成为政策性金融机构产生的理论基础。

然而，当代表政府意愿的政策性金融机构试图弥补市场失灵的时候，由于政府或政策性金融机构自身的局限性，仍然可能存在一些问题。尤其是，政策性金融机构对政府财政补贴的严重依赖，不仅会导致其投资资金供给不足，财务缺乏可持续性，而且会导致其只以国家政策为准，不重视投资盈亏，出现道德风险，此时就会产生政府失灵问题。也就是说，市场失灵和政府失灵同时出现。

所谓政府失灵，就是政府在干预经济、社会生活，以期弥补市场失灵的过程中，由于自身治理能力的局限性或者客观因素的影响，又出现了新的问题（如腐败、寻租等），导致社会资源无法达到最优配置。当出现政府失灵，或者市场失灵和政府失灵同时存在时，就需要开发性金融机构发挥作用①。因为开发性金融机构兼具"政策性"和"商业性"双重性质，它不仅可以弥补商业性金融机构功能不足导致的市场失灵，而且能够弥补政策性金融机构功能不足导致的政府失灵。

---

① 赖溟溟，马力．论开发性金融治理模式及其在中国的创新［J］．辽宁大学学报（哲学社会科学版），2007（4）：119－124．孙国峰．开发性金融的逻辑［J］．清华金融评论，2014（7）：73－77．

开发性金融机构的业务范围

简单来讲，开发性金融机构的业务范围就是指开发性金融机构要开展哪些业务、从事哪些活动，业务范围限定了开发性金融机构应该做什么、不应该做什么，或者说应该进入哪些领域、不应该进入哪些领域。

最核心的问题是，如何清晰界定政策性金融机构、开发性金融机构和商业性金融机构之间的业务界限。很多国家会通过独立的立法来界定开发性金融机构的业务范围，这有利于协调各类金融机构之间的市场行为，推进它们合作共赢，这也是推动开发性金融机构法治化的必要条件之一。但立法的根本前提仍然是明晰各类金融机构之间的特征差异，尤其是功能或职责的差异，开发性金融机构的政策性、引导性和补充性功能直接决定了其特殊的业务范围。

开发性金融机构的业务范围可以从宏观和微观两个层面来界定。宏观层面是指开发性金融机构在产业或项目选择方面应该遵循哪些标准，微观层面是指开发性金融机构具体的市场运作方式有哪些，这些标准和运作方式与政策性和商业性金融机构有何差别。

宏观层面：进入标准

目前，大多数法律以进入的领域或产业来界定开发性金融机构的业务范围，如规定开发性金融机构应支持基础设施建设、基础产业发展、城镇化建设等具有公共产品性质的领域。然而，在界定开发性金融机构的业务范围时，不宜单纯以进入的行业或领域作为标准，而应具体分析产业或项目的盈利能力、实施主体、持续期限、行业成熟度、发展阶段等。

例如，城镇化建设是开发性金融机构的主要投资领域之一，其中的交通、电力等基础设施建设属于开发性金融机构的业务范围，但住房改造、医疗条件改善、供水等在很大程度上属于商业性金融机构的业务范围，尤其是其中盈利性较强的项目贷款，或者中短期的批发零售贷款业务。

界定开发性金融机构业务范围需要一套系统的指标体系，可供参考的指标至少有以下 4 个方面：

一是盈利能力。开发性金融机构坚持保本微利的原则，其主要目标是支持国家的发展政策或战略性发展目标，而不是追逐利润；相反，商业性金融机构以营利为目的，其首先考虑的就是自身的成本和收益，不会参与那些利润较低甚至没有盈利的项目；政策性金融机构完全是由政府财政支撑的，其并不关心盈利问题。

因此，对于那些无论是短期还是长期都不会盈利的项目，应该由政策性金融机构进入，完全依靠政府财政补贴给予支持；对于那些在短期和长期都可能盈利的项目，宜由商业性金融机构予以支持；对于那些短期不会盈利，但是长期会盈利的项目，则由开发性金融机构进入负责开展相关业务。

二是实施主体。一般而言，大型企业尤其是国有企业因具备"国有"背景和规模优势，容易获得商业性金融机构的信贷支持，而中小企业和民营企业往往较难获得金融机构贷款，但它们对经济和产业发展不可或缺，甚至在某些产业更具有比较优势。因此，对于大型企业实施的项目，可考虑由商业性金融机构进入，而中小企业和民营企业实施的项目，则由开发性金融机构予以支持，鼓励中小企业、民营企业的发展，增强其市场竞争力，从而提高各类企业的运作效率。

三是持续期限。开发性金融机构的成立就是为了满足国家或地区的中长期投融资需求，而商业性金融机构倾向于进行中短期贷款，以避免长期的不确定导致的收益损失。因此，对于超过一定期限（如 10 年或 20 年以上）的长期贷款项目，可考虑由开发性金融机构或政策性金融机构进入，而对于持续期限较短（如 10 年或 5 年以下）的项目，则由商业性金融机构进入。

四是行业成熟度和发展阶段。开发性金融机构的政策性目标之一就是支持新兴产业或弱势产业的发展，这些产业或行业在起步阶段缺少各种发展资源和条件，发展很不成熟，此时开发性金融机构进入开展业务，可以起到"催化剂"的作用，当发展到一定阶段后，开发性金融机构又将通过自身的引导性功能吸引商业性金融机构进入，开展相关业务。由于行业成熟度是随着时间不断变化的，因此应动态地划分开发性金融机构和商业性金融机构之间的业务范围。

当然，上述指标只起到一定的参考作用，具体应该选取哪些指标，以及标准如何设定，还需要开展深入系统的研究。当指标体系和具体标准设定后，就可以制定相关的法律法规，以法律的形式规范开发性金融机构的业务范围，以防止开发性金融机构挤占商业性金融机构的业务，导致不公平竞争[1]。

---

[1] 因为开发性金融机构是以国家信用为依托开展投融资活动的，所以其在债券市场上更有融资优势，而且由于融资成本低，贷款利率也较低，这就容易导致商业性金融机构的竞争力受挫，危害其发展。

微观层面：运作方式

政策性金融机构完全按照政府指令开展中长期信贷业务，满足项目的资金需求，其资金也完全来源于政府财政，因而除贷款业务以外，并不存在其他业务运作方式，更不涉及任何市场化的业务。

商业性金融机构以短期零散投融资为主要业务，其资金来源主要是居民储蓄，因此商业性金融机构的主要市场运作方式就是存款和中短期贷款。当然，商业性金融机构也可以发行债券，但是其发行债券的融资成本要远高于吸收储蓄，不符合经济效益原则。

开发性金融机构的主要业务是提供中长期贷款（不提供居民储蓄业务），但是，与商业性金融机构相比，开发性金融机构的贷款不仅期限长，而且利率很低，带有明显的优惠和扶持性质，充分体现了其政策性、引导性功能。

更重要的是，虽然开发性金融机构和政策性金融机构都会提供中长期贷款，但是由于开发性金融机构的主要资金来源不是政府财政，而是在资本市场发行债券，所以它在资本市场上非常活跃。

正因如此，开发性金融机构开展的业务除了中长期贷款之外，还涉及股权投资、风险投资、债券承销、保险和租赁等多样化的资本运作业务品种。不仅如此，政策性金融机构只是强调满足国家战略性项目的资金需求，而开发性金融机构不仅强调为项目建设提供资金，更强调运用开发性方法，开展咨询服务、技术援助、PPP① 等"软"业务，主动推进市场建设、信用建设和制度建设，提高国家和私营部门的治理能力。其中，咨询服务包括发展规划咨询、企业业务（如上市、并购重组、资产评估等）咨询等。

开发性金融机构的经营业绩考核

开发性金融机构具有"政策性"和"商业性"双重性质，即它虽然采取市场化的业务运作方式，但其业务却带有很强的政策目的，因此在考核其经营业绩时，不能仅仅像考核商业性金融机构那样，只关注利润率、资本充足

---

① PPP（Public – Private Partnership），即政府和社会资本合作，是公共基础设施建设的一种项目运作模式。——编者注

率、净资产收益率、不良资产比率等微观的业绩考核指标，同时还要考察其贷款或其他活动对整个国民经济、投资、居民生活条件等宏观指标的促进作用。

更何况，开发性金融机构建立和开展业务的初衷并不是盈利，而是服务于国家政策，所以在确保自身可持续运行的基础上，其推动国家发展目标的实现情况才是经营业绩考核时更应被关注的方面。

宏观层面：发展促进绩效

如前文所述，引导性是开发性金融机构非常重要的功能之一。虽然，与商业性金融机构巨额的市场投资无法直接匹敌，但开发性金融机构能够间接引导商业性金融机构资金和其他社会资本的流向，因而其实际调动的投资额远高于它们起初的资金投入。

更重要的是，在投融资过程中，开发性金融机构还会起到优化结构、培育市场、推进体制机制建设等重要作用，其对整个社会、经济发展的贡献将被无限放大。鉴于此，从宏观层面考察开发性金融机构的经营绩效不应被忽略，因为这实质上是其市场运作绩效的价值转移效应和价值扩大效应。

具体而言，可以从两个方面来考察开发性金融机构对国民经济、社会发展的促进绩效。其一是开发性金融机构对发展指标（如经济增长、居民收入水平提高、消费、投资、基础设施、减贫、就业、环境可持续发展等）的促进作用，即开发性金融机构的贡献度指标体系。其二是开发性金融机构与国家发展目标的吻合程度，即开发性金融机构的契合度指标体系。

上述两方面分别从总量和相对量的角度衡量开发性金融机构的发展促进绩效。由于开发性金融机构投资的大多是一些中长期的基础设施项目，短期之内很难产生明显的效果，所以开发性金融机构的贡献度指标在核算时难度相对较大，且容易出现偏差。而契合度指标相对简单，依据开发性金融机构的资金流向、结构、具体项目的性质等，可以采用赋值的方法予以衡量。当然，如果想要进一步考察开发性金融机构对社会、经济发展等的实际贡献与国家设定的政策目标之间的吻合程度，则会面临同贡献度指标体系一样的困境。

微观层面：市场运作绩效

开发性金融机构需要确保本机构至少保本微利，以实现自身可持续发展，尽可能地减少政府财政支持；而且，开发性金融机构的良性发展、盈利能力的提升，可以增强其对国家政策的支持力度，因此必须对开发性金融机构的市场运作绩效予以定期考核。目前，对开发性金融机构的考核主要还是依据商业性金融机构的指标来进行的，以《巴塞尔协议》为参照。反映金融机构市场运作绩效的指标有：资产总额、资本充足率、所有者权益、净利润、不良资产率、不良贷款率、流动性等。

需要指出的是，由于开发性金融机构采取市场化运作方式，因此在指标选取、标准设定等方面与商业性金融机构存在一定的相似性。然而，开发性金融机构的职能、业务范围和市场运作方式与商业性金融机构存在较大差异，两种金融机构采用同样的市场绩效考核指标和标准并不合适。

例如，对于流动性指标，商业性金融机构为规避风险，从事的主要是中短期信贷业务，对流动性的要求很高。但是，开发性金融机构从事的主要是国家政策要求的中长期投资，长期贷款的占比很高，因而其资本流动性必然较差。但这种低流动性是由开发性金融机构的功能和职责决定的，从根本上来讲是国家政策要求决定的，而不是其自身经营存在问题，所以在设定流动性指标时，对两种金融机构的要求必须不同。

再如，对于净利润或盈利性指标，商业性金融机构的逐利性导致其对利润率的要求必然很高，而开发性金融机构开展业务的目的是实现国家的战略性发展目标，并非盈利，所以利润率不能成为开发性金融机构绩效考核的重点指标，至少在标准上相对要低。同样地，资本充足率、不良贷款比率等指标在设定标准时也应考虑不同金融机构在职能、业务范围等方面的差异性。

此外，可能还会存在一些商业性金融机构尚未考虑，但对于开发性金融机构却非常重要的指标，如政策风险类指标，因为开发性金融机构受国家政策变动的影响较大，这类指标就需要纳入考量范围，但商业性金融机构一般无须考虑（系统性风险除外）。

总而言之，现有的开发性金融机构的市场运作绩效指标具有一定的合理性，但并不完全适用。社会各界需要进一步深入探究，设计出一套专门的、适合开发性金融机构的业务绩效评价指标体系，尤其要与商业性金融机构的评价指标体系区分开来。

基于上述分析，我们认为，开发性金融机构的经营业绩考核需要同时考虑其发展促进绩效和市场运作绩效，唯有如此，才能更加全面地衡量开发性金融机构的实际贡献，否则便可能反向激励其偏离"政策性"特性，一味关注本机构的盈利。更何况，有很多研究系统考察了全球主要的开发性金融机构的市场运作绩效，发现大多数开发性金融机构的不良贷款率很低（低于5%），基本上都实现了盈利，至少达到了盈亏平衡，很多机构的资本充足率达到8%以上，高于《巴塞尔协议 III》对商业银行资本充足率不低于6%的要求①，其他市场运作指标的表现也很好。

这表明，开发性金融机构的市场运作绩效普遍很好，并不存在各界担心的一些问题②，反而是开发性金融机构对经济社会发展的实际贡献，即发展促进绩效几乎没人关注，而这其实是开发性金融机构开展市场业务、提高市场运作绩效的根本目的。

开发性金融机构的监管体系

现有监管体系

大部分发达国家都在关于开发性金融机构的专门法律中规定了开发性金融机构的监管问题，如监管部门、监管内容、监管指标等。尽管如此，它们设定的监管体系并不是专门针对开发性金融机构的，而且大多遵从了与商业性金融机构一致的监管标准。

整体来讲，3/4 以上的开发性金融机构与本国的商业性金融机构有着共同的监管者，通常是中央银行或银行业监管机构（如银行业监督管理委员会或者金融监管委员会），其余的则以提供战略指引的政府部门（如财政部门）作为监管者③。

在监管指标方面，约60%的开发性金融机构遵从与本国商业性金融机构同样的审慎监管标准，即以财务报表为基础，以《巴塞尔协议》为参照，对市场运作指标进行管理和评估，包括资本充足率、流动性、资产收益率、透明度等。

所以，对开发性金融机构的市场运作绩效进行考核，实际上是对其进行

---

① 王剑. 开发性金融机构的国际比较［J］. 金融发展评论，2014（8）：129－135.

② 由于开发性金融机构不以营利为目的，且有国家的信用支持，所以很多人担心开发性金融机构会因此不注重自身的市场运作，可能存在较高的不良贷款率或者亏损等问题。

③ 益言. 开发性金融机构发展历程及面临挑战［J］. 金融发展评论，2016（7）：20－28.

监管的重要方式之一。此外，几乎所有的开发性金融机构都设有风险管理部门，通过风险监控和管理，确保机构的稳健经营。

纵观现有开发性金融机构的监管体系可以发现，现有的开发性金融机构监管体系在独立性、适用性、全面性等方面存在不足。

其一，独立性。现有开发性金融机构的监管者大多是政府部门，而开发性金融机构本身又受到政府部门发展政策的约束，这就意味着，投融资政策的制定者和监管者都是政府部门，甚至是同一部门，这就导致监管很难做到独立、客观。因此，在内部自我监管的同时，成立独立的开发性金融机构监管部门十分必要。

其二，适用性。虽然商业性金融机构与开发性金融机构在监管手段、指标设定等方面有很多的相似之处，但开发性金融机构与商业性金融机构在职能、业务、目标等方面又存在很大差异，所以开发性金融机构不能直接套用商业性金融机构的监管指标和标准，否则会导致监管无效。然而，目前很多开发性金融机构采用与商业性金融机构类似甚至相同的监管指标，其风险管理体系也是参照《巴塞尔协议》对商业性金融机构的要求而设置的，其适用性令人质疑。

其三，全面性。一方面，目前监管关注的都是开发性金融机构的市场运作绩效，但其经营绩效并不单单反映在市场运作业务绩效上，还包括其发展促进绩效。因此，开发性金融机构的监管工作应全面考虑其发展促进绩效和具体业务运作绩效，全面设定监管指标体系。另一方面，目前对开发性金融机构的监管主要还是集中在对结果（即经营业绩）的评估，而对于开发性金融机构的合规性监管，包括其业务范围是否合法、贷款投向是否合理（是否反映国家政策）、贷款规模和条件是否符合规定等，则一直被忽略。

监管体系改革

提高监管的独立性和有效性

首先，设立独立的开发性金融机构监管委员会，由它统一调动监管资源，通盘考虑和制定金融监管法规、监管政策和监管标准，综合评估项目的可行性、贷款额度、贷款期限和利率的合理性等。该监管委员会可由来自相关政府部门的人员构成，直接受国务院管理，定期对开发性金融机构的市场活动和经营业绩进行监管，并发布监管报告。

其次，如有必要，还应建立独立的外部专家委员会，由智库、权威专家和学者、研究机构等组成，为监管委员会提供政策建议和独立的监督评估，确保监管委员会的监督工作客观、公正、有效。

最后，提升开发性金融机构的信息透明度，定期向社会公众真实、全面地披露其经营活动信息，通过公众、新闻媒体以及社会组织的监督与约束，确保监管的有效性。

构建合理的监管指标体系

基于开发性金融机构特定的职能和特性，构建一套不同于商业性金融机构的开发性金融机构监管指标体系很重要。该指标体系应包括：政策性指标、安全性指标、合规性指标、流动性指标、盈利能力指标、资本充足率指标等，且监管标准应区别于商业性金融机构的监管标准。

其中，政策性指标监督开发性金融机构的投融资活动对经济社会发展的促进作用；安全性指标监督开发性金融机构的投融资活动受国家或政府政策变动的影响程度，以及应对能力；合规性指标监督开发性金融机构的业务范围、贷款投向、贷款条件是否按计划进行，其业务开展过程和操作方法、财务和会计制度是否规范、合法等；流动性指标、盈利能力指标、资本充足率指标等主要监督其能否实现财务可持续发展。

注重监管结果的使用

对开发性金融机构进行监管的目的是提高其经营绩效，而不是为了监管而监管，因此监管结果或监管报告必须得到重视。

一方面，建立监管报告的反馈机制。监管委员会将监管报告以及据此提出的政策建议下发给开发性金融机构，并要求开发性金融机构在一定期限内提交反馈报告，就其未来可能的改进政策提交一份方案，监管委员会将依据该方案为政府部门下一年度的拨款和其他支持性政策提出建议。只有这样，监督过程才会真正起到约束和督促开发性金融机构的作用。

另一方面，及时向社会公布监管报告，这不仅有利于发挥社会监督的作用，而且有助于其他金融机构以此为鉴，改进自身的经营活动，同时也便于其他金融机构制订和调整与开发性金融机构之间的合作计划，推进各金融机构间更好的合作。

第二章　国外开发性金融立法体系和
治理结构比较

引言

　　促进经济包容性增长、维护金融稳定、推动区域和产业均衡发展是政府的重要职责，同时也是政府进行宏观调控的重要目标。肇始于美国次贷危机的全球金融危机爆发以来，各国都开始重新审视政府与市场的关系，普遍利用政府信用锚定市场信心，稳定金融体系，促进本国经济的复苏与重振，在此过程中，开发性金融发挥了重要作用。开发性金融作为一种介于政府和市场之间的金融形态，是政策性金融的深化和发展，它以服务国家战略为宗旨，以中长期投融资为载体，以国家信用为依托，通过把国家信用和市场化运作相结合，承担实现政府的发展目标、弥补市场失灵、提供公共产品、提高社会资源配置效率以及熨平经济周期性波动的重要职能，它是各国经济金融体系中不可替代的重要组成部分，也日益成为政府和市场之间的桥梁和纽带。

　　如何最大限度地发挥开发性金融在国民经济发展中的作用，是摆在各国政府面前的关键性问题。根据制度经济学的经典理论，基础性制度会对经济行为和经济发展产生重要作用，其完善与否直接关系到经济发展的内在驱动力和外部性影响。因此，建立健全开发性金融的基础性制度就显得非常必要和迫切。"法者，治之端也"①，法律制度作为基础性制度的重要组成部分，无疑发挥着更为关键的作用。法律作为一种强制性秩序，具有严肃性、权威性、规范性和约束性，对于维护经济金融稳定，建构审慎有效的监管体系至关重要。立法是法律制度建设的第一个环节，也是最为重要的步骤，制定系统完备的法律规范是完善法律制度建设的根本前提。纵观全球范围内开发性金融起步较早、

――――――――――

　　①　参见《荀子·君道》。

发展较为稳健成熟的国家，无一例外地注重立法工作，在开发性金融发展伊始，就通过制定、颁行单独性法律法规实施金融监管，在开发性金融机构的资金来源和投向、投融资结构、会计制度、资本约束以及公司治理结构等方面进行规制，全面审慎地加强宏观管理和微观监管。

概括而言，开发性金融的法律制度是指，关于开发性金融机构创设的目的、资金来源渠道、资金运用和业务范围、政府信用支持和优惠政策、组织架构、公司治理结构以及监督机制等内容的法律规范的统称。建构开发性金融的法律制度，特别是制定针对开发性金融机构的法律法规，是明确其战略地位和基本职能、协调开发性金融机构与其他金融主体的外部关系、规范开发性金融机构内部运行机制的基石，是保障其高效运行的基础性条件，同时也决定了开发性金融机构能否持续、稳健发展。就其法律属性而言，开发性金融机构法的本质是"以社会责任为本位，贯彻平衡协调、责权利效相统一的法律价值观"的经济法。第一，开发性金融机构法归属于经济法范畴，就应当体现经济法的本质，即"社会责任本位法"，所以开发性金融机构法是在对社会尽责的前提下行使其权利及获取利益的，需要全面贯彻"权利与义务相统一"的原则；第二，开发性金融机构法是一种在国家利益与金融企业利益、长远效益与当前效益、国家干预与市场调节、公平与效率之间不断协调的特殊的经济法，所以具有鲜明的协调与平衡特质。①

从国外相关国家的发展实践来看，开发性金融机构一般都坚持"立法先行"的基本路径，通过长时期的探索实践，逐渐建立了较为成熟的法律制度，不仅保证了开发性金融机构在成立之初就有法可依，而且还根据现实条件和实际运行中遇到的问题，动态调整法律规范，真正做到与时俱进。国外在开发性金融领域的立法经验和探索实践，值得我国深入学习与科学借鉴。

国外开发性金融立法概述

立法形式

在开发性金融立法形式方面，以专门性、单独性立法为主；在立法层级

---

① 白钦先，李军. 我国政策性金融立法及相关问题研究［J］. 上海金融，2005（11）：4－7.

方面，以位阶较高的专门性法律为主，很少以行政法规或者部门规章等位阶较低的法律形式出现。大多数国家，特别是市场经济相对成熟、法律制度比较完善的发达国家，都是由国家立法机关研究制定并颁布实施单独的开发性金融机构法等专门性法律。从世界各国的开发性金融机构的构成体系来看，融资专业领域的细分形成了种类繁多的开发性金融机构，由于不同机构具有差异化的业务范围及运作规则，因而各国对不同的开发性金融机构进行单独立法，并且以一般法律而非条例等行政法规或部门规章的形式予以确立，每家开发性金融机构都相应制定了专门的法律，有的国家则是一个类型（如开发银行）由一部法律（如"开发银行法"）来规范，作为其设立和运作的法律依据。这些法律大多以所调整的开发性金融机构的名称来命名，如调整美国农产品信贷公司法律关系的是《农产品信贷公司特许法》，调整日本政策投资银行法律行为与关系的是《日本政策投资银行法》，调整日本国际协力银行法律关系的是《日本国际协力银行法》，等等。

立法的主要特点及规制内容

明确创设目的和宗旨

阐释法律调整对象的创设目的，明确其设立的政治和经济愿景，并将其作为正式条款列于法律之首。比如，《日本开发银行法》第一条就明确规定，"日本开发银行的目的在于通过提供长期资金，促进产业的开发和社会经济的发展，补充并奖励一般金融机构"；《哈萨克斯坦开发银行法》第三条第1款规定，"开发银行业务活动的宗旨是改善并提高国家投资业务活动的有效性，发展生产基础设施和制造业，并促进国民经济吸引国内外投资"；《巴西开发银行内部规章》第三条规定，"巴西开发银行是实施并开展联邦政府投资政策的主要机构，其首要的任务是为国家经济和社会发展相关的计划、项目、建设和服务提供支持"。从上述规定可以看出，各国设立开发性金融机构的主要目的基本一致，即促进本国产业的开发和社会经济的发展，同时更好地吸引国内外资本进行投资。

明确法律性质和法律地位

关于开发性金融机构的法律性质或者法律地位、法人资格问题，各国开发性金融机构法中大都明确指出该机构属于特殊公法法人，即不是以追求利润最大化为唯一目标的一般公司或企业法人，也并非不注重经济效益和经营质量的政府机关，而是代表国家利益、公众利益的特殊公法法人。例如，《日本开发银行法》第一章第二条规定，"日本开发银行为公法法人"；《德国复兴信贷银行法》第一章第一条规定，"德国复兴信贷银行是依公法设立的法人团体"。有些国家虽然只是将开发性金融机构简单概括为"法人"，但也并非指一般的法人，而是一种特殊的法人。如在韩国，《韩国产业银行法》《韩国进出口银行法》《韩国住宅银行法》分别在其第二条中规定，这些开发性银行的法律性质都为法人。

明确资金来源

开发性金融机构的资金主要包括初始资本金和日常运营资金两部分，对于初始资本金的来源，各国立法一般都有非常明确和严格的规定。国外立法大多允许开发性金融机构以发行特别债券或者以政府贷款的方式募集资金。以《日本政策投资银行法》为例，该法第五条明确规定："政策投资银行可以通过发行日本政策投资银行债券募集资金。"《德国复兴信贷银行法》第四条规定："（1）为了筹集必要资金，尤其可发行债券和进行贷款；（2）短期债务不得超过中长期债务的10%；（3）使用本国货币发行的债券适用于地方选区货币的投资。"《韩国产业银行法》第二十五条明确规定："（1）产业银行可发行产业金融债券以募集开展第十八条规定的贷款和还款担保等业务所需的资金；（2）产业银行具有发行产业金融债券的专属权利。"

确定资金运用和业务范围

明确开发性金融机构的资金运用和业务范围，是立法的重要内容，对于开发性金融机构的业务运作和资金使用都具有重要的规制和约束作用。例如，《日本政策投资银行法》第三条以列举的形式，对政策投资银行的业务范围进行了厘定："吸收存款业务（仅限于可转让存款及其他政策规定的存款）；进行资金的放款业务；进行资金的出资业务；对债务进行担保的业务；进行有价证券的放款业务；进行取得货币债权……进行金融及其他与经济相关的调查、研究或培训业务；进行以上各项所规定的业务的附带业务。"《韩国产业银行法》第十八条规定，"为达成第一条规定的目的，产业银行从事以下业务：发放贷款或贴现票据；认购、承销及/或投资；担保或承担债务；通过吸收存款，发行产业金融债券、其他证券和债务票据，从政府、韩国银行和其他金融机构借款以及借入国外资本等方式，为前三项规定的业务获得必要的资金；办理国内外汇兑业务等。"《哈萨克斯坦开发银行法》第七条对开发银行的业务范围进行了界定，业务范围非常多元化，既有传统信贷业务，也涉及资本市场业务，其主要业务内容包括：借贷业务，接受存款，开立并管理接收资金的银行账户，为本国和外国法人履行货币债务提供银行担保，出具并保兑信用证，租赁业务，证券发行，以及提供夹层融资等。

确定特殊的融资原则

开发性金融机构特殊的融资原则主要有：第一，充当"最后出借人"原则，即在融资条件或资格上要求融资对象必须是从其他金融机构不易得到所需融通资金的条件下才给予最后支持。例如，《德国复兴信贷银行法》第二章规定，该银行只对那些重建和促进德国经济发展的项目发放贷款，并且这些项目所需的资金，其他信贷机构无能力筹集。第二，非竞争性原则，该原则的目的是规范开发性金融机构与商业性金融机构的关系，维护市场经济秩序。例如，《日本开发银行法》在第三章第二十二条"禁止同金融机构竞争"中规定，鉴于其目的，日本开发银行"不得通过业务经营，与其他银行及金融机构竞争"。第三，倡导性原则，即对其他金融机构自愿从事的符合国家政策目标的放款给予偿付保证或者再融资，以支持、鼓励、吸引和推动更多的金融机构开展政策性融资活动。例如，《日本开发银行法》中就有"对与开发资金有关的债务提供保证"的规定。①

明确公司治理结构及高管职责

开发性金融立法中必须明确开发性金融机构的公司治理结构，并就机构的管理层构成予以说明，在"产权清晰"的基本条件下，明确管理层的权责。② 比如，根据《韩国产业银行法》的相关规定，总裁代表产业银行，并负责管理产业银行整体的业务运营；产业银行以总裁（也称为董事长兼首席执行官）、执行董事和审计师为其高管，产业银行设一位总裁和一位审计师，此外根据章程的规定，需要设立若干执行董事的席位；董事会应包括总裁和执行董事，审计师可出席董事会会议，并表达意见，但无表决权。又比如，

---

① 白钦先，王伟. 中外政策性金融立法比较研究 ［J］. 金融理论与实践，2005（12）：3－6.

② 李志辉，武岳. 开发性金融机构监管体系的构建研究 ［J］. 现代财经，2007（2）：20－27.

根据日本开发性金融的相关法律规定，开发性金融机构的权力主体主要由总裁、副总裁、理事和监事等构成。总裁代表银行或者公库总理业务；副总裁辅助总裁开展日常管理和业务；理事协助总裁、副总裁工作；监事负责对业务进行监督检查；参事接受总裁的咨询，同时在重大议题和决策问题上，享有建议权。《德国复兴信贷银行法》第五条规定，"银行的主体机构为执行董事会和监事会"；第六条规定，"执行董事会至少由两名成员构成，由监事会任免执行董事会的成员；执行董事会负责开展银行的业务和管理资产"；第七条就监事会的构成进行了规定，同时明确"监事会有责任慎重考虑和持续监督银行的业务开展和资产管理"。

明确监督管理机制

各国的法律都对开发性金融机构的监管机制有明确的规定。例如，《日本政策投资银行法》第二十六条规定，"主务大臣根据本法律所规定的内容监督政策投资银行"；第二十七条规定，"主务大臣认为有必要为了确保公司业务的健全及恰当的运营以及其他认为有必要实施本法律时，可以让政策投资银行报告，或者要求其职员进入政策投资银行的营业场所和其他设施对业务的状况或账本、文件和其他必要的物品进行检查"。《韩国产业银行法》第四十七条规定，"金融服务委员会应根据本法的规定监督产业银行，并可下达监督所需的命令；金融服务委员会还应根据总统令的规定开展监督以确保产业银行管理良好，并可下达此类监督所需的命令"。同法第四十八条还授予金融服务委员会特定的监督和检查权限，即要求产业银行提交关于必要事项的报告或指示本部的主管官员或金融监督委员会的官员检查产业银行的经营状况、账簿、记录和其他必要事项。

日本开发性金融立法与治理体系

作为中国"一衣带水"的邻邦，日本在开发性金融的发展、立法体系的建构方面积累了丰富的经验，也取得了良好的效果。"二战"后，日本制定并实施了高起点、快节奏的"赶超型战略"："高起点"是指借鉴其他国家经济发展的成功经验，充分发挥政府在经济发展中的引领性作用，并以法律的形式予以确定和规范；"快节奏"是指短期内高效率地颁行相关法律法规，创立各类开发性、政策性金融机构，为经济重振和产业升级提供强力支撑。①

日本开发性金融体系概述

以 1950 年日本输出入银行的建立为标志，日本开启了建构开发性金融体系的新阶段，到 20 世纪 80 年代，日本初步建立了以"两行十库"② 为代表的开发性金融体系。自 20 世纪 50 年代开始，日本先后经历了经济复兴期、经济高速增长期、经济稳定期和经济结构调整期等历史阶段，但无论历史的车轮行进到哪个阶段，日本的开发性金融机构都在经济稳定和社会发展方面发挥了重要作用。按照相关法律的规定和政府的战略规划，各开发性金融机构分别从事特殊领域的金融活动，经营商业性金融机构不愿意或者无力经营的金融业务，弥补市场失灵，发挥政府引导性作用，进而成为电力、海运、煤炭、钢铁等基础产业和电子工业、防止公害、高新技术开发及知识产权保护等特定产业发展和振兴的主力军，有效推动了新技术的研究、开发和应用，促进了产业结构的优化升级，为实体经济的投融资活动提供了金融便利，承担起经济和金融稳定器的使命。

日本开发性金融体系的转型与再造

20 世纪 90 年代，日本泡沫经济破灭，加之随后发生的亚洲金融危机，日本传统的财政投融资体系暴露了很多显性的问题，为了稳定经济和金融系统，日本政府开启了针对开发性金融机构的调整、重组和再造的改革浪潮：1999年 6 月，日本国会通过《日本政策投资银行法》；1999 年 9 月，经国会批准，日本政府将日本开发银行和北海道东北开发金融公库合并，成立日本政策投资银行（Development Bank of Japan，DBJ）；此后，日本政府又颁布了《国际协力银行法》，并以此为依据，将日本进出口银行和海外经济协力基金合并重组为"国际协力银行"；将国民金融公库和环境卫生金融公库合并，创设新的国民生活金融公库等。经过这一阶段的重组和再造，日本的开发性金融体系

---

① 刘孝红. 我国政策性银行转型研究［M］. 长沙：湖南人民出版社，2010：180.

② "两行"是指日本开发银行和日本输出入银行；"十库"是指国民金融公库、商工组合中央金库、中小企业金融公库、中小企业信用保险公库、环境卫生金融公库、农林渔业金融公库、住宅金融公库、公营企业金融公库、北海道东北开发金融公库、冲绳振兴开发金融公库。

由之前的"两行十库"变为"两行七库"①。2007 年 5 月，日本参议院通过《日本政策金融公库法》，根据该法案，国民生活金融公库等 5 家开发性金融机构和政策性金融机构合并为一家机构——"日本政策金融公库"，改革的目的是提高开发性金融机构的运行效率，剔除一般性贷款和投资金融业务，突出开发性融资的特质。

日本开发性金融机构的市场化、民营化改革

在日本传统的财政投融资体制下，开发性金融机构和政策性金融机构的资金来源主要是邮政储蓄上缴财务省（旧称"大藏省"）资金运用部的资金，只有少量资金来源于债券市场等。但是，随着 2005 年 10 月《邮政民营化法案》在日本众议院通过，邮政储蓄资金这一最重要的融资渠道被堵死，开发性金融机构和政策性金融机构的资金来源失去保障，因此市场化改革势在必行。2005 年 11 月，日本经济财政咨询会议明确提出了开发性金融和政策性金融改革的基本原则、业务范围、功能分类和组织形式等内容，并确定了"融资改革方案"，自此开启了开发性金融和政策性金融市场化和民营化改革的新阶段。"市场化"主要体现在，开发性金融和政策性金融的资金来源不再依赖邮政储蓄，而是可以通过市场化和多元化的融资渠道募集资金。例如，可以通过公募的方式发行政策性金融债，或者通过财政投融资特殊账户发行财投债，还可以在海外资本市场发行有政府担保的债券。"民营化"则体现在，将日本政策投资银行、商工组合中央金库以及公营企业金融公库 3 家由政府所有的开发性金融机构逐步进行私有化改革，最终实现彻底的民营化。②

日本开发性金融立法体系

日本作为大陆法系国家，在立法体系的建构中特别注重对成文法的制定，对于涉及国计民生的重要领域，大多以成文法或者法典的形式进行规范和约

---

① "两行"是指日本政策投资银行和国际协力银行；"七库"是指国民生活金融公库、商工组合中央金库、住房金融公库、农林渔业金融公库、中小企业金融公库、公营企业金融公库、冲绳振兴开发金融公库。

② 刘孝红. 我国政策性银行转型研究［M］. 长沙：湖南人民出版社，2010：183 - 186.

束，从而构建了较为完整的成文法体系。在开发性金融领域，日本也是遵循上述惯例，采取由国家立法机构制定和颁行单独的开发性金融成文法的立法形式。

日本国内的金融体系大致分为政府金融（国家金融）和民间金融两类，政府金融的载体主要是各类开发性、政策性金融机构，民间金融的载体则以商业性金融机构为主。需要特别强调的是，日本在立法和监管过程中，严格将商业性金融和开发性金融、政策性金融加以区分，针对不同类型的金融机构制定不同的法律规范加以规制。比如，普通的商业性金融机构受《银行法》的规制，同时需要接受中央银行和金融监督厅的监管；而开发性金融机构和政策性金融机构除发行债券业务需要遵照《银行法》的规定外，其他内容均不受《银行法》的约束，而是适用具有独立性的专门性法律，如《日本开发银行法》《日本政策投资银行法》《冲绳振兴开发金融公库法》等。同时，开发性金融机构原则上也不需要接受日本中央银行和金融监督厅的监管，而是受财务省和财务大臣的独立监管，从而在立法和监管领域自成一体。此外，在业务活动方面，两者也不会发生交叉和竞争，而是彼此分离和互相补充。经过漫长的重组、市场化改革和再造过程，目前，日本的开发性金融体系已初步建成，按照"一机构一法"的原则，开发性金融法律体系也基本完成，主要包括《日本政策投资银行法》《日本政策金融公库法》《国际协力银行法》《商工组合中央金库法》《公营企业金融公库法》等法律规范以及与其相适应的补充性规定等。①

日本开发性金融机构的运作理念和治理体系

1. 担纲政府宏观调控的重要工具。《日本政策投资银行法》第一条规定，"日本政策投资银行为实现完全民营化的同时确保经营的自主性，通过经营与使用一体的出资和融资方法……向长期需要资金供给的企业顺畅地提供资金"。该条款明确了日本政策投资银行的定位和宗旨，即依法向特定企业提供信贷支持，担纲政府宏观调控的重要工具。

2. 依法组建完善的公司治理结构，并接受相应的监管。针对不同开发性金融机构和政策性金融机构的专门性法律都明确要求其必须建立完善

---

① 白钦先，王伟. 政策性金融概论［M］. 北京：中国金融出版社，2013：203－205.

的公司治理结构，并将任命权赋予政府的相关部门。以日本政策投资银行为例，《日本政策投资银行法》规定，日本政策投资银行的董事长或者执行代表、监事会成员、董事等重要部门的人员由财务大臣任命，"在未得到财务大臣认可前，不发生任何效力"。该法同时规定财务大臣负责对日本政策投资银行进行监督和管理，如果财务大臣认为有必要，可以要求日本政策投资银行或其受托机构递交报告，或者进入日本政策投资银行的营业场所或其他设施对业务状况、账本、文件和其他必要物品进行现场检查。

3. 按照金融治理规范和要求开展业务，坚持审慎经营，严格防范金融风险。日本的开发性金融机构一般都在保证财务稳健、不亏损和合理盈利的前提下自主决策、独立经营，因此需要其在项目考察、决策、投资以及贷后管理等环节，严格遵照资产负债管理和风险管理等方面的规范和要求审慎开展工作。在实际运行中，为了有效规避风险，降低不良贷款率，日本的开发性金融机构都建立了完善的信用风险管理职能部门，制定了完备的信用评级制度、贷款项目审查制度以及贷后跟踪和管理机制，多管齐下，确保贷款的安全性和经营的稳健性。①

日本的开发性金融机构虽然几经调整和变革，但其设立的宗旨以及承担的使命并没有改变。随着法律治理和监管体系的日臻完善，日本的开发性金融机构遵循各自对应的专门性法律，以市场融资为手段，以国家信用为依托，以市场化的经营理念为原则，积极参与金融市场活动，在可以预见的未来，将更好地发挥引导性和建设性职能，为日本经济的发展和金融稳定提供强有力的支撑。

德国开发性金融立法与治理体系

德国是世界上最早创设开发性金融机构的国家之一。"二战"结束以后，德国经济百废待兴，实体经济和基础产业亟须信贷资金支持，而商业性金融机构出于自身利益和能力的考虑，往往不愿或者没有实力支持本国需要优先

---

① 白钦先，王伟. 各国开发性政策性金融体制比较［M］. 北京：中国金融出版社，2005：169 - 174.

发展的产业和领域，在此背景下，德国最早的开发性金融机构——德国复兴信贷银行（Kreditanstalt für Wiederaufbau，KfW）应运而生。1948 年 11 月 5 日，《德国复兴信贷银行法》颁布实施，此后德国政府依据该法创立了德国复兴信贷银行。随着开发性金融立法体系的不断完善，德国的开发性金融机构步入规范发展的快车道，为德国本土的百业振兴和经济发展奠定了良好的基础。

德国开发性金融立法体系概述

德国也是大陆法系国家之一，因此也极为重视成文法的作用，在实际的立法工作中，更加强调法律的系统化、法典化。德国国内的法律主要分为公法和私法两类，这一点在金融机构的划分以及相应的立法中也有明显的体现。根据相关的金融立法规定，德国的金融体系主要包括三类金融从业机构：第一类是根据私法成立的商业性金融机构；第二类是根据私法创立的合作性、互助性银行；第三类是根据公法设立的开发性金融机构（公立银行）。不同类型的金融机构都有相应的、专门的成文法予以规制。例如，德国国内的商业性金融机构都必须按照《银行监管法》《金融集团监管法》以及欧盟的部分金融监管法律的规定开展业务，接受中央银行的监管。但是，德国的开发性金融机构，比如复兴信贷银行就无须接受上述法律法规的监管（个别条款除外），而只接受专门性法律——《德国复兴信贷银行法》的监管和约束，其监管主体也并非德国中央银行或者欧盟的金融监管组织，而是德国联邦财务部和联邦经济与技术部共同履行法律监督职责。《德国复兴信贷银行法》对 KfW 的资金来源、股权结构、法律地位、职能业务、主体机构、财务制度、利润分配以及监管框架等内容有明确的规定，为 KfW 业务的开展及功能的发挥提供了法律依据和制度性保障。

目前，德国国内的开发性金融机构的股东基本都是联邦政府和州政府，它们不以营利为目的，根据专门性金融立法从事特定领域、特定性质的资金融通业务。目前，德国的开发性金融机构主要包括复兴信贷银行、不动产抵押贷款银行以及经济发展均衡银行等，其中复兴信贷银行是德国最重要的开发性金融机构。

不动产抵押贷款银行是以不动产或者类不动产性财产（比如，大型船舶、航空器等）为抵押品，向德国地方政府或者其他具有公共性质的机构发放长期贷款的专业性银行，它主要通过在资本市场发行债券来募集信贷资金。1990 年，德国政府颁布《抵押银行法》，正式将抵押银行及其业务纳入监管框架。《抵押银行法》规定了一系列关于抵押银行开展业务的基本原则：第一，保证金原则。该法规定，所有抵押债券和市政债券的发行，必须有同等数量或者等值的抵押品或者市政贷款做保证，目的是防范信用风险，守护好投资的安全边界。第二，一致性原则。该法要求抵押银行发行的抵押债券和市政债券必须与其所持有的保证贷款期限一致，杜绝期限错配问题的出现。第三，优先赔偿原则。该法规定，在银行因资不抵债或其他原因申请破产时，抵押债券和市政债券的持有者对抵押贷款索赔享有绝对优先权。①

经济发展均衡银行的资金来源主要是长期借款和发行债券。它设立的主要目的是向德国国内的贫困人口等特殊群体提供贷款，以及处理联邦清算局信托或者委托的金融业务。此后，随着国内经济形势和金融需求结构发生变化，该银行的业务重心转为向中小微企业提供信贷、向环保项目提供融资、扶持社会性信贷行动以及向高新技术创业等活动提供信贷支持。经济发展均衡银行在缩小群体间收入差距、促进中小企业成长以及维护地区间、产业间的生态平衡和共同发展等方面发挥了重要作用。

德国复兴信贷银行作为德国最早成立运行的开发性金融机构，在德国战后经济重建、再工业化以及促进经济均衡、持续和健康发展过程中都发挥了关键性作用。根据《德国复兴信贷银行法》的规定，KfW 是一个"公共法律机构"，其主要作用是对"联邦政府有特殊政治或经济利益的项目"提供信贷支持。KfW 的主要职能有：对有益于战后重建和促进德国经济发展的项目发放贷款，对从事出口贸易的德国本土企业发放贷款，对以上两类经济活动提供担保。随着德国经济的恢复和发展以及产业结构的调整，KfW 的资金投放重心也在悄然发生转变。20 世纪 50～60 年代，资金重点流向基础设施和电力、煤炭和钢铁等基础性工业部门；60～70 年代，资金投放的重点转向对外发展援助项目；70～90 年代，资金重点支持中小企业、环保、高新技术、住房以及出口等产业，尤其注重对中小企业的信贷支持，为中小企业的技术创新和产品出口提供了强大的资金保障；90 年代以来，资金投放的目标群体更

---

① 白钦先，王伟. 各国开发性政策性金融体制比较［M］. 北京：中国金融出版社，2005：175－177.

加多元化，个体经营者、初创企业、地方和市政当局、市政企业和其他类型的社会机构、联邦各州的发展机构和信用机构以及开展国际业务的大中型企业都是其目标群体，信贷投放的领域涉及住宅物业、教育、市政能源供应和城市节能改造、气候和环保项目以及出口金融和对外投资等国际业务。KfW不仅拉动了国内需求，促进了德国国内经济的发展，同时有力地推动了德国企业"走出去"战略的实施，加快了德国企业的国际化进程。

经营理念和治理体系——以德国复兴信贷银行为例

自主决策，自主经营

在创立伊始，德国复兴信贷银行的"政策性"特征非常明显，突出表现在资金的投放领域和信贷规模方面，即必须严格遵循政府的指令和政策要求，更加注重扶持性和援助性。自20世纪80年代以来，随着国内外经济和金融形势的变化，KfW也逐步走上了市场化转型和改革的道路，其政策性和商业性业务被拆分，拆分后成立的商业银行不再享受政府的优惠待遇，而是作为独立的商业性金融机构独立运行，而保留的政策性业务也更加突出"开发性"的特征，政策性业务虽然不以营利为目的，但是在实际的业务运作中，严格遵循金融治理和风险管理的要求，在项目审核、信贷资金投放方面更加具有独立性，在保证财务稳健和风险可控的前提下，自主决策，自主经营，不需要相关政府部门的审批，政府不再进行干预。

市场化的融资模式

经过市场化改革，KfW的信贷资金由最初的政府注入变为通过发行债券从国际、国内货币市场和资本市场获得。目前，KfW已经成为国际资本市场中最大和最活跃的债券发行人之一，由于其发行的债券长期稳定地获得国际权威信用评级机构的3A级评级，因此KfW债券也成为国际市场机构投资者选择和认可的重要资产类别。KfW通过发行债券募集的资金以欧元和美元为主，此外澳元和英镑也是重要的货币单位。根据KfW官方统计数据，2016年其总共发行了超过700亿欧元的债券，所募集的资金极大地提高了其信贷投放能力，增强了经营的稳健性和可持续性。

政府给予必要的信用支持和担保

根据《德国复兴信贷银行法》的规定，对于向KfW提供的贷款和由其所发行债券相关的所有债务、由KfW签订的定期远期交易合约或确定的交易权、向 KfW 发放的其他贷款以及由 KfW 明确担保向第三方提供的贷款，均由德国政府无条件提供担保。KfW 的债权人有权向德国联邦政府直接提出索赔。《德国复兴信贷银行法》还明确规定，联邦政府对 KfW 承担"机构责任"，即保证其具有健全的经营基础，并在其发生财务困难时提供资金或以其他方式提供必要支持。KfW 代表政府承担 50% 的贷款风险，在操作中，政府通过两种方式进行补偿：第一，政府从预算中向 KfW 的风险基金以 1% 的利差拨付现金；第二，政府和 KfW 各承担 25% 的第一债务人风险。虽然政府是银行债务的最终承担者，但是在实际运行中，只有政府指定的业务产生的亏损才能享受政府的补贴，其他业务则由 KfW 自负盈亏，自行承担后果。此外，根据德国行政法的相关规定，德国政府有保障 KfW 经济基础的义务，即必须保证 KfW 正常运营并按时履行契约义务。

治理结构和监督机制

经过数十年的发展，KfW 已经形成了较为完善的银行治理结构。KfW 的治理主体机构为执行董事会和监事会。根据《德国复兴信贷银行法》的规定，除法律或章程另有规定外，由执行董事会负责开展 KfW 的业务和管理 KfW 的资产，董事会主席原则上由政府授权的财政部部长担任，董事会成员中必须有 7 名政府官员。监事会负有持续监督业务开展和资产管理、任免执行董事会成员、批准年度财务报表、任命审计人员等职责。监事会由 37 名成员组成，构成主体包括：联邦财政部部长、联邦经济事务和能源部部长；联邦议院和联邦参议院任命的成员；抵押银行、储蓄银行、合作银行、商业银行和在工业贷款领域表现突出的信贷机构委派的代表；来自工会、市政、工业、农业、商业以及住房等行业的代表。其中，监事会主席和副主席由联邦财政部部长、联邦经济事务和能源部部长分别担任，每年交换一次职位。KfW 作为依据独立性、专门性公法而设立的开发性金融机构，除个别业务指导、人事参与等内容外，不受德国中央银行即德意志联邦银行的监管，而是由德国财政部、联邦经济事务和能源部联合监管，且监管的范围仅限于"法律监管"。此外，KfW 还必须接受独立的审计人员的审计以及政府指定的监察机构的监察。

各国开发性金融立法和治理探索达成的共识

开发性金融在促进经济包容性增长和均衡发展，提高资源配置效率等方面的成效有目共睹，无论是发达国家，还是发展中国家，都意识到发展开发性金融的必要性和迫切性。同时，经过几十年的探索实践，各国关于开发性金融机构的立法、运作机制、治理结构以及监管等问题达成了一定的共识。

保持开发性金融立法与商业性金融立法的协同性和一致性

各国政府，尤其是市场经济高度发达的国家，都非常注重开发性金融的专门性立法，并严格地将金融类法规区分为针对商业性金融的一般性银行法、证券法等法律法规，以及针对开发性金融的单独的开发银行法、农业发展银行法、进出口银行法、住房银行法、中小企业银行法等法律法规两大类。比如，在日本的金融法律体系中，不仅有适用于普通商业银行的《银行法》，而且还包括分别适用于各类开发性金融机构的专门性法律。德国复兴信贷银行之所以被世界银行称为"健康的开发性银行"，根本原因在于《德国复兴信贷银行法》的有力保障与规范约束，业务开展有法可依、有据可查，既有充分的自主权，又接受政府部门的监督，同时其与商业性金融机构建立了融洽的业务合作关系，形成了和谐的互补机制。

立法先行——开发性金融机构依法设立和运行

在开发性金融领域，无论是发达国家还是发展中国家，"先有立法，后创制机构"是通行的国际惯例，即使是由其他机构转型而成的开发性金融机构，也必须遵循这项原则。以韩国为例，"二战"以后，韩国的现代金融制度逐步确立和完善，开发性金融机构（其前身为"专业银行"）与普通商业银行一起构成韩国金融体系的"第一金融圈"，韩国国内主要的几家专业银行都是根据相应的专门性法律创立的：集中为韩国产业投资提供信贷支持的韩国产业银行是根据 1953 年颁布的《韩国产业银行法》创立的；专门为韩国国民发放长期住房贷款的韩国住房银行是根据 1967 年颁布的《韩国住房银行法》创立的。再以美国为例，美国的联邦土地银行是根据 1916 年通过的《联邦农业信贷法》设立的，联邦住房贷款银行是根据 1932 年颁行的《住房贷款银行法》创设的，美国进出口银行是根据 1945 年颁行的《进出口银行法》设立的。而国际性或区域性的开发性金融机构，其成立更是遵循已有的法律，不过这里所提到的"法"是指国际法而非国内法。例如，世界银行和亚洲开发银行是分别通过缔结《国际复兴开发银行协定》和《亚洲开发银行协定》而成立的。①

组织结构和业务运作应当成为立法重点关注的内容

各国针对开发性金融机构的立法和规制的重点是机构组织与业务运作两方面。开发性金融法律规范不仅对机构的组织结构，如法律地位、法律性质、职责权限、组织形式、内部机构设置、人事安排、机构变更、终止的条件与程序、权利与义务、法律责任与处罚、监督机制等做出规定，而且对开发性金融机构的业务范围、资产与负债业务、经营原则、财务与会计、外部关系等问题做出规范与限定，是开发性金融机构组建与开展业务活动，实现其既定目的与宗旨，发挥其职能作用的法律依据，是处理开发性金融机构与商业性金融机构业务关系的法律依据，同时是国家对开发性金融机构进行监督、管理的法律依据。因此，在立法时应当重点关注开发性金融机构的组织结构和业务运作问题。

注重开发性金融的公共性与市场性的动态平衡

开发性金融既不同于传统的政策性金融，又有别于商业性金融，它是兼具公共性和市场性的一类特殊的金融业态和金融活动。随着金融深化的逐步推进，金融业态日益多元化，私人金融和公共金融的边界更加难以厘清，进而对于金融的公共性和市场性的界定和划分也更加困难。开发性金融的一个重要职能是发挥引导性作用，弥补市场失灵和提供公共产品，促进金融资源的优化配置。而在一个开放的金融生态中，哪些金融具有商业性和市场性，哪些具有公共性，在实务中是非常难以界定的，因此很可能造成开发性金融的"越位"或者"缺位"，出现开发性金融与商业性金融业务交叉，或者因为分工不明而出现相互推诿，使得部分领域无法及时获得信贷资源，影响经济的稳定和可持续发展。因此，应当格外重视开发性金融的市场性和公共性的平衡，以法律规范的形式确定相关标准、边界和业务细则，并根据宏观调控的要求、产业政策的变化以及金融需求结构的变迁适时进行调整，达到两

---

① 邢会强. 我国政策性银行向开发性金融机构的转型及其立法［J］. 法学杂志，2007（1）：65 - 68.

者的动态协调和平衡，最终促使私人金融产品和公共金融产品都实现帕累托最优。

对开发性金融机构实施差异化监管

开发性金融机构在法律地位、设立宗旨和目标导向、资金来源和负债结构以及经营原则等方面都显著区别于商业性金融机构，因此对开发性金融机构的监管应当有别于传统的商业性金融机构。但从各国针对开发性金融机构的法律治理、监管政策和监管实践来看，还未形成科学审慎的差异化监管体系。在实际运作中，大部分开发性金融机构主要参照商业性金融机构的监管指标和监管手段进行风险管理和流动性管理，因此其监管效果很可能大打折扣，同时也不利于建构宏观审慎的金融监管体系。对于开发性金融机构而言，实施差异化的监管有助于提高其监管的有效性、针对性和科学性。鉴于此，各国监管当局应当根据本国金融结构特点，开发性金融机构的发展程度、组织形式以及业务范围等因素，建立与本国开发性金融机构相适应的，包括安全性指标、合规性指标、流动性管理指标、信用风险管理指标、资本充足率指标在内的一揽子监管指标体系，对本国的开发性金融机构进行分类指导和差异化监管，引导开发性金融机构确立符合自身发展的定位和目标，走出一条特色化、差异化的发展道路。

法律的修订和完善要做到与时俱进、动态调整

开发性金融机构立法与国家对经济的宏观调控密切相关，随着不同时期政府政策目标的不同，许多国家也适时地对开发性金融法律进行修改、补充乃至重大调整，以适应新形势的发展。与之相对应的是，开发性金融机构的业务也根据修改后的法律要求而有所调整和转向，以及时应对复杂的社会经济变化，实现国家的政策意图与目标。以德国为例，自1948年11月5日颁布《德国复兴信贷银行法》开始，根据国内、国际经济金融形势的变化以及政府政策目标的调整，德国政府相继于1949年8月18日颁布《德国复兴信贷银行相关法律修订与补充法案》、1951年12月4日颁布《德国复兴信贷银行相关法律第二次修订法案》、1961年8月16日颁布《德国复兴信贷银行相关法律修订法案》、1969年5月20日颁布《德国复兴信贷银行相关法律修订法案》、2003年8月15日颁布《有关联邦共和国

促进性银行重组的法律——促进性银行重组法案》以及 2013 年 7 月 4 日颁布《德国复兴信贷银行相关法律和其他法律修订法案》，真正做到法律的与时俱进和动态调整。

市场化运作和风险防控是开发性金融机构发展的重要保障

对开发性金融机构而言，其稳健运行的关键是优良的业务，因此应当坚持市场化的运作模式，以保本微利为原则；同时，强调整体的业务平衡，不断完善经营管理，构建科学合理的风险管控以及项目开发和评审制度，只有这样才能为开发性金融的发展奠定良好的基础。

我国开发性金融立法和监管

以国家开发银行为代表的开发性金融机构，在我国经济发展和产业结构优化方面发挥了重要作用，特别是在消除"两基一支"① 及其配套领域的发展瓶颈方面起到了不可替代的作用。虽然开发性金融在业务实践中取得了良好的成效，但是仍然存在许多问题，突出表现为立法的缺失和监管的缺位。

在立法方面，我国应当学习和借鉴他国在开发性金融立法领域较为成熟的经验，并结合我国经济金融运行的环境和本土资源禀赋，统筹规划、分别立法，在法律的内容上应当既体现普遍性原则，又考虑基本规则与不同机构业务特殊性、规范性要求的有机统一，真正走出一条有中国特色的开发性金融可持续发展道路。从我国目前开发性金融机构和政策性金融机构的发展状况来看，可以考虑采取单一、分散的立法模式，以现有开发性金融机构和政策性金融机构为基本主体，由其单独的法律规范组成我国独具特色的、初步的开发性金融法律体系。在立法步骤方面，可以考虑先由国务院制定和颁行《国家开发银行条例》等行政法规，对开发性金融机构创设的目的、法律地位、资金来源、业务范围、财务会计制度、税负减免以及公司治理结构等内容进行明确的界定和规范，使开发性金融机构真正有法可依。待时机更为成熟时，再行考虑由全国人大常委会制定和颁行法律位阶更高的一般性法律，

① "两基一支"是指基础设施投资、基本建设投资和支柱产业。

这实际上也符合开发性金融立法的动态调整规律和基本要求。①

在监管方面，应当坚持差异化监管的监管策略，针对开发性金融机构的特点，制定更具适用性的监管规则和监管标准，提高监管的科学性和有效性。在监管机构方面，应当设立一个专门的监管机构——开发性金融监管委员会，由其行使监管职责，负责制定相应的金融监管规范和监管标准，加强宏观审慎监管，监测和评估开发性金融机构运行的潜在风险；注重微观审慎监管，细化监管指标，集中收集监管信息，统一调动监管资源，全面加强对开发性金融机构的信用风险监管、合规性监管以及流动性监管等，保证其稳健运行，不发生系统性和区域性金融风险。② 此外，还应当加强金融监管协调机制的建设，完善开发性金融监管委员会与"一行三会"及财政部、发展和改革委员会等主管机构的常态化协调沟通机制，信息及时共享，有效解决开发性金融机构日常运行中遇到的问题，推动其持续、稳健发展。

---

① 邢会强．我国政策性银行向开发性金融机构的转型及其立法［J］．法学杂志，2007（1）：65 – 68.

② 李志辉，黎维彬．中国开发性金融理论、政策与实践［M］．北京：中国金融出版社，2010：362 – 365.

第二篇　国际开发金融机构特性

第三章　多边开发性金融机构

世界银行集团

世界银行集团（World Bank Group，WBG）下属的国际复兴开发银行（IBRD）与国际开发协会（IDA）是集团内部主要负责向发展中国家提供贷款和赠款的机构。IBRD 作为全球最大的发展银行，共有 188 个成员。IBRD 有两大目标：2030 年前消除绝对贫困和持续地促进共同繁荣。IBRD 主要通过为中等收入国家与资信可靠的低收入国家提供贷款、担保、风险管理产品和发展经验，协调区域与全球行动，应对挑战，实现目标。

资金来源和主要经营数据

2015 年，IBRD 共发行 21 种货币债券，筹集了相当于 577 亿美元的资金。同时，IBRD 具有强劲的资本实力和股东支持。根据 2011 年 3 月 16 日世界银行集团理事会通过的普遍与选择性增资决议，IBRD 的认购资本预计将增加 870 亿美元，其中 51 亿美元将在 6 年时间内缴付。截至 2015 年 6 月 30 日，IBRD 的总认购资本达 627 亿美元，与增资相对应的实缴资本达 37 亿美元。

按照 IBRD 的发展宗旨，IBRD 承担的金融风险主要是其贷款和担保项目中所隐含的国别信用风险。衡量 IBRD 风险的一个总体指标是股本占贷款比例。IBRD 根据其财务和风险严格控制这一比例。截至 2015 年 6 月 30 日，这一比例为 25.1%（见图 3.1）。

IDA 的主要资金来源是合作伙伴政府捐款，其他资金来源包括 IBRD 净收入转移、国际金融公司（IFC）赠款和借款国偿还 IDA 信贷的回流资金。国际开发协会第 17 次增资（IDA 17）所含的时间范围是 2015～2017 年，总资金为 337 亿特别提款权（相当于 508 亿美元）。50 个伙伴国（包括 4 个新捐资国）提供 172 亿特别提款权（相当于 261 亿美元）捐款，其中 7 亿（相当于

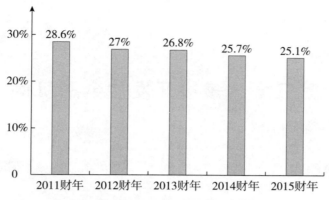

图 3.1 国际复兴开发银行股本占贷款比例

11 亿美元）以优惠贷款中所含赠款成分提供。伙伴国提供 29 亿特别提款权（相当于 44 亿美元）优惠贷款或 22 亿特别提款权（相当于 33 亿美元）的扣除赠款成分的贷款。出资伙伴还将提供 30 亿特别提款权（相当于 45 亿美元）补偿多边债务免除倡议的债务豁免。IDA 接受国的信贷回流提供了 92 亿特别提款权（相当于 139 亿美元）。世界银行集团内部通过 IBRD 与 IFC 收入转移及相应投资收入共计 21 亿特别提款权（相当于 32 亿美元）。

　　IDA 第 17 次增资的主题是实现最大化发展成效，帮助 IDA 国家更好地利用私营部门与公共部门资源及知识，更强调结果有效性与成本有效性。而 IDA 将秉承第 17 次增资的宗旨，与 IBRD 合作在全球、区域与国家层面开展工作。

　　2015 年，国际复兴开发银行新增承诺贷款 235 亿美元，涉及 112 个项目。欧洲和中亚（67 亿美元）与拉丁美洲和加勒比地区（57 亿美元）获得的新增贷款最多，随后是东亚和太平洋地区（45 亿美元）。按承诺部门划分，公共管理、法律与司法获得承诺贷款最多（43 亿美元），随后是金融（34 亿美元）以及能源与采矿（32 亿美元）。除贷款外，IBRD 还向客户国提供金融产品，帮助各国提高发展项目资金的使用效率，管理货币、利率、大宗商品价格和自然灾害等风险。世界银行司库执行了相当于 33 亿美元的对冲交易，4 300万美元的灾害风险管理交易以及分别用于管理 IBRD 资产负债表风险与 IDA 资产负债表风险的 240 亿美元和 7.27 亿美元的调期交易。

　　国际开发协会同样承诺资金 189 亿美元，包括 159 亿美元信贷、24 亿美元捐款及 6 亿美元担保。非洲地区获得的承诺资金（104 亿美元）最多；南亚（58 亿美元）、东亚和太平洋（18 亿美元）也获得了较大份额资金承诺；随后是欧洲和中亚（5.27 亿美元），拉丁美洲和加勒比地区（3.15 亿美元）以及中东与北非（1.98 亿美元）。孟加拉（19 亿美元）与印度（17 亿美元）是 IDA 最大的受援国。

IDA 承诺资金中用于基础设施的为 58 亿美元，其中包括能源与采矿、交通、供水、环境卫生与防洪、信息通信等。大量承诺资金投向公共管理、法律与司法（39 亿美元）及医疗卫生与其他社会服务领域（37 亿美元）。按主题划分，获得承诺资金最多的依次是人力资源开发（41 亿美元）、农村发展（33 亿美元）及社会保障与风险管理（32 亿美元）。

工作亮点

国际社会在 2015 年所做决定对全球是否有能力实现 2030 年前消除绝对贫困的目标产生了深远影响。世界银行集团向其成员和私营企业承诺了大约 600 亿美元贷款、赠款、股权投资和担保。其中，IBRD 承诺资金总额为 235 亿美元，IDA 承诺资金总额为 189 亿美元。国际金融公司为私营部门发展提供了 177 亿美元，多边投资担保机构为紧急的基础设施项目等各类投资提供政治风险和信用增级担保 28 亿美元。世界银行集团全部工作都是围绕两大目标展开：可持续地消除极端贫困和促进共享繁荣。在全球各个洲，世界银行集团的工作都取得了相应成果。

在非洲，2015 年度世界银行集团共批准了非洲项目 103 个，总价值 116 亿美元，其中包括 IBRD 贷款 12 亿美元，IDA 承诺资金 104 亿美元。投入最多的领域依次是：公共管理、法律和司法（30 亿美元），医疗卫生和其他社会服务（28 亿美元），以及交通运输（12 亿美元）。世界银行集团在非洲的业务主要包括支持区域一体化发展，应对灾害与冲突对发展的影响，提高电力使用，支持小农发展，提高农业生产率，以及为受到埃博拉疫情影响的国家设计并实施经济复苏计划。

在东亚和太平洋，世界银行集团为该地区批准了 57 个项目，共计 63 亿美元，其中包括 IBRD 贷款 45 亿美元，IDA 承诺资金 18 亿美元。重点投资领域包括：水、卫生和防洪（12 亿美元），公共管理、法律和司法（12 亿美元），交通运输（12 亿美元）。世界银行集团在该地区重点关注五大领域：包容与赋权、就业与私营部门发展、治理与机构建设、基础设施与城镇化、气候变化与灾害风险管理。世界银行集团同样关注对性别歧视、灾害应对和冲突与贫困等跨领域问题的分析。

在欧洲和中亚，世界银行集团为该地区批准了 54 个项目，共计 72.27 亿美元，其中包括 IBRD 贷款 67 亿美元，IDA 承诺资金 5.27 亿美元。投入最多的领域依次是：能源和采矿（14 亿美元），交通（11 亿美元），公共管理、法律和司法（11 亿美元）。世界银行集团与该地区 9 个国家签署了 19 项可补偿咨询服务（RAS）协议，总价值 1 600 万美元。RAS 协议为医疗卫生与教育体系改革、公共部门治理与机构能力建设、投资气候改革、基础设施投资计划与管理等问题提供了技术建议。世界银行集团在本地区的战略重点包括两方面：以就业、环境、社会、财政可持续性及气候行动提高竞争力，实现共享繁荣。公共部门治理与性别问题是两大战略重点中的优先领域。

在拉丁美洲和加勒比地区，世界银行集团为该地区提供了 60.15 亿美元，支持了 33 个项目，其中包括 IBRD 贷款 57 亿美元，IDA 承诺资金 3.15 亿美元。投资最多的领域依次是：医疗卫生与其他社会服务（16 亿美元），公共管理、法律与司法（13 亿美元）以及教育（10 亿美元）。世界银行集团根据该地区迫切的需要为其提供了多种量身定制的金融、知识与服务，包括提高生产力，加强贸易一体化，加强灾害风险管理，以及营造高质量的教育与就业环境。世界银行集团通过多种方式满足这些需求，包括建立项目融资、气候投资基金等创新机制；开展深入研究，例如，编写了研究报告《伟大的教师：如何加强拉丁美洲与加勒比海地区学生的学习》《拉丁美洲与崛起的南部：改变世界，变革重点》。

在中东和北非，世界银行集团为该地区批准项目 17 个，总计 34.98 亿美元，其中包括 IBRD 贷款 33 亿美元，IDA 承诺资金 1.98 亿美元。世界银行集团还为西岸和加沙地带的 6 个项目批准了 7 500 万美元作为特殊融资资金。投入最多的领域依次是：能源与采矿（10 亿美元），水、公共卫生与防洪（6.11 亿美元），以及医疗卫生和其他社会服务（6 亿美元）。

未来，世界银行集团声明仍将秉持在 2030 年前消除绝对贫困和可持续地促进共同繁荣的目标，积极探索新途径，加强与各成员和私人投资机构的合作，共同促进世界的发展。

专栏3－1 世界银行集团结果导向型融资工具

当代社会发展更强调结果的实现和制度的强化。无论是政府官员、社会成员，还是私人企业家，都希望社会发展项目能提供可持续性结果并建立相应高效的制度。为了满足这项日益增长的需求，世界银行集团率先提出了结果导向型融资工具。

与传统的建设拨款或者低于市场利率的优惠贷款不同，结果导向型融资模式以提高政府和企业的效率与绩效为主要目的。施贷方和受贷方事先约定一定的条件或达标准则，根据企业运营的效率与绩效，给予相应比例的资金支持，资金并非一步到位，这样可以较好地避免贷款人在获得资金后不履行承诺的现象。不过，结果导向型融资也存在项目数据获取困难，对项目监控和检测执行不利等问题。根据世界银行集团的研究，虽然结果导向型融资方式与传统融资方式相比难度大，但它的边际效益远远超出边际成本，值得推广和借鉴。

一、结果导向型融资工具的特点和评估方法

由世界银行集团倡导的结果导向型融资工具具有以下5个特点：

1. 资金支持贷款人的项目。结果导向型融资工具可以支持整个项目或其中的子项目，新项目或现有项目，国家项目或地方政府项目，单个部门项目或多部门项目。结果导向型融资通过促进合作伙伴关系、调整合作伙伴的目标和结果，使得世界银行集团的发展援助得到充分利用，从而进一步提高发展的效益。

2. 依据项目取得结果支付资金。结果导向型融资工具将资金支付与特定项目结果的实现情况直接挂钩。世界银行集团在商定的结果取得并确认后向项目支付资金。结果的评价标准在结果导向型融资的准备阶段商定。

3. 专注于制度设计能力的提升和项目流程的强化。结果导向型融资工具将帮助项目实施国进行能力建设，提高其效率与绩效，使项目实施国达到实际的、可持续性的项目结果。能力建设和制度强化被整合到政府项目中。当能力提升后，项目结果也更可能有显著持久的影响。

4. 保证银行资金使用得当。结果导向型融资工具将保证项目相关的环境和社会问题得到妥善处理。为此，世界银行集团要进行适当的尽职调查、评估和监测，保证对项目实施进行实时监管。

5. 向所有成员提供。结果导向型融资向世界银行集团所有成员提供，并且与投资项目融资及发展政策性融资一起作为世界银行集团三大融资工具。对融资工具的选择取决于贷款者的需要和所面临的发展问题。

目前，世界银行集团使用结果导向型融资工具支持贷款国项目一般会对以下 4 个方面进行评估：

1. 确定对政府项目的支持范围。

2. 识别项目的关键目标和衡量这些目标的指标。

3. 评估项目的技术可靠性，项目受托的容量和能力，项目的环境、社会和制度安排，以及其他可能影响项目发展目标实现的因素。

4. 锁定可以提高项目能力和改善制度安排表现的措施，并将这些措施贯穿到项目实施过程中。

世界银行集团通过对项目相关因素进行评估，使结果导向型融资工具更好地推动项目结果的取得以及相关制度的建立和改进。结果导向型融资工具的实施包括监督制度安排的表现，监督和核查项目实施的结果两个方面。

二、结果导向型融资工具已在全球广泛使用

自 2012 年世界银行集团提出结果导向型融资工具以来，该融资机制取得了巨大成果。结果导向型融资工具在全球不同类型国家中均有使用（从经济脆弱型国家到中等收入国家），并涉及非常广泛的领域。截至 2016 年 7 月 7 日，全球共有 46 个项目使用了结果导向型融资工具，总值达 116 亿美元，支持了总值达 551 亿美元的政府项目。

摩洛哥国家人类发展倡议是首个使用结果导向型融资工具的项目。该项目致力于改善当地居民获得参与地方治理机制、基础设施使用、社会服务和就业机会的途径。埃塞俄比亚卫生领域也是一个使用结果导向型融资工具的例子。国家支持卫生部门发展计划的实施，优先帮助埃塞俄比亚实现了与健康相关的联合国千年发展目标。该项目的实施展示了结果导向型融资工具对推动与其他发展伙伴（例如，英国国际发展署和联合国儿童基金会）合作所发挥的作用。越南农村供水和环境卫生项目则在结果导向型融资工具的支持下，实现了向红河三角洲地区的 8 个省的居民提供充足的水源、良好的卫生条件和卫生服务的目标。

三、京津冀空气污染治理创新融资计划

京津冀空气污染治理创新融资计划是世界银行集团在中国及其能源行业首次使用结果导向型融资工具。该计划旨在通过提高能源效率和增加使用可再生能源，减少空气污染和碳排放，而结果导向型融资工具将使资金支付与项目实际取得的结果更好地联系起来。该计划的投资总额预计为 14 亿美元，其中世界银行集团提供贷款 5 亿美元，华夏银行投入配套资金 5 亿美元，其余 4 亿美元为子项目借款人的股权出资。该计划主要在以下 3 个领域开展工作：

1. 提高工业和建筑业的能源效率，降低煤炭消耗，通过采用太阳能、风能和生物质能技术增加可再生能源供应等。

2. 采取污染治理措施，减少污染空气排放。这些措施包括：安装末端设备用于微粒去除，烟气脱硫、脱硝；煤改气；用电动车和压缩天然气动力汽车替代柴油车辆等。

3. 提高华夏银行的机构组织能力，包括设立绿色信贷中心，设立内部绿色信贷程序，开发和试行创新融资模式与产品，为员工提供有关能源效率和清洁能源融资的培训等。

该计划于 2016 年 5 月 22 日实施，预计 2022 年 6 月 30 日结束。该计划设定 9 项评估标准，其中主要包括碳排放减少量、二氧化硫排放减少量，建立使用识别系统、风险评估系统和绿色贷款系统的绿色融资中心等。世界银行集团在评估标准达到预期目标后才会批准对项目支付资金。该计划将为我国国务院制定的《大气污染防治行动计划》设定的目标助力，帮助商业银行推进绿色信贷的主流化。这体现了结果导向型融资工具支持贷款国项目，调整项目与贷款国发展目标相一致，从而使项目更好发挥效益的特点。

根据世界银行集团结果导向型融资工具对项目实施的促进作用、对结果取得的持续性作用，以及对项目国能力和制度的提升作用，我国可以在生态环保、工业技术改进、农业生产等领域积极采用结果导向型融资工具，加强项目结果取得的可持续性，提高相关领域的制度能力和效益。

亚洲开发银行

近年来，全球发展呈现动荡趋势，亚洲开发银行（简称"亚行"）始终致力于减少贫困、推动可持续发展以及控制气候变化等。为了面对亚太地区发展所面临的挑战，亚行显著增加了自身的行动，践行着"更强、更好、更快"的理念。

资金来源和主要经营数据

亚行的资金来源分为普通资金（OCR）、专项基金以及联合融资。普通资金包括实收资本、营业余额和债券发行收益。2015 年，亚行的法定股本为 1 475.5 亿美元，认缴资本为 1 470.5 亿美元（见图 3.2）。OCR 的收益及未实现收益为 10.96 亿美元。专项基金达到了 8.12 亿美元，其中大部分来自亚洲开发基金（Asian Development Fund，ADF）。值得一提的是，在 2015 年 4 月，亚行通过了将亚洲开发基金中的贷款资产组合与 OCR 在资产负债表中进行合并的决议，这将大大提高亚行的所有者权益。亚行在 2015 年共筹集 189.5 亿美元的中长期资金和 40.8 亿美元的短期资金。

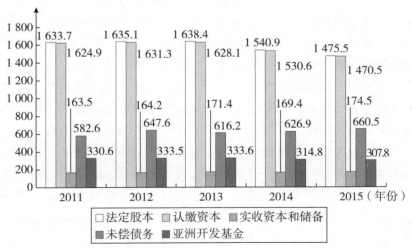

图 3.2　亚行 2011～2015 年资金来源（单位：亿美元）

2015 年，亚行批准投资项目总额达到271.71 亿美元。其中，164.36 亿美元由亚行自行承担，107.35 亿美元由联合融资伙伴承担。亚行发放给发展中国家的贷款和补助金为162.9 亿美元（包括主权投资项目和非主权投资项目），这笔资金由亚行普通资金、亚洲开发基金以及其他专项基金提供，其中专项基金提供了1.41 亿美元的技术援助款项。除此之外，联合融资伙伴提供了107.35 亿美元。亚行贷款及补助金支出总额为122.3 亿美元，借款（来自OCR）为202.7 亿美元，这一项较2014 年增加约38%。运营收入（来自OCR）为3.4 亿美元，较2014 年减少近40%（见图3.3）。

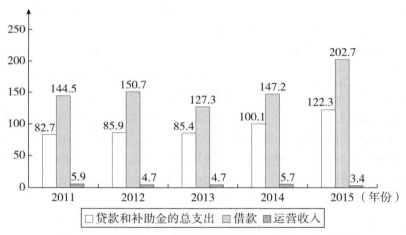

图 3.3　亚行 2011～2015 年支出和收入（单位：亿美元）

工作亮点

推动绿色可持续发展

2015 年，联合国可持续发展目标获得通过；2015 年 12 月，在第 21 届联合国气候变化大会上，195 个国家一致通过了《巴黎协定》。未来，亚行将致力于在这两个成果的资金支持方面发挥核心作用，继续促进亚太地区的包容性经济增长以及环境可持续发展。2015 年，亚行在清洁空气、交通、城镇发展、水源、教育等领域的投资均超过了 20 亿美元。同时，亚行持续关注气候变化，并发挥着领导作用。

支持区域发展与合作

西亚与中亚。由于受到全球经济下行以及大宗商品价格下跌的影响，西亚与中亚地区增长乏力。亚行致力于加强当地的基础设施建设、促进区域合作和一体化，以及加快包容性增长。2015年，亚行在提高当地民生方面批准了54.2亿美元的贷款，这些贷款主要用于能源、交通以及公共部门管理等领域。2015年，亚行支持了该地区大量知识共享计划，尤其是在能源、环境和交通领域。在区域合作及一体化方面，亚行在2015年投资了38亿美元，这将带来联合融资方面约4.06亿美元的杠杆效应，使发展成果惠及更多的人。

东亚。2015年，亚行向东亚地区提供了20亿美元的贷款，主要用于农村及农业发展、能源以及基础设施建设等领域。其中，亚行向中国提供了17.3亿美元，包括农村地区基础设施建设、道路建设、农业、自然资源、气候变化和教育等方面的12个项目。环境和气候变化、包容性增长和社会保护、政策支持和发展伙伴关系是亚行支持该地区的三大重点。亚行向中国批准了第一个基于政策的贷款，用于减少京津冀地区的污染。与此同时，亚行继续支持中亚区域经济合作（CAREC）项目，促进地区合作。

太平洋地区。2015年，太平洋地区经济增速放缓。亚行向该地区批准了1.78亿美元的贷款，其中大部分被用于交通领域。亚行在该地区重点关注基础设施建设、环境及气候变化、减少贫困及包容性增长等方面。通过太平洋基础设施咨询中心（PRIF），亚行与世界银行集团、欧洲投资银行一道，帮助该地区解决环境治理问题和基础设施问题。

南亚。2015年，南亚成为亚太地区经济增长最为迅速的地区。这一年，亚行向该地区批准了38亿美元的贷款及补助金，其中对印度的援助占48%，对孟加拉国和斯里兰卡的援助分别占30%和13%。这些款项主要用于交通、能源和金融领域。基础设施建设、减少贫困和包容性增长、环境和气候变化是该地区的三大重点。亚行提供2亿美元用于尼泊尔震后学校、道路以及政府的重建。

东南亚。2015年，亚行向东南亚地区提供了34.7亿美元的贷款，主要用于能源、金融和基础设施建设等领域。预计在接下来的3年中，亚行将把该地区投资的44%用于交通、能源和城市的基础设施建设。同时，亚行继续推进东南亚地区的教育计划，金融包容性将成为亚行在该地区的关注重点。

提升私营部门竞争力

2015年，亚行私营部门业务在投资方面达到历史最高的26.3亿美元，较

2014 年提高了 37% 。在商业联合融资以及官方联合融资方面，私营部门业务也分别积累了 45.6 亿美元和 2 490 万美元。亚行相信，私营部门是增长的关键动力，也是减轻贫困问题的重要途径。通过改善商业环境、扩大融资方式，亚行帮助私营部门创造了更多工作岗位，提高了亚太地区人们的生活水平。亚行私营部门业务主要聚焦于能源（特别是可再生能源和清洁能源）、设立小额信贷的金融机构以及中小企业融资。

机构改革

由于全球经济增长引擎在变化、亚太地区需求增加等原因，在亚行《2020 战略》中期检查的指导下，亚行进行了一系列机构改革。2015 年，亚行继续推进 2014 年引入的采购改革，这些改革措施减少了采购时间，提高了执行效率。1 000 万美元以上的业务办理时间缩短了 14 天。亚行致力于培养高能力、高潜力、高水平的员工，这将保障亚行始终充满活力和创新力，始终以结果为导向。

美洲开发银行

美洲开发银行（Inter-American Development Bank，IDB）近几年主要面临两大挑战：保障 IDB 成员在过去数十年取得的经济和社会发展成果，协助其尽快从发展的泥淖中走向繁荣的正轨。拉美和加勒比地区的经济总量依旧在缩水，部分经济体的缓慢增长并没有改变其余经济体衰退的颓势。在这样的背景下，美洲开发银行坚持与其成员进行双边对话，并竭力在多年调查研究的经验中寻求发展的道路并与之分享。

主要经营数据

相较于 2014 年，2015 年年末美洲开发银行的资产总额从 1 062.3 亿美元上升至 1 112.4 亿美元。从资产负债表来看，资产总额的上升主要源于贷款损失准备金的上升，这有可能是因经济不景气使违约增加所致。

在 2015 年，美洲开发银行的资产负债表虽然依旧在扩张，但其中一些数据值得关注，部分甚至预示着潜在的风险。经其批准的贷款额已经连续第二年下降，仅为 104 亿美元，而这一数值仅和 2011 年水平相当。其投资收益虽然在 2012 年达到了 3.82 亿美元的巅峰，但是在 2015 年仅为 6 000 万美元，这也反映了当地经济不景气的状况。

工作亮点

2015 年，美洲开发银行共批准通过了 171 项、总价值 112 亿美元的项目计划。其中 151 项投资性运作价值 76 亿美元，20 项政策性贷款价值 36 亿美元。2011 ~ 2015 年美洲开发银行的年均批准项目金额达到 123 亿美元，超过 2006 ~ 2010 年的年均 109 亿美元。

美洲开发银行于 2015 年批准的 171 项计划分布于多个领域，包括能源、交通、金融、城市发展等。这些项目可划分为四大类，其中社会类 21 项，资金占比 22%；贸易相关 52 项，资金占比 8%；基础设施和环保建设计划 52 项，资金占比 39%；发展机构计划 46 项，资金占比 31%。而在私营部门和非主权担保项目中，有 88 个是非主权担保项目，总计 22 亿美元。

在捐赠和无偿技术合作方面，美洲开发银行遭遇一定的挫折——业务发生一定的缩水。2015 年，银行运作 71 项捐赠和贷款基金，其中包括 19 项普通资本特别项目/捐赠，42 项个人和多方信托基金，以及 10 项金融中介基金。在 2015 年年底，这些基金总值为 8.94 亿美元，相比 2014 年下降 22%。但美洲开发银行在 2015 年创立了两项新的捐款方的信托基金：双边韩国基础设施发展联合融资基金和多方捐赠拉美和加勒比农业基金。此外，美洲开发银行技术合作业务的 61% 用于支持客户对贷款操作的准备、执行和评估，另有 30% 用于金融研究和宣传其产品。

2015 年，美洲开发银行通过和 69 个积极合作伙伴的 121 笔交易，共筹资 38 亿美元，其中超过 2.69 亿美元属于捐赠融资，剩余 35 亿美元源于共同融资。来自韩国战略与金融部、中国人民银行以及巴西国家银行经济和社会发展担保委员会的融资占总筹资的 93%。2015 年，美洲开发银行与其合作伙伴在公共和私营部门的合作也有显著的进步。美洲开发银行与其合作伙伴的长期合作，譬如和北欧发展基金在可持续发展方面的合作，旨在整合再循环利用的包容性区域循环，并提出倡议，为拉美和加勒比地区的发展提供了支持和帮助。

作为区域政策性银行，美洲开发银行的主要目标仍然是提高本区域居民的生活水平。在宽带业务、居民安全、城市可持续发展等需要各个部门高效合作的领域，美洲开发银行取得了骄人的成绩。

1. 宽带业务：美洲开发银行继续推进宽带业务的发展。该项目将促进区域间创新，争取实现区域内全民覆盖和全民享有相关服务。而互联网的普及给各国带来了诸多附加价值，墨西哥的医疗健康项目、多美尼加的金融包容工作、加勒比地区工业生产的扩张都从中获益。此外，当地居民、企业和公共机构获取数字服务的渠道也借此得以完善。

2. 居民安全：美洲开发银行改进了相关数据库和数据平台。犯罪和暴力相关数据的录入、整合和分析全部在新平台 DataSeg 上进行，并作为居民安全指数向公众开放。这一数据平台可以帮助政府当局、学界和社会分析了解犯罪的起因，也有利于相关政策的制定。

3. 城市可持续发展：通过将更多的城市纳入新兴和可持续城市倡议，美洲开发银行推动了城市可持续发展。截至 2015 年年底，已有 55 座城市被纳入该计划，总人口达到 5 700 万。而新兴和可持续发展城市倡议带来的资本撬动则更引人瞩目，每 1 美元的银行储备资本能带来 2.25 美元的杠杆，而这些城市获得的技术援助总计达到 6 500 万美元。

在拉美和加勒比地区的快速发展中，各国的借贷需求也随之增长。为此，美洲开发银行重新评估了银行的资本状况并且对资本进行了一定程度的扩张。这项工作自 2010 年开始，被称为"第九次资本扩增"［Ninth Capital Increase (IDB-9)］。2015 年，拉美和加勒比地区面临出口萎缩、经济下行的新挑战。为了应对这一情形，同时为了提高工作的相关性、效率和效用，美洲开发银行在 IDB-9 的框架下推行了一些新的计划。

自从通过第九次资本扩增的决议后，美洲开发银行逐步开始获得资本注入。2015 年年底，第一轮资本、第二轮资本、94% 的第三轮资本和 84.7% 的第四轮资本已全部支付，总额接近 13 亿美元，这也使得银行特殊项目基金（FSO）新增 4 730 万美元。

此外，美洲开发银行在海地地震后的灾后重建工作也值得关注。震后至今，银行为海地提供了接近 13 亿美元的项目捐助，使海地经济、生产和社会状况均有显著改善。银行董事会连续 5 年特批从普通资本中转移 2 亿美元至项目赞助账户。这不仅显著带动了当地的投资发展，也有利于海地经济和社会的可持续发展。

美洲开发银行继续落实其发展战略。战略的两大支柱——消除贫困和社会不公，以及支持经济、社会和环境可持续发展——均要求美洲开发银行在现有的制度和技术基础上继续发展。

部门框架文件（Sector Framework Documents，SFDs）为银行制定新的战略和规范性工具提供了指导。这些于 2012 年设立的文件，为美洲开发银行及其成员应对大范围的挑战提供了一个多变的框架，也为相关项目组提供了富有意义的战略指导。到 2015 年，美洲开发银行于 2012 年设定的 20 个SFDs目标全部完成。

在协助弱小国家和不发达国家方面，美洲开发银行承诺，每年贷款总额的35%将发放给这些国家。此外，在 2015 年，美洲开发银行近50%的新开发项目都旨在改善这些国家的经济社会状况。FSO 和普通账户发放给这些国家的贷款总额已经达到53 亿美元。与此同时，美洲开发银行还为东加勒比地区的国家通过了可持续发展能源项目，以提高当地能源使用的多样性。据估计，该计划将提高相关国家的竞争力和宏观经济稳定性。

在私营部门方面，美洲开发银行持续关注 IDB-9 设定目标的完成情况。2015 年，美洲开发银行通过的大多数减贫和提高社会公平的项目都重点支持中小企业和住房。此外，美洲开发银行也为可再生能源、能源使用率、绿色金融项目进行融资。在私营部门融资中，26% 用于区域一体化，57% 用于减贫。

第九次资本扩增的会议议程提出建设更好的美洲开发银行，其内容包含改革和主动求变，旨在 3 个方面——执行效率、工作效果和透明度——进行审慎思考并提高。为了达到这些要求，一方面，美洲开发银行研发了一些新型工具。发展效用矩阵（Development Effectiveness Matrix，DEM）为银行用于公共和私营部门的操作提供了保障。这些操作的深度逻辑性、循证解决性将被考量，同时其目标也将和美洲开发银行以及各成员的优先需求相匹配。另一方面，美洲开发银行更新了其宏观可持续性评估系统，以提高对债务、财政和货币变量的分析能力。在环保、社会安全保障、提高性别平等等方面，美洲开发银行都有所建树。

事实上，拉美和加勒比地区资本流入依旧有"骤停"的危险，考虑到与金融危机前相比，政府在财政策略上有更多的掣肘，美洲开发银行及其成员在这方面的紧迫感要求其在促进经济与生产方面做出更多努力。未来，美洲开发银行依旧将确保银行对拉美和加勒比地区的资金投入，同时保障当地的金融稳定。

专栏 3-2　　美洲开发银行的可持续发展融资项目

　　美洲开发银行是拉丁美洲和加勒比地区重要的开发性金融机构，IDB 有六大目标：减少贫困和社会不平等、解决小国弱国的需求、通过私营部门促进发展、应对气候变化、促进可再生能源和环境可持续发展、推动区域合作和一体化。

　　IDB 作为联结 48 个成员的多边开发性金融机构，自成立以来就持续关注拉美和加勒比地区的能源状况、环境保护、创业就业、教育发展等可持续发展议题。通过在拉美和加勒比地区开展的 26 个借款国的经济发展项目，美洲开发银行每年在成员创造了 20 000～30 000 个商业合同与咨询的机会，向那些对社会和经济发展有积极影响的企业项目提供资金和技术援助。

一、成立女性创业基金，为女性企业家提供金融服务

　　小型企业常年因融资难问题无法充分发挥潜力，其中女性企业家更是如此。企业家的性别所导致的贷款额度差距可以通过提供专业化的金融产品缩小。因此，美洲开发银行近年来致力于为女性企业家提供相对优厚的金融环境。

　　2013 年，"扩大对厄瓜多尔女企业家的金融服务"项目获得批准。该项目是美洲开发银行的多边投资基金（MIF）与厄瓜多尔 Banco Pichin-cha 银行在 2008 年建立的合作伙伴关系的延续。作为向拉美和加勒比地区的民营企业提供技术援助的牵头者，MIF 通过提供无偿技术合作资金，加强对厄瓜多尔女性领导的中小企业的融资支持。这将促使厄瓜多尔改进风险分析工具，开发针对女性企业家的专业化金融产品及服务。同时，MIF 通过提供无偿技术合作资金支持 Banco Pichincha 银行扩展面向小企业的融资服务。IDB 将小额信贷的对象扩展到 32 465 家中小企业，远超项目的原定目标。

　　2016 年 2 月，美洲开发银行与美国国务院及在线小额贷款机构 Ki-va. org 联合成立女性创业基金，贷款将被用于发掘女性创业者的经济潜能，为其筹融资提供方便。接下来的 5 年，美洲开发银行将以 Kiva. org 为平台，利用 Kiva 众筹的风险承受力高的社会资本，为 100 万女性创业者提供人均 450～10 000 美元的贷款。

二、推动可再生能源开发，助力城市可持续发展

2016 年 2 月，美洲开发银行宣布为哥伦比亚共和国的可再生能源私人投资项目提供 930 万美元的贷款。此前，哥伦比亚国土的 60% 无法连接到本地电网，而 IDB 的贷款将帮助私营企业为哥伦比亚提供公共电力设施，推动可再生能源科技的开发。该项目贷款来自气候投资基金，贷款的利率固定为 0.75%，投资回收期为 5 年，宽限期为 10.5 年。IDB 的贷款通过哥伦比亚国民外贸银行（Banco de Comercio Exterior de Colombia S. A.）发放。

2016 年 3 月，美洲开发银行参与世界银行启动的"可持续城市全球平台"（Global Platform for Sustainable Cities，GPSC）项目。该项目由世界银行联合非洲开发银行、亚洲开发银行、南部非洲开发银行、美洲开发银行、联合国环境署、联合国开发计划署和联合国工业发展组织共同实施，旨在提供最先进的工具，推广可持续城市规划和融资的综合性方法。预计未来 5 年内，GPSC 可筹集 15 亿美元用于资助 11 个发展中国家的城市可持续发展规划。通过共享数据、经验、理念和城市问题的解决方案，推动加强城市的长期可持续性，从而惠及更多的城市。

同年 4 月，美洲开发银行发布报告，呼吁联合国应优先将迫切的住房问题列入新城市发展议程。近期由美洲开发银行与国际仁人家园组织共同发布的住房研究报告表示，世界各国政府应当达成具有纲领性及财务性的承诺以保证提供足够的、可负担及安全的住房。该研究报告认为，为了改善到 2030 年全球将有 8.81 亿人居住的简陋住房，以及额外提供给 11.8 亿人的基本住房需求，将住房问题列入各国政府优先议程是当务之急。

三、关注气候变化，提高气候变迁项目融资

2016 年 4 月，美洲开发银行年会在巴哈马首都拿骚召开，年会重点讨论了气候变迁对拉丁美洲和加勒比地区各国经济的负面影响，以及加强投资对抗气候变迁的相关计划。美洲开发银行气候变迁及永续组组长强调，该行非常重视气候变迁对区域经济的影响，该行评估，到 2050 年，海平面上升、全球气温升高或气候高度不可预测性将导致拉丁美洲和加勒比地区各国国内生产总值（GDP）平均下降 2%~4%，2020~2030 年，拉丁美洲和加勒比地区的气候变迁投资每年仍有 750 亿~800 亿美元的缺

口，而该地区目前的相关投资额还不到缺口的 1/3。因此，美洲开发银行和美洲投资公司（IIC）设立目标：2020 年前增加气候变迁相关项目融资，该目标预计每年将为气候变迁有关项目增加 40 亿美元的融资。该目标与 2015 年联合国举办的巴黎气候变化大会目标完全一致，美洲开发银行将优先协助各国执行《巴黎协定》，并帮助各国将其转化为实体投资项目。

欧亚开发银行

2015 年，受国际原材料商品价格下跌以及西方对俄制裁等因素的影响，欧亚开发银行（EDB）各成员的经济普遍遭受重创，6 个成员的 GDP 较 2014 年总体下降 3.2%（2014 年同比增长 1.1%），各国在整体投资下滑、国家预算紧缺、国际收支恶化、通货膨胀加速等方面都面临着不同程度的困难和挑战。经济上的这一总体趋势也体现在 EDB 的各项经营数据中。

主要经营数据

2014 年，EDB 盈利 0.06 亿美元，2015 年，EDB 未能实现盈利，共亏损 1.39 亿美元。2015 年，EDB 总资产为 28.8 亿美元，较 2014 年减少 13.5 亿美元；流动资产投资总额为 22 亿美元，同比减少 9.56 亿美元；所有者权益为 1.5 亿美元，同比减少 8.5%；资产收益率（ROA）和净资产收益率（ROE）分别为 -3.89% 和 -9.09%。EDB 的亏损和总资产的减少主要与债券的提前偿还、资产减值准备金的增加以及俄罗斯卢布和哈萨克斯坦坚戈兑美元汇率大幅走低等因素有关。

2016 年，EDB 的净收入为 1.63 亿美元，而 2015 年净亏损为 143.6 亿美元。减值利息损失条款确立前的净利息收入为 1.092 亿美元，同比增加 1 630 万美元。这一改变得益于银行采取的以下措施：

由于 2015 年年末及 2016 年该行的证券被回购，利息支出由 1.331 亿美元大幅减少至 0.843 亿美元（36.7%）。

银行可供出售金融资产的利息收入从 2015 年的 490 万美元增加到 2016 年的 1 850 万美元。

2016 年，EDB 致力于提高其贷款组合的可靠性，恢复了 5 450 万美元的减值损失拨备。

2016 年，由于与世界银行国库资产交易的回报增加，EDB 的非利息净收入达到 3 020 万美元。而 2015 年，由于设立了高达 6 439 万美元的权益工具减值亏损拨备和其他资产减值拨备，非利息净收入为负数。通过优化运营费用的使用模式，严格预算纪律，2016 年运营费用同比减少 12.3%。

截至 2016 年 12 月 31 日，EDB 的资产增加了 3.74 亿美元（13.0%），达到 32.6 亿美元。客户贷款总额为 14.8 亿美元，较上年同期减少 1 720 万美元。期末发行债务证券为 11.6 亿美元，较 2015 年年底减少 3.4%。股本增加 1.678 亿美元（11.2%），达到 16.7 亿美元。

工作亮点

在信贷和投资领域，2015 年 EDB 的流动资产投资涵盖了 6 个成员的 62 个项目，其中包括 3 个新增项目（两个实体经济项目，一个金融行业的项目，其投资总额为 0.59 亿美元），其中哈萨克斯坦和俄罗斯的投资项目分别占投资总额的 39.6% 和 31.9%。此外，共有 21 个项目处于审核阶段（已通过预先批准阶段），30 个项目处于项目建议书分析阶段，各成员项目数量占这部分项目总数的比重和 2014 年相比没有太大变化，排名前三的成员分别是哈萨克斯坦、俄罗斯、白俄罗斯。根据 EDB 在 2013～2017 年的发展战略，EDB 重点关注的投资领域仍然是能源、机械制造、化工、采矿、油气工业和基础设施，其中能源领域所占比重最大，占总投资额的 25.1%。在选择优先发展项目时，EDB 始终秉持着把成员经济需求和竞争力与银行自身资源和任务结合起来考虑的原则，制定适合每一个成员的切实目标。

EDB 成立的主要任务是通过投资活动促进成员市场经济的发展，实现经济可持续增长并且不断扩大成员之间的经贸往来。EDB 一切经营活动的宗旨是为一体化进程的深化和经济可持续发展的实现创造条件，从而为成员带来社会经济效益。

促进欧亚一体化进程仍然是 EDB 的基本目标。EDB 高度重视投资项目中的一体化项目，并期望通过实施这些项目在欧亚一体化方面取得成效。根据 EDB 在 2013～2017 年的发展战略，至 2017 年年底，具有一体化成效的项目应当不少于投资总额的 50%，而 2015 年，这一比重达到了 53.85%。自 EDB

开始运行以来，由投资组合项目带来的相互投资的总增长量为 18.99 亿美元。通过分析这一数据，EDB 便能够利用投资项目评估和监测系统定期对投资项目是否符合 2013~2017 年发展战略做出评估。

促进经济可持续发展是 EDB 的另一个重要目标，它决定了产量的增长、就业率的提高、预算的有效性、投资的启用和民间资本的流入、市场经济制度的建立和基础设施的开发。可以说，EDB 参与实施的项目具有巨大的社会经济效益，这些项目平均每年可以创造 46.66 亿美元的总产值。同时，EDB 投资组合具有乘数效应，它能够促进产量的增长和相关行业附加值的增长。2015 年，EDB 项目为可持续发展做出的最显著贡献之一就是为各成员创造了或计划创造近 2.3 万个就业岗位。同时，国家预算也通过税收的增长得到一定程度的补充。此外，EDB 的经营活动都建立在社会生态责任的基础之上，旨在提高自然资源利用率和保护生态环境。在选择和实施项目时，EDB 始终遵循 2012 年出台的《欧亚开发银行生态与社会责任政策》中对投资活动的社会生态因素进行监控和考量的相关规定，这使得 EDB 借款人能够参与社会生态问题管理体系的研究和协助工作，最大可能地避免出现社会生态不良后果，保障融资项目对可持续发展的贡献。2015 年，EDB 继续参与各个多边金融机构的生态与社会标准工作小组，并且积极与各方就投资活动中的生态与社会责任问题交换经验。

欧亚一体化与发展基金（EFSD）是 EDB 的下属机构，其资金由 EDB 管理，主要目标是确保成员长期经济稳定和促进经济一体化。EFSD 通过贷款支持预算、收支和本国货币平衡，并提供投资信贷为国际项目融资。2015 年，EFSD 为总额 34.7 亿美元的 12 个项目融资，同比增长 11%。

2015 年，EDB 继续与各大国际组织保持密切合作，如联合国开发计划署（UNDP）、世界银行（WB）、亚洲开发银行（ADB）、欧洲复兴开发银行（EBRD）等。这些卓有成效的合作对 EDB 成员经济发展问题的解决做出了巨大贡献。同时，EDB 还积极参与达沃斯世界经济论坛、博鳌亚洲论坛、彼得堡国际经济论坛、金砖国家与上合组织金融论坛等大型国际论坛和会议。

非洲开发银行集团

面对全球范围内严峻的经济形势，非洲开发银行集团（AfDB）以实现经济的包容性增长和绿色增长为主要发展目标，深化实施"十年优先战略"，并将"五年优先发展计划"（High 5s）作为战略优先发展领域，致力于"点亮非洲，为非洲提供足够的食物，实现非洲工业化、区域一体化，以及提高非洲人民的生活水平"，助力非洲经济的持续增长。AfDB所提出的"十年优先战略"指明了非洲10年内的发展目标和发展方向，成为非洲发展道路上的一盏指明灯。

主要经营数据

AfDB由3个机构组成：非洲开发银行、非洲发展基金会和尼日利亚信托基金会。其法定资本由80个成员认缴，其中包括54个非洲国家和26个非洲以外的国家。截至2015年12月31日，AfDB的法定资本共计928亿美元，认缴资本共计907亿美元，已缴资本共计68亿美元，通知即缴的资本共计840亿美元，总准备金共计40亿美元。2015年，AfDB投资共计88亿美元，其中63亿美元由非洲开发银行提供、21亿美元由非洲发展基金会提供、1 732万美元由尼日利亚信托基金会提供。

AfDB在2015年批准了241项业务，批准了100项共计66亿美元的贷款，批准了87项共计6.5亿美元的拨款。在2015年AfDB批准的业务中，基础设施建设部门占48.9%，共计43亿美元；财政部门占21.6%，共计19亿美元；交叉部门占12.5%，共计11亿美元；社会部门占9.1%，共计8亿美元；农业与农村发展部门占7.9%，共计7亿美元。

AfDB通过绑定全球大型基准债券与满足特定需求业务的方式发行中长期债券，并与多边合伙人、双边机构、政府和当地企业开展联合融资业务。

工作亮点

2015年，基础设施建设（主要是运输和能源领域）依然是AfDB支持的重点。

"十年优先战略"重点支持的部门

AfDB"十年优先战略"重点支持的部门主要包括基础设施建设部门（能源、运输、水资源与环境卫生以及通信领域）、私营部门、区域一体化部门、管理部门以及技能与人类发展部门。

能源部门。2015年，AfDB批准能源部门的业务共计12亿美元，占基础设施建设的28.3%，其中贷款和拨款共计11.6亿美元，占能源部门业务总额的96.7%。

环境与气候变化部门。2015年，AfDB的工作重点之一就是加强非洲对气候变化的适应能力，并缓和非洲的气候变化。AfDB宣布将增加其对气候变化应对的资金支持，预计于2020年达到每年50亿美元的资金支持。

交通运输部门。2015年，AfDB批准交通运输部门的业务共计24亿美元，占所有基础设施建设业务的55.9%，在基础设施领域的所有部门中居于首位。

水资源与公共卫生部门。2015年，AfDB继续加大对水资源与公共卫生领域的投入，在该领域批准业务共计5.5亿美元，同时继续主办并且支持3个相关项目：农村水资源供应和公共卫生项目（RWSSI）、多方捐助者水资源合作伙伴项目（MDWPP）、非洲水利设施项目（AWF）。

区域一体化部门。2015年，AfDB批准区域一体化部门的业务共计20亿美元，相较2014年增长了33.3%。在其所批准的所有地区性业务中，交通运输所占比重达到了40.2%，居于首位，其次是财政部门、贸易部门和能源部门。2015年11月，AfDB董事会批准了新区域一体化政策和战略，旨在创造一个更大的、更有吸引力的市场。

私营部门。2015年，AfDB批准的由私营部门支持的业务共计22亿美元，比2014年下降了1.9%，其中金融部门所占比重最大，达到42.9%。2013年，CEC Africa（CECA）公司作为一个泛非洲的私营公司成立，致力于推动南撒哈拉非洲的电力项目的运转。

经济改革和管理改革部门。截至2015年12月底，AfDB所批准的与管理相关的业务共计10.9亿美元。其中两项比较重要的业务包括对尼日尔财政改革和食物安全支持项目的共计2 000万美元的资助以及对马里应急管理和经济恢复支持项目的共计1 500万美元的资助。

技能与人类发展部门。2015年，AfDB批准了共计8亿美元以支持人类发展和社会救济，其中一项重要的业务是给予几内亚、利比里亚和塞拉利昂3 312万美元的拨款以支持其在"后埃博拉时期"的经济恢复。

"十年优先战略"重点支持的领域

农业发展。AfDB重点关注农业部门的发展，2015年批准农业部门业务共计7亿美元，并于2015年10月组织了以非洲农业转型为主题的达喀尔高层会议，包括155名政府高层代表在内的600余名各界人士参加了会议，该会议为非洲农业转型的长期战略铺平了道路。

性别问题。2015 年 4 月，AfDB 组建了由 85 个性别焦点问题组成的网络，标志着其性别战略的加速实施。在 AfDB 于 2015 年 10 月举办的达喀尔高层会议上，AfDB 主席阿肯乌米·阿德西纳（Akinwumi Adesina）宣布要为非洲妇女提供充足的财政支持。

对形势脆弱国家的支持。2015 年，AfDB 批准了 5 亿美元以支持 16 个形势脆弱国家的发展。

AfDB 新的业务战略方向。AfDB 第八任主席阿肯乌米·阿德西纳提出了"High 5s"的战略目标，即"点亮非洲，为非洲提供足够的食物，实现非洲工业化、区域一体化，以及提高非洲人民的生活水平"。"High 5s"以 AfDB 现有的战略和政策为基础，致力于推动非洲经济的快速、可持续和包容性增长。

专栏 3-3　AfDB 的"五项优先发展计划"及行动

2015 年 9 月 1 日，AfDB 第八任主席阿肯乌米·阿德西纳在其就职演说中指出，将以正在执行的 2013~2022 年战略发展计划为基础，为 AfDB 制订新的发展计划。其中，最引人关注的当数"五项优先发展计划"（High 5s），涉及能源、粮食、工业化、非洲一体化和改善非洲人民生活条件 5 项内容。这些内容对于改善非洲人民生活至关重要，与联合国可持续发展目标（SDGs）进程表也是一致的。"五项优先发展计划"提出后，AfDB 在非洲各国积极推进相关计划的实施，朝着既定的目标迈进。

一、促进非洲能源开发

非洲大陆虽然拥有丰富的资源，但是由于缺乏足够的资金和技术，一直以来，丰富的资源无法得到开采和利用。"五项优先发展计划"提出后，AfDB 通过提供贷款融资的方式，积极解决这一问题。

1. 提供一笔价值 2 400 万美元的贷款，支持跨国鲁齐齐三期水电工程项目。该项目源于三大湖区国家——布隆迪、刚果民主共和国和卢旺达的联合倡议，项目建成后将增加约 50 兆瓦的清洁能源发电能力，为该地区乃至更大范围提供充足的电力。

2. 提供一笔价值 2 亿美元的资金，支持科特迪瓦—利比里亚—塞拉利昂—几内亚区域的电力联网工程建设。工程完工后，预计将增加该区域的电力接入率，并显著降低发电成本。

二、改善非洲粮食供应

多数非洲国家仍然依赖粮食进口，成千上万的非洲孩子长期遭受饥饿、营养不良等问题的困扰，相较于其他国家同龄的孩子，他们显得更加瘦弱、矮小，在智力发育上也相对不足。粮食供应问题的解决不仅是出于人道主义的关怀，也是为非洲国家建设和经济发展提供人力和智力支持。AfDB致力于通过农业转型升级、资金支持等方式，帮助非洲国家解决粮食供应问题。

1. 2016年4月16日，AfDB主席阿肯乌米·阿德西纳在由盖茨基金会举办的有关全球营养的会议上提出了AfDB致力于解决非洲面临的营养挑战的办法。银行将首先实施一项名为"喂饱非洲"的计划，以期在10年内将非洲大陆由粮食净进口转变为粮食自给自足并有出口。银行还将利用即将于5月召开的AfDB 2016年年会，倡导有关非洲领导人采用创新、有效的金融方法增加粮食供应。

2. 2016年3月22~23日，AfDB内部农业与工业部门（OSAN）和转型支持部门（ORTS）在科特迪瓦首都阿比让组织了一场题为"农业与工业一体化平台（Agropoles）和农业加工地带（Agro-Processing Zones, APZ）在解决非洲粮食问题和促进工业化进程中发挥的作用"的研讨会。本次研讨会的目的在于分享成功经验并开发最佳实践方案，以解决农业转型中所面临的挑战。

三、促进非洲工业化进程

促进工业化能够推动经济增长并提供更多就业岗位，由于非洲的工业化在目前仍处于较低水平，因此AfDB大多通过支持基础设施建设来推动工业化进程，或是通过支持非洲各国经济模式多样化，达到扶持各国工业，进而推动工业化进程的目的。

1. 2016年4月，非洲可持续能源基金（SEFA）支持坦桑尼亚JUMEME农村供电公司建设300个左右的太阳能混合动力微型电网，使得坦桑尼亚农村超过10万人和2 340家小型企业能够使用电力。

2. 2016年3月初，AfDB第一副主席博阿马（Charles Boamah）与通用电气董事长兼首席执行官杰夫·伊梅尔特（Jeff Immelt）展开会谈，博阿马指出，私营企业，如通用公司，可以在缩小非洲基础设施差距和推动工业化进程中起到至关重要的作用。近年来，通用公司在非洲一些关键领域的投资持续增长，如医疗保健、基础设施、能源、石油和天然气等。

3. 2016 年 4 月 19～20 日，AfDB 主席阿肯乌米·阿德西纳访问阿尔及利亚，承诺将制定一项政策，通过创新性融资工具调动外部资金，支持三大领域发展：能源领域，尤其是可再生能源；工业化以及经济多样化；农业转型。

四、促进非洲一体化进程

AfDB 主席阿肯乌米·阿德西纳提出，通过基础设施建设，加强各国更加密切的交流，并逐步消除各国之间的贸易壁垒，促进各国更加便利地开展经济及贸易往来。

1. 2016 年 2 月初，AfDB 与非洲联盟委员会（AUC）、联合国非洲经济委员会（UNECA）联合主办了一场专家会议，讨论建立非洲大陆自由贸易区的相关事宜。该会议是正式启动非洲大陆自由贸易区谈判系列准备工作的一部分。有关非洲大陆自由贸易区路线图的谈判暂定于 2017 年结束，谈判的主要议题是改善非洲贸易现状，培育非洲自由贸易体系，深化非洲区域一体化。

2. 作为衡量非洲区域一体化进程的首次尝试，2016 年 4 月 2 日，AfDB、非洲联盟委员会和联合国非洲经济委员会共同推出了非洲区域一体化指数（ARII）报告。ARII 涵盖了生产一体化、贸易一体化、金融一体化、区域基础设施、人口自由流动五大方面，涉及 16 个指标。迄今为止，还没有一种机制能够系统地衡量非洲不同国家和地区的发展情况，ARII 系统评估了非洲大陆的现状，并指出不同国家和地区的差距，以及缩小这种差距的最佳方案。

五、改善非洲人民生活条件

除了融资支持能源、农业、工业等重点领域，推进非洲一体化进程外，AfDB 在改善非洲人民生活条件方面也做出了积极的努力。以下是 2016 年以来 AfDB 采取的一些行动。

1. AfDB 在 3 月 8 日国际妇女节当日召开研讨会，着重讨论了在交通基础设施的设计与规划方面考虑女性的需求及处境。安全问题是女性对于交通工具最大的担心所在，推广既安全又能负担得起的交通工具是城市和农村妇女共同关注的核心问题。

2.4 月 7 日世界卫生日，AfDB 重申将帮助非洲国家进一步加强医疗体系建设，更好地防治非传染性疾病，如糖尿病等。AfDB 已通过东非卓越中心计划介绍了防治非传染性疾病的关键技术，并加强了东非的医疗体系建设。

3.2016 年 3 月，AfDB 批准了一项价值 100 万美元的拨款用于即将推出的利比里亚青年就业和创业项目。该项目将支持新建 40 家可持续企业，其中 40% 由妇女拥有。该项目还将对 2 400 名学生进行培训，为他们进入劳动力市场提供更好的基础。

欧洲复兴开发银行

2015 年，欧洲复兴开发银行（EBRD）在 35 个经济体投资 381 个项目，投资总额达 90.4 亿欧元，在支持私人企业发展、加快可持续发展与包容性增长方面表现突出。2016 年，EBRD 加紧投资重点战略领域，全年共投资 378 个项目，投资总额达 94 亿欧元。EBRD 的当地货币融资项目在 2016 年达到了 93 个，2015 年这一数据是 80 个。同时，EBRD 保持对中小企业的投资力度，因为中小企业被视为潜在的经济发展力量，并能提供大量就业机会。EBRD 的转型项目也从 2015 年的 102 个发展到 2016 年的 114 个。2016 年 11 月，该行确定了最新的转型理念：使项目所在国充满竞争、包容、治理良好、绿色、弹性和集成的市场氛围，迎接 21 世纪所面临的新挑战。

主要经营数据

2015 年，EBRD 在各区域投资呈现一定的差异（见图 3.4）。在中欧和波罗的海三国、中亚、地中海东南四国、土耳其、希腊，EBRD 的投资较上一年有所增长，尤其在中亚地区，其投资额为 14.02 亿欧元，同比增长高达 74.6%。相反地，在东南欧、东欧和高加索、塞浦路斯、俄罗斯，EBRD 的投资较上一年有所下降，尤其在俄罗斯，其投资额为 1.06 亿欧元，同比减少 82.57%。此外，欧盟负债最多的成员希腊于 2015 年 3 月 29 日开始至 2020 年，可以从 EBRD 获得融资，以推进希腊经济改革，2015 年希腊从 EBRD 获得融资 3.2 亿欧元。

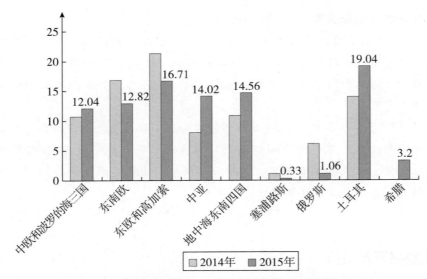

图 3.4 2014～2015 年 EBRD 在各区域的投资额（单位：亿欧元）

从投资领域来看，2015 年 EBRD 总投资项目达 381 个，32% 的投资额用于支持中小企业项目，27% 的资金投到了能源领域，22% 的资金流向农业、制造业、服务业和信息通信技术产业，19% 的资金投入城市基建与环境交通改善项目（见图 3.5）。在 2015 年新签署的项目中，5% 表现卓越，19% 表现优秀，71% 表现良好，5% 被评估为较好（见图 3.6）。

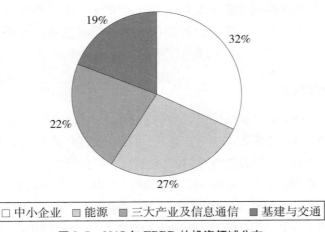

图 3.5 2015 年 EBRD 的投资领域分布

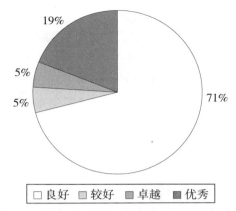

图 3.6　2015 年 EBRD 新签署项目的评估结果

工作亮点

EBRD 在应对区域危机、推进可持续发展及信息公开、创新融资渠道等方面的举措都具有重大战略意义。

援助希腊，支持希腊银行业重组

源于 2009 年 12 月的希腊债务危机已经持续多年，对希腊经济造成了巨大的打击，民众生活陷入困境。为了支持希腊国内经济改革、银行业重组以及改善希腊银行的内部治理，2015 年 EBRD 购买了希腊四大银行价值 2.5 亿欧元的股份，包括阿尔法银行（Alpha Bank）6 500 万欧元股份、欧银耳嘎斯银行（Eurobank Ergasias）6 500 万欧元股份、希腊国家银行（National Bank of Greece）5 000 万欧元股份和 Piraeus 银行 7 000 万欧元股份。希腊银行业的稳定和结构调整需要恢复储户和投资者信心，恢复信贷流动和改善对实体经济的金融支持。而 EBRD 对希腊国内银行的增资使希腊银行拥有更强大的资本实力以应对经济严重低迷时期遭遇的冲击。

推动改革进程，帮助乌克兰度过危机

2015 年乌克兰经济面临严重困难，GDP 缩水 11%，在这种情况下，EBRD 仍坚定履行支持乌克兰的承诺，帮助乌克兰度过经济危机。EBRD 致力于促进乌克兰政治对话的努力也推动了该国改革进程，并显著改善了乌克兰的商业环境和出口形势。该行签署了对乌克兰的 29 笔交易协议，价值近 9.97 亿欧元，最新签署的协议是 EBRD 与乌克兰国家油气公司 Naftogaz 关于购买冬季采暖设备的 3 亿美元贷款协议。EBRD 在乌克兰交通领域的投资表现较为活跃，与乌克兰签署的 5 项交易协议总额高达 3 830 万欧元。与此同时，EBRD 还努力促进乌克兰农业的现代化，最大限度地提高其出口潜力，中国也是乌克兰农产品主要出口国，2015 年中国占乌克兰农产品出口总额 8% 以上。该行除了用自有资金为乌克兰提供援助外，还帮助乌克兰寻找其他的融资渠道，例如促进国有企业私有化。在环境保护与区域安全方面，EBRD 除了管理切尔诺贝利核电站捐献基金外，还承诺调拨 6.75 亿欧元的自有资金支持切尔诺贝利项目。

改造供水基础设施，应对约旦难民危机

2015 年，大量叙利亚难民涌向邻国约旦，尤其是约旦北部，据统计，进入约旦的难民人数大约 140 万，相当于约旦总人口的 20%。"难民潮"给当地的基础设施造成了严重的负担。为了缓解难民用水问题，EBRD 提供资金支持约旦供水设施现代化，向约旦水务局提供 1 290 万欧元贷款用于污水管网的改造升级，这笔贷款中，460 万欧元是由该行"股东特别基金"资助的。作为辅助，欧盟居民投资机构（NIF）向约旦提供了技术援助和环境评估。

签署第 1 000 份可持续发展资源投资协议

在可持续发展方面，EBRD 对土耳其第二大 PVC 塑料门窗系统制造商 EgeProfil 的贷款标志着 EBRD 第 1 000 份可持续发展资源投资协议生成。该公司将利用 EBRD 和"清洁技术基金"（CTF）提供的 2 600 万欧元融资计划在伊兹密尔省建立一个全新的、先进的、环境友好的生产厂。该厂将集成光伏太阳能电池、废水处理、复合冷却和加热发电等功能。这笔贷款在 EBRD "零浪费计划"下使用，预计 EgeProfil 每年将回收至少 800 吨 PVC 塑料。

加入"全球援助透明度倡议"

透明度和问责制是 EBRD 自 1991 年成立以来关键的工作指导原则和主要的公共信息政策。2015 年，EBRD 在这一方面迈出了重要的一步，加入"国际援助透明度倡议"（IATI），开始与 IATI 标准保持一致。IATI 的宗旨是使有关援助项目的信息更易于被包括民间社会组织在内的公众知晓，它为 300 多家机构提供通用定义和信息发布标准，其中就包括 EBRD。EBRD 在官网上发布的工作信息采用 IATI 建议的电子格式，并能链接到 IATI 的官网上。

成立"参股基金"

EBRD 继续深化其参与股权融资的角色，为融资者提供多元化的融资选择，改善被投资企业的公司治理。"参股基金"（Equity Participation Fund）的成立获得了 EBRD 董事会的批准，该机构的设立将为全球机构投资者提供了直接参与 EBRD 项目的渠道。

EBRD 确立了 2016～2020 年三大战略方向：坚持增强投资地区的经济弹性、促进成员经济体融入区域与全球经济一体化进程、应对诸如气候变化和能源安全问题的全球区域挑战。为达成战略目标，EBRD 将坚持三大原则：发挥转型影响力、建立健全的银行体系和采用额外激励因素。为了增强自身影响力，EBRD 董事会于 2015 年通过了"绿色经济转型计划"（GET），以期在 2020 年之前 EBRD 的环境投资项目占总投资额的 40% 以上。此外，董事会还通过了"推进性别平等计划"，在未来几年着力提高女性的影响力和平等就业机会。

专栏 3-4　EBRD 的中小企业发展融资经验

2015 年以来，欧盟联手 EBRD 扶持中小企业动作频频。EBRD 与 ABC Pharmacia 公司（格鲁吉亚大型医药供应商）合作，推动该公司业务拓展；与 Autocool 公司（埃及车用空调制造商）合作，帮助 Autocool 公司重新建构公司组织结构与财务系统；帮助 Belausian 公司（白俄罗斯儿童衣食销售商）拓展业务，现在 Belausian 公司的分支机构遍布白俄罗斯主要城镇；向埃及 Europack 公司（为货物提供听装制造与包装方案服务）发放 178 万欧元贷款。

EBRD 是"二战"后美国、日本及欧洲一些国家政府联合发起成立的开发性金融机构，主要任务是帮助欧洲战后重建和复兴。自 1991 年成立以来，EBRD 在 36 个国家开展投资，总额达 954.04 亿欧元，仅 2014 年投资额就达 88.54 亿欧元，所有投资项目中仅 6% 存在风险预警。其中，向中小企业提供贷款是 EBRD 颇为成功的一个方向，资助模式通常是由欧盟提供资金，项目包括多项服务计划，主要为中小企业提供技术和必备技能，以及协助其培养商业领导人才。EBRD 的资金援助通常是直接或间接通过当地银行以及投资基金等中介机构提供，技术援助通常是利用商业开发计划帮助受惠国发展新领域，或通过商业顾问计划帮助中小企业经营者提升经营管理能力。

EBRD 向中小企业提供融资的主要做法有：

1. EBRD 通过代理行向中小企业发放贷款，代理行对此业务单独考核、单独记账，加强管理，核销坏账。

2. EBRD 根据客户的经营规模设计了相应的产品，在贷款金额、利率和期限等方面有所差异。10 个雇员以下的企业能获得 8 000 欧元以内的小微贷款。8 000 欧元的发放需要经过一段时间的审核，但是 2 500 欧元可以在小微企业提交申请后的一天内发放。雇员在 100 人以内的中小企业可以获得 160 000 欧元的小额贷款。在设置贷款利率方面，EBRD 设置了固定利率和浮动利率，小企业贷款利率要高于当地银行的其他贷款利率，但仍远低于民间借贷利率。贷款的条件也不是固定不变的，可根据项目考察和客户谈判结果对贷款条件做出一定的调整。贷款抵押物选择空间较大，土地、设备动产、公司年收入、股票等都可以作为抵押物。需要注意的是，EBRD 不接受第三方担保，因为接受担保意味着银行必须对担保人进行评估，这将影响贷款发放的效率，增加银行成本，还可能导致还款约束弱化。EBRD 的还款周期为半年一次，较为宽松的周期减轻了中小企业的还款压力。

3. EBRD 中小企业贷款审批程序相对完善。从贷前调查到贷款发放不超过一个星期的时间，从贷款发放到偿清一般为 1 ~ 15 年，基建项目清偿周期更长。贷款审批包括拟订贷款方案草案、草案再度审核、董事会审核、签署有法律效力的协议、选择贷款方式等程序。

4. 在信贷员管理方面，EBRD 规定，信贷员的收入由基本工资和奖金组成，奖金与业绩挂钩。业绩考核指标由每月新发放贷款笔数和质量构成。对于每笔新贷款，EBRD 的合作银行都有一定金额的奖励，但如果某个信贷员名下的贷款本息出现逾期情况，会视逾期严重程度决定是否扣减该信贷员的奖金，在一定程度上控制了贷款风险。信贷员的奖金一般不超过基本工资的 50%。EBRD 还建立了完善的信贷员培训机制，一名成熟的信贷员最长需要一年左右的反复培训，并经考试合格后持证上岗。小企业融资项目办公室常年举办针对不同类型人员的培训班，如微型金融初级班、快速贷款班、小型贷款班等。

EBRD 通过代理行发放贷款，根据客户规模设计不同贷款产品，建立完善的贷款审批程序和高素质的信贷队伍，以资金援助和技术援助相结合的方式帮助中小企业成长，其相对成熟的中小企业融资经验值得我国借鉴。

欧洲投资银行

欧洲投资银行（EIB）以其丰富的专业知识，坚持通过创新的手段开发新的应对方法，坚定不移地推动欧洲经济的发展和人类生存环境的改善。

主要经营数据

EIB 的贷款资金主要来自国际资本市场的债券发行。2015 年 EIB 总投资额为 775 亿欧元，旗下拥有 59.15% 股份的"欧洲战略投资基金"（EFSI）全年投资 75 亿欧元。其中，187 亿欧元用于创新及教育领域、284 亿欧元用于资助中小企业发展、191 亿欧元用于基础设施建设、196 亿欧元用于环境领域①（见图 3.7）。EIB 批准签署了 126 个项目，50% 集中在气候及环境领域，涉及欧盟 22 个国家，81 000 家中小企业从中获益。2016 年，EIB 有效地吸引了投资者，迎来投资高峰：融资 838 亿欧元，支持了 2 800 亿欧元的总投资。330 亿欧元贷款被提供给中小企业，惠及 30 万家小型公司，这些小型公司雇用了 440 万人。2016 年，EIB 筹资近 200 亿欧元用于支持基础设施建设，筹资约 170 亿欧元用于环境项目。

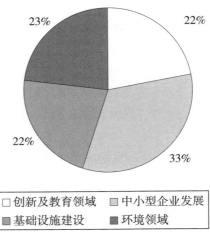

图 3.7 2015 年 EIB 各区域投资比例

---

① 由于各领域投资存在交叉，因此分领域投资额相加多于总投资额。——编者注

EIB 的原始资金来自欧盟成员的分摊，此后，发行债券成为其主要资金来源。2015 年 EIB 支持了 12 种货币交易并发行了 16 种货币的债券，89% 的债券为欧元、英镑及美元。债券的 63% 在欧洲资本市场发行，21% 发行于亚洲资本市场、14% 发行于北美洲资本市场，另有 2% 发行于中东及非洲资本市场（见图 3.8）。目前，EIB 已经成为继英国政府后最大的英镑发行者，并且是土耳其里拉、加拿大元、挪威克朗、南非兰特的市场领导者。

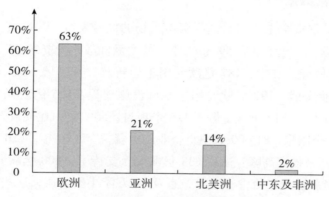

图 3.8 2015 年 EIB 债券发行市场分布

工作亮点

使命——成立欧洲战略投资基金（EFSI）

2015 年，对于 EIB 来说，意义最为重大的事件当属"欧洲战略投资基金"的成立。2013 年以来，欧盟经济年均增长率只有 0.1%，欧元区下滑了 0.4%，失业率高达 11.5%。面对如此严峻的局面，欧盟委员会主席容克携手 EIB 于 2014 年 11 月 26 日提出"欧洲投资计划"（EIF）。这项投资计划主要包含 3 个方面：提供资金担保、开发可供投资的项目、改善投资环境。2015～2017 年，该计划每年将为欧盟经济增长提速 1 个百分点，使欧盟区域内生产总值增加 3 300 亿～4 100 亿欧元，并且创造 130 万个就业机会。

为落实"欧洲投资计划"，欧盟委员会提出建立"欧洲战略投资基金"，并于 2015 年 6 月 25 日获得欧盟理事会通过，EIB 出资 160 亿欧元作为种子基金并负责管理该基金，欧盟委员会从欧盟预算中拿出 80 亿欧元为该基金提供担保。"欧洲战略投资基金"预计将以 15 倍的杠杆率撬动来自私营和公共领域的约 3 150 亿欧元的投资。

绿色——投资欧洲的未来，世界的未来

EIB 是世界上最大的气候资金提供者。自成立以来，EIB 在气候领域的投资及活动超过其余五大多边开发银行的总和。2015 年 12 月巴黎气候大会上签署的协议无疑为 EIB 未来的工作提出了新的要求，EIB 承诺为气候项目提供至少 1/4 的资金，2015～2020 年将向气候项目投入 1 000 亿欧元。

2015 年 EIB 向气候领域提供了 207 亿欧元资金，圆满完成了任务，并计划对发展中国家的气候项目增加 35% 的投资。在气候领域的投资中，33 亿欧元用于可再生能源领域、36 亿欧元用于提高能源效率、16 亿欧元用于科研创新、103 亿欧元用于低碳及环境友好型交通系统建设、9 亿欧元用于气候变化适应、10 亿欧元用于绿化及废物废水处理（见图 3.9）。

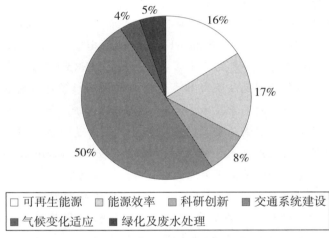

图 3.9 EIB 气候领域投资分布

EIB 希望维护自然界的生态平衡，支持促进空气清洁，维护生物多样性，致力于新能源的研发与推广，旨在保护未来孩子们的生存环境，并通过不断创新使他们的未来更加繁荣。

责任——难民问题的解决

近年来难民问题十分突出，EIB 对此反应迅速，在第一时间积极地组织难民住房建设，并在难民国家或地区增加融资项目。例如，大量叙利亚难民涌入约旦，给当地饮用水供应造成巨大压力，引发了难民与约旦原住民之间的冲突。EIB 于 2015 年 11 月同约旦签署了一份 5 000 万欧元的供水管道建设投资协议，该项目将有效缓解约旦的饮用水供应压力，并减少地区冲突。

除进行经济救助外，EIB 还支持欧洲国家加强边境建设，鼓励难民到就近国家避难，减少欧洲的外来难民数量，以缓解欧洲各国压力。

EIB 的影响力是全球性的，所以它始终肩负着应对国际挑战、助力欧洲经济发展的重任。EIB 的作用和实力正在逐年稳步增长，这一趋势在 2016 年更加明显。EIB 表示，未来还将为人类社会的发展贡献更大的力量。

专栏 3-5　EIB 集团的 InnovFin 咨询业务

为了推动科技创新和技术研发，EIB 推出了一款专为创新者融资提供帮助的金融工具 InnovFin。这款产品被设计成体系化的综合金融工具，包括中小企业担保金、中小企业创业投资金、中型企业担保金、中型企业成长金、大型项目贷款和担保产品、能源示范项目产品、传染病金融支持便利，以及 InnovFin 咨询 8 项产品。其中 InnovFin 咨询业务具有一定的特殊价值。

InnovFin 咨询业务产生的原因在于，人们认识到市场上有很多基础很好，却因为各种原因无法获得融资支持的科技创新项目。金融机构很难对这些未经市场证实的复杂技术和无形资产进行判断，但更多时候是因为科技创新项目本身难以满足融资的各项条件，或者是科技公司不知道自身适用于哪种类型的金融工具，产生融资畏惧心理。InnovFin 咨询业务专门为科技创新型企业和项目提供专业的融资建议，帮助它们充分发挥潜力。

在 InnovFin 咨询业务的组织下，来自 EIB 和欧盟委员会的专家，亲自指导客户，使得他们更容易获得融资。该服务帮助企业利用自己的特长，通过改善商业模式、治理结构、资金来源和融资结构等提高资本进入的便利性。从长远来看，这也增加了这些科技创新型项目走向市场的机会。具体来说，InnovFin 咨询业务提供如下服务：

1. 战略规划；
2. 商业模式塑造；
3. 资本结构、债务和风险分配；
4. 经典或者创新的金融工具；
5. 公司治理；
6. 股东结构；
7. 公共金融工具的有效使用。

InnovFin 咨询还包括改善创新项目融资环境的一系列活动，为特定的创新项目建立一套全新的融资机制，或者通过研究改进已有的金融工具来增加其支持创新项目的精准性和有效性。例如，InnovFin 系列第七项产品 InnovFin 传染病金融支持便利（IDFF）就源自 InnovFin 咨询的创新。InnovFin 咨询发现，传染病的防治离不开新疫苗、药物、医疗诊断设备的研发，然而这些研发活动通常投入很大、风险很高，金融机构根本无法对这些研发活动提供支持。在与欧盟委员会、多家制药公司和行业代表进行深入讨论后，InnovFin 咨询准备了一份概念文件，向欧盟委员会提出针对传染病防治研发新的融资工具，即 IDFF。该产品由欧盟预算资金作为引导资金，承担前期投资风险，待项目成熟后吸引更多社会资本进入。随后，InnovFin 咨询的工作人员与各利益相关者协同工作，深入挖掘 ID-FF 的概念，设计其运作模式和运行机制。经过设计，IDFF 包含了大量的金融工具，有标准的债务工具（如优先级债务、次级贷款和夹层融资），也有风险分担工具，金额为 750 万 ~ 7 500 万欧元，融资期限最长 7 年，由项目自身提供担保，直接向 EIB 提交融资申请。IDFF 诞生后，吸引了很多的社会资金，影响力逐步扩大。

值得一提的是，InnovFin 咨询服务独立于 EIB 的贷款或投资决策，也就是说，InnovFin 咨询不限于向客户推荐 EIB 的资金，也为客户推荐其他潜在可获得的资金，这使得创新项目和企业能够有机会得到更多的金融支持，从而获得充足的资金。

InnovFin 咨询服务的对象十分广泛，涵盖大型和小型企业、行业协会、金融市场协会等私营部门，欧盟委员会、成员、政府机构等公共部门，研究机构、基金会、非政府组织等半公共部门。

在中国，像 InnovFin 咨询这样为科技创新型企业量身打造融资方案，承担政府、金融机构、科技企业和社会资本四者之间的桥梁纽带作用，并且具备号召力的中介机构并不多见。中国的创新驱动发展战略和《中国制造 2025》战略规划的实施仅靠政府、金融机构、企业的单打独斗难以快速实现，市场需要一种黏合剂，把这些利益相关者联系起来，共同推动科技创新和技术创新。InnovFin 咨询由政府信用带动、财政资金支持、开发性金融机构运作、社会机构参与的方式以及成功的案例，为我们提供了一个很好的范例。

加勒比开发银行

作为一家致力于加勒比地区借贷成员经济发展的多边金融机构，加勒比开发银行通过为相关国家的政府、公共机构和其他团体提供项目贷款与技术援助，促进该地区的经济可持续发展与减贫。成立 45 年来，加勒比开发银行的成员总数从 19 个上升至 28 个。2015 年年末，巴西成为加勒比开发银行在加勒比地区第四个非借贷成员。

目前，加勒比开发银行正在执行新一轮五年战略计划（2015—2019 年），其项目运行进入了新篇章。2015 年，加勒比开发银行的活动主要围绕新一轮战略计划展开，旨在帮助借贷成员更好地实现联合国新议程中的可持续发展目标。2015 年，加勒比开发银行共通过贷款和捐款 2.94 亿美元，相比去年同期增加 0.24 亿美元。其中，1.97 亿美元来自"普通资金"，0.97 亿美元来自"特别资金"（SFR）。在 2015 年的机构评级中，加勒比开发银行的标准普尔评级为 AA，穆迪评级为 Aa1。

主要经营数据

普通资金

截至 2015 年 12 月 31 日，加勒比开发银行 OCR 总资产为 14.071 亿美元，比 2014 年同期增长 2.1%（0.286 亿美元）。2015 年，其资产收益率和净资产收益率分别为 1.20% 和 1.90%；共通过贷款 9.925 亿美元，其中不良贷款率为 0.54%（540 万美元）；总负债从 2014 年的 5.57 亿美元减少到 5.33 亿美元；总收益为 850 万美元。

特别发展基金（SDF）

截至 2015 年 12 月 31 日，加勒比开发银行 SDF 总资产为 9.941 亿美元，比上年同期增长 4.1%（0.393 亿美元）。2015 年，SDF 年度净亏损为 330 万美元，其中平均流动资产收益率为 0.41%，贷款收入 1 250 万美元，现金与投资收入 140 万美元，总支出为 1 720 万美元。

其他特别基金（OSF）

截至 2015 年 12 月 31 日，加勒比开发银行 OSF 的总资产为 2.651 亿美元，比 2014 年同期减少 1 440 万美元。2015 年，OSF 年度净收入为 400 万美元，其中贷款收入为 250 万美元，现金和投资收入为 330 万美元。

项目运作

在 2015 年，加勒比开发银行共通过 2.942 亿美元的贷款与拨款，其中贷款额为 2.615 亿美元，拨款额为 0.327 亿美元。2015 年贷款支出总额为 1.353 亿美元，拨款支出总额为 0.261 亿美元。

工作亮点

基础设施

2015 年，加勒比开发银行进行的基础设施项目包括：惠及 3 万余人、长约 84 公里的道路建设和翻修，以及长 12 公里的供水管的安装。同时，有 17 个新的资金与技术干预项目通过，将在安圭拉、巴哈马、巴巴多斯、伯利兹、格林纳达、多米尼加和圣卢西亚等地展开，涉及领域包括能源、交通、水、卫生和灾后应急。

技术合作

加勒比开发银行技术合作司作为连接银行和外部伙伴的重要技术合作与援助部门，在 2015 年继续通过多模块项目运作，为借贷成员提供发展支持：

1. 区域合作与一体化。加勒比开发银行向加勒比单一市场和经济（CSME）指导委员会递交的 11 个项目获批，获得 346 万美元项目款项；向加勒比论坛与欧盟“经济伙伴协定”递交的 14 个项目获批，加上之前已获批的 4 个项目，共获得 371 万美元项目款项。这些资金将作为拨款投入所有符合条件的国家，支持其贸易推广、福利改进和服务业发展，提高其在劳动力自由流动中的竞争力。

2. 加勒比贸易和区域一体化信托基金（CARTFund）。CARTFund 是由英国国际发展署委托加勒比开发银行管理的，旨在通过贸易发展和区域一体化促进加勒比与欧盟经济伙伴关系成员的经济发展和减贫。2015 年，CARTFund 的投资组合包括 14 个国家共 32 个项目，其中 18 个项目是在该年度开始的，并在年末全部完工。

3. 加勒比技术咨询服务网络（CTCS）。针对中小微企业项目，加勒比开发银行通过了 110 万美元款项，设立加勒比技术咨询服务网络体系，用于更好地提供技术援助。截至 2015 年 12 月 31 日，已有 68.2 万美元（占通过款项的 55%）被投入到 26 个技术援助项目中，包括 23 个国家和地区的培训地和 3

个直接技术援助项目，共有 480 位商界人士参与，共同探讨解决借贷成员中小微企业面临的管理、技术和运行挑战。

4. 提高卫生饮水系统覆盖率。1990～2012 年，海地的供水系统覆盖率从 19% 上升至 24%，但它仍然是加勒比开发银行 18 个借贷成员中供水系统覆盖率最低的国家。2015 年，加勒比开发银行继续与海地国家饮用水供应与卫生局（DINEPA）合作，组织为期 5 个月的治理和卫生培训项目，为来自该国环境健康相关部门与非政府组织的 41 位技术和管理人员提供网络课程与实地培训，更好地帮助海地提高卫生饮水系统覆盖率。

环境可持续性

加勒比开发银行将环境可持续性纳入其业务项目的考虑中，通过强化社区功能、增强应对气候变化韧性、降低灾害风险、加强能力建设与知识学习，以及建立伙伴关系等，在地区与国家层面强化环境治理、管理能力和公众认知。

应对气候变化：2015 年 10 月，加勒比开发银行将气候风险评估和筛查工具的使用情况设为各借贷成员提交的国家战略报告中的必需内容。

防灾减灾：加勒比开发银行为多米尼加提供了 3 000 万美元帮助其完成热带风暴艾瑞卡过后的迅速恢复，以及长期灾后重建和安置工作；为海地政府提供了 240 万美元以缴纳加勒比灾害风险保险业务的年费；加勒比灾害应急管理机构（CDEMA）得到了加勒比开发银行 9.83 万美元的技术援助资金以改善机构采购和合同管理系统。

能力建设：加勒比开发银行举办了一系列认知与宣传气候变化和自然灾害风险的培训活动，加勒比开发银行的员工和来自借贷成员相关机构的技术人员参与了这些培训。

伙伴关系：2015 年 1 月，加勒比开发银行与世界银行合作共同组织和赞助了区域研讨会。作为世界银行环境与社会保障政策修订的第二阶段磋商的一部分，本次研讨会邀请了来自 19 个借贷成员和 8 个非政府组织的代表参加。2015 年 5 月，两家银行再次联合举办了一场培训，为加勒比开发银行员工介绍了世界银行针对气候变化与灾害风险的筛查工具。此外，加勒比开发银行还与世界银行共同完成了巴哈马、巴巴多斯、圣基茨和尼维斯、伯利兹、圭亚那和苏里南的"气候风险与适应国家简况"项目。

社会发展

加勒比开发银行的社会发展项目主要分布在教育、农业与食品安全，以及性别平等等领域。在教育方面，加勒比开发银行通过了 0.705 亿美元款项（2011 年以来最高水平），用于帮助借贷成员继续发展基础教育和加大对职业技术教育培训的投资。在农业与食品安全方面，加勒比开发银行发起了数个活动和项目，旨在推动与食品安全相关的基础设施建设，改善借贷成员的食品合规评估系统。2015 年，加勒比开发银行与格林纳达政府和国际贸易中心合作开展了针对鲜果行业的食品安全合规审计，旨在帮助行业识别食品质量弱点，提出解决方案。在促进性别平等方面，加勒比开发银行 2015 年度项目中明确提及性别平等问题的项目占比 57%，比 2014 年同期增长 14%。

此外，通过基本需求信托基金（BNTF），加勒比开发银行与当地政府和社区团体合作，回应贫困地区居民需求，继续将社区赋权、性别平等、环境可持续性和整体发展作为关注重点。目前，加勒比开发银行与 BNTF 执行机构进入了第七轮和第八轮脱贫项目，表 3.1 列出了 BNTF 第七轮和第八轮项目投资分布。

表 3.1　基本需求信托基金第七轮和第八轮项目投资分布　　　　　（单位：百万美元）

基本社区设施		教育与人力资源		饮水与卫生系统	
国家	金额	国家	金额	国家	金额
多米尼加	0.923	伯利兹	3.922	伯利兹	1.150
圭亚那	1.404	格林纳达	2.453	多米尼加	0.570
牙买加	1.45	圭亚那	2.247	圭亚那	1.966
蒙特塞拉特	0.635	牙买加	3.004	蒙特塞拉特	0.534
		圣文森特和格林纳丁斯	1.555	圣卢西亚	1.136
		特克斯和凯科斯群岛	0.731		
总计	4.412	总计	13.912	总计	5.356

私营部门发展

加勒比开发银行继续把金融中介贷款作为支持借贷成员私营部门发展的

首选方式，并结合能力建设项目，更好地解决私营部门发展的几大困境，如融资、创新和企业家能力等。2015年，加勒比开发银行通过了总计为1 775万美元的两笔贷款，用于巴巴多斯的高校学生贷款和格林纳达各行业的保障性项目贷款。据估计，这两笔贷款将保证大约75家中小微企业（包括初创和已有企业）的资金需求，并为320名学生尤其是低收入家庭学生提供贷款上学的机会。

另外一个发展性干预是加勒比开发银行与世界银行、牙买加政府合作发起的培训项目，旨在促进区域内从事信息通信技术工作的青年的成长、就业和薪金提高，共有来自12个借贷成员和16个金融机构的59人参加了这个培训。

区域公私伙伴关系

为应对借贷成员政策制定者在基建方面对政府与社会资本合作的高度需求，加勒比开发银行和世界银行、公私合营基础设施咨询机构（PPIAF）、美洲开发银行、多边投资基金（MIF）合作，共同成立了区域公私伙伴关系支持部门。通过训练营、加勒比PPP工具箱开发和PPP咨询台搭建，显示了加勒比开发银行在加勒比地区基建服务传递方面的持续努力。

可再生能源与能效

为促进能源转型和发展可持续能源，2015年6月和10月，加勒比开发银行在欧盟—加勒比海投资基金和英国国际发展部倡议下分别通过了两个重要项目，445万欧元和250万英镑将对应投入东加勒比海可持续能源计划（SEEC）。目前，通过SEEC，加勒比开发银行已经为两家金融中介提供了50万美元的信贷额度，用于支持中小企业可持续能源发展。

另外，加勒比开发银行继续鼓励可替代能源的使用，并将可持续能源与能效纳入其6个项目中。例如，2015年12月通过的BWA项目，将550千瓦时的太阳能光伏板放置在4个地点，预计每年生产855兆瓦时的电力（相当于这些地点15%的现电力消耗量），并减排温室气体909吨。

伊斯兰开发银行

伊斯兰开发银行（IsDB）是伊斯兰会议组织（OIC）领导下的政府间金融合作机构，是目前伊斯兰世界评级最高的多边开发性金融机构。IsDB成立于1973

年，于 1975 年 10 月正式运营，总部位于沙特阿拉伯吉达。IsDB 的资金主要来自各成员认购的股份。截至伊历 1437 年，持股最多的 5 个国家依次为沙特阿拉伯（23.52%）、利比亚（9.43%）、伊朗（8.25%）、尼日利亚（7.66%）和阿拉伯联合酋长国（7.51%）。

主要经营数据

在伊历 1437 年，IsDB 净核准了总计为 121 亿美元的项目，比上一财年增长 13%。在上述核准资金中，国际伊斯兰贸易金融公司与 IsDB 普通资金的出资比例分别为 52.9% 与 40.6%，伊斯兰私营部门发展集团出资占比 5.5%，其他基金，如单元投资基金与宗教财产投资基金，投资额占比 0.9%，特别援助业务占比 0.1%（见图 3.10）。

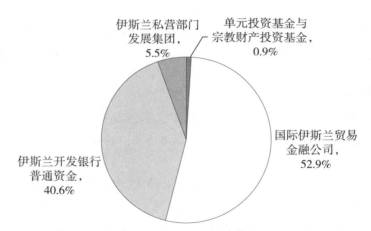

图 3.10　伊历 1437 年 IsDB 核准项目金额出资比例

在区域方面，中东与北非获得了 IsDB 54 亿美元的投资，占总投资额的 44.6%；撒哈拉以南非洲获得 36 亿美元，占总投资额的 29.8%；亚洲（除西亚地区以外）获得 25 亿美元，占总投资额的 20.6%；独联体国家获得 3.828 亿美元，占总投资额的 3.2%（见图 3.11）。在上一财年，IsDB 资助金额最多的 5 个国家分别为：埃及、土耳其、孟加拉国、巴基斯坦和塞内加尔，这 5 个国家获得的资金总额以及所占该财年 IsDB 资助总额的比例分别为：20.1 亿美元，16.6%；19.6 亿美元，16.2%；12 亿美元，9.9%；11 亿美元，9.1%；4.696 亿美元，3.9%。

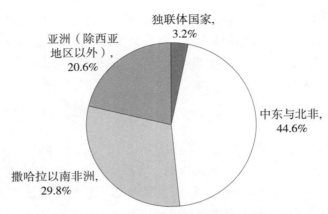

图 3.11   伊历 1437 年 IsDB 核准项目金额区域分配

在伊历 1437 年，IsDB 共支付 69 亿美元，比上一财年增加 38%。而 IsDB 在伊历 1437 年收到的还款为 28 亿美元。自成立以来，IsDB 累计支付总额为 714 亿美元，累计收到还款总额为 549 亿美元，净资源转移为 165 亿美元。

工作亮点

伊历 1437 年，在 IsDB 净批准项目中，基础设施项目所占比例最大，为 78.4%；其次是农业和农村发展项目，占 8.5%；教育项目占 6.9%，卫生项目占 4%，其余项目占 2.1%。

在基础设施领域，交通运输项目占比最大，为 46%，其次分别是能源 (29%)、水资源与城市发展 (10%) 和工业 (4%)。交通领域共有 19 个项目，总计 16 亿美元；能源领域共有 20 个项目，总计 11 亿美元；城市发展领域共有 6 个项目，总计 3.68 亿美元。

在教育领域，共有 17 个项目获批，总金额为 3.392 亿美元，比上一财年增长 75%。其中，贝宁高等教育发展项目占比最大，占总批准额的 45%。此外，IsDB 还与世界银行合作发起了"教育促进竞争力计划"，该计划涵盖 3 个方面：终身学习教育、就业教育与转型教育。

在医疗领域，共有 12 个项目获批，总金额为 1.983 亿美元，其中包括一项涵盖预防和控制传染病的奖学金项目。

其他批准的项目主要包括：若干 PPP 项目，金额总计为 7.4 亿美元；31 个农业项目，总计 4.19 亿美元；67 个科技合作项目，总计 170 万美元。

此外，IsDB 的特色运营机制在伊历 1437 年取得较好的成效。"双向链接"是 IsDB 引入的一个新概念，指的是两个发展中成员在合作互助中实现知识、技术和资源的双向流动，以达到优势互补、互利共赢的目的。在伊历 1437 年，IsDB 共发起 10 个双向链接提议，其中 3 个提议被董事会通过，分别为塞内加尔和印度尼西亚的洪水灾害风险管理合作项目、吉布提和摩洛哥的高风险怀孕和分娩监测合作项目以及苏里南共和国与马来西亚水稻生产合作项目。另外，两个合作伙伴关系也被列入双向链接的框架，包括 IsDB 与埃及发展合作委员会以及 IsDB 与阿拉伯非洲经济开发银行之间的合作项目。

在伊历 1437 年，IsDB 在组织架构调整和国际合作方面取得了显著成果：

1. 成立总裁顾问小组。该高级别小组成立于 2015 年 3 月 19 日，由 13 名成员组成，任期为 3 年，为 IsDB 以及成员的发展提供建议。

2. 财年调整。IsDB 董事会通过决议，决定将该行的财年调整为伊斯兰阳历，而保留伊斯兰阴历作为其官方日历。该调整将从 2016 年开始实施，调整后 2016 年财年的长度将会增加至 14.5 个月，于公历 2016 年 12 月 31 日结束。财年调整使得 IsDB 与世界其他主要金融机构的财年起止时间统一，便于工作与交流。

3. 提出深潜倡议（Deep Dive Initiative）。该倡议促成了 IsDB 集团与世界银行集团之间历史性的战略伙伴关系框架协议。该协议于 2015 年 10 月在华盛顿特区发布，旨在加深 IsDB 和世界银行集团在促进其共同成员经济社会发展方面的合作。

4. 建立生活与生计基金。基金总额为 5 亿美元，其中 IsDB 与盖茨基金会各出资 1 亿美元，剩余资金来自捐助者。该基金将主要用于应对成员的贫困与卫生问题。

5. 成员伙伴战略。在伊历 1437 年，IsDB 与 9 个成员更新了合作战略。其中，与印度尼西亚、土耳其和塞内加尔开展第二期战略合作；与阿富汗、喀麦隆、吉尔吉斯共和国、尼日利亚、苏丹和也门开展第一期战略合作。

IsDB 作为伊斯兰世界评级最高的多边开发性金融机构，成立 40 多年来，一直致力于促进成员以及非成员穆斯林社群的经济与社会发展，获得了稳健的经济效益与良好的社会效益，为伊斯兰开发性金融机构提供了发展的范例，也为其他国家发展多边开发性金融机构提供了有益的借鉴。

专栏 3-6　**IsDB 助力土耳其新能源发展**

推动清洁能源与节能减排项目的发展，不仅能够提高国家能源的独立性，减少对他国的能源依赖，还能够降低能源成本，提高企业的竞争力，为全球应对气候变化做出贡献。同时，还会产生促进社会发展、带动就业等一系列附加效应。土耳其政府认识到推广新能源发展的重要性，计划到 2030 年拥有 10 000 兆瓦的太阳能发电容量和 16 000 兆瓦的风能发电容量，并在其他产业领域推广节能项目。土耳其作为伊斯兰会议组织与 IsDB 的成员，其推动可再生能源发展的战略获得了 IsDB 的支持。

一、注资可再生能源与节能项目

土耳其的化石燃料储量有限，在传统能源方面对外依赖较为严重，但在包括水能、太阳能与风能在内的新能源开发方面具有巨大的潜能。在 2012~2015 年，IsDB 与土耳其工业发展银行合作进行了项目开发。

IsDB 共对 4 个可再生能源发展项目提供了资助，包括两座水力发电站、一座太阳能发电站和一座风力发电站，此外还有 6 个节能项目也获得了资助。10 个项目的投资额总计为 6.422 亿美元，其中 IsDB 投入 1 亿美元的资金。这些项目的综合收益远远超出了预期。其中，4 座新能源发电站原计划的总装机容量为 150 兆瓦，实际达到了 370 兆瓦。截至 2016 年 2 月，6 个节能项目已经减少了 100 600 吨温室气体的排放，对土耳其温室气体减排做出了 50% 的贡献。

二、修筑能源配套设施，促进居民就业

IsDB 资助建设的圭克塔什一期和二期水电站坐落于土耳其阿达纳北部的山谷深处。为配合水电工程建设，项目修建了一条总长为 52 公里的公路，为山区 7 个村镇的居民打开了通向外部世界的大门；同时，项目还修建了 3 座跨越扎曼提河的大桥，将山区与包括阿达纳和科赞在内的大城市连接起来，平均通行时间由 4 个小时缩短到 1.5 个小时。

负责建设大坝的贝拉克能源公司积极为当地居民创造工作岗位，在两个水利工程的建设过程中，有 60% 的临时雇工来自项目附近的村镇。在工作中，当地居民可以获得相关的技能培训，而此前，他们中的大多数只能依靠放牧和矿山工作维持生计。

三、帮助企业实现电能自给

除了大型的可再生能源项目，IsDB 还支持了一些小型项目，包括帮助企业实现电能自给。位于土耳其首都的博康工程与制造公司就是项目的受益者之一。2013年3月，在IsDB主导的节能减排项目的资助下，博康公司在一家工厂的屋顶安装了2 040块太阳能板，这是同等规模的太阳能板在土耳其的首次安装。得益于土耳其丰富的太阳能资源，博康公司的太阳能板在光照最为充足的7月和8月拥有75～95兆瓦的发电容量。2013年4月～2016年2月，博康公司通过太阳能板共生产出1 835兆瓦时的电能，并将超出自用范围的电能转卖给土耳其国家电力公司。截至2016年2月，博康公司已通过太阳能板项目获益25万美元。

从可再生能源中获益的博康公司已将太阳能设备的开发和生产纳为新业务，该公司目前开发了"太阳能跟踪"技术，能够使太阳能板跟随阳光转动，以最大限度地利用太阳能，这一技术将提高15%～18%的电能产量。

四、促进企业能源重复利用

目前，土耳其的能源密度（衡量一个国家能源效率的指标，指的是每单位国内生产总值所需要的能量）是欧盟国家平均值的两倍，能源使用效率不高。土耳其政府致力于降低本国能源密度，提高企业的竞争力。在IsDB主导的节能减排项目的资助下，一家名为巴提索克的土耳其水泥公司在其位于爱登附近的工厂安装了废热回收系统。这个系统利用水泥生产过程中产生的热量来发电，发电容量为5.5兆瓦，到2015年，废热回收系统已经能够为该工厂提供30%的电能，平均每天能够节省9 000美元的开销，一年能够节约300万美元的成本。巴提索克公司已经决定在该工厂附近新建一座工厂，并为其安装废热回收系统。

推广可再生能源与促进节能减排是一条漫长的道路，我们可以看到，IsDB帮助土耳其成功地迈出了关键一步。

阿拉伯非洲经济开发银行

阿拉伯非洲经济开发银行（Arab Bank for Economic Development in Africa，ABEDA）是根据1973年11月举行的第六次阿拉伯国家首脑会议的决议成立的，并于1975年3月开始运营，总部位于苏丹共和国的首都喀土穆。ABEDA

是一家独立的金融机构，享有完整的国际法律地位以及管理和财务方面的自主权，其所有者为阿拉伯国家联盟中的 18 个国家。该行的宗旨是加强阿拉伯和非洲国家之间的经济、金融及技术合作，增进阿拉伯和非洲国家之间基于平等和友谊的团结。该行理事会拥有 ABEDA 的最高管理权，理事会由来自每个成员的一位理事和一位副理事组成，其中理事通常由成员财政部长兼任。董事会则由来自持股最多的 9 个国家的 9 位常任董事和来自其他成员的两位董事组成。该行总干事由理事会任命，并出任首席执行官。

2015 年是 ABEDA "第七个五年计划"（2015—2019 年）的开局之年，"第七个五年计划"旨在进一步促进该行作为开发性金融机构的作用，满足非洲国家的发展需要，帮助非洲国家减轻贫困和实现可持续发展。该计划还向私营领域项目提供资金，鼓励阿拉伯国家的对非投资和产品出口，并为其提供技术援助。此外，ABEDA 还将继续为受援的非洲国家提供债务减免。

主要经营数据

ABEDA 主要基于"第七个五年计划"的原则和受益国政府的优先考虑来发放贷款。2015 年，ABEDA 的贷款承诺总额为 4.1 亿美元，同比增长 205%。其中，2 亿美元用于公共领域，同比增长 4.2%，共为 19 个发展项目提供资金；5 000 万美元用于私营领域，为 4 个非洲银行提升信贷限额；1.5 亿美元用于资助阿拉伯国家向非洲国家的出口；1 000 万美元用于技术援助业务，技术援助业务资金所占比例同比增长 25%。

公共领域的贷款承诺包括 4 个部分，分别为基础设施领域、农业和农村发展领域、社会发展领域以及小微贷款领域，具体分配情况如下：基础设施领域所获拨款为 1.128 亿美元，占贷款承诺的 56.4%，其中道路方面的 5 个项目占 53.2%，供水和卫生方面的 4 个项目占 37.1%，电力项目占 9.7%。农业和农村发展领域所获拨款为 3 560 万美元，占贷款总额的 17.8%，其中包括两个农村电气化项目和一个农村发展项目。社会发展领域所获拨款为 4 660 万美元，占贷款总额的 23.3%，其中包括 4 个教育项目和一个卫生项目。小微贷款领域所获拨款为 500 万美元，占贷款总额的 2.5%，由当地政府发放以抗击贫困。

私营领域贷款承诺在借款国的经济发展中发挥着重要作用，因此 ABEDA 对该领域给予越来越多的关注。1975~2014 年，ABEDA 在私营领域发放的贷款共 45 笔，资金总额为 1.169 3 亿美元，惠及工业、农业、农村发展和交通运输等领域的许多小型项目。2015 年，ABEDA 拨款 5 000 万美元，扩大了 3 家多边金融机构和一家非洲跨国银行的信贷限额，这一举动主要服务私营中小型项目和基础设施项目，旨在为当地创造就业机会，增加收入，减少贫困。

在支持进出口贸易方面，ABEDA 特别重视促进阿拉伯国家和非洲国家之间的贸易交流。2015 年，该行出资 1.5 亿美元支持阿拉伯国家向非洲国家出口，并与非洲开发银行、欧佩克国际发展基金（OFID）、IsDB 以及国际开发协会等机构开展合作。截至 2015 年年底，ABEDA 已在阿拉伯出口融资项目中投入 3.995 亿美元，其中 1.87 亿美元用于资助 29 个项目，受惠的非洲国家包括坦桑尼亚、几内亚、毛里求斯、津巴布韦、塞舌尔、赞比亚、科特迪瓦、肯尼亚、塞内加尔和冈比亚等。

在技术援助业务方面，ABEDA 向非洲国家提供了培训课程、专家支持、硬件设备等支持，并组织阿拉伯国家和非洲国家之间的经贸论坛及会议。2015 年，该行核准的技术援助业务共 35 项，拨款总额为 1 000 万美元。其中，378.5 万美元用于支持 9 个可行性研究项目，包括 7 个基础设施项目和两个农业和农村发展项目；621.5 万美元用于支持 26 个机构项目，这些机构支持项目包括采购、财政、规划、金融、农业、管理和人力资源等领域的 14 个区域性培训课程，还包括水资源、环境、农业和港口领域的阿拉伯专家服务，以及支持妇女、协助组织阿拉伯—非洲贸易展览会等相关活动。

考虑到资助项目的性质和借款国的经济情况，ABEDA 继续为资助项目和借款国提供优惠贷款。2015 年，ABEDA 贷款利率的加权平均值为 1.14%，略高于 2014 年的 1.11%；贷款期限的加权平均值为 29.94 年，略长于 2014 年的 29.47 年；而贷款宽限期的加权平均值则由 2014 年的 9.70 年缩短至 2015 年的 9.48 年。

2015 年年底，ABEDA 的净资产与 2014 年相比增加了 1.171 亿美元。但由于 2015 年全球金融市场表现不佳，证券组合的市场价值下降，ABEDA 的净收入从 2014 年的 1.892 亿美元降至 2015 年的 1 540 万美元。

2015 年，ABEDA 与其他阿拉伯金融机构合作资助了 19 个核准项目中的 14 个，合作机构包括沙特开发基金、科威特阿拉伯经济开发基金、阿布扎比发展基金和欧佩克国际发展基金等。ABEDA 共投入 6.454 22 亿美元，占项目总融资额的 24.92%，其他金融机构的投资约占 61.62%，当地政府和受益人的投资约占 13.46%。

ABEDA 一直十分重视与其他开发性金融机构，特别是阿拉伯开发性金融机构的协调，以增强项目效力并扩大自身影响：2015 年 1 月，ABEDA 参加了阿拉伯协调小组与发展援助委员会和经济合作与发展组织举行的高级别会议；2 月参加了国际农业发展基金理事会会议；10 月参加了世界银行集团和国际货币基金组织年会等高级别会议。这些会议为 ABEDA 协调项目方案、商定合作安排，以及更新自身观念提供了宝贵机会。

ABEDA 作为阿拉伯地区和非洲地区重要的开发性金融机构，为非洲国家的经济发展提供了关键的金融支持和技术援助，建立了阿拉伯国家与非洲国家之间合作的桥梁，积极促进阿拉伯资本参与非洲发展，取得了经济效益与社会效益的双赢。

拉美开发银行

2015 年，拉美经济整体呈现放缓态势。拉美开发银行（CAF）强化其反周期角色，通过 24 亿美元的快速支付与配额项目运转，以及 122 亿美元的资金批放，继续成为拉美地区，尤其在基础设施建设方面，最主要的多边资金提供方之一。作为国际发展金融俱乐部的 23 家发展银行成员之一，CAF 不断深化国际关系，推进与全球高校、智库和金融发展机构的合作网络构建，目前已经成为联结拉丁美洲和世界其他地区的重要枢纽，在国际发展尤其是环境、气候变化方面发挥了很大作用。

2015 年，CAF 批准资金 122 亿美元，创历史最高纪录，股东国家的缴入资本增额为 45 亿美元，使得 CAF 在 2016～2022 年可为拉美地区提供的贷款总额达到 1 000 亿美元；受到多家风险评级机构的认可，CAF 在主要资本市场发放了 13 只总价值达 304.4 万美元的债券；巴巴多斯成为 CAF 的 C 系列股东成员。同时，CAF 推进与"相遇学校"基金会和"美洲十万强计划"的合作，旨在促进拉美地区青少年的教育普及与社会融合；与古巴的机构及学术界开展沟通交流，并在技术方面启动相关合作。

主要经营数据

贷款： CAF 为公共和私营实体提供短期、中期和长期贷款，为项目、周转、贸易活动等提供资金，以便对投资机会进行可行性研究，同时能够更好地发展在股东国家的一体化计划和项目。为了达到信用风险管控的目的，CAF 将其贷款组合划分为主权贷款和非主权贷款。

- 主权贷款：包括给予国家、区域或地方政府或权力下放机构的贷款以及由国家政府充分担保的其他贷款。
- 非主权贷款：包括授予公司和金融部门的贷款，其中不受国家政府（公共和私营部门）保证。

股权投资：股权投资是指中远基金投资公司和基金在（CAF）战略部门的股本证券，目标是促进这些公司和基金的发展及参与证券市场，并作为催化剂从股东国家吸引资源。

借款：包括以摊余成本记录的本地或外国金融机构和商业银行的债务，除去使用利率掉期作为经济对冲的一些借款。发行以美元计值的借款相关的前期成本和费用将在资产负债表中作为直接扣除项从借款的面值中扣除并在借款期间摊销为利息费用。

信用评级：基于 CAF 在通过持续增资和更加多元化、通过扩大股东基础和股东支持巩固的股权加强的信用投资组合方面的表现，惠誉和穆迪等各大信用评级机构对 CAF 的偿付能力表示了肯定（见表 3.2）。目前，CAF 是拉丁美洲评级最高的债券发行人之一。

表 3.2　各评级机构对 CAF 的评级

评级机构	信用评级
惠誉	AA －
日本信贷评级机构	AA
穆迪	Aa3
标准普尔	AA －

重点项目运营情况

在拉丁美洲经济放缓的态势下，2015 年，CAF 共批准了 152 个项目，资金总投入 122 亿美元。相较往年，因为原材料价格下降、国际资金成本增加和门槛提高以及中国等新兴经济体发展减速，CAF 本年度的项目总量较少。

面对这一形势，CAF 及其股东国家达成共识，优先运作充足预算支持的项目，同时推动在公共领域方面的投资，取得较好效果。

CAF 本年度的经营管理具有灵活、财政实力强和反周期性支持等特点。在提高干预质量与效率的理念下，银行启动了数个战略性业务举措。在与私营部门的合作方面，CAF 积极推动生产转型，促进高质量劳动力和高附加值产业生成，注重提高生产力和创新。为此，CAF 将交通基建、能源与金融发展、农业及工业都被定义为发展干预的重点领域，继续履行其对于地区社会融合和环境保护的使命。

在项目方面，CAF 积极运用新的第三方融资机制，吸引多元股东。2015年，银行的主权项目联合融资达 2.7 亿美元，融资机构包含法国开发署（AFD）和石油输出国组织（OPEC）国际发展基金（OFID）。此外，在乌拉圭和哥伦比亚等国家，CAF 推动主题投资工具等创新产品的开发。以哥伦比亚为例，CAF 获得该国养老基金 4.117 亿美元的借款，用于发展关键项目，缩小基础设施差距，促进国家经济发展。2015 年，为应对基础设施项目的融资需求，CAF 成立了名为"拉美开发银行资产管理公司"的子机构，旨在管理直接或间接来自投资者的基金，并将它们用于机构有专业性和比较优势的领域，比如基建项目 PPP 模式或纯私人项目。

2015 年，CAF 继续在中美洲与加勒比地区积极建立伙伴关系，巴巴多斯成为机构的第 19 个股东国家。业务的地理扩展和运营项目的多样化给 CAF 带来诸多挑战。面对这一形势，CAF 也积极优化其主要的信贷流程，并巩固机构的传统优势，如敏锐、灵活和客户导向，从而优先促进区域发展的项目。与此同时，与内部信贷周期次数和 CAF 贷款的发展贡献评估相关的信息和指标项目也在开展，用于补充机构的发展策略，更准确定位机构的优势和机遇。

第四章　高收入国家的开发性金融机构

德国复兴信贷银行

正如德国复兴信贷银行（KfW）提出的要在德国、欧洲和世界范围内持续促进人们生活条件的改善，KfW 一直致力于从社会经济的各个方面提高人们的生活水平。KfW 的中心议题是全球化，工作重心是确保德国和欧洲的市场竞争力和促进其技术进步，因此 KfW 投资于蓬勃发展的科技公司，积极参与容克投资计划。2015 年，KfW 的另一个挑战是为躲避战争和恐怖主义的难民提供安身之所。

主要经营数据

KfW 银行成立时的原始股本来自德意志联邦共和国和联邦政府的财政预算，其中联邦政府占 80%，各州政府占 20%。2015 财年，德国复兴信贷银行提供的资金总额为 795 亿欧元，其中 505 亿欧元用于支持国内建设，由旗下做银行 KfW 中小企业银行与 KfW 区域和私人银行负责；279 亿欧元用于国际业务，由其子银行 KfW 国际项目融资和出口信贷银行、旗下子公司德国投资与开发有限公司（DEG）承担；另有 11 亿欧元用于商业领域的资本市场（见图 4.1）。

2015 财年，KfW 的总利润为 21.71 亿欧元（不包含 KfW 的援助项目），这主要得益于不断攀升的国外信贷利率、美元汇率的发展及对 KfW 长期有利的融资条件。2015 财年，KfW 的总资产达 5 030 亿欧元，贷款总额为 4 470 亿欧元，总股本达 252 亿欧元。2015 年，KfW 的核心资本充足率为 18.3%，资本充足率为 18.4%，相比 2014 年同期，提高了 3 ~ 4 个百分点。

2015 年，KfW 总投资量为 793 亿欧元，2016 年总投资量达到 810 亿欧元，显示出市场对其金融产品的强劲需求。2016 年，551 亿欧元注入本国市

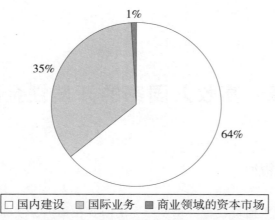

图 4.1　2015 年德国复兴信贷银行投资资金分布

场，强有力地促进了德国经济的发展。其中，214 亿欧元进入国内中小银行商业领域，107 亿欧元进入环境和能源重点领域。此外，住房建设领域投资增长也十分令人瞩目，达到了 208 亿欧元，比同期增长 26%。

工作亮点

2015 年是全球化趋势和技术进步浪潮不断加深的一年，KfW 从德国国内与国际视角出发，重点关注三个板块的内容，分别是"科技进步与生产创新""气候变化与环境"和"个人发展和难民援助"。

科技进步与生产创新

2015 年，KfW 对中小企业的贷款承诺达 204 亿欧元，相比 2014 年的 199 亿欧元达到了新的高度。其中，用于支持环境保护和气候变化的中小企业贷款承诺达 93 亿欧元，占中小企业银行总贷款的 46%。同时，KfW 对环保和可再生能源给予了极高的关注。此外，KfW 还倡导企业在生产过程不断创新，这也是近几年医疗技术发展的重要理念。以巴伐利亚医疗科技集团（FIT）为例，该企业用 10 年时间完成了生产流水线的数字化，实现 3D 打印，使得生产过程更加快捷、高效和高质。KfW 在两年前开始重点支持 FIT 集团，对其生产过程的优化做出很大贡献。实际上，通过 KfW 的"ERP① 创新计划"，类

---

① ERP 指的是企业资源计划，即建立在信息技术基础上，以系统化的管理思想，为企业决策层及员工提供决策运行手段的管理平台。——编者注

似的中小企业可以向 KfW 申请低利率贷款。而 2015 年，KfW 通过 "ERP 创新计划" 共投入了 6.2 亿欧元支持中小企业的生产创新。此外，通过 "ERP 创立基金"，KfW 还资助了很多生物技术领域刚起步的科技公司，帮助其增加自有资本。

气候变化与环境

通过子公司德国投资与开发有限公司，KfW 持续支持发展中国家的可持续发展。德国公司 Mobisol（太阳能发电系统供应商）一直接受 KfW 的资金支持，在非洲投资分布式太阳能，其业务已经遍布坦桑尼亚、卢旺达、肯尼亚等多个国家，非洲用户可以通过分期付款方式购买家用太阳能系统，大约 15 万人可以因此通过 Mobisol 的设备使用电能，极大方便了普通家庭的生活。

帮助发展中国家改善交通系统和气候环境，是 KfW 为世界气候和环境做出的一份贡献。中国和巴西都面临人口急剧增长的问题，低效的交通基础设施与严重的空气污染在大城市里屡见不鲜。在巴西，KfW 与巴西国家开发银行为建设大城市环境友好型的交通系统达成合作，共同投资数额累计达 10 亿美元。在中国，KfW 为中国淮南的 "智能交通系统" 项目提供了高达 1 500 万欧元的援助资金。

个人发展和难民援助

2015 年，KfW 投入 505 亿欧元用于德国国内经济建设，相比 2014 年提高了近 6%。这些项目既包括中小企业发展，也包括个人住房建设。2015 年，KfW 对私人客户的支持达到 191 亿欧元，相比 2014 年增加了 13%，其中在住房领域的援助达 165 亿欧元。实际上，住房一直是 KfW 关注的重要领域。在 2015 财年，这一问题和难民及社会团结问题紧密地联系在一起。在对德国国内和国际直接的难民援助中，KfW 投入了总额为 30 亿欧元的资金。2015 年 9 月～2016 年 1 月，KfW 陆续拿出 15 亿欧元用于德国国内难民住所的建设，大约 15 万人由此受益。同时，通过 KfW 开发银行、KfW 子公司 DEG 及 KfW 基金会，KfW 对与德国有发展合作关系的国家也进行了与难民有关的支持，其中包括 KfW 投入 9 000 万欧元对叙利亚 36 个难民相关项目的支持（如学校建设、约旦河供水系统建设等），投入 8.75 亿欧元对危机多发地区和边境地区的支持等。

由于最新涌入德国的难民生存及其社会融入是个长期问题，KfW 正在计划投资涉及 20 个国家的与难民相关的 70 个计划，项目总额高达 14 亿欧元。

而 KfW 目前承诺的 38 个与难民直接相关的项目，将涉及 5.7 亿欧元的资金。KfW 也表示将在难民问题上给予持续关注和长久的支持。

专栏 4-1　从立法看德国复兴信贷银行的中小企业融资

中小企业融资难一直是不争事实，而中小企业在经济发展中又起着非常重要的作用，世界各国为解决此问题采取了不同措施，通常是财政政策与其他经济政策相结合。开发性金融机构如何引导商业银行支持中小企业？下面从立法角度来分析德国的开发性金融机构——德国复兴信贷银行的做法。

德国复兴信贷银行是根据 1948 年颁布的《德国复兴信贷银行法》成立的，是一家由德国联邦政府和州政府全资拥有的开发性金融机构。成立至今，《德国复兴信贷银行法》历经多次修改，使 KfW 的运行和业务开展享有充分的自主权。该法第一条规定："联邦共和国为 KfW 提供的贷款和发行的债券、签订的定息远期合约或期权、获得的其他贷款以及由 KfW 提供明确担保的给予第三方的贷款提供担保。"德国政府以立法形式给予 KfW 国家担保，为其在资本市场建立了良好的信用基础。

作为国有性质的开发性金融机构，扶持中小企业是 KfW 非常重要的职能。《德国复兴信贷银行法》第二条第一款规定，根据国家授权，KfW 在中小型企业、自由职业者和新创企业、住宅、环境保护、基础设施、技术进步等方面拥有执行促进性任务（融资方面）的职权，其中第一个融资支持对象就是中小型企业、自由职业者和新创企业。为促进德国中小企业发展，KfW 对中小企业在国内外投资项目提供长期优惠信贷。

为更好地完成上述目标，2003 年 8 月，KfW 兼并了负责中小企业金融业务的德国清算银行（Deutsche Ausgleichs Bank，DtA）。DtA 成立于1950 年，是国家机构，主要职责是对中小企业和起步项目发放贷款并行使调控银行的职能。合并后，KfW 和 DtA 将各自负责的中小企业业务统一转给新成立的 KfW 中小企业银行（KfW - Mittelstands - Bank），专门负责中小企业金融服务，并加以法律保障。《德国复兴信贷银行法》第二条第二款规定，针对中小型企业、自由职业者和新创企业，由 KfW 的促进性机构"KfW 中小企业银行"进行融资支持。该规定明确了 KfW 中小企业银行的职责，这种"行中行"的管理模式优化了 KfW 的组织结构，使

KfW 中小企业银行在为中小企业、自由职业者和新创企业提供金融服务时，能够更好地提高经营效益。

那么，KfW 是如何引导商业性金融机构支持中小企业发展的呢？《德国复兴信贷银行法》第三条第一款规定，信贷机构或其他融资机构须参与到针对包括中小型企业、自由职业者和新创企业在内的融资服务中。这一条款规定了 KfW 必须通过完全市场化运作的商业银行直接面对中小企业，为中小企业提供融资服务。KfW 以政府信用从资本市场筹集资金，在某些情况下政府还给予适当利息补贴。由于 KfW 信用等级高，筹资成本低，加之政府给予的利息补贴，保证了 KfW 能够以非常低的利率向转贷银行或中小企业提供资金。在实际操作中，KfW 的资金通常以转贷方式发放，首先选择地方银行（通常以中小企业的主控银行作为转贷银行），通过转贷银行向中小企业发放贷款并由转贷银行承担最终贷款风险（也有共同承担的情况），从而引导商业性金融机构广泛参与支持中小企业发展。

北莱茵威斯特法伦州银行

北莱茵威斯特法伦州银行（NRW）作为德国北莱茵—威斯特法伦州的一家地方银行，自 2002 年成立以来，一直致力于北莱茵—威斯特法伦州的地方建设。2015 年，NRW 面临的两大挑战分别是难民数量的急剧增长和德国社会的数字化需求。NRW 在 2015 年的信贷承诺高达 97 亿欧元，更加强有力地支持了国民经济发展。

主要经营数据

2015 年，北莱茵—威斯特法伦州银行的总资产为 1 411.75 亿欧元，自有资金达 200.63 亿欧元，资本储备为 7.26 亿欧元，利息和佣金收入为 5.46 亿欧元，经营收入达 3.64 亿欧元，企业员工有 1 309 人。在资本市场，由于受金融市场危机的影响，NRW 在 2015 年相应地调整了相关活动，减少了计划中的总资产和业务量。同时，因为其良好的信用等级和活跃的投资活动，NRW 在有利的条件下发行债券，从而稳固了其长期的资金基础。2015 财年，

NRW 的佣金收入为 1.095 亿欧元，较上一年增长了 620 万欧元。

工作亮点

NRW 主要针对 3 个领域提供优惠政策，分别是住房与民生、支持新兴企业、发展与保护。2015 年，NRW 共提供 96.77 亿欧元的资金推动这 3 个领域的发展，分别是 51.48 亿、33.44 亿和 11.85 亿欧元（见图 4.2）。2015 年，NRW 给信贷机构贷款 334 亿欧元，其中近一半是超过 5 年的长期贷款；给私人客户贷款 602.74 亿欧元，近 400 亿欧元是超过 5 年的长期贷款；NRW 发放债务证券及其他固定收益证券共计 394.34 亿欧元。

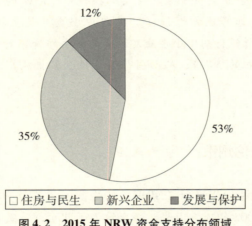

图 4.2　2015 年 NRW 资金支持分布领域

住房与民生

建设居民可承担的住房及提高住房品质，是 NRW 促进住房建设的两大目标。2015 年，住房依旧是 NRW 支持的重要领域。这一年，NRW 在居民住宅及社区建设上分别投入了 16 亿欧元和 28 亿欧元。NRW 的社会住房推广计划针对的是收入较低的人群。由于社会住房的高质量要求，NRW 对旧建筑的翻新和新住房的建设都给予了相应支持。同时，随着 2015 年难民数量的增多，社区住房建设的信贷需求也急剧增加。NRW 投入大量资金支持难民的临时收容处和长期住所建设。

例如，针对难民住房的需求，NRW 提供了"NRW 银行难民住房"项目的支持手段。它是一个纯粹的市政项目，由北莱茵—威斯特法伦州的市和县政府共同支持。同时，该贷款项目无利息且年限为 20 年，真正帮助难民购买拥有现代化装备的住宅。在 2015 财年的前 11 个月，NRW 的这一项目就达到了 1.22 亿欧元的贷款承诺。

支持新兴企业

2015 年，NRW 投入 27 亿欧元用于支持中小企业的发展，另有 5.82 亿欧元用于企业创立。NRW 设立了"NRW 广义信贷项目"和"NRW 中小企业信贷项目"，通过这两个支持项目为中小企业、自由职业者等提供资金。低利率贷款项目使中小企业获得运营资本和再融资成为可能。此外，NRW 还通过投资购买新兴中小企业的股份来支持有潜力的中小企业的发展。

发展与保护

气候变化和环境保护是全球关注的重要问题。NRW 在 2015 年投入 10 亿欧元用于保护环境、气候和节约能源，该数额几乎占 NRW 信贷承诺的 1/3。但与 2014 年相比，这个数据下降了近 22 个百分点。在能源问题方面，NRW 的着重点是节约能源和提高能源效率，通过低息贷款支持节能增效的相关项目。例如，NRW 投资了北莱茵—威斯特法伦州的电动交通项目和热电联产的升级项目；在基础设施和节水系统建设方面，NRW 也投入了大量资金。此外，在鼓励创新和支持教育方面，NRW 也分别投入了 400 万和 1.44 亿欧元。

法国储蓄托管机构

自 1816 年创立至今，法国储蓄托管机构（CDC）一直坚持发展四大主题，即生态和能源转型、数字化转型、人口和社会转型、土地资源转型，长期致力于推动社会经济发展、改善人居环境、分享科技成果，是当之无愧的公众利益发言人。此外，随着世界各大经济体交流合作日益频繁，全球化进程加快，CDC 也将目光投向了世界，试图在更广阔的土地上留下法国人的足迹。

主要经营数据

2015 年，CDC 经常性收入比同期增长 3.9%，自有资本增加 20 亿欧元。集团本身盈利逾 5 亿欧元，其旗下子公司及战略性参股共创造收益 8.64 亿欧元。另外，它开设的储蓄基金也经营良好，贷款发放量逐年递增，由 2014 年的 204 亿欧元增加至 2015 年的 211 亿欧元（涨幅 3%），其中 172 亿欧元用于资助居民住房，31 亿欧元拨给地方公共职能机构。

工作亮点

生态和能源转型是 21 世纪一大主题。CDC 作为绿色金融的引领者，不断创新，为应对全球气候变暖贡献了自己的智慧和力量。2015 年，CDC 共发放 30 亿欧元生态和能源转型贷款，同时发起免息绿色发展贷款以及净化、保护生物多样性主题的贷款，改善居民住房生态翻新工程的融资环境（免息），并为致力于生态和能源转型的企业提供 12.6 亿欧元的融资。为响应第 21 届联合国气候变化大会（巴黎气候变化大会，COP 21），CDC 集团做出承诺，立志在 2020 年之前将其上市公司股票碳足迹减少 20%，同时在 2030 年之前实现建筑能耗降低 38%。

CDC 作为法国国家现代化的主要推动力之一，一直鼓励国家数字化发展，在发展新科技方面从未松懈。全民数字化是一次科技革命，为了让全体民众享受到科技成果，CDC 大力推进建设智能城市、智能校园，为地方行政机构提供安全保障服务，比如交易过程有形化、数据保存，并创立数据区块链技术实验室，专门研究交易信任与安全问题。此外，CDC 也是《法兰西高网速方案》主要实施者之一，该方案旨在 2022 年实现高速无线网全法覆盖。为了发展数字化经济，它鼓励相关企业积极创新，积极响应法国公共科技创议（PIA），并由此获得 PIA 项下的生态科技基金的资助。

秉承"更好生活在一起"的理念，CDC 几乎出现在法国人生活的方方面面。CDC 管理着法国 1/5 人口的退休计划，并在 2014 年发起养老改革，给法国养老体制松绑；建立了惠及 2 300 万法国老年人的继续教育账户，帮助他们随时了解自己的权益和可获得的培训资源。此外，CDC 集团极为关注养老经济，专门设立了一项"银色经济荣誉贷款"，为 2016 年前 42 个项目提供无息融资服务。同时，CDC 投资城镇改造计划，为促进代际和平共处研究创新方案。

2015 年，CDC 集团在增加地区吸引力方面做了大量的工作，尤其在土地资源转型上。所谓土地资源转型，就是协调地方小城镇和大都市之间的发展，开展居民区建设，大力发展就业，改善人民生活。2015 年，CDC 和法国（市、省、大区）各大行政机构共签订了 40 余项框架协议。在 2015 年 11 月，

CDC 和国家城镇翻新署（ANRU）合作投资 2.5 亿欧元以实现城市社区房屋改造工程。而在重组地区管理模式和公共机构方面，为增加地区吸引力，CDC 向"法国旅游资源开发"平台投资了 10 亿欧元；在改善住房方面，CDC 在一年内共建造、收购居民住房 134 000 处，为 311 000 处住房提供地暖，其制定的《过渡性住房方案》预计在 2020 年之前建成 35 000 处住房（共投资 63 亿欧元），其中 10 307 处住房将在 2015 年年末完成订购，并正式施工，即 800 处工地动工，总投资额将达 15 亿欧元。

2015 年，CDC 集团开始部署全球发展战略，注重维护与国际投资者和公共机构的关系，积极参与鼓励长期投资的倡议。CDC 也是长期投资者俱乐部（LTIC，聚集了 18 个国际组织机构）、欧盟长期投资者协会（ELTI，机构成员包含 27 个欧盟国家）、储蓄所世界论坛的发起人之一。它曾在 2015 年投资两只投向可再生能源计划的国际基金，分别是玛格丽特和 InfraMed。截至目前，玛格丽特已经投入 2.87 亿欧元用于资助在法国和欧洲的 10 个计划方案，总价值达 47 亿欧元，即创造了 16 倍的杠杆效应；InfraMed 已在埃及、约旦、土耳其投资了 4 个项目（2.26 亿欧元），其产生的杠杆效应将高达 19 倍。

为促进经济发展和环境能源转型，CDC 采取了更加主动的战略。一是在未来 5 年，CDC 集团将继续加大投资和贷款的力度与广度；二是加强集团的国际影响力，在全球范围内建立合作伙伴关系，进一步加强与法国发展署的关系以及大力发展容克（Juncker）计划，加强与欧盟各国家银行之间的合作；三是在经济转型方面始终保持高度热情，在集团上下实行《两个层面路线图》，做到生态能源转型从己做起，同时把环境保护理念延伸至金融账户（委托管理、创新融资、私人股权、债券交易）；四是促进数字化转型，推动智能城市建设和争取 2024 奥林匹克运动会，投资数字化基础设施以及数据区块链技术；五是加快土地转型，特别是大巴黎定位；六是推动人口和社会转型，推出个人账户和业务账户（2017 年 1 月 1 日实行）以及设立社会集体经济基金。

专栏 4-2　法国储蓄托管机构引领创新发展

法国储蓄托管机构创立于 1816 年，受法国议会管辖，是欧洲唯一一个受公众保护的能独立开展金融业务的机构。作为法国政策性开发银行，CDC 一直以国家利益、公众利益为己任，致力于创新和可持续发展。作为公共投资者，它以长期贷款的形式向有创新精神的资金需求者提供融资渠道，为发展法国企业、缓解法国住房问题、促进环境能源转型做出了重要贡献，对法国经济社会发展有着深刻的影响。

2016 年，对法国而言，是非常关键的一年。一方面，连续的恐怖袭击加之近年来法国经济停滞不前、失业率逐年攀升、劳动力成本居高不下、产业连续外迁、投资幅度下降，增加了法国经济的不确定性；另一方面，法国政府正因筹备申奥，6 月 9 日号召所有的企业、机构、创新者、创造家为 2024 年申奥成功一起出谋划策，希望能在智能城市、智能组织、智能体验、智能出行和智能体育五大板块寻找创新方案。法国储蓄托管机构发挥开发性金融引领作用，积极响应国家号召，在其重点支持领域，支持实施创新工程，扶持创新企业，极大地推动了经济社会的发展。

土地资源转型

为了增加城市中心的吸引力和巩固地区经济发展的成果，2015 年 6 月 10 日，卡奥尔市的市长、大卡奥尔主席以及法国储蓄托管机构土地和渠道处负责人签订了首个国家级别的建立示范中心的协议。三方决定开设城市试点，开放实施一系列创新方案，使人口在 1.5 万~10 万之间的二、三线城市重新恢复活力。基于自愿的原则，法国储蓄托管机构筛选出 10 个实验城市：卡奥尔、维耶尔宗、讷韦尔等，并将在这几个城市展开为期一年的试点活动。在卡奥尔，工作重点将放在国王城堡路一带商业区的整顿、戴高乐广场附近电影院的建设和瓦伦悌桥街区的旅游建设。除此之外，对于大卡奥尔之前承诺的改善住宅区和城镇翻新的项目，法国储蓄托管机构也将加大支持力度。为了使 500 座翻修房顺利投放到市场，CDC 制定、跟进改造旧城方案，并充分调动地方金融机构的投资积极性。该试点工程主要分为两个阶段：第一阶段主要是在全国和全世界范围内征集城市中心具体改造方案；第二阶段就是正式试验阶段，最后总结试验结果并在全国其他有相同特征的中等城市推行该成果。

生态和能源转型

2015 年 6 月 7 日，法国大东区落成世界上首个深层地热发电站，该项目由法国储蓄托管机构、罗盖特集团和斯塔斯堡电力公司发起，受国家环境和能源控制机构与大东区补贴，总耗资约 5 500 万欧元。该发电站预计每年产热量为 24 兆瓦,相当于 10 万兆瓦时,能为 27 000 所住房供暖;每年能减少二氧化碳排放 39 000 吨,相当于 25 000 辆小汽车一年的尾气排放量。此外,由于该发电站使用了生物质能锅炉,其可再生能源使用率从 50% 上升至 75%(包括 50% 生物质能,25% 深层地热能)。该工程的竣工预示着法国在环境能源转型方面又迈进了一大步,展现了其在深层地热开发方面独一无二的科技成果,同时提升了法国在世界范围的环保成就。

数字化转型

6 月 21 日,法国巴黎银行安全部、法国储蓄托管机构、欧洲债券结算系统、泛欧证券交易所等在巴黎金融市场委员会的支持下宣布了研究面向欧洲中小企业的数据区块链基础设施建设的协定。这一创新方案将增加交易的安全性和透明度,因此有利于中小企业进入资本市场。该协定的首要目标是充分发挥协议签订方的融资能力和专业技术来推动企业创新。企业因此可以把数据区块链技术成果运用到创新方案的设计、发展和实施上。同时,中小企业的筹资效率也得以提高,因为在保证安全的前提下下降了交易成本。此外,数据区块链使交易程序大幅度简化而加强了欧洲市场证券交易登记,保证了实时结算—配送的执行效率。

人口和社会转型

6 月 21 日,法国劳工部部长、投资委员会主席和法国储蓄托管机构总经理共同庆祝《职业培训和就业合作伙伴关系》(PFPE)计划的顺利实行。该计划处于未来投资项目之下,由法国储蓄托管机构全权负责管理。其初始资本为 1.26 亿欧元,将为 15 个创新方案提供融资服务。例如,Tech'Indus 方案,旨在建立一个培养工业人才的校园,其设计理念主要由三方面构成:一是先进电子和自动化方面的专业创新培训平台,二是提供可选大学生活或继续教育的实体校园,三是企业和大学合作的长短期培训。而 Open Source University(OSU)这个方案则是希望在不同的城市设立开放性资源大学,提供开放性软件资源领域的专业培训。该资助计划旨在解决法国现下就业岗位快速变化而相关合格资质劳动力匮乏的问题。通过不同体量的企业和培训机构（高校、中学或者私立培训机构）建立长久的合作伙伴关系来实现教学内容和人力资源管理的协同发展，PFPE 既有利于企业，也有利于职员：企业能够因此预测经济变化，而职员能借这个机会掌握专业知识，提高自身就业竞争力。

事实上，PFPE 是在《交替投资职业培训》计划的基础上加以创新的结果，鼓励有创造力的企业和培训机构为面临职业变化的工作者量身定制职业培训方案。而这些方案再经过层层筛选，最终入围的职业培训发展方案将获得 CDC 管理的项目拨款。这是 CDC 作为法国社会和人口转型的首要推动者之一，着眼于当下法国就业形势发起的又一次投资活动。这也宣告了继续教育时代的到来，CDC 提出用继续教育来弥补校内职业教育的不足，并举国收集创新培养方案，使求职者更能满足职业、行业需要，推动个人职业发展，同时促使企业更好地适应快速变化的经济环境，从而推动整个经济社会良性发展。

日本国际协力银行

日本国际协力银行（JBIC）作为日本政府全资创立的政策性金融机构，积极推动资源能源与基础设施领域的投资，协助日本中小企业发展海外市场，基本完成了对其他金融机构进行补充的作用，确保了日本能源资源的稳定，提高了日本产业的国际竞争力。

主要经营数据

2015 财年（2015 年 4 月 1 日~2016 年 3 月 31 日），JBIC 整合后的总资产为 175 806 亿日元（约 1 709 亿美元），有价证券总值为 2 366 亿日元（约 23 亿美元），总负债为 123 223 亿日元（约 1 198 亿美元），担保和保证金总额为 23 974 亿日元（约 233 亿美元），共参与投资 298 个项目。借贷和公司债券分别为 95 369 亿日元、27 219 亿日元。经常利润为 2 400 亿日元（约 23 亿美元），其中国内投资 423 亿日元，大洋洲 275 亿日元，亚洲 547 亿日元，欧洲、非洲、中东共计 598 亿日元，北美、中南美 558 亿日元（见图 4.3）。穆迪评级 A1，标准普尔评级 A +。

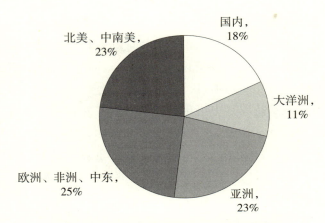

图 4.3　2015 财年 JBIC 投资地域分布情况

工作亮点

加大海外资源投资

在资源投资领域，2015 年 JBIC 共参与 12 个相关项目，担保和保证金总额为 4 892 亿日元，整体低于 2014 年。主要原因有：在石油等资源价格低迷的背景下，日本企业投资更加谨慎；2014 年投资比较多的大型资源项目，2015 年则出现了反弹下降。其中重点项目有：为强化与资源大国的关系，对阿布扎比国家石油公司进行投资；为特立尼达岛和多巴哥提供项目贷款，在国家风险管理领域也承担责任；积极参与有利于降低液化天然气输送的项目。

加大基础设施建设投资

在基础设施建设领域，特别是在电力基础设施和通信基础设施建设领域，JBIC 积极向日本大型民营企业进行投资，大力推进可再生能源发电机械和通信技术的出口，拓展海外市场，提高国际竞争力。电力基础设施建设的重点项目有：支持日本企业出资筹备的卡塔尔天然气火力发电、淡化海水事业；支持日本企业参与荷兰海洋风力发电事业；协助日本企业向孟加拉国电力开发公社、冰岛国营电力公社、土耳其地热发电机器市场基础设施投资。通信基础设施建设的重点项目有：通过向安哥拉开发银行提供外贸贷款，推动海底光缆设施的投资，该项目将建成北美和南美之间第一个横跨南大西洋的海底光缆；积极参加缅甸土瓦经济特区的建设，为其提供必要资金支持和指导通信技术。

支持企业海外并购

近年来，在支持企业并购方面，日本向海外投资和并购的需求旺盛，JBIC 充分利用"支持海外开发融资设施"这一专项融资渠道，在 2015 财年共参与出资 105 个企业海外并购项目，担保和保证金总计达 10 233 亿日元。这是日本企业海外开发支持项目中历年最高值。JBIC 在帮助日本企业海外拓展时，重点地域主要放在东南亚、中南美等新兴国家，并购企业从事的领域主要包括农业、食品、信息技术及大数据等，其中重点项目有：帮助日本企业并购缅甸啤酒生产、销售公司；支持日本企业收购新加坡物流公司。

推动中小企业发展

在推动中小企业发展方面，JBIC 加强同地区金融机构合作，积极响应货币融资日益增长的需求。2015 财年，JBIC 共参与出资 133 个加强中小企业建设的项目，担保和保证金总计为 429 亿日元，这也是 JBIC 在该领域投资的历年最高值。在推动中小企业发展方面，JBIC 结合自身优势，重点推动中小企业的海外市场拓展，进一步帮助日本中小企业走出国门。

增加环境保护融资

在环境领域，根据日本政府于 2015 年 12 月颁布的"美丽星球行动 2.0"（Actions for Cool Earth：ACE 2.0）计划，JBIC 积极协助发展中国家落实气候变化对策。提出"保护地球环境计划"（Global Action for Reconciling Economic Growth and Environmental Preservation，GREEN），并向巴西国立经济社会发展银行、墨西哥外国贸易银行、安第斯开发协会提供融资，为中南美洲有效利用可再生资源提供资金支持。

日本政策投资银行

安倍经济学已实行 4 年，由于 2015 年石油等资源价格持续回落，亚洲新兴发展中国家及资源型国家经济增速放缓，全球经济从整体上来说不太景气。日本国内经济回升不稳，个人收入、就业环境虽有所改善，但国民仍陷入通货紧缩思维模式，消费市场持续低迷；企业收益虽有所改善，但设备投资增加缓慢。在这一背景下，日本政策投资银行（DBJ）继续发挥政策性开发银行的作用，在投资、融资、危机应对、推动企业持续发展等方面做出重要贡献。

主要经营数据

2015 财年（2015 年 4 月 1 日～2016 年 3 月 31 日），DBJ 整合后总资产为 159 071 亿日元。2015 年财年，DBJ 的净资产收益率和资产收益率分别为 0.80% 和 4.60%，不良资产率为 0.64%。有价证券总值为 18 030 亿日元，比 2014 财年减少 4.5%；总负债为 130 229 亿日元；借贷和公司债券分别为 78 922 亿日元、32 219 亿日元；净利润为 1 291 亿日元；投融资总额为 30 277 亿日元，比 2014 财年增加 19%；经常利润为 3 586 亿日元。穆迪评级 A1，标准普尔评级 A。DBJ 的主要资金来源是政府资金支持和债券发行，2015 财年政府出资 650 亿日元。

工作亮点

支持融资、投资项目

在融资方面，2015 财年 DBJ 的融资总额为 28 613 亿日元，除了传统的与其他金融机构合作的项目外，2015 财年还增加了无追索权贷款、结构融资等多种融资方式，以满足日益多样化的融资需求。在投资方面，2015 年 5 月 20 日，DBJ 成立了"特定投资业务"，以提高日本海外竞争力、促进地区发展为目标。2015 财年 DBJ 投资额为 1 663 亿日元。在咨询业务方面，DBJ 利用常年积累的社会网络及广泛的业务经验，向企业和其他金融机构提供咨询服务，2015 财年咨询业务利润达到 101 亿日元。

危机应对业务

早在 2008 年金融危机和 2011 年日本大地震以后，DBJ 就建成了危机应对网络。根据《日本公共金融公司法案》，特定金融机构的成立意义是在自然灾害及重大危机之后提供信贷，DBJ 便是其中之一。DBJ 帮助企业建立灾后应对措施以抵御灾难风险，并提供应急资金，从业务持续性计划、抗震设施建设到 IT 备份系统等多方面入手应对灾难。除了继续帮助因 2011 年日本大地震受损的企业恢复发展以外，2015 财年 DBJ 还主要应对了如下灾害：口永良部岛火山喷发，台风 18 号、21 号带来的大暴雨，2016 年 4 月的熊本地震以及地震中汽车供应链受损的中小企业支援对策等。2015 财年，DBJ 危机应对业务的融资总额为 56 019 亿日元，提供损害担保金 2 683 亿日元，购买商业票据 3 610亿日元。

增强日本企业的海外竞争力

随着新兴国家发展和全球化带来的激烈竞争，以及低出生率、人口老龄化带来的国内市场饱和、经济发展低迷的现象，DBJ努力提升日本企业的竞争力，特别是推动日本中小企业充分利用自身技术和管理经验，进入国际市场。为此，DBJ设立了专项"竞争力提升基金"，截至2016年3月末，该专项基金已累计投资12个项目，金额累计达1 290亿日元。投资的公司有SF Solar Power、日本电气株式会社、Maritime Innovation Japan等开发新能源、新技术，努力创新的日本公司。

特定投资业务

"特定投资业务"是指2015～2020年这5年内专门为提升地方活力和企业竞争力而设立的专项投资业务，主要目的是调动民间金融机构的投资积极性，用该项资金为民间金融机构投资做保障。为此，2015年6月DBJ专门设立了"投资本部"部门，制定了"日本再兴战略修改2015"、"城市、居民、工作创生基本方针2015年修订版"等方针政策。DBJ还同地方金融机构组成共同基金（2015年度共设立6只共同基金），通过合作，充分发挥日本政策投资银行和地方金融机构的知识、经验。

除特定投资业务外，为了进一步推动迅速发展的新兴资金市场，DBJ还制订了"成长协创设施"计划，为相关企业提供咨询建议，还可以同企业、金融机构、投资家一起为地方企业发展提供各方面支持。其中，增强地方活力项目为重中之重。具体来说，DBJ设立了"增强地方活力计划"，为优秀的地方企业提供资金支持；设立"地方未来建设大学"，以培养地方优秀人才，其中值得一提的是"创新中心"的设立，2015财年DBJ共投资43个创新项目；设置"企业民间资金活用事业推进机构"（PFI机构），并定期举办"PPP/PFI课堂"；另外，设立"地方贡献型并购项目"，为有利于地方经济发展的企业提供资金和技术支持。

总体来说，2015年，DBJ基本完成了政府给其设定的任务，提高了日本企业的竞争力，并提升了地方经济的活力，维护了自然灾害等危机下日本经济的稳定。这些都给我们带来了宝贵的经验。

专栏4-3　　"DBJ环境评级"制度助力日本企业可持续发展

DBJ是以《株式会社日本政策投资银行法》为基础，受日本财务省直接管理，注册资本超过 100 亿美元的一家大型国有综合政策性金融机构。DBJ 的投融资方向主要集中在政府确定的政策性重点项目，其经营不以营利为目的，不参与市场竞争。作为综合政策性金融机构，DBJ 主要向对日本经济社会发展有利的项目提供长期稳定的资金。

"DBJ 环境评级"是 DBJ 独创的评级体系，即根据企业对环境友好程度来决定融资优先级。2004 年，为了更好地促进企业的环保工作发展，日本政策投资银行推出了此制度。该制度以支持减轻环境压力、促进企业环保投资为最终目标。通过其自行开发制定的环境经营评价系统，对申请环保贷款企业的环境绩效予以评分，根据评价结果，将环保方面表现优异的企业根据评价等级提供不同程度的环保专项低息贷款，支持企业增加环保投入。

一、"DBJ 环境评级"的特征

1. 分级评定。"DBJ 环境评级"融资业务的最大特点是根据贷款目标企业的环境评级结果确定贷款对象及利率。低息贷款被规定主要用于企业环境保护相关软件、硬件设备的购买及研发投入等。DBJ 在收到企业的环保专项贷款申请后，将通过评级系统对申请企业进行环境评级，并根据评级结果确定相应的贷款利率。

2. 基于国际国内环保动向设立的公正、中立的评价体系。每年，在由相关领域专家组成的 DBJ 环境评级制度志愿委员会上，参会人员都会结合当年的国际国内的环保动态，修订并发布每年的环保检查报表。

3. 与企业面对面的调查评价。

4. 对企业管理者直接进行访谈。

5. 丰富的评价经验。

6. 服务客户多样化。从制造业到非制造业，大型企业到地域集中型企业均有涉及。

7. DBJ 标识的使用。获得"DBJ 环境评级"融资服务的企业，被允许在官网和宣传品中自由使用日本政策投资银行标识，以显示自身的环保能力及可持续发展能力。

二、"DBJ 环境评级"的方法

"DBJ 环境评级"分别从"环境保护型经营体制"、"企业涉及全领域的环境投入和对策"、"针对主要环境问题的处理能力"三个角度设定了定性与定量两方面的 120 个评价指标，满分为 250 分。其中，120 分以上为合格（中型企业为 110 分以上）。合格的企业会根据得分的高低被分成三个不同的档次，DBJ 以此为依据，确定低息贷款的利率。针对不同的行业，评价指标会有所差异，现行体系可对应 13 种不同行业。

三、"DBJ 环境评级"的流程

"DBJ 环境评级"的流程为：一次筛查——企业环境问题问答——二次检查（公布结果）（见图 4.4）。一次筛查，是指在 DBJ 内部对审核企业的报表信息、公开资料进行检查。企业环境问题问答是指 DBJ 与企业负责人针对企业公开信息中无法判断的事项进行确认，并听取企业有特色的环保措施，针对企业未来的发展方向、政策交换意见。二次检查（公布结果），是评价项目组以外的 DBJ 工作人员，在对前两项流程、企业状况以及在 DBJ 内部召开的评价会议进行认真审议后，发布审核企业的"DBJ 环境评级"结果。DBJ 将根据评级结果进行融资，并向审核企业发放环境评级报告书。

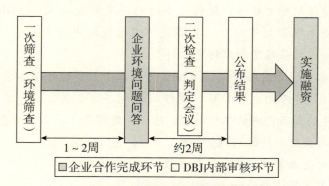

图 4.4　DBJ 环境评级流程图

日本境内所有满足 DBJ 融资要求的企业，都可以成为"DBJ 环境评级"的服务对象。在资金运用原则上，与一般性融资相同，不包括特殊的利息补给政策。"DBJ 环境评级"制度自创建以来，到 2015 年 3 月月末为止已成功完成融资服务 472 次，资金流量达到约 8 000 亿日元。

韩国产业银行

作为韩国境内第一家人民币境外投资者，韩国产业银行（KDB）成为韩国的"全球先行者"；而通过为工业基金注入前所未有的超过 67 万亿韩元的资金，它也成为"经济促进者"；此外，KDB 通过巩固韩国基础债券发行人的地位，还巩固了自己"市场领导者"的地位；最后，以"全球合作基金 II"资助新兴公司，KDB 还扮演了"创新孵化者"的角色。

着眼于"韩国金融发展引擎、全球化的韩国产业银行"这一终极目标的 KDB，2015 年为自己设立了 5 个中长期规划的战略目标：促进创新经济发展，领导金融产业进步，夯实市场安全网络，建立持续发展金融基础。如今，KDB 旨在为促进韩国经济发展扮演更多重要的角色。

主要经营数据

截至 2015 年年末，KDB 的资产已达到 309.492 万亿韩元，比 2014 年增长 11.8%。这一增长主要来自其他资产的增加。由于大宇造船和海洋有限公司以及其他企业最近被 KDB 纳为子公司，KDB 的负债也增加了 11.6%，达到 275.549 万亿韩元，这主要源于债券和其他负债的增加。同时，由于已发行资本和留存收益均有所增加，KDB 股本增加至 33.942 万亿韩元，比 2014 年增长了 14.3%（见表 4.1）。2015 年，韩国政府通过额外注资，使得 KDB 的发行资本增加了 2.55 万亿韩元。

表 4.1　韩国产业银行 2014～2015 年的资产负债情况　　　　　　（单位：10 亿韩元）

	2015 年	2014 年
总资产	**309 491.70**	**276 704.80**
现金及同业存款	7 894.70	10 895.30
证券	82 107.20	94 267.60
贷款	142 440.20	143 484.40
其他	77 049.60	28 057.50

（续表）

	2015 年	2014 年
总负债	**275 549.40**	**247 004.20**
交易性金融负债	—	394
存款	41 431.50	41 665.80
借贷	33 576.20	37 814.40
债券	121 617.00	120 731.30
其他	78 924.70	46 398.70
权益（股本）	**33 942.30**	**29 700.60**
发行资本	17 235.40	15 180.40
资本盈余	1 579.20	1 621.60
留存收益	9 266.40	7 577.00
资本调整	225.5	223.7
其他	4 763.80	4 411.00
累计其他综合所得	872	686.9

　　由于家庭贷款的减少与公司和公共贷款的增加相抵消，KDB 的贷款总额仅增长 4.4%，为 128.926 万亿韩元。同时，2015 年 KDB 对大型企业的贷款增长了 1.5%，对中小型企业的贷款大幅增加 17.2%，从而使其企业贷款比 2014 年增加了 4.5%，达到 124.914 万亿韩元（见表 4.2）。

表 4.2　韩国产业银行 2014～2015 年贷款情况　　　　　　（单位：10 亿韩元）

	2015 年	2014 年	变动	
			额度	百分比（%）
企业贷款	124 914	119 514	5 400	4.5
大型企业	97 670	96 275	1 395	1.5
中小企业	27 244	23 239	4 005	17.2
家庭贷款	3 135	3 238	-103	-3.2
公共和其他部门	877	717	160	22.3
总贷款	**128 926**	**123 469**	**5 457**	**4.4**

2015 年，KDB 存款和借款额分别下降 0.6% 和 11.2%，但债券发行量上升 0.7%（见表 4.3），债券占总资金比例从 2014 年的 60.3% 增加到 2015 年的 61.9%。

表 4.3　韩国产业银行 2014～2015 年储蓄情况 　　　　　　　（单位：10 亿韩元）

	2015 年	2014 年	变动	
			额度	百分比（%）
存款	41 432	41 666	-234	-0.6
借款	33 576	37 814	-4 238	-11.2
债券	121 617	120 731	886	0.7

考虑到 KDB 的业务扩张，其基金的主要收入来源工业金融债券（KDB 债券）发行量的增大巩固了 KDB 在经济增长中的地位。2015 年发行的 KDB 债券金额为 33.7 万亿韩元，另外还发行了 35 亿美元的外币计价债券。与 2014 年相比，其余额分别增加 47 万亿韩元和 44 亿美元。

2015 年年底，KDB 债券在韩国国内的发行量排名第三。考虑到全球经济放缓，韩国央行在 2015 年两次下调利率，新发行的 KDB 债券的平均融资成本也下降了 0.8%。虽然 KDB 债券的利率大大低于其他公共机构债券的利率，但它的规模保证了其所起的关键基准利率的作用。

伴随存款业务扩张的还有 KDB 对公司存款和支票账户的重视，这些举措可以降低资金成本，最大限度地减少市场摩擦。

工作亮点

在企业领域，KDB 通过向陷入流动性困境的企业、中小企业和信用社提供 1.5 万亿韩元的紧急资金作为信用增级，防止其陷入财务困境。此外，对具有成长潜力的公司，KDB 通过"企业投资刺激计划"为其提供了 4.8 万亿韩元的资金，累积总额达到 15.6 万韩元。而为了先行管理风险，KDB 加强了其定期流动性检查，并鼓励流动性短缺的公司提高其财务稳健性。这些举措的主要目的在于防止金融风险的蔓延。

同时，KDB 向中小企业提供了 37 万亿韩元资金，占资金总供应的 54.7%。旨在促进中小企业发展的共同增长基金，其总额连续第三年保持在

5 000亿韩元以上，达到约 5 180 亿韩元。此外，KDB 还向 3 846 家中小企业提供了 6.4 万亿韩元的贷款以改善其财务状况。在这笔资金中，有 71% 用于促进技术融资。

KDB 还在韩国国内的重组业务方面加强了其市场安全网的功能——通过采取紧急行动尽可能减少大型企业陷入财务困境的可能。在经济增长减缓的预期将持续到 2016 年的背景下，KDB 将继续重视企业重组。同时，通过 KDB 丰富的知识积累和有经验的专业人士的协助，自愿重组和改进等先期措施也将被鼓励实施。

作为韩国国内唯一一家获许发行公司债券的银行，KDB 在投资银行业务中仍然保持领先地位。例如，来自新加坡的 Nomura 国际融资、来自中国的平安租赁等大型企业都通过 KDB 成功融资。2015 年，KDB 衍生品交易额达到 957.0 万亿韩元，年末余额为 475.0 万亿韩元，被视为"最佳衍生品供应商"。此外，2015 年年末，KDB 在韩元兑人民币直接交易市场发挥其做市商的角色，占据了 8.6% 的份额。同年，KDB 还完成了一些并购业务。对正在进行重组和需要起诉人的公司客户，KDB 也为它们提供咨询服务，并为通过并购寻求业务扩张的客户完成了多项融资项目。

为了提高技术优势公司的竞争力并协助创业公司和新兴企业发展壮大，KDB 长期以来在技术金融领域积累了相当丰富的专业知识和富有经验的人力资源。2015 年，KDB 开发了行业领先的知识产权融资产品，为创意融资奠定了基础，并开展了多元化咨询服务。这些服务已向有需求的公司提供了超过 5 000亿韩元的资助，其中 2015 年达到 1 657 亿韩元，比 2014 年增长 78.7%，领先国内技术金融市场。

在另类投资领域，KDB 关注国内社会组织资本和市政发展项目。2015 年，KDB 通过了 15 个社会组织资本和 49 个地区项目，项目总额为 13 万亿韩元，这证明了其另类投资领导者无可挑剔的地位。KDB 名下 16 只私募股权基金在 2015 年年末的资本承担总额为 8.154 万亿韩元，占市场份额的 13.9%。

KDB 的海外业务也在 2015 年迅速扩大。7 月，KDB 成为韩国第一家获得人民币合格境外机构投资者（RQFII）资格和中国银行间债券市场（CIBM）资质的银行。KDB 中国青岛分行的开业，支撑了其在中国市场的业务。KDB 还在伦敦和北京新设立两个办事处，专门从事船舶和飞机的结构性融资业务。KDB 作为牵头银行，在 2015 年安排的海外贷款总额中，船舶/飞机融资占

47.9%，一般公司贷款占 39%。

在其他方面，KDB 的养老金资产比 2014 年增加了 19.7%，2015 年年底达到 4.1 万亿韩元。其托管资产结余为 21.244 万亿韩元，增长 27.9%。而 KDB 更广泛、更多样化的研究也促进了韩国工业的可持续发展。通过建立债务人财务状况模型，识别潜在风险和对宏观经济金融环境的冲击，KDB 能够更加全面、系统地对隐患进行识别，并且尽早地意识到金融风险。而科技评估手段则为 KDB 提供韩国各个产业的发展全景，助其对相关行业进行竞争力评估，并整合最新的消息和焦点以指导行业的发展。

但是 2015 年对于 KDB 而言并非一帆风顺。造船业的低迷使其债权人和相关政策银行受到不小打击。大宇造船、现代商船和三星重工由于产能过剩和需求萎缩而连续陷入危机。为应对这些问题，KDB 鼓励现代商船加入新成立的集装箱航运联盟，并参与了三星重工的重组。2016 年 6 月，KDB 和韩国进出口银行通过韩国政府和韩国银行建立的基金为这些造船巨头提供资金帮助其处理债务等问题，总额达 99 亿美元。

专栏 4-4　韩国产业银行在新一轮韩国造船业危机下的应对举措与结构调整

造船业是韩国最主要的支柱产业之一，20 世纪 70 年代起韩国就提出了"战略引导、企业精进、造船立国"的目标。然而在近几年，世界航运和造船行业持续低迷，由于海工市场异常惨淡、新造船需求疲软，韩国也在这轮风暴中摇摇欲坠，2015 年韩国造船业仍面临困境，盈利能力继续恶化。在如此危机时期，为了挽救造船业，韩国产业银行及政府、金融界出台了多项政策和支援计划，企业自身也为了摆脱困境公布了包括裁员、重组、抛售非核心资产等多种自救方案，将首先分析韩国造船业的危机现状，再解读现阶段韩国产业银行作为主要债权人针对造船业调整出台的各项政策。

一、韩国造船业现状

1. 总体情况

综合韩国造船业近 10 年来的三大指标和人员结构情况来看，2008 年的金融危机让韩国造船业经历了第一次结构调整，生产指标和人员增长都出现了不同程度的下滑和停滞，但经过"大并小"的重组调整后，韩国造船业很快恢复了高速上升势头。2015 年，在船舶市场仍旧处于低谷的情况下，全球海工市场急剧萎缩，韩国船企在海工领域损失惨重，现代商船、三星重工和大宇造船为首的"BIG 3"亏损超过50亿美元。至2015年一季度，韩国三大造船企业经营亏损高达近80亿美元。BIG 3新接订单更是雪上加霜，第一季度韩国三大船厂除现代商船接到两艘苏伊士型油船外，三星重工和大宇造船的接单量均为零；第一季度的订单量仅为20万修正总吨（CGT），同比下降90％。

2. 韩国三大造船企业具体现状

截至2015年年底，韩国三大船企的负债情况为：大宇造船负债比率高达4 266％；三星重工负债比率为306％，未偿还债务总计13.3万亿韩元；现代商船负债比率为221％，未偿还债务总计34.2万亿韩元。

（1）韩国大宇造船最先告急。韩国产业银行指出，由于行业不景气，韩国大宇造船海洋株式会社一直因海工业务延期和撤单而严重亏损。作为大宇造船的股东，韩国产业银行及其他债权人已经注入了4.2万亿韩元（约合37亿美元）现金援助。韩国产业银行表示，2016年2月起，大宇造船将不会得到任何来自债权人的现金注入。

（2）现代商船遭受重创。2016年4月，继大宇造船后陷入困境的现代商船为避免破产，申请成为韩国产业银行的子公司，并按7∶1的比例将股本无偿转移给韩国产业银行。韩国金融监管机构和现代商船债权人同意将该公司债权转为股权，以维持其运转，直到现代商船规范化。

（3）三星重工艰难自救。2016年5月底，三星重工向主债权银行韩国产业银行提交"自救计划"，在行业危机中试图艰难自救。具体措施包括：通过出售三星宾馆和斗山发动机股份筹资2 200亿韩元（约合1.8亿美元）、暂时关停部分造船设施、改组管理层等。据悉，三星重工自2015年9月就已经开展自救行动，通过出售资产获得1 000亿韩元，并裁员500人。

二、危机下的应对举措和结构调整

在全球和韩国造船产能过剩的大背景下，统筹规划船企的结构调整问题，压缩造船产能以适应需求萎缩，是韩国船企此轮结构调整的重点，也是韩国政府和金融界对韩国国内造船行业未来走向的基本判断。在此基础上，韩国产业银行针对不同船企和配套企业的实际情况进行了多项调整。具体包括：

1. 运用政府设立的 11 万亿韩币（约合 99 亿美元）基金向船企融资

2016 年 6 月 9 日，韩国政府和央行宣布将成立一个规模 99 亿美元的基金，用于购买两家国有银行——韩国产业银行和韩国进出口银行（KEXIM）发行的混合债券。这些债券将为处于困难中的造船和航运公司提供融资。这两家银行作为对造船业曝险最高的国有银行，在船企和航运公司的不良贷款高达 470 亿美元。韩国产业银行是正在重组的主要造船厂和航运公司的主要债权人，这些公司包括大宇造船和现代商船。韩国三大造船巨头正加速推动整顿。海工政府称，现代商船、三星重工及大宇造船已向债权人提交筹资方案，计划通过出售资产与裁员等减支措施，合计筹措 8.41 万亿韩元（约合 73 亿美元）。

2. 针对 BIG 3 采取不同策略，鼓励船企探寻复苏道路

2016 年 5 月初，韩国产业银行表示会继续为三大船企提供财政资助，债务偿还期限也将延长，为三大船企吃上"定心丸"，也是作为政府鼓励船企探寻复苏道路的策略之一。

（1）力促现代商船加入世界集装箱航运联盟"THE Alliance"：5 月初，赫伯罗特、韩进海运、阳明海运、商船三井、日本邮船、川崎汽船 6 家集装箱航运公司正式宣布组建全新的联盟 THE Alliance。同时，全球运力排名第 15 的现代商船的大股东韩国产业银行正在力促其加入 THE Alliance，以实现航线和挂靠港口互补、船期协调、舱位互租、信息互享、共建共用码头和堆场、共用内陆物流体系。

（2）参与探讨三星重工的自救计划：5 月，三星重工向其主要债权人韩国产业银行提交了重组计划，承诺通过处置非核心资产筹资 3 000 亿韩元，并承诺将解雇 500 名员工，暂停一些造船业务。韩国产业银行参与自救计划的探讨，并希望三星重工促进一系列彻底的重组步骤，从而重振其举步维艰的造船业务。韩国产业银行尤为希望三星集团也参与到自救项目中。

此外，韩国中央和地方两级政府也出台了大量应对措施，包括：出台《企业特别活力法》等支援法律促进产业结构优化；联合金融界支援监督造船企业结构调整，优化韩国整体造船业竞争力；加大技术研发，促使船企转型为全周期服务型企业。比如研发新一代智能型商船、节能

减排船和数字化造船厂；庆尚南道等地方政府推出金融支援计划，包括下调中小船配企业的地方税率、延长交税期限等税金减免措施。

综上所述，目前全球海工市场急剧萎缩，韩国船企在海工领域损失惨重，以现代商船、三星重工和大宇造船为首的"BIG 3"亏损巨大。2016 年，韩国造船业第二次徘徊于结构调整的十字路口，BIG 3 共同的债权人，即韩国开发性金融领导者韩国产业银行，从金融手段和企业建制方面积极为韩国造船业的危机处理贡献力量；同时，以"造船立国"为口号的韩国政府、社会和企业也都在讨论造船业的出路并开始了积极的应对。

第五章　中低收入国家的开发性金融机构

俄罗斯发展与对外经济事务银行

2015 年，受欧美制裁、贸易减少、能源价格和卢布汇率大幅下跌等不利因素的影响，俄罗斯投资整体下降了 8.4%。在国内经济形势悲观的背景下，俄罗斯发展与对外经济事务银行（VEB）肩负着抵御危机的重大使命，也面临着前所未有的挑战。这一年中，VEB 积极发挥开发性金融的功能，整合各方资源，在应对危机、促进国民经济发展和增加就业方面发挥了巨大的作用。其工作重点包括资助长期投资项目、发展基础领域和国民经济的重要部门、促进地区经济发展、支持高科技和创新产业、支持中小企业和出口、行使联邦政府代理人职能等。

主要经营数据

到 2015 年年底，VEB 从资本市场募集的各种货币资金中，美元由 180 亿减少到 158 亿，欧元由 23.3 亿减少到 20.4 亿，卢布由 3 742.4 亿增加到 3 848.9 亿。

从资金来源看，2015 年 VEB 主要通过增发国内债券来弥补从其他银行获得的信贷资金的减少。在俄罗斯资本市场投资不景气的背景下，VEB 于 2015 年共发行了 150 亿卢布的国内债券，并将之前发行的债券进行再融资，再融资债券名义价值为 790 亿卢布。由于受到欧盟和美国的制裁，欧洲债券和欧洲商业证券未能发行。截至 2015 年，VEB 从其他银行获得的中长期信贷资金共计 88 亿美元。部分欧洲的银行同意为从欧洲进口的项目提供不超过项目总价值 85% 的贷款，前提是由俄罗斯国家出口保险公司提供担保。基于此，2015 年 VEB 与法国、意大利、德国、丹麦、捷克的银行完成了金融合作。

2015 年 VEB 与中国国家开发银行（CDB）签署了价值 100 亿人民币的贷款协议，贷款将用于支持有中国公司参与的 VEB 在俄罗斯的投资项目和俄罗斯向中国出口的项目，这也是 VEB 和 CDB 签署的第一个以人民币交易的贷款项目。

工作亮点

支持投资项目

支持具有国家意义的投资项目一直是 VEB 的使命之一。VEB 以提供贷款、投资股份和为项目参与者提供担保三种方式参与支持投资项目，其中提供贷款是最主要的方式。2015 年，VEB 新参与了总额达 1 622 亿卢布的 6 个投资项目，其中 929 亿卢布由 VEB 出资，到年末共有 241 亿卢布已到账。同时，该年度共有 8 个 VEB 参与的投资项目竣工。

截至 2015 年年末，VEB 累计参与了 159 个投资项目。在提供贷款方面累计出资 13 592 亿卢布，在股份投资方面累计出资 354 亿卢布，在保证金方面累计出资 15 亿卢布。贷款总额中，1 996 亿卢布（占 14.7%）用于支持俄罗斯经济现代化建设的优先发展方向，以提高能效和节约能源，促进医药学、航天科技和通信发展。贷款总额中，4 690 亿卢布（占 34.5%）用于推动创新。2015 年，VEB 发放贷款增长最快的领域是冶金、油气化工和电子工业，它们的贷款额分别增长了 43.3%、38.1% 和 37.6%。新建的一批现代化企业正在成为新的经济增长点，提供了新的高科技工作岗位，并增加了政府的税收收入。

VEB 参与的部分投资项目如下：

1. 博古昌铝工厂。项目总价值 504 亿卢布，VEB 出资 15 亿美元。博古昌铝工厂更新了电解铝的设备，于 2015 年 8 月重新恢复生产。项目创造了 4.47 亿卢布税收，新增 391 个工作岗位。

2. 氨、甲醇和尿素综合工厂。项目总价值 22 亿美元，VEB 提供了 18 亿美元的贷款和 15 亿卢布的股权投资。2015 年年末工厂正常开工，并与世界领先交易商签署了 50 万吨氨、甲醇和尿素生产合同。项目创造了 16 亿卢布的税收，新增 356 个工作岗位。

3. 库鲁莫奇国际机场。项目总价值 75 亿卢布，VEB 出资 46 亿卢布。2015 年完成了该机场的重修工程，新建面积为 4.2 万平方米的航站楼和货运装置。新的候机厅专门为 2018 年世界杯重建。项目创造了 9.655 亿卢布的税收。

支持优先发展地区

2015 年之前，VEB 已经和 58 个联邦主体签署了合作协议。2015 年，VEB 与萨拉托夫州政府和俄联邦克里米亚事务部签署了合作协议，旨在促进这两个地区的经济发展。

在完善与地区的协作方式方面，VEB 进行了创新性的实践，即与联邦区的总统全权代表建立合作伙伴关系。在北高加索地区，截至 2015 年年末，VEB 为 6 个投资项目提供了 235 亿卢布。在该地区，与 VEB 协作的机构还有北高加索地区开发公司（North Caucasus Development Corporation，NCDC），NCDC 参与了北高加索地区的 6 个投资项目，截至 2016 年 1 月 1 日，NCDC 共投资了 54 亿卢布。在远东联邦区，VEB 的项目投资总额达 506 亿卢布，股份投资总额达 259 亿卢布，共支持了 10 个投资项目。在该地区，远东和贝加尔地区开发基金也承担着国家支持地区发展的责任。2015 年，该基金会共批准了总价值达 740 亿卢布的 6 个优先投资项目，其中该基金会提供 95 亿卢布。

VEB 于 2014 年年末新建了非商业机构"俄罗斯支持产业城发展基金会"，该机构的工作于 2015 年步入正轨，在俄罗斯产业城的发展和复兴方面发挥了巨大的作用。2015 年，VEB 共出资 603 亿卢布支持产业城发展。截至 2016 年 1 月 1 日，支持产业城发展方面的投资额累计达 2 373 亿卢布，共支持了 19 个项目。

支持中小企业发展

2015 年，在 VEB 的支持下，俄罗斯支持中小企业发展银行（SME Bank）启动了《支持中小企业发展项目》，重点关注国家优先发展经济部门的中小企业。该项目提供的贷款期限较长，利率相对较低，为中小企业带来很大帮助。受益于该发展项目，俄罗斯中小企业获得贷款的比例大大提高。

截至 2016 年 1 月 1 日，VEB 提供给该项目的资金总额达 567 亿卢布。截至 2015 年年底，俄罗斯中小企业通过该项目获得的贷款总额达到 1 057 亿卢布。2015 年，VEB 的合作银行为中小企业提供的贷款年加权平均利率为 13.2%，远低于市场利率。在 VEB 提供给中小企业的贷款中，年限超过 3 年的中长期贷款项目占比提高了 7 个百分点，到 2016 年 1 月 1 日增加到 83.9%。

支持出口

支持俄罗斯非原料产品出口是 VEB 的基本任务之一，然而 2015 年，挑战尤为巨大。一方面因为欧美制裁限制了俄罗斯公司的出口，另一方面全球经济形势不乐观，地缘政治也带来负面影响。为了对冲环境带来的负面影响，2015 年 VEB 以支持出口为目的共发放贷款 324 亿卢布，是 2014 年的 1.6 倍。到 2015 年年末，VEB 支持出口的贷款累计达 866 亿卢布。2015 年，VEB 以支持出口为目的共提供了 79 项保证金，总额 993 亿卢布，几乎增加了一倍。到 2015 年年末，VEB 支持出口的保证金累计达 3 975 亿卢布。2015 年 VEB 共完成了俄罗斯产品出口超过 20 个国家的投资项目。VEB 支持的出口产品大部分隶属于高科技范畴，包括交通、汽车制造、原子能、飞机制造和太空火箭项目等领域。此外，2015 年，VEB 新设立了专业化子机构"俄罗斯出口中心"，其职责是通过为出口商提供综合的专门化支持来促进出口。

行使俄联邦政府代理人职能

1. 提供和使用国家担保资金。2015 年，VEB 共代表俄罗斯联邦政府签署了 111 项担保协议，使用了 2 114 亿卢布的国家担保资金。国家担保资金来自政府财政拨款，为投资项目提供担保，从而撬动更多投资资金，推动项目实施。截至 2015 年年底，VEB 累计签署 614 项国家担保协议，总额为 31 237 亿卢布。2015 年，VEB 审查了 115 家受国家担保的委托方的财务状况。

2. 退休金管理。俄罗斯的居民退休金由两部分组成——劳动退休金和储蓄退休金。其中劳动退休金由退休金基金会管理，储蓄退休金由居民自愿选择交由政府或私营管理公司管理。自 2003 年起，VEB 代表政府管理退休金，为那些选择由政府管理退休金的居民设计了两种投资组合——政府有价债券组合和扩展后的投资组合。2015 年年末，扩展后的投资组合的市场价值为 19 902 亿卢布（年初为 18 923 亿卢布），政府有价债券投资组合的市场价值为 227 亿卢布（年初为 105 亿卢布）。2015 年，VEB 将储蓄退休金投放于这两种投资组合的年收益率分别为 13.2% 和 15.3%，这两项数据比该年度通货膨胀率分别高出 0.25% 和 2.41%。

2015 年，俄罗斯联邦退休金基金会将 21.66 亿卢布的支付储备金和 3.212 亿卢布的定期支付退休金转交 VEB 管理，从而使 VEB 的支付储备金（按市场价值）的总量从 25.63 亿卢布增加到 49.16 亿卢布，定期支付退休金总量从 2.47 亿卢布增加到 5.65 亿卢布。VEB 管理这两类资金的主要任务是保值。这两类资金的投资年收益率在 2015 年分别为 11.59% 和 11.28%。

2014 年 10 月，VEB 观察委员会制定了《2015—2020 年发展战略》。截至 2015 年年底，VEB 在很多方面超额完成了上述《战略》所设目标。其中，贷款总额达到 24 328 亿卢布，超出目标 24.8%。到 2015 年年底，支持出口的贷款总额为 866 亿卢布，低于目标 40.2%。VEB 投入支持中小企业发展的资金为 1 057 亿卢布，超出目标 5.7%。到 2015 年年末，VEB 通过市场和政府财政共获得资金 25 186 亿卢布，符合原定目标范围。其中，来自资本市场的资金为 15 680 亿卢布，超出目标 39.4%，从政府和俄罗斯央行获得的资金为 9 506 亿卢布，低于目标 34.6%。在受到欧美国家制裁、发放外债受阻的情况下，VEB 成功通过国内资本市场筹资，展示了其不断进步的能力和实力。总体来说，2015 年 VEB 通过筹资，支持各类项目、发展基础设施和创新产业、支持中小企业和出口，在俄罗斯应对危机和促进国民经济发展方面发挥了独特和重要的作用。

专栏5-1　俄罗斯产业城发展基金会推动产业城改革

产业城的发展困境是个世界性问题，在很多工业发达国家都发生过类似的情况。起初在一个地区建立大型工业企业，它的周边逐步形成工人聚居地，随着企业发展和时间的推移，这里慢慢形成一座城市。当市场环境发生变化、原材料耗尽，企业经营陷入困境，或是技术进步使人工使用率降低，都会导致居民失业。由于城市产业结构单一，居民再就业十分困难，整座城市经济面临瘫痪。美国的汽车制造之都底特律曾是规模巨大的工业中心，如今却彻底破产。

一、俄罗斯的产业城困境及改革

俄罗斯的产业城问题具有俄罗斯国家特色，是计划经济的产物。苏联时期，大批工业企业建立在人烟稀少的原材料产地，由于地域过于广阔，加上长久以来道路等基础设施建设不足，产业城的发展趋于封闭。现在，俄罗斯共有 319 座产业城，居民 1 400 万，占俄罗斯总人口的 10%。只有 71 座产业城的经济状况相对正常，其余城市都经历着不同的经济发展困难。

为了协助产业城经济多元化、创造更多工作岗位和吸引投资，解决产业城发展落后的问题，在俄罗斯总统普京的关心下，俄罗斯产业城发展基金会（FDM）于 2014 年成立，它是俄罗斯发展与对外经济银行集团旗下子公司之一。两年来，基金会通过投资产业城基础设施和创建大型投资项目，带动民间投资，为产业城经济发展注入了活力。基金会的运作得到了政府的财政支持，2014 年基金会获政府财政补贴 30 亿卢布（约合 4 695 万美元），2015 年获政府财政补贴 45 亿卢布（约合 7 042 万美元），2016 年和 2017 年预计分别获得 108 亿卢布（约合 1.69 亿美元）的补贴。2016 年 6 月 22 日，俄罗斯总理梅德韦杰夫签署了政府第 549 号决议，决定将基金会的职责范围扩展到全部 319 座产业城。目前，基金会和各地方政府共签署了 17 项综合协议，并在 10 个地区进行了投资和基础设施建设项目有效性评估。基金会观察委员会批准了一系列项目申请，并在 18 座城市开展了前期准备工作。根据计划，在 3~5 年内，基金会将投资约 300 亿卢布（约合 4.74 亿美元），用于改善 30~35 座产业城的状况。据估算，这些投资还将吸引超过 940 亿卢布（约合 14.86 亿美元）的私人投资。

二、俄罗斯产业城发展基金会的运作方式

产业城中的地方政府和企业最有意愿启动经济改革项目，但它们缺乏资金和联邦政府支持，而且薄弱的基础设施限制了它们的发展能力。在这种情况下，基金会所起的作用至关重要。

（一）组织作用

俄罗斯产业城发展基金会根据当地特点，组织政府、VEB、基金会和企业共同致力于地区改革方案的制定。改革方案由基金会观察委员会审核通过后，便可启动。各个产业城设有联邦政府认可的社会环境监测机构，各级机构协同 VEB 的代表、产业城发展基金会的代表共同了解产业城的情况。从 2015 年起，一些落后的产业城获得了"优先发展区域"地位，得到了重点关注并享受优惠税收政策。

（二）融资作用

基金会主要通过两大途径推动产业城改革——完善基础设施和建立农工业产业园以吸引民间投资。基金会对于产业城投资项目的申请程序和审核条件有明确规定：

1. 新投资项目的业务应与原产业城支柱企业无关，新项目所用原料中来自原支柱企业的份额不超过 50%，新项目为原支柱企业提供的商品

或服务不超过总产出的 50%，原支柱企业在新项目中控股不超过 50%。

2. 新投资项目应兼具经济效益与社会效益，致力于提供独立于原支柱企业的新工作岗位，并为产业城吸引投资。

3. 基金会将为每个项目提供 1 亿~10 亿卢布（约合 157.8 万~1 578 万美元）的资金支持，且投资金额不超过项目总值的 40%。投资周期不超过 3 年，贷款需要 8 年内还清。

4. 使用基金会资金的成本为支付年利率 5% 的利息。

5. 基金会在项目运行期间承担项目管理者的角色。

纵观基金会成立以来重点支持的项目可以发现，入驻工业园的企业主要是中小企业和从事废物利用加工、金属加工企业和高科技企业。值得一提的是，基金会尤其重视通过发展中小企业活化地方经济，对单个小型创业公司的补助可达 50 万卢布（约合 7 891 美元）。

（三）培训作用

制订并实施产业城经济改革方案并非易事，当地居民面临失业、生活窘迫时，政府和企业的权威性也遭到质疑，这对由政府和企业组成的地方领导团队提出了更高的能力要求。为了提高当地政府和企业人员在行政和发展规划等各个方面的能力，基金会还设立了培训项目，帮助政府和企业人员同居民建立良好对话机制，扎实论据，规划前景，立足民生，讨论改革方案。

三、产业城改革项目实例

1. 2015 年，基金会启动了鞑靼斯坦共和国卡马河畔切尔尼的改革项目。此地建有大型汽车制造企业卡玛斯公司。该公司为提升自己的竞争力和利润率，一直致力于提高生产力、优化生产模式和降低成本。随着生产力的提高，该公司开始出现劳动力过剩，导致其大幅裁员，并将厂房占地面积缩小约 4 000 公顷。许多居民面临失业。基金会到来后，这座产业城现在正在进行 5 个新的项目，分别是利用废料生产钢筋的企业"TEMPO"、香肠加工企业"卡姆斯基"、"海尔"空调工厂、服务于中小企业发展的联合信息站"MASTER"、生产人造蓝宝石的公司"卡玛水晶科技"。此外，基金会和鞑靼斯坦共和国政府还致力于基础设施的建设和完善。2016 年 7 月，城市电力网的问题已全部解决，道路基础设施还有待完善，基金会已拨款超过 6.27 亿卢布（约合 991 万美元）用于修路，另外的 1.98 亿卢布（约合 313 万美元）来自地方财政拨款。在 2015～2020年实施期间，这些投资项目计划在当地新增 3 438 个工作岗位，吸引投资86.24 亿卢布（约合1.35 亿美元）。

2. 2015 年，基金会投资了斯维尔德洛夫斯克州的克拉斯诺图灵斯克的改革项目，主要包括投资基础设施建设（建立工程管道）和建立"博戈斯洛夫斯基"工业园以吸引新的投资者。工业园计划包含以下投资项目：铝工件制造工厂，氧化铝废料再加工工厂，钻探设备生产厂，去污剂生产厂，氧化铝废料制作矿物补充剂工厂，氧化铝废料制作无机颜料工厂，土壤改良剂和吸附剂生产厂，利用聚合物和木材废料再生产复合材料工厂。

3. 2016 年 1 月，基金会与车里雅宾斯克州州长鲍里斯·杜布罗夫斯基签订了有关阿沙城市发展的协议。该协议计划建设占地150 公顷的农工业园区，这一计划将在未来 4 年为阿沙提供 1 500 个工作岗位。该项目总投资将超 70 亿卢布（约合1.09 亿美元）。

4. 2016 年 3 月，基金会在哈巴罗夫斯克边疆区建立了 Chegdomyn 工业区，且实施的项目已卓有成效。Chegdomyn 有 1.25 万居民，2015 年基金会投资了约 5 亿卢布（约合789 万美元），创造了 615 个工作岗位，现在那里有 5 个投资项目在进行，已有 3 家电枢企业入驻。

5. 2016 年 6 月，基金会计划投资 2.8 亿卢布（约合442 万美元）支持基洛夫州白霍卢尼察市建立工业园和基础设施建设，该工业园已入驻10 家公司，计划重点发展林业和化工业。

类似的改革实例不胜枚举。然而，这些改革措施的效果并非立竿见影，产业城发展的问题也并非一朝一夕能够解决的。但值得肯定的是，启动资助项目、联合政府和企业的力量、吸引投资、建立有效的监管框架有助于未来这些发展困难的地区变为新的经济增长点。

蒙古开发银行

作为蒙古政府全资建立的政策性金融机构，蒙古开发银行（DBM）长期致力于基础设施领域的投资、贷款以及协助政府完成战略性方案。2015 年，国际市场的原材料价格严重下跌，中国经济发展放缓以及外商对蒙古的直接投资下降，导致蒙古遭遇金融危机。在这一背景下，DBM 作为蒙古政府直属的金融机构，在投资、融资、危机应对、推动企业持续发展等方面做出了重要贡献。

主要经营数据

2016 年上半年，DBM 的总资产为 6.62 万亿图格里克（MNT）（约 26.98 亿美元），总负债为 6.36 万亿 MNT（约 26.24 亿美元）。DBM 的总股本为 0.26 万亿 MNT（约 1.06 亿美元），净利润为 390 亿 MNT（约 0.16 亿美元）。资本充足率为 11.0%，资产收益率为 0.61%，净资产收益率为 15%。2016 年 8 月 19 日标准普尔评级机构将蒙古的主权信用评级下调至 B－，前景稳定。穆迪评级机构于 2016 年 8 月将蒙古的主权信用评级从 B2 下调至 B3。

DBM 主要资金来源包括向国内外发放的债券、中期票据及政府借款。银行存款为 153 亿 MNT。放置其他银行的存款为 0.44 万亿 MNT。2015 年 5 月 26 日以 6.10% 票息，为期 125 日，在蒙古贸易发展银行存放 5 000 万美元，双方首次签署回购合同，于 2016 年 4 月 4 日到期。

截至 2015 年 12 月 31 日，DBM 向国内贸易银行以 4% 的票息发放了 0.15 万亿 MNT 债券，为迎接亚欧峰会（ASEM）代表，其债券融资将用于建设或改善住宿。DBM 以 4% 的年息发行 1 年票息，向蒙古贸易发展银行融资 1 705.95 亿 MNT，用于向 ETT 公司发放贷款，购买道路和基础设施。2014 年 2 月 DBM 以 4.25% 年息发放给 ETT 公司 1 705.95 亿 MNT 贷款资金。

截至 2015 年 12 月 31 日，DBM 政府借款融资总额为 2.563 9 万亿 MNT（约 11.25 亿美元），银团借款融资 0.60 万亿 MNT（约 2.62 亿美元），中国国家开发银行借款融资达到 0.302 2 万亿 MNT（约 1.33 亿美元），国际投资银行借款融资 423.64 亿 MNT（约 0.19 亿美元），VEB 借款融资达到 351.62 亿 MNT（约 0.15 亿美元），德国商业银行借款融资 237.33 亿 MNT（约 0.104 亿美元）（见图 5.1）。

可售投资证券是指投资蒙古证券有限责任公司（MIK）的 DBM 自有资产。2015 年 12 月 3 日，MIK 将公司所有权更改为股份公司，其公司名更换为 MIK 股份有限公司。2014 年 3 月，DBM 投资蒙古证券有限责任公司 100 亿 MNT（约 438.60 万美元），并签署了持该公司 14.88% 股份的合同，MIK 股份有限公司于 2015 年第三季度宣布股份利润分红消息，DBM 获得 23.64 万美元分红利润。

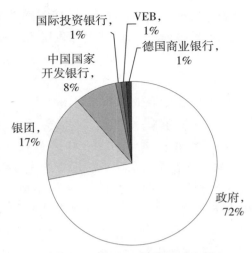

图 5.1　2015 年 DBM 借款融资情况

2015 年年末，MIK 在证券交易所以每股 12 000 MNT（约 5.26 美元）的价格交易成功。为维持其现持有的 MIK 14.88% 股份，DBM 被提议按上述价格额外购买 462.294 次股，2015 年 12 月 31 日每股 9 000 MNT（约 3.95 美元），投资额升值为 105 亿 MNT（约 460.53 万美元）。

工作亮点

DBM 协助蒙古经济可持续发展，在更多的领域寻求多样化发展，支持增值产品。DBM 有如下重要方案：蒙古政府对铁路运输的政策性方案；赛音山工业区方案；通过债券融资，完工后偿还的方式修建道路、能源设施等。

战略改革：蒙古政府为了提高 DBM 的竞争能力以及其在国际市场上融资能力，逐渐减少政府担保及由国家预算偿还的贷款，建设能在国际市场上独自融资的高效率金融机构。DBM 将贷款项目由国家预算偿还、政府担保改为由公司偿还、无政府担保。DBM 计划于 2018 年全部还完政府担保的资金，并从 2018 年以后减少贷款量。蒙古政府保持对社会效益高的方案直接投资的政策。

2015 年 2 月 18 日，蒙古通过了《债务管理法》，依据该法 DBM 是唯一有权获得政府 100% 的担保发放贷款的银行，而其他银行有权获得政府 85% 的担保。

2015 年 6 月 11 日，为了偿还 2014 年 0.17 万亿 MNT 债务支付，DBM 将 0.55 亿美元和 0.35 亿 MNT 政府债券以 0.14 万亿 MNT 的价格转移到蒙古央行，其余部分用现金支付。2015 年 12 月 27 日，DBM 以 6 000 万美元的政府债券作为抵押，与蒙古贸易开发银行签订了出售及回购合同。

DBM 向 ETT 提供的贷款由公司偿还。DBM 向 ETT 发放了 2 亿美元的贷款（截至 2015 年年末，贷款资金达到 0.40 万亿 MNT，约 1.75 亿美元）。这些贷款在往期的贷款上进行调整，还款推迟到 2017 年。这些贷款由政府担保，如果 ETT 公司未能履行其合同义务，相应贷款将全部由国家预算偿还（包括应急利息）。

DBM 发放给 ETT 的 3 项贷款的贷款利息及贷款逾期导致的额外利息，由蒙古政府支付了 100.27 万亿 MNT。通过这种调整，DBM 获得了 10 万亿 MNT 政府债券，也提前注册了未来应收所得税的 902.69 亿 MNT。

2015 年 DBM 董事会决定建立国家出口保险有限责任公司。DBM 于 2016 年 1 月入股国家出口保险有限责任公司，投资 50 亿 MNT，此外，2016 年 DBM 规划入股投资"融资租赁发展"有限责任公司，投资 10 亿 MNT。

马来西亚开发银行

马来西亚开发银行（BPMB）成立于 1973 年 11 月 28 日，由马来西亚财政部成立并全权管理。其成立初衷是，通过提供各种融资设施、企业家培训和咨询服务等，帮助马来西亚中小型企业的管理者。除了提供直接的金融服务外，马来西亚开发银行也通过旗下的子公司促进马来西亚战略经济部门的增长。

在商品价格的波动和不确定性，金融市场以及全球经济高度竞争的经营局势下，贷款增长缓慢，融资成本较高，继续拖累银行业表现。尽管面临此逆境，马来西亚开发银行表现相对较好，并将继续致力于为利益相关者创造长期价值。

主要经营数据

鉴于全球经济动荡，石油价格暴跌引发马来西亚货币贬值，马来西亚开发银行处于艰难的经营环境中。在整个银行业利润率及资本回报率低下的挑战下，BPMB 在 2015 年的税前利润达 12 480 万令吉，与 2014 年的 30 640 万令吉相比，跌幅达 59.3%。BPMB 的总资产从 292 亿令吉下降到 267 亿令吉，跌幅达 8.6%，下降原因主要是贷款、预付款和融资的减少。由于借款减少，其总负债下降了 24 亿~194 亿令吉。

工作亮点

在支持国家发展议程和促进经济增长方面，2015 年 BPMB 共批准了 23 个贷款项目，总金额达 35 亿令吉。在银行业增长放缓的背景下，该项审批金额比 2014 年下降 35.2%，2015 年，BPMB 向基础设施部门划拨了 28 亿令吉（80.0%），向科技部门划拨了 5 亿令吉（14.3%），剩余的 2 亿令吉（5.7%）划拨给海运部门，同时没有拨款给石油和天然气部门。BPMB 收紧了贷款审批流程，贷款多针对有健康财务状况的借款人。此外，BPMB 一直专注于与政府发起的项目有关的贷款和具有良好支付记录的借款人。

1. 基础设施。基础设施项目仍是 BPMB 主要的资金去向。截至 2015 年 12 月 31 日，BPMB 批准了 18 个基础设施项目的融资/贷款，占全部融资/贷款的 80%。随着政府进一步改善国家基础设施建设，这些基础设施融资/贷款中有 15.4% 用到公路/高速公路项目，52.6% 用于区域发展，13.9% 用于旅游业，剩余的 18.1% 分配给了公用事业和港口（见图 5.2）。基础设施部门批准的融资/贷款总额中 67.5% 用于政府支持的项目，其中"私人融资计划"（PFI）下有两个项目。PFI 是政府推动的一种机制，旨在促进私营部门参与提供公共服务，BPMB 积极参与了该计划。截至 2015 年 12 月 31 日，BPMB 资助了 33 个 PFI 项目，金额达 62 亿令吉。

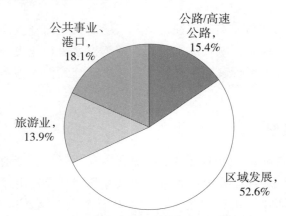

图 5.2　2015 年基础设施部门投资构成

2. 科技。2015 年，BPMB 共拨款 5 亿令吉给科技部门。其中，先进制造业占 28.1%，信息通信技术占 47.3%，剩余的 24.6% 用于环境保护行业（见图 5.3）。

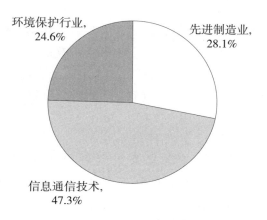

图 5.3　2015 年科技部门投资构成

3. 海运。缓慢的全球经济增长和持续交付新船只导致航运容量过剩，限制了海运公司提高运费收费的能力，进而限制了收入和盈利增长。由于不利的环境，BPMB 在 2015 年没有为船舶业融资。BPMB 在海运部门资助的唯一一个项目是融资价值为 2 亿美元的造船厂。

4. 石油、天然气。由于全球油价下跌，国内发展缓慢，项目规模持续缩小，海运租船费率持续下降，海外制造业企业的竞争日益激烈以及区域前景的可见度不断下降等原因，马来西亚石油和天然气部门波动频繁。较慢的项目产出和新投标的延误已经导致当地石油和天然气运营商收入下降。在市场疲软的环境下，2015 年 BPMB 并未批准石油及天然气部门的贷款请求。

未来几年，航运业仍然疲软，船舶供应仍将高于需求。考虑到过去 5 年中建成的船舶供应过剩，预计当前租船费率将至少持续两年以上，因为市场正在努力寻找新的均衡。预计 2017 年航运业将有更多的贷款重组，股权掉期债务或将强制销售。石油和天然气部门持续疲软，普遍的低油价将继续在中期造成黯淡的前景。因原油市场波动造成收入下降，马来西亚国家石油公司将进一步降低其资本支出。

土耳其工业发展银行

近年来，全球经济增速令人失望，美国、欧洲和日本等发达经济体呈温和复苏态势，中国经济增速放缓，巴西、俄罗斯和其他商品生产国则经历了深度衰退。尽管全球经济波动，土耳其宏观经济仍保持协调。2015 年，土耳其银行业扩张 10.5%，总贷款额同比增长 13.5%，土耳其本币里拉贷款增长 15%，外币贷款增长 9.9%，不良贷款同比增长 30.2%，增速较上年有所放缓。

2015 年对土耳其银行业而言是不幸的一年。由于"大国民议会"选举，政治不稳定因素造成土耳其投资者心理出现波动，股指大跌 6%，里拉贬值 4.5%，投资者投资欲望严重下降。然而，土耳其工业发展银行（TSKB）通过多样化投资有效地分散风险，并为其股东创造了价值。

主要经营数据

截至 2016 年年末，TSKB 资产总额达 240 亿里拉（约 64.5 亿美元），同比增长 15.8%；净利润 4.764 亿里拉（约 1.28 亿美元），同比增长 17.1%；股东应享权益 29 亿里拉（约 7.8 亿美元），同比增长 17.7%；现金贷款达 173 亿里拉（约 46.5 亿美元），同比增长 26.7%。TSKB 年平均总资产收益率为 2.1%，净资产收益率为 17.6%。此外，TSKB 资产质量保持相对稳定，不良贷款率仅为 0.3%。

2015 年，该行 93% 的贷款由外币贷款组成，美元计价贷款占 57%，欧元计价贷款占 36%。里拉贷款占比从 2014 年的 10% 降至 2015 年的 7%，不良贷款率为 0.4%，远低于土耳其银行业平均水平。由于贷款货币与借款货币一致，该行的汇率风险敞口接近零。截至 2015 年年末，该行有息资产占总资产的比例为 93%，如此高的比例是增强银行偿付能力的一个因素。此外，在与超国家组织建立长期密切关系的背景下，该行在资本市场中的积极作用及长期可持续的资金结构，将对其盈利能力和偿付能力产生持续的积极影响。

工作亮点

TSKB 的使命是支持土耳其可持续发展。2015 年，土耳其工业发展银行获得了来自国际市场的 9.5 亿美元资金，用于支持私营部门发展。该行发放了 6 亿美元现金贷款，用于可再生能源、能源和资源使用效率、环境、可持续旅游、医疗保健、教育和中小企业融资。该行大部分融资项目为能源电厂项目，其次是配电、其他私有化部门、物流和房地产等领域。

支持低碳排放制造业发展

2015 年，TSKB 贷款总额中具有可持续发展主题的贷款所占比例为 50%。在应对气候变化和促使土耳其向低碳经济转型的过程中，有效、准确地利用可再生能源具有极其重要的意义。在过去 6 年中，TSKB 为土耳其私营部门提供中期和长期融资，以支持其提高资源使用效率。在能源和资源使用效率方面，TSKB 为旅游、化工、汽车、钢铁、采矿、水泥和纺织等部门的 103 个项目提供融资，融资金额占该行总贷款的 10%。

到 2015 年年底，TSKB 在制造过程、废物管理以及能源和资源效率范围内已为 133 个可再生能源项目和 100 多个能源和资源节约举措提供贷款。因此，土耳其工业发展银行在应对气候变化和满足土耳其不断增长的能源需求方面发挥了重要作用。此外，作为土耳其第一个实现碳中和的银行，该行还鼓励股东在其影响力范围内采取有利于可持续发展的相关举措。

支持工业公司的建立及私营部门的发展

在过去的一年中，TSKB 在许多工业企业的建立中发挥了关键作用，这些工业企业被视为国家私营部门的基石。截至 2015 年年底，该行向中小企业发放的贷款金额占到贷款总额的 16%。

2015 年，TSKB 获得了来自日本国际协力银行的 1.5 亿美元可再生能源和能源效率贷款，来自欧洲投资银行的 1 亿欧元中小企业贷款，TSKB 发行的 3.5 亿美元欧洲债券以及来自国际金融公司的 7 500 万美元可再生能源和能源效率贷款。

支持艺术和文化发展

2015 年，TSKB 继续为伊斯坦布尔文化艺术基金会组织的伊斯坦布尔音乐节中的部分音乐会提供赞助。2015年6月8日，伊斯坦布尔音乐节上，TSKB赞助的"舞蹈巴黎"活动，得到了广泛赞誉。

自2014年起，该行定期为参与音乐会的音乐家和观众抵消碳足迹，这是该行将可持续发展原则与艺术赞助相结合的创举。该行的具体做法是将个性化定制的黄金标准（GS）自愿减排量证书（VER）送给商业伙伴及客户作为新年礼物，有效地中和他们在日常交通、取暖等活动中产生的碳足迹。VER是作为奖励颁发给全球实现二氧化碳减排项目的一种证书，是《联合国气候变化框架公约》清洁发展机制减排量之外自发的、公益的、可认证的减排信用额度证明。

专栏5-2　土耳其银行信用评级的影响因素

近年来，土耳其经济持续增长，银行业监管良好、资产规模不断扩大、净利润不断增长。根据土耳其银行监理署发布的数据，2016年1~8月，土耳其银行业净利润同比增长63.4%，达88.5亿美元；总资产达8 358亿美元，贷款金额达5 299.7亿美元；银行资本充足率为16.03%，核心资本充足率为13.80%。然而，2016年土耳其银行信用评级却频繁变动。土耳其农业银行、TSKB等运营良好、财务健全，保持着可持续的盈利能力且拥有庞大的分行网络，其评级为何也遭到下调？

一、土耳其农业银行和土耳其工业发展银行的评级变动

2016年对于土耳其而言可谓是多事之秋。伊斯兰国和库尔德极端组织多次在土耳其境内制造恐怖袭击、"七一五"未遂政变和日益棘手的叙利亚难民问题等均对土耳其的安全局势和经济形势造成冲击。土耳其经济风险的负面趋势给土耳其银行的信用评级带来不利影响，使银行个体信用状况面临压力。目前，土耳其财政风险、安全风险、政治不稳定性和地缘政治局面恶化，主权信用评级被穆迪、惠誉、标准普尔等多家评级机构下调，其中穆迪更是将土耳其主权信用评级下调至垃圾级。相应地，包括土耳其农业银行、TSKB在内的10余家银行的评级也受此影响发生了变化（见表5.1及表5.2）。

表 5.1　土耳其农业银行评级变化

评级机构	类别	2015 年 10 月	2016 年 10 月
惠誉评级	长期外币发行人违约评级	BBB	BBB –
	展望	稳定	负面
	短期外币发行人违约评级	F3	F3
	长期本币发行人违约评级	BBB	BBB –
	展望	稳定	负面
	短期本币发行人违约评级	F3	F3
	国家长期评级	AAA（tur）	AAA（tur）
	展望	稳定	稳定
	支持评级	2	2
	支持评级底线	BBB –	BBB –
	生存力评级	bbb –	bbb –
穆迪评级	展望	负面	稳定
	长期外币存款评级	Baa3	Ba2
	短期外币存款评级	P – 3	非优质
	长期本国货币存款评级	Baa3	Ba1
	短期本国货币存款评级	P – 3	非优质
	基准信用评估等级	ba1	ba2
	调整基准信用评估等级	ba1	ba2

表 5.2　土耳其工业发展银行评级变化

评级机构	类别	2015 年 10 月	2016 年 10 月
惠誉评级	**外币信用评级**		
	长期	BBB –	BBB – –
	展望	稳定	负面
	短期	F3	F3

（续表）

评级机构	类别	2015 年 10 月	2016 年 10 月
惠誉评级	**本币信用评级**		
	长期	BBB	BBB –
	展望	稳定	负面
	短期	F3	F3
	其他		
	支持评级	2	2
	支持评级底线	BBB –	BBB –
	长期国家评级	AAA（tur）	AAA（tur）
	展望	稳定	稳定
穆迪评级	基准信用评估评级	ba2	Ba2
	长期外币发行人评级	Baa3	Ba1
	长期本币发行人评级	Baa3	Ba1
	展望	负面	稳定
	短期外币发行人评级	P – 3	非优质
	短期本币发行人评级	P – 3	非优质

二、土耳其银行信用评级变动的影响因素

（一）财政风险

2015 年土耳其举行了两次有争议的议会选举，但政府财政基本稳定，中央政府赤字略微收窄到 GDP 的 1.2%，2015 年年底政府债务占国内生产总值的比重下降到 32.6%。然而，为兑现选举前的承诺，2016 年政府财政状况更加恶化，难民安置和安全开支也给财政支出造成较大压力。进入 2016 年以来，从表面上看土耳其经济仍然保持增长，但其通胀率高达 8%，可以说土耳其经济实际上已经开始衰退。

此外，长达 20 多年的巨大贸易逆差，使土耳其背负了沉重的外债负担。2015 年年底土耳其经常项目赤字占 GDP 的 38.4%。有专家指出，土耳其投资资金的流入为经常项目赤字和外债偿付融资，该国是 20 国集团中经常项目赤字最高的国家之一。虽然油价下跌推动了经常项目赤字的

周期性下降，但没有证据表明土耳其的外债状况有所改善。同时，土耳其里拉一路贬值，美元对里拉的汇率从2015年年底的2.8一路涨至目前接近3.5的水平。

受政治不稳定因素等影响，土耳其外部融资脆弱性不断突显，导致债务/国内生产总值下降趋势逆转，国际收支不平衡不断恶化。

（二）政治不稳定性

土耳其长期的、日益深化的政治不稳定性有损于经济表现，对经济政策可信度构成威胁。军事政变使土耳其的政治环境更加动荡，土耳其政府为应对政变所采取的措施更深化了土耳其的政治风险，对其主权信用状况造成影响。有媒体报道称，政变后政府马上逮捕了6 000多人，其中包括法官和检察官等公职人员。随后政府彻底清查葛兰信徒，到8月19日已有7万多人因此停工。埃尔多安还计划立法加强总统职权，这可能给体制的完整性带来进一步的压力。政变后，土耳其政府虽然迅速控制局面，但如果政治因素导致国际投资者信心显著下降，土耳其的外部融资需求就会受到影响。

长期以来，土耳其在世界银行治理指标中政治稳定方面得分一直较低，这是土耳其主权信用状况的一个特征。国内冲击会影响投资者对土耳其主权信用的看法。而如果政治不确定性使投资环境进一步恶化，使财政收支压力进一步加大，那么土耳其的经济、财政和债务指标可能超预期恶化，成为影响主权信用评级和金融机构评级的不稳定因素。

（三）地缘政治局面恶化，安全风险日益突显

由于库尔德问题、邻国叙利亚问题和伊斯兰国势力的侵扰，土耳其安全风险日益加深。2016年，在伊斯坦布尔和安卡拉发生的恐怖袭击造成多人死亡。而军事政变后大量高级军官被撤，这也可能影响土耳其应对安全问题的能力。2015年11月与俄罗斯发生军事冲突后，俄罗斯已对土耳其采取经济制裁，虽然目前俄土关系升温，但冲突造成的影响并未完全消失。

恐怖袭击对土耳其旅游业造成重大冲击，来自国外游客的旅游收入同比下降41%。土耳其旅游业约占GDP 3%，占当前外资收入的13%。与俄罗斯的外交和解使土耳其旅游业稍稍回暖，但只要安全条件没有显著的改善，土耳其旅游业就不可能完全恢复。

2014年11月土耳其大国民议会选举后正发党继续执政，缓解了国内

政治不确定性，但将来为了加强总统权力而进行的宪法改革将给土耳其带来新的政治不确定性。

（四）银行机构所受到的影响

主权信用评级是大多数土耳其银行评级的关键影响因素。土耳其银行的信用状况与国家风险、外部融资渠道和里拉汇率等有着密切的联系。

未遂政变可以说是诸多问题的导火索，直接导致土耳其银行信用评级下行风险增加。虽然土耳其银行部门基本健全，短期内银行的财务指标也未出现急剧变化，并未导致存款不稳定，中央银行也表示愿意向该部门提供支持，但政变后里拉大幅下跌突显了银行部门面临的外币贷款风险。外币贷款占银行业总贷款组合的1/3，近来里拉大幅贬值可能使银行遭受损失。此外，里拉进一步贬值将增加银行资产质量的风险。随着政治不稳定性进一步加剧，土耳其旅游业在一段时间内都不景气，个别银行的资产质量比率也可能受到新的压力。所幸土耳其银行旅游贷款份额很小（约占贷款的3%），土耳其与俄罗斯关系解冻也可以使土耳其旅游业得到喘息的机会。

事实上，国际评级机构的评级结果常常具有政治动机，所以仅凭信用评级并不能全面反映土耳其的投资贸易环境。但随着评级下调，土耳其将面临难以吸引外资以弥补其经常项目赤字的困境。由于土耳其政局、地缘政治局面及安全风险等因素具有不确定性，受其影响的土耳其主权评级及金融机构评级也具有不确定性，甚至频繁变动。

土耳其农业银行

2015 年土耳其经济深受国际经济形势影响。美联储利率决议、欧洲央行扩张性货币政策、通货膨胀、地缘政治风险等均对土耳其经济造成不利影响。然而，面对这些困境，土耳其经济仍实现了增长。2015 年，土耳其农业银行（TCZB）总资产同比增长 22.3%，达到 3 028 亿里拉。由于大力发展可持续的盈利能力和生产力，TCZB 净利润达 52 亿里拉，同比增长 27.5%。除了为农业生产、农业工业部门提供资金等核心业务活动外，贸易融资最近也成为TCZB 增强其竞争力的业务之一。TCZB 的实体部门融资增长快于行业平均水平，对公司细分客户的现金贷款增长 44%，达到 680 亿里拉，非现金信贷增长 45%，达到 530 亿里拉。此外，该行新开设了 112 家国内分行，进一步扩大其在国内市场的地域覆盖面。

主要经营数据

TCZB 的战略目标是：实现客户关系管理可持续化，致力于与所有客户培养创造价值的、可持续发展的关系；不断改进和发展业务流程并将业务流程制度化，以提高生产效率；加强综合子公司管理，通过扩大土耳其农业银行财团，强化国内和国际子公司、关联公司和国际分支机构之间的协同作用；优化运营，快速适应新技术，实现运营高度数字化、集中化；人力资源管理客观透明，提高现有员工工作能力，同时不断引进人才，以确保商业模式的可持续性；最大限度地利用信息技术，以确保竞争优势；优化资产负债表，使其结构更加以客户为本，并在不影响收入增长的情况下控制支出。

TCZB 致力于通过可持续增长、盈利能力和生产力来加强其财务结构。该行继续通过自身所遵守的资产负债管理策略，加强股本资产负债表结构，在资本充足程度、盈利能力及生产效率方面保持良好。

TCZB 继续成功保持土耳其政府债券市场指定主要交易商这一地位，在初级市场和二级市场发挥积极作用。根据伊斯坦布尔证券交易所债务证券市场的交易总量衡量，2015 年土耳其农业银行外汇交易量上升 29%，交易表现排名第二。

截至 2016 年年末，该行总资产达 3 577.6 亿里拉（约 985 亿美元），同比增长 18.1%；净利润 65.8 亿里拉（约 18.2 亿美元），同比增长 27%（见表 5.3）。2016 年该行提供的农业贷款额增长了 25%，增至 420 亿里拉（约 116 亿美元）。

表 5.3 TCZB 2015～2016 年主要经营数据　　　　　　　　（单位：百万里拉）

	2015 年 12 月	2016 年 9 月	2016 年 12 月
贷款	186 813	209 966	232 644
存款	186 469	204 516	223 019
股东权益	31 546	37 266	38 382
总资产	302 848	329 749	357 761
净利润	5 162	5 009	6 576

工作亮点

与法国开发署签署信贷协议

TCZB 从法国开发署获得了 12 年期 1 亿欧元的贷款，这笔货款将主要为从事动物源食品生产的非畜牧业中小企业提供支持，帮助其实现生产现代化并使其生产符合欧盟卫生和环境标准及土耳其有关法律法规的要求。

与欧洲开发银行签署信贷协议

2014 年，TCZB 与欧洲开发银行签署了一份为期 7 年的协议，欧洲开发银行通过土耳其农业银行租赁子公司提供总额为 5 000 万欧元的信贷。2015 年这笔信贷转入土耳其农业银行，总额中至少 15% 将贷给在土耳其优先发展区域从事经营的企业，帮助这些企业创造新的就业机会，提高他们保护现有企业的能力。

与世界银行签署信贷协议

该协议最初于 2010 年签订，协议金额 2 亿美元，在 2015 年第一季度圆满完成。土耳其农业银行从世界银行获得的资金用于支持中小型企业发展，满足其投资需求和流动资金需求，同时资助中小企业和大型企业进行能源效率投资。

与欧洲投资银行签署对中小企业和大型企业的信贷融资协议

2015 年，土耳其农业银行从欧洲投资银行获得协议金额 2 亿欧元中的第二笔贷款，金额 1 亿欧元，用于为中小型企业和大型企业提供投资资本和运营资本，帮助其增加产出，提高生产力和就业能力，从而实现增长。此外，贷款的另一个明确目标是帮助缩小区域间发展水平的差异。

与沙特出口计划署签署信贷协议

2013 年，土耳其农业银行从沙特出口计划署获得 5 000 万美元的信贷额，以资助沙特阿拉伯产品进口到土耳其。2015 年融资持续进行，根据沙特出口计划署要求，从沙特阿拉伯进口除石油以外的大量商品的客户可获得低成本融资。

与德国开发银行签署信贷协议

2014 年，土耳其农业银行与德国开发银行签署了一项为期 10 年的协议，向位于农村地区或处于农业生产价值链中的中小企业提供总额 1.5 亿欧元的融资。

与土耳其中小企业发展联盟支持计划签署协议

土耳其农业银行与土耳其中小企业发展联盟签署的这项协议，可使联盟中的企业更容易获得贷款融资。

药房支持计划

2015 年 3 月 23 日，土耳其农业银行推出了"药房支持计划"，该计划向药剂师提供药品，其所在社会保险公司通过土耳其农业银行收款和付款。这一综合性优惠信贷产品和服务旨在为土耳其的药房和药剂师提供帮助，并提升银行在这一业务领域的领导力。

女企业家支持计划

2015 年 12 月 4 日，土耳其农业银行推出"女企业家支持计划"，其目的是通过支持女企业家的商业活动，帮助其在国民经济中发挥更大的作用。

推出 7 只新的共同基金

为使客户投资选择多样化，土耳其农业银行增加了 7 只新的共同基金。包括：对冲基金、基金中的基金、房地产投资信托基金、符合伊斯兰教法的对冲基金、符合伊斯兰教法的股本基金、符合伊斯兰教法的外汇基金和符合伊斯兰教法的租赁证书参与基金等。后 4 个基金是为偏好无息集体投资计划的客户提供的。

发放银团贷款

2015 年土耳其农业银行进行了第三次银团贷款，由来自 19 个国家的 41 家银行在 4 月联合发行，由美银美林国际有限公司牵头。该交易承诺分两期为土耳其农业银行提供 11 亿美元资金。土耳其农业银行将利用这笔资金，通过其更广泛、更多样化的外贸金融产品和服务，有效地支持客户。

为农业部门融资

为农业部门提供资金支持一直是土耳其农业银行最基本也最重要的任务，土耳其农业银行致力于提供与国家农业政策相适应的金融解决方案。土耳其农业银行以可持续的资金模式为客户提供支持，使参与农业生产的企业能够提高其生产能力、现代化水平和盈利能力，并创造附加价值。

2015 年，土耳其农业银行为农业部门提供的贷款总额为 358 亿里拉。截至 2015 年年底，该行农业信贷客户达到 634 689 户。土耳其农业银行根据政府法令向从事各方面农业生产的客户提供补贴信贷，这类贷款的利率一般每年在 0 ~ 8.25% 之间变动。

巴西国家开发银行

2015 年，世界总体宏观经济状况依然延续了缓慢的发展趋势，世界主要经济体也依旧面临着经济发展停滞期。这使得国际贸易经济持续放缓，商业和消费者信心指数创下历史新低。同时，雷亚尔兑美元的汇率下降也给巴西带来通胀压力。这些因素导致标准普尔和惠誉国际评级机构于 2015 年 12 月降低了对巴西投资能力的评级；企业的盈利能力停留在历史平均值以下，借贷成本升高，股票的投资风险也因为宏观经济情况的不确定性而增加。尽管面临着不利的经济态势和来自社会与监管机构的压力，巴西国家开发银行（BNDES）在推动巴西境内外投资和促进当地经济发展方面依然取得较好成绩。

主要经营数据

至 2015 年，BNDES 拥有总资产共计 9 306 亿雷亚尔（约 2 909.2 亿美元）。2015 年 BNDES 的净利润达到了 62 亿雷亚尔（约 19.37 亿美元），相较于上年同期的 86 亿雷亚尔（约 26.9 亿美元）减少了 5.4%。经证实，自 2015 年 12 月起，366 亿雷亚尔（约 114.37 亿美元）可作为核心资本的金融资产将不再作为净权益列出，而是整合至国库负债。此外，BNDES 在 95 万余项目上共支出 1 359 亿雷亚尔（约 420 亿美元），相较上一年减少了 28%。其主要投资领域集中在电气、交通物流和绿色经济方面。

工作亮点

改善问责和透明机制

为响应来自社会与人民的压力和监管机关的要求，BNDES 不断致力于问责和透明机制的改善。自 2008 年以来，BNDES 便已将公开运营信息作为特色服务的一部分。2015 年 6 月，BNDES 在原有基础上进一步完善了透明公开制网站，使得信息易于获取，并对信息数据库进行了补充。最新的运营信息包括主要金融概况，如利率和财务担保信息等。

承担环境责任

在环境领域，BNDES 努力在投资项目分析和本土公司行为准则方面达到最严格的国际可持续环境标准。除了成立亚马逊基金（Amazon Fund）外，BNDES 还为与大西洋森林生物群落区（Atlantic Forest Biome）相关的 7 个项目提供了 2 000 万雷亚尔（约 624. 98 万美元）的融资。同时，BNDES 还扶持了多个"从蔗糖废料中提炼乙醇作为新能源"的项目，以帮助巴西政府实现至 2025 年减少 35% 温室气体排放量的目标。

扶持基础设施建设

2015 年，BNDES 为能源和物流领域的金融项目投入为 294 亿雷亚尔（约 91. 87 亿美元）。同年，主要用于农商业贸易运输的两段高速公路项目的资金获批。随着 BNDES 基础设施建设业务的扩展，圣保罗国际机场和坎皮纳斯国际机场的项目进入最后的支付阶段。在城市机动性和卫生领域，BNDES 则投入了 104 亿雷亚尔（约 32. 5 亿美元）。其中，在里约热内卢市数个城镇开展的水供应和卫生系统项目得到了约 2. 956 亿雷亚尔（约 9 237 万美元）的融资。其他的基础设施建设还包括奥运地铁四号线、轻轨铺设、快速公交等项目。

推动创新型中小微企业发展

2015 年度，BNDES 创新型中小微企业项目（BNDES Innovative MSME Program）共批准了 66 个运营项目，总投资额达到 1. 015 亿雷亚尔（约 3 200 万美元）。另一个重点项目 BNDES ProBK Program 在开展一年以来已经在各个签约项目上投入了 2. 3 亿雷亚尔（约 7 200 万美元），其中一半的项目是与中小微企业的合作。

另外，作为 BNDES 主要负责资本市场运营和金融产品完善的重要附属机构，2015 年，其下属机构共资助超过 1 000 家创新型公司，尤其是科技创新型公司。

南部非洲开发银行

南部非洲开发银行（DBSA）成立于 1983 年，是一家由南非共和国政府所有的国有银行，也是南部非洲地区占据领导性地位的开发性金融机构。南部非洲开发银行致力于推动南非乃至整个非洲经济的发展、人力资源的优化以及机构能力的建设，助力南部非洲地区经济社会的发展。2015 年，DBSA

继续加大对基础设施建设项目的资金扶持，协助南非政府向民众提供高质量的基础设施服务。

主要经营数据

截至 2015 年年底，DBSA 拥有发展资金 631 亿兰特，遍布 13 个南部非洲发展共同体的国家，主要集中在能源、道路、水资源、交通和社会基础设施部门。DBSA 坚持践行"高效率、共同愿景、诚信、创新、服务导向"的价值理念，旨在将南部非洲建设成为一个繁荣、和谐、没有贫困的地区。DBSA 不断扩大其发展资金的覆盖范围，致力于通过社会基础设施建设提高人民的生活水平，通过对经济基础设施的投资支持经济增长，并支持区域一体化。

DBSA 主要拥有四方面的资本，包括社会资本、智力资本、财务资本和人力资本。在社会资本方面，DBSA 强调与客户、合作伙伴以及政府的关系，与 13 个国家存在业务关系。在智力资本方面，DBSA 在基础设施建设方面有 31 年的经验，并得到了南非政府的智力支持。在财务资本方面，其资金主要来自债务、资产净值等财务资源以及业务、投资所得。2015 年，DBSA 的资本和准备金共 237 亿兰特，从政府部门获得的发展资金共 25 亿兰特，带息债务共 462 亿兰特，业务运营带来的资金共 27 亿兰特。在人力资本方面，工作人员的健康、知识和技能构成了其主要的人力资本。2015 年，DBSA 员工数量达到了 459 人，专门支持基础设施建设的合同制员工共计 88 人。

工作亮点

为了更好地适应自身的战略转型，DBSA 升级了战略目标。2015 年，DBSA 主要有 3 个战略目标：一是推动各项业务扩张，最大化发展成果；二是为南部非洲的基础设施建设提供完整的解决方案；三是实现财务的可持续性，维持盈利能力，提高业务效率，增加资产净值。为了实现这 3 个战略目标，DBSA 提出了以下几项战略举措：

为南部非洲的基础设施建设提供创造性解决方案

基础设施建设是 DBSA 的工作重点。2015 年，DBSA 投资南非基础设施建设项目累计 1 亿欧元，批准项目共计 64 亿兰特，尚处于准备中的投资项目共计 2 600 亿兰特，多集中在能源和交通部门。2015 年，DBSA 在基础设施建设上共投入 130 亿兰特，其中能源部门 70 亿兰特、水资源部门 21 亿兰特、交通部门 13 亿兰特、通信部门 3.5 亿兰特，共计 113 个基础设施项目。在基础设施的投入中，54 亿兰特投资流向了城市地区。在城市地区，DBSA 完成了 3 个关于基础设施建设项目的总体规划，累计完成 60 个项目，27 个项目正处于规划阶段，84 个项目正在执行。在非城市地区，DBSA 完成了 15 所学校的修建，48 所学校正在修建，建造了 1 128 套房屋，修建了 60 个医生咨询室、26 个卫生诊所。DBSA 通过创新更高效地解决市场和客户的需求问题，用产品的多元化获得更大的竞争优势，加速基础设施的建设并扩大基础设施的覆盖面。

创造并维持高效的文化氛围

对于 DBSA 而言，人力资源是最有价值的资源。DBSA 致力于通过构建一个充满挑战性并且令人振奋的工作环境来吸引、壮大、维系并奖励最优秀的工作人员，增强凝聚力，促进发展。为了协调人力资源，DBSA 董事会成立了 HRNSE 委员会，主要负责执行其人力资本战略，协调包括人事任免在内的多项管理、社会和伦理问题。

发展并利用其战略合作伙伴关系

DBSA 致力于通过发展同其他机构的战略合作伙伴关系来扩展并深化对所选市场部门和地域市场的占有和渗透。这些战略合作伙伴关系让 DBSA 获得更多的信息和项目资金，增强了其竞争优势。DBSA 积极地与客户和发展伙伴发展战略合作关系，制订发展计划并且推动基础设施项目实施。例如，2015 年，DBSA 积极与国际发展融资俱乐部（IDFC）开展合作，并继续积极参与世界经济论坛（WEF）的活动，加速基础设施建设项目的执行。

推动业务的发展和扩张

DBSA 致力于建设其业务运营模型，更加高效地为发展提供资金支持并提高项目执行能力。DBSA 加大对教育、医疗、卫生等领域的投入，兴建学校，完善学校基础设施，改善居民的住房条件，修建诊所和医生咨询室，并对诊所的设施进行了修缮。

成立绿色基金，支持南非绿色经济的发展

绿色基金于 2013 年成立，旨在支持南非的经济转型，引导南非走上一条低碳的绿色发展道路。2015 年，绿色基金批准了 15 个项目，资金共计 4.551 亿兰特，主要集中在可再生能源领域，其次是废物管理和循环利用领域。

成立就业基金，创造更多的就业岗位和就业机会

就业基金于 2012 年成立，致力于为以创造就业机会为导向的项目提供资金支持。2015 年，就业基金共投资 5.138 亿兰特，创造了 401 217 个永久性工作和 9 468 个临时性工作，6 551 人完成了短期实习工作，66 483 人接受了职业培训。

哈萨克斯坦开发银行

由国企公司控股的哈萨克斯坦开发银行（DBK）在 2015 年卓有成效地完成了它的战略任务。虽然哈萨克斯坦金融部门在该年度遭遇了严重的危机，但 DBK 仍成功实现了 57 亿坚戈（约 1 761 万美元）的净利润。

DBK 的宗旨是，在国家规划的框架内行使国家投资机构的职能，为私有和国有部门（包括基础设施部门）的非原料生产领域提供中长期、低利率的贷款支持。根据哈萨克斯坦共和国法律《关于哈萨克斯坦的银行和银行事务》，DBK 并非二级银行，它拥有特殊的法律地位。DBK 并不接受来自国家监管部门的管理，其业务受《关于哈萨克斯坦开发银行》这一特殊法律约束。

DBK 的股份完全由国家控股股份公司 Baiterek 持有，其注册资本也完全由国家持有。截至 2015 年 12 月 31 日，DBK 注册资本为 3 536.68 亿坚戈（约 10.93 亿美元）。

主要经营数据

截至 2015 年 12 月 31 日，DBK 总资产达 21 280 亿坚戈（约 65.76 亿美元），相比 2014 年增长了 63%（见图 5.4）。

截至 2015 年 12 月 31 日，DBK 总负债达 17 720 亿坚戈（约 54.76 亿美元），相比年初增长了 78%（见图 5.5）。

截至 2015 年 12 月 31 日，DBK 股东权益达 3 560 亿坚戈（约 11.00 亿美元），相比 2014 年增加了 43 亿坚戈（约 1 328 万美元）。

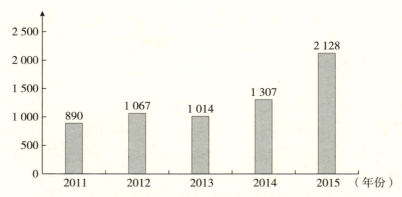

图 5.4 2011～2015 年 DBK 总资产情况（单位：10 亿坚戈）

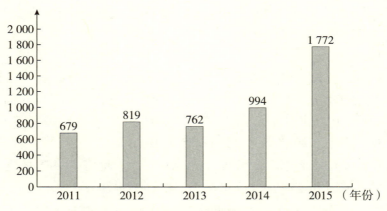

图 5.5 2011～2015 年 DBK 总负债情况（单位：10 亿坚戈）

据 2015 年统计结果，DBK 净盈利 57 亿坚戈（约 1 761 万美元），比 2014 年减少了 49%（2014 年净盈利 113 亿坚戈）。净利息收入为 310 亿坚戈（约 9 580 万美元），比 2014 年增加了 50 亿坚戈（约 1 545 万美元），即增加了 19%。

2015 年 DBK 贷款组合总计 14 520 亿坚戈（约 44.87 亿美元），相比 2014 年增长了 78%。

工作亮点

贷款发放

2015 年，DBK 大幅提高了哈萨克斯坦经济中的借贷量，超额完成了重要的计划指标。DBK 的合并贷款组合总额在两年间增加了 3 倍，2013 年年末为3 780亿坚戈（约11.68亿美元），2015年年末达到1.45万亿坚戈（约44.81亿美元）。DBK所资助项目的经济部门范围愈发广泛，如今接受该行贷款的项目来自冶金、石油化工、汽车制造、食品加工、建筑和交通等多个部门。

2015年DBK在非原料经济部门发放直接贷款总计2 623亿坚戈（约8.11亿美元），相当于所有二级银行在该领域发放贷款总量的66%。在制造业发放贷款总计2 165亿坚戈（约6.69亿美元），相当于所有二级银行在该领域发放贷款总量的82%。

截至2015年年末，DBK发放贷款总量为14 520亿坚戈（约44.87亿美元），相当于二级银行在非原料部门发放长期贷款总量的96%。DBK在制造业部门发放贷款总量为11 800亿坚戈（约36.46亿美元），相当于二级银行在制造业发放长期贷款总量的151%。

项目融资

自成立之日起，DBK共批准了111个投资项目，总价值48 978亿坚戈（约151.35亿美元），其中DBK参与投资24 692亿坚戈（约76.30亿美元）；DBK共批准了95项出口业务，总价值6 135亿坚戈（约18.96亿美元），其中DBK参与投资3 739亿坚戈（约11.55亿美元）。

14年来DBK共支持投放了79个产能项目，总价值16 487亿坚戈（约50.95亿美元），DBK参与投资7 862亿坚戈（约24.30亿美元）。这些产能项目包括：

- 55个加工类项目，总价值5 274亿坚戈（约16.30亿美元）。
- 6个电能生产和配置类项目，总价值779亿坚戈（约2.40亿美元）。
- 11个交通和后勤类项目，总价值1 289亿坚戈（约3.98亿美元）。
- 5个通信类项目，总价值272亿坚戈（约8 405万美元）。
- 2个旅游基础设施类项目，总价值248亿坚戈（约7 664万美元）。

新建并投入运行的企业共创造了20 400个工作岗位。

以下列举了2015年DBK批准的一些投资项目的相关信息：

在喀拉塔巫市建设年产量为1.5万吨氰化钠的工厂。需要指出的是，氰化钠目前在哈萨克斯坦仍为进口产品，该项目将有助于促进进口替代和国产商品出口。该工厂创造了约500个工作岗位。

在现有的Condensate炼油厂新建欧洲标准5号机动车燃料的生产线，年产量为 11.4 万吨 AI – 92 号汽油和 8.6 万吨 AI – 95 号汽油。该项目将有助于解决国内燃料市场的短缺，摆脱进口依赖和促进燃料出口

在克孜勒奥尔达的工厂建设平板玻璃的生产和加工项目。这是最为重要的工业—创新发展项目之一，该工厂将 100% 打开国内市场需求。

在埃基巴斯图兹建设铁路车轮生产厂。项目在国家的第二个五年工业化规划内进行，新工厂有望在 2017 年投入生产。工厂的年产量将由 7.5 万增长到 20 万，其中 60% 的产品计划出口。

DBK 批准的投资项目和出口业务中占据较大比例的是以下领域：石油化工（41%），冶金（22%），汽车制造（16%）和建材生产（13%）。

筹资

为保障自身资金来源，DBK 在国内外资本市场以多种方式筹资：债券发行和募集，银行间贷款和政府预算贷款，银团贷款，吸收存款等。

2015 年，DBK 通过 Baiterek 集团内部融资获得了 127 亿坚戈（约 3 925 万美元）。

DBK 在"Light Road"项目中从哈萨克斯坦国家基金中分得 850 亿坚戈（约 2.63 亿美元），以支持国内生产商和出口商：其中 300 亿坚戈（约 9 271 万美元）用于支持国产汽车制造业，50 亿坚戈（约 1 545 万美元）用于支持客运车厢生产，500 亿坚戈（约 1.55 亿美元）用于支持出口企业。

2015 年 3 月 13 日，为落实政府第 124 号令，哈萨克斯坦共和国国家基金向 DBK 拨款 500 亿坚戈（约 1.55 亿美元），以保障对大型加工企业的资金支持。

在 2010 年发行的欧洲债券框架内，2015 年 12 月 18 日 DBK 兑现了第五批总价值约 2.85 亿美元的债券，其中包括 2.77 亿美元的主要债务和 760 万美元的第十次利息。

2015 年 3 月，在哈萨克斯坦总理访华期间，DBK 与中国国家开发银行签署了 6.5 亿美元的借贷条约，资金将支持以下领域的项目：能源、运输、基础设施、工业、信息技术、农业和其他。此举在保障双方利益的同时拓宽了中哈两国在经济—贸易领域的合作。

2015 年 3 月同期，DBK 与三菱东京 UFJ 银行签署了 1 000 万美元的贷款条约，资金将用于哈萨克斯坦矿业公司"Kazzinc"的出口前投资。

根据 2014 年 DBK 与汇丰银行（HSBC）签署的支持阿克托别钢梁轧机厂

建设的贷款条约，2015 年 6 月 DBK 再次获 HSBC 的 470 万欧元贷款支持。

据 2015 年综合数据，DBK 在债权人处共借贷 57.8 亿美元。

DBK – 租赁

根据 2015 年统计数据，在 DBK – 租赁的资助下成交了 27 笔租赁交易，总额为 357 亿坚戈（约 1.10 亿美元）。

这些项目包括：

- 哈萨克斯坦机车向阿塞拜疆铁路公司的出口（国际租赁）。
- 汽车制造厂 Kazakhmys 的生产技术革新。
- 铁路公司 Istkomtrans 对车厢的售后回租。

DBK – 租赁资助的交易主要来自以下领域：加工制造（46.9%）、交通运输和仓储（39.6%）。

DBK – 租赁需要在国家投资规划框架内参与政府项目，包括"交通规划 – 2020"和"产能 – 2020"。

DBK 的使命和愿景被写入该行 2014～2023 年的发展战略中，该战略于 2014 年 7 月经董事会批准通过。DBK 的使命是促进国民经济稳定发展，其主要通过对非原料经济部门进行投资以实现该使命。根据 DBK 的使命，其优先投资的项目来自非原料经济部门：冶金、化学和石油化工、汽车制造、农产品加工，此外还包括基础设施生产（能源、运输、电视通信和服务业）。

DBK 有以下发展愿景：

- 成为全国领先的评估机构和执行者，专为私营部门和政府的大型基础设施及工业项目服务。
- 成为专业化的国家开发性机构，为工业和基础设施领域项目提供及时和充足的资金。
- 成为以本国货币提供最佳融资的金融机构。
- 成为在国家市场享有盛誉的、资产庞大的哈萨克斯坦领先金融机构。
- 成为为公司类客户吸引长期、低成本贷款的重要机构。

乌兹别克斯坦共和国国家对外经济活动银行

乌兹别克斯坦的银行—金融系统发展战略以国家参与为主要特色，以

（前）总统卡里莫夫制定的国家发展的关键原则为基础，目标是使该国完全适应自由市场环境。

乌兹别克斯坦经济改革的优先方向之一是创造良好的商业和投资环境，吸引外国资本。乌兹别克斯坦采取的稳定的、有针对性的经济政策使得投资量连年增长，其中就包括直接的外国资本。对银行系统在本国经济发展中的参与分析表明，商业银行所关注的放贷领域与保障国家经济完全独立所需要的关键领域恰好一致。

主要经营数据

乌兹别克斯坦共和国国家对外经济活动银行（NBU）是乌兹别克斯坦银行系统的领头羊。根据 2015 年统计结果，乌兹别克斯坦银行业总资产的 25% 由 NBU 控制。NBU 净资产等价为本国货币 16.07 万亿苏姆（约 49.2 亿美元）。在 2010~2015 年期间增加了 1.3 倍，增加了 9.08 万亿苏姆（约 27.8 亿美元），在 2015 年间增加了 3.152 万亿苏姆（约 9.65 亿美元）（+24.4%）。

银行股本等价为本国货币 2.124 万亿苏姆（约 6.50 亿美元）（已考虑次级证券和其他次级负债），在 2010~2015 年间增加了 1.6 倍。

由于 2015 年 10 月 26 日总统签署 ПП－2420 号法令《关于进一步促进银行资本化和增加其资产投资的补充办法》，以及 2015 年 12 月 18 日乌兹别克斯坦共和国部长办公室签署了 367 号法令《关于对乌兹别克斯坦国家对外经济活动银行章程的改进》，NBU 注册资本于 2015 年增加了 350 亿苏姆（约 1 071.8 万美元）。截至 2015 年 12 月 31 日，NBU 注册资本为 1 609 460 亿苏姆，比 2014 年增加了 28%。

根据乌兹别克斯坦中央银行最新规定的阶段性引入的巴塞尔协议 Ⅲ 的要求，NBU 资本充足率为 18.9%，核心资本率为 14.2%，杠杆率为 7.0%，当前流动性比率为 101.8%，乌兹别克斯坦中央银行的标准化要求中，这 4 项数据的最低值分别为 10%、7.5%、6% 和 30%。受益于高度的资本化，NBU 贮存了大量准备金用以扩大客户基础。流动性库存使银行不仅能及时和足量地在国内外市场完成支付，而且满足了银行及其客户在发展金融和经济事务方面的要求。NBU 盈利较 2014 年增加了 23.4%。资产收益率为 0.6%，净资产收益率为 5.3%。资产收益率像往年一样并不高，因为银行投入大量资金为指令性项目提供优惠贷款，以促进经济基础领域和小私企业的发展，以及资助社会项目等。

资产负债管理的主要目标是通过管控受外部环境和资产负债结构影响的风险，保障当前和战略性目标的实现。NBU 在资产负债管理方面的基本目标为：实现高效、稳定的财务业绩，扩大资本化，保持一定水平的流动性，为每一位顾客提供高质量和可靠的金融服务，在可接受的风险条件下增加资金投放的收入，按期达到资产和负债结构平衡。在 2015 年 NBU 并未出现使商誉受损的风险因子。

NBU 的生息资产占净资产的 83%，比上一年增加了 27.6%，超过总的净资产增速 24.4%。

在 NBU 的资产结构中，信贷业务占了相当大的比例（61%）。NBU 在以下方面提供全面的贷款支持：经济基础领域的现代化和技术更新；刺激小企业发展；服务业和居家工作；促进地区社会经济发展的项目等。NBU 在乌兹别克斯坦央行的同业往来账户上存有余额，这是必要的负债储备，用以支付可能的资产损失，这部分资金占总资产的 14%。此外，净资产中 NBU 在其他银行的存款占 13%，股票和证券占 5%，固定资产和其他财富占 1%（见图 5.6）。

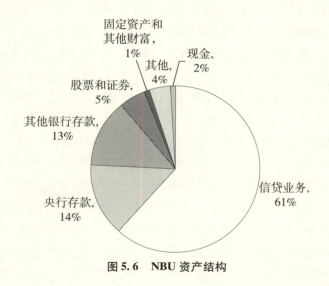

图 5.6　NBU 资产结构

银行负债的 90% 由负债资金组成，10% 由权益资金组成。其中应付借款占 50%，这些借款被 NBU 用来再融资，以完成作为乌兹别克斯坦政府在吸收国外资金方面的代理人角色。此外，客户存款占 36%，发行债券占 1%，其他银行存款占 2%，银行自有资金占 10%（见图 5.7）。

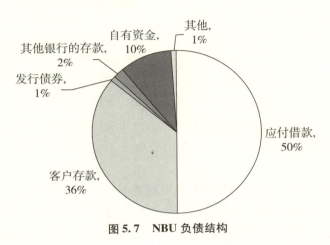

图 5.7 NBU 负债结构

工作亮点

国际舞台上的 NBU

银行系统应当承担起促进本国与其他国家合作的责任。在这方面，NBU 不断发展与国外银行和金融机构的联系，积极促进乌兹别克斯坦与国际金融社会的一体化。

与 NBU 合作的银行中不乏世界各地的大型银行：德国商业银行和德意志银行，美国摩根大通银行、花旗银行和纽约梅隆银行，瑞士信贷银行，日本三井住友银行和东京三菱日联银行等。

在国际金融机构和开发性银行中，NBU 有以下重要合作伙伴：中国国家开发银行，中国进出口银行，韩国进出口银行，韩国开发银行，伊斯兰开发银行，亚洲开发银行，日本国际协力银行，国际金融公司等。如今，NBU 的合作网络包括 80 个国家的 667 家银行，其中包括 24 家乌兹别克斯坦的银行。

NBU 在 2015 年签署了一系列双边合作协议，包括：与日本三井住友银行签署的 1 亿美元合作协议；与德国商业银行签署的 2.5 亿欧元框架借贷协议；与德意志银行签署的 8 亿美元谅解备忘录等。

自 2007 年 12 月起，银行积极与穆迪国际评级机构合作，自 2008 年 11 月起也开展了与标准普尔评级机构的合作。各机构对该行的预测均为"稳定"。

发放贷款

乌兹别克斯坦（前）总统卡里莫夫在自己的演讲中不止一次强调，必须扩展银行在吸引投资方面的业务，其中既包括为大型企业融资，也包括为小企业和私人企业融资。为实现既定目标，NBU 重点资助了以下几个方面的项目：现代化建设、现有工厂的技术更新和引进新的生产设备。

2015 年 NBU 共发放贷款 9.975 万亿苏姆（约 30.55 亿美元），比 2014 年增加 24%。外汇贷款资金来源包括国外银行资金的再融资、乌兹别克斯坦改革和发展基金以及银行自有资金，本币资金来源包括银行自有资金以及吸收央行和财政部的资源。

受益于 NBU 的支持，乌兹别克斯坦新建了一批高科技生产企业，积极生产在国内外市场兼具竞争力的产品。此举不仅优化了经济和工业结构，而且优化了出口品名表，表现为增加成品出口来代替原料出口，同时也在一定程度上解决了该国非常严重的就业问题。

在 2015 年，NBU 依照 2010 年 11 月 26 日签署的第 ПП – 1438 号总统令，"关于在 2011～2015 年间进一步改革和提高金融—银行系统稳定性，达到高水平国际评级指标的优先方向"，继续提供贷款。截至 2016 年 1 月 1 日，投资贷款在总信贷组合中占比 86%。

根据 2015 年 1 月 7 日签署的第 ПП – 2282 号总统令，NBU 为农村地区的住宅统一建造项目提供资金支持。

在支持小企业发展方面，NBU 主要为以下几个领域的项目提供了贷款支持：掌握奶制品、畜牧业产品和其他农业产品的加工工艺，发展包括旅游业在内的服务业、畜牧副产业，扶持农场经济和女性企业家等。

此外，为提高居民的物质生活条件，NBU 提供了可用于购买本国生产的家具、电子设备和家用电器的消费贷款，以及用于支付学费的助学贷款。这类贷款总额在 2015 年增长了 121%。

截至 2016 年 1 月 1 日，银行为青年家庭的住房建设项目提供了总计 353 亿苏姆（约 1 084.05 万美元）的贷款。

2015 年 NBU 为实体经济部门发展做出了自己的贡献，它通过发放贷款支持优先发展领域、小私企业和农场经济，帮助实现政府的经济发展计划，促进地区的社会经济发展和保障就业。

项目融资

乌兹别克斯坦共和国独立后，国家在新经济立法以及建立良好的商业和投资环境方面投入大量工作，而这些工作的落实急需一个现代化的国家金融系统。在独立初期，NBU为政府在此方面的工作提供了可靠的支持。乌兹别克斯坦（前）总统卡里莫夫为NBU设定了以下目标：建立世界级的金融机构，有能力服务国企的外贸事务，开发本国出口潜力，为本国经济吸引外资和先进的技术。

NBU如今是乌兹别克斯坦最大的投资银行。它积极参与推动很多国家和区域项目，这些项目主要来自以下领域：燃料和供能、农业综合生产、纺织工业、交通和通信业、采矿业。该行积极寻求一切可能为企业和组织提供长期贷款，用以新建项目、引进先进技术和生产有竞争力的产品。

NBU提供的贷款主要针对优先经济领域的发展、提高生产效率、支持小型企业、建立和发展进口替代产品。

为落实第 ПП-2264 号总统令《关于2015年乌兹别克斯坦共和国的投资计划》，NBU参与推进了一系列大型投资项目，其中包括在乌兹别克斯坦政府担保下吸引外国资金的项目。在推进大型投资项目的框架内，2015年NBU的总融资额为8.21亿美元。其中包括以下大型投资项目：

1. 国家控股企业 Uzbekneftegaz 公司（乌兹别克斯坦石油天然气）：建设乌斯秋尔特天然气化工厂，融资额2.95亿美元，其中1亿美元来自乌兹别克斯坦改革和发展基金，1.95亿美元来自准备基金。

2. 乌兹别克斯坦铁路运输公司：建设电气化铁道运输线路 Angren-Pap，融资额3.5亿美元，来自中国进出口银行的借款。

3. 乌兹别克斯坦铁路运输公司：机车园更新，购进11台货运电力机车，融资额4 217万美元，来自中国进出口银行的借款。

4. 乌兹别克斯坦铁路运输公司：购进两辆高速客运电力火车TALGO-250（西班牙），融资额1 900万欧元，来自乌兹别克斯坦改革和发展基金。

5. 无线电通信、广播和电视中心：乌兹别克斯坦共和国地面数字广播网络的发展项目，融资额6 259万美元，来自日本国际协力银行的借款。

6. Kuriliş 服务公司：在塔什干的纳沃伊大街建酒店综合体，融资额4 200万美元，来自乌兹别克斯坦改革和发展基金。

7. 乌兹别克斯坦农业和水资源部：重建纳曼干州的 Kukumba 泵站，融资额 378 万美元，来自中国进出口银行的借款。

支持小型企业发展

小型企业发展一直都是乌兹别克斯坦经济改革优先发展方向。2015 年，NBU 为支持小型企业共发放贷款 1.8 万亿苏姆（约 5.512 亿美元）。这些贷款主要用于以下几个领域的项目投资：掌握奶制品、畜牧业产品和其他农业产品的加工工艺，发展包括旅游业在内的服务业、畜牧副产业，扶持农场经济、家族企业和女性企业家等。

NBU 是乌兹别克斯坦共和国可靠和稳定的金融机构，在促进该国社会经济发展方面发挥着巨大的作用。它协助落实政府的方针政策，深化市场改革和提高经济自由度，加快现代化和多样化进程，保障本国产品和服务在国内外市场的竞争力。

在国际金融—银行体系迅速发展的背景下，NBU 需要利用现代化和高效的方法对大环境的变化做出准确反应。因此，银行还须进一步改进法律框架，引进先进的银行管理方法，采取措施保障竞争力。

第六章　中国及与中国相关的开发性金融机构

国家开发银行

近年来国际形势错综复杂，经济下行压力加大。2015 年我国 GDP 同比增长 6.9%，经济运行呈现缓中趋稳、稳中向好的发展态势。国家开发银行（CDB）对接国家宏观政策，服务国家战略，助力稳增长、调结构、惠民生，发挥开发性金融逆周期调节作用，参与国家"十三五"规划、"一带一路"、京津冀协同发展、长江经济带等重大战略规划和政策的制定实施，发挥金融引擎和先导作用。

2015 年 3 月，国务院批复国家开发银行深化改革方案，明确国家开发银行的开发性金融机构定位和相关政策支持、制度安排，提出国家开发银行要紧紧围绕服务国家经济重大中长期发展战略，进一步发挥开发性金融在重点领域、薄弱环节、关键时期的功能和作用。此次深化改革对于国家开发银行提高可持续发展能力，更好地支持国民经济持续健康发展，具有重大意义。

主要经营数据

截至 2015 年年末，CDB 资产总额为 12.62 万亿元，贷款余额为 9.21 万亿元，不良贷款率为 0.81%；累计本息回收率为 98.78%，连续 16 年保持高位；净利润为 1 027.88 亿元，资产收益率为 0.90%，净资产收益率为 11.74%，资本充足率为 10.81%，可持续发展能力和抗风险能力进一步增强（见表 6.1）。

表 6.1　2015 年国家开发银行财务数据　　　　　　　　　（单位：10 亿人民币）

	2015 年	2014 年	2013 年	2012 年	2011 年
总资产	12 619.70	10 317.00	8 197.20	7 534.90	6 252.30
贷款余额	9 206.90	7 941.60	7 148.30	6 417.60	5 525.90
不良贷款率	0.81%	0.65%	0.48%	0.30%	0.40%
贷款拨备率	3.71%	3.43%	3.05%	2.82%	2.22%
总负债	11 549.40	9 636.20	7 627.80	7 025.10	5 807.00
发行债券余额	7 301.40	6 353.60	5 840.60	5 302.20	4 476.40
股东权益	1 070.30	680.8	569.4	509.9	445.3
资本充足率	10.81%	11.88%	11.28%	10.92%	10.78%
净利润	102.8	97.7	80	63.1	45.6
利息净收入	158.4	178.7	171.5	154.4	116.5
平均资产收益率	0.90%	1.06%	1.02%	0.92%	0.80%
平均净资产收益率	11.74%	15.63%	14.82%	13.21%	10.76%

工作亮点

鼎力支持实体经济发展

2015 年，国家开发银行优化资源配置，加大中长期投融资支持力度，发挥开发性金融在增加公共产品供给中的作用，新增人民币贷款 8 892 亿元，贷款余额中铁路 1 216 亿元，公路 2 730 亿元，电力 1 371 亿元，水利 797 亿元，石油石化 2 789 亿元，公共基础设施 1 606 亿元，有力保障了"两基一支"重点领域和重大项目的融资需求（见图 6.1）。

全力保障棚户区改造

2015 年，国家开发银行持续加大棚户区改造融资支持力度，全年发放贷款 7 509 亿元，是 2014 年贷款发放的 1.84 倍，贷款余额 1.31 万亿元，为提前完成全国 580 万套棚户区改造年度任务和保障续建项目资金需求提供有力支持（见图 6.2）。深化与住房和城乡建设部的协作机制，做好与地方棚户区

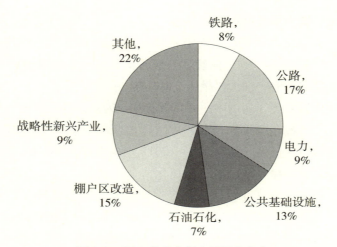

图 6.1　CDB 贷款余额主要行业分布

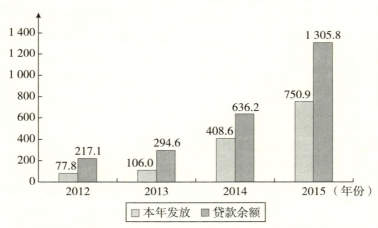

图 6.2　棚户区改造贷款发放及余额情况（单位：10 亿元人民币）

改造计划对接。加大对困难地区棚户区改造支持力度，积极推进货币化安置。研究推动融资模式创新，拓展债贷组合、银团贷款等渠道。在黑龙江"四煤城"采煤沉陷区、吉林省吉林市、河南开封等地区棚户区改造项目中取得明显成效。中低收入家庭生活质量得到改善，居民安居置业，幸福指数提高。注重发挥棚户区改造"一发多动"效应，改善棚户区居民住房条件，推动新型城镇化建设、环境综合治理、文化古城保护性开发等领域综合发展。

促进区域协调发展和产业转型升级

2015 年，国家开发银行围绕新型城镇化、城乡一体化等重点领域，"中国制造 2025""互联网＋"等产业转型升级方向，以及京津冀协同发展、长江经济带等重大发展战略，加大投融资支持力度。

支持区域协调发展，新增中西部贷款 5 494 亿元，新增东北老工业基地贷款 774 亿元。支持援疆援藏取得新进展，新增新疆贷款 228 亿元，新增西藏和四省藏区贷款 160 亿元。明确 2015～2017 年向京津冀协同发展领域提供融资总量 2.1 万亿元。深入推进新型城镇化，全力支持"以人为核心"的新型城镇化建设，探索建立多元可持续资金保障机制，有力支持综合交通、产业园区、城乡一体化等领域重大项目，保持城镇化建设骨干银行地位。

大力支持产业结构调整与优化升级，以集成电路、平板显示、新能源、新材料等领域为重点，支持"补短板"，促进产业发展迈向中高端。密切与工业和信息化部、国家发展改革委等部门合作，参与集成电路相关产业政策研究。全年发放战略性新兴产业贷款 2 530 亿元。截至 2015 年年末，战略性新兴产业贷款余额为 7 957 亿元。

积极服务绿色发展，重点支持污染防治、土壤修复、循环经济、清洁能源等领域，推动生态文明建设。截至 2015 年年末，绿色信贷贷款余额 1.57 万亿元。

支持扶贫开发，助力保障和改善民生

国家开发银行与国家有关部门和地方政府合作，创新融资模式，引导社会力量共同支持扶贫开发、农业和新农村建设、中小企业、教育等民生领域发展。深化银政合作，密切与国务院扶贫办、中央农办、国家发展改革委、交通运输部等部门合作，加大融智支持。探索支持城乡统筹发展助推扶贫开发新模式，积极推进易地扶贫搬迁、乡村基础设施建设、教育医疗和特色产业发展。创新服务"三农"融资模式，加大对农业农村建设的中长期信贷投放。重点支持扶贫开发、创新创业等领域中小企业发展。进一步扩大助学贷款覆盖面，实现全国县区覆盖率 70%，高校覆盖率 100%。

2015 年向连片特困地区县和国家级贫困县发放贷款 2 122 亿元，为 4 个定点扶贫县和 1 个对口支援县安排捐赠资金 1 140 万元。截至 2015 年年末，扶贫开发贷款余额 9 623 亿元。发放现代农业贷款 326 亿元，贷款余额 654 亿元。发放新农村建设贷款 2 625 亿元，贷款余额 8 557 亿元。发放给中小企业

的贷款余额 2.82 万亿元，其中，小微企业贷款余额 1.12 万亿元。发放助学贷款 187 亿元，贷款余额 562 亿元。

深入推进国际合作，服务"一带一路"

国家开发银行服务国家经济外交战略，推动重大项目实施；以开发性金融的力量带动中国企业"走出去"；推动国际业务管理体制改革，完善境外机构布局，成立伦敦代表处；大力开展跨境人民币贷款业务，推进人民币国际化。

2015 年，国家开发银行开发了一批"一带一路"重大项目并推动实施，发放相关贷款 149 亿美元。积极配合我国与"一带一路"国家的高层互访，全年共签署合作文件 70 份，涉及融资额超过 650 亿美元，涵盖能源、矿产、交通基础设施、产能合作、金融和高新技术等领域，有力推动了国家间的务实合作不断深化。推进多双边合作机制和各种专项贷款，为"一带一路"项目打造优势平台。国家开发银行积极参与和推动中哈产能合作机制、中蒙俄经济走廊建设；借助上合银联体、东盟银联体、金砖国家银行合作机制、欧亚经济论坛及中俄等多双边合作机制谋划项目，推动业务进展；设立 APEC 中小企业专项贷款，推动设立中国—东盟基础设施专项贷款、中国—东欧专项贷款，为"一带一路"建设提供精准支持。截至 2015 年年底，国家开发银行在"一带一路"沿线国家累计承诺贷款近 1 900 亿美元，累计发放贷款约 1 556 亿美元，余额 1 114 亿美元，占全行国际业务余额的1/3。

完善债券筹资体系，提升综合金融服务

推进国开债一、二级市场建设，建立"基准债＋浮息债＋超长债"全产品、"银行间＋柜台＋交易所"全场所发行机制。全年累计发行人民币债券11 361 亿元，历史累计发行人民币债券 11.8 万亿元。多元化外币筹资取得新突破，在境外资本市场成功发行 10 亿美元债券和 5 亿欧元债券，并在伦敦证券交易所上市。推进子公司协同发展，为重点领域、重大项目提供多元化服务。加大证券化产品发行力度，共发行 11 单产品，合计 1 013 亿元。保持债券承销市场领先地位，累计承销债券 7 596.5 亿元，平均发债利率低于市场23 个基点（BP），助力降低实体经济融资成本。

2016 年，国家开发银行继续秉持"增强国力、改善民生"的使命，服务供给侧结构性改革，着力保障棚户区改造、铁路、水利等重点领域和国家重大工程项目建设，支持产业创新发展和转型升级，助力打好脱贫攻坚战，大力推动国际合作重大项目，做好"一带一路"金融服务。深化综合经营，发挥集团跨市场多元化融资优势，推广投贷、债贷、租贷组合等协同模式，提供多元化金融服务，带动社会和同业资金支持实体经济发展。强化资产负债管理，拓展多元化筹资渠道，强化财务预算统筹，加强内外部定价管理，积极推进中间业务发展，提升综合收益水平。严格风险管控，严控项目入口关，加强风险预研预判预警，稳步推进风险责任认定工作，守住资产质量底线。

中国进出口银行

中国进出口银行（Chemix）成立于 1994 年，主要职责是为扩大我国机电产品、成套设备和高新技术产品进出口，推动有比较优势的企业开展对外承包工程和境外投资，促进对外关系发展和国际经贸合作，提供金融服务，发挥在稳增长、调结构、支持外贸发展、实施"走出去"战略中的功能和作用。

2015 年，中国进出口银行落实国家对外战略，围绕"一带一路"、非洲"三网一化"等重大战略部署，推进一批重大项目签约，加强与周边国家互利合作，进一步拓展与中东欧、拉丁美洲、大洋洲等国家多领域务实合作。推动外贸优进优出，大力支持成套设备、高新技术、"两自一高"等优势产品出口，积极扩大先进技术和关键设备等产品进口，推动外贸稳定增长和结构优化，积极扶持企业"走出去"，带动过剩产能转移和海外项目并购与开发。支持实体经济发展，助力结构调整和转型升级，加快推进"中国制造"优化升级，支持企业开展自主创新和技术升级改造，提高资源利用效率和重大技术装备国产化水平，推动战略性新兴产业发展。

主要经营数据

2015 年，中国进出口银行全年共批准表内贷款 11 016 亿元，签约贷款 11 809 亿元，发放贷款 10 774 亿元。年末，表内贷款余额 21 482 亿元，表外转贷余额 146 亿美元，表内外资产总额 29 352 亿元。全年共支持了 3 912 亿美元的机电产品和高新技术产品出口以及对外承包工程和境外投资项目，此外还支持了 2 005 亿美元的技术装备和资源类产品进口。

2012～2014年营业收入及支出持平，2015年，由于汇兑收益比2014年增加2107%，营业收入比2014年增加111.8%；同时由于资产减值损失或呆账损失比2014年增长168%，营业支出也上升119.3%；净利润增长27.5%（见表6.2及图6.3）。2012～2015年中国进出口银行年末资产、负债和贷款总额稳定上升（见表6.2及图6.4），2015年年末，对外贸易贷款余额、对外投资贷款余额、对外合作贷款余额和境内对外开放支持贷款余额均比年初有约20%的增长（见图6.5）。国际信用评级继续与中国主权信用评级一致。

表6.2 2015年中国进出口银行财务概要　　　　　　　　（单位：1 000元人民币）

全年度	2015
营业收入	48 430 437
营业支出	44 520 715
年底	**2015**
资产总额	2 833 473 408
负债总额	2 524 005 049
贷款总额	2 052 496 636
净利润	5 142 943

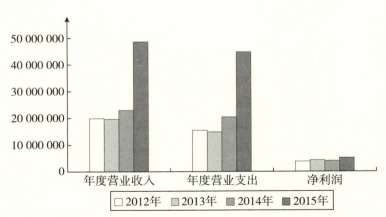

图6.3 2012～2015年中国进出口银行年度营业收入与支出
（单位：1 000元人民币）

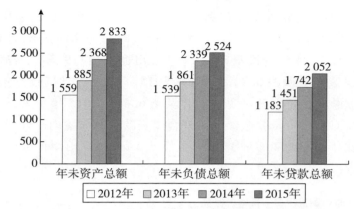

图6.4 2012～2015年中国进出口银行年末资产、
负债、贷款总额（单位：10亿元人民币）

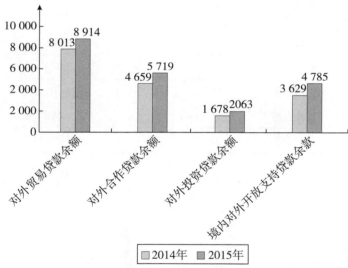

图6.5 2014～2015年中国进出口银行核心数据
（单位：亿元人民币）

工作亮点

落实国家对外战略

2015年，中国进出口银行紧紧围绕"一带一路"、国际产能和装备制造合作等重大战略部署，积极推进一批重大项目签约、落地取得新成效。加大对周边共同体建设支持力度，加强与周边国家互利合作，推动同周边国家互联互通和产能合作项目建设。积极扶持企业"走出去"，进行海外项目并购与开发。

埃塞俄比亚阿达玛风电项目是中国企业在海外实施的第一个风电总承包项目，并且全部使用中国设备和采用中国相关设计与施工标准，对推动中国风电标准"走出去"意义重大。项目的实施改善了埃塞俄比亚电网的电源结构，缓解了当地电力供应紧张的状况，并且促进了就业、经济发展和社会稳定。

为落实"一带一路"政策，中国进出口银行相继开展了巴基斯坦卡西姆港燃煤应急电站项目及孟加拉希拉甘杰 220 MW 联合循环电站项目等，有力促进了中国技术、标准"走出去"和国际产能合作。

白俄罗斯是丝绸之路经济带向欧洲延伸的重要节点，白俄罗斯引进中国制造高端智能化电力机车和铁路电气化改造项目于 2015 年成功推进，有利于深化中白经贸与金融合作，推动中国铁路装备和服务"走出去"进入欧洲市场，同时项目运营后将进一步提高白俄罗斯铁路运输能力，促进当地就业。

推动外贸优进优出

2015 年，中国进出口银行大力支持成套设备、高新技术等优势产品出口，重点支持装备制造产品及相关技术、服务和标准出口，积极扩大先进技术和关键设备等产品进口。积极推动船舶、航空业发展，帮助船舶企业抓订单、稳生产、脱困境、谋转型，加大对飞机制造企业自主创新、进口航材和技术、实施境外并购、出口国产飞机的支持力度。

为进一步推动"大飞机"战略实施，中国进出口银行与中国商用飞机有限责任公司签署 500 亿元人民币融资框架协议，支持中国商飞国产民机研发、制造及销售环节的资金需求。

中国船舶重工国际贸易有限公司医疗船项目是我国建造出口的首个符合国际新规范的大型客船项目，也是全球首个大型民用医疗船项目。该项目的实施，可为我国未来建造类似的功能船以及豪华邮轮提供宝贵的技术经验，提升中国船舶企业国际声誉和核心竞争力。

英国海事装备（SMD）公司是具有国际领先水平的工作级深海机器人和海底工程机械制造商，主要产品是适应深海极端恶劣环境的工作级机器人、挖沟铺缆设备。2015 年，株洲南车时代电气股份有限公司收购英国 SMD 公司深海机器人，有利于中国企业获得海洋工程装备制造业高端技术和市场，将其核心技术向深海机器人及其他深海高端装备领域延伸，填补目前国内深海装备产业多项空白。

支持实体经济发展

中国进出口银行积极推进"中国制造"优化升级，支持企业开展自主创新和技术升级改造，提高资源利用效率和重大技术装备国产化水平，推动战略性新兴产业发展。加大对绿色、循环和低碳经济的金融支持力度，支持"三高"行业开展节能环保改造，推进新能源和可再生能源利用。加强银政与同业合作，推进小微企业转贷款业务创新。

2015 年，沈阳鼓风机集团股份有限公司（简称沈鼓集团）营口新建大型透平压缩机组制造和试验基地项目顺利实施，这标志着我国在超大型空分装置关键设备配套方面跻身世界前列，我国高端装备制造业重大技术装备国产化实现零的突破。

中国进出口银行支持企业开展自主创新，促进了中国船舶（香港）航运租赁有限公司 3 艘 18 000 箱集装箱船项目顺利实施。中国船舶（香港）航运租赁有限公司 18 000 箱船舶是我国企业首次自主研发、设计并建造的全球最大箱位级集装箱船，一举打破国外船企在该领域的垄断局面。

对外交往

2015 年 4 月，中国进出口银行与巴基斯坦签署了一批互联互通和能源类项目的合作协议，以缓解巴基斯坦电力紧缺和改善基础设施状况，促进区域互联互通，推进中巴经济走廊建设。2015 年 5 月，中国进出口银行与俄罗斯和白俄罗斯签署能源、互联互通及工业制造领域协议共 9 项，金额逾 11 亿美元，将直接促进当地经济发展，有力支持我国与有关国家产能合作，顺利推进"一带一路"建设及与沿线国家发展战略的对接。2015 年 12 月中非合作论坛约翰内斯堡峰会期间，中国进出口银行与肯尼亚、塞内加尔和加蓬政府签署了基础设施建设领域的若干合作协议，总金额达 196.8 亿元人民币。

2015 年，中国进出口银行继续深化与多边机构和国际组织的合作。6 月，与联合国工业发展组织签署了《谅解备忘录》。11 月，与东南非贸易与开发银行（PTA Bank）签署了《谅解备忘录》。9 月，中国进出口银行增持非洲进出口银行 C 类股份 2 529 股，在该行持股总计 5 151 股。2015 年，中国进出口银行出席了美洲开发银行、亚洲开发银行、非洲开发银行、东南非贸易与发展银行等多边金融机构的年会。

社会责任

中国进出口银行积极履行社会责任，开展扶贫济困活动，关心支持社会公益事业，在节能环保、三农、扶贫等领域实施了多个项目，努力推动经济可持续、社会可持续和环境可持续发展。

中国进出口银行大力支持绿色、循环和低碳经济发展，支持了钢铁等一批高耗能、高排放企业回收利用工业废物等技术改造项目和秸秆、污水等处理利用项目，支持了风电、光伏、新能源汽车等一批清洁能源开发应用项目。

重点支持农业科技引进及研发、现代种业、农机装备制造等现代农业项目，农产品出口基地及物流基地建设项目和农业境外投资合作项目等。截至 2015 年 12 月，中国进出口银行涉农贷款余额 2 114.06 亿元，占全行表内贷款余额的 9.84%，其中农业"走出去"项目贷款余额 1 369.4 亿元，项目覆盖 57 个国家和地区。

积极加强与国务院扶贫办合作，深入贫困地区发掘区域特色和产业潜力，依托地方特色帮助贫困地区人民脱贫增收。截至 2015 年年末，中国进出口银行累计在全国 28 个省（区）、14 个集中连片特困地区支持了 200 多个金融扶贫项目，其中支持国务院扶贫办推荐的金融扶贫重点项目 143 个，批贷金额近 134 亿元，贷款余额 83 亿元，带动数十万农户脱贫。

中国农业发展银行

中国农业发展银行（ADBC）是我国直属国务院领导的唯一一家农业政策性银行，成立于 1994 年，主要职责是按照国家的法律法规和方针政策，以国家信用为基础筹集资金，承担农业政策性金融业务，代理拨付财政支农资金，为农业和农村经济发展服务；保障国家粮食安全、保护农民利益、维护农产品市场稳定、促进城乡发展一体化。

2015 年，ADBC 外部改革正式启动，确立了"一二三四五六"总体发展战略，进一步明确了 ADBC 的职能定位、现代化建设目标和实施路径。"一二三四五六"总体发展战略是指牢牢抓住发展这个第一要务，强化从严管党、从严治行两大根本保障，坚持执行国家意志、服务"三农"需求和遵循银行规律"三位一体"，拓展改革、创新、科技、人才四条路径，全力服务国家粮食安全、脱贫攻坚、农业现代化、城乡协调发展和国家重点战略五大领域，统筹推进治理结构、运营模式、产品服务、管控机制、科技支撑、组织体系六个现代化建设。

ADBC 始终坚持政策属性，全力服务国家粮食安全、农业现代化、城乡发展一体化、国家区域发展战略、扶贫攻坚。2015 年，ADBC 全力支持粮棉油收储，为经济发展和社会稳定托底；支持农村土地流转和规模经营、高标准农田建设、种业工程、农业科技推广；积极支持脱贫攻坚，为全面建成小康社会补短板，率先组建扶贫金融事业部，研究推出易地扶贫搬迁贷款；大力支持重大水利工程建设，强化公共产品供给；创新支持新型城镇化，促进城乡协调发展；快速推进重点建设基金工作，加大对重大水利、易地扶贫搬迁、棚户区改造等支持力度，支持项目 4 338 个，可拉动社会投资 3～5 倍，从而更好地在农村金融体系中发挥主体和骨干作用，促进国民经济平稳健康发展。

主要经营数据

2015 年年末，ADBC 本外币贷款余额 34 410.4 亿元，比上年年末增加 6 096.7 亿元，同比增加 2 810.2 亿元，增速 21.53%。全年对"三农"领域净投入资金 7 803.4 亿元，是 2014 年投入量的 2.4 倍，创历史最高纪录，全行总资产迈上了 4 万亿元的新台阶。全年发行债券 8 649.7 亿元，年末债券余额 27 467.4 亿元，存款余额 9 375 亿元。在利差缩窄形势下，ADBC 继续实行优惠利率，让利于农，通过向内挖潜、降控成本，实现拨备前利润 351.4 亿元。2015 年年末，ADBC 不良贷款率 0.83%，保持较低水平；所有者权益 986.36 亿元，比年初增加 253.39 亿元，增长 34.57%；实收资本由年初的 200 亿元增至 570 亿元，资本实力不断增强（见表 6.3）。

表 6.3 2015 年 ADBC 财务概况　　　　　　　　　　　　（单位：亿元）

项目	2014 年	2015 年
总资产	31 420.31	41 831.32
贷款余额	28 313.51	34 410.37
总负债	30 687.35	40 844.96
向央行借款	3 220.00	3 058.00
发行债券	21 188.56	27 467.36
所有者权益	732.97	986.36
实收资本	200	570
利润总额	140.79	207.84
拨备前利润	441.6	352.51
所得税费用	63.09	54.45
净利润	77.7	153.39
资产利润率	1.53%	0.96%
资本利润率	64.36%	40.88%

工作亮点

信贷业务

1. 服务国家粮食安全。ADBC 严格履行政策性银行职能，全力服务国家粮食安全，支持粮棉油收储，维护粮油市场稳定，保护广大农民利益，实现了粮油信贷业务的健康发展。全年累计投放粮油收储贷款 5 737.95 亿元。2014 棉花年度，临储政策取消，棉花产业全面市场化，ADBC 按照市场化原则积极支持企业随行就市进行棉花收购，全行共发放棉花收购贷款 464 亿元。

2. 支持脱贫攻坚。2015 年，ADBC 易地扶贫搬迁信贷业务实现了从无到有的快速发展，政策性金融扶贫工作顺利开局。自 2015 年 8 月启动以来，审批易地扶贫搬迁贷款项目 491 个，涉及搬迁人口 577 万人，其中建档立卡贫困人口 361 万人。易地扶贫搬迁贷款余额 808 亿元。

3. 服务农业现代化。2015 年，ADBC 全力推进农村土地流转和规模经营贷款业务，优先支持政府委托代建及特许经营融资模式，助力现代农业的发展。2015 年，ADBC 共发放农村土地流转和规模经营贷款 21.37 亿元。在积极支持粮棉油产业化龙头企业的同时，审慎稳健支持糖、丝、麻、烟、毛绒产业化龙头企业，以及林业、水果、中药材、园艺、茶叶等产业化龙头企业，全年累计发放非粮棉油产业化龙头企业贷款 328.28 亿元，支持龙头企业 678家。同时，ADBC 积极支持农业科技创新领域，围绕提高农业综合生产能力，重点支持种业、农机、节水灌溉等领域农业科技成果的推广应用，并提供相应信贷资金，全年累放农业科技贷款 68.18 亿元，支持企业 196 家。

4. 促进城乡协调发展。ADBC 着眼于促进城乡公共资源均衡配置、城乡要素平等交换，加快补齐农业农村短板。重点支持棚户区改造、农村公路和改善农村人居环境建设，积极支持整体城镇化、农民集中住房建设等。截至 2015 年年末，ADBC 棚户区改造贷款余额 498.14 亿元，全年累计发放棚户区改造贷款 283.83 亿元，支持拆迁建筑面积 5 862 万平方米，新增安置住房建筑面积 5 302 万平方米，惠及棚户区居民 39 万户、136 万人。2015 年年末，农村土地整治贷款余额 4 272.71 亿元，比年初净增 433.4 亿元，增幅11.29%。全年累计发放农村土地整治贷款 1 808.6 亿元，支持复垦土地 79.5万亩，新增耕地 116.1 万亩，置换城镇建设用地 88.8 万亩，整治村庄 7 984个，促进了土地资源的集约节约利用。农村路网贷款余额 1 997 亿元，比年初净增 395 亿元，增幅 24.66%。全年累计发放农村公路中长期贷款 792 亿元，比 2014 年净增 402 亿元，增幅 103%。

5. 服务国家重点战略。2015 年，ADBC 专项过桥贷款共支持国家 172 项重大水利工程中的 49 个项目。其中，贷款投放大中型灌区续建配套节水改造骨干工程 89 亿元，南水北调东中线一期工程 48 亿元，引江济淮工程 38 亿元，长江中下游河势控制和河道整治工程 29 亿元，田间高效节水灌溉工程 15 亿元。截至 2015 年年末，ADBC 水利贷款余额 3 589 亿元，较 2014 年年末增加1 047 亿元，增长 41.2%；2015 年实际发放贷款 1 625 亿元，较 2014 年增加892 亿元，增长 121.69%。全年共支持病险水库除险加固 43 座，增加蓄水8.57 亿立方米，增加或改善灌溉面积 1 594.4 万亩，修缮疏浚河道沟渠 6 646公里，解决了 2 105.7 万人的饮水问题。

投资业务

ADBC 注重发挥政策性金融逆周期调节作用，设立中国农发重点建设基金，并全力做好基金投资工作，同时抓好中间业务、投行业务、资管业务、股权投资业务的发展，取得了明显成效。

1. 重点建设基金。ADBC 投资范围涉及民生改善、"三农"建设、城市基础设施、重大基础设施和转型升级 5 大类 34 个专项基金。专项基金投资有效解决了制约投资增长的突出问题，为"促投资，稳增长"发挥了重要作用，探索出经济新常态下更好发挥政策性金融战略服务供给侧结构性改革的新模式。

2. 中间业务。2015 年，ADBC 实现中间业务收入 10.52 亿元，较 2014 年增加 0.93 亿元，在减费让利的基础上继续稳步增长。

3. 投行业务。成功发行 2015 年第一期发元信贷资产支持证券 33.57 亿元。

4. 资管业务。全年共发行 7 单理财产品，规模合计 14.8 亿元，批复 8 个省级分行开办企业理财业务。正式获得期货保证金存管业务资格，并做好了开业准备工作。

5. 股权投资业务。截至 2015 年年末，中国农业产业发展基金和现代种业发展基金累计实现投资项目 32 个，投资金额 37 亿元。

信息化建设

2015 年，ADBC 有序推进软件研发工作，完成对公网银系统涉及的综合业务系统配套改造、信贷管理系统优化升级、期货保证金存管业务系统等研发工作；优化综合业务、二代支付、银企直联等系统以及开放式接入平台。完成软件测试体系建设，开展 CMMI 3 级认证达标建设，加强研发管理和质量管控。此外，ADBC 积极开展科技创新研究，开展核心系统建设、IT 架构规划、农业政策性银行数据仓库建设、惠农互联网平台建设、信贷管理系统知识转移接收以及计算"资源池"等创新研究，开展数据治理和发掘应用创新研究，明确 ADBC 推进大数据发掘和应用的总体思路、目标和主要任务。

亚洲基础设施投资银行

自 2013 年 10 月中国国家主席习近平提出筹建亚洲基础设施投资银行（AIIB，简称"亚投行"）的倡议以来，AIIB 一直是国际社会关注的焦点。历经 800 余天紧锣密鼓的筹备工作，由 57 个创始成员共同筹建的 AIIB 于 2015

年 12 月 25 日正式成立［17 个意向创始成员已批准《亚洲基础设施投资银行协定》（以下简称《协定》）并提交批准书，其股份总和占比 50.1%，达到了《协定》规定的生效条件］，并于 2016 年 1 月 16～18 日在北京举行了隆重的开业仪式暨理事会和董事会成立大会。开业以来近 10 个月内，AIIB 凭借其倡导的高标准、高效、廉洁、绿色等理念获得了国际社会的广泛认可，吸引了 30 多个国家申请加入。首批总额为 5.09 亿美元的 4 个项目已于 2016 年 7 月 12 日得到正式批准，第二批总额为 3.2 亿美元的 2 个项目也于 2016 年 9 月 28 日获得董事会批准，实现 2016 年贷款总额 12 亿美元的目标指日可待。

2016 年，AIIB 的重点发展领域是基础设施建设及其他生产性行业的发展，主要包括公路、电力、棚户区改造等项目，这很好地体现了 AIIB "向亚洲地区在发展基础设施、推进互联互通方面提供融资支持" 的宗旨以及 "高效"、"绿色" 的发展理念。

已于 2016 年 7 月 12 日得到正式批准的首批总额为 5.09 亿美元的 4 个项目包括：

1. 孟加拉国电力输送升级和扩容贷款项目，项目总额为 1.65 亿美元。

2. 印度尼西亚国家贫民窟升级项目，此项目为 AIIB 与世界银行（WB）联合融资的项目，其中 AIIB 提供贷款 2.165 亿美元。

3. 巴基斯坦 M4 国家高速公路（绍尔果德与哈内瓦尔段）贷款项目，是 AIIB 与亚洲开发银行（ADB）联合融资的项目，AIIB 与 ADB 分别提供 1 亿美元的贷款，英国国际发展部还为该项目提供了 3 400 万美元的援助（该项目已于 2016 年 8 月 13 日正式动工）。

4. 塔吉克斯坦首都杜尚别到塔吉克斯坦与乌兹别克斯坦边境的公路改善项目，是 AIIB 与欧洲复兴开发银行联合融资的项目，两个银行分别为项目提供 2 750 万美元的贷款，项目总额 5 500 万美元。

于 2016 年 9 月 28 日获得批准的第二批总额为 3.2 亿美元的两个项目则包括：

1. 巴基斯坦水电站扩建工程，贷款额 3 亿美元，由 AIIB 与世界银行联合融资。

2. 缅甸 225 兆瓦联合循环燃气轮机发电厂项目，贷款额 0.2 亿美元，由 AIIB 与其他多边开发银行和商业银行联合融资。

一些向 AIIB 递交贷款申请的项目包括（不完全统计）：

1. 2016 年 3 月，印度寻求从 AIIB 贷款，以支持总理莫迪将太阳能装机容量到 2022 年增加至 100 千兆瓦的计划。

2. 2016 年 5 月，俄罗斯向 AIIB 递交了 16 个远东项目，提议 AIIB 参加北方海路开发项目，总投资额为 80 亿美元。

3. 2016 年 8 月，印尼政府申请为北干巴鲁—杜迈高速公路项目筹集贷款 16.2 万亿印尼盾（约 82.39 亿元人民币）。

4. 2016 年 9 月，蒙古向 AIIB 寻求融资多个铁路项目，包括兴建 550 公里连接中国与欧洲的铁路线。

由此可见，AIIB 是一个真正的、极具吸引力的国际大型金融开发机构。除了可以在知识共享、能力建设、人员交流等方面相互借鉴，还可以直接在项目融资方面与世界银行、亚洲开发银行、欧洲投资银行和欧洲复兴开发银行等多边开发机构开展实质性合作。与此同时，加拿大养老基金投资公司（CPPIB）、香港"基建融资促进办公室"（IFFO）等商业机构和事业单位也表示愿意与 AIIB 建立长期合作机制。这将有助于 AIIB 在较短时间内积累经验，提升管理能力，降低运营风险，对于提升 AIIB 工作效率和行业形象以及 AIIB 在国际舞台树立信心奠定了基础，极大地保障了亚洲地区大型基础设施建设项目的顺利开展，进而促成和加强世界范围内的基础设施投资。

从 2016 年 AIIB 的总体表现来看，AIIB 在治理和运营模式上与已有多边开发银行具有明显的差别，它具有自己鲜明的特点和独特的优势。

AIIB 的治理和运营是开放的、包容的

第一，《协定》规定 AIIB 在其贷款项目中将进行全球采购，而不限于成员采购，这就使得受援国能够在项目实施过程中购买到最适合自己的产品，获取最大的利益。

第二，中国作为 AIIB 发起国和最大股东国，在投票权中不谋求长期拥有一票否决权。根据《协定》确立的股权结构，中国目前实占 AIIB 股权 30.34%，为第一大股东，比第二至第五大股东股权总和（23.4%）还高出 6.94 个百分点。按照国际惯例，中国 30.34% 的股权可相应获取大体同等的投票权，但为了体现团结共筹之诚意，中国对投票权做了适度削减（中国实有投票权 26.06%）。

第三，AIIB 欢迎来自五大洲各地区的新成员加入，而不仅仅限于亚洲国

家。9月，AIIB 已经启动有关希腊、加拿大等 30 多个国家提交的成员资格申请审议程序（其中，加拿大 8 月 31 日宣布正式申请加入 AIIB 具有重大意义，它是第一个申请加入 AIIB 的北美国家，这将有助于实现中加两国的双赢和中美关系的升温），新成员最早有望在 2017 年年初正式加入 AIIB，届时，AIIB 成员总数将突破 90 家。

AIIB 的治理和运营是高效的、高标准的

第一，AIIB 未设常驻执董会，由董事会直接监督管理层，职责分工明确，运作高效。总行在中国之外仅设几个办事处，员工人数目前只有 500 ~ 600 人，大约为亚洲开发银行和世界银行员工人数的 1/6 和 5%。

第二，AIIB 在贷款审批流程上进行了简化。在成立初期，AIIB 已经深刻意识到现有国际金融机构烦琐苛刻的规则对其长期发展的不利影响，因此在项目审批方面进行了改革，包括缩短项目审批流程、提高审批效率等，从而建立了一个架构简单、运作高效的金融机构。

第三，AIIB 目前所拥有的高度多元化的股东结构，以及由理事会、董事会和管理层所形成的三层组织架构，已经形成了良好的现代治理模式，为AIIB 始终如一地坚守高标准奠定了制度保障。目前，AIIB 正在筹建一个由国际前政要和知名学者组成的顾问团，负责为 AIIB 的发展策略和日常运营提供政策建议。

AIIB 的治理和运营是务实的、灵活的

开业以来，AIIB 计划采用的是银行贷款、股权投资和担保业务 3 种投资模式同时运作。除去传统的主权信用担保贷款外，根据《协定》，AIIB 还将进行直接投资，即对公共部门和私营部门进行股权投资。这一模式的灵活度高，更有利于采用 PPP 模式，并且在某些情况下能够通过承担较高风险而获取较高回报。另外，AIIB 也可以作为担保人，为资金需求方和供给方提供中间业务以促进投资。3 种投资模式的配合使用，能够大大增强 AIIB 的市场适应能力，为区域发展融资做出更大贡献。通过推进 PPP 模式，整合市场资源参与基础设施建设，发挥 AIIB 的杠杆效应，增强基础设施项目对私营部门投资者的吸引力。

总的来说，2016 年的 AIIB 秉持精简、清廉和绿色发展的原则，切实考虑

发展中国家的实际需要，稳步推进各项机构建设、业务经营和基础设施领域的项目融资，积极与各大国际多边开发机构开展互利合作，赢得了国际社会的广泛认可与好评。在众多国际多边开发机构中，AIIB 展现出独特的优势和潜力，它的治理和运营是开放、包容的，是高效、高标准的，是务实、灵活的。作为一个新兴金融开发机构，它的吸引力和影响力正在不断扩大，其全球性金融机构地位正日益形成并不断得到巩固。

专栏6-1	**AIIB 步入国际合作密集对接期**

随着全球经济陷入低增长状态，中国"一带一路"倡议下的沿线基础设施项目引发各方关注，欧洲投资银行、欧洲复兴开发银行、亚洲开发银行、世界银行等机构以及俄罗斯、印度、欧盟等主要经济体，近期正抓紧与 AIIB 进行项目对接，数个重量级项目逐渐进入全球资本市场的视野。

一、国际金融机构与亚投行的合作意愿强烈

亚投行成立后，国际金融机构纷纷表现出加强与亚投行进行项目对接及金融合作的意愿，这些国际金融机构主要包括：

1. 欧洲投资银行。EIB 是欧盟各成员共同成立的多边融资机构，既为欧盟成员中具有可持续发展能力和创新特质的中小企业提供融资，也在欧盟以外地区，包括土耳其及非洲等国家和地区，有不少投资项目。EIB 内部围绕 AIIB 有不少讨论，并很早就与中国多家银行及 AIIB 接触。EIB 总裁霍耶尔于 2016 年 5 月访问北京时，就未来双方在能源和节能等产业领域合作的可能性，尤其是在极端气候、污染治理等问题上进行了讨论。可以说，EIB 所表现出的积极性，与中国政府表示要参与欧盟执委会主席容克提出的投资复苏计划以及中国对投资欧洲表示出极大兴趣密切相关。

2. 欧洲复兴开发银行。EBRD 主要为中东欧国家经济复兴提供支持，随着上述国家向市场经济转型，EBRD 支持对象扩大至中东、北非、希腊和中亚等基础设施需求旺盛的周边国家。这意味着，EBRD 支持中亚各国的计划与中国提出的"一带一路"倡议紧密相关。2016 年 1 月，中国正式加入 EBRD，此举为中欧双方推进"一带一路"倡议、基础设施建设领域合作奠定了坚实的基础。

3. 金砖国家新开发银行（NDB）。NDB 和 AIIB 作为两家"姐妹机构"，都将基础设施建设作为投融资项目的重点领域，在中国、俄罗斯等发展中国家为主的亚洲地区存在诸多共同利益。但两者在规则和商业模式上不是竞争关系，而是积极寻求联合融资项目。2016 年 3 月，俄罗斯政府已正式批准 AIIB 和 NDB 在俄罗斯境内发行有价证券。此举旨在推动俄罗斯基础设施建设和金融市场的发展。两家银行已经确定了卢布贷款项目，这一项目将成为双方未来行动计划的重要方向之一，同时双方还计划在俄罗斯金融市场吸引更多融资。虽然 NDB 在 4 月发放的第一批贷款中没有与 AIIB 直接合作的项目，但两家银行行长和官员都已释放出积极寻求合作并实现区域合作互补的信号。

4. 亚洲开发银行。以日本和美国为主导的 ADB 也表达了与 AIIB 合作的兴趣，并期待为区域发展带来互补共赢效应。2016 年 3 月，ADB 行长中尾武彦表示，AIIB 希望在 2016 年第二季度批准一个投资项目，目前正以 ADB 和 AIIB 合作融资为前提积极推进。ADB 的一大优势在于，它以亚洲为中心，开设了 29 家办事机构，这为当地政府和民众对话带来便利，将有利于项目成立和环境保护，而 AIIB 没有这些地区办事机构，从长期发展来看，双方可以更多地进行互补合作。

5. 世界银行。世界银行则表现出更为强烈的合作意愿，并已于 2016 年 4 月中旬与 AIIB 签署了首份联合融资框架协议，为双方的合作打下基础。WB 与 AIIB 已就 12 个联合融资项目进行了商讨，主要涉及中亚、南亚和东亚地区的交通、水利、能源等项目。根据协议，WB 将为双方联合融资的项目提供采购、环保、社会保障等方面的支持，并将在 AIIB 的各联合项目中发挥主导作用。

总的来说，欧洲投资银行、欧洲复兴开发银行正逐步加深同亚投行的高层联系，显示出积极合作的姿态；金砖国家新开发银行与亚投行在共同发行有价债券的基础上，进一步寻求项目联合融资；亚洲开发银行、世界银行积极与亚投行商讨和签署联合融资框架协议，推动亚投行治理体系的建设，有利于亚投行提升运行效率和树立国际形象，保障其在亚洲地区大型基础设施建设项目融资的顺利开展。

二、亚投行首批融资项目初见端倪

2016 年 4 月 19 日，亚投行公布的首批贷款项目一时成为公众关注的热点。首批贷款主要是为中亚三条公路建设提供融资支持：一是巴基斯坦肖克特至哈内瓦尔的公路，该项目将由亚投行、亚洲开发银行和英国国际发展部联合提供建设资金；二是从塔吉克斯坦杜尚别至图尔孙扎德的高速公路，该项目将由亚投行、亚洲开发银行和欧洲复兴开发银行联合提供资金；三是哈萨克斯坦阿拉木图的一条环路，这一项目将由亚投行、世界银行和欧洲复兴开发银行共同融资。

除此以外，俄罗斯和印度也相继透露亚投行今年进行融资项目的计划。据印度官员称，亚投行或于 2016 年向印度提供 5 亿美元的首批贷款用于发展太阳能项目。俄罗斯远东发展基金总经理阿列克谢·切昆科夫也表示，该基金将向亚投行提出为俄罗斯 19 个项目进行共同融资，其必要的投资额为 90 亿美元，用于西伯利亚和远东地区资源开采领域的基础设施、国际交通走廊、港口与机场建设。

三、亚投行的吸引力和包容性

亚投行行长金立群早前透露，亚投行在努力接纳一些新成员，目前有 57 个创始成员。3 月，波兰正式成为亚投行创始成员，出资额约占总股本的 0.83%。加拿大哈珀政府曾拒绝加入亚投行，导致加拿大未能成为亚投行创始成员，而现在的加拿大则表示出加入亚投行的意愿，金立群对此表示欢迎。潜在的新成员还包括中国香港和中国台湾：香港加入亚投行指日可待，台湾目前虽因申请程序而拒绝加入，但相信未来双方会有妥善的解决方案。

亚投行首批项目备受全球瞩目，产生国际示范效应，中国和亚洲更广泛的合作机遇展现在世界面前。随着各方与亚投行密切沟通，许多当初对亚投行有所质疑的西方国家开始动摇，可以预计，随着亚洲投资项目的开启，透明、公平的运行机制展现给世人，更多的合作模式将接踵而至，亚投行的发展将展现更大的包容性和吸引力。

金砖国家新开发银行

金砖国家新开发银行成立于 2015 年 7 月 21 日，是历史上第一个由新兴市

场国家自主成立并主导的国际多边开发银行，是对全球增长和发展领域的现
有多边和区域金融机构的有力补充。它的发展宗旨是支持金砖国家及其他新
兴市场和发展中国家的基础设施建设和可持续发展，同时减少对美元、欧元
的依赖。2016 年 1 月，NDB 董事会会议通过了银行运作的主要政策和章程。
2 月，NDB 先后与中国政府签订了总部协定以及与上海市人民政府签订谅解
备忘录，从而开始了全面运作。2016 年对于 NDB 来说是起步的一年，也是成
就辉煌的一年。NDB 至少在两方面取得了积极进展：第一，共批准了 7 个绿
色可再生能源项目，总额超过 15 亿美元；第二，成功发行了首批 30 亿元人
民币绿色债券。

2016 年 NDB 批准通过的 7 个项目

4 月 15 日，NDB 批准了该行成立以来的首批贷款项目，总规模为 8.11 亿
美元，用于支持成员 2 370 兆瓦的可再生能源发电能力，每年可避免排放二氧
化碳 400 万吨。首批 4 个项目分别为：巴西的可再生能源发电项目、中国上
海临港弘博新能源发展有限公司的太阳能屋顶发电项目、印度的可再生能源
发电项目、南非的输电网络建设项目。

7 月中旬，NDB 决定为俄罗斯卡累利阿水电站项目提供融资，该项目总
投资额为 118 亿卢布（约 1.9 亿美元）。俄罗斯直投基金和中国能源工程集团
有限公司是项目股本的投资方。该项目已于 10 月 17 日正式启动，计划于
2019 年完工。

11 月 22 日，NDB 董事会又批准了其在中国和印度的两个新项目：福建
莆田平海湾风电项目（20 亿元人民币）和中央邦道路项目（3.5 亿美元）。
福建莆田平海湾风电项目每年预计发电 8.73 亿千瓦时，每年预计减排 87 万
吨二氧化碳；而中央邦道路项目支持建设的道路具有交通枢纽的作用，对印
度中央地区及沿海地区起到连接作用，促进相关区域发展升级。

金砖国家等一些发展中国家都亟须进行能源结构转型，但是目前新能源
以及其他高新技术产业的发展依赖于风险投资，因此，需要开发性金融机构
提供有力支撑。而 NDB 就将在其中起到桥梁和金融杠杆的作用，将金融部门
和能源部门结合起来，撬动资金投入能源部门，加快新兴经济体和发展中国
家的能源结构转型。这些项目将为金砖国家提高能源利用率、应对环境气候
变化和生态环境恶化、平衡发展与环境、节能减排等做出巨大贡献，完全符

合 NDB 金融支持可持续发展的宗旨。由此可见，绿色金融是 NDB 着力发展的重点领域，也是国际社会优化发展模式的重要前沿领域。

2016 年 NDB 发行的首批人民币绿色债券

7 月 18 日，NDB 成功发行了首批 30 亿元绿色金融债券，债券期限为 5 年，发行利率 3.07%，认购倍数 3.1 倍，吸引了境内外多元化的投资者踊跃认购，募集资金将专项用于金砖国家、其他新兴经济体以及发展中国家的绿色产业项目，即 2016 年 4 月批准通过的首批绿色能源项目、俄罗斯西部卡累利阿水电站项目、向南非提供兰特贷款以应对美元波动的敞口等其他项目。经评定，这一绿色金融债券的主体及债项评级均为 AAA 级。

此次债券发行是 NDB 在资本市场上的首次亮相，也是多边开发银行首次获准在中国银行间债券市场发行人民币绿色金融债券。此次债券发行既反映了 NDB 自身的特点，也体现了国际开发性金融的理念和实践创新。一方面，以人民币计价体现了中国作为世界第二大经济体和金砖银行东道国的独特优势，反映了 NDB 管理层的稳健与务实，也表明了国际金融市场对人民币国际化的信心；另一方面，绿色金融债券突出了绿色可持续的发展理念，填补了现行国际开发性金融机构的业务空白。

未来发展重点

开业一周年以来，NDB 一步一个脚印，走出了一条高效稳健之路。可以说，通过发行绿色债券来为成员提供稳定、成本低廉的资金筹措渠道，体现了 NDB 的投融资方向突出绿色可持续的发展理念。同时，NDB 也面临着一些困难和挑战，例如 NDB 未获得国际评级、存在流动性风险、金砖国家存在利益冲突、银行相关制度尚不完善等问题。面对接下来的挑战和机遇，NDB 将从战略高度和长远角度谋划未来，既借鉴现行多边开发银行的成熟经验和做法，坚持国际性、规范性和高标准，不断提高运营的透明度，同时对现有的政策和制度体系等方面进行适当的改进和创新。

拓展金砖国家合作新空间，创新发展融资新模式。近年来国际资本市场动荡不安，为发展中国家利用外资造成不少困难，一方面，NDB 应当进一步发展本币业务，为成员提供稳定、成本低廉的资金筹措渠道，据悉，NDB 已计划在其他金砖国家陆续发行本币债券；另一方面，NDB 还应当广泛动员政策性金融机构、商业银行、保险基金、私营部门等参与基础设施项目投资，积极稳妥运用公私合作伙伴关系模式，帮助成员实现经济社会可持续发展。

构建全方位合作伙伴关系新格局，壮大多边开发机构整体力量。从世界层面来看，由新兴经济体主导的 NDB 应当和世界银行以及其他多边开发银行在发展减贫、维护世界经济秩序、基础设施建设等领域展开合作。从地区层面来看，NDB 也应当积极寻求合作，形成优势互补的全方位合作关系格局，例如我国倡议实行的"一带一路"愿景与规划。

完善全球经济治理新秩序，提高新兴经济体的话语权。NDB 极有潜力被认为是金砖国家和新兴经济体的"准中央银行"，并和"应急储备基金"相互配合，形成新的全球性金融稳定网络，为发展中国家稳定货币和金融体系提供帮助。NDB 的成员间互相平等，凸显新型国际经济秩序的民主平等特征，反映出国际关系民主化的大趋势。

2017 年，NDB 将参与 15 个基础设施项目，贷款规模将达到 25 亿美元。此外，NDB 2017 年还将参与国际市场评级，未来考虑在国际市场上发债。从人员扩充角度来看，虽然目前 NDB 主要依靠借调 5 个成员的专业人员，但2017 年第一季度会有 10 名局长到位，加上新聘请的专业人员，将会形成100～150人的团队。从申请贷款流程来看，目前不同国家申请贷款程序不一样，一般来说从项目申请到批准需要 6 个月的时间，NDB 今后也会致力于提高效率，缩短项目申请受理时间。2018 年则可能引入第一批新成员。

一年以来，NDB 可谓低调地完成了诸多重大任务——确定了银行管理团队、运营模式，批准了 7 个绿色可再生能源项目，成功发行首笔人民币计价的绿色债券。迈向未来，NDB 还将面临更多机遇和挑战。相信 NDB 这个完全由新兴经济体创建的多边开发机构能够秉持可持续发展的宗旨继续成长，焕发出无限的生机和活力，并且朝着专业、高效、透明、绿色的目标不断迈进。

丝路基金

2014 年 11 月 4 日，中国国家主席习近平在中央财经领导小组第八次会议上首次提出"丝路基金"（The Silkroad Fund）的概念。同年 11 月 8 日，习近平主席正式宣布中国将出资 400 亿美元成立丝路基金。丝路基金作为"一带一路"战略"保驾护航"的三大机构之一（丝路基金、亚洲基础设施投资银行和金砖国家新开发银行），受到不少国家欢迎。对于一些"重债穷国"来说，因为主权信用评级低、贷款成本高，过去采用的主权融资模式已难以为继，而股权融资配合债权、贷款等新型融资模式更为便利。

完善治理

2015 年以来，丝路基金在公司的治理结构方面做了很多努力，公司的董事会、监事会和高管团队完成搭建，日常运行已经走向正轨。一是明确了中长期开发投资基金的功能定位；二是搭建了比较科学高效的治理结构，组建董事会、监事会和管理层，设立了战略规划委员会、投资委员会、审计委员会等若干专业委员会，并不断健全完善相关工作机制；三是搭建了比较规范有序的投资管理框架，坚持"对接、效益、合作、开放"的投资原则；四是引导培育积极向上的企业文化，确定了扁平化的管理架构和以人为本的管理理念，倡导开拓进取、协同高效的团队合作精神。

业务拓展

2015 年，丝路基金项目投资取得实质性进展。2015 年 4 月 20 日，丝路基金与三峡集团、巴基斯坦私营电力和基础设施委员会在中国国家主席习近平和巴基斯坦总理纳瓦兹·谢里夫的见证下签署了合作备忘录，启动首单对外投资；6 月 5 日，丝路基金与中国化工签署了合作投资协议，联合投资意大利倍耐力公司；8 月 31 日，丝路基金与哈萨克斯坦出口投资署在中国国家主席习近平和哈萨克斯坦总统纳扎尔巴耶夫的见证下签署了建立中哈产能合作专项基金的合作备忘录；9 月 3 日，丝路基金与俄罗斯诺瓦泰克公司交换了购买俄罗斯亚马尔液化天然气一体化项目部分股权的框架协议；12 月 14 日，丝路基金与哈萨克斯坦出口投资署签署了设立中哈产能合作专项基金的框架协议；12 月 17 日，丝路基金与俄罗斯诺瓦泰克公司签署了亚马尔液化天然气一体化项目交易协议。丝路基金成立一年多以来，已经成功启动了五单跨境直接投资项目。以上项目分别代表了丝路基金在绿地项目开发、国际市场并购以及支持能源合作等重点领域的积极尝试。

丝路基金所采取的投资模式主要有 3 种。一是开展股权投资，支持企业海外运营方式和激励机制转型。通过股权投资，帮助企业解决对外投资中资金瓶颈问题，支持企业在境外的项目拓展和运营。二是提供贷款融资，配套股权提供更多融资便利。在参与股权投资的基础上，还可以通过参与银团贷款等形式对项目提供进一步融资支持。此外，还可以投资项目主体发行的各类债券工具等。三是建立子基金或专项基金，对特定领域的投融资提供支持。如在 2015 年，为支持中哈产能合作，丝路基金与哈萨克斯坦有关政府部门就设立产能合作专项基金进行了积极探讨。

国际交流方面，丝路基金也多次参与国际论坛。2015 年 3 月 20 日，丝路基金董事长金琦与会"2015 中国境外中资企业年会"；5 月 28 日出席亚欧互联互通产业对话论坛；6 月 27 日出席陆家嘴金融论坛；12 月 14 日，丝路基金与哈萨克斯坦巴伊捷列克国家控股公司在北京签署了合作备忘录，双方商定，综合运用金融、信息、法律、组织等资源，以股权、债权等多种方式，在中哈产能合作专项基金框架下开展合作，共同寻求产能、信息技术等优先领域的合作机会；12 月 21 日，金琦董事长会见了尼泊尔驻华大使马赫什和尼泊尔政府前秘书长；2015 年 12 月 10 日，王燕之总经理会见了来访的格鲁吉亚经济与可持续发展部部长。

金融合作方面，丝路基金和境内外多家金融机构签订了合作意向书。2015 年 9 月 3 日，在国家主席习近平与俄罗斯总统普京的共同见证下，丝路基金同俄罗斯发展与对外经济事务银行、俄罗斯直接投资基金在北京签署了关于开展投资合作的备忘录。根据合作备忘录，丝路基金将与俄方在基础设施、产业合作、电力和能源等领域共同实施投资项目；2015 年 12 月 4 日，金琦董事长会见了香港金融管理局总裁和香港银行公会主席率领的香港银行公会代表团一行，就合作一事展开讨论；12 月 9 日，丝路基金与香港银行公会签署了《关于服务"一带一路"战略和支持企业"走出去"的合作框架协议》，标志着双方在海外市场开发、境外项目投融资和风险管理等方面建立长期稳定的战略合作关系，这将有助于更好地发挥各自优势，为中国企业"走出去"提供更全面的投融资服务。

经营理念

一年以来，丝路基金颇有建树，这与其一以贯之的 4 个原则和 3 种思维分不开。一是对接原则。丝路基金的投资首先要与各国的发展战略和规划相衔接。"一带一路"没有严格的地域界限，只要有互联互通的需要，丝路基金都可以参与相关的项目。二是效益原则。丝路基金的资金都有相对应的人民币负债，丝路基金不是援助性或捐助性的基金，运作上必须坚持市场化的原则，投资于有效益的项目，维护股东的权益。三是合作原则。丝路基金不是多边开发机构，需遵守中国和投资所在国家或地区的法律法规，维护国际通行的市场规则和国际金融秩序。四是开放原则，丝路基金愿意与国际和区域的多边金融机构开展投融资的项目合作。

3 种思维的第一种是对接思维，着眼宏观层面。要推动资源要素在更广阔的范围进行配置和结构优化，实现需求、责任和利益的对接。第二种是着眼产业层面，形成产业链思维。在"一带一路"框架下，金融机构要支持企业实现海外投资由单纯的工程承包为主向以"BOT"（建设－经营－移交）为主转型，通过装备"走出去"和产能合作，带动产业资源整合和技术的升级换代，实现向全球产业价值链高端升级。第三种是着眼金融层面，形成资本思维。以资本"走出去"助推企业"走出去"，通过创新投融资支持方式，综合运用股权、债券、基金及本币外币等多种融资方式和多币种组合，为各类项目提供有效的资金组合支持，加速资金循环和提高投资效率。

风险管理

丝路基金"走出去"，面临着国别风险、地缘政治风险（全球重大地缘政治风险都集中在中东、南亚、东欧和东北亚 4 个地区）、恐怖主义风险、经营风险、市场风险及国际项目运营经验缺失造成的风险等各类风险。因此，丝路基金建立了相对完善的风险防控机制：一是建立激励约束机制，与企业共担风险。建立产权清晰、责任明确的治理结构，明确出资各方的经营管理责任。二是设计合理的风险缓释和补偿机制。开展项目评估和尽职调查时要全面梳理风险，投资方案中充分设计规避风险机制。三是设计合理的退出机制。对商业性较强的项目，通过上市并实现投资回报后退出，对于基础设施建设类的项目，可以选择在项目建成并运营后，通过向当地政府转让、公开上市、股权转让等方式退出，并实现合理收益。四是注意遵守投资所在国社会文化和法律法规，选择项目时，必须充分评估投资项目与所在国的各类政策规范的一致性，避免发生不当投资风险。

　　未来，丝路基金将继续定位于中长期开发投资基金，秉承"开放包容、互利共赢"的理念，致力于为"一带一路"框架内的经贸合作和双边、多边互联互通提供投融资支持，与境内外企业、金融机构一道，促进中国与"一带一路"沿线国家和地区实现共同发展繁荣。

第七章　国别开发性金融协会

亚洲和太平洋发展融资机构协会

亚洲和太平洋发展融资机构协会（ADFIAP）通过加强融资职能和机构、提高成员能力和人力资源能力以及推动融资创新来促进可持续发展。ADFIAP通过其成员来提供融资发展服务，亚洲发展基金希望未来该地区在经济、环境和社会方面进行可持续发展和增长，以人民为最终受益者。

协会成员

各行业从事金融发展的金融机构/银行均可获得成员资格，无论是工业、服务业，还是其他生产性经济行业。协会应拥有以下各类型的成员：

普通成员：位于亚洲及太平洋地区的以融资发展为重要活动的机构。

特别成员：位于亚洲及太平洋地区的区域性或亚区域性金融机构；位于亚太地区以外的协会可能建立或保持合作关系的金融机构；区域以内或以外的其他金融机构，由 ADFIAP 董事会根据具体情况定位为"观察员身份"。

赞助方/维护方：公共和私有机构，非政府组织和个人，拥护 ADFIAP 的宗旨和使命，并愿意支付会费或做出贡献以在经济上协助协会。

机构伙伴：根据本国成员机构的建议，在省级或州级范围内进行经营的机构。

其他组织和金融机构：包括商业银行、其他单位或部门负责以发展为导向的活动，比如中小企业银行、小额信贷、环境贷款、住房贷款及相关业务。

荣誉成员：在发展银行领域服务表现突出，或与开发银行相关工作有密切联系，或多年来一直服务于亚太发展银行的个人，将由 ADFIAP 授予荣誉会员资格。

截至 2015 年 3 月，协会共有 110 余名成员。其中绝大多数分布在亚洲和大洋洲，在北美地区和欧亚交界地带也有少量成员。我国国家开发银行是协会成员，且是中国唯一的成员。亚洲地区，日本有 4 家机构，分别是日本融资公司微型企业及个人部分、日本发展银行、日本国际协力银行和日本经济研究所。韩国有生态前沿和韩国发展银行两家机构。此外，印度有 18 家机构，澳大利亚和加拿大各有一家机构是协会成员。

历史

1969 年，亚洲开发银行在马尼拉召开了亚洲及太平洋融资发展机构第四次区域会议，并提出了建立发展银行家协会的想法。1970 年，在巴黎召开的联合国工业发展组织银行家会议期间，这一想法得到了进一步体现。据了解，在加拉加斯举行的最后一次联合国工业发展组织会议上，成立了两个区域协会，分别是拉丁美洲和非洲区域协会。据加拉加斯的相关报告，阿拉伯国家和东欧国家也设立了类似机构。来自亚太地区的发展金融机构参加了加拉加斯会议，并同意组建亚太地区发展融资机构协会。

在 1976 年 10 月 1 日第六次区域会议结束时，31 个发展机构在亚洲开发银行主持下参加了马尼拉会议，并共同签署了一项协议备忘录，通过了"章程"，即成立了亚洲和太平洋发展融资机构协会，并确认愿意成为协会成员。

协会的治理结构

大会：最高机构每两年举行一次会议，选举协会董事会成员并对相关组织事项进行决议。董事会：对政策性事项进行决议的理事机构。协会选出具有表决权的成员不超过 30 名，并从中选出主席，3 名副主席和财务部长。秘书长是董事会的当然委员。该协会由秘书长进行管理，并由秘书处的服务部负责人进行协助。秘书处：秘书处设有一个负责全面运作的商业中心以及专职工作人员，以落实相关方案、工作和任务。其主要服务面是：会员、项目、培训和认证、信息、财务以及行政管理。该协会的亚太发展金融机构定期举办培训课程，并对协会的资格认证进行管理。

董事会对协会的未来进行设定，负责制定协会愿景、使命和经营目标。协会由一个不超过 30 名普通会员组成的董事会进行管理。董事会任命一名主席，不超过 3 名副主席以及一名财务部长。董事会从无表决权的成员中任命不超过 3 名顾问，即特别顾问、合作顾问以及协理顾问，作为董事会的当然成员。董事会成员应致力于达成协会的使命，并愿意拿出足够的时间和资源来帮助实现协会使命并履行其相关责任。秘书长应设为董事会具有表决权的成员。为了进行重大审议，并考虑到多样性，委员会由选举产生的成员机构组成，并以其指定的首席执行官和/或主席为代表。根据协会章程确定董事的任职期限。理事会成员不因其所提供的服务而获得任何报酬。董事会提名程序将向协会的普通会员公布，感兴趣的成员可以提名自己或其他任何人。

信息交流活动

ADFIAP 及其合作伙伴欧洲可持续发展组织（EOSD）于 2016 年 7 月 14 ~ 15 日在德国卡尔斯鲁厄成功举办了第六届全球可持续金融会议（GSFC 6）。来自全世界 35 个国家的 100 多名代表参加了此次会议。GSFC 的总体目标是为金融服务行业的可持续转型做出贡献，通过国际论坛让来自世界各地的主要利益相关者分享知识和经验，并通过共同努力建立一个强大、公平、安全且有弹性的金融服务行业，能够与自然环境相协调。会议涉及一系列可持续性金融主题，包括未来可持续性银行和金融创新，各个国家可持续性银行和金融业务最佳实践，如俄罗斯、巴基斯坦、尼日利亚和马来西亚，气候行动和金融机构，金融机构对 2010 年可持续发展目标（SDGs）的作用，以及可持续性金融机构和地方政府单位。该计划还包括对德国最大和最知名的应用研究机构之一 Fraunhofer 研究所进行参观，并召开"绿色"启动会议。该会议负责颁发了 2016 年全球可持续金融奖。

ADFIAP 与位于柏林的可再生能源学院（RENAC）在德国联邦环境部的国际气候倡议下以及德国驻马尼拉大使馆的支持下，于 2016 年 1 月 26 日在菲律宾马卡蒂市新世界酒店提出了一项合作项目，即"绿色银行 – 绿色能源和气候融资能力建设"。该能力建设三年（2015 ~ 2018 年）计划的主要目标是支持金融机构建立新的业务线，为可再生能源和能效项目提供资金，并利用国际性气候融资工具。该计划是对 RENAC 的 CapREG（可再生能源和电网集成产能发展）项目的补充。该项目设立奖学金，为印度、印度尼西亚、泰国、越南和菲律宾的专业人士提供不同类型的培训（在线和面对面课程）、游学课程、网络活动和经验交流，它旨在开发"绿色银行专家"学位课程。

非洲发展筹资机构协会

非洲发展筹资机构协会（Association of African Development Finance Institutions，AADFI）致力于通过银行与金融机构的合作促进非洲经济与社会发展；加强促进经济与社会发展的融资方面的合作；构建成员机构之间信息交换的系统化机制；加速非洲地区经济一体化进程；鼓励有关共同利益问题的学术研究与共识达成。

协会成员

截至 2016 年 10 月，非洲发展筹资机构协会共有 79 名成员，分为 3 种，其中普通成员 59 名，特别成员 14 名，荣誉成员 6 名。

普通成员：所有非洲地区的全国性金融机构，包括阿尔及利亚发展银行、（安哥拉）储蓄信贷银行、埃及工业发展工人银行、加纳农业发展银行等。特别成员：所有非洲地区的地方性和区域性机构，包括非洲担保经济合作基金会、中部非洲国家银行、协约委员会、非洲进出口银行、非洲经济委员会、东南非贸易与开发银行、非洲共济基金会、阿拉伯非洲经济发展银行、西非发展银行、非洲发展银行和东非发展银行等 14 家机构。荣誉成员：所有非洲或非洲以外的国际性机构组织，包括印度进出口银行、世界中小企业协会、佐丹奴德拉莫尔基金会、葡萄牙投资银行、国际重建与发展银行等机构。

非洲开发银行第一次董事会议于 1969 年 8 月在塞拉利昂共和国弗里敦召开。非洲开发银行召集会议旨在确定各机构和银行之间进行合作的方式和方法。1970 年 5 月在阿比让举行了进一步会议，来自 23 个非洲国家的发展银行以及各地方机构（如东非发展银行和非洲发展银行）的各个代表出席了会议。各国际银行和其他金融机构的代表也出席了该会议，并就国家开发银行的组织、管理和资源调动有关的一系列问题进行了讨论。1975 年 3 月 4~7 日在阿比让召开的会议取得了一定的成果，在非洲开发银行的主持下成立了非洲发展筹资机构协会。协会的成立符合整个非洲大陆的协调和经济团结需要。在阿比让举行的开幕式期间设立了一个联络委员会，负责起草和指定协会相关法律文件。这些法律文件是在协会第一届大会期间通过的，出于此目的，于 5 月 2 日和 3 日在塞内加尔达喀尔召开了此次会议。

组织架构

该协会由大会、执行委员会和总秘书处组成。大会是负责制定政策、确定条例和其他必要规定的最高机构,大会每年在其成员所在的某个非洲国家举行其常规会议。根据协会的规定,还可召开特别大会。大会由该协会的所有成员参加。执行委员会负责协会活动的开展并对总秘书处进行监督。其主席团由主席和两名副主席组成。还有 5 名成员分别代表联合国非洲经济委员会所定义的大陆 5 个分区,或者由大会根据需要对 5 个分区进行确定;另外一个成员由特别名誉委员会选举产生。总秘书处负责协会日常活动的落实和管理,通过其礼宾服务协助科特迪瓦的商业活动,特别是与非洲开发银行进行合作,通过非洲发展筹资机构协会的出版活动进行机构推广。

信息交流活动

非洲发展筹资机构协会于 2016 年 5 月 22～24 日在赞比亚共和国的卢萨卡举行了第 42 届常规会议。开幕式、工作会议以及闭幕式均在赞比亚共和国卢萨卡的穆隆古希国际会议中心举行,由南部非洲发展银行(DBSA)首席执行官兼 AADFI 主席德拉米尼主持。来自 39 家成员机构的 91 名代表以及合作机构的观察员参加了 AADFI 第 42 届常规会议,通过了 13 项重要决议,反映了 AADFI 成员机构对协会可持续性发展的诚意与愿景。

中国开发性金融促进会

中国开发性金融促进会(CAPDF)于 2013 年成立,会员主要包括在开发性领域开展活动的企事业单位,以及从事开发性金融理论研究的专家学者和相关科研院所。CAPDF 服务于中国开发性金融领域的各类市场主体,建立开发性领域的广大企业与各级政府、金融机构、科研院所的交流合作平台,促进政府、市场、企业、金融合作,更好地运用开发性金融方法推动市场建设、信用建设和制度建设,服务中国工业化、信息化、城镇化和农业现代化同步发展。

2016 年,CADDF 致力于推动绿色发展、生态旅游开发和特色小镇建设,促进中国及东北亚地区乃至全球的绿色发展合作;建设技术评价鉴定中心,在技术和金融之间建立信用基础，推动各类金融形态对技术型企业进行支持，促进实体经济与金融体系紧密结合；积极促进开发性金融领域的国际交往和经济合作；建设开发性、普惠性金融服务机制，支持扶贫开发，为贫困地区、战略成长型行业和困难群体创造公平的融资机会。

推动绿色发展，培育生态经济

目前制约一些大城市发展的不是土地资源，而是城市快速扩张带来的生态承载能力不足。这种生态约束在一定程度上抵消了城镇化带来的诸多优势。无论土地价值有多高，一旦生态环境恶化，传统的基础性土地地价和各种资本关系，都会遭到破坏性和颠覆性重组，因此需要探索绿色发展和生态经济。南北"4+8"地区（内蒙古、黑龙江、吉林、辽宁、福建、江西、湖南、四川、广东、广西、贵州、云南）森林遍布，水源充裕，没有遭受过度开发，其高质量、稀缺性的生态资源正是其价值所在。中国开发性金融促进会致力于推动中国生态资源优越的地区转变传统发展模式，发展生态财政和绿色金融，把生态优势转化为发展竞争力。

2016年，中国开发性金融促进会与江西省赣州市、黑龙江大兴安岭地区等地方政府联合举办了绿色发展座谈会、东北亚绿色发展（漠河）论坛等系列活动，推动"4+8"绿色发展平台建设及项目落地。组织及参与了一系列绿色发展相关会议，包括2016中国工业产品生态设计与绿色制造年会、2016年度特色小镇发展研讨会、中国产学研合作创新大会等。协同地方政府、企业、金融机构等，搭建"4+8"绿色发展平台，建立地方政府间协作机制，启动中国绿色产业投资基金、中国特色小（城）镇产业投资基金，推动绿色金融资产交易中心、消费金融公司等平台的建设。

落实创新发展，建设产业金融

技术进步、科技创新是推动经济长期可持续发展的根本动力，但由于社会缺少促进技术进步的氛围，传统金融对技术的重视程度不够，经济管理中的专业技术人才越来越少，金融对产业发展的理解和支持不足。中国民营企业日益成为推动技术进步的重要力量，但能够获得的支持非常有限，技术型民营企业的发展受到制约。2016年，中国开发生金融促进会组织建立专家库，对有一定技术专长的民营企业项目进行评估，由上海远东资信评估公司评估科技型企业的市场价值，促进各金融形态支持技术型企业。

2016 年 8 月，中国开发性金融促进会组织召开全国首次"技术评价鉴定会议"，对集成精密成型、生物环保消防、互联网＋社区健康医疗、海上生命搜救领域的 4 项特色技术进行评价鉴定，并推动相应投融资工作。此外，积极推动专家库、网络平台和项目库建设，研究技术评价指标体系和大数据建设。11 月，中国开发性金融促进会和西安交通大学共同主办"一带一路质量高端论坛"，研讨经济与产业质量管理法规，智能制造与质量创新等，推动"一带一路"沿线国家的交流合作，加快制造业转型升级。

促进开发性金融国际合作

经中国外交部授权，中国开发性金融促进会成为亚信金融领域协调国活动承办单位。与德国能源署合作设计以能源节约额度作为还款来源的融资模式，推动德国先进技术和模式支持河北等地的节能减排和雾霾治理工作，并筹划中德绿色发展国际论坛。举办系列国际论坛：3 月与中国民营经济国际合作商会举办"第三届中国境外中资企业年会"；6 月举办"首届跨境电子商务国际论坛"；先后于 2016 年 1 月和 2017 年 1 月举办两届"空中丝绸之路国际论坛"，组织会员参与"一带一路"建设。

推动开发性、普惠性金融服务机制建设

中国开发性金融促进会积极为贫困地区、战略成长型行业和困难群体创造公平的融资机会：

第一，推动生态扶贫，调研贫困地区基本情况，包括南北"4＋8"12 个省区 592 个县市地区的生态农业、生态旅游等基础资料，组织专家研究资源要素禀赋，挖掘这些地区的发展优势，建立贫困地区绿色发展资源库。与中国扶贫开发协会合作推动山西沁县农业扶贫项目，开展扶贫开发课题研究，为扶贫项目提供融智支持。

第二，中国开发性金融促进会与黑龙江大兴安岭地区签署《漠河生态建设与特色小镇综合体示范项目合作协议》，探索以 PPP 模式支持林区旅游及生态经济发展的道路，帮助漠河打造国际旅游休闲度假城市，为偏远地区创造融资机会。

建设开发性金融特色智库

中国开发性金融促进会积极打造开发性金融特色智库，2016 年出版《全球开发性金融发展报告》及智库系列丛书，包括《国外开发性金融法律汇编》《丝路经济文化前沿》等。构建开发性金融资讯体系，发布《开发性金融国际通讯》《"一带一路"伊斯兰地区和国家金融动态》等。搭建行业专家研讨平台，组织开发性金融法治国际研讨会，与俄法德日等国开发性金融机构建立直接联系，与国家信息中心合作组织 2016 年行业发展报告会，策划并举办了非洲电力和农业投资交流会等。

第三篇　开发性金融机构的分析与展望

第八章　开发性金融机构的
结构与发展趋势[*]

本章将对 30 家开发性金融机构，包括 12 家多边开发银行，以及 18 家国别开发性金融机构进行分析。在 18 家国别开发性金融机构中，包括 6 家高收入国家开发银行，以及 12 家中低收入国家开发银行；而 12 家多边开发银行中，也是既包括高收入国家主导的多边机构，又有中低收入国家主导的区域性多边机构。因此本章将从国别和多边，以及高收入和中低收入国家这两个维度，对这 30 家开发性金融机构的总体结构和发展趋势进行比较分析。

美国和地区大国主导的全球开发性金融体系

中低收入国家影响力迅速上升

如果我们将时间划分为以下 3 个阶段：1965 年以前、1965～2000 年、2000 年以后，我们会发现，新成立的机构以中低收入国家为主。1965 年以前，高收入国家凭借自身的经济优势，成立了多个国别及区域性开发性金融机构，以充分支持本国及本地区的经济发展；1965 年以后，尤其是 2000 年以来，随着中低收入国家经济的增长以及经济转型时期经济发展的需要，中低收入国家陆续成立各自的开发性金融机构。

图 8.1 显示，在 1965 年以前，全球范围内共成立了 12 家开发性金融机构，1965～2000 年成立的开发性金融机构数量达到了 20 家，而从 2000～2015 年的

---

　　* 样本中共有 30 家开发性金融机构，总资产、总权益、ROA、ROE 指标所用数据为 26 家机构，最长贷款年限所用数据为 22 家机构，其余指标所用数据均为 27 家机构。

15 年间，又新成立了 10 家开发性金融机构，其中 8 家由中低收入国家成立，占比 80%，仅有两家来自高收入国家。这表明，中低收入国家普遍认识到，单纯依靠市场并不能完全实现社会资源的有效配置和经济的协调发展，通过开发性金融机构进行有效的资源配置，对本国乃至区域间的经济发展有着至关重要的作用。

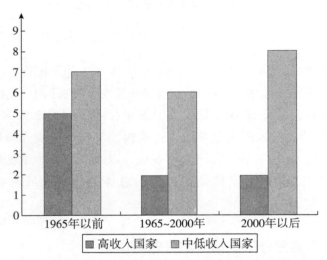

图 8.1　高收入国家与中低收入国家主导的开发性金融机构成立时间对比

从 1965 年起，高收入国家主导设立的开发性金融机构的增量明显放缓。在过去的 50 年间，高收入国家主导设立的开发性金融机构仅有亚洲开发银行、欧洲复兴开发银行、北莱茵威斯特法伦州银行和日本政策投资银行 4 家。这同时也有另外一个背景，就是高收入国家主导的开发性金融机构体系已经进入相对成熟阶段。

中国经济的高速发展，也在很大程度上扩大了中低收入国家开发性金融机构的总体规模。如果剔除中国，从其他中低收入国家的开发性金融机构来看，其发展水平仍远不及高收入国家的开发性金融机构。

全球开发性金融体系仍以国别开发银行为主体

从资产总量、权益总量来看（见图 8.2），国别开发性金融机构规模，都远远高于多边开发性金融机构。这表明，全球开发性金融机构体系仍然以支持本国经济为主。其中，中国国家开发银行规模巨大，总资产和总权益超过全球开发性金融机构总量的 1/3，在贯彻宏观经济政策、引导社会投资等方面发挥着重要作用。另外，德国复兴信贷银行、北莱茵威斯特法伦州银行和法国储蓄托管机构的经济体量也相对较大。而在多边开发性金融机构中，世界银行的经济体量位列第一，在世界范围的贷款援助中发挥着不可替代的作用。

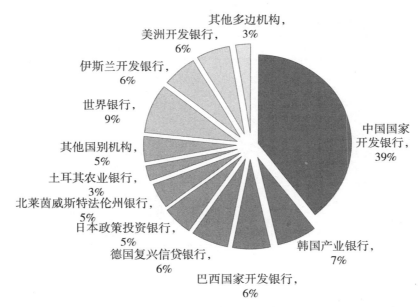

其他多边机构，3%
美洲开发银行，6%
伊斯兰开发银行，6%
世界银行，9%
其他国别机构，5%
土耳其农业银行，3%
北莱茵威斯特法伦州银行，5%
日本政策投资银行，5%
德国复兴信贷银行，6%
巴西国家开发银行，6%
韩国产业银行，7%
中国国家开发银行，39%

图 8.2　国别开发性金融机构与多边开发性金融机构总权益对比

国别开发性金融机构多以支持本国经济发展为主要目标，而多边开发性金融机构的主要目标是满足区域或全球的发展需要。在经济全球化的大背景下，各国需要加强沟通与交流、促进合作共赢、共同应对风险与挑战，以满足区域性的经济发展要求。中国在这方面做出了重要贡献：2000 年后新成立的 4 家多边开发性金融机构中，亚投行、金砖国家新开发银行均与中国的积极推动有关，这也凸显了中国在世界金融市场上日益增长的影响力。

从成立时间来看，在 30 个样本机构中，国别开发性金融机构在 1965 年之前成立的有 8 家，1965~2000 年成立 4 家，2000 年之后成立 6 家，而在上述 3 个阶段，多边开发性金融机构新设立的数量都是 4 家。在上述每一个阶段，新成立的国别开发性金融机构的数量均大于或等于多边开发性金融机构的数量。这从另一个侧面体现出开发性金融机构在设立阶段就更多侧重于本国的发展。

多边开发性金融机构的股权结构

表 8.1 列出了 30 个样本机构中多边开发性金融机构的股权构成。

表 8.1　多边开发性金融机构股权结构

中文名称	国家收入组别	总部	所有权结构（2015 年）
世界银行	高收入	美国华盛顿	美国，15.85%；日本，6.84%；中国，4.42%；德国，4.00%；英国，3.75%；法国，3.75%
欧洲复兴开发银行	高收入	英国伦敦	美国，10.1%；法国，8.6%；德国，8.6%；意大利 8.6%；日本，8.6%；英国，8.6%
美洲开发银行	高收入	美国华盛顿	美国，29.34%；阿根廷，10.77%；巴西，10.77%；墨西哥，6.92%；加拿大，6.29%
亚洲开发银行	高收入	菲律宾马尼拉	日本，15.67%；美国，15.56%；中国，6.47%；印度，6.36%；澳大利亚，5.81%
亚洲基础设施投资银行	中低收入	中国北京	中国，28.7%；印度，8.3%；俄罗斯，6.5%；德国，4.6%；韩国，3.7%
金砖国家新开发银行	中低收入	中国上海	中国，20%；俄罗斯，20%；巴西，20%；印度，20%；南非，20%
欧亚开发银行	中低收入	哈萨克斯坦阿拉木图	俄罗斯，65.97%；哈萨克斯坦，32.99%；白俄罗斯，0.99%；亚美尼亚，0.01%；塔吉克斯坦，0.03%；吉尔吉斯共和国，0.01%
非洲开发银行	中低收入	科特迪瓦阿比让	尼日利亚，9.320%；美国，6.6%；日本，5.5%；埃及，5.4%；南非，4.8%

（续表）

中文名称	国家收入组别	总部	所有权结构（2015 年）
加勒比开发银行	中低收入	西印度群岛巴巴多斯	牙买加，18.62%；特立尼达和多巴哥，18.62%；加拿大，10.02%；英国，0.02%；德国，6.00%；中国，6.00%
伊斯兰开发银行	中低收入	沙特阿拉伯吉达	沙特阿拉伯，23.52%；利比亚，9.43%；伊朗，8.52%；尼日利亚，7.66%；阿拉伯联合酋长国，7.51%

高收入国家主导的多边机构中美国占股比例高

美国作为世界银行、美洲开发银行、欧洲复兴开发银行的第一大股东，亚洲开发银行的第二大股东，在高收入国家主导的多边开发性金融机构中具有较高的话语权。其中，世界银行和美洲开发银行的总部均设在美国华盛顿，美国作为主要牵头人，在这些开发性金融机构中扮演着重要角色。日本、德国作为仅次于美国的大股东，也占据着重要地位。

此外，高收入国家主导的多边开发性金融机构股权相对分散，其控制权由几个大股东（多为高收入国家）分享，既保留了股权相对集中的优势，又使得股权制衡程度较高。以欧洲复兴开发银行为例，其主要股东为美国（10.1%）、法国（8.6%）、德国（8.6%）、意大利（8.6%）、日本（8.6%）和英国（8.6%）（见表8.1），均为高收入国家且持股比例相当均衡，既保留了高收入国家总体的控制权，又使股东之间相互制约，协调各方利益。

中低收入国家中，地区大国在区域性多边开发性金融机构中占主导地位

亚洲基础设施投资银行（亚投行）、金砖国家新开发银行、欧亚开发银行、非洲开发银行、加勒比开发银行、伊斯兰开发银行均为区域性多边开发性金融机构，以本地区成员为主，同时与其他地区国家积极合作，股权结构也呈现多元化特点。

其中，中国倡议设立的亚投行意向创始成员囊括了欧洲、美洲、大洋洲、非洲等多个地区的 57 个国家，主要股东为：中国（28.7%）、印度（8.3%）、俄罗斯（6.5%）、德国（4.6%）、韩国（3.7%）。而伊斯兰开发银行的主要成员则均为中东国家，沙特阿拉伯（23.52%）、利比亚（9.43%）、伊朗（8.52%）、尼日利亚（7.66%）、阿拉伯联合酋长国（7.51%）。欧亚开发银行的股权集中度较高，俄罗斯以65.97%的股权对欧亚开发银行拥有绝对控制权，哈萨克斯坦以32.99%的股权比例位居第二大股东。总体而言，中低收入国家主导的多边开发性金融机构以区域性合作为主，主要股东为本地区大国。不过与高收入地区国家相比，中低收入地区国家的整体融合程度较弱，地区间的互通互联和贸易投资有待进一步整合协作。

业务模式：相同的主权信用基础，不同的资金运作模式

资金来源以借款发债和政府拨款为主

与传统商业银行相比，开发性金融机构有较强的政策性，吸收公众存款较少，但大多数机构都能获得政府的资金支持，尤其是获得政府的信用支持，利用市场运作模式，从其他金融机构借款、在国内和国际资本市场上发行债券，这些是开发性金融机构最普遍的筹资方式（见图8.3）。

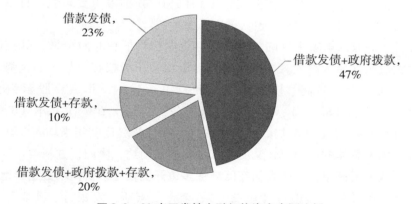

图 8.3　30 家开发性金融机构资金来源比例

在30家开发性金融机构中，所有机构都用到了借款、发债的融资方式，其中有20家机构可以得到政府的直接拨款（俄罗斯发展与对外经济事务银行和菲律宾开发银行两家机构未获得政府是否直接拨款的数据），仅有9家机构将从公众吸收存款作为资金来源（见表8.2）。而这9家机构中只有北莱茵威斯特法伦州银行、法国储蓄托管机构、韩国产业银行3家属于高收入国家的

开发性金融机构，其他 6 家均来自中低收入国家。

表 8.2　30 家开发性金融机构资金来源

借款发债	政府拨款	吸收存款
所有	除了美洲开发银行、欧亚开发银行、非洲开发银行、伊斯兰开发银行、法国储蓄托管机构、土耳其工业开发银行、土耳其农业银行、委内瑞拉经济社会发展银行	北莱茵威斯特法伦州银行、法国储蓄托管机构、韩国产业银行、乌兹别克斯坦共和国国家对外经济活动银行、印度工业开发银行、菲律宾开发银行、埃及工业发展和工人银行、土耳其农业银行、马来西亚开发银行

从多边和国别层面的角度来看，在 12 家多边开发性金融机构中，除美洲开发银行、欧亚开发银行、非洲开发银行、伊斯兰开发银行 4 家没有获得政府的直接拨款外，其余 8 家均可以从政府拨款获得资金，同时，所有多边机构无一向公众吸收存款。由此可以看出，多边机构及大部分高收入国家的国别开发性金融机构较少开展吸收存款业务，且多边机构大多能获得政府的资金支持。

金融产品渐次多元

高收入国家与中低收入国家开发性金融机构金融产品比较

高收入国家开发性金融机构的金融产品种类较为多元，这是因为其金融市场较为发达和完善。而中低收入国家开发性金融机构的金融产品以传统的存贷款和现金转账业务为主，这源于其金融市场成熟度较低，金融体系尚未健全。

从图 8.4 来看，发放贷款是最普遍的金融业务，拥有贷款担保业务的机构也在 70% 以上，其次是信托服务、存款账户和储蓄账户，开展小额保险业务的开发性金融机构占比最低。

在高收入国家开发性金融机构中，信托服务、小额保险等非传统银行业务开展相对较多。其中，信托服务在高收入国家开发性金融机构的比重要比中低收入国家开发性金融机构高出 34 个百分点，而小额保险业务仅存在于高收入国家开发性金融机构。而存款账户、现金转账业务则在低收入国家开发性金融机构中占比更高。由此可以看出，高收入国家开发性金融机构

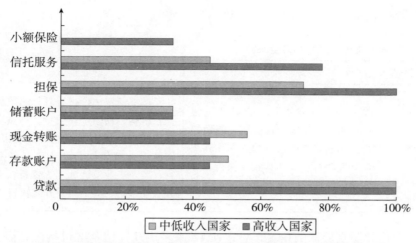

图 8.4　中低收入国家与高收入国家开发性金融机构业务模式对比

的金融产品更为灵活和丰富，而中低收入国家开发性金融机构提供的产品则相对传统。

多边开发性金融机构业务模式相对简单

多边开发性金融机构的宗旨是发展和减贫，其职能注重对发展中国家的经济发展提供国家层面的资金支持，因此其业务比国别开发性金融机构更为集中。80% 以上的多边开发性金融机构都开展了贷款和担保业务，而开展信托服务、现金转账业务的多边开发性金融机构仅占 25%（见图 8.5）。

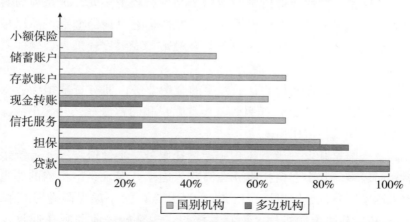

图 8.5　国别开发性金融机构和多边国家开发性金融机构业务模式对比

除了上述 4 项业务之外，多边开发性金融机构并没有提供其他的银行业务，而国别开发性金融机构还提供存款账户、储蓄账户、小额保险等服务，其业务模式与多边开发性金融机构相比更为丰富。由此可见，国别开发性金融机构主要是为本国经济发展提供更多支持和便利，因此其开展的业务也更加灵活和多元；而多边开发性金融机构因其直接针对国家层面的业务，其业务模式相对简单集中。

产业投向相对集中

开发性金融机构贷款覆盖领域众多，其资金的产业投向相对集中。其中，绝大多数开发性金融机构（95% 以上）都向建筑、基础设施和能源行业提供贷款（见图 8.6 及图 8.7）。

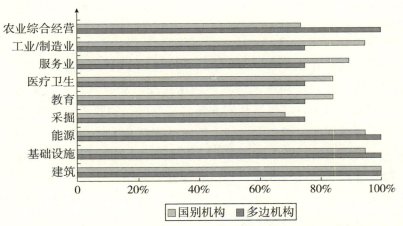

图 8.6　国别开发性金融机构与多边开发性金融机构的资金产业投向

多边开发性金融机构更偏向于投资额巨大的资本密集型行业，国别开发性金融机构则更注重对本国国内经济社会发展型项目的投入。图 8.6 显示，相较于国别开发性金融机构，更多的多边开发性金融机构将资金投向农业综合经营、采掘、基础设施和能源行业，主要因为这些外部性较强的项目投资期限长、资金需求量大且收益不确定性高，市场化资金投入少，因此更容易得到多边开发性金融机构的资金支持。而国别开发性金融机构则更侧重于工业制造业、服务业、教育和医疗卫生等行业。此类项目投资额相对较小，且各国差异性较大，不利于多边开发性金融机构进行评估，因而多由各国的国

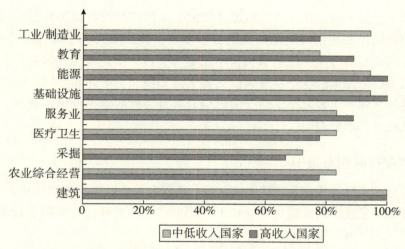

图 8.7　中低收入国家与高收入国家开发性金融机构的资金产业投向

别开发银行投资。

　　从国别角度来看，中低收入国家开发性金融机构的投资更关注与当前阶段发展相关的领域，而高收入国家则向增值型产业投入更多。图 8.7 显示，中低收入国家开发性金融机构在农业综合经营、工业制造业、采掘和保健等领域的业务开展程度，均大于高收入国家开发性金融机构，这些确实也是发展中国家亟待完善的领域。而高收入国家开发性金融机构则更侧重于在教育、能源、服务业和基础设施等增值领域开展业务。不过总体而言，各类开发性金融机构的资金投向产业仍较为集中，一类是具有外部性的公共产品，一类是特定经济发展阶段的瓶颈领域。

目标市场

多边开发性金融机构更注重国家层面的资金支持

　　大多数开发性金融机构均选择中小微企业、大型民营企业作为目标市场。但多边开发性金融机构和国别开发性金融机构的目标市场有所不同，多边开发性金融机构更加注重国家层面的资金支持，样本中可获得数据的 8 家多边开发性金融机构都对其成员提供了国家层面的资金支持（见图 8.8）。

　　多边开发性金融机构的主要目标就是促进成员的经济发展，对成员的资

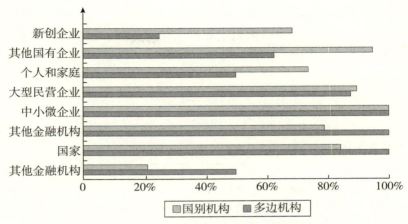

**图 8.8 国别开发性金融机构与多边开发性金融机构
对不同市场主体的资金支持**

金支持主要体现在发放贷款和提供拨款。通过向成员提供低利率信贷，支持其国内众多领域的投资；同时，多边开发性金融机构还会向发展中国家提供一些无偿援助，支持这些国家的经济社会发展。

国别开发性金融机构则更关注国有企业、新创企业与个人家庭

国别开发性金融机构在支持国有企业、大中型企业发展的同时，还会关注新创企业和个人家庭。95％和89％的国别开发性金融机构为本国国有企业和大型民营企业提供贷款，68％的国别开发性金融机构能够满足风险企业、新创企业的融资需求，同时74％的国别开发性金融机构也会为个人及家庭提供资金支持，为个人及家庭的住房民生教育等问题提供保障（见图8.8）。

贷款产品：高收入国家开发性金融机构对创新、创业类高风险企业支持更多

高收入国家开发性金融机构提供更加多样化的贷款产品，样本中所统计的所有高收入国家开发性金融机构都向客户提供创业贷款，运营资本贷款，长期贷款和银团贷款，而只有50％的中低收入国家开发性金融机构提供创业贷款。56％的高收入国家开发性金融机构提供风险极大的无担保贷款，而只有33％的中低收入国家开发性金融机构提供无担保贷款（见图8.9）。说明高

收入国家开发性金融机构对创新、创业等风险较高企业的贷款支持力度更大，而中低收入国家开发性金融机构则主要提供长期贷款、短期贷款等传统的贷款产品。

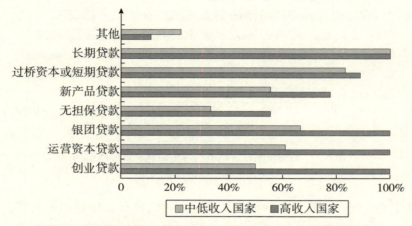

图 8.9　中低收入国家与高收入国家开发性金融机构贷款产品对比

这从另一个角度说明高收入国家开发性金融机构更加支持创新型经济发展，通过发放创业贷款、新产品贷款等方式来支持风险企业、新兴企业的发展，使高收入国家的弱小企业逐渐壮大从而带动弱势产业迅速发展，有利于经济转型及创新型经济发展。而大多数中低收入国家开发性金融机构贷款产品种类较少，以传统贷款为主，说明其承担风险意愿低于高收入国家开发性金融机构。

贷款期限：高收入国家和多边开发性金融机构贷款平均期限较长

高收入国家开发性金融机构的最长贷款期限要长于中低收入国家开发性金融机构，这主要因为高收入国家的风险承受能力更强。高收入国家开发性金融机构最长贷款期限中最短的为 6～10 年，拥有最长 20 年以上贷款的机构占比高达 67%；而中低收入国家开发性金融机构的最长贷款年限则相对较短，提供 20 年以内贷款的机构有 75%，其中最长年限为 11～20 年的机构最多，占比达到了 50%，而仅有 6% 的机构提供的最长贷款年限在 30 年以上。

多边开发性金融机构因其具有更强的风险抵御能力，其最长贷款期限要大于国别开发性金融机构。多边开发性金融机构的最长贷款期限都大于 10 年，最长贷款期限在 11～20 年、21～30 年和 30 年以上的机构各占1/3。国别开发性金融机构的最长贷款期限都在 30 年以内，其中，提供 11～20 年贷款的机构最多，占比达到47%，最长贷款年限小于及等于 5 年、6～10 年和 21～30 年的开发性金融机构占比分别为13%、20%和20%。

盈利能力：中低收入国家开发性金融机构运营状况良好

资产收益率用来衡量每单位资产创造多少净利润，净资产收益率则反映股东权益的收益水平，这两个指标共同反映了开发性金融机构的盈利能力。虽然开发性金融机构不以利润最大化为经营目标，但盈利能力仍然可以反映其运营状况以及抵御风险的能力。

图 8.10～图 8.13 显示，由俄罗斯主导的欧亚开发银行，由于国际油价的持续低迷导致成员经济严重下滑，资产收益率及净资产收益率均为负值，其余可获得数据的 25 家开发性金融机构的这两个指标均为正值，说明多数机构运营状况良好。

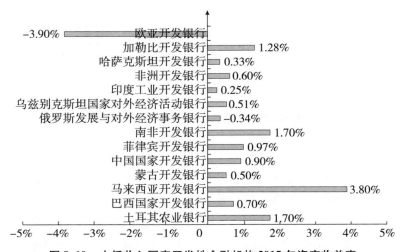

图 8.10　中低收入国家开发性金融机构 2015 年资产收益率

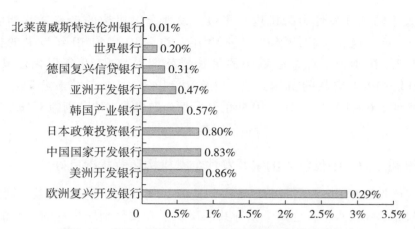

图 8.11　高收入国家开发性金融机构 2015 年资产收益率

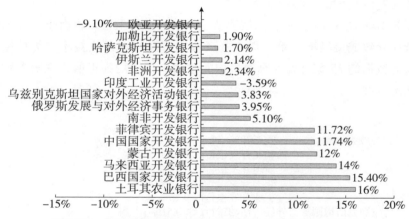

图 8.12　中低收入国家发性金融机构 2015 年净资产收益率

　　另一方面，资产收益率排在前十位的机构中，只有欧洲复兴开发银行和法国储蓄托管机构属于高收入国家开发性金融机构，其余 8 家均为中低收入国家开发性金融机构。而净资产收益率排在前十位的开发性金融机构中，只有欧洲复兴开发银行一家属于高收入国家开发性金融机构，这表明整体上中低收入国家主导的开发金融机构的盈利能力优于高收入国家主导的开发性金融机构。

　　根据前文对贷款产品的数据分析可以看出，高收入国家开发性金融机构对创新、创业等风险较高企业的贷款支持力度更大，这也在一定程度上导致

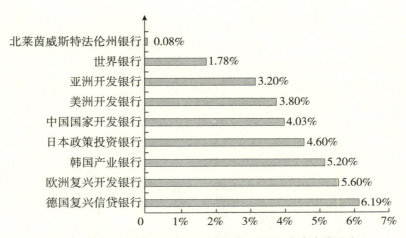

图 8.13　高收入国家开发性金融机构 2015 年净资产收益率

了其承担的风险更大，并且高收入国家开发性金融机构的资产规模也远远高于中低收入国家（除中国国家开发银行外），因此其资产收益率和净资产收益率明显低于中低收入国家开发性金融机构。

中低收入国家开发性金融机构运营状况良好，有利于其抵御风险，因而承受高风险支持性贷款的潜力更强。中低收入国家开发性金融机构通过创新变革，开发新的金融产品，找到新的盈利模式，将有助于为创新创业等高风险企业提供更多的资金支持，推动创新型经济的发展。

发展趋势

中低收入国家主导的开发性金融机构发展势头迅猛

高收入国家得益于 1965 年以前的资本积累以及先发优势，在开发性金融体系中占据了主导地位，进入 2000 年以后，已经达到相对成熟的阶段，因而发展势头比较平稳，处于稳步上升的状态；而中低收入国家在 1965 年以后，经济发展增速加快，陆续成立了支持本国发展的开发性金融机构。后者仍处于上升阶段，其总体规模已经超过高收入国家主导的开发性金融机构。尤其是 2000 年以后，全球范围内成立的 10 家开发性金融机构中，8 家来自中低收入国家。

其中，中国国家开发银行的强势崛起，对于中低收入国家开发性金融总规模的提升起到了极大的推动作用。图8.14、图8.15显示，2006～2015年，高收入国家开发性金融机构的总资产从1.55万亿美元上升到2.09万亿美元，年均增长3.48%；总权益从0.23万亿美元上升到0.29万亿美元，年均增长2.61%，总体处于稳步上升状态。

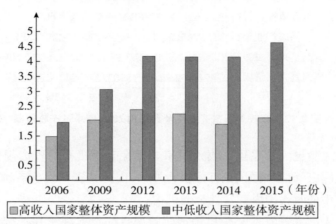

图8.14　高收入国家与中低收入国家开发性金融机构的资产总量（单位：亿万美元）

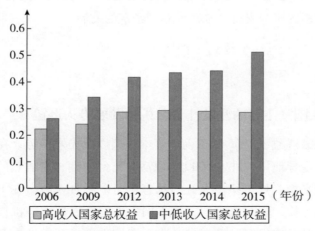

图8.15　高收入国家与中低收入国家开发性金融机构的总权益（单位：亿万美元）

与此同时，中低收入国家开发性金融机构的总资产从 2.03 万亿美元上升到 4.60 亿美元，年均增长 12.66%；总权益从 0.27 万亿美元上升到 0.51 万亿美元，年均增长 8.89%。无论是总资产还是总权益，中低收入国家主导的开发性金融机构，其规模都增长了 50% 左右，总体发展势头迅猛。另外，从图中还能发现 2012 年以后，无论是中低收入国家还是高收入国家开发性金融机构，其总资产都呈现先回落后上升的现象。我们认为，造成这一现象的主要原因是欧债危机，2014 年以后危机初步消除，全球范围内的开发性金融机构的总规模都又处于上升态势。

开发性金融机构整体盈利能力趋弱

2006 ~ 2015 年，开发性金融机构的盈利能力整体上下降，资产收益率的（简单算术）平均值从 2006 年的 2.01% 下降到 2015 年的 0.83%，净资产收益率的（简单算术）平均值从 2006 年的 9.25% 下降到 2012 年的 6.69%，之后回升至 2015 年的 8.13%（见图 8.16 及图 8.17）。

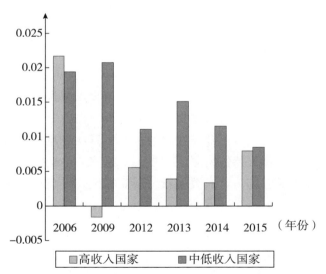

图 8.16　高收入国家与中低收入国家开发性金融机构的资产收益率

金融危机后，全球经济不景气，经济复苏较为缓慢，导致开发性金融机构的盈利能力下滑。其中，高收入国家开发性金融机构的盈利能力下降更为明显。由于受到全球金融危机的冲击，2009 年高收入国家开发性金融机构的

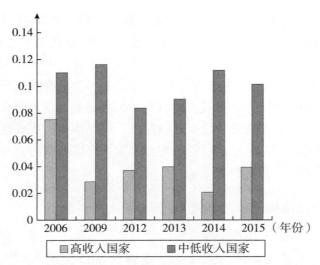

图 8.17　高收入国家与中低收入国家主导机构的净资产收益率

资产收益率仅为 −0.16%。近几年，其运营状况较 2009 年有所改善，2015 年的资产收益率为 0.81%，是 2009 年以来的最高值，但高收入国家开发性金融机构的资产收益率和净资产收益率还是低于中低收入国家开发性金融机构。这说明，中低收入国家开发性金融机构盈利能力和运营状况相对好于高收入国家开发性金融机构。

　　除了金融危机和全球经济不景气的影响，高收入国家开发性金融机构对创新、创业等风险较高企业的贷款支持力度更大，也一定程度上导致其承担的风险更大。而中低收入国家开发性金融机构运营状况良好，有利于抵御风险，所以其承受高风险支持性贷款潜力更强。未来，中低收入国家开发性金融机构可以通过改革创新，对本国创新、创业等风险较高企业提供更多的资金支持，更好地服务于创新驱动型经济发展。

总结

　　高收入国家主导的开发性金融机构体系相对成熟，整体规模发展平稳，中低收入国家影响力迅速上升，总体规模增速迅猛，地区大国在区域机构中占主导地位。

　　开发性金融机构的资金来源主要以其他金融机构借款、发行债券和政府拨款为主，辅以吸收存款。

开发性金融机构的资金流向渠道呈现多样化，其中高收入国家开发性金融机构提供的金融产品种类丰富，包括保险、信托等非银行业务，而中低收入国家开发性金融机构则仍以传统银行存贷、现金业务为主要业务，多边开发性金融机构相比国别开发性金融机构其业务模式更为简单和集中。

开发性金融机构资金支持的产业覆盖面广，多边开发性金融机构更偏向于投资额巨大的资本密集型行业，中低收入国家开发性金融机构更关注与当前阶段本国发展相关的领域，而高收入国家开发性金融机构则向增值型产业投入更多。

多边开发性金融机构更注重国家层面的资金支持，国别开发性金融机构则更侧重于国有企业、新创企业与个人和家庭，其中高收入国家开发性金融机构对创新、创业类高风险企业支持力度更大。

开发性金融机构的最长贷款期限与其风险承受能力成正比，高收入国家及多边开发性金融机构的最长贷款期限要长于中低收入国家及国别开发性金融机构。

开发性金融机构整体盈利能力趋弱，中低收入国家开发性金融机构运营状况优于高收入国家开发性金融机构。

第九章　开发性金融机构的投资与合作

　　本章概述了全球各大开发性金融机构在 2016 年的投资与合作情况。一方面，我们希望可以借此分析与当前开发性金融机构重点关注领域及地区相关的现象；另一方面，我们也试图对开发性金融机构在全球和区域的合作关系做出考察。

　　本章使用的数据全部来自由中国开发性金融促进会创立的《国际开发性金融通讯》。该通讯为半月刊，实时跟踪、收集并汇总世界银行、亚洲开发银行、亚洲基础设施投资银行等近 50 余家金融机构在国际交流、金融合作、区域发展、重点领域项目等方面的最新信息，每期信息总量超过 100 条。我们对每条消息中涉及的金融机构、投资金额、投资领域、涉及地区、项目类型等都进行了重新编码以形成所需的可分析数据。

　　需要特别说明的是，本章的分析只是基于 2016 年 20 期《国际开发性金融通讯》的统计，并不能代表 2016 年各开发性金融机构在各地区、各领域全部的投资与合作情况。后文的所有结论都只针对 20 期《国际开发性金融通讯》所列出的信息。

开发性金融机构的资金投资状况

资金领域流向

资金领域流向呈"三段式"阶梯状分布

　　基于对 20 期《国际开发性金融通讯》的统计可以看到，当前开发性金融机构在各领域①的全球性投资整体呈现出长尾分布的格局，即主要的几个重点领域占据了投资的绝大部分，剩下相对较少的投资分散在了其余各领域。投

---

　　① 领域分类依照《国际开发性金融通讯》中的划分。

资数额最大的 4 个领域投资总和占全部投资的 55%。

具体而言，电力通信（14.77%）、扶贫（14.77%）、能源资源（13.36%）、交通运输（12.38%）构成了第一梯队，它们是当前开发性金融机构最主要的投资领域，也往往是开发性金融机构资本长久以来关注的传统领域。社会发展（7.38%）、中小企业（6.81%）、科技创新（4.69%）、工业进步（3.95%）构成了第二梯队，这一梯队往往是近几年开发性金融机构的资本逐渐涉足的热点领域。剩下的生态环保、政府治理、农林牧渔、城市建设等领域构成了第三梯队（见图 9.1）。

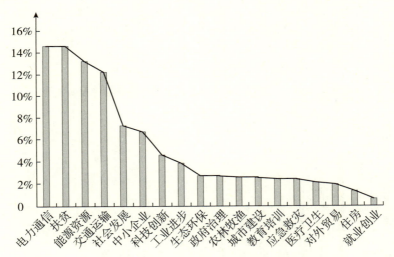

图 9.1　2016 年开发性金融机构各领域投资占总投资比例

不同类型开发性金融机构关注领域有所不同

在全球开发性金融机构的总体格局中，工业进步、扶贫、医疗卫生、住房等领域集合了更多的多边性金融机构的力量，就业创业、应急救灾、生态环保等领域则以国别开发性金融机构为主，农林牧渔、社会发展、交通运输等领域的差异并不明显（见图 9.2）。

关于投资领域，不同收入国家主导的开发性金融机构同样呈现出巨大的差异。中低收入国家更关注扶贫、社会发展、医疗卫生、农林牧渔等领域；高收入国家则更关注生态环保、教育培训、工业进步和城市建设等领域（见图 9.3）。这和不同国家所处的发展阶段有关，毕竟不同的发展阶段面临着不同的社会与经济问题。

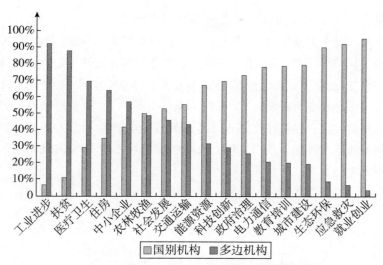

图 9.2　2016 年国别与多边开发性金融机构各领域投资占比

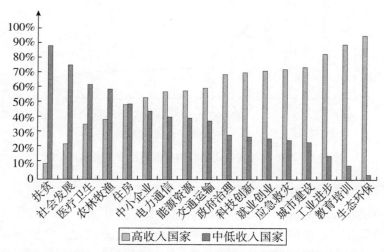

图 9.3　2016 年高收入与低收入国家开发性金融机构各领域投资占比

投资领域集中度不同

多边开发性金融机构一般投资更多的领域，但也出现了少数投资较为多元的国别开发性金融机构。

一般而言，多边开发性金融机构更可能在更多的领域投资，而由于主要服务于各国的具体问题，国别开发性金融机构更可能聚焦于某几个特定领域。

样本资料中的数据基本支持了这一判断，平均而言，多边开发性金融机构会比国别开发性金融机构多涉足 3 个领域。样本中投资领域排名前 6 位的均为多边开发性金融机构。不过值得注意的是，德国复兴信贷银行、中国国家开发银行、日本国际协力银行 3 家国别开发性金融机构也都分别涉足了 8 ~ 9 个投资领域，投资多元化程度较高。

资金国家流向

资金国家流向在不同地区的差异程度不同，并形成了几个热点的投资区域

根据样本中的数据，2016 年开发性金融机构在多达 128 个国家和地区都有投资，涵盖了当今世界上的大部分国家和地区。在不同的地区，投资的集中程度不同。比如在整个非洲、北欧、加勒比海地区，开发性金融资本的布局都十分分散；但在亚洲的大部分地区、拉丁美洲和西欧的部分地区，都形成了开发性金融资本重点投入的国家。

总体而言，中国、俄罗斯、埃及、印度尼西亚、菲律宾、印度、哈萨克斯坦和巴西是当前的热点投资国家。非洲的投资虽然较为分散（除去几内亚湾附近的几个国家），但总体的体量仍然很大。

不同地区主要投资领域不同

总体上，各地区的投资领域分布存在鲜明的异质性（见图 9.4 及图 9.5）。在不包括其他领域的几个重点领域，西欧、东欧、拉丁美洲的投资分布都较为平均；但其他地区都存在一个或几个重点的投资领域，比如中亚的能源资源领域、东南亚和非洲的电力通信领域、南欧的中小企业；而有的地区各领域的投资规模则相对较为平均，比如拉美和西欧，都有相对分散的多个重要投资领域。这种现象一方面与各地区的资源禀赋有关，比如中亚有丰富的能源储存，存在一定的利用潜力；另一方面也与各地区的经济发展现状有关，比如相比发展中国家更为集中的拉丁美洲和非洲，西欧在教育培训、城市建设就明显有更大规模的投入。

开发性金融机构的合作概况

在世界金融体系中，不同类型的组织具有不同的资源积累和领域专长。对于开发性金融机构而言，如何在世界范围内加强与其他金融机构、非金融

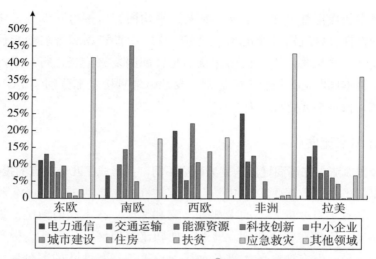

图 9.4 2016 年开发性金融机构各地区^①投资领域占比（第一部分）

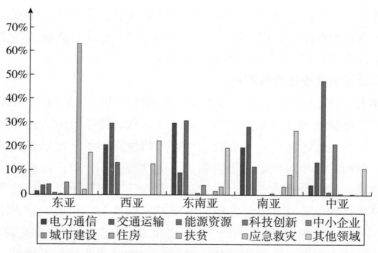

图 9.5 2016 年开发性金融机构各地区投资领域占比（第二部分）

性的企业乃至政府及区域性国际组织等开展多边合作，从而更好地发挥不同组织的比较优势、实现资源的有效整合，是开发性金融机构在发展中必须面

---

① 图中没有展示北欧和北美两个地区的分布情况，是因为这两个地区的国家数目和涉及开发性金融资本投入的事件或项目都很少，导致开发性金融机构在这两个地区的投资很少。

对和思考的问题。基于 2016 年 20 期《国际开发性金融通讯》的统计，2016
年开发性金融机构一共开展了 207 项合作。

总体上，可以将开发性金融机构的合作对象分为 5 类：其他开发性金融
机构；商业银行、保险、信托、投资管理公司等其他非开发性金融机构；非
金融性企业，以各领域的实业企业为主；政府（部门）及国际组织，包括区
域性的和全球性的；教育机构、行业协会、基金会等非营利性社会组织。图
9.6 展示了开发性金融机构与各种类型机构合作的次数及比例。

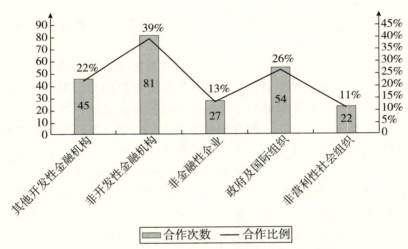

图 9.6　2016 年开发性金融机构合作次数与比例①

涉及开发性金融机构的合作以其与其他非开发性金融机构之间的合作为主

在数量上，尽管高于同非金融性的实业企业、非营利性社会组织的合作，
但开发性金融机构之间的合作（22%）与开发性金融机构与其他非开发性
金融机构的合作（39%）相比还有不小的差距，后者几乎是前者的两倍。
其他非开发性金融机构的合作仍然是开发性金融机构最为主要的合作对象。
另外，开发性金融机构之间的合作也少于开发性金融机构与政府及国际组
织的合作。

———————————

① 由于部分合作会涉及超过两类的合作对象，所以各类合作的次数相加会超出 207。

一方面，上述现象与开发性金融机构在世界金融体系中扮演的角色密切相关，即开发性金融机构肩负着实现公共政策和政府发展目标的使命，而并不以营利为最终目标，依托政府信用，在基础性、公共性领域引导商业银行等其他非开发性金融机构投入更大规模的资本，是其实现自身目标的重要方式；另一方面，上述现象也说明了开发性金融机构间的相互信任、多边协作和沟通仍然有进一步深化的空间。

不同类型的开发性金融机构有着不同的主要合作对象和合作倾向

多边开发性金融机构更广泛地开展合作，且更倾向于和开发性金融机构开展合作

总体上，多边开发性金融机构尽管绝对数量更少，却表现出了更强的合作倾向。就合作对象的类型而言，多边开发性金融机构与国别开发性金融机构也有所分化。前者更紧密地与非开发性金融机构及其他开发性金融机构开展合作，与非金融性实业企业的合作相对较少；相比之下，后者除去与非开发性金融机构的合作，还明显更重视与政府部门及国际组织、非金融性实业企业的合作（见图9.7）。这与多边开发性金融机构所开展的业务往往涉及多重主体，需要与各个国家和地区的资本彼此协调联动有关。而国别开发性金融机构主要为本国经济发展提供更多支持和便利，因此与本国国内的实业企业和金融机构联系更为紧密。由此我们也可以透视两种类型的开发性金融机构在经济体系中扮演的不同角色。

高收入国家的开发性金融机构更倾向于与非开发性金融机构合作，中低收入国家的开发性金融机构则更倾向于与政府部门及国际组织合作

在我们的样本中，高收入国家的开发性金融机构更重视合作的开展，它们最主要的合作对象是非开发性金融机构。相比而言，中低收入国家的开发性金融机构与政府部门及国际组织的合作更为紧密（见图9.8）。另外，尽管从次数来看，高收入国家的开发性金融机构与其他开发性金融机构开展了更多的合作，但从比例上看，低收入国家的开发性金融机构却更为依赖与其他开发性金融机构的合作。

开发性金融机构与其他机构的合作业务较为多元，形式也不尽相同

开发性金融机构与其他非开发性金融机构之间的合作以联合投资为主，

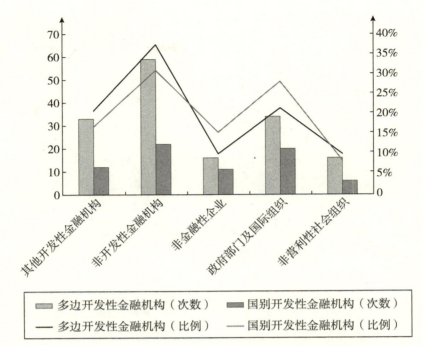

图 9.7　2016 年多边与国别开发性金融机构与不同类型机构
合作次数及比例对比

具体形式多样，包括联合融资、共同出资设立基金、创立公司等，在风险分担、数字化管理业务咨询等方面也有少量的合作。典型案例如下：

- 德国复兴信贷银行和黑森—图灵根州银行 Helaba 合作出资近 1.6 亿美元，以支持德国风力涡轮机制造商 ENERCON 将产品出口到乌拉圭，在当地建设最先进的风力发电厂 Peralta Ⅰ－Ⅱ；
- 日本政策投资银行与三菱 UFJ 租赁株式会社共同出资设立日本最大规模的医疗看护特殊投资基金；
- 国际金融公司、欧洲投资银行、泛非经济银行签署了标志性风险分担协议，后两家银行共同参与国际金融公司现有的风险管理。

开发性金融机构与非金融性企业（实业企业）之间的合作以综合性商业服务和联合投资为主。典型案例如下：

- 美洲开发银行与马士基（Maersk）、海陆（SeaLand）集团共同签署协议，3 家机构将以 Connect Americans 为平台，为中小企业提供商业、融资、培训机会；

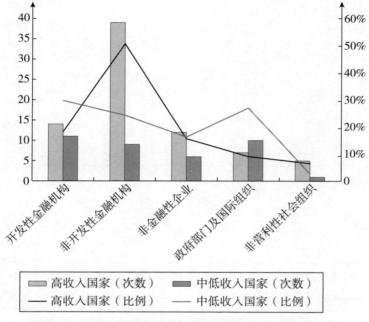

**图 9.8 2016 年高收入与中低收入国家开发性金融机构与
不同类型机构合作次数及比例对比**

- 丝路基金与欧洲能源利用有限公司、北京控股有限公司在北京签署了三方框架性合作协议，将欧洲固废环保业务的先进技术及管理经验引入中国；
- 法国储蓄托管机构、罗盖特公司和斯塔斯堡电力公司共同出资设立世界首个深层地热发电站。

开发性金融机构与政府及国际组织的合作涵盖范围较广，既有联合投资、贷款等金融业务，也有一定比例的技术应用、模式推广、经验研究等非金融业务。典型案例如下：

- 中国国家开发银行与工信部签订《共同推进实施"中国制造 2025"战略合作协议》，双方将建立沟通机制，选取试点示范，加强补贴、贷款、投资联动；
- 欧洲投资银行、欧盟及法国开发署共同提供 1.06 亿欧元贷款开展"卡巴拉工程"项目，通过从卡巴拉调取饮用水以满足马里首都巴马科的用水需要；

● 美洲开发银行与经济合作与发展组织发展中心、拉丁美洲及加勒比地区经济委员会合作出版拉美经济报告。

开发性金融机构与非营利性社会组织之间的合作以人才支持培养为主，也出现了少量的金融业务合作。典型案例如下：

● 拉美开发银行组织、哥伦比亚罗萨里奥大学和伊塞西大学协办的首届拉美开发银行管理与领导力培训项目；

● 欧洲复兴开发银行和克罗地亚雇主协会联合开展"私营企业青年计划"；

● 美洲开发银行与拉美和加勒比地区一体化研究所举办创意产品比赛，旨在寻找科技创新型企业家人才。

在 207 项合作中，有 22 项合作（约为 10%）涉及了至少 3 个类型的组织机构。这类合作虽然绝对数量不多，但在实践中常常能突破固有的合作模式，将国有资本与社会资本之间的联动、实业企业在本领域的经验技术积累等各方优势有机结合起来，对未来开发性金融机构合作模式的探索具有一定的启发性。如法国储蓄银行集团、农业信托公司、法国国家人寿保险、Natixis 资产管理公司、OCTO 技术公司 4 家公司利用区块链技术联手开发了证券借贷的非现金抵押管理实验平台，用以测试智能合同的使用、金融中介职能执行情况，实现了合同执行的自动化，对优化金融业务的合作流程、提高流程监管效率都做出了有益的探索。

未来，开发性金融机构与其他各种类型组织机构密切合作将是大势所趋，而要实现共赢发展不仅需要各方加强战略对话、勇于尝试不同的合作模式，国际性、区域性等各个层面的规则激励与制度保障也将是必不可少的。

开发性金融机构之间的合作业务较为单一

不仅合作的次数较少，开发性金融机构之间的合作形式相对也更为单一。基于《国际开发性金融通讯》的统计，开发性金融机构之间在 2016 年一共开展了 45 项合作。在这些合作中，有 20 项（44%）合作是谅解备忘录或框架协议的签订，其余 25 项（56%）合作为实际开展或协议生效的项目。

就合作类型而言，有 34 项（76%）合作为联合融资。无论是签订协议，还是已经开展实际项目的合作，联合融资都是当前开发性金融机构间最为主要的合作形式。这些联合融资主要投放到了大型基础设施的建设及能源的可持续发展中，如亚洲开发银行与亚洲基础设施投资银行对巴基斯坦高速公路项目的投资、世界银行和亚洲基础设施投资银行对南亚水电能源延伸项目的投资、亚洲开发银行同日本国际协力银行共同出资用于东帝汶的公路升级等；也有极少量的联合融资投向了实体企业，如韩国产业银行与韩国进出口银行在大宇造船债务重组项目中的联合注资。

相比与其他类型机构的合作，开发性金融机构之间的合作业务还略显单一。不过积极的现象是，一些开发性金融机构已经开始逐步突破已有的合作模式，试图从不同的维度中寻找深化协作的可能。比如在金融领域，我们能看到包括德国复兴信贷银行在内的多国开发银行与欧洲投资基金一起启动了 ENSI 项目，推广对中小企业有利的证券化市场；而在非金融领域，美洲开发银行联合拉丁美洲开发银行共同着手建立 INFRALATAM 数据库也是整合资源搭建平台以促进信息共享的重要举措。未来，合作业务领域的延展可能仍将是开发性金融机构实现广泛共赢、建立伙伴关系的重要途径。

开发性金融机构之间的合作较为稀疏和分散，但也出现了一些积极开展多边合作的开发性金融机构

根据 45 次合作事件，我们还绘制了开发性金融机构的合作网络图（见图 9.9）。

通过对 45 项合作进行分析，开发性金融机构之间的合作呈现出以下几个特征：

第一，开发性金融机构之间的合作较为稀疏。整体来看，合作网络的连通程度较低，许多开发性金融机构只与其余 1 ~ 2 家开发性金融机构存在合作关系。根据计算，两家开发性金融机构之间只有 11% 的可能性建立合作关系。

第二，开发性金融机构之间的合作较为分散。除去少数开发性金融机构之间有一定数量的合作（如欧亚开发银行与亚洲开发银行），我们很少能观察到有两家或几家开发性金融机构之间发生较为频密的合作。无论是世界范围内抑或区域范围内都没有形成稳定、聚集的合作集团。

第三，合作网络中出现了一些非常重视开展多边合作的开发性金融机构，在沟通世界范围内的开发性金融业务方面发挥了重要作用。这类机构是当前世界开发性金融体系的关键节点和中坚力量，它们以世界银行、亚洲基础设施投资银行、欧洲投资银行、美洲开发银行等多边开发性金融机构为主，但也包括中国国家开发银行、日本国际协力银行等国别开发银行。

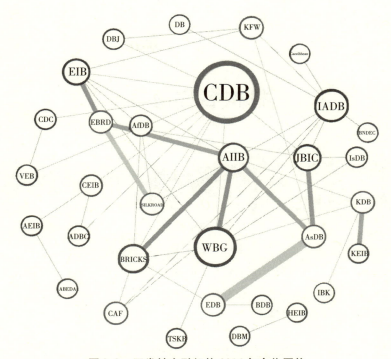

图 9.9　开发性金融机构 2016 年合作网络

　　注：在上图中，点的面积越大表示该开发性金融机构在 2016 年的合作次数越多；两点之间的连线表示两家开发性金融机构之间的合作，连线越粗表明这两家开发性金融机构在 2016 年的合作次数越多。

　　开发性金融机构之间的合作在近年来多次被各大机构强调，全球基础设施互联互通需要开发性金融提供资金支持和市场建设，其市场之大、项目之多、资金之巨，已不是单独一两个机构可以承担的。结合上述 3 个特征，就现状而言，持续深化开发性金融机构之间的对接，构建整体性的多边合作网络以实现机构之间的聚集效应，仍然具有不小的空间和潜力。在这个过程中，如何更好地发挥开发性金融体系中那些关键节点和中坚力量的作用，从而使其真正成为沟通整个合作网络的引导者和桥梁，如何让那些游离在合作体系之外的边缘化机构更深入地参与进来，将是值得所有开发性金融机构进一步思考的问题。

机构名称简写

英文简写	中文全称
多边开发性金融机构	
WBG	世界银行集团
AsDB	亚洲开发银行
IADB	美洲开发银行
EDB	欧亚开发银行
AfDB	非洲开发银行
EBRD	欧洲复兴开发银行
EIB	欧洲投资银行
Caribbean DB	加勒比开发银行
IsDB	伊斯兰开发银行
ABEDA	阿拉伯非洲经济开发银行
CAF	拉美开发银行
国别开发性金融机构	
KfW	德国复兴信贷银行
NRW. BANK	北莱茵威斯特法伦州银行
CDC	法国储蓄托管机构
DBJ	日本政策投资银行
KDB	韩国产业银行
DBM	蒙古开发银行
BPMB	马来西亚开发银行

（续表）

英文简写	中文全称
国别开发性金融机构	
DBP	菲律宾开发银行
IDBI	印度工业开发银行
VEB	俄罗斯发展与对外经济事务银行
DBK	哈萨克斯坦开发银行
NBU	乌兹别克斯坦共和国国家对外经济活动银行
TSKB	土耳其工业发展银行
TCZB	土耳其农业银行
BNDES	巴西国家开发银行
DBSA	南部非洲开发银行
有中国因素的开发性金融机构	
CDB	国家开发银行
Chexim	中国进出口银行
ADBC	中国农业发展银行
AIIB	亚洲基础设施投资银行
NDB BRICS	金砖国家新开发银行
Silkroad Fund	丝路基金
国别开发性金融协会	
ADFIAP	亚洲和太平洋发展融资机构协会
AADFI	非洲发展筹资机构协会
CAPDF	中国开发性金融促进会

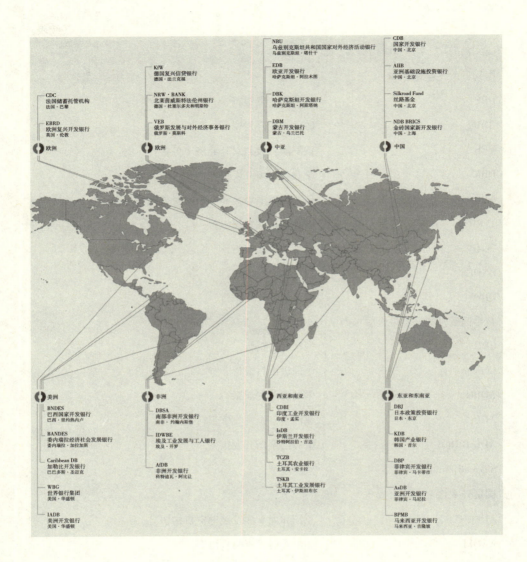

NBU
乌兹别克斯坦共和国国家对外经济活动银行
乌兹别克斯坦·塔什干

EDB
欧亚开发银行
哈萨克斯坦·阿拉木图

DBK
哈萨克斯坦开发银行
哈萨克斯坦·阿斯塔纳

DBM
蒙古开发银行
蒙古·乌兰巴托

中亚

CDB
国家开发银行
中国·北京

AIIB
亚洲基础设施投资银行
中国·北京

Silkroad Fund
丝路基金
中国·北京

NDB BRICS
金砖国家新开发银行
中国·上海

中国

KfW
德国复兴信贷银行
德国·法兰克福

NRW·BANK
北莱茵威斯特法伦州银行
德国·杜塞尔多夫和明斯特

VEB
俄罗斯发展与对外经济事务银行
俄罗斯·莫斯科

欧洲

CDC
法国储蓄托管机构
法国·巴黎

EBRD
欧洲复兴开发银行
英国·伦敦

欧洲

美洲

BNDES
巴西国家开发银行
巴西·里约热内卢

BANDES
委内瑞拉经济社会发展银行
委内瑞拉·加拉加斯

Caribbean DB
加勒比开发银行
巴巴多斯·圣汊克

WBG
世界银行集团
美国·华盛顿

IADB
美洲开发银行
美国·华盛顿

非洲

DBSA
南部非洲开发银行
南非·约翰内斯堡

IDWBE
埃及工业发展与工人银行
埃及·开罗

AfDB
非洲开发银行
科特迪瓦·阿比让

西亚和南亚

CDBI
印度工业开发银行
印度·孟买

IsDB
伊斯兰开发银行
沙特阿拉伯·吉达

TCZB
土耳其农业银行
土耳其·安卡拉

TSKB
土耳其工业发展银行
土耳其·伊斯坦布尔

东亚和东南亚

DBJ
日本政策投资银行
日本·东京

KDB
韩国产业银行
韩国·首尔

DBP
菲律宾开发银行
菲律宾·马卡蒂市

AsDB
亚洲开发银行
菲律宾·马尼拉

BPMB
马来西亚开发银行
马来西亚·吉隆坡

致　谢

　　本报告由中国开发性金融促进会编写。编写过程中，北京大学外语学院、北京大学法学院、北京外国语大学的同学们承担起收集各开发性金融机构基础数据和资料的重任，他们是安梦琪、陈希、王诗敏、哈斯高娃、李麟寅、李芊芊、宋高、汤晨、唐姗、王紫、杨挺、张寒露、赵盈盈、刘夕冉、齐涵博、孔金磊、孙凌凌、沙凡、王聪、姜宛如、赵玥辉、陈庄、邓海默。中国社会科学院的董维佳、徐奇渊、朱丹丹老师撰写了第一章和第八章，北京大学的李真博士撰写了第二章，罗祎撰写了第九章。中国开发性金融促进会的张桦成、薛天忆等担任组织、校对工作，中信出版社在报告审核阶段，为完善报告提出了重要建议。

　　报告是集体智慧的结晶，融合了上述所有人员的创意和扎实工作，感谢他们展现出的专业精神和团队合作，感谢他们在面对开创性工作时迎接挑战的勇气，感谢他们对开发性金融国际合作的信念和为此做出的所有努力。

　　由于时间仓促和经验不足，报告难免有不当和错误之处，恳请读者批评指正。

PREFACE

Global Development Financing Report 2016 is a ground-breaking and forward-looking report. It is of great significance for enhancing our knowledge of development financing and its trends. Development financing institutions were originated from Europe two hundred years ago, with a long history. With official support, it has been booming since World War II, and has made great contributions to promoting national economic growth, sustainable development, and maintaining economic and financial security. According to rough estimates, the members of the World Federation of Development Financing Institutions (WFDFI) number as many as 328. They play a decisive role in the international financial system. Currently, global development requires that development financing play a more and more important role. Yet our knowledge about development financing is far from comprehensive, and our understanding of its working principles and main functions is insufficient. In this sense, this timely report is of great importance, for it sets out the overall pattern and future trends of development financing institutions.

Meanwhile, this report also provides a great opportunity for mutual exchange and learning. The major purpose of development financing is to help governments achieve their development targets. Through medium-/long-term financing backed by sovereign creditworthiness, development financing can leverage financial market operations to mitigate the bottlenecks in social and economic development and maintain financial stability. Due to differences in political institutions, legal systems, economic policies, and development missions and priorities, development financing institutions differ from each other in many aspects, such as operational modalities, practical experiences and specialized advantages. These diversities inspire innovations in international development financing. In order to jointly promote the healthy development of global development financing, all development financing institutions need to learn from each other. This report is a step towards mutual learning among development financing institutions.

Enhanced mutual trust and cooperation among development financing institutions have become more and more important, particularly as countries are increasingly inter-connected and interdependent with each other, as regional or inter-regional cooperation is booming, and as the construction of interconnections and intercommunications speeds up. Mutual trust and cooperation are the key pillar for both maintaining regional financial stability and financial security and enhancing the medium-/long-term momentum of economic development. Furthermore, mutual trust and cooperation among development financing institutions are the driving force behind constructive interactions and coordinated development among Asian economies - a community of common destiny. In the past twenty years, development financing institutions in China, represented by the China Development Bank, have provided Chinese experiences and wisdom in an effort to innovate development financing worldwide, by combining international experiences with China-specific circumstances at different development stages. Looking forward, development financing will experience further significant growth, because it will be increasingly emphasized by governments, and demanded by capital markets. Meanwhile, the inconsistency of national market rules and incompleteness of market systems call for more integrated cooperation among development financing institutions, in order to jointly incubate markets, respond to risks and challenges, and shape the future. This is the goal pursued by the report, and the ultimate driving force for carrying on further research.

I sincerely hope that all development financing institutions will make new contributions to promoting global sustainable development and improving human well-being.

Vice Chairman of the National
Committee of Chinese People's Political Consultative Conference

Chairman of China Association for the Promotion
of Development Financing

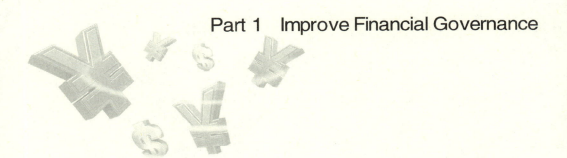

Part 1　Improve Financial Governance

Chapter 1   Roles and Responsibilities of DFIs

Development financing institutions face a number of fundamental questions regarding their roles and responsibilities. These include what should be the scope of business? How to evaluate their performance? How to construct the inner risk control mechanism and the exterior supervisory system that is consistent with its position and business scope as well? Before coming to a conclusion for these, we should clarify a primary concern, that is, what role does a development financing institution play in an economy? Only when we understand the central role of development financing institutions we can address other questions.

Globally, most developed economies have established a legal system, which specifically applies to the development financing institutions. Within such a system, a development financing institution is defined in terms of its basic orientation, rights and obligations, and its business scope. From the perspective of China, we should not only figure out the aforementioned points, but also even more practical and dynamic concerns. More specifically, China is the largest developing economy in the world, with considerable regional disparity. Besides this, a wide range of structural problems leads to tough challenges, which calls for corresponding structural solutions. Meanwhile, China's fiscal system and financial market are still on the way to further marketization. China's development financing institutions operate exactly against the background of a developing economy and a developing financial system as well. Before we come back to shed light on China's features, it is necessary to clarify the role of development financing institutions from a general point of view.

Role of Development Financing Institutions

Development Financing Institutions (DFIs) are financial institutions that rely on sovereign credit, deploy market mechanisms, and aim to realize public policies or strategic targets of countries or regions by promoting institutional and market building. DFIs are different from traditional policy financing institutions and commercial financing institutions, which can be seen as the intersection of those two. They have the policy and market dual nature. DFIs are dedicated to providing medium- and long-term development funds to meet the strategic capital needs of countries and regions by policymaking, guidance, and support.

Policy Role

The most fundamental characteristic of DFIs is that they are driven by policy. That is, DFIs are tools serving state policies. DFIs aim to realize specific strategic targets of countries, other than profit like commercial financing institutions. Therefore, DFIs inevitably remain strongly politically driven. That is why they can conduct financing business in capital markets relying on state credit. The policy role of DFIs mainly reflects in the following respects:

First, DFIs provide public goods. Public goods have the "free-riding" problem owing to their strong external and non-exclusive features, so private sectors pursuing profit maximization do not want to invest in relevant fields. The most evident fields are large infrastructure projects and social sectors such as health care, education and so on.

Actually, it is not just DFIs that provide public goods, but so do policy financing institutions. Panizza (2004) defines policy financing institutions as: financial institutions that provide long-term financing for projects having a positive externality but cannot be met by commercial credit. [1] Therefore, the government is the provider of public goods naturally, and policy financing institutions will be the main capital provider. However, the most outstanding characteristic of policy financing institutions is completely political. That is, policy financing institutions have no profitable businesses, and their operations completely rely on financial allocations and subsidies, which are far from the huge need of public goods. More importantly, once the financial fund is insufficient or the state financial situation becomes worse, those policy financing institutions will lose funding, and cannot further satisfy the financing of public goods.

The main goal of the state is to gradually reform these policy financing institutions into development financing institutions which are encouraged to use market mechanisms. The features of DFIs ensure they will and can contribute to the supply of na-

---

[1] Panizza U., Eduardo L., Alejandro M., "Should the Government be in the Banking Business? The Role of State-owned and Development Banks", Inter-American Development Bank Working Paper, 2004, P. 15.

tional public goods. On one hand, the policy nature of DFIs determines that they will invest in fields in which the government is concerned, rather than in fields to maximize profits, so they will invest into public goods; on the other hand, the market or commercial mechanism of DFIs, such as issuing bonds, ensures they are able to get enough funding from capital markets to meet the need of public goods.

Second, DFIs support emerging or vulnerable industries. For some strategic emerging industries, there is so much uncertainty at the initial stage of their development that the private sector is reluctant to invest, and commercial financing institutions also have little willingness to provide loans. Therefore, these industries need early support from DFIs.

DFIs can become involved in process of states developing early plans, DFIs investing early, and the private sector and commercial financing institutions entering later to enhance emerging industries. Furthermore, states or governments make up the national plan for the development of potential strategic emerging industries first; then based on the national plan, DFIs conduct feasibility research, invest into appropriate projects and develop relevant market mechanisms. DFIs will gradually exit from the projects on certain conditions, while the private sector will manage these emerging industries independently, and be supported by commercial financing institutions.

The support of DFIs to strategic emerging industries most evidently reflects their "development" nature. The "development" nature is not only capital support, but also the building and improvement of market mechanisms and the institutional environment for industry development. DFIs will also support some vulnerable industries (such as agriculture) with the goal of balancing the development among industries. Consequently, DFIs play the policy role of enhancing efficiency of resource allocation and optimizing the industrial and economic structure by supporting certain industries.

Third, DFIs moderate economic fluctuations. The core business of DFIs is medium- and long-term financing, so they can adjust the amount and structure of financing and investment according to the economic situation. By this, DFIs can influence investment activities of the economy, so as to ease the impact of economic cycles. For example, when the economy is too hot, DFIs could shrink investment, reduce the support for industries, increase bond issuing to withdraw currency at the same time, and finally reduce the economic heat. On the contrary, when the economy is in recession, DFIs could expand investment, increase support to relevant industries, and reduce bond issuing and operations on the capital market, so as to play a counter-cyclical role.

Guiding Role

The guiding role of DFIs is to indirectly attract social capital flows into specific industries or fields. Specifically, they can attract the private sector and commercial financing institutions to invest in industries conforming to policy intentions or long-run development targets of state or regions.

DFIs conduct business based on national credit and aim to realize national strategic development targets. This virtually gives a hint to the private sector and commercial financing institutions, that is, the industries that DFIs support must be industries that the state will encourage to develop in the future. National credit undoubtedly provides a guarantee for the uncertain risk of industries, and enhances the investment intention of the private sector and willingness to lend of commercial financing institutions.

Meanwhile, the early inputs of DFIs have already laid the foundation for further development of industry, which will attract the private sector and commercial financing institutions and allow them to free-ride and enter at lower costs. Hence, if governments intend to prioritize some industries, such as heavy industry or an environmentally friendly industry, they can instruct DFIs to increase investment to these industries, which could attract investment from the private sector and commercial financing institutions, and guide economic development.

Complementary Role

Development financing institutions, policy financing institutions, and commercial financing institutions are complementary, not substitutive and competitive. It is considered that the fundamental function of DFIs is to solve market failure. From this perspective, DFIs are to complement the shortcomings of commercial financing institutions, and provide concessional medium- and long-term loans for industries that commercial financing institutions are unwilling to involve. However, solving market failure should be the responsibility of government first, and the direct way to solve it is to require policy financing institutions to interfere in the market on behalf of the state. Therefore, market failure becomes the theoretical basis of policy financing institutions.

Nevertheless, when policy financing institutions try to remedy market failure on behalf of the government, there are still some problems because of their limitations. In particular, policy financing institutions heavily rely on fiscal subsidies. This reliance not only leads to a shortage of funding and a lack of fiscal sustainability, but also gives rise to "moral hazard" because the DFIs take national policy as the only benchmark and disregard investment profits and losses. Then this will result in a "government failure" problem. That is, there are both market failure and "government failure" problems at the same time.

"Government failure" is when governmental interference in economic and social activities to offset the market failure causes some new problems to arise (such as corruption and rent-seeking) because of its limited governance capacity or other external factors. In the presence of "government failure", social resources will not be optimally allocated. When "government failure" arises, DFIs are needed. [1] Due to their policy and market dual nature, DFIs can make up the market failure caused by the incapacity of commercial financing institutions on one hand, and also can remedy the "government failure" caused by the incapacity of policy financing institutions on the other hand.

Business Scope of Development Financing Institutions

In short, the business scope of DFIs defines which activities they conduct, what DFIs should and should not do, and which fields they could and could not become involved in.

The most essential problem is how to clearly define business lines among DFIs, policy financing institutions, and commercial financing institutions. Many countries define the business scope of DFIs by independent legislation, which helps to coordinate the market behavior of all kinds of financial institutions, enhance the cooperation among them, and also is one of the requirements to promote the rule of law in DFIs. The precondition of legislation of DFIs is still to clarify the differences between them and other types of financial institutions, especially the differences of their functions or responsibilities. The role of DFIs directly determines their special business scope.

We can define the business scope of FDIs from both a macro and a micro level. From a macro level, what criteria should DFIs follow when they choose industries or pro-

---

① Mingming Lai and Li Ma, On Development Financial Governance Models and Innovation in China, Journal of Liaoning University (Philosophy and Social Sciences), 2007 (4): 119 – 124; Guofeng Sun, Theory of Development Financing Institutions, Tsinghua Financing Review, 2014 (7): 73 –77.

jects to finance? From a micro level, what specific market operation methods do DFIs have? And what are the differences of these criteria and methods from policy financing institutions and commercial financing institutions?

Macro Level: Entrance Criteria

Most laws define business scope of DFIs by field or industry. For example, these laws state that DFIs should support infrastructure projects, fundamental industries, urbanization, etc. Nevertheless, it is not suitable to define the business scope of DFIs simply by industries or fields they should enter. It is also necessary to analyze the characteristics of profitability, operating actor, duration, maturity, development stage in detail for each individual project or industry.

For instance, urbanization is one of the main investment fields of DFIs, and therein infrastructure like transport, electricity, etc. are businesses of DFIs. But businesses like housing transformation, health care, water supply, etc. are businesses of commercial financing institutions to a large extent, especially loans to projects with stronger profitability or medium- and long-term loans to wholesale and retail businesses.

Defining the business scope of DFIs requires an index system, and indicators for reference involve the following four aspects:

1) Profitability. DFIs insist the principle of break-even and meagre profit, and their main target is to support national development policies or strategic development goals, not to pursue profit. On the contrary, commercial financing institutions aim to profit, so they will first consider their own cost and benefit, and not become involved in projects with little or no profit. Policy financing institutions are entirely supported by governmental finance and do not care about profit.

Therefore, for those projects with no profit in the short-term or long-term, policy financing institutions should enter and be supported entirely by governmental subsidy. For those projects that will be profitable in the long-term and also short-term, commercial financing institutions are appropriate to support. For those projects that will not profit in short-term but profit in long-term, DFIs could enter to support.

2) Operating actor. In general, large enterprises, especially state-owned enterprises, have easy access to loan support from commercial financing institutions as their "state-owned" background and scale advantage. However, small- and medium-sized enterprises and private enterprises often have a hard time getting loans from financing institutions, but they are indispensable to economic and industrial development, and even have more comparative advantages than large enterprises in certain industries.

Therefore, for projects implemented by large enterprises, commercial financing institutions could enter; but for projects implemented by small- and medium-sized enterprises and private enterprises, DFIs could provide support. It could encourage the development of small- and medium-sized enterprises and private enterprises, so as to increase market competition and improve operational efficiency of all kind of enterprises.

3) Duration. DFIs aim to meet the medium- and long-term financing and investment needs of nations or regions, while commercial financing institutions tend to provide short and medium loans to avoid losses in the long-term because of uncertainty. Therefore, for project loans over a period of 10 or 20 years, DFIs or policy financing institutions could enter. For project loans with shorter periods of less than 10 or 5 years, commercial financing institutions could enter.

4) Maturity and development stage of industries. One of DFIs' policy targets is to support the development of emerging or vulnerable industries which lack the resources and conditions for development and are immature in their early stages. Hence, if DFIs enter and conduct businesses then, they will play a "catalyst" role. After a certain phase of development, DFIs will attract commercial financing institutions to enter and conduct relevant businesses through their guiding role. The maturity of industries gradually changes over time, so DFIs and commercial financing institutions should dynamically divide the business between them.

Of course, these indicators above are just for reference. What indicators should be chosen, and how to set criteria, still need systematic and thorough study. After setting up an index system and detail criteria, states can make relevant laws and regulations to stipulate the business scope of DFIs, so as to avoid DFIs occupying businesses of commercial financing institutions and unfair competition. [1]

Micro Level: Business Model

Policy financing institutions rely entirely on administrative command to conduct medium-and long-term businesses and are all financially dependent on government to subsidize their operations. Therefore, they do not have other business except loans, let

---

[1] DFIs conduct investment and finance businesses by relying on national credit, so they have more advantages in the bond market, and lower financing costs and lending rates, which lead commercial financing institutions to lose their competitive edge, lose relevant business, and harm their development.

alone any market-oriented business.

Commercial financing institutions mainly conduct short-term retail investment and financing business, and their main capital sources are household savings, so most of their business is in deposits and short- and medium-term loans. Commercial financing institutions surely could issue bonds, but the cost will be much higher than attracting deposits, which is not in accord with the principle of economic benefit.

The main business of DFIs is medium- and long-term credits (not household deposits), but loans of DFIs have longer maturities and lower interest rates compared to commercial financing institutions, which shows the supportive feature and fully reflects the policy and guiding roles of DFIs.

More importantly though, DFIs and policy financing institutions both provide medium- and long-term credits. The main funding source of DFIs is not governmental finance, but capital from bonds issue in capital markets, so they are very active in capital markets.

Because of this, the operation of DFIs involves diverse capital operation methods except for medium- and long-term loans, such as equity investment, risk investment, bond underwriting, insurance, lease, etc. Furthermore, policy financing institutions emphasize meeting the capital needs of national strategic objectives, while DFIs emphasize the need to not only provide funds for projects, but also to conduct such "soft" businesses as consulting services, technical assistance, public-private partnership (PPP). By these "soft" businesses, DFIs promote market formation, credit building and institutional formation actively, and enhance governmental capacity in the public and private sectors. Consulting services include development plan consulting, enterprise business consulting like listing of enterprises, mergers and acquisitions, assets evaluation, etc.

Business Performance Evaluation of Development Financing Institutions

DFIs have a dual "policy" and "commercial" nature. That is, although DFIs conduct businesses through market mechanism, their businesses have strong policy objectives. Therefore, when evaluating their business performance, we should not only just pay attention to such micro market operation indicators as profit margin, capital adequacy ratio, return on equity, bad asset ratio, etc., but also study the effect they have on macro indicators, like the overall economic growth, investment, resident living condition, etc.

Moreover, DFIs aim to serve national policies instead of profit, so under the premise of their sustainable development, we should pay more attention to the achievement of the national development objectives they promote.

Macro Level: Development Promoting Performance

As mentioned above, the guiding role is one important function of DFIs. DFIs' investment cannot compare directly with the large magnitude of investment from commercial financing institutions, but DFIs could indirectly guide capital flows of commercial financing institutions and other actors. Hence DFIs' actual investments are much higher than their initial capital input.

More importantly, DFIs will play significant roles in structure optimization, market incubation, institutional formation during financing and investment, so their contribution to the whole society and economic development will be magnified. Given this importance, evaluating the business performance of DFIs from the macro level should not be neglected, as it actually is the reallocation effect and magnification effect. Specifically, we can evaluate the promoting performance of DFIs on economic and social development from two aspects. One is indicators that check the promoting performance of DFIs to development, such as economic growth, investment, infrastructure, poverty reduction, employment, environmental sustainable development, etc. That is DFIs' contribution index system. The other is indicators checking the gap between DFIs' activities and national development objectives. That is DFIs' fit index system.

These two aspects respectively evaluate the development promoting performance of DFIs from the total amount and relative amount perspectives. DFIs mostly invest in medium- and long-term infrastructure projects, which are hard to gain evident benefits from the short-term. Therefore, DFIs' contribution index system is very difficult to evaluate. But the fit index system is simpler, which can be measured with assignment methods according to capital flows, structure, and the characteristics of projects. Surely, we will face the same difficulties as the contribution index system if we want to further evaluate the actual consistency of DFIs' contributions to social and economic growth with national policy targets.

Micro Level: Market Operation Performance

DFIs should ensure that they break even or earn meagre profits to realize sustainable development goals and to reduce governmental support. Moreover, DFIs working well and improving profitability could increase their support to national policies, so it is

239

necessary to evaluate regularly the market operation performance of DFIs. Currently, evaluations of DFIs are done according to the index of commercial financing institutions based on Basel Accords. Indicators reflecting DFIs' market performance include: total assets, capital adequacy ratio, ownership interest, net profit, bad asset ratio, ratio of non-performing loans, liquidity, etc.

The point is that DFIs operate with market mechanisms, so they share some features with commercial financing institutions in indicators chosen, criteria, and so on. However, there are large differences in the roles, business scopes, and business models of DFIs and commercial financing institutions, so it is not suitable for these two institutions to adopt the same market performance index and criteria.

Consider liquidity for instance. Commercial financing institutions mainly conduct short- and medium-term credit operations to avoid risks, so they have very high demand for liquidity. However, DFIs mainly conduct medium- and long-term investments required by national policies, so the ratio of long-term loans is very high, inevitably resulting in low capital liquidity. Nevertheless, this low liquidity of DFIs is decided by the function and role of DFIs, which is fundamentally decided by national policies, not a problem caused by their operation. Therefore, the liquidity criteria for these two institutions must be different.

Also, for net profit or profitability indicators, commercial financing institutions require high profit margin, but DFIs aim to realize national strategic development targets, but not profit. So profit margin should not be a key indicator when evaluating DFIs' business performance. Likewise, the use of other indicators such as capital adequacy ratio or the ratio of non-performing loans should also consider the differences of functions and objectives among various types of financing institutions.

In addition, there may be indicators that commercial financing institutions have not considered but are very important for DFIs. For example, because DFIs are affected by national policies, DFIs should allow for policy risk indicators, which commercial financing institutions need not consider generally (except for systematic risk).

All in all, current indicators for DFIs to evaluate their market operation performance are reasonable, but not totally appropriate. We should further study and design a special index system suitable to evaluate operation performance of DFIs, which especially must be different from the index system of commercial financing institutions.

Based on the above analysis, we think evaluating the business performance of DFIs should consider both development promoting performance and market operation performance. Only in this way could we fully evaluate actual contributions of DFIs. Otherwise, it will encourage DFIs to deviate from their "policy" feature, just paying attention to profit. Furthermore, many researchers systematically exam market operation performances of global major DFIs, and show that the ratio of non-performing loans of most DFIs is very low (less than 5%); nearly all DFIs gain profit or at least break-even; many DFIs' capital adequacy is over 8% , higher than 6% required on commercial financing institutions by *Basel III*;[1] and other market operation indicators also do well.

These indicate that market operation performances of DFIs are very good in general without problems people worry about.[2] On the contrary, the development promoting performance of DFIs is rarely considered, despite it being the fundamental goal for which DFIs conduct market businesses and improve market operation performance.

Reshape the Regulatory System of DFIs

The Problems in the Existing Regulatory System

In the legal system applying to development financing institutions, most developed countries have specified the regulatory authority, the boundary of regulation, and the supervisory indicators. Despite this, sometimes the regulatory systems are not exactly based on the special features of development financing, but more closely follow the regulatory framework of commercial banks.

From a global perspective, three quarters of DFIs share the same regulatory authority with the commercial banks in the same country. Usually, the central bank or the banking regulator plays the role as the common regulatory authority. For the latter case, the banking regulatory commission or the financial supervision committee acts as the banking regulator. For the remaining quarter of institutions, they are supervised by the relevant government departments, such as the ministry of finance.[1]

---

① Jian Wang, International Comparison among Development Financing Institutions, Financial Development Review, 2014 (8): 129 – 135.

② DFIs are not for profit and supported by national credit, so some people worry that DFIs would not pay much attention to their own market operation, hence have higher rates of non-performing loans or losses.

③ Yi Yan, The History of Development Financing Institutions and the Challenges, Review of Financial Development (in Chinese), 2016 (7): 20 – 28.

For the supervisory indicators, about 60% of DFIs follow the same prudential standards as the commercial banks in the same country. The prudential standards require the supervision be based on the financial statements, while at the same time, applying the framework of the Basel Accords to direct and evaluate their performances, such as indicators of capital adequacy ratio, liquidity, return on asset, transparency.

A crucial part of supervision is to evaluate the market performances of DFIs. In addition, almost all DFIs have set up their inner risk management department so as to ensure prudential operation.

From an overview of the existing development financing regulatory system, there are deficiencies in at least the three following aspects: the independence of the regulator, the applicability of the system, and the coverage of the supervision.

1) The independence of the regulator. For the existing regulatory authorities, most of them are government divisions, while DFIs are restricted by development policies made by the government. This leads to a dual role for the government. On one hand, it makes investment and financing policy; on the other hand, it plays the role of regulator. Sometimes, these two roles are even performed by the same department in the government. This undermines the independence and the objectivity of the regulator. Therefore, it is necessary to found an independent regulatory institution.

2) The applicability of the system. There are quite a few similarities between commercial financing institutions and DFIs. These two share some similarities in regulatory means and indicators. But a development financing institution differs from a commercial institution remarkably in many ways, such as the function, scope of business, and its objectives. Consequently, we cannot apply the regulatory indicators and standards of commercial financing institutions mechanically to the DFIs. Otherwise, the supervisions could be ineffective. But so far, in many economies the development financing system shares the same regulatory system with commercial banks. In some cases, the inner risk control system is also borrowed from the Basel Accords, which is specifically designed for the commercial banks. For such a kind of regulatory system, its applicability questionable.

3) The coverage of the supervision. Now, almost all the supervisors evaluate DFIs from the perspective of market-oriented performances. Whereas the performance of a development financing bank lies not only in the profits, returns, and its business sustainability, but also, to some extent more meaningfully, lies in positive external spillovers and the promotion of regional development. For this reason, the supervising authority should consider not only the development financing banks' self-per-

formance, but also the additional and inherent contributions to the region and the society. In contrast to the ideal framework, the fact is that the existing regulatory system still focuses mainly on the business performances, but the compliance regulatory is to some extent neglected. The latter includes the constraints of business scope, the rationality of the loan's direction, the scale and the conditions of the loans, and so on. Comparing with the former performance supervision, the latter is more process-oriented.

Reform the Regulatory System

Improve the Independence and Effectiveness of the Supervision

Primarily, the regulatory committee should be set up with complete independence. In this way, the committee could uniformly mobilize the regulatory resources, taking all things into consideration and make proper regulatory rules, policies, and standards. Consequently, the committee would be able to make comprehensive evaluations for the development financing institutions, including the project feasibility, lending quota, and the rationality of the interest rate level and so on. The staff of the regulatory committee could be drawn from the related government departments. The committee should publish the business activities, performances, and supervision reports of DFIs directly under the lead of the state council or the congress.

Then, if it is necessary, an independent external committee of experts should also be established. This committee could consist of specialists from think tanks, scholars from academic institutions, and professionals from other institutions. Based on this, the committee could provide policy proposals and supervision evaluations independently, so as to ensure that the supervision is objective, impartial and effective.

At last, the regulatory committee can improve the information transparency of DFIs. This kind of information should be published publicly, regularly, and comprehensively. By these means, the news media, social organizations, and the public can implement their supervisory and restrictions on DFIs and ensure the effectiveness of the supervision.

Construct a Index-system of Supervision

The regulatory index system of DFIs should differ from commercial banks. The differences should be based on the objectives and functions of DFIs. Such a index-system should include: policy index, resilience index, compliance index, liquidity index, profitability index, capital adequacy index, and so on. Besides, these supervision standards should differ from those of commercial banks.

Amongst the indexes, each one targets a certain area: the positive external spillovers and promotions to the social development would be measured by the policy index; the resilience index monitors the capacity of responding to policy changes from the government; compliance index will cover business scopes, loan directions and conditions, business operations, and legitimacy of accounting; liquidity index, profitability index, capital adequacy index will reflect the financial sustainability.

Make Full Use of the Regulatory Outcomes

The purpose of supervision is to improve the overall performances of DFIs, rather than the supervision itself. Therefore, full use should be made of the regulatory outcome or reports.

Specifically, the regulatory committee could set up feedback mechanisms of supervision report. Within the feedback mechanisms, the committee can send its reports and recommendations to DFIs and demand that the DFIs submit before a deadline their feedback report that includes the feasible improvement approaches. Based on the feedback report, the committee will suggest on next year's appropriation and other supportive policies for the DFIs. Through these interactions, the supervision could be really effective and constructive.

Besides, there should be interactions between the regulatory committee and the public as well. The committee could publish the supervision report publicly. By these means, society would be enabled to play the supervisory role. In addition, all the other financial institutions could learn from the report and improve their business. Meanwhile, the report will also facilitate further collaboration between other financial intuitions and development financial banks.

Chapter 2   Comparative Study on Overseas Legislation Systems and Governance Structures of Development Financing Institutions

Introduction

The primary responsibilities of government and goals of macroeconomic policy include maintaining financial stability and promoting inclusive regional, industrial, and economic development. Since the outbreak of the global financial crisis, most countries have begun to re-examine the relationship between the government and the market, utilize government credit to anchor market confidence, stabilize the financial system, and promote the recovery and revitalization of the domestic economy. Development financing has played an important role during the process. As a financial agency between government and market, development financing is the deepening and development of policy financing. It aids the national strategy by providing medium- and long-term investments and financing that is supported by sovereign guarantees combined with market-oriented measures. Development financing objectives include correcting market failures, providing public goods, improving the efficiency of social resource allocation, and smoothing the economic cycle. Development financing is an irreplaceable and important part of the national economic and financial system and is also becoming a bridge between the government and the market.

A key issue for governments is to consider how to maximize the contribution of development financing in the development of the national economy. According to the classic theory of institutional economics, the institutional foundation plays a vital role in determining economic behavior and economic development, and its improvement is directly related to the internal momentum of the economy and the external influence of economic development. Therefore, it is necessary and urgent to establish and perfect the institutional foundation of development financing. The legal system, as an important part of the institutional foundation, no doubt plays a critical role. As a compulsory order, law is serious, authoritative, normative, and binding. It is very important to maintain the economic and financial stability of the system and to construct a prudent and effective supervision system. As the first and most important component of the legal system, the legislative system is a prerequisite for developing a comprehensive system of legal norms. Throughout the world, those countries that developed early and have mature development financing systems attach greater importance to legislation. These countries initially promulgated the specialized laws and regulations to implement financial regulation, especially with regards to defining the sources and uses of funds, regulating the accounting system, imposing capital restraints, and imposing corporate governance structure of the development financing institutions. These comprehensive and prudent laws strengthened macro-management and micro-regulation.

Generally, the legal system of development financing refers the legal norms regarding such issues as the purpose, source of funds, use of funds, scope of business, government credit support and preferential policies, organizational structure, corporate governance structure, and supervision mechanism of development financing institutions. The development of the legal system for development financing, especially the development of specific legislation for development financing, is the cornerstone for clarifying its strategic position and basic functions, coordinating the external relations between development financing institutions and other financial entities, and regulating the development of financial institutions within the operating mechanism to ensure the efficient operation of the basic conditions. Developments in the development financing legal system determine the development of financial institutions can be sustained and steady development. In terms of its legal attributes, the essence of development financing law is the economic law which is based on social responsibility and carries out the legal values balancing and coordinating obligations, rights, benefits, and duties. First, development financing law belongs to the category of economic law. It should reflect the nature of economic law, that is, the law of social responsibility, so the law of development financing requires DFIs to exercise their rights and access to benefits under the premise that they carry out their social responsibility. Second, the legislation of development financing is a special economic law which seeks to strike a balance between national interests and financial enterprise interests, long-term and current efficiency, state intervention and market regulation, and fairness and efficiency. Therefore, the law of development financing is characterized by coordination and balance.

Based on the development practice of foreign countries, development financing institutions adhere to the basic principle of "legislation first". Through a long period of exploration and practice, these countries gradually established a mature legal system, not only to ensure the development of financial institutions in the establishment, but also make dynamic adjustments of legal norms in accordance with actual conditions and problems encountered during operation. Examining how other countries have developed their DFI legal systems could be worthwhile for China.

Overview of Foreign Development Financing Legislation

The Form of Legislation

When it comes to the form of development financing legislation, most laws are specialized and distinct. From the perspective of legislative levels, most of the laws related to development financing are at a higher level than administrative regulations or departmental rules. Most countries, especially developed countries where the market economy are relatively mature and the legal system is relatively comprehensive, formulate and promulgate development financing legislation in the state legislature to enact separate laws on the development financing institutions. From the point of view of development financing institutions around the world, because different institutions have different scopes of business and operational rules, most countries make distinct sets of laws applying to each DFI. These laws are general laws rather than administrative or departmental rules or regulations. Some countries also make laws based on the type of DFI involved. Most of these laws are named after the DFI they apply to, such as the Law of Agricultural Credit Company Franchise, the Japan Policy Investment Bank Law, the Japan Bank for International Cooperation Law, and so on.

The Main Features of Legislation and the Main Content of Regulation

Clarify the Purpose of Establishing Development Financing Institutions

Explanations for the purpose of creating development financing institutions, clarifications of their political and economic visions, and formal terms are listed at the beginning of the law. For example, Article 1 of the Japan Development Bank Act clearly stipulates that "the purpose of the Japan Development Bank is to supplement and reward general financial institutions by providing long-term funds to promote industrial development and socio-economic development". Article 3 (1) of the Kazakhstan Development Bank Law states that "the purpose of the activities of a development bank is to improve and enhance the effectiveness of national investment operations, develop production infrastructure and manufacturing, and promote the national economy to attract domestic and foreign investment". Article 3 of Internal Regulations of the Brazilian Development Bank states that "the Brazilian Development Bank is the main body for the implementation of the federal government investment policy whose primary purpose is to provide support for national economic and social development-related programs, projects, construction and services". The above provisions show that the establishment of development financing institutions basically serve the same purpose: promoting the development of domestic industries, socio-economic development, and attracting domestic and foreign capital investment.

Clarify the Legal Identity and Legal Status of DFIs

With regard to the legal identity or legal status of development financing institutions, most laws have pointed out that these institutions are special public legal persons, not general corporations with the sole objective of maximizing profits. This type of legal person is also not a government agency without consideration for financial efficiency and operation feasibility. However, these DFIs are special legal persons acting on the behalf of national interests. For example, Article 1 of Chapter 1 of the Japanese Development Bank Act states that "the Japanese Development Bank is a public corporation". Article 1 of Chapter 1 of the German Reconstruction Credit Institute Act stipulates that "the KfW is a legal person established by public law group". Some countries define DFIs as a legal person, but they are not ordinary legal persons. Instead, they are special legal persons, as defined by the second article in Korea Industrial Bank Law, Export Bank Act, Korean Residential Banking Act in South Korea.

Clarify the Sources of Funding

The two main funding sources of development financing institutions are initial capital funds and daily operating funds. For the source of the initial capital, different countries generally have very clear and strict requirements. Their legislation mostly allows development financing institutions to issue special bonds or government loans to raise funds. Take the Japan Policy Investment Bank Act as an example. Article 5 of the Act clearly states that "policy investment banks may raise funds through the issuance of Japanese policy investment bank bonds". Another example comes from the Law of the German Reconstruction Credit Institute. Article 4 states that "in order to raise the necessary funds, in particular to issue bonds and loans; short-term debt may not be over 10% of long-term debt; bonds issued in local currency for the local constituency currency investment". Another example, Article 25 of the Korea Industrial

Bank Law clearly stipulates that "an industrial bank may issue industrial financial bonds to raise funds necessary for the business such as loans and repayment guarantees provided in Article 18; the Industrial Bank has the exclusive right to issue industrial financial bonds".

Determine the Use of Funds and Business Scope

It is a critical function of the legislation to clarify and regulate the capital operation and business scope of development financial institutions. For example, Article 3 of the Japanese Policy Investment Bank Law defines the scope of business of the Policy Investment Bank: "deposit business (only deposits that are transferable or are allowed by other policies); lending business; capital investment business; guarantee business; securities; securities lending business; obtain monetary claims for financial and other economic-related investigations, research, or training business; carry out the above-mentioned business of the incidental business. " Article 18 of the Korean Industrial Bank Law states that "for the purposes set forth in Article 1, the Industrial Bank undertakes the following business: issuance of loans or discounted bills; subscription, underwriting and/or investment; guarantees or liabilities; debt collection, issuance of industrial financial bonds, other securities and debt instruments, borrowing from the government, Bank of Korea, and other financial institutions, and borrowing foreign capital, etc. , for the first paragraph to the provisions of paragraph 3 to obtain the necessary funds; for domestic and foreign exchange business". Article 7 of the Law of Kazakhstan Development Bank Law defines the business scope of the Bank. Its business scope is very diversified. It covers both traditional credit business and capital market business. Its main business activities includes loan business, taking deposit, opening and managing bank accounts to receive funds for domestic and foreign legal entities to perform monetary obligations to provide bank guarantees, issuing and confirming letters of credit, leasing, issuing securities, and providing mezzanine financing.

Establish the Special Financing Principles

Development financing institutions have special financing principles. The first is the "lender of last resort" principle. That is, DFIs will offer loans to recipients who are experiencing financial difficulty and cannot obtain funds from other financial institutions. For example, Chapter 2 of the Law of the German Reconstruction Credit Institute stipulates that "the bank is lending to projects that rebuild and promote economic development in Germany, and the funds required for these projects are not available to other credit institutions. " The second is the non-competitive principle. This principle mainly regulates development and commercial financial institutions, and thus maintains the order of the market economy. For example, the Japan Development Bank Act, in Chapter 3 Article 22: "Prohibition of Competition with Financial Institutions" stipulates that, in view of its purpose, the Japan Development Bank may not "compete with banks and other financial institutions through business operations". The third is the principle of advocacy. DFIs provide financial guarantees and refinancing to other lending institutions that are voluntarily pursuing projects aligned with the national strategy. In addition, DFIs are supporting, encouraging, attracting, and promoting more financial institutions to carry out policy-oriented financing activities. One example is the Japan Development Bank Act in the "development of funds related to the provision of debt guarantee" requirement.

Clarify the Corporate Governance Structure and Executive Responsibilities

In the development financing legislation, it is necessary to clarify the corporate governance structure and to explain the management structure of the organization. Under the basic conditions of "clear property rights", these laws require that DFIs clarify the powers and responsibilities of the executives. For example, according to the relevant provisions of the Korean Industrial Bank Law, the president represents the Bank and is responsible for managing the overall operations of the Bank. The Korean Industrial Bank is headed by a president (also known as the chairman and chief executive officer), an executive director, and an auditor. In addition, according to the Articles of Association, there are also a number of executive directors. The board of directors shall include the president and the executive director, who may attend the meetings of the board and express their opinions without the right to vote. According to Japan's laws and regulations related to development financing, the main power of development financing institutions belongs to the president, vice president, director, supervisors, and others. The president is responsible for the supervision and inspection of the business. The vice president assists the president with the daily operations and management. The director assists vice president and president. The supervisors oversee the completion of these operations. The counselor provides advices to the president on major issues and decisions. Another example, Article 5 of the Reconstruction Credit Institute Law stipulates that "the main body of the bank is the executive board and the board of supervisors". Article 6 stipulates that "the executive board shall be composed of at least two members, and the board of supervisors shall appoint and remove the members of the executive board; the executive board is in charge of the Bank's business and management of assets." Article 7 stipulates the composition of the board: "the board of supervisors has the responsibility to carefully consider and continue to monitor the Bank's business development and asset management. "

Clarify the Supervision and Management Mechanisms

The laws of foreign countries all have clear regulations on the regulatory mechanism of development financing institutions. For example, Article 26 of the Japan Policy Investment Bank Act provides that "the Secretary of State shall supervise the Policy Investment Bank in accordance with the provisions of this Law". Article 27 states that "the Secretary of State considers it necessary to ensure that, the soundness of the business and the proper operation of the business and any other activities deemed necessary to implement this law, the Policy Investment Bank may be required to report or require its staff to enter the Policy Investment Bank's business premises and other facilities in respect of business conditions or books, the necessary items to be checked". Article 47 of the Korean Industrial Bank Law provides that "the Financial Services Commission shall supervise the Industrial Bank in accordance with the provisions of this Law and may issue such orders as may be required by the Superintendent; and the Financial Services Commission shall, in accordance with the provisions of the Presidential Decree, the Bank is well managed and may issue such orders as may be necessary for such supervision". Article 48 also grants the Financial Services Commission specific supervisory and inspection powers to require the Korean Industrial Bank to submit a report on the necessary matters or to direct this department's officials or officials of the Financial Supervisory Commission to examine the operating conditions, books, records, and other necessary matters of the Korean Industrial Bank.

Japan's Development Financing Legislation and Governance System

As a neighbor of China, Japan has accumulated rich experience in the development of development financing and the construction of the legislative system, and has also achieved great results. After the Second World War, Japan developed and implemented a kick-started and fast-paced catch-up strategy. "Kick-started" refers to the fact that the Japanese government could emulate the successful experience of other countries and play a leading role in economic development. "Fast-paced" refers to the short-term efficient implementation of relevant laws and regulations and the creation of various types of development, policy-oriented financial institutions. These institutions will provide strong support to economic revitalization and industrial upgrading.

An Overview of Japan's Development Financing System

In 1950, the establishment of Japan's Export-Import Bank indicated Japan had begun a new stage of the development financing system. By the 1980s, Japan had initially established a development financing system represented by "two banks and ten storehouses". Since the 1950s, Japan has experienced an economic recovery period, a period of rapid economic growth, economic stability, a period of structural adjustment, and other historical stages, but regardless which of these phases the economy is in, Japan's development financing institutions have played an important role in promoting economic stability and social development. In accordance with the provisions of relevant laws and the government's strategic plan, development financing institutions are engaged in special areas of financial activities that commercial financing institutions are unwilling or unable to perform. DFIs correct this market failure and play a guiding role in the marine, coal, steel, and electronics industries by preventing pollution, developing high-tech products, and protecting intellectual property. DFIs are the vanguard of rejuvenating specific industries, promoting new technology research and development, optimizing and upgrading industrial structure, and providing financing for the real economy. With these activities, DFIs serve as economic and financial stabilizers.

The Transformation and Restoration of Japan's Development Financing System

In the 1990s, Japan's "bubble economy" burst, along with the subsequent Asian financial crisis, led to many explicit problems for Japan's traditional financial investment and financing system. In order to stabilize the economic and financial system, the Japanese government initiated reforms that adjusted, restructured, and reconstructed development financing institutions. In June 1999, the Japanese parliament passed the Japan Policy Investment Banking Act. In September 1999, with the approval of the Congress, the Japanese government merged the Japan Development Bank and the Hokkaido Northeast Development Finance Corporation, establishing the Development Bank of Japan (DBJ). The Japanese government also issued the Law on International Cooperation Banks. With this law, the Japan Export-Import Bank and the Overseas Economic Cooperation Fund were reorganized into "International Cooperation Bank". The national financial public storehouse and environmental health financial storehouse combined, creating a new financial storehouse for citizens. After this period of reorganization and restoration, Japan's development financing system changed from the previous "two banks and ten storehouses" to "two banks and seven storehouses". In May 2007, the Japanese Senate adopted the Japan Policy Financing Public Bank Law. In accordance with the contents of the bill, the National Life Finance Bank and five other development financing and policy financing institutions merged into one organization—Japan Policy Financing Corporation. The purpose of the reform was to improve the operational efficiency of development financing institutions, exclude general loans and investment finance in their business scope, and highlight the characteristics of development financing.

The Marketization and Privatization of Japan's Development Financing Institutions

Under the traditional fiscal investment and financing system in Japan, the sources of funds for development financing and policy-oriented financing institutions were mainly postal savings turned over to the Ministry of Finance funds, with only a small amount of funds coming from the bond market. However, with the adoption of the Post Office Privatization Act in October 2005, the most important source of funds, postal savings was blocked, and the sources of funds for development financing and policy financing were no longer available. Reform is imperative. In November 2005, the Japan Economic and Financial Consultative Conference clearly set forth the basic principles, scope of business, functional classification, and organizational form of development financing and policy-oriented financing reforms, as well as the "financing reform plan". Since then, Japan has opened a new stage of market-oriented and privatization reforms of development financing and policy financing institutions. "Market" is mainly reflected by the fact that development financing and policy financing no longer rely on postal savings as a source of funds, but instead on market-oriented and diversified financing channels. For instance, government bonds can be issued in overseas capital markets by issuing policy financial bonds through public offerings, or issuing financial bonds through special accounts for financial investment and financing. "Privatization" is reflected in the fact that investment banks, commercial banks, and industrial banks all underwent a gradual reform from being state-owned to completely privatized.

Japan's Development Financing Legislation System

As a country with civil law, Japan has paid special attention to the enactment of statute law in the construction of the legislative system. The most important areas concerning the national economy and peoples' livelihoods are regulated and constrained in the form of statute law, so as to construct a complete system of written law. In the field of development financing, Japan also follows the above-mentioned practice and has adopted a special form of legislation enacted and promulgated by the national legislature as separate developmental financial law.

Japan's domestic financial system is divided into government finance (national finance) and private finance. The main body of government finance includes all kinds of development, policy-oriented financing institutions. The main body of private finance includes commercial financing institutions. It is important to emphasize that in terms of legislation and supervision, Japan strictly differentiates commercial financing from development and policy financing, and sets different legal norms for the different types of financing institutions. For instance, ordinary commercial financing institutions are subject to the "Banking Law" regulation and supervised by the Central Bank and Financial Supervision Department. In addition to issuing bonds in accordance with the provisions of the "Banking Law", development financing and policy financing institutions are also subject to independent specialized laws, such as the Japan Development Bank Law, Japan Policy Investment Bank Law, and so on. At the same time, in principle, they do not need to accept the supervision of the Central Bank and the Financial Oversight Office of Japan, but accept the supervision of the Ministry of Finance and the Finance Minister's independently. So, in the field of legislation and regulation, development and policy financing institutions are self-contained. In addition, these two do not have overlapping or competing business scopes, but instead separate and complementary. After a long period of restructuring, market-oriented reforms, and restoration, Japan's development financing system has been basically completed. In accordance with the principle of "one institution, one law", the development financing legal system is basically completed, including the Japan Policy Investment Bank Law, Japan Policy Financing Public Bank Law, Central Bank of Commerce and Industry Combination Law, other legal norms and their corresponding complementary provisions.

The Operating Concept and Management Systems of Development Financing Institutions

First, DFIs is an important tool for the government's macro-control. Article 1 of the Law of Policy Investment Bank of Japan stipulates: "in order to achieve full privatization while ensuring the autonomy of business, Japan Policy Investment Bank provide funding to enterprises which need long-term loans through the operation and use one of the funding and financing methods." The terms make clear the position and purposes of the Bank. According to the law, the Bank provides credit support to specific enterprises, being an important tool for government macro-control.

Second, DFIs form a sound structure of corporate governance and accept the appropriate supervision. Specific laws for different development financing and policy-oriented financing institutions clearly require the establishment of a sound corporate governance structure and enfranchising the relevant government departments. In the case of DBJ, the Japan Policy Investment Bank Act stipulates that DBJ's chairman or executive representative, members of the board of supervisors, directors, and other important departmental personnel shall be appointed by the finance minister. "These appointments are not effective until they are approved by the finance minister." The Act also provides that the finance minister is responsible for the supervision and management of DBJ. If the finance minister finds it necessary, he or she can ask DBJ or its trustee to submit a report or provide access to DBJ's business premises or other facilities to inspect the business conditions, books, documents, and other necessary items.

Third, DFIs, in accordance with the norms and requirements of financial management, carry out business, adhere to prudent management, and strictly guard against financial risks. Japan's development financing institutions are generally independently-operated decision-makers with the goals of ensuring financial stability, not making losses, and earning reasonable profit. Therefore, they need to strictly follow the norms and requirements for balance sheet management and risk control in project inspection, decision-making, investment, and post-loan management. In addition to these requirements, they must also work with prudence. In practice, in order to effectively avoid risks and reduce the rate of bad loans, Japan's development financing institutions have established sound credit risk management departments and developed a comprehensive credit rating system, loan project review system, and post-loan tracking and management mechanism. This multi-pronged approach ensures the safety of loans and robustness of business activity. Despite repeated adjustments and changes, the purpose and commitment to the mission of the development financing institutions in Japan have not changed. With improved legal governance and regulation, Japan's development financing institutions follow corresponding specialized laws, provide market financing supported by a sovereign guarantee with a market-oriented business philosophy as the principle, and actively participate in financial markets. In the foreseeable future, DFIs will better play the government's guiding and constructive functions for Japan's domestic economic development and financial stability.

Germany's Development Financing Legislation and Governance Systems

Germany was one of the first countries in the world to create development financing institutions. At the end of World War II, the German economy was in full swing. The real economy and basic industries demanded credit support, but commercial financial institutions were unable or unwilling to meet these financing demands in important industries and fields. In this context, Germany's first development financing institutions—the German Reconstruction Credit Institute (Kreditanstalt für Wiederaufbau, KfW) —came into being. On November 5, 1948, the German government passed the "German Bank of Restoration Credit Law", establishing the Reconstruction Credit Institute. With the continuous improvement of the development financing legislation system, the German development financing institutions are on the fast track to revitalize German local industry and lay the foundation for economic development.

An Overview of the German Development Financing Legislation System

German is also a country with civil law, and therefore also attaches great importance to the role of statutory law. In the actual legislative work, more emphasis was placed on legal systematization and codification. German domestic law is divided into public law and private law. This division is reflected in the legislation for financial institutions. According to the relevant provisions of the financial legislation, the German financial system consists mainly of three types of financing institutions. The first is commercial financing institutions established under the private law . The second is cooperative banks also based on private law, such as credit unions. The third is the development financing institutions (public banks) based on public law. Different types of financing institutions have corresponding, specialized statutory laws they must follow. For instance, German commercial financing institutions must be regulated by the Central Bank in accordance with the Banking Supervision Act, the Financial Group Regulatory Law, and some of the European Union's financial regulatory laws. However, Germany's development financing institutions, such as KfW, do not fall under the purview of the above laws and regulations (except for individual articles). German DFIs are only regulated by the special law— "the Law of Reconstruction Credit Institute" . The regulatory body is not the German Central Bank or the European Union's financial regulatory organization. Instead, the German Federal Ministry of Finance and the Federal Ministry of Economic Affairs and Technology jointly perform the legal supervision duties. The KfW Law clarifies the sources of capital, ownership structure, legal status, functional business, main body, financial system, profit distribution, and regulatory framework of KfW, as well as the development and function of KfW business. This law provides a legal basis and a safeguard for the system.

As far as development financing is concerned, the shareholders of development financing institutions in German are basically federal and state governments. They engage in certain areas of specific financial intermediation business under specific financial legislation, but not for profit. At present, the development financing institutions in German mainly including the KfW, real estate mortgage banks, and the Balanced Economic Development Bank, etc., of which the KfW is the most important development financing institution in German.

Take the real estate or real estate-like property (such as large ships, aircraft, etc.) as collateral, real estate mortgage banks provide long-term loans to German local governments or other institutions of public nature. Real estate mortgage banks operate mainly through issue bonds in the capital market to raise credit funds. In 1990, the German government promulgated the Law on Mortgage Bank, which formally incorporated mortgage banks and their businesses into the regulatory framework. The Law on Mortgage Bank provides a set of basic principles on the operation of mortgage banks:

1) The principle of margin. The Act stipulates that all mortgages and municipal bonds must be issued with collateral of equal value or municipal loans as a guarantee against credit risks, safeguarding the investment.

2) The principle of consistency. The Act requires mortgage banks to issue mortgage bonds and municipal bonds with the same maturities, in order to avoid the problem of term mismatch.

3) The principle of priority compensation. The law provides that holders of mortgage bonds and municipal bonds have absolute priority in claims for mortgages when banks claim bankruptcy due to insolvency or any reason.

Balanced Economic Development Bank's funding sources are mainly long-term loans and issue bonds. It was established to provide loans to special groups, such as the poor in Germany, as well as to deal with trusts or entrusted financial services of the Federal Clearing House. Since then, with the domestic economic situation and changes in financial demand structure, the Bank's business has focused on providing credit to small- and medium-enterprises, financing environmental projects to support social credit operations, and providing credit to high-tech entrepreneurship and other activities. Balanced Economic Development Bank plays an important role in bridging the income gap between groups, promoting the growth of small- and medium-sized enterprises, and maintaining the ecological balance and common development among regions and industries.

As one of the earliest development financing institutions in Germany, KfW has played a key role in the post-war economic reconstruction and re-industrialization of Germany, and the promotion of balanced, sustained, healthy economic develop- ment. Under the KfW Act, KfW is a "public legal institution" whose primary role is provide credit to "projects with special political or economic interests of the federal government". KfW's main functions are benefit the post-war restoration and the pro- motion of economic development projects in Germany, lend to German exporting firms, and provide guarantees for these two economic activities. With the German e- conomic recovery, development, and industrial structure adjustment, the focus of KfW's capital investment has been quietly changing. In the 1950s and 1960s, fun- ding focused on infrastructure, power, coal, steel, and other basic industries. In the 1960s and 1970s, the focus of capital investment shifted to financing foreign devel- opment assistance projects. In the 1970s and 1990s, it focused on supporting small- and medium-enterprises (SMEs), environmental protection, high-tech, housing, and export industries, with particular emphasis on credit to small- and medium-sized enterprises. They provided financial guarantees for SMEs engaged in technological innovation and exporting. Since the 1990s, capital investment target groups are more diversified, including individual operators, start-ups, local and municipal authori- ties, municipal enterprises, other types of societal institutions, federal development agencies, and credit institutions. KfW's credit field involve residential property, ed- ucation, municipal energy supply, urban energy efficiency, climate and environmen- tal projects, export finance, foreign investment, and other international business. KfW supported the development of the German economy not only by boosting domes- tic demand, but also by providing a strong impetus for German firms to export, speeding up the internationalization of local enterprises.

Business Ideas and Governance System—Taking KfW as an Example

Independent Decision-making and Self-management

Since its founding, the "policy-oriented" nature of KfW has been obvious. It mani- fested in the fields of funds and the scale of credit. KfW must strictly follow the government's directive and policy requirements, with an emphasis on support and as- sistance. Since the 1980s, with the changes in domestic and international economic financial situations, KfW has gradually embarked on a market-oriented transformation and reform. Its policy-oriented business and commercial business were separated. After the split, the commercial business operated independently, no longer enjoying preferential treatment from the government. The policy-oriented business retained the more prominent "development" features. That is, it was not for profit. Nonetheless, the business must operate strictly in accordance with the requirements of financial management and risk management. On the condition that the Bank is financially stable and risk is controllable, the Bank has more discretion in project auditing and lending without needing the intervention and approval of the government.

Market-oriented Financing Model

After market-oriented reform, KfW's credit funds switched from the injection of government to the issuance of bonds in international and domestic money markets and capital markets. At present, KfW has become one of the largest and most active bond issuers in the international capital market. KfW has also become an international market institutional investor choice because of its long-term stable AAA rating from authoritative international credit rating agencies. KfW's bond has become recognized as an important asset. The funds raised by KfW's bond issuance are mainly euros and dollars, with the Australian dollar and the pound of secondary importance. Official statistics show that KfW issued a total of more than 70 billion euros bonds in 2016. These raised funds improved its credit capacity and enhanced the stability and sustainability of operations.

The Government Gives the Necessary Credit Support and Guarantees

The KfW Act stipulates that the federal government of Germany unconditionally guarantees loans provided to KfW, all liabilities relating to bonds issued by KfW, regular future transactions or definitive transaction rights signed by KfW, other loans issued to KfW, and loans issued by KfW. KfW creditors have the right to file a claim directly with the federal government of Germany. The KfW Act also explicitly states that the federal government assumes "institutional responsibility" for KfW by ensuring that it has a sound operating base and providing funding or otherwise providing the necessary support in the event of financial difficulties. KfW, on behalf of the government, assumes 50% of the loan risk. The government compensates KfW for this assumption of risk in two way. First, the government will appropriate cash to KfW's risk fund with an interest rate of 1%. Second, the government and KfW bear 25% of the first debtor risk. Although the government is the ultimate guarantor commitment of bank debt, but in actual operation, only losses incurred by government directive business are compensated with government subsidies. KfW is responsible for all other business losses. In addition, according to the relevant provisions of German administrative law, the German government has the obligation to protect the KfW economic base. That is, the government is responsible for maintaining the normal operation of KfW and timely fulfillment of contractual obligations.

Governance Structures and Oversight Mechanisms

After several decades of development, KfW has formed a relatively comprehensive banking governance structure. KfW's governing body includes the Executive Board and the Supervisory Board. In accordance with the provisions of the Act, the Executive Board shall be responsible for the conduct of the business of KfW and the management of the assets of KfW. In principle, the chairman of the Executive Board shall be the Minister of Finance authorized by the Government, and the members of the Board must be 7 government officials. The Board of Supervisors has the responsibility of continuously supervising the conduct of business and management of assets, appointing and removing members of the Executive Board, approving annual financial statements, and appointing auditors. The Board of Supervisors consists of 37 members, including the Federal Minister of Finance, the Federal Minister for Economic Affairs and Energy, member appointed by the Bundestag and the Federal Senate, and representatives from mortgage banks, savings banks, cooperative banks, commercial banks, and well-performing industrial lending agencies, and representatives from trade unions, municipalities, industry, agriculture, commerce, and housing. The positions of Chairman and Vice-Chairman of the Supervisory Board are held by the Federal Minister of Finance and the Federal Minister for Economic Affairs and Energy, and the positions are exchanged once a year. KfW, as a development financing institution established on the basis of independence and special public law, is not subject to the supervision of the German Central Bank, the Federal Bank of Germany, except for individual business guidance and personnel participation, but is regulated jointly by the Ministry of Finance, the Federal Economic Affairs, and DOE. The scope of regulation is limited to "legal supervision". In addition, KfW is subject to independent auditors' audits and government-appointed inspections.

The Consensus of Foreign Development Financing Legislation and Governance

Development financing has made remarkable achievements in promoting inclusive economic growth, balanced development, and improving the efficiency of resource allocation. Both developed and developing countries are aware of the necessity and urgency of developing development financing. At the same time, after decades of exploration and practice, countries have formed a consensus on the legislative, operation, and governance structures of development financing institutions.

Keep DFI Legislation Consistent and in Sync with Commercial Financing Legislation

The legislative authorities of most countries, especially the countries with highly developed market economies, attach great importance to the development of specialized financial legislation, and strictly separate two types the financial laws and regulations. The first is commercial financing legislation, which includes commercial banking law, securities laws, and other laws and regulations. The second is DFI legislation, which includes the Agricultural Development Bank Act, the Export and Import Bank Law, the Housing Bank Law, the Small and Medium Business Banking Law, and so on. For instance, in Japan's financial legal system, there are not only the banking laws applicable to ordinary commercial banks, but also specific laws applicable to various types of development financing institutions. Germany's Reconstruction Credit Institute was called a "healthy development bank" by the World Bank. The fundamental reasons for this claim include the fact that the law provides strong protection and normative constraints, strictly guides business practices, allows both full discretion and supervision of government departments, and allows KfW to establish harmonious cooperation and complementary relationships with other commercial financing institutions.

Establish "Legislation First" —Development Financing Institutions Should Set Up and Run According to Laws

In the field of development financing, "legislation first" is an international practice in both developed and emerging countries. Even other institutions becoming development finance institutions have to follow this principle. In Korea, for example, after the Second World War, Korea's financial system was gradually established and improved. Development financing institutions (formerly known as " specialized banks") and ordinary commercial banks constituted the "first financial circle" of the Korean financial system. The specialized banks are created based on the corresponding specialized. For example, the Korean Industrial Bank was created to provide loans to domestic industries in accordance with the 1953 "Korea Industrial Bank Act". The Housing Bank of Korea was founded based on the 1967 "Korean Housing Bank Act" to issue long-term housing loans. Considering the United States, the

United States Federal Land Bank was created based on the 1916 adoption of the "Federal Agricultural Credit Law". The Federal Housing Loan Banking System is based on the 1932 "Housing Loan Act". Finally, the US Import and Export Bank was established in accordance with the Import and Export Bank Act of 1945. On the international or regional development financing institutions, their establishment is always based on pre-existing international laws. For example, the World Bank and the Asian Development Bank were established in accordance with the International Bank for Reconstruction and Development (IBRD) Agreement and the Asian Development Bank (AsDB) Agreement respectively.

Focus Legislation on Organizational Structure and Business Operations

Foreign legislation concerning development financing institutions is mainly focused on organization and operation. The development financing legal norms not only concern the organizational structure of the organization, such as the legal status, legal nature, rights and responsibilities, organizational form, internal institutions, personnel arrangements, institutional changes, termination conditions and procedures, rights and obligations, legal liability and punishment, and supervision mechanism, but also regulate the business scope, assets and liabilities, business principles, finance and accounting, external relations and other issues of DFIs. It is the legal basis for handling the business relationship between development financing institutions and commercial financing institutions. It is also the legal basis for the state to supervise and manage the development financing institutions. Therefore, the legislation should focus on the organizational structure and operational issues of the development financing institutions.

Pay More Attention to the Dynamic Balance between Public and Commercial Components of Development Financing

Development financing is different from traditional policy financing and commercial financing. It is a special kind of financing with both public and market characteristics. With increased financial deepening, the financial industry is becoming more diversified and the boundary between private finance and public finance is obscured. An important function of development financing is playing a guiding role to correct market failures, providing public goods, and optimizing the allocation of financial resources. In an open financial environment, it is difficult to ascertain which financing is public and which is commercial. This difficulty is likely to cause either an absence or overreaching of development financing, so that some areas do not have access to timely credit resources, affecting economic stability and sustainable development.

Therefore, it is necessary to pay special attention to the balance between the commercial and public components of development financing, set relevant standards, borders, and business rules in the form of legal norms, and make timely changes in industrial policy and financial demand structure. DFIs try to achieve the dynamic coordination and balance of the two components, ultimately promoting private financial products and public financial products realize Pareto optimal.

Implement Differentiated Supervision for Development Financing Institutions

Development financing institutions are significantly different from commercial financing institutions in legal status, purpose of establishment, goal orientation, funding sources, liabilities structure, and operating principles. Therefore, the regulation governing development financing institutions should be different from the regulation of traditional commercing financing institutions. However, in terms of legal governance, regulatory policies, and regulatory practices of development financing institutions, there is no scientifically prudent and differentiated regulatory system. In practice, most of the development financing institutions manage risk and liquidity based on indicators and methods of commercial financing institutions. Therefore, the regulatory effect of DFI legislation is likely to be greatly reduced, which is detrimental to the construction of a macro-prudent financial regulatory system. For the development financing institutions, the implementation of differentiated supervision will make the supervision more effective, targeted, and scientific. In this view, national regulation should be based on the characteristics of the local financial structure, and the maturity, organizational form, and business scopes of development financing institutions. National regulation should establish and develop a supervision system that includes safety indicators, compliance indicators, liquidity management indicators, credit risk management indicators, and capital adequacy index indicators. National regulation also needs to provide differential guidance and supervision for directing the development financing institutions to establish and develop goals in line with their reality and objectives.

Promptly Revise and Perfect the Law

The law of development financing institutions is rooted in the fundamental duties of government macroeconomic policies to oversee the basic functioning of the national economy. These laws should adapt to the changes of a dynamic economy. Correspondingly, the operations of the development financing institutions are also adjusted and shifted in accordance with the revised legal requirements, so as to respond to complex socio-economic changes and achieve the national policy intentions and objectives. Take the Law of Germany's Reconstruction Credit Institute as an example, since the promulgation of the law on November 5, 1948, in accordance with the changes in global economic and financial situations and the adjustment of government policy objectives, the German government promulgated the "Law on Revising and Supplementing of the Germany's Reconstruction Credit Institute Law" on August 18, 1949, "the Second Amendment Law of the Germany's Reconstruction Credit Institute" on December 4, 1951, the "Law of Germany's Reconstruction Credit Institute Amendment Act" on August 16, 1961, as well as the "German Law on the Restoration of Credit and Other Acts" on July 4, 2013. These illustrate that DFIs evolve with the times.

Guarantee the Growth of Development Financing Institutions through Market Operations and Risk Control

For the development financing institutions, the key to sound operation is good business. Therefore, the development financing institutions should adhere to market-oriented operation to ensure minimal, albeit positive, profits. At the same time, DFIs should emphasize the overall business balance, constantly improve the management, and establish a scientific system for project evaluation and risk control.

Conclusion: China's Development Financing Legislation and Regulatory Approach

In China, development financing institutions, represented by the China Development Bank (CDB), have played a significant role in economic development and optimizing industrial structure, especially in eliminating the bottleneck in "infrastructure, basic industries, and pillar industries". Although development financing has achieved good results, there are still many problems, such as the lack of legislation and the absence of supervision.

In the area of legislation, China should learn from the successful experiences of other countries in the development financing legislation. Combining these experiences with China's economic endowments and financial environment, the overall planning, legislation, and content of the law should reflect both the universality principles and the idiosyncratic natures of different institutions. Reflecting these two principles will make Chinese DFI legislation sustainable. From the development of China's current development financing institutions and policy-oriented financing institutions, we could consider a single, decentralized legislative model, with the existing development financing and policy-oriented financing institutions as the basic unit of construction. Other specialized laws will combine with this basic unit to form a complete DFI legal system. In terms of legislative steps, the State Council may enact and promulgate administrative regulations such as the "Regulations of the State Development Bank" stipulate that the purpose, legal status, sources of funds, scope of business, financial and accounting systems, tax deduction and exemption status, and corporate governance structure of the development financing institutions should be clearly defined and standardized. In this view, development financing institutions will have rules and regulations to follow. When the time is right, we could consider re-enactment by the Standing Committee of the National People's Congress and the enactment of a higher legal level of general law.

In the aspect of supervision, we should insist on differentiated supervision. In view of the characteristics of development financing institutions, we should formulate more applicable regulatory rules and supervisory standards so as to ensure scientific and effective supervision. In the case of regulators, a special regulatory body, the "Development Financing Regulatory Commission", should be established to exercise regulatory responsibility, to establish appropriate financial regulatory and regulatory standards, to strengthen macro-prudential management, to monitor and evaluate the overall risks of development financing institutions. The commission should also focus on micro-prudential supervision, refinement of regulatory indicators, centralized collection of regulatory information, and unified mobilization of regulatory resources, so as to strengthen the development financing institutions' credit risk regulation, regulatory compliance, and liquidity regulation to ensure its stable operation without posing systemic and regional financial risks. In addition, we should strengthen the financial supervision and coordination mechanisms, improve the communication among the development financing supervision committee, the People's Bank of China, the Banking Regulatory Commission of China, the Securities Regulatory Commission of China, the Insurance Regulatory Commission of China, the Ministry of Finance, the Development and Reform Commission, and other regulatory agencies to effectively solve the problems encountered by development financing institutions in their daily operation and to promote sustainable development.

Part 2 The Characteristics of the Global Development Financing Institutions

Chapter 3   Multilateral DFIs

World Bank

Two of the World Bank Group's institutions—the International Bank for Reconstruction and Development (IBRD) and the International Development Association (IDA) —are partnering with countries to end extreme poverty by 2030, promote shared prosperity, and support the global sustainable development agenda.

Main Business Data

IBRD is a global development cooperative owned by its 188 member countries. As the largest development bank in the world and part of the World Bank Group, IBRD has two main goals: to end extreme poverty by 2030 and to promote shared prosperity in a sustainable manner. It seeks to achieve these goals primarily by providing loans, guarantees, risk management products, and expertise on development-related disciplines, as well as by coordinating responses to regional and global challenges. In fiscal year 2015, IBRD raised $ 57. 7 billion by issuing bonds in 21 currencies. IBRD currently enjoys a robust capital position and shareholder support. Under the terms of the general and selective capital increase resolutions approved by the Board of Governors on March 16, 2011, subscribed capital is expected to increase by $ 87. 0 billion, of which $ 5. 1 billion will be paid over a six year period. As of June 30, 2015, the cumulative increase in subscribed capital totaled $ 62. 7 billion. Related paid-in amounts in connection with the capital increase were $ 3. 7 billion.

Consistent with IBRD's development mandate, the principal financial risk it takes on is the country credit risk inherent in its portfolio of loans and guarantees. One summary measure of IBRD's risk profile is the ratio of equity to loans, which is closely managed in line with its financial and risk outlook. This ratio stood at 25. 1% as of June 30, 2015 (see Figure 3. 1).

IDA is financed largely by contributions from partner governments. Additional finan-

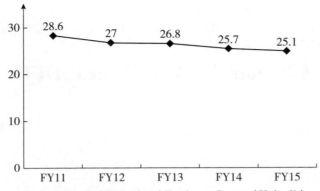

Figure 3. 1   IBRD Ratio of Equity to Loans (Unit: %)

cing comes from transfers from IBRD's net income, grants from the International Finance Corporation (IFC), and borrowers' repayments of earlier IDA credits. Under the IDA17 Replenishment, which covers fiscal years 2015 – 2017, total resources amount to 33. 7 billion in Special Drawing Rights (SDR) (equivalent to $ 50. 8 billion). 50 partners, four of which are new contributing partners, are providing SDR 17. 2 billion (equivalent to $ 26. 1 billion) in grants, of which SDR 0. 7 billion (equivalent to $ 1. 1 billion) is the grant element from concessional partner loan contributions. Partners are providing SDR 2. 9 billion (equivalent to $ 4. 4 billion) in concessional partner loans or SDR 2. 2 billion (equivalent to $ 3. 3 billion) excluding the grant element of the loans. Credit reflows from IDA recipients are providing SDR 9. 2 billion (equivalent to $ 13. 9 billion). Contributions from World Bank Group resources, through transfers from IBRD and IFC, including associated investment income, amount to SDR 2. 1 billion (equivalent to $ 3. 2 billion).

Anchored in the World Bank Group Strategy, the ambitious IDA17 policy package includes a range of policy commitments and performance indicators under IDA's four-tier Results Measurement System. The IDA17 overarching theme of maximizing development impact focuses on helping IDA countries better leverage private resources, public resources, and knowledge, with a greater emphasis on both results and cost-effectiveness.

New lending commitments by IBRD were $ 23. 5 billion in fiscal year 2015 for 112 operations. Europe and Central Asia ($ 6. 7 billion) and Latin America and the Caribbean ($ 5. 7 billion) received the largest shares of new lending, followed by East Asia and the Pacific ($ 4. 5 billion). Public administration, law, and justice projects received the largest sectoral commitments ($ 4. 3 billion), followed by finance ($ 3. 4 billion) and energy and mining ($ 3. 2 billion). IBRD also offers financial products that allow clients to efficiently fund their development programs and manage risks related to currency, interest rates, commodity prices, and disasters. In fiscal 2015, the Bank's Treasury executed U. S. dollar equivalent (USDeq) 3. 3 billion in hedging transactions, a $ 43 million transaction in disaster risk management, transactions totaling USDeq 24 billion to manage the risks of IBRD's balance sheet, and USDeq 727 million to manage the risks of IDA's balance sheet.

IDA commitments amounted to $ 18. 9 billion in fiscal 2015, including $ 15. 9 billion in credits, $ 2. 4 billion in grants, and $ 600 million in guarantees. The largest share of resources was committed to Africa, which received $ 10. 4 billion. South Asia ($ 5. 8 billion) and East Asia and the Pacific ($ 1. 8 billion) also received large shares of committed funding, followed by Europe and Central Asia ($ 527 million), Latin America and the Caribbean ($ 315 million), and the Middle East and North Africa ($ 198 million). Bangladesh ($ 1. 9 billion) and India ($ 1. 7 billion) were the largest country recipients.

Commitments for infrastructure—including energy and mining; transportation; water, sanitation, and flood protection; and information and communications—reached $ 5. 8 billion. Significant support was also committed to the sectors of public administration, law, and justice ($ 3. 9 billion) and health and other social services ($ 3. 7 billion). The themes receiving the highest share of commitments were human development ($ 4. 1 billion), rural development ($ 3. 3 billion), and social protection and risk management ($ 3. 2 billion).

Highlights of the Year

Overall, 2015 was set to be a pivotal year in global development aspirations. That year, the World Bank Group committed nearly $ 60 billion in loans, grants, equity investments, and guarantees to its members and private businesses. IBRD delivered record amounts of financing for any year except at the height of the global financial crisis, with commitments totaling $ 23. 5 billion. And IDA, the World Bank's fund for the poorest, has just had the strongest first year of a replenishment cycle ever, committing $ 18. 9 billion. This year, IFC provided about $ 17. 7 billion in financing for private sector development, about $ 7. 1 billion of which was mobilized from investment partners. The Multilateral Investment Guarantee Agency (MIGA) issued $ 2. 8 billion in political risk and credit enhancement guarantees underpinning various investments, including much-needed infrastructure projects. In different areas of the world, the World Bank Group achieved great successes.

Africa. The Bank approved $ 11. 6 billion to the region for 103 projects in fiscal year 2015. Support included $ 1. 2 billion in IBRD loans and $ 10. 4 billion in IDA commitments. The leading sectors were public administration, law, and justice ($ 3. 0 billion); health and other social services ($ 2. 8 billion); and transportation ($ 1. 2 billion).

World Bank activity in Africa included supporting regional integration, addressing development-related drivers of fragility and conflict, increasing access to power, supporting small farmers and boosting agricultural productivity, as well as designing and implementing economic recovery plans in the countries affected by the Ebola epidemic.

East Asia and Pacific. The Bank approved $ 6. 3 billion to the region for 57 projects in fiscal year 2015. Support included $ 4. 5 billion in IBRD loans and $ 1. 8 billion in IDA commitments. The leading sectors were water, sanitation, and flood protection ($ 1. 2 billion); public administration, law, and justice ($ 1. 2 billion); and transportation ($ 1. 2 billion).

The Bank's strategy in the region focuses on five priority areas: inclusion and empowerment, jobs and private sector-led growth, governance and institutions, infrastructure and urbanization, and climate change and disaster risk management. The Bank also focuses on the cross-cutting themes of gender, fragility and conflict, and poverty analytics.

Europe and Central Asia. The Bank approved $ 7. 2 billion in lending to the region for 54 projects in fiscal year 2015. Support included $ 6. 7 billion in IBRD loans and $ 527 million in IDA commitments. The leading sectors were energy and mining ($ 1. 4 billion); transportation ($ 1. 1 billion); and public administration, law, and justice ($ 1. 1 billion). The Bank also signed 19 Reimbursable Advisory Services (RAS) agreements with nine countries for a total amount in the region of $ 16 million. The agreements provide technical advice to health care and education systems reform, public sector governance and institutional capacity building, investment climate reform, planning and management of infrastructure investments, and other issues.

The Bank's strategy for the region focuses on two main areas of intervention: competitiveness and shared prosperity through jobs, and environmental, social, and fiscal sustainability, including climate action. Governance and gender are thematic priorities under both areas.

Latin America and the Caribbean. The Bank approved $ 6. 0 billion to the region for 33 projects in fiscal year 2015. Support included $ 5. 7 billion in IBRD loans and $ 315 million in IDA commitments. The leading sectors were health and other social services ($ 1. 6 billion); public administration, law, and justice ($ 1. 3 billion); and education ($ 1. 0 billion). The Bank tailors its diverse financial, knowledge, and convening services to the region's pressing needs, which include raising productivity, increasing trade integration, better managing disaster risk, and creating high-quality education and jobs. It addresses these needs through project financing; innovative mechanisms, such as the Climate Investment Funds; and in-depth reports, such as *Great Teachers: How to Raise Student Learning in Latin America and the Caribbean* and *Latin America and the Rising South: Changing World, Changing Priorities.*

Middle East and North Africa. The Bank approved $ 3. 498 billion to the region for 17 projects in fiscal year 2015, including $ 3. 3 billion in IBRD loans and $ 198 million in IDA commitments. It also committed $ 75 million in special financing for six projects in the West Bank and Gaza. The top three sectors were energy and mining ($ 1. 0 billion); water, sanitation, and flood protection ($ 611 million); and health and other Social services ($ 600 million).

In the past year, The World Bank Group achieved great success in different areas. The World Bank Group leveraged its strengths, expertise, and resources to help countries and other partners make a real impact on development by driving economic growth, promoting inclusiveness, and ensuring sustainability.

Column 3 –1　Program-for-Results (PforR) of the World Bank

The development of contemporary society requires results and the strengthening of the system. Not only government officials, but also members of the community and private entrepreneurs, want social development projects to deliver sustainable results and create efficient institutions. To meet with this growing demand, the World Bank pioneered Program-for-Results.

Unlike traditional construction appropriation or preferential loans at sub-market rates, Program-for-Results aims at improving the efficiency and performance of governments and firms. The debtor and the lender agree to certain conditions or standards in advance, the debtor gives the corresponding proportion of financial support, instead of one large transfer, according to the efficiency and performance of business operations. This can avoid the lender from breaching the commitment after the financing. However, Program-for-Results has difficulties in acquiring project data, monitoring, and inspecting the project. According to the World Bank, although Program-for-Results is more difficult than traditional financing methods, its marginal benefits can be far greater than marginal cost, making it worthwhile to promote and expand.

The Characteristics and Evaluation Methods of the Program-for-Results

Program-for-Results initiated by the World Bank has five characteristics as follows:

1) Fund the lenders' project. Program-for-Results can support the entire project or its sub-projects, new or existing projects, national or local government projects, individual sector projects or multi-sector projects. Program-for-Results makes the World Bank's development assistance fully leveraged by promoting partnerships and aligning development partner goals and outcomes, to further development gains.

2) Provide payments based on the project results. Program-for-Results links the payment of funds directly to the achievement of specific project results. The funds are disbursed to the project after the agreed results have been obtained and confirmed. The evaluation criteria of the results were agreed in the preparation of the Program-for-Results stage.

3) Focus on the improvement of institutional capacity and strengthening of the project process. Program-for-Results helps the project implementation countries with capacity-building, efficiency and effectiveness to achieve practical and sustainable project outcomes. Capacity building and institutional strengthening are integrated into government projects. Project results are also more likely to have a significant lasting impact when they are upgraded.

4) Ensure proper use of bank funds. Program-for-Results ensures that the project-related environmental and social issues should be properly addressed. Thus, appropriate due diligence procedures, evaluation, and monitoring arrangements are needed to ensure real-time monitoring of project implementation.

5) Serve all member countries of the World Bank. Program-for-Results is available to all member countries and serves as one of the three major financing vehicles of the World Bank along with Investment Project Financing and Development Policy Financing. The choice of financing tools depends on the needs and

the developmental issues of the borrowers.

The World Bank typically evaluates the following four areas before using Program-for-Results to support lending countries' projects:

1) Define the support scope of government projects.

2) Identify the key objectives of the projects and indicators to measure the objectives.

3) Assess the technical reliability of the projects, the capacity and ability entrusted to the projects, the environmental, social and institutional arrangements for the projects, and other factors that may affect the achievement of the projects' development objectives.

4) Lock down measures that can improve projects' capabilities and improve institutional performance, and use the measures throughout the implementation of the projects.

Through the assessment of project-related factors, the World Bank will enable Program-for-Results to facilitate the acquisition of project results and the establishment and improvement of related systems. The implementation of Program-for-Results includes two aspects: monitoring the performance of institutional arrangements, and monitoring and verifying the results of the implementation of projects.

Program-for-Results Financing Instrument has been Widely Used around the World

Since its introduction by the World Bank, Program-for-Results has yielded significant results. Program-for-Results has been used in different types of countries around the world (from economically vulnerable countries to middle-income countries) and covered a wide range of areas. Since its introduction in 2012, the use rate of Program-for-Results has continued to increase. Through July 7, 2016, a total of 46 projects around the world worth $ 11.6 billion have used Program-for-Results to support government projects worth $ 55.1 billion.

The National Human Development Initiatives of Morocco was the first project to use Program-for-Results of the World Bank. The project aimed to improve local governance mechanisms, infrastructure use, and access to social services and employment opportunities for local residents. The Ethiopian health sector was also an example of the use of Program-for-Results. The implementation of the national health sector development plan gave priority to helping Ethiopia achieve the health-related Millennium Development Goals (MDGs). The implementation of this project demonstrated the capacity of Program-for-Results to facilitate collaboration with other development partners such as the Department for International Development (DFID) of UK and the United Nations Children's Fund. The Viet Nam Rural Water Supply and Sanitation Project, with the support of the World Bank's Program-for-Results, has achieved the goal of providing adequate water supply, good sanitation, and sanitation services to the eight provinces of the Red River Delta.

The Innovative Financing for Air Pollution Control in Jing-Jin-Ji (JJJ)

The Innovative Financing for Air Pollution Control in Jing-Jin-Ji (JJJ) is the World Bank's first use of Program-for-Results in China and its energy industry. The program aims to reduce air pollution and carbon emissions by increasing energy efficiency and increasing the use of renewable energy sources. The goal of Program-for-Results was to create better linkages between the disbursement of funds and the results achieved on the ground of the project. Total investment in the program is estimated at $ 1.4 billion, with the World Bank providing $ 500 million in loans, Huaxia Bank matching funds of $ 500 million, and the remaining $ 400 million coming from equity contributions by sub-project borrowers. The program work is in three main areas:

1) Improve the energy efficiency in industry and construction, reduce coal consumption, and increase the supply of renewable energy through the use of solar, wind, and biomass technologies.

2) Take pollution control measures and reduce air pollution emissions. These measures include the installation of end equipment for particle removal, flue gas desulfurization and denitrification; coal to gas; the replacement of diesel vehicles with electric vehicles and compressed natural gas powered vehicles.

3) Improve Huaxia Bank's institutional capacity by establishing green credit centers, establishing internal green credit procedures, developing and piloting innovative financing models and products, and providing training on energy efficiency and clean energy financing for the staff.

The project was implemented on May 22, 2016, and the end of the plan is June 20, 2022. The project set nine assessment criteria, including coal emission reduction, sulfur dioxide emission reduction, the establishment of the use of i-dentification systems, risk assessment systems, and the Green Financing Center, etc. The World Bank approves the payment to the project when the assessment criteria meet the expected targets. The project will assist the objectives of the Air Pollution Prevention and Control Action Plan formulated by the State Council and help the commercial banks promote the mainstreaming of green credit. This reflects the fact that Program-for-Results supports the lending country project, aligns the project with the development goals of the lending countries, and makes the project more effective.

Taking into account the role of the World Bank's Program-for-Results in project implementation, the sustained impact on results, and the enhancement of the capacity and system of the project countries, China can make progress by actively using Program-for-Results. This progress can be made in the fields of eco-environmental protection, industrial technology improvement, agricultural production, among others. Program-for-Results will help to enhance the sustainability of the project results and improve institutional capacity and effectiveness in related areas.

Asian Development Bank

Asian Development Bank (AsDB) made great progress in 2015. In that year, the world witnessed a seismic shift in the global development agenda. AsDB worked on poverty reduction, sustainable development, and climate change. Facing the challenges in Asia-Pacific, AsDB scaled up operations and practiced the slogan— "stronger, better, faster".

Main Business Data

The sources of funding for AsDB included ordinary capital resources (OCR), special funds (including Asian Development Funds), and co-financing partners. OCR included subscribed capital, operation balances, and bond yields. Authorized and subscribed capital stocks respectively amounted to $ 147.55 billion and $ 147.05 billion in 2015 (See Figure 3.2). Other resources in OCR—revenue and net realized gains—amounted to $ 1.09 billion. Resources in AsDB's special funds—contributions and revenue—totaled about $ 812.37 million and were mainly from Asian Development Fund (ADF). The approval in April 2015 of the merger of AsDB's concessional ADF loan portfolio with its ordinary capital resources balance sheet became effective in January 2017. Combining these resources would almost triple AsDB's equity base from about $ 17. 5 billion to about $ 49 billion. In 2015, AsDB raised $ 18. 95 billion as medium- and long-term funds and $ 4. 08 billion as short-term funds.

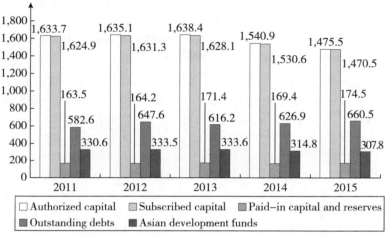

Figure 3. 2   Funding Resources as of 31 December 2015
(Unit: Hundred Million Dollars)

The total approvals of AsDB in 2015 reached $ 27. 17 billion, of which $ 16. 44 billion was from AsDB and $ 10. 74 billion was from co-financing partners. $ 16. 29 billion was for sovereign and non-sovereign project approvals financed by AsDB ordinary capital resources (OCR), Asian Development Fund (ADF), and other special funds; $ 141 million was for technical assistance financed by special funds; and $ 10. 74 billion by co-financing partners. In 2015, loan and grant disbursements totaled $ 12. 23 billion. Borrowings (form OCR) in 2015 amounted to $ 20. 27 billion, an increase of almost 38% compared to the previous year. Operating income (form OCR) was $ 340 million, a decrease of almost 40% compared to 2014 (see Figure 3. 3).

Highlights of the Year

Promoted Green and Sustainable Development

In 2015, the international community adopted a new global development agenda— the Sustainable Development Goals (SDGs), and a new climate deal was forged dur-

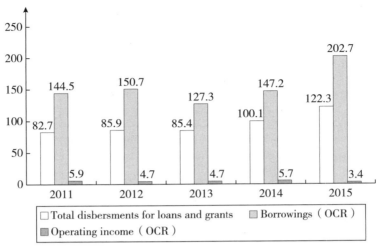

Figure 3. 3   Income and Expenditure of AsDB, 2011—2015
(Unit: Hundred Million Dollars)

ing the 21st Conference of Parties on Climate Change (COP 21) in Paris. 195 countries signed a legally binding agreement to keep global warming below 2°C. As-DB is fully committed to playing a central role in financing the SDGs and supporting the COP21 agreement. In 2015, AsDB continued to strive for inclusive economic growth and environmentally sustainable growth across Asia and the Pacific. AsDB has been playing a leading role in addressing climate change, with more than $ 2 billion invested in each of the following fields: clean energy, transport, urban development, water, and education.

Supported Regional Development and Cooperation

Countries in Central and West Asia were affected by the continued economic slow-down of the region's major trading partners and slumping global commodity prices in 2015. AsDB focused on infrastructure, inclusive growth, and regional cooperation and integration. In 2015, AsDB approved $ 5. 42 billion worth of loans to improve the lives of people in Central and West Asia, key targeted sectors of which were energy, transport, and public management. In 2015, AsDB funded or supported a variety of knowledge-sharing initiatives across Central and West Asia, focusing on energy, the environment, and transport. AsDB invested $ 3. 8 billion—which leveraged $ 406 million in co-financing—for regional cooperation and integration projects. Furthermore, AsDB contributed to notable achievements under the Central Asia Regional Economic Cooperation (CAREC) Program in 2015.

In 2015, AsDB provided $ 2 billion for 16 loans and grants to East Asia, distributed across the sectors of agriculture, natural resources and rural development; energy; water; and other urban infrastructure and services. AsDB's assistance to the People's Republic of China (PRC) totalled $ 1.73 billion for 12 projects in urban and road infrastructure, agriculture and natural resources, climate change, and education. The three priorities of AsDB to the area were climate change and environment, inclusive growth and social protection, and policy support and development partnership. As-DB approved its first-ever policy-based loan to the PRC. It committed $ 300 million to help reduce air pollution in the Beijing-Tianjin-Hebei region.

Declining momentum in the Pacific's larger economies saw the region's growth slow to 7.0% in 2015. In 2015, AsDB approved outlays of $ 177.80 million for 18 loans and grants in the Pacific, most of which were invested in the transport sector. In this area, AsDB focused on infrastructure development, environment and climate change, and poverty reduction and inclusive growth. Regional assistance administered by AsDB covers climate change, education, energy, gender equity, and core government services.

In 2015, South Asia became the fastest-growing region in Asia and the Pacific. AsDB's assistance to South Asia approached $ 3.80 billion in 2015. AsDB provided the most support to India (48%), followed by Bangladesh (30%) and Sri Lanka (13%). It provided the largest share of its assistance to the transport sector, followed by the energy and finance sectors. Infrastructure development, poverty reduction and inclusive growth, and environment and climate change were also priorities in the area. In 2015, AsDB extended $ 200 million in earthquake emergency assistance to Nepal. This funding was to help rebuild schools, roads, and district-level government buildings.

AsDB supported its members across Southeast Asia in 2015 with $ 3.47 billion in loans and grants, which assisted the energy, finance, and water sectors. During 2016 – 2018, AsDB expects to commit 44% of its total investment in the region to infrastructure development, with a focus on large projects and programs in the transport, energy, and urban sectors. AsDB is expanding its education program in Southeast Asia. Financial inclusion will be at the heart of AsDB operations in Cambodia, Indonesia, the Lao People's Democratic Republic, Myanmar, the Philippines, and Viet Nam.

Developed the Private Sector

Private sector operations in AsDB achieved a record level of investments in 2015 of

$ 2. 63 billion (37% higher than 2014). Private sector operations also generated $ 4. 56 billion in commercial co-financing and $ 24. 9 million in official co-financing in 2015. AsDB believed that the private sector was a key engine of growth and a critical partner in alleviating poverty. By promoting an improved business climate, with enhanced access to more flexible financing solutions and trade facilitation tools, AsDB helped the private sector create high-quality jobs and increase living standards across Asia and the Pacific. In 2015, the AsDB portfolio of private sector projects continued to expand, with a strong focus on infrastructure (particularly renewable and clean energy), financial institutions engaged in microfinance, and the financing of small- and medium-sized enterprises (SMEs).

Delivered Institutional Reform

In 2015, AsDB carried out far-reaching organizational reforms. These reforms responded to the changing dynamics of global development and the expanding needs of Asia and the Pacific. The changes were also guided by the Midterm Review of Strategy 2020 Action Plan (MTR Action Plan). AsDB continued to implement procurement reforms introduced in August 2014. These measures have reduced procurement time and increased administrative efficiency. The time taken to process transactions above $ 10 million was reduced from 58 days in 2014 to 44 days in the first half of 2015. In 2015, AsDB continued to build a strong mix of high-performing and high-potential staff with the right balance of skills to carry the organization into the future. These initiatives are part of broader efforts to ensure that AsDB remains dynamic, agile, innovative, and strongly focused on results.

Inter-American Development Bank

In 2015, Inter-American Development Bank (IDB) faced two major challenges: defending the social and economic gains that IDB member countries made over the past decade, and helping them to return more quickly to a path to ward prosperity. The regional GDP shrank in 2015, with several economies facing recessions and others managing only modestly positive growth. IDB maintained continuous dialogue with member countries, and strived to share insights gained from years of investigating the nature of development.

Main Business Data

Compared to 2014, IDB's assets increased from $ 106. 23 billion to $ 111. 24 billion, which mainly resulted from the growth in allowance for loan losses in preparation for possible default.

In 2015, IDB approved a program of 171 projects with a total value of $ 11. 112 billion, including 151 investment operations for $ 7. 6 billion and 20 policy-based loans approved for a total of $ 3. 6 billion. Average annual approvals have increased over the last five years as compared with the previous five-year period, increasing from $ 10. 9 billion in 2006 – 2010 to $ 12. 3 billion in 2010 – 2015.

Highlights of the Year

The 171 approvals, distributed into various sectors, including energy, transport, financial markets, urban development, and so on, can be categorized into four big sectors. With 46 projects approved, 32% of approved financing was allocated to institutional support for development, amounting to $ 3. 57 billion. 38% of financing, as well as 52 projects, was allocated to the infrastructure and environment sectors. 22% of the financing went to social sector programs, and 8% went to integration and trade programs.

Considering the private sector and non-sovereign guaranteed activities, we can see that among the 151 investment operations, 88 of them were non-sovereign guaranteed (NSG) operations, totaling $ 2. 2 billion.

In grants and non-reimbursable technical cooperation business, IDB experienced setbacks and shrank. In 2015, the IDB managed 71 funds for grant and loan financing operations, including 19 OCR (Ordinary Capital Resources) Special Programs/Grants, 41 single and multi-donor trust funds, and 10 Financial Intermediary Funds. The total level of fund resources managed by the Bank in 2015 amounted to nearly $ 894 million, a decrease of 22% compared to 2014. But IDB created two new donor trust funds: bilateral Korean Infrastructure Development Cofinancing Fund (KIF) and the multi-donor Agro LAC 2025 (MAG) fund. On the other hand, 61% of its Technical Cooperation (TC) business approvals were used to support clients' preparation, execution, and evaluation of loan operations, while 30% were used to finance research and product promotion.

With 121 transactions and 69 active partners, IDB mobilized resources totaling $ 3. 8 billion in 2015. More than $ 269 million was attributable to the mobilization of grant financing while $ 3. 5 billion resulted from co-financing. With contributions from Korea's Ministry of Strategy and Finance, The People's Bank of China, and Brazil's Banco Nacional de Desenvolvimento Economico e Social and Finnvera,

IDB's co-financing accounted for 93% of the Bank's total mobilization. With respect to IDB's partnerships, it expanded and deepened them with both the public and private sectors. Its longtime partnership with the Nordic Development Fund in the field of sustainable development and the Inclusive Regional Recycling Initiative aiming at integrating recyclers into formal supply chains, for instance, supported development in Latin America and Caribbean region.

As a development bank, the primary objective of IDB is improving People's living standards. IDB achieved success in areas like increasing broadband access, citizen security, and sustainable cities, which were of crosscutting nature and required collaboration among different divisions.

First, IDB continued the Broadband Special Program in 2015 to support the development of intersectional innovations aimed at universal coverage, adoption, and use of broadband services in the region. This program supported health initiatives in Mexico, promoted financial inclusion in the Dominican Republic, boosted industries' productivity in the Caribbean, and assisted achieving universal access to digital services for citizens, firms, and public administrations.

Second, IDB improved its database and information platform concerning citizen security. The production, compilation, and analysis of data on crime and violence was centralized on an interactive platform, DataSeg, serving as a repository for citizen security indicators. By supporting pilot projects in groundbreaking areas, the program also helped strengthen innovation and knowledge generation.

Third, KDB also drove the development in the sector of sustainable cities by including more cities in the Emerging and Sustainable Cities Initiative (ESCI). By the end of 2015, 55 cities had been included, representing a population of approximately 57 million. The ESCI program has leveraged $ 2. 25 for every $ 1 of the Bank's ordinary capital contribution, for a total of $ 65 million in technical assistance to cities. To execute the program in the 55 cities, the initiative mobilizes around professionals, including 200 staff and consultants from the Bank.

With demand for development lending by Latin America and the Caribbean countries increasing, IDB reevaluated the Bank's capital levels and started the expansion of resources, the Ninth Capital Increase (IDB-9), since 2010. In 2015, Latin American experienced shrinking exports and an economic downturn. In response, the Bank made plans within the framework of IDB-9 to strengthen the relevance, efficiency, and effectiveness of Bank interventions.

After obtaining the minimum number of votes to approve the IDB-9, IDB gradually received capital installments. 100% of the first and the second capital installments had been paid by the end of 2015, as well as 94% of the third and 84.7% of the fourth installment, amounting to nearly $ 1.3 billion. This makes $ 473 million worth of new contributions to the Fund for Special Operation.

It is worth taking a moment to introduce the IDB's support of Haiti's economic, productive, and social development through the placement of $ 1.3 billion from the Grant Facility after the 2010 earthquake. In 2015, the Board of Governors approved the transfer of $ 200 million from ordinary capital to Grant Facility for the fifth consecutive year. This commitment was not only translated into a significant investment of resources, but also into support for the government in implementing a long-term vision of sustainable economic and social growth.

Besides, IDB also implemented its institutional strategy in 2015. The two pillars of its strategy, reducing poverty and inequality, and supporting sustainable development of economic, social and environmental, required IDB to define several targets and actions in the new era.

The Sector Framework Documents (SFDs), under which the Bank has been reformulating the strategic and normative instruments since 2012, provides a flexible framework to accommodate the range of challenges and institutional contexts faced by members, and meaningful strategic guidance for projects teams. In 2015, IDB completed its goal made in 2012 to settle 20 SFDs.

In supporting smaller and less developed countries, IDB made a commitment to allocate 35% of its lending to small and vulnerable countries. 50% of the new approvals were aimed at this group of countries. The aggregate amount of combined FSO (Fund for Special Operations) and ordinary capital loans was $ 5.3 billion for these countries. Besides, IDB approved the Sustainable Energy Facility (SEF) for the Eastern Caribbean, which aimed to help diversify energy usage in the region. This program was designed to help countries of the region to enhance their competitiveness and macroeconomic stability.

In the private sector, IDB continued to focus on attaining the objectives of the IDB-9. Most of the projects approved in 2015 in the area of poverty reduction and equity enhancement focused on SMEs or housing. The Bank also financed renewable energy, energy efficiency, and green financing projects. 26% of financing provided for regional integration and 57% for poverty reduction.

The Agenda for a Better Bank contained reforms and initiatives in three areas, including efficiency, effectiveness, and transparency. To achieve the goal of becoming a better bank, IDB developed several initiatives. The Development Effectiveness Matrix (DEM) ensured both public-sector and private-sector operations supported by the Bank are designed taking sound project logic and evidence-based solutions into consideration. Furthermore, these projects are evaluated at completion to ensure they are aligned to both the IDB and country priorities. Improving the analyses of debt, fiscal, and monetary variables, IDB also renovated its Macroeconomic Sustainability Assessment. Further, strengthening environmental and social safeguards and promoting gender equality were successfully achieved, too.

Actually, Latin America and the Caribbean are still vulnerable to "sudden stops" in capital inflows, and have less fiscal margin to maneuver than they had before the 2008 global crisis. With a sharpened sense of urgency, IDB's member countries need to boost the economic productivity. As it did in 2015, IDB shall make every effort to ensure a positive flow of resources from the Bank to the region in future years as well, while safeguarding financial strength and stability.

Column 3 –2　The Inter-American Development Bank's Sustainable Development Financing Project

The Inter-American Development Bank (IDB) is an important development funding source for Latin America and the Caribbean. IDB has six main objectives: to reduce poverty and inequality, to address the needs of small and weak countries, to promote development through the private sector, to address climate change and promote renewable energy and environmentally sustainable development, and to promote regional cooperation and integration.

IDB is a multilateral development financing institution linking 48 countries. IDB has been paying close attention to sustainable development issues such as energy, environmental protection, employment, and education development in Latin America and the Caribbean since its establishment. IDB has created 20,000 to 30,000 business contracts and consultations per year in member countries, through economic development projects in 26 borrowing countries in Latin America and the Caribbean. In addition, IDB has provided money and technology support to enterprises that have a positive impact on social and economic development. This article states a brief overview of the basics of these projects.

Establish the Women's Entrepreneurship Fund to Provide Financial Services to Women Entrepreneurs

Small businesses, especially led by women entrepreneurs, are limited by financing difficulties and unable to maximize their potential. The gap in the amount of credit resulting from the sex of the entrepreneur can be reduced by providing specialized financial products. Thus, IDB has been committed to providing a relatively favorable financial environment for female entrepreneurs in recent years.

In 2013, the project "Expanding the financial services for women entrepreneurs in Ecuador" was approved. This project is a continuation of the partnership established between IDB Group's Multilateral Investment Fund (MIF) and the Banco Pichincha region in Ecuador in 2008. As the lead provider of technical assistance to private enterprises in Latin America and the Caribbean, MIF has strengthened the financial support for women-led SMEs in Ecuador through the provision of gratis technical cooperation funds. This has led Ecuador to improve its risk analysis tools and develop specialized financial products and services for women. At the same time, MIF supported Banco Pichincha's expansion of financial services for small businesses through providing gratis technical cooperation funds. IDB has extended the targets of microcredit to 32,465 SMEs, far exceeding the project's original target.

In February 2016, IDB, the United States Department of State, and the online microfinance institution Kiva. org, set up a Women's entrepreneurship fund, whose loans will be used to explore the economic potential of women entrepreneurs to facilitate their financing. Over the next five years, IDB will use Kiva. org as a platform to provide $ 450 to $ 10,000 loans to one million women entrepreneurs with high risk-bearing social capital raised by Kiva.

Promote the Development of Renewable Energy and Help Urban Sustainable Development

In February 2016, IDB announced a $ 9.3 million loan to the Republic of Colombia for private investment in renewable energy. Prior to this, 60% of Columbia could not connect to the local power grid, and loans of IDB would help the private sector provide public power facilities and promote the development of renewable energy technology. The loans of this project from the Climate Investment Funds, with the loan interest rate fixed at 0.75%, an investment recovery period of 5 years, and a grace period of 10.5 years. IDB's loans were issued through the Banco de Comercio Exterior de Colombia S. A.

In March 2016, IDB participated in the launch of the "Global Platform for Sustainable Cities" (GPSC) project held by the World Bank. Jointly implemented by the World Bank, the African Development Bank, the Asian Development Bank, the South African Development Bank, the Inter-American Development Bank, the United Nations Environment Program, the United Nations Development ment Program, and the United Nations Industrial Development Organization, the project would provide the most advanced tools to promote integrated approaches for sustainable urban planning and financing. GPSC was expected to raise $ 1. 5 billion over the next five years to finance urban sustainable planning in 11 developing countries. Through sharing data, experience, ideas, and solutions of urban problems, GPSC would promote the long-term sustainability of cities and benefit more cities.

In April 2016, IDB issued a report calling on the United Nations to prioritize urgent housing issues on the New Urban Agenda. A recent housing research report issued by IDB and Habitat for Humanity stated that governments around the world should reach a programmatic and financial commitment to ensure more affordable and safe houses. According to the report, it was imperative to include urgent housing issues on national priorities, in order to improve basic shelter demands for people that expected to reach 881 million worldwide by 2030, as well as additional basic housing needs for 1. 18 billion people.

Pay Attention to Climate Change and Improve Financing of Climate Change Projects

In April 2016, the annual meeting of IDB was held in Nassau, Bahamas. The annual meeting focused on the negative impacts of climate change on Latin American and Caribbean economies, and the related plans to invest in climate change. Amal-Lee Amin, head of the Climate Change and Sustainability Group of IDB, stressed that IDB attached great importance to the impact of climate change on the regional economy. The Bank assessed that between then and 2050, the sea level would rise, global temperatures would increase, and the unpredictability of climate would cause the average GDP of Latin American and Caribbean countries fall by 2% to 4% ; from 2020 to 2030, there would still be an annual gap of $ 75 billion to $ 80 billion of the investment in Latin America and the Caribbean climate change projects, but the region's current investment is far less than one-third of the gap. Thus, IDB and the Inter-American

Investment Corporation (IIC) set the target of increasing climate-related project financing by 30% by 2020, which was expected to increase $ 4 billion per year for climate change-related projects. This goal was fully in line with the goals of the 2015 UN Conference on Climate, and IDB would give priority to assisting countries in implementing the Paris Agreement and helping countries to transform their commitment into physical investment projects.

Eurasian Development Bank

In 2015, influenced by factors like raw material prices fell and Western sanctions a-gainst Russian, the economies of the Eurasian Development Bank (EDB) member countries had been hammered heavily. The GDP of the six member countries de-clined by 3. 2% compared to 2014 (the year-on-year growth in 2014 was 1. 1%). All member countries were facing different levels of difficulty due to various degrees of investment declines, tightening national budget, balance of payments deteriora-tions, and inflation acceleration. The general economic trends are also reflected in EDB's operating data.

Main Business Data

In 2015, the EDB failed to earn a profit, with losses totaling $ 139 million (how-ever it earned $ 6 million in 2014). That year, the total assets of EDB amounted to $ 2. 88 billion, which was a reduction of $ 1. 35 billion compared to 2014; the to-tal amount of current assets invested was $ 2. 2 billion, which was down $ 956 mil-lion year on year; the ROA and ROE were-3. 89% and-9. 09% respectively. EDB's loss and the reduction of total assets were mainly relative to the prepayment of bonds, the increase of the provision for assets impairment, and the sharp decline in the exchange rate of the Russian Ruble and the Kazakhstan Tenge against the US dollar.

In 2016, Eurasian Development Bank's net income totaled $ 163. 5 million, com-pared to a net loss of $ 14. 36 billion in 2015.

The net interest income before provisions for impairment losses on interest bearing as-sets amounted to $ 109. 2 million, a $ 16. 3 million increase year-on-year. This change due to:

1) A significant decrease of interest expenses, from $ 133. 1 million to $ 84. 3 mil-

lion (36. 7%), as a result of the repurchase of the Bank's securities in the end of 2015 and during 2016.

2) The interest income of financial assets available for sale increased from $ 4. 9 million in 2015 to $ 18. 5 million in 2016.

In 2016, EDB worked to improve the reliability of its loan portfolio. As a result, EDB recovered the previously created provisions for impairment losses in the amount of $ 54. 5 million.

The net non-interest income in 2016 reached $ 30. 2 million due to the increased return on transactions with the Bank's treasury portfolio. In 2015, this figure was negative because of a $ 64. 3 million provision for impairment losses on equity instruments and other assets was created.

The operating expenses reduced $ 4. 2 million, or 12. 3% year-on-year, to $ 30 million, by optimizing the usage model of operating expenses and a stricter discipline.

As of 31 December 2016, EDB's assets grew by $ 374. 4 million (13. 0%) to $ 3. 26 billion. Loans to customers totaled $ 1. 48 billion, down $ 17. 2 million or 1. 1% over the period. Issued debt securities stood at $ 1. 16 billion at the end of the period, which is 3. 4% less compared to the end of 2015. The Bank's equity increased by $ 167. 8 million (11. 2%) to $ 1. 67 billion.

Highlights of the Year

In credit and investment areas, EDB's current assets covered 62 projects in six member countries in 2015, including three new projects (two industrial projects and one finance project with total investments amounting to $ 59 million), and the investment projects from Kazakhstan and Russian accounted for 36. 9% and 31. 9% in the total investment respectively. Besides, there were 21 projects in the audit stage (had already passed the pre-approval stage) and 30 projects in the project proposal analysis stage. The proportion of the quantity of each member countries' projects in this part did not change much compared to 2014, the top three countries were Kazakhstan, Russia, and Belarus. According to EDB's development strategy in 2013 – 2017, the focal areas in 2015 were still energy, machinery manufacturing, chemicals, mining, oil and gas, and infrastructure. The energy field received the highest proportion of total investment, which was 25. 1% .

The main mission of EDB is through investment activities to promote the development of market economies in member countries, realize sustainable economic growth, and continuously expand economic and trade interactions among the member countries. The purpose of all EDB's operating activities is to set the stage for deepening the integration process and realizing sustainable economic growth, thus bringing social and economic benefits to every member.

Accelerating the process of Eurasian integration was still the primary target of EDB. EDB paid great attention to the integration projects in the investment projects, and expected to gain some achievements in Eurasian integration through the implementation of these projects. According to EDB's 2013 – 2017 development strategy, by the end of 2017, the integration projects should receive no less than 50% of total investment. In 2015, this proportion reached 53. 85%. Since EDB started operating, the total amount of mutual investment brought by portfolio projects has grown by $ 1. 899 billion. By analyzing these statistics, EDB will be able to use the investment projects evaluating and monitoring system to estimate periodically whether the investment projects meet the requirements of its 2013 – 2017 development strategy.

Promoting sustainable economic growth was another important goal of EDB in 2015. Sustainable growth is associated with a growth of production, an increase in employment, more effective spending, the implementation of investment, the inflow of private capital, the establishment of a market economy system, and the development of infrastructure. The projects in which EDB was involved had enormous social and economic benefits, and these projects could create $ 4. 666 billion gross output on average per year. At the same time, EDB's portfolio also had the multiplier effect, which increased the production growth and value added of certain industries. In 2015, one of the most significant contributions in sustainable development of EDB's projects was the creation or planned creation of nearly 23 ,000 jobs in member countries. In the meantime, the national budget had also been supplemented in some degree by the growth of tax revenue. In addition, all of EDB's operating activities were based on social and ecological responsibility and aimed at improving the utilization of natural resources and protecting the ecological environment. When selecting and implementing projects, EDB followed the relevant provisions in *The Eurasian Development Bank Ecosystems and Social Responsibility Policy* released in 2012: regarding the monitoring and assessing of socio-ecological effects of investment activities. This protocol made EDB's borrowers better able to participate in the research and assistance of social ecology problem management, avoid undesirable consequences as much as possible, and ensure the contributions of finance projects for sustainable development. In 2015, EDB continued to take part in the working groups of various multilateral financial institutions in the fields of ecological and social standards, and exchanged experiences on ecological and social responsibility in investment activities with other groups.

Eurasian Fund of Stability and Development (EFSD) is a subsidiary of EDB, whose funds are arranged by EDB and whose main objective is to ensure long-term economic stability and promote economic integration in member countries. EFSD offers loans to ensure national budgets are balanced, stabilize BOP, and provides investment credits to finance for international projects. In 2015, EFSD financed 12 projects totaling $ 3.47 billion, with year-on-year growth of 11%.

In 2015, EDB closely cooperated with major international organizations, including the United Nations Development Program (UNDP), the World Bank (WB), the Asian Development Bank (AsDB), and the European Bank for Reconstruction and Development (EBRD). The fruitful cooperation contributed to solving economic development problems in member countries. At the same time, EDB also actively participated in the Davos Economic Forum, Boao Forum for Asia, Petersburg International Economic Forum, the BRICS countries, the SCO Financial Forum, and other large international forums and conferences.

African Development Bank

African Development Bank Group experienced great achievements in 2015. Confronted with the economic depression, African Development Bank Group was dedicated to the inclusive and sustainable growth of African economies, further carrying out the Ten-Year Strategy (TYS). African Development Bank Group prioritized "High 5s" as its preferential strategy, committing itself to lighting up and powering Africa, feeding Africa, industrializing Africa, integrating Africa, and improving the quality of life for the people of Africa. The Ten-Year Strategy clearly pointed out the developmental goals and direction of Africa, enlightening Africa's future road.

Main Business Data

African Development Bank Group is composed of three institutions: the African Development Bank (AfDB), the African Development Fund (AfDBF) and the Nigeria Trust Fund (NTF). Its legal capital was contributed by 80 member countries including 54 African countries and 26 non-African countries. By the end of 2015, its authorized capital amounted to $ 92.8 billion. Subscribed capital amounted to

$ 90. 7 billion. Paid-up capital amounted to $ 6. 8 billion. Callable capital amounted to $ 84 billion. Total reserves amounted to $ 4 billion. By the end of 2015, total approvals of Bank Group operations amounted to $ 8. 8 billion. Total Bank Group approvals for 2015 were made up of total African Development Bank (AfDB) public and private approvals ($ 6. 3 billion), African Development Fund (AfDBF) approvals ($ 2. 1 billion) and Nigeria Trust Fund (NTF) approvals ($ 17. 32 million).

By the end of 2015, Bank Group had approved 241 operations of which loans accounted for 100 operations ($ 6. 6 billion), grants accounted for 87 operations ($ 650 million). In terms of approvals by sector, infrastructure accounted for 48. 9% ($ 4. 3 billion), finance accounted for 21. 6% ($ 1. 9 billion), 12. 5% ($ 1. 1 billion) went to projects spanning multiple sectors, the social sector accounted for 9. 1% ($ 800 million), agriculture and rural development accounted for 7. 9% ($ 700 million).

ADB issues mid-term and long-term bonds by binding global large-scale benchmark bonds and meeting the demands of specific operations. In addition, it actively carries out co-financing operations by cooperating with multilateral partners, bilateral institutions, governments, and local companies.

Highlights of the Year

As in the previous year, infrastructure operations, mainly in the field of transport and energy, received the bulk of the resources.

Ten-Year Strategy Priority Sectors

The TYS emphasizes priority sectors comprising infrastructure (energy, transport, water and sanitation, and communications), private sector development, regional integration, governance, and skills and human development.

Energy. The Bank Group's total approvals for the energy sector in 2015 amounted to $ 1. 2 billion, made up of loan and grant approvals of $ 1. 16 billion (96. 7%). The energy sector approvals represented 28. 3% of total Bank Group infrastructure approvals.

Environment and Climate Change. One key area of the Bank Group's activities in 2015 was the support towards climate-change adaptation and mitigation issues. The Bank Group announced that it would triple its financing for climate-change initiatives to reach $ 5 billion per year by 2020.

Transport. In 2015, the Bank Group total approvals for transport sector operations amounted to $ 2. 4 billion. Approvals for the transport sector represented the largest share (55. 9%) of the total Bank Group approvals for all infrastructure operations.

Water and Sanitation. During 2015, the Bank Group's interventions contributed to the development of the water supply and sanitation sector, with total approved operations of $ 550 million. The Bank Group continued to host and support three special and complementary initiatives: the Rural Water Supply and Sanitation Initiative (RWSSI), the Multi-Donor Water Partnership Program (MDWPP), and the African Water Facility (AWF).

Regional Integration. In 2015, total approvals for regional (multinational) operations amounted to $ 2 billion, a 33. 3% increase from the 2014 approvals . In the total regional approvals, the largest share (40. 2%) was allocated to transport. This was followed by the finance sector (25. 3%) for lines of credit and trade finance, and the energy sector (23. 8%). In November 2015, the board approved new policies and strategies of regional integration, aiming to create a bigger and more attractive market.

Private-Sector Operations. Total Bank Group approvals of private sector-financed operations in 2015 amounted to $ 2. 2 billion, a marginal decline of 1. 9% from 2014. In 2015, in the total private sector, finance sector approvals accounted for the largest share (42. 9%). In 2013, CEC Africa (CECA) was established in 2013 as a pan-African company with a mandate to develop, finance, and operate power projects across sub-Saharan Africa.

Supporting Economic and Governance Reforms. At the end of 2015, total approvals for governance-related operations amounted to $ 1. 09 billion. Two of the approved operations included Niger's Financial Reforms and Food Security Support Program (PAREFSA I) for $ 20 million and Mali's Emergency Governance and Economic Recovery Support Program (EGERSP) for $ 15 million.

Promoting Skills and Human Development. The sum of $ 800 million was approved to support various human development and relief operations during 2015. One of the operations highlighted is a grant of $ 33. 12 million approved for the Post Ebola Recovery Social Investment Fund Project (PERSIF) in the three worst-affected West African countries (Guinea, Liberia, and Sierra Leone).

Areas of Ten-Year Strategy Special Emphasis

Agriculture. In 2015, the Bank Group placed much emphasis on the development of the agriculture sector. The Bank Group approvals in the agriculture sector amounted to $ 700 million. In line with the TYS, the Bank Group organized the Dakar High-Level Conference on Agricultural Transformation in October 2015 for over 600 participants, including 155 high-level government representatives. This conference guided the preparation for the continental long-term strategy of agricultural transformation.

Gender. Implementation of the Bank Group's Gender Strategy was accelerated in April 2015 with the establishment of a network of 85 gender focal points throughout the Bank. During the Dakar High-Level Conference on Agricultural Transformation in Africa in October 2015, AfDB President Akinwumi Adesina announced that Bank Group would provide African women with adequate financial support.

Countries under Fragile Situations. In 2015, the AfDBF Board approved $ 500 million in support of 16 countries considered to be in fragile situations.

The Bank Group's New Operational Strategic Orientation. The eighth President of the Bank Group Adesina laid out a new strategic operational agenda for the Bank Group, outlined in the "High 5s". The "High 5s" are to: light up and power Africa; feed Africa; integrate Africa; industrialize Africa; and improve the quality of life for the people of Africa. These operational priorities were based on the past policies and strategies of Bank Group, and aimed at promoting the quick, sustained, and inclusive growth of African economies.

| Column 3 –3 | Five Priority Development Plans and Actions of the African Development Bank |

On September 1, 2015, Akinwumi Adesina, the eighth president of the AfDB, in his inaugural address, developed a new development plan for the AfDB based on the ongoing 2013 – 2022 Strategic Development Plan. The most compelling components of the plan are the "High 5s", covering energy, food, industrialization, African integration, and improving the living conditions of the people of Africa. These elements are essential for improving the lives of people in Africa and consistent with the United Nations SDGs process. After the "High 5s" proposal, the African Development Bank actively brought the plans into effect in Africa to achieve the established goals.

Promoting Energy Development in Africa

The African continent, which is rich in resources, has not been able to exploit and use its abundant resources due to the lack of adequate financial and technical resources. After the "High 5s" were announced, the AfDB actively sought to provide loan financing.

1) Provide a $ 24 million loan to support the transnational Luzizi III Hydro-power Project. The project is a joint initiative of the countries of the Great Lakes region—Burundi, the Democratic Republic of the Congo, and Rwanda, which will add about 50 megawatts of clean energy generation capacity to the region and provide an adequate supply of electricity for the region and beyond.

2) Provide a $ 200 million fund to support the construction of a power grid in the Côte d'Ivoire-Liberia-Sierra Leone-Guinea region. The completion of the project is expected to increase the area's power access rate and significantly re-duce the cost of electricity generation.

Improving Food Supply in Africa

The majority of African countries still rely on food imports and thousands of Af-rican children have suffered from hunger and malnutrition for a long time. Compared to their peers, they are much thinner, shorter, and less intellectually developed. Solving the problem of food supply is not only a humanitarian con-cern, but also provide human and intellectual support for state construction and economic development. African Development Bank is committed to help Afri-can countries solve the problem of food supply by agricultural transformation and upgrading, financial support, etc.

1) On April 16, 2016, AfDB's President Akinwumi Adesina presented the Bank's approach to address the nutritional challenges faced by Africa at a global nutrition conference organized by the Gates Foundation. The Bank would first implement a plan called "Feeding Africa" to transform the continent from a net food importer to food self-sufficiency and exports within a decade. The Bank would also use the African Development Bank Annual Conference 2016, which would be held in May, to advocate for African leaders to adopt innovative and effective financial methods to increase food supply.

2) On March 22 – 23, 2016, the African Development Bank's Department of Agriculture, the Bank's agro-industrial sector (OSAN), and the Bank's transi-tional support sector (ORTS) organized a lecture entitled "The function of Agropoles and Agro-Processing Zones (APZ) in addressing African food prob-lem and promoting the industrialization process" in Abidjan, Cote d'Ivoire. The purpose of this symposium was to share successful experiences in implemen-

ting Agropoles and Agro-Processing Zones (APZs) and to develop best practices to address the challenges of agro-industrial transformation.

Promoting Industrialization in Africa

The promotion of industrialization can promote economic growth and provide more jobs. As Africa is still at a low level of industrialization at present, the AfDB supports the national industries and thus promotes the process of industrialization by supporting infrastructure construction and supporting diversification efforts within African countries.

1) In April 2016, the Sustainable Energy Fund of African (SEFA) supported JUMEME Rural Power Supply Company in Tanzania to construct about 300 solar hybrid mini-grids, enabling more than 100,000 people and 2,340 small businesses in the Tanzanian countryside to use electricity.

2) In early March 2016, Charles Boamah, first vice-chairman of the African Development Bank, met with Jeff Immelt, chairman and chief executive officer of General Electric. Boamah pointed out that private companies such as General Motors could play a vital role in bridging Africa's infrastructure gap and industrialization. In recent years, General Motors' investment in some key areas in Africa continues to grow, such as health care, infrastructure, energy, oil and gas.

3) On April 19 and 20, 2016, the President of the African Development Bank Group Akinwumi Adesina visited Algeria and committed to formulate a policy, through innovative financing instruments, to mobilize external funds to support the development of three areas: the energy sector, with particular emphasis on renewable energy; industrialization and economic diversification; and agricultural transformation.

Promoting African Integration

AfDB's President Akinwumi Adesina proposed to promote more convenient economic and trade exchanges between countries by constructing infrastructure and gradually eliminating trade barriers between countries.

1) In early February 2016, the African Development Bank, the African Union (AU), and the United Nations Economic Commission for Africa (ECA) co-sponsored an expert meeting to discuss the establishment of the African continent free trade zone. The meeting is part of a series of preparations for the formal launch of the African Free Trade Area negotiations. Negotiations on the African continent's free trade zone roadmap are tentatively scheduled to end in

2017. The main tasks of the negotiations are to improve the trade situation in Africa, foster a free trade system, and deepen regional integration in Africa.

2) The African Regional Integration Index (ARII) report was launched by the AfDB, the African Union Commission (AUC) and ECA on April 2 as the first attempt to measure Africa's regional integration process. ARII covers 16 indicators, including production integration, trade integration, financial integration, regional infrastructure, and free movement of the population. So far, there is no mechanism to systematically measure the development of different countries and regions in Africa. ARII assesses the status of the African continent, the gap between different countries and regions, and the best way to bridge this gap.

Improving the Living Conditions of the African People

In addition to providing financial support to energy, agriculture, industry, and other key areas' development and promoting the integration process in Africa, the African Development Bank has also made positive efforts in improving the living conditions of African people. The following are some of the actions taken by the African Development Bank in 2016.

1) AfDB convened a seminar on March 8, 2016, International Women's Day, to discuss and consider Women's needs in the designing and planning of transport infrastructure. Safety was the biggest concern for women, and the promotion of safe and affordable means of transport was a central concern to both urban and rural women.

2) On April 7, 2016, World Health Day, the African Development Bank reiterated that it would help African countries to further strengthen their health care systems to better address non-communicable diseases such as diabetes. The banking industry has introduced key skills in tackling non-communicable diseases through the East Africa Centers for Excellence project and strengthened the health system in East Africa.

3) In March 2016, the African Development Bank approved a $ 1 million grant for the forthcoming Liberia Youth Employment and Entrepreneurship Program. The project will support the creation of 40 new sustainable enterprises, of which 40% will be owned by women. The program will also train 2,400 students to be better prepared when they enter the labor market.

European Bank for Reconstruction and Development

2015 was a special year for the European Bank for Reconstruction and Development (EBRD). It marked a quarter-century of helping its member countries to make the transition to more market-based, sustainable economies. In 2015, EBRD invested € 9. 4 billion in 381 projects. It showed outstanding performance in supporting the private sector as well as accelerating sustainable development and inclusive growth. The European Bank for Reconstruction and Development continued to deliver strong support for its regions in 2016 with a powerful program of investments that helped modernize economies and make them more robust and resilient. In 2016, the EBRD invested in 378 individual projects worth € 9. 4 billion, matching the previous record set in 2015. The EBRD stepped up its financing in local currencies with 93 local currency projects in 2016 compared with 80 a year earlier. The EBRD maintained a strong level of investment in small businesses that are seen as key to ensuring underlying economic strength and providing job opportunities. The EBRD increased the number of its projects in the least advanced transition countries to 114 in 2016 compared with 102 a year earlier. The Bank's updated transition concept was approved in November and seeks to make the Bank's countries of operations competitive, inclusive, well-governed, green, resilient and integrated, equipping them for the challenges of the 21st century.

Main Business Data

Investments were made to 381 operations in 2015, compared to 377 in 2014. In February 2015, the EBRD welcomed Greece as a temporary recipient country and in November the Bank signed its first transaction in Greece by taking stakes worth a total of € 250 million in its most important banks. In December 2015, shareholders approved a request for membership by China. They also approved a request for membership by Lebanon with a view to conducting operations in the future. The EBRD continued to increase its investment levels in central Europe and the Baltic states, investing close to € 1. 20 billion in 2015. Year on year the investments rose by 12. 73%. Investment in South-eastern Europe exceeded € 1. 28 billion, a decline of 23. 26 % compared with the last year. EBRD invested € 1. 67 in Eastern Europe and the Caucasus, a 21. 32% decline year on year; € 1. 40 billion in Central Asia, an increase of 74. 6% ; € 1. 46 billion in the Southern and Eastern Mediterranean, an increase of 36. 07% ; € 33 million in Cyprus, dropping form € 108 million in 2014 (see Figure 3. 4). Business activity was strong in Turkey during 2015, with € 1. 9 billion invested and 43 transactions signed across a wide range of sectors. While the Bank made no new investments in Russia, with € 106 million invested, Russia witnessed a huge decline of 82. 57% compared with the last year.

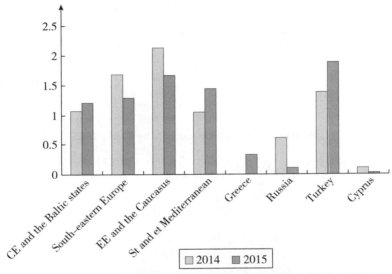

Figure 3. 4   EBRD Investments in Different Regions: 2014—2015
(Unit: Billion Dollars)

Altogether, the EBRD invested in 35 countries in 2015, with investments by field as follows: 32% in supporting SMEs, 27% in the energy sector, 22% in the industry, commerce, and agribusiness sectors, and 19% in the infrastructure sector (see Figure 3. 5). Of all the projects, 95% were assessed as good, very good, or excellent (5% excellent, 19% very good and 71% good) transition impact potential. 5% of projects were assessed as having moderately good transition impact potential. Assessments by field are shown in the Figure 3. 6.

In 2015, the European Bank for Reconstruction and Development took significant measures to address regional crises, insisting on sustainable development and promoting the spread of information.

Highlights of the Year

EBRD Sought to Boost the Greek Banking Sector

As part of efforts to strengthen Greece's banking sector and support the recovery of

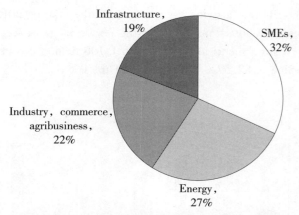

Figure 3. 5　EBRD Investments by Field: 2015

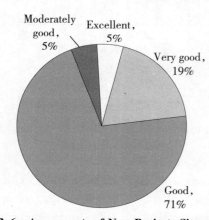

Figure 3. 6　Assessments of New Projects Signed by EBRD

the wider Greek economy, the EBRD purchased equity stakes worth a total of € 250 million in the country's four systemic banks. It invested € 65 million in Alpha Bank, 65 million in Eurobank, € 50 million in the National Bank of Greece, and € 70 million in Piraeus Bank. As a shareholder, the EBRD would play an active role, in particular by enhancing the banks' corporate governance.

The investments will give the banks a more robust capital base and facilitate their return to private ownership. The stabilization and restructuring of the Greek banking sector was needed to restore depositor and investor confidence, re-establish credit flows, and improve access to finance for the real economy. The financing assistance provided to Greece's four systemic banks was an effort strengthen their capital base to levels prescribed by the Single Supervisory Mechanism and the Bank of Greece. It complemented a memorandum of understanding between the Greek authorities and the European Commission.

Ukraine Crisis Response

The EBRD maintained its strong commitment to supporting Ukraine, which experienced ongoing difficulties and saw its GDP shrink by 11% in 2015. The Bank signed 29 transactions worth almost € 997 million while its policy dialogue efforts contributed to the reform process and a significant improvement in Ukraine's business climate and export potential. The largest deal was a $ 300 million (equivalent to € 276 million) loan to the national gas and oil company Naftogaz for winter heating purchases. Substantial investments were also made in the agribusiness sector (€ 184 million) and the financial sector (€ 386 million), including through the Bank's Trade Facilitation Program as well as several equity transactions. The EBRD remained active in transportation (€ 17 million) and the municipal and environmental infrastructure sector, signed 5 transactions worth a total of € 38.4 million, and approved a € 100 million facility for public transport improvements in Ukrainian municipalities.

The Bank provided its own funds and helped secure donor funding for essential undertakings such as the Business Ombudsman Council for Ukraine, which became operational in 2015 and the National Reform Council. Significant resources were committed to supporting a transparent and competitive legislative regime for the privatization of state-owned enterprises. The EBRD also pursued the modernization of Ukraine's agribusiness sector and maximization of the country's export potential. These resulted, among other achievements, in Ukrainian companies obtaining permission to export dairy products to China.

Lastly, the EBRD continued to administer donor funds to make the Chernobyl site safe and secure. Construction of the New Safe Confinement reached a major milestone last year when the two halves of the structure were joined together. In addition to its role as fund manager, the Bank has committed € 675 million of its own resources to support Chernobyl projects.

Helped Jordan's Water Infrastructure Cope with the Refugee Crisis

The EBRD responded to the refugee crisis in the Middle East by financing the upgrade of Jordan's water infrastructure, which was struggling to cope with the influx of people from neighboring Syria. A loan of € 12.9 million to the Water Authority of Jordan (WAJ) would support the urgently needed modernization of the sewage network. An estimated 1. 4 million people have fled from Syria to Jordan, mainly to the north of the country. This is equivalent to nearly 20% of Jordan's total population before the refugee crisis and has put a serious burden on the kingdom's resources and infrastructure.

The EBRD investment would enable the WAJ to construct a wastewater pipeline from East Zarqa pumping station to As-Samra Wastewater Treatment Plant and reha-bilitate an existing water pipeline and related infrastructure. The loan was co-financed by an investment grant of € 4. 6 million from the Bank's Shareholder Special Fund. The EU Neighborhood Investment Facility (NIF) funded associated technical assis-tance and environmental assessments.

EBRD Signed 1000th Sustainable Resource Investment

A loan to Ege Profil, the second-largest maker of polyvinyl chloride (PVC) window and door systems in Turkey, marked the 1000th EBRD investment in the area of en-ergy and resource efficiency. Ege Profil received a € 26 million financing package from the Bank and the Clean Technology Fund (CTF) to construct a new, state-of-the-art, environmentally-friendly production plant in Izmir Province.

The facility would feature photovoltaic solar panels, wastewater treatment facilities, and a combined cooling, heating, and power plant as well as infrastructure that would enable Ege Profil to carry out more recycling.

The loan was extended under the EBRD's Near-Zero Waste program in Turkey and Ege Profil is expected to recycle at least 800 more tons of PVC per year as a result of the investment.

EBRD Joins Global Transparency Initiative

Transparency and accountability have been key principles guiding the EBRD's work since the establishment of the institution in 1991. They occupied a prominent place in EBRD's public information policy.

In 2015, the EBRD took a big step forward as it disclosed information about its op-erations by starting to comply with the standard of the International Aid Transparency Initiative (IATI). IATI aims to make information about aid and development spend-ing easier to be accessed by the general public, including civil society organizations. It provides common definitions and publishing standards for the activities of more than 300 institutions, including the EBRD and other development financing institu-tions (DFIs). The EBRD now publishes information about its work in IATI's a-greed electronic format (XML) and links it to the IATI registry.

Create an Equity Participation Fund

In 2015, the EBRD continued to strengthen its engagement in equity financing to help provide diversified funding options and improve the corporate governance of invested companies. The institution received Board approval to create an Equity Participation Fund that would provide global institutional investors with access to the EBRD's portfolio of direct equity investments across the region. In order to guide investment and policy activities towards their goals, in 2015 the Bank introduced, with shareholder approval, a Strategic and Capital Framework for the period 2016 – 2020. This roadmap focuses on three main themes: fostering the economic resilience of countries; improving their integration into the regional and global economies; and addressing global and regional challenges, such as climate change and energy security. To meet these objectives, the EBRD will continue to be guided by its key operating principles of facilitating transitions, sound banking, and additional incentives. To equip the EBRD with the additional tools required to deliver greater impact, last year the Board approved a Green Economy Transition (GET) approach, which sought to raise the level of environmental investment to 40% of total EBRD financing by 2020. It also approved the EBRD's first strategy for the promotion of gender equality, which set out how the Bank would seek to increase Women's empowerment and equality of opportunity in the future.

Column 3 –4	EBRD's Experience in the Development of Financing for SMEs

In 2016, EU together with EBRD took frequent action to support small- and medium-sized enterprises (SMEs): EBRD cooperated with ABC Pharmacia (a large, Georgian pharmaceutical supplier) to expand pharmacy chains across the country; with Autocool (an Egyptian car air-conditioning manufacturer) to help the company rebuild its corporate structure and financial system; with Belausian (a Belarusian children's food and clothing vendor) to expand its business, whose branches cover almost all of the major cities and towns throughout Belarus now; and with Egyptian Europack by issuing € 1. 78 million worth of loans (to provide canned manufacturing and packaging solutions for goods).

EBRD, was established by the US, Japan, and some European countries after World War Ⅱ, to help build a new, post-Cold War era in Central and Eastern Europe. Ever since its establishment in 1991, EBRD has invested € 95. 404 billion in 36 emerging economies. In the year 2014 alone, it increased its total annual investment to € 8. 9 billion and signed 377 projects, according to its annual report. Among all of its investments, only 6% were under risk warning.

SMEs are an important source of jobs and growth, and an essential part of a healthy modern economy. At the same time, they are particularly vulnerable to some of the transition gaps that exist in the EBRD region, such as financing constraints and difficult business conditions. Offering loans to SMEs is what EBRD succeeds in doing, and it usually get funds from EU. In 2014, the EBRD extended € 1. 34 billion worth of loans to small businesses in 126 transactions, accounting for 33% of its projects. The project includes multiple items, mainly aiming to provide SMEs with technology and necessary skills and to help cultivate talents in the field of business management. EBRD provides finance directly or indirectly through agents like local banks, partner institutions, and investment funds. Technical aids are allocated to help the beneficiary country develop emerging areas through business protocols or to help small enterprises' owners develop their management abilities.

EBRD's main approaches to small business financing include:

1) The basic operation mode of loans to SMEs is loans through agency banks which are separated from EBRD in terms of assessment, accounting, managing, and writing-off bad debts.

2) EBRD has designed its products according to the business scope of its customers, which vary in terms of loan amounts, interest rates, and maturities. Companies with fewer than 10 employees can get micro-level loans which stay at less than € 8,000. The full payment will take some time to be reviewed and allocated, but € 2,500 is issued within one day after applying. SMEs with fewer than 100 employees are eligible for a loan of € 160,000. In terms of lending rates, EBRD sets fixed and floating interest rates separately. Although the rates for SMEs are higher than those of local banks, they are still far below private lending rates. The maturity is not fixed, that is to say, certain changes are allowed according to project inspection and negotiation. Loan collaterals are varied, but include land, equipment, movable property, the company's annual income and stocks, etc. It is important to note that EBRD does not accept third-party guarantees, as the acceptance of a guarantee means that a bank must assess the guarantor, which will affect the efficiency of loan issuance, increase the cost to the bank, and is likely to weaken the repayment constraint. EBRD's repay-

ment period is semiannual, for a comparatively relaxing period helps to reduce repayment pressure for SMEs.

3) The approval procedure of EBRD-SMEs-loan is relatively comprehensive, with the period from pre-loan investigation to loan issuance lasting no more than a week. The payment period is generally 1 to 15 years, but infrastructure projects can enjoy longer cycles. The loan approval process is as follows: preparation of the draft loan plan, draft re-examination, board review, signing a legally binding agreement, and selecting a loan mode.

4) In terms of loan officer management, EBRD stipulates that loan officer's income is composed of basic salary and incentives. The latter is linked to performance. Performance evaluation indicators consist of the quantity and quality of new loans on a monthly basis. For each new loan, cooperative banks will be rewarded. However, if any principal or interest is overdue, the corresponding loan officer's income will be reduced in accordance to the overdue severity. Thus, the risk of loans is controlled to some extent. Loan officers' incentives generally do not exceed 50% of the basic salary. EBRD also established a thorough loan officer training mechanism. To train a mature loan officer, up to about a year of repeated training is needed, and an examination is required before working in the field. The Small Business Financing Project Office organizes different types of training courses, including micro-finance junior courses, fast loan courses, small loan courses, etc.

EBRD grants loans through agencies and designs different loan products according to the size of customer, establishing a sound loan approval process and high-quality credit team. The combination of financial assistance and technical aids help SMEs develop. EBRD's relatively mature SMEs-financing experience is noteworthy.

European Investment Bank

In 2015, European Investment Bank (EIB) witnessed great achievements. However, it faced many challenges at the same time. EIB persisted in finding innovative ways with its professional knowledge to strengthen Europe's economy and improve the human living environment.

Main Business Data

In 2015, EIB loan investment achieved its annual peak, with total investment reaching € 77. 5 billion. European Fund for Strategic Investments (EFSI), in which EIB holds 59. 15% of its share, invested € 7. 5 billion in 2015. Among total investment (85 billion) in 2015, € 18. 7 billion was used for innovation and education, € 28. 4 billion for financing the development of small- and medium-sized enterprises, € 19. 1 billion for infrastructure, and € 19. 6 billion for the environmental sector[①] (see Figure 3. 7). In 2015, climate and the environment accounted for almost 50% of EIB approved projects, involving 22 countries in the European Union, thereby leading 81,000 small- and medium-sized enterprises to benefit from the financing.

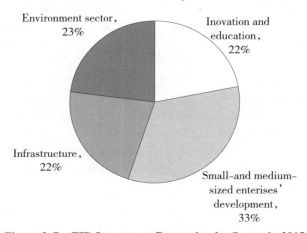

Figure 3. 7   EIB Investment Proportion by Sector in 2015

In 2016, the EIB Group was effectively attracting other investors: € 83. 8 billion financing supports a total investment of € 280 billion. The lending activities of EIB are mainly funded via bond issuance in the international capital markets, and the Bank successfully raised € 66. 4 billion from investors around the world.

A record € 33 billion were delivered in SME financing to the benefit of 300,000 smaller companies, which employ 4. 4 million people. The EIB Group supported close to € 20 billion for infrastructure, and some € 17 billion went to environmental projects, in 2016.

---

① There were overlap in the investments for the abovementioned sectors.

The EIB's original funding comes from the EU members' assessment. After that, the issuance of bonds became its main funding source. In 2015, the EIB supported transactions in 12 different currencies and issued bonds in 16 currencies, 89% of which were issued in euros, pounds and dollars. 63% of the bonds were issued in Europe, 21% in Asia, 14% in North America, and 2% in the Middle East and Africa (see Figure 3.8). At present, the EIB has become the UK's largest issuer of sterling, and the market leader of the Turkish lira, the Canadian dollar, the Norwegian krone, and the South African rand.

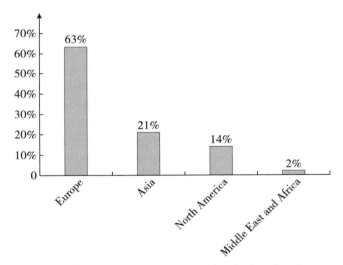

Figure 3.8   EIB Bond Market Distribution Graph

Highlights of the Year

Mission—the Foundation of EFSI

The most important event for the EIB in 2015 was the establishment of the European Fund for Strategic Investments (EFSI). Since 2013, the EU average annual economic growth rate has been 0.1%, the euro area GDP shrunk by 0.4%, and the unemployment rate has been as high as 11.5%. Facing such a dire situation, on November 26, 2014, Jean-Claude Juncker, the European Commission President, and EIB proposed the "European Investment Plan" (EIP). This plan mainly includes three measures, namely to promote financial security, to develop investment projects, and to improve the investment environment. Between the years 2015 and 2017, the plan will accelerate EU economic growth by 1 point each year, thus increasing the EU's GDP by € 330 billion to € 410 billion and creating 1.3 million jobs.

To implement the European Investment Plan, the European Commission proposed to found the EFSI, which was approved by the European Council on 25 June, 2015. The EIB financed € 16 billion to the seed fund and was responsible for the Fund. The European Commission appropriated € 8 billion from the EU budget as collateral for the Fund. The EFSI is expected to mobilize around € 315 billion from private and public sources with a 15-fold leverage ratio.

Green—Invest not only the Europe's Future but also the World's

The EIB is the world's largest climate fund provider. Since its inception, investment and activities in the climate field have outstripped the sum of the five largest multilateral development banks. The ambitious agreement signed at the Paris Climate Conference in December 2015 undoubtedly sets new demands on the future work of the EIB—the EIB will be committed to providing at least a quarter of its funding for climate action projects, and in the years from 2015 to 2020, the EIB will invest € 100 billion in climate projects.

In 2015, the EIB provided € 20.7 billion worth of financing to the climate sector, successfully fulfilling its objectives, and it plans to invest 35% more in climate projects in developing countries. In the climate sector, € 3.3 billion was spent on renewable energy, € 3.6 billion spent on energy efficiency, € 1.6 billion spent on research and innovation, € 10.3 billion spent on low carbon and environmentally friendly transport systems, € 9 billion spent on climate change adaptation, and € 1 billion spent on greening and waste treatment (see Figure 3.9).

EIB, which is eager to maintain the ecological balance of nature, supports the promotion of clean air, the maintenance of biodiversity, devotion to new energy research and development. It aims to protect the future living environment of the next generation, and make a more prosperous future through continuous innovation.

Responsibility—the Resolving of Refugee Problem

The year 2015 marked a very prominent year for the refugee issue. The EIB responded quickly, in actively organizing refugee housing construction, and increased financing projects in the refugee countries or regions. For example, the influx of Syrian refugees into Jordan poses a severe strain on local drinking water supplies, triggering a conflict between the refugees and the indigenous Jordanian people. The EIB signed a water pipeline investment agreement with Jordan in November 2015 to fi-

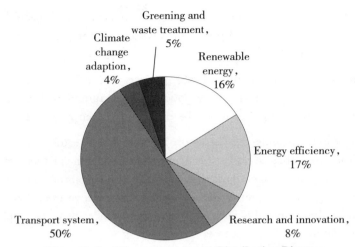

Figure 3. 9 **Climate Investment Distribution Diagram**

nance € 50 million, which will effectively alleviate the current pressure on drinking water supplies in Jordan and reduce regional conflicts.

In addition to economic aid, the EIB also supports European countries in border construction strengthening, and encourages refugees to evacuate to neighboring countries, to reduce the number of foreign refugees in Europe and alleviate the pressure of European countries.

EIB has a global influence, so it always has the responsibility to cope with international challenges and help with the European economic development. The influence and strength of the EIB shows a steady growth year by year. This trend became even more pronounced in 2015 with the EIB contributing more to the development of human society in the future.

Column 3 –5 European Investment Bank's InnovFin Advisory

Under Horizon 2020, the new EU research program for 2014 – 2020, the European Commission and the European Investment Bank Group (EIB and EIF) have launched a new generation of financial instruments and advisory services to help innovative firms access finance more easily. InnovFin financing was designed as a series of integrated and complementary financing tools, consisting of eight products including InnovFin SME Guarantee, InnovFin SME Venture Capital, InnovFin MidCap Guarantee, InnovFin MidCap Growth Finance, InnovFin Large Projects, InnovFin Energy Demonstration Projects, Infectious Diseases Finance Facility, and InnovFin Advisory. Among them, InnovFin Advisory has special value.

Many research and innovation (R&I) projects face difficulties in securing finance, despite being fundamentally good projects. InnovFin Advisory supports these projects and companies make the most out of their potential.

InnovFin Advisory guides its clients on how to structure their R&I projects in order to improve their access to financing. The service helps them to capitalize on their strong points and adjust elements such as their business model, governance, funding sources, and financing structure to improve their access to financing. In the long run, this increases a project's chances of being implemented. InnovFin Advisory offer 7 services:

1) Strategic planning.

2) Business modeling.

3) Capital structure, debt and risk allocation.

4) Classic or innovative financial instruments.

5) Governance.

6) Management of stakeholders.

7) More "efficient usage" of public financial instruments.

InnovFin Advisory also provides advice to improve investment conditions through activities that are not project-specific. This includes things such as developing a business case for new financing mechanisms and preparing studies on increasing the effectiveness of financial instruments to address specific R&I needs.

For example, the naissance of Infectious Diseases Finance Facility is ascribed to the InnovFin Advisory's Development of new financing mechanisms. Following discussions with the European Commission, pharmaceutical companies, and industry players, InnovFin Advisory prepared a concept paper covering the latest trends in innovative financing instruments for Infectious Diseases R&D. The paper outlines the need for a new, higher risk-taking, Infectious Diseases Finance Facility ("IDFF"). This facility is expected to be funded by EU budgetary resources and, potentially, to be a catalyst for attracting additional resources from other funders.

InnovFin Advisory has met with various pharmaceutical companies and stake-holders to check the IDFF concept and contribute to the development of a potential investment pipeline. Going forward, InnovFin Advisory will work to attract additional resources from other entities/ donors to invest in IDFF to enhance the impact of the facility.

It is worth mentioning that InnovFin Advisory provides services independently of the EIB's lending/investment decisions. The staff will assess all potential financing sources including, but not limited to, EIB funding.

Building on the support, networks, and expertise of the EIB Group and the European Commission, InnovFin Advisory has clients in:

• The private sector (large and small corporations, RDI clusters, industry associations, financial market associations, etc.).

• The public sector (European Commission, member states, government agencies, etc.).

• Public-private and semi-public institutions (research institutes, foundations, NGOs, etc.).

In China, there are no intermediary institutions like InnovFin Advisory playing a role in improving the bankability and investment-readiness of large projects that need substantial, long-term investments. China's innovation-focused development strategy and the implementation of the "Made in China 2025" plan need the government, financial institutions, and enterprises to work together. InnovFin is the adhesive that can bring together the different types of market participants to jointly promote technological innovation. InnovFin Advisory, driven by government credit, supported by developmental financial institutions, and operated by social institutions, provides a good example for us.

Caribbean Development Bank

As a multilateral financial institution, Caribbean Development Bank (Caribbean DB) is dedicated to the economic development of its Borrowing Member Countries (BMCs). Through project loans and technical assistance to the government, public agencies, and other entities, Caribbean DB aims at promoting sustainable economic development and poverty reduction in Caribbean countries. Since establishment, the past four and half decades Caribbean DB witnessed the expansion of its membership from 19 to 28 countries. Just at the end of 2016, Caribbean DB welcomed Brazil as the fourth regional, non-borrowing member.

While celebrating the achievement, Caribbean DB was starting a new chapter in its operations with the launch of the Strategic Plan 2015 – 2019. In this initial year, the Bank directed its operations and activities towards implementing the new Plan to better assist BMCs with preparations to meet their obligations under the United Nation's new agenda on Sustainable Development Goals (SDGs).

In 2015, Caribbean DB approved loans and grants amounting to $ 294 million, up from $ 270 million in 2014. Among them, $ 197 million came from the ordinary capital resources (OCR), and $ 97 million was from the special funds resources (SFR). During 2016, the rating agency Standard and Poor's reaffirmed Caribbean DB's long-term rating as AA, while Moody's Investor Services reaffirmed Caribbean DB's long-term issuer rating as Aa1, both with a stable outlook.

Main Business Data

Ordinary Capital Resources (OCR)

On December 31, 2015, Caribbean DB's total assets were $ 1,407. 1 million, representing an increase of $ 28. 6 million (2.1%) from $ 1,378. 5 million in 2014. The Returns on Assets (ROA) and the Returns on Equity (ROE) were 1. 20% and 1. 90% respectively. Among the total loan portfolio of $ 992. 5 million, 0. 50% ($ 5. 4 million) was in non-performing loans. The total liabilities decreased from $ 557. 0 million in 2014 to $ 533. 1 million in 2015. The comprehensive income is $ 8. 5 million.

Special Development Fund (SDF)

On December 31, 2015, the total assets of the SDF were $ 994. 1 million, representing an increase of $ 39. 9 million (4. 1%) from $ 954. 8 million at the end of 2014. There was a net loss of $ 3. 3 million in 2015. The income represented a return of 0. 41% on average liquidity. The income from loans was $ 12. 5 million, the income from cash and investments was $ 1. 4 million, and the total expenses were $ 17. 3 million.

Other Special Funds (OSF)

On December 31, 2015, the total assets of the OSF were $ 265. 1 million, representing a decrease of $ 14. 4 million from $ 279. 5 million at the end of 2014. In 2015, the net income was $ 4. 0 million, among which the income from loans accounted for $ 2. 5 million and the income from cash and investments was $ 3. 3 million.

Operations

In 2015, Caribbean DB approved $ 261. 5 million in loans and $ 32. 7 million in grants, totaling $ 294. 2 million. During the year, there were loan disbursements of $ 135. 3 million and grant disbursements of $ 26. 1 million.

Highlights of the Year

Economic Infrastructure

Ongoing infrastructure projects during the year 2015 included the construction and upgrading of approximately 84 km of roads, benefitting some 30,000 people, and the installation of 12 km of supply mains. 17 new capital and Technical Assistance (TA) interventions were approved for economic infrastructure development in Anguilla, the Bahamas, Barbados, Belize, Grenada, Dominica, St. Lucia, and others. Interventions were made in the energy, transportation, water, and sanitation sectors, as well as in post disaster response.

Technical Cooperation

As the focal point for Technical Cooperation and TA within the Bank and among its external partners, in 2015, the Technical Cooperation Division (TCD) continues to provide adequate support to BMCs through its various units.

1) Regional cooperation and integration. During 2015, the TCD submitted 11 projects to the Steering Committee of the Caribbean Single Market and Economy (CSME) Standby Facility for Capacity Building and they were all approved. This brings to $ 3. 46 million funds committed under the Facility. Besides, 14 projects were approved by the Steering Committee for the EPA (Environmental Protection Agency) Facility. This brought the total number of approvals under the Facility to 18, with a total value of $ 3. 71 million. Funds and grants, approved for all eligible countries, focused on trade facilitation, stakeholder welfare advancement, as well as the development of the services sector, to improve the regional competitiveness under the free movement of labor and people.

2) Caribbean Aid for Trade and Regional Integration Trust Fund (CARTFund). The CARTFund is a trust fund, financed by the United Kingdom government's De-

partment for International Development (DFID) and administered by Caribbean DB. Its overall aim is to assist CARIFORUM (the Caribbean Forum) countries in boosting growth and reducing poverty through trade and regional integration. In 2015, the CARTFund portfolio included 32 projects in 14 countries. 14 of these projects were implemented prior to 2015. The 18 remaining were all concluded at the end of the year.

3) Caribbean Technological Consultancy Services (CTCS) Network. Caribbean DB approved $ 1.1 million for TA interventions under its MSME program, known as the Caribbean Technological Consultancy Services (CTCS) Network in 2015. By December 31, a total of $ 682,000, approximately 55% of the approved amount, was disbursed for the implementation of 26 TA activities. These included 23 regional and national workshops and 3 direct TA interventions, which involved 480 business people, and addressed critical managerial, technical, and operational challenges affecting MSMEs in BMCs.

4) Increasing access to safe sanitation. Although the coverage rate of safe sanitation facilities in Haiti increased from 19% in 1990 to 24% in 2012, it remained the lowest among Caribbean DB's 18 BMCs. In 2015, Caribbean DB partnered with the National Directorate of Water Supply and Sanitation (DINEPA) to coordinate the Governance and Sanitation training program, which began in December 2015 and continued through April 2016. The program comprises the delivery of online courses and a workshop to 41 technical and management-level sanitation professionals to help Haiti improve its sanitation system coverage.

Environmental Sustainability

The Bank continues to ensure the full integration of environmental sustainability considerations in its operational work program. To this end, Caribbean DB is strengthening environmental governance, management capacity, and public awareness at national and regional levels through the following efforts:

1) Climate change resilience. Approved in October 2015, climate change assessment and the use of related screening tools are now mandatory in the preparation of country strategy papers (CSP) for each BMC.

2) Disaster risk reduction. In response to the catastrophic damage caused by Tropical Storm Erika, Caribbean DB provided $ 30 million to Dominican Republic to help with immediate recovery efforts, as well as long-term reconstruction and rehabilitation. Caribbean DB also allocated $ 2.4 million to help the government of Haiti

pay its annual insurance premium to the Caribbean Catastrophe Risk Insurance Facility. The Caribbean Disaster Emergency Management Agency (CDEMA) also received TA support of $ 98, 313 to improve its procurement and contract adminis-
tration system.

3) Capacity building. In 2015, Caribbean DB hosted a range of training activities to
strengthen skills, improve knowledge, and facilitate the dissemination of information
for enhance awareness of climate change and disaster risk reduction issues. Caribbean
DB's staff and technical personnel from several BMC institutions attended these activities.

4) Partnership and external representation. In January, Caribbean DB co-hosted and
co-financed a regional workshop with the World Bank as part of the second phase of
consultations on the revision of the World Bank's Environmental and Social Safeguards. Representatives from 8 non-government organizations and Caribbean DB's
19 BMCs attended the workshop. In May, the two institutions again jointly sponsored a workshop to introduce the World Bank's Climate and Disaster Risk Screening
tools to Caribbean DB's staff. Caribbean DB teamed up with the World Bank to develop Climate Risk and Adaption County Profiles for the Bahamas, Barbados, Belize, Guyana, St. Kitts and Nevis, and Suriname.

Social Sector

In 2015, Caribbean DB's social sector projects mainly focused on education, agriculture and food safety, and gender. In education, Caribbean DB approved $ 70. 5
million to assist with continued development of basic education and investment in
Technical and Vocational Education and Training (TVET), representing the highest
level over the five-year period starting from 2011. As for agriculture and food safety,
Caribbean DB initiated a range of activities to improve food safety and infrastructure
quality as well as conformity assessment systems across BMCs. This year, partnered
with International Trade Centre (ITC) and the government of Grenada, Caribbean
DB undertook a food safety compliance audit of the fresh fruit industry to help identify weaknesses and recommend remedial action to ensure that Grenada's trade in fresh
produce is compliant with international requirements. In terms of gender, the percentage of projects that explicitly addressed gender issues was 57% , an increase of
14% over the same period in 2014. There was also a marked improvement in the
number of pro-gender equality TA grants.

The Bank, through the Basic Needs Trust Fund (BNTF), continued to cooperate
with governments and community groups in responding to citizens' needs in impov-

erished areas. The Bank also kept prioritizing fields like gender equality, environmental sustainability, community empowerment, and holistic development. In 2015, Caribbean DB and BNTF Implementing Agencies (IAs) entered the preparation and implementation of the Seventh (BNTF 7) and Eighth (BNTF 8) Programs. Figure 3. 10 is the sector portfolio distribution of BNTF 7 & 8.

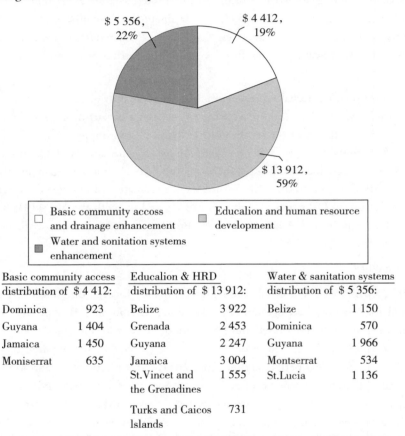

Basic community access distribution of $ 4 412:		Educalion & HRD distribution of $ 13 912:		Water & sanitation systems distribution of $ 5 356:	
Dominica	923	Belize	3 922	Belize	1 150
Guyana	1 404	Grenada	2 453	Dominica	570
Jamaica	1 450	Guyana	2 247	Guyana	1 966
Moniserrat	635	Jamaica	3 004	Montserrat	534
		St.Vincet and the Grenadines	1 555	St.Lucia	1 136
		Turks and Caicos Islands	731		

Figure 3. 10   BNTF 7&8 Sector Portfolio Distribution (Unit: Thousand Dollars)

Private Sector Development

Caribbean DB continued to view financial intermediary lending as the preferred mode of supporting private sector development in the Bank's BMCs. Along with the capacity building projects, it aims at addressing major constraints that the private sector faces, such as financing, innovation, and entrepreneurship. In 2015, Caribbean DB approved two lines of credit totaling $ 17. 75 million, one dedicated to student loan financing in Barbados, and the other one offering financing across a wide range of sectors in Grenada on affordable terms. It is expected that approximately 75 MSMEs, including start-ups and existing enterprises, will be able to secure funding, and a-round 320 student loan beneficiaries will get opportunities to keep pursuing study programs, including those from low income households.

The other intervention was implemented in partnership with the World Bank and Government of Jamaica. It aimed at encouraging growth and employment, in addition to increasing income earning opportunities for young persons in the region's information, communication, and technology industry. The training program attracted a total of 59 participants from 12 BMCs and 16 financial institutions.

Regional Public-Private Partnership Support Facility

Given the high infrastructure needs, policy-makers in the BMCs are increasingly resorting to public-private partnerships (PPPs). In response to this need, Caribbean DB, in co-operation with its development partners the World Bank, the Public-Private Infrastructure Advisory Facility (PPIAF), the IDB, and the Multilateral Investment Fund (IMF), launched a regional PPP support facility. Through initiatives such as PPP Boot Camps, Caribbean PPP Toolkit Development, and PPP Help Desk Building, Caribbean DB demonstrated its ongoing commitment to the delivery of infrastructure services in the region.

Renewable Energy and Energy Efficiency

To promote energy transformation and sustainable energy development, in June and October of 2015, Caribbean DB approved two important initiatives under the agreements with EU-CIF and UK-DFID. € 4. 45 million and € 2. 5 million respectively was set aside for the Sustainable Energy for the Eastern Caribbean (SEEC) Program. Through SEEC, Caribbean DB has already provided lines of credit of $ 500,000 to two financial intermediaries for lending to small- and medium-sized enterprises.

Besides, the Bank continued to encourage the use of alternative energy, with RE/EE components included in 6 projects. For example, the BWA project approved, in December 2015, includes installation of 550 kWh of solar photovoltaic power at 4 locations, projected to produce 855 MWh per year (equivalent to about 15% of the current consumption at those sites), and will reduce greenhouse gas emissions by a-bout 909 tons annually.

Islamic Development Bank

The Islamic Development Bank (IsDB) is a multilateral development financing institution located in Jeddah, Saudi Arabia. It was founded in 1973 by the Finance Ministers at the first Organization of the Islamic Conference and began its activities on 20 October 1975. Ranked on the basis of paid-up capital as of Islamic calendar year 1437H, major shareholders include: Saudi Arabia (23. 52%), Libya (9. 43%), Iran (8. 25%), Nigeria (7. 66%) and United Arab Emirates (7. 51%).

Main Business Data

In the Islamic calendar year 1437H, the net approvals of the Islamic Development Bank Group were $ 12. 1 billion, an increase of 13% compared to the previous year. In terms of the members' shares in the total approvals, 52. 9% and 40. 6% were funded respectively by the International Islamic Trade Finance Corporation (ITFC) and ordinary capital resources (OCR), followed by the Islamic Corporation for the Development of the Private Sector (ICD) at 5. 5%. Other funds, such as the Unit Investment Fund (UIF) and the Awqaf Properties Investment Fund (APIF), accounted for 0. 9% and the Special Assistance Operations accounted for 0. 1% (see Figure 3. 11).

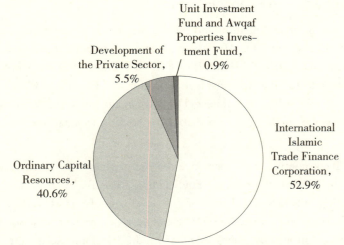

Figure 3. 11　Proportion of the Capital Contribution for Approved Projects in the Islamic Calendar Year 1437H

Regionally, the Middle East and North Africa received the largest share of IsDB Group net approvals with $ 5. 4 billion, 44. 6% of all approvals. Sub-Saharan Africa ranked the second with $ 3. 6 billion (29. 8%), followed by Asia with $ 2. 5 billion (20. 6%), and the Commonwealth of Independent States with $ 382. 8 million (3. 2%) (see Figure 3. 12). Among all the countries of the IsDB Group, the top 5 financing recipients were Egypt, Turkey, Bangladesh, Pakistan, and Senegal. The total funding and shares received by the 5 countries were 16. 6% , $ 2. 01 billion; 16. 2% , $ 1. 96 billion; 9. 9% , $ 1. 2 billion; 9. 1% , $ 1. 1 billion; and 3. 9% , $ 469. 6 million.

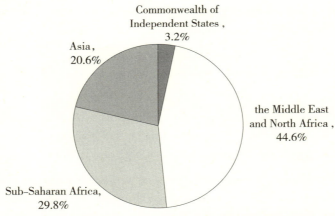

Figure 3. 12   Regional Allocation for the Amounts of Approved Projects in the Islamic calendar year 1437H

The disbursements of the Bank in 1437H totaled $ 6. 9 billion, an increase of 38% compared to the previous year, while the Bank received repayments of $ 2. 8 billion. Since the establishment of the Islamic Development Bank, the disbursements of the Bank cumulatively total $ 71. 4 billion, with the repayments totaling $ 54. 9 billion and the net resource transfer totaled $ 16. 5 billion.

Highlights of the Year

In 1437H, infrastructure projects accounted for 78. 4% of the total in the Islamic Development Bank Group's net approved projects, followed by agriculture and rural development projects at 8. 5% , education at 6. 9% , health programs at 4% , and the remaining sectors accounted for 2. 1% .

In the field of infrastructure, the transportation projects accounted for the largest proportion at 46% , followed by energy at 29% , water, sanitation and urban develop-ment at 10% and industry at 4% . 19 projects in the transportation sector were ap-proved worth a total of $ 1. 6 billion; 20 projects in the energy sector were ap-proved totaling $ 1. 1 billion; and 6 projects of urban development operations were approved worth a total of $ 368 million.

In the field of education, 17 operations were approved totaling $ 339. 2 million, with an increase of 75% over the previous year. Among them, the Higher Educa-tion Development Project in Benin accounted for 45% of the total approval. Be-sides, IsDB and the World Bank jointly launched the education for competitiveness (E4C) initiative, which covered three dimensions: education for lifelong learning, education for employment, and education for transformation.

In the health sector, 12 operations were approved worth $ 198. 3 million, including teaching assistant grants covering areas of prevention and control of communicable diseases.

Other approved operations included several public-private partnership projects totaling $ 740 million, 31 agriculture projects totaling $ 419 million, 67 operations under the Technical Cooperation Program for a total of $ 1. 7 million.

In addition, the Islamic Development Bank achieved better results in its special oper-ating mechanism in 1437H. "Reverse Linkage Program" (RL) is a new concept in-troduced by the Islamic Development Bank, which refers to when two developing member countries of the IsDB realize a mutually-beneficial, two-way flow of knowl-edge, technology, and/or resources through cooperation. In 1437H, 10 new Re-verse Linkage projects were initiated, of which 3 were approved. The first was a Re-verse Linkage project between Senegal and Indonesia in Flood Disaster Risk Manage-ment. The second was a Reverse Linkage project between Djibouti and Morocco in the monitoring and surveillance of high-risk pregnancies and childbirth. The third was a Reverse Linkage project between the Republic of Suriname and Malaysia in the area of rice production. The cooperation between the Islamic Development Bank and the Egyptian Agency of Partnership for Development (EAPD), and the cooper-ation between the IsDB and the Arab Bank for Economic Development in Africa (ABEDA) were also included in the Reverse Linkage Program.

In 1437H, the Islamic Development Bank achieved remarkable results in its organiza-tional restructuring and international cooperation, as illustrated by the following:

1) The establishment of the President Advisory Panel. Introduced on 19 March

2015, this high-level panel is composed of 13 eminent personalities for a three-year term. This panel provides external, independent, and objective perspectives on the development of the Islamic Development Bank and its member countries.

2) The adjustment of the fiscal year. The Board of Governors of the Islamic Development Bank passed a resolution approving an adjustment of the fiscal year of IsDB Group to the Solar Hijri calendar, while retaining the Lunar Hijri as its official calendar. This adjustment was to be implemented during 2016, which means that the length of the adjusted fiscal year 2016 will increase to 14.5 months, ending on December 31, 2016 by the Gregorian calendar. The adjustment will make the Islamic Development Bank begin and end its fiscal year at the same date as other major financial institutions in the world to make work and communication easier.

3) Deep Dive Initiative. This initiative gave rise to a historic strategic partnership framework (SPF) agreement between the Islamic Development Bank Group and the World Bank Group (WBG). The SPF agreement was launched in Washington DC in October 2015 to deepen the cooperation between the Islamic Development Bank and the World Bank in promoting economic and social development in their common member countries.

4) Lives and Livelihoods Fund. The total amount of this fund is $ 500 million, of which the Islamic Development Bank and the Bill & Melinda Gates Foundation funded $ 100 million, with the remaining funds coming from other donors. The Lives and Livelihoods Fund will be used primarily to address poverty and health-related challenges in the member countries of IsDB.

5) Member country partnership strategy. In 1437H, the Islamic Development Bank updated its cooperation strategy with 9 member countries. With Indonesia, Turkey, and Senegal, the partnership strategy was in its second generation; with Afghanistan, Cameroon, the Kyrgyz Republic, Nigeria, Sudan, and Yemen, the partnership strategy was in its first generation.

As one of the world's highest rated multilateral development financing institutions, the Islamic Development Bank has been committed to promoting economic and social development in its member countries as well as the Muslim communities in non-member countries, with sound economic returns and good social benefits. The Bank and its operations provide a model for the development of Islamic finance and a useful reference for the development of multilateral development financing institutions in other countries.

Column 3 −6	Islamic Development Bank Supports the Development of New Energy in Turkey

Promoting the development of clean energy and energy saving, emission reduction projects can not only improve the energy independence of a nation and reduce the energy dependence on other countries, but also has a series of peripheral effects including promoting social development and employment.

The Turkish government has realized the importance of promoting the development of new energy and aims to increase its production of solar power up to 10 gigawatts (GW) by 2030 and increase its wind power up to 16 GW by the same year. This comes alongside efforts to promote energy-saving projects in several productive sectors. As a member country of the Organization of the Islamic Conference and the Islamic Development Bank, Turkey has received support from the Islamic Development Bank for its plans to develop renewable energy.

Investment in Renewable Energy and Energy Saving Projects

As the fossil fuel reserves of Turkey are limited, the country is strongly dependent on other countries in terms of traditional energy. However, Turkey has great potential in the field of new energy including water, solar, and wind energy. From 2012 to 2015, the Islamic Development Bank cooperated with the Industrial Development Bank of Turkey on the project development. The Industrial Development Bank of Turkey is one of the most important development banks and investment banks in Turkey, as well as the first bank to support the renewable energy development projects in the country.

The Islamic Development Bank has provided support to 4 renewable energy development projects in Turkey, including two hydroelectric power stations, one solar power station, and one wind power station. Besides, 6 energy-saving projects also received support from the Islamic Development Bank. The investment in the 10 projects totaled $ 642.2 million, of which the Islamic Development Bank invested $ 100 million. The combined benefits of these projects far exceeded expectations: the 4 new energy plants have the capacity to provide 370 megawatts (MW) against a target of 150 MW. In addition, the 6 energy-saving projects have already saved 1,006,000 tons of greenhouse gases through February 2016, and the combined contribution to Turkey's overall reduction in greenhouse gas emissions is 50%.

Building the Supporting Facilities for Energy Projects and Promoting Employment of Local Residents

The two hydroelectricity dams—Gökta I and Gökta II - lie in a valley deep in the mountains north of Adana. A 54-km road was built as an auxiliary project for the hydroelectricity dams and it opened up the gate to the outside world for the local residents. Besides, 3 new bridges that cross the Zamantl River were built to connect the mountainous areas to big cities including Adana and Kozan, with the average transit time reduced from 4 hours to 1.5 hours.

The Bereket Enerji Company, which was in charge of building the dams, actively created jobs for local residents. In the process of building the two hydroelectricity dams, 60% of the temporary workers were from nearby villages and towns. The residents received relevant skill training at work, while in the past they could only make a living by grazing and mine work.

Supporting Enterprises to Realize Self-sufficiency for Electrical Energy

In addition to large-scale renewable energy projects, the Islamic Development Bank also provides assistance to small-scale projects to help enterprises realize power self-sufficiency. One of the beneficiaries is Prokon, an engineering and manufacturing company located outside Ankara. In March 2013, with the support of an energy-saving project led by the Islamic Development Bank, Prokon installed 2,040 solar panels on the roof of its workshop, which was the first solar-power project of this scale in the country. Owing to the rich solar energy resources in Turkey, these panels generated around 75 – 95 MW during the peak months of July and August. From April 2013 to February 2016, Prokon has generated 1,835 MWh from the panels in total, and it even sold the excess clean energy back to the national grid of Turkey. Through February 2016, Prokon has obtained a benefit of $ 250,000 from the solar-power project.

Benefiting from the renewable energy, Prokon has taken the development and production of solar equipment as its new business. The company has currently developed a solar-tracking system, which can make the panel rotate and "follow" the sun to maximize the absorption of solar energy and produce 15% – 18% more power.

Promoting Energy Recycling among Private Enterprises

The energy intensity[①] of Turkey is around twice that of the European Union average. The Turkish government is committed to reducing the energy intensity of the country to improve the competitiveness of Turkish enterprises. With the support of an energy-saving project led by the Islamic Development Bank, a Turkish cement company named Batlsöke Çimento installed a waste heat recovery system at its plant near Aydln. This system utilizes the heat produced in the process of producing cement to generate electricity with a capacity of 5.5 MW. Up to 2015, it can meet 30% of the plant's electricity needs, and save $ 9,000 in costs per day or $ 3 million per year. Batlsöke Çimento has decided to build a new plant near this one and install a waste heat recovery system for the new plant as well.

All in all, the promotion of renewable energy, energy conservation, and emission reduction has a long way to go. During this process, the Islamic Development Bank supports Turkey to succeed in taking a crucial step.

Arab Bank for Economic Development in Africa

The Arab Bank for Economic Development in Africa (ABEDA) was established pursuant to the resolution of the 6th Arab Summit Conference at Algiers in November 1973 and began its operations in March 1975. Its headquarters are located in Khartoum, the capital of the Republic of Sudan. ABEDA is an independent financial institution, which has full international legal status and autonomy in administrative and financial matters. It is owned by 18 member countries of the League of Arab States (LAS). ABEDA aims at strengthening economic, financial, and technical cooperation between Arab and African countries and the embodiment of Arab-African solidarity on the basis of equality and friendship. The Board of Governors is the highest authority in the Bank, which consists of a Governor and a deputy Governor from each member state. The Governors are usually the Ministers of Finance of the member states. The Board of Directors of the Bank is composed of 9 permanent members of the 9 largest contributors to the Bank's capital and two non-permanent members from

① Energy intensity is an indicator measuring a country's energy efficiency, which indicates the energy required per unit of GDP.

other countries. The Board of Governors appoints the Director General of the Bank, who is also the chief executive officer responsible for the management of the business of the Bank.

The year 2015 represented the first year of the Seventh Five-Year Plan (2015 – 2019) of the Bank. This plan aims at further promoting the role of the Bank as a developmental financial institution, responding to developmental needs of African countries and contributing to poverty alleviation and the realization of sustainable development. The Seventh Five-Year Plan also aims at expanding finance to private sector projects, encouraging Arab investments in Africa, financing Arab exports to African countries, and providing technical assistance. In addition to these objectives, the Bank will continue its contribution to the relief of the debt burden of African countries receiving aid from the Bank.

Main Business Data

In 2015, loan commitments and allocations to sectors were essentially based on the principles of the Seventh Five-Year Plan and the priorities expressed by the governments of the beneficiary countries. ABEDA's commitments during 2015 stood at $ 410 million and exceeded those of 2014 by 205%. Of the financing commitments in 2015, $ 200 million was earmarked for the public sector to finance 19 development projects, an increase of 4.2% compared to 2014. $ 50 million was earmarked for the private sector, extending lines of credit to 4 African banks. $ 150 million was allocated to finance Arab exports to African countries, and $ 10 million was allocated to technical assistance operations, an increase of 25% compared to the previous year.

The commitments in the public sector covered 4 fields, namely, agriculture and rural development, infrastructure, and the social sector and small and micro loans. The infrastructure sector received $ 112.8 million, representing 56.4% of the total. 53.2% of this sum was distributed to the roads sub-sector, 37.1% to the water supply and sanitation sub-sector, and 9.7% to an electricity project. Commitments for agriculture and rural development sector in 2015 amounted to $ 35.6 million, about 17.8% of the total, consisting of two rural electrification projects and one rural development project. Commitments in the social sector amounted to $ 46.6 million, or about 23.3% of the total projects commitments, and was earmarked to 4 education projects and one health project. Commitments in the small and micro loans amounted to $ 5 million, or about 2.5% of the total, was for anti-poverty by the government.

The ABEDA continued to devote growing attention to the private sector in its funding operations due to the important role played by that sector in the economic development of the countries eligible for ABEDA assistance. Thus, during the period 1975 – 2014, the number of credits targeting the private sector totaled 45. The net total volume of these commitments totaled $ 116. 931 million, benefiting small projects in the industrial, agriculture and rural development, and transport sectors. Besides, the Bank extended a total of $ 50 million of credit lines to 3 multilateral financing institutions and to a transnational African Bank. This initiative mainly served small- and medium-sized private projects and infrastructure projects, aiming at creating jobs, increasing income, and reducing poverty in the region.

The Bank accorded a special priority to the promotion of trade exchanges between Arab and African countries. An amount of $ 150 million was allocated to finance Arab exports to African countries. ABEDA also cooperated with other developmental financial institutions, such as the African Development Bank, the OPEC Fund for International Development (OFID), the Islamic Development Bank Group, and the International Development Association (IDA). Since the beginning of the implementation of Arab Exports Financing Program and through the end of 2015, approvals totaled $ 399. 5 million, of which $ 187 million was used to finance 29 operations benefiting 10 African countries: Tanzania, Guinea, Mauritius, Zimbabwe, Seychelles, Zambia, Cote d'Ivoire, Kenya, Senegal, and Gambia.

As for the technical assistance operations, ABEDA provided African countries with training courses, expert support, and equipment. The Bank also organized forums and meetings for economic actors in Africa and the Arab world. The number of technical assistance operations approved during 2015 totaled 35 worth $ 10 million. The sum approved for feasibility studies amounted to $ 3. 785 million to finance 9 studies: 7 in the infrastructure sector and two in the agriculture and rural development sector. In addition, 26 institutional support operations were approved at a total cost of $ 6. 215 million. These operations included 14 regional training courses in the fields of procurement of goods and services, finance, planning, funding, agriculture, management, and human resources development. The institutional support operations during 2015 also included financing the services of Arab experts in the fields of water, environment, agriculture and ports, supporting Women's activities, organizing the Arab-African trade fair, etc.

Considering the nature of the funded projects and the economic realities of the borrowing countries, ABEDA continued to extend loans in concessionary terms in 2015.

The weighted-average interest rate charged on ABEDA's loans stood at 1. 14% in 2015, a little higher than 1. 11% in 2014, while the weighted average of the loan period was 29. 94 years in 2015 compared to 29. 47 years in 2014. The weighted average for the loan's grace period was 9. 48 years in 2015, representing a slight decrease from the average of 9. 70 years recorded in 2014.

The net assets of ABEDA increased by $ 117. 1 million during 2015. However, it is worth noting that the net revenue decreased from $ 189. 2 million in 2014 to $ 15. 4 million in 2015, due to the decline in market value of securities portfolios as a result of poor performance in global financial markets during 2015.

During 2015, ABEDA co-financed 14 projects out of 19 approved projects with other Arab financing institutions, such as Saudi Fund for Development, Kuwait Fund for Arab Economic Development, Abu Dhabi Fund for Development, and OPEC Fund for International Development. The percentage of ABEDA's financing in relation to the total cost of these projects ($ 645. 422 million) stood at 24. 92%. The contribution of other Arab funds amounted to about 61. 62%, while the local governments and beneficiary entities contributed about 13. 46%.

Coordination with other development financing institutions, particularly the Arab ones, has always been at the top of ABEDA's agenda, to enhance project effectiveness and increase development impacts. In 2015, ABEDA participated in high level meetings that Arab Coordination Group Institution, Development Assistance Committee (DAC), and Organization of Economic Cooperation and Development (OECD) held in January, IFAD (International Fund for Agricultural Development) Board of Governors Meetings in February, and the Annual Meetings of the World Bank Group and the International Monetary Fund in October. These meetings provided valuable opportunities for ABEDA to coordinate activities and programs, make co-financing arrangements, and to experience a new revolution of ideas.

As an important developmental financial institution in the Arab region and Africa, ABEDA provides key financial support and technical assistance to the economic development of African countries, building a bridge for Arab-African cooperation. It actively promoted the participation of Arab capital in African development and achieved both economic and social benefits.

Development Bank of Latin America

Faced with the loss of economic dynamism in Latin America in 2015, the Development Bank of Latin America (CAF) took actions to step up its anti-cyclical role with fast-disbursing and contingent operations of $ 2. 4 billion, having more than $ 12. 2 billion in total approvals over the course of the year. This level of operations confirms the institution as one of the main sources of multilateral financing in the region, especially in infrastructure. As one of the 23 development banks involved in the International Development Finance Club (IDFC), CAF continued to deepen its international relationships and build connections with an extensive global network of universities, think tanks, and financial and development institutions. In addition to becoming an important link between Latin America and the rest of the world, and the CAF plays a significant role in international development, with specific progress in environmental and climate change issues.

In 2015, CAF's approvals in the region hit a new milestone: $ 12. 2 billion. The shareholder countries approved a paid-in capital increase of $ 4. 5 billion. This increase will allow CAF to provide up to $ 100 billion in loans to the region over 2016 – 2022.

CAF signed agreements with the non-profit organization Fundación Scholas Ocurrentes and collaborated with the "100,000 Strong in the Americas" campaign, with the aim of promoting education and social inclusion among Latin American youth. The institution received the ratification of its ratings by the main credit rating agencies and completed 13 bond issues in the most prestigious capital markets for a total amount of $ 3 million. Cooperation with Cuban institutions and academia created technology improvements within Cuba.

Main Business Data

CAF classifies its investments into the following categories:

Marketable Securities

Trading marketable securities are mainly bought and held with the purpose of selling them in the short term.

Loans

CAF grants short-, medium- and long-term loans to finance projects, working capital, trade activities, and to undertake feasibility studies for investment opportunities. These loans are to both public and private entities, with the intention of funding development and integration programs and projects in stockholder countries. For credit risk purposes, CAF classifies its portfolio into sovereign and non-sovereign loans.

1) Sovereign loans: include loans granted to national, regional, or local governments or decentralized institutions and other loans fully guaranteed by national governments.

2) Non-sovereign loans: include loans granted to corporate and financial sectors, among others, which are not guaranteed by national governments (public and private sectors).

Equity Investments

CAF invests in equity securities of companies and funds in strategic sectors with the objective of promoting the development of such companies and funds and their participation in the securities markets to serve as a catalytic agent in attracting resources to stockholder countries.

Borrowings

The borrowings account includes those obligations with local or foreign financial institutions and commercial banks which are recorded at amortized cost, except for some borrowings that are hedged using interest rate swaps as an economic hedge. The up-front costs and fees related to the issuance of borrowings denominated in US dollars are deferred and reported in the balance sheet as a direct deduction from the face amount of borrowings and amortized during the term of the borrowings as interest expenses.

Credit Ratings

The credit rating agencies, including Fitch and Moody's, have recognized the excellent solvency of CAF, which is based on the strengthening of equity that was consolidated through the expansion of the shareholder base and support by the shareholders, through continued capital increases, and greater diversification of the credit portfolio (see Table 3. 1). In fact, CAF ratings are among the highest of debt issuers in Latin America.

Table 3. 1　CAF Credit Ratings by Varieus Rating Agencies

Credit Rating Agencies	Credit Ratings (Long Term)
Fitch Ratings	AA –
Japan Credit Rating Agency	AA
Moody's Investor Service	Aa3
Standard & Poor's	AA –

Highlights of the Year

In 2015, under the deceleration of Latin American economies, CAF approved 152 operations worth a total of $ 12. 2 billion in financing. Compared to previous years, due to the decline in prices of raw materials, lower availability, rising cost of international funding, and the slowdown in emerging economies like China, the activity level this year is relatively low. Facing this situation, CAF reached a consensus with its shareholder countries to prioritize freely available budgetary support operations and to promote the investment in the public sector. Overall, it has achieved positive results.

CAF's operational management in 2015 was characterized by the institution's flexibility, financial strength, and the counter-cyclical role it played. With the intention of improving the quality and efficiency of its interventions, CAF put into action several strategic and operational initiatives. In this regard, a corporate strategy for the private sector was drafted over the course of the year. The main components of the strategy include playing a central role in the generation of high-skilled labor and high value-added industries to increase productivity and innovation. To do this, 3 crosscutting platforms—transport infrastructure, energy and financial development—and the agro-industrial sector were defined as strategic areas of intervention, with which CAF maintained its commitment to social inclusion and the preservation of the environment.

At the operational level, CAF is actively using new mechanisms to attract resources from third parties and bring together multiple stakeholders. In 2015, co-financing for sovereign projects totaled $ 270 million, with proceeds from the French Development Agency (AFD) and the OPEC Fund for International Development (OFID). Furthermore, in countries like Uruguay and Colombia, CAF drove the development of innovative products such as thematic investment vehicles. In Colombia, for example, the institution was able to channel $ 411. 7 million from Colombian pension funds with a debt instrument to promote the development of key projects aimed at closing the infrastructure gap and supporting national economic growth. With the intention of addressing demand for infrastructure project financing, CAF established a subsidiary called CAF-Asset Management Company (CAFAM) in 2015. The objective is to manage and administer funds from investors, directly or indirectly, and focus them on projects in which the institution has expertise and comparative advantage, such as infrastructure projects executed via PPP or exclusively private operations.

CAF continued its process of expanding partnership with the countries of Central A-
merica and the Caribbean. In this regard, the institution embraced Barbados as the
nineteenth shareholder country this year. The geographical expansion of interventions
and the variation of operations pose challenges to the Bank. Facing this situation,
CAF launched the optimization process of its main credit processes. This is intended
to strengthen the institution's traditional advantages such as agility, flexibility, and
costumer orientation, reinforcing the prioritization of operations that contribute to regional development.

Chapter 4　National DFIs in High
Income Countries

KfW

In addition to being committed to improving the living conditions of people in Germany, Europe, and around the world, KfW is also devoted to raising People's living standards in all other social and economic aspects. For KfW, the core theme for 2015 was globalization, with a focus on securing market competitiveness in Germany and Europe and promoting technological advancement. Therefore, KfW has been invested in thriving technology companies and actively involved in Juncker's investment program. Another challenge for KfW in 2015 was to provide shelter for refugees from war and terrorism.

Main Business Data

When KfW was founded, its initial equity came from the budgets of the federal government (80%) and from state governments (20%). In FY 2015, KfW provided a total of € 79. 5 billion in lending. Of that total, € 50. 5 billion was used in domestic promotional business conducted by KfW SME Bank and KfW Municipal and Private Client Bank, € 27. 9 billion was used in international business conducted by KfW IPEX-Bank and KfW's subsidiary DEG, and another € 1. 1 billion was used in business sector capital markets (see Figure 4. 1).

In FY 2015, KfW's consolidated profit was € 2,171 million (excluding KfW's assistance), mainly due to rising foreign credit rates, the appreciation of the dollar, and long-term favorable financing conditions for KfW. In 2015, KfW's total assets reached € 503 billion, its total loans reached € 447 billion, and the total equity reached € 25. 2 billion. In 2015, KfW's tier 1 capital ratio was 18. 3% and the total capital ratio was 18. 4%, an increase of 3 − 4 percentage points over the same period in 2014.

KfW Group registered very strong demand for its financing products again in financial

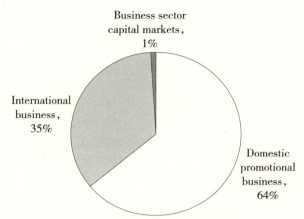

Business sector
capital markets,
1%

International
business,
35%

Domestic
promotional
business,
64%

Figure 4. 1 KfW Investment Pie Chart

year 2016. The volume of promotional commitments rose to a total of € 81 billion (2015: € 79. 3 billion, +2%). With a volume of commitments totalling € 55. 1 billion (2015: € 50. 5 billion, +9%), domestic promotional business spurred the growth of the German economy. Among the total volume, € 21. 4 billion went to the new business in the Mittelstandsbank business sector, € 10. 7 billion in the environment and energy priority sector. Growth was very strong in the housing priority area in particular. Commitments reached a volume of € 20. 8 billion. The increase is above all due to very strong demand for housing finance, combined with robust demand for finance from industry.

Highlights of the Year

The year 2015 was a time of accelerated globalization and technological advancement. Thinking globally and acting locally, KfW focused on three areas, namely "globalization and scientific and technological progress", "climate change and the environment", and "individual development".

Technological Progress and Innovation in Production

In 2015, KfW vowed to support SMEs with loans of € 20. 4 billion, a new high compared to € 19. 9 billion in 2014. Of these loans, € 9. 3 billion worth of loans was meant to help SMEs with environmental and climate protection, accounting for 46% of the total. In addition, KfW attached great importance to ecological protection and renewable energy. It also advocated for continuous innovations in production, which has been an important philosophy in the development of medical technologies. For example, FIT, a medical corporation in Bavaria, took 10 years to automate its production lines and realize 3D printing, which made its production more efficient and optimized.

KfW began to support FIT two years ago and has made an important contribution in bettering its production. Actually, through KfW's "ERP Innovation Program", SMEs like FIT can now apply for low interest rate loans. In 2015, KfW supplied € 620 million through the "ERP Innovation Program" to support production innovation of SMEs. In addition, through the "ERP Start-up Fund", KfW also funded many biotech start-ups to increase their equity capital.

Climate Change and the Environment

Through its subsidiary DEG, KfW supports sustainable development of developing countries. A German company Mobisol has been constantly receiving financial support from KfW to invest in distributed solar systems in Africa. The businesses of Mobisol have extended to Tanzania, Rwanda, Kenya, etc. African users can purchase solar home systems in installments. About 150,000 people can access power through Mobisol products, which has greatly improved the lives of local people.

Helping developing countries improve transportation systems, climate, and the environment is one of KfW's contributions to addressing global climate and environmental concerns. China and Brazil both face the problem of rapid population growth. low-efficiency transport infrastructure and severe air pollution are common in big cities. In Brazil, KfW and the Brazilian Development Bank have collaborated to build an environmentally-friendly transport system in big cities, with a joint investment amounting to $ 1 billion. In China, KfW has provided up to € 15 million in assistance to the "Intelligent Transport System" project in Huainan, China.

Individual Development and Refugee Aid

In 2015, KfW invested € 50. 5 billion for domestic economic construction, nearly a 6% increase compared to 2014. These domestic projects include both SME development and individual housing construction. In 2015, KfW's support to private clients reached € 19. 1 billion, an increase of 13% from 2014, with assistance in the housing sector amounting to € 16. 5 billion. In fact, housing has been a focus of KfW. In FY 2015, this issue was closely linked to refugee and social unity issues. KfW invested a total of € 3 billion in direct refugee assistance domestically and internationally.

From September 2015 to January 2016, KfW successively supplied € 1. 5 billion to the construction of refugee homes in Germany, from which about 150,000 people benefited. At the same time, through the KfW Development Bank, KfW DEG, and

KfW Stiftung, KfW has also provided refugee-related support to countries with development cooperation with Germany. The support includes € 90 million for 36 refugee-related projects in Syria (eg. school building, construction of the Jordan River water supply system) and € 875 million for crisis-prone and border areas.

2015 was a bumper year for KfW in which it launched a number of projects to support innovation, development, and climate protection in Germany, Europe, and around the world. But that year also posed the biggest challenge for decades, as the latest influx of refugees and their social inclusion presented a long-term problem. KfW is planning to invest in 70 refugee-related projects involving 20 countries worth a total of € 1.4 billion. KfW is currently committed to 38 projects worth € 570 million directly related to refugees. KfW also said it would give sustained attention and long-term support to the refugee issue.

| Column 4 – 1 | Observing KfW's SME Financing from the View of Legislation |

Financing SMEs is a notoriously difficult, but crucial aspect of economic development. As such, many countries have adopted various policies to provide funding to SMEs, usually by combining fiscal and other economic policies. However, how do the development financing institutions actually guide commercial banks to support SMEs? In the following, we describe how Germany's development financing institutions KfW approaches this problem from a legislative point of view.

KfW, established based on *Kreditanstalt fuer Wiederaufbau Law* issued in 1948, is a development financing institution wholly owned by the federal government and state governments. Since KfW was established, *Kreditanstalt fuer Wiederaufbau Law* has been revised many times, providing KfW with more and more autonomy in its operation and business development. As the first article of this Act stipulates, "the Federal Republic provides guarantees for the loans KfW offered, the bonds KfW issued, the fixed-rate forward contracts or options KfW signed, other loans KfW acquired, and the third-party loans KfW clearly guaranteed". The German government gave a national guarantee to KfW through legislation, which built a good credit basis in the capital market for KfW.

As a state-owned development financial institution, supporting SMEs is a very important function of KfW. The 2 (1) article in *Kreditanstalt fuer Wiederaufbau Law* stipulates, according to national authorization, KfW has the power to promote SMEs, freelancers, start-ups housing, environment protection, infrastructure, technical progress, and so on. The first priority of all those financing support objectives is lending to SMEs, freelancers, and start-ups. In order to promote the development of SMEs in Germany, KfW provides long-term preferential credit to their domestic and foreign investment projects.

For implementing the above objectives better, in August 2003, KfW merged with Deutsche Ausgleichs Bank (hereafter referred to as DtA) who was in charge of SMEs' financial business. Founded in 1950, DtA was a national institution whose primary responsibility was issuing loans to SMEs and start-ups projects and executing the functions of regulating banks. After the merger, KfW and DtA transferred their SME business to the newly established KfW-Mittelstands-bank, which specialized in providing financial services and legal protection to SMEs. Article 2 (2) of *Kreditanstalt fuer Wiederaufbau Law* stipulates that, it is KfW's government-sponsored enterprise, KfW-Mittelstands-Bank's duty, to provide financing support to SMEs, freelancers, and start-ups. This article defined the duty of KfW's KfW-Mittelstands-bank, and the "bank-in-bank" management model that optimized KfW's organizational structure, enabling KfW-Mittelstands-bank to improve their operating efficiency, especially when providing financing services to SMEs, freelancers, and start-ups.

So, how does KfW guide commercial banks to support SMEs' development? Article 3 (1) of *Kreditanstalt fuer Wiederaufbau Law* commands that, credit institutions and other financing institutions have to offer financing services aimed at SMEs, freelancers, and start-ups. This article means that KfW must interact with SMEs directly and provide financing services to them through fully market-based commercial banks. Depending on government credit, KfW raises money from the capital market, and in some cases, the government even gives appropriate interest subsidies. Because of KfW's high credit rating and low financing costs, coupled with the interest subsidies given by the government, KfW is able to provide money to lending banks and SMEs with very low interest rates. In practice, KfW usually provides the money by lending; the first choice is local banks (usually chooses SMEs' major holding banks as the lending banks). Then KfW issues loans to SMEs through lending banks and in the end, it is the lending banks that undertake the final risk (but in some cases, they undertake the risk together). Thus, commercial financial institutions are encouraged to participate widely in supporting SMEs' development.

NRW

North Rhine-Westfalen Bank (NRW BANK) is a development bank owned by the North Rhine-Westphalia state and has supported local construction in the state since 2002. In 2015, the rapid increase of refugees and the demand for digitalization of German society had become the most challenging issues for NRW. In 2015, the Bank had over € 9. 7 billion in committed investments, compared to € 8. 9 billion in 2014. In 2015, NRW Bank undoubtedly reached a higher level in promoting the German economy.

Main Business Data

According to the financial report of NRW, it had € 141. 2 billion in total assets, € 20. 63 billion in equity funds, € 726 million in capital reserves, € 546 million in interest and commission income, € 364 million in operating income, and 1,309 employees. In the capital markets sector, NRW adjusted its operations and reduced the planned total assets and business volume in response to the financial market crisis in 2015. At the same time, because of its good credit rating and active investment activities, NRW could issue bonds under relatively favorable conditions, thereby solidifying its long-term capital base. NRW's commission income for fiscal year 2015 was € 109. 5 million, generating an increase of € 6. 2 million from the previous year.

Highlights of the Year

NRW mainly promoted development in the areas of housing & living, seed & growth, and development & protection. In 2015, the total net volume of new commitments in the three fields was € 9. 677 billion and the volumes in each field were € 5. 148 billion, € 3. 344 billion, and € 1. 185 billion (see Figure 4. 2).

Housing & Living

NRW designed its Housing & Living programs to support, in particular, the creation of affordable, high-quality housing for residents. In 2015, NRW separately invested € 1. 6 billion and € 2. 8 billion in the areas of Housing and Municipalities. In the field of social housing, NRW mainly focused on low- income households. In order to fulfill the high demand of social housing, NRW supported not only the renovation of aged buildings, but also new construction. In response to the growing num-

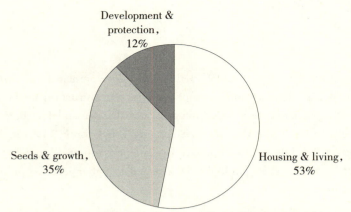

Figure 4. 2   Proportion of the NRW Promotion Offerings

ber of refugees and the resulting challenges for the housing market, a new social housing service project was launched last year to encourage investors to create and provide housing for refugees.

For example, in order to provide support for the accommodation of refugees, a separate promotion program NRW "Refugee Housing" was launched, which was a municipal program supported by North Rhine-Westphalian local and regional governments. This program offers interest-free loans with a maturity of 20 years to help refugees acquire housing with modernized facilities. 11 months before fiscal year 2015, NRW had already provided € 122 million worth of commitments for this program.

Seeds & Growth

In 2015, NRW offered € 2. 7 billion to improve small- and medium-sized enterprises and another € 582 million to support "start-ups". Two promotion programs of NRW provided loans for small- and medium-sized enterprises and the self-employed. NRW's low- interest loans allow the SMEs to finance or refinance. In addition, NRW supports promising start-ups by purchasing their shares via a separate fund.

Development and Protection

Climate change and environmental protection are worldwide concerns. In 2015, NRW invested a total amount of € 1 billion in environment, climate, and energy, which accounts for about one third of the reported net volume of new commitments. However, in comparison to the year 2014, the proportion declined 22%. In terms of energy, NRW has focused on energy saving and energy efficiency in private companies and public programs through offering low- interest loans for relative investments.

NRW launched projects for upgrading electric vehicles and co-generation of heat and power in North Rhine-Westphalia. NRW also injected significant capital in energy infrastructure construction and water-saving systems. Additionally, it has invested € 4 million and € 144 million to support innovation and education, respectively.

CDC

Main Business Date

The year 2015 was fruitful for Caisse des Dépôts et de Consignations (CDC): annual income grew by 3.9% and its capital had an increase of € 2 billion. The savings deposit business of the group had generated more than € 500 million of profits, along with the Group's subsidiaries and strategic equity, which created benefits of € 864 million. In addition, it also set up a savings fund which made significant contributions to French social and economic development. The volume of loans increased from € 14.4 billion in 2014 to € 21.1 billion in 2015 (+3%), of which € 17.2 billion was allocated to subsidize residential housing and € 3.1 billion was allocated to local public authorities.

Highlights of the Year

Since its establishment in 1816, CDC has focused on 4 major themes: ecological and energy transition, digital transition, population and social transition, and land resource transition. CDC is an advocate for the public interest, which has devoted itself to promoting socio-economic development, improving living environments, and sharing scientific and technological achievements. Furthermore, with frequent communication and cooperation with the world's major economies and the acceleration of globalization, CDC Group is also looking toward the world and attempting to leave footprints of the France in a broader area. Here are some highlights of the Group's accomplishments in major areas:

Ecological and Energy Transition

Ecology and energy transformation is a major theme in the 21st Century. As a green asset leader, CDC reacted to global warming and has been contributing its wisdom and strength. Savings Fund issued a total of € 3 billion in loans in 2015. In addition to interest-free green development loans and purification, CDC also launched loans targeting the protection of biodiversity. CDC engaged in improving the financial environment (interest-free) for residential renovation projects as well as in financing the innovative green companies with € 1,260 million.

In response to the Paris Climate Change Conference (COP 21), the CDC Group committed to reducing the carbon footprint of its listed companies by 20% before 2020, while reducing building energy consumption by 38% before 2030.

Digital Transition

CDC, as one of the main driving forces of French national modernization, has been encouraging the development of national digitalization and has never slackened in the development of new technologies:

CDC has been actively promoting the construction of intelligent cities and intelligent campuses, providing security services for local administrative organizations, such as the materialization of the transaction process, the preservation of data, and the creation of a data block chain technology experiment for transaction security. It is a real scientific and technological revolution for humans. In addition, the CDC was one of the main implementers of the French High Speed Internet Program, which aims to achieve full coverage of high-speed wireless networks by 2022. In order to develop the digital economy, it has been encouraging enterprises to actively innovate and respond to the French Public Technology Initiative (PIA), thus these enterprises could get the support of the Ecological Science and Technology Fund under the PIA.

Population and Social Transition

Adhering to the concept of "better living together", the CDC is present in all aspects of French life. It manages retirement plans for one fifth of the population in France and initiated pension reform in 2014, loosening the pension system in France. CDC established personal training accounts for the benefit of 23 million French people to help them keep abreast of their own interests and access to training resources. On the other hand, the CDC Group is very concerned about the pension economy and specifically set up a "silver honorary loans to the economy" for 42 plans by 2016 (interest free). At the same time, it invested in urban transformation plans to promote intergenerational peaceful coexistence.

Land Resources Transition

In 2015, the CDC Group coordinated the development of local and metropolitan areas in order to increase regional attractiveness. It did this by adjusting its institutions to local geography and strengthening its local team construction. In 2015, CDC and major administrative agencies (cities, provinces, and regions) signed more than 40 framework agreements, and CDC also participated in residential construction, vigorously increasing employment and improving People's living. In November 2015, the Group and the National Urban Refurbishment Agency (ANRU) jointly invested a total of € 250 million to achieve the urban community housing renovation project.

On reorganization of regional management and public institutions, CDC invested € 1 billion in the "French Tourism Resource Development" platform to increase regional attractiveness. In the improvement of housing, the CDC built and acquired 134,000 residential buildings in one year (+7 %) of the total number of housing units, and provided heating to 311,000 homes. Its transitional housing program was expected to establish 35,000 housing units (a total investment of € 6. 3 billion) by 2020, of which 10,307 houses would be ordered by the end of 2015 and the construction would officially begin, involving 800 sites. The total investment would reach € 1. 5 billion.

Global Strategy

The year of 2015 saw the CDC Group deploy its global development strategy. It focused on maintaining relationships with international investors and public institutions and was actively involved in initiatives to encourage long-term investment. It was also one of the founders of Long-Term Investor Club (LTIC, with 18 international organizations), the European Long-Term Investors Association (ELTI, which has 27 European Union member countries), and the World Bank Forum.

CDC Group has been investing in two international funds for renewable energy projects over the past 15 years: Margaret and InfraMed. Until now, the first one has received € 287 million to finance 10 projects in France and Europe, worth a total of € 4. 7 billion with a leverage ratio of 16. The second has supported 4 projects (worth € 226 million with a leverage ratio of 19) in Egypt, Jordan, and Turkey.

These are some of the achievements of the CDC Group, whose projects were executed steadily and carefully. In 2016, the Group has underlined 6 major directions: First, to promote economic development and environmental energy transformation, it will take a more active strategy. Precisely, in the next 5 years, CDC will continue to increase investment. The total investment will be as high as € 26. 3 billion. The CDC will allocate € 100 billion in loans and also launch the 200th anniversary of the program. This includes providing € 3 billion to finance residential and environmental energy transformation. Second, to strengthen the Group's international influence, CDC International Capital will establish a global partnership and will further narrow the relationship with the French Agency for Development and vigorously develop the Juncker plan to strengthen cooperation between the EU national banks. Third, the Group will enthusiastically pursue economic transformation. On one hand, it has implemented the "two-level roadmap" to achieve eco-energy transformation. On the other hand, the Group has extended the concept of environmental protection to financial accounts (entrusted management, innovative financing, private equity and bond trading). Fourth, in order to promote the digital transition, CDC is engaged in the construction of smart cities and the preparation of the 2024 Olympic Games. It will pour investment into digital infrastructure and data block chain technology. Fifth, CDC will accelerate the transformation of land, especially the Paris. Last, the Group will promote population and social transition, including the introduction of personal accounts and business accounts (beginning January 1, 2017) and the establishment of social collective economic fund.

Column 4 -2   CDC Leading Innovative Development

CDC, founded in 1816 and governed by the French parliament, is the only institution in Europe that is supported by the public and provides financial service independently. As a policy development bank, CDC has been devoted to innovative and sustainable development. It always puts national interests and People's interests first. As a public investor, CDC provides financing channels in the form of long-term loans to innovative capital borrowers. CDC has made great contributions in promoting French companies' development, mitigating housing problems, and facilitating energy transformation. The CDC played a crucial role in influencing French economic and social development.

The year of 2016 was crucial for France. On one hand, constant terrorist attacks increased uncertainties about the French economy, as well as the increasing unemployment rate, high labor costs, constant outsourcing of enterprises, decreasing investments, and economic stagnation. On the other hand, the French government was busy preparing the Olympic bid. On 9 June, all institutions and innovators were called on to offer ideas for the 2024 Olympic bid. They expected to innovate in 5 areas: smart cities, smart organizations, smart experience, smart trip, and smart sport. CDC, as a developmental financial institution, actively responds to the nation's call and plays a leading role in supporting the major fields and innovative enterprises, thereby promoting economic and social development.

Land Use Transition

On 10 June, in order to increase the attraction of urban centers and to consolidate economic growth, the mayor of Cahors, the President of Grand Cahors, and the CDC Director of Territory and Network signed an agreement to build the first national demonstration center. The three sides decided to apply pilot cities and implement a series of innovation programs to revitalize second- and third-tier cities with populations between 15,000 and 100,000.

CDC chose 10 voluntary pilot cities including Cahors, Vierzon, and Nevers to carry out a 1-year pilot program. In Cahors, the focus would be reorganizing the Chateau du roi Street shopping center, building movie theatres around Charles de Gaulle Square, and developing tourism in Pont Valentre. In addition, CDC would increase its assistance to the housing improvement and urban renewal project that the President of Grand Cahors had promised to support. To ensure putting 500 renovated houses into market, CDC designed urban renewal programs, followed up on these projects, and stimulated the local financial institutions' investment enthusiasm. There were two phases of the pilot program: collecting urban center reconstruction designs worldwide; and carrying out experiments and summarizing the results, then generalizing the design to other similar medium-sized cities.

Environmental Power Transition

On 7 June, the first deep geothermal power station in the world was completed in French Grand East. This project, initiated by CDC, Roquette Group, and Strasbourg Electricity, cost € 55 million. It was funded by the French Department of Environment and Energy and the Grand East. The power station was estimated to produce 24 MW of heat per year (100,000 W per hour), which could provide 27,000 houses' heat supply. This would reduce carbon dioxide emissions by nearly 39,000 tons each year, which roughly equals the emissions of 25,000 cars each year. Additionally, since the application of the biomass furnace, the proportion energy coming from renewable sources increased from 50% to 75% (50% biomass plus 25% deep geothermal power). This project indicated substantial progress in the transition of French environmental power and its unique scientific progress in deep geothermal power exploitation. The achievement of protecting the French environment was recognized worldwide.

Digital Transition

On 21 June, CDC, along with Banque Nationale de Paris (BNP) Safety Department, Euroclear, and Euronext, etc. , under the support of Paris Europlace, announced an agreement to investigate blockchain infrastructure construction for European small- and medium-enterprises. This program would increase the safety and transparency of transactions, thereby helping small- and medium-enterprises enter the capital market.

The first priority of this agreement was to make full use of the financing capabilities and technical skills of their partners to promote innovation. Companies could apply blockchain technology to innovative project design and development. Meanwhile, fund raising efficiency of small- and medium-enterprises would increase as a result of decreasing transaction costs, and safety would be ensured. Moreover, blockchain technology significantly simplified transaction procedures, thereby strengthening the European securities trading registration and ensuring the executive efficiency of real time settlement and distribution.

Social Human Resources Transition

On 21 June, the French Labor Minister, the Chairman of the Investment Committee, and the CDC general manager together celebrated the smooth implementation of the project "Vocational Training and Employment Partnership" (Partenariat de Formation Professionnelle et d'emploi, PFPE), which was under the "Future Investment Program" . CDC was in full charge of the project. The initial capital, € 126 million, would provide financing for 15 innovation projects. For example, the project Tech'Indus aimed at establishing a school that trains industrial talents had 3 main ideas: build professional training platforms for innovation in the fields of advanced electronics and automation; build a physical campus that has both college and continuing education; organize long- and short-term training programs to foster the collaboration between university and industry. However, project "Open Source University" (OSU) proposed to set up open source universities in various cities to provide training programs in the area of open source software. OSU aimed at solving the issue of qualified labor shortage due to fast-changing requirements of jobs. By establishing long-term cooperation between enterprises and training institutions (colleges, high schools, and private training organizations), HR management and the content of training courses could develop synergistically. This plan was beneficial to both enterprises and employees. Enterprises could predict economic changes while employees could learn specialized skills and improve their competence.

In fact, PFPE was an innovation on the basis of "Alternating vocational training investment". It encouraged creative enterprises and training institutions to make individualized programs for people who face career moves. Through layers of screening, shortlisted programs would receive funding from CDC. As one of the major propellers of French human resources transition, CDC launched PFPE to solve the issue of low employment, which announced the arriving of continuing education era. CDC proposed to cover the shortage of career education inside school by continuing education, and collected innovative training programs nationwide. The ultimate goal was to make job seekers better fit in the job and industry and improve their career development, meanwhile facilitating enterprises to better adapt to the rapidly changing economic environment, thereby promoting positive economic development for all of society.

Japan Bank for International Cooperation

In 2015, Japan Bank for International Cooperation (JBIC), a policy financial institution wholly-owned by the Japanese government, actively promoted investment in the fields of resources, energy, and infrastructure, helped Japanese SMEs to develop overseas markets, and achieved good results. It basically played the supplementary role for other financial institutions, ensuring the stability of Japan's energy resources and improving the international competitiveness of Japanese industry.

Main Business Data

After integration in fiscal year 2015 (April 1, 2015—March 31, 2016), the total assets of the Japan Bank for International Cooperation were 17.08 trillion yen (about $ 170.9 billion), total value securities was 236.6 billion yen (approximately $ 2.3 billion), total liabilities were 1,322.33 billion yen (approximately $ 119.8 billion), guarantees and deposits were 2,397.4 billion yen (approximately $ 23.3 billion), and the Bank participated in 298 projects. Borrowing and corporate bonds totaled 9,536.9 and 2,721.9 billion yen respectively. Regular profits were 240 billion yen (about $ 2.3 billion), of which 42.3 billion yen was from domestic investment, 27.5 billion yen was from Australian investment, 54.7 billion yen was from Asian investment, 59.8 billion yen was from Europe, Africa and the Middle East,

345

and 55. 8 billion yen was from North America, Central America, and South America (see Figure 4. 3). JBIC was rated A1 by Moody's Ratings and A + by Standard & Poor's Ratings.

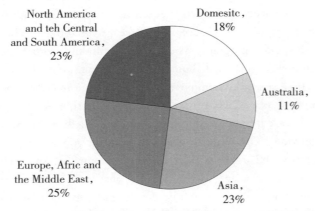

Figure 4. 3   **The Regional Distribution of JBIC Investments in Fiscal Year 2015**

Highlights of the Year

Overseas Resource Investment

In the field of resource investment, JBIC participated in 12 related projects with guarantees of 489. 9 billion yen, which was lower than the previous year. The following are reasons that help to account for this difference. First, Japanese enterprises were more cautious about investment when resource prices such as oil had been falling. Second, there had been more large-scale investments in resource projects in the previous year but a decline this year. Of the 12 related projects, key projects included investment in Abu Dhabi National Oil Company to strengthen relations with major resource countries; providing project loans to Trinidad and Tobago to help in the area of national risk management; and active participation in projects in favor of reducing liquefied natural gas transportation.

Increase Investment in Infrastructure Construction

In the field of infrastructure construction, especially in the field of electric power infrastructure and communication infrastructure construction, JBIC actively invested in large-scale private enterprises in Japan, vigorously promoted the export of renewable energy power generation machinery and communication technology, expanded overseas markets, and enhanced international competitiveness. The focus projects in the field of electric power infrastructure included supporting the participation of Japanese companies in the Dutch ocean wind farm business, and assisting Japanese companies in exporting to the Bangladesh Electric Power Development Corporation, the Iceland State Power Corporation, and Turkey Geothermal Power Company. The key projects in the development of the communications infrastructure included promoting the export project of undersea fiber optic cable facilities by providing foreign trade loans to the Angolan Development Bank. This would be the first submarine cable network in North and South America crossing the South Atlantic. Key projects also include actively participating in the construction of special economic zones, and providing necessary financial support and communication technology guidance.

Support Overseas Mergers and Acquisitions

In recent years, in terms of M&A support, there has been strong demand for overseas investment, mergers, and acquisitions in Japan. JBIC has made full use of the special financing channel of "supporting overseas development financing facilities". In 2015, JBIC invested in 105 overseas M&A projects, providing guarantees and deposits of 1,023.3 billion yen. This value was the highest for any single year for Japanese companies in overseas development and support projects. When helping Japanese companies expand overseas, JBIC focused on emerging countries in Southeast Asia, Central America, and South America, mainly in the fields of agriculture, food, and IT (large data, etc.), which had been developing stably and rapidly. The key projects included helping Japanese companies merge and acquire beer manufacturing and sales company in Myanmar and supporting Japanese companies in acquiring a Singapore logistics company.

Promote the Development of SMEs

In promoting the development of small- and medium-enterprises, JBIC strengthened cooperation with regional financial institutions and actively responded to the growing demand for local currency financing. In fiscal year 2015, JBIC contributed 133 projects to strengthen SME construction, with a total of 42.9 billion yen in guarantees and bonds, which was the highest value of JBIC's investment in this field. In promoting the development of SMEs, combined with their own advantages, JBIC focused on promoting the expansion of overseas markets for SMEs, and further helped Japanese SMEs go abroad.

Environmental Protection Financing

In the area of the environment, JBIC is actively assisting the implementation of climate change measures in developing countries in accordance with the "Actions for Cool Earth: ACE 2.0" program, which the Japanese government promulgated in December 2015. JBIC came up with "Global action for Reconciling Economic growth and Environmental preservation" ("GREEN"), provided financing to the Brazilian National Development Bank, the Mexican Foreign Trade Bank, and the Andean Development Association, and provided financing to support the effective use of resources in Central and South America.

Development Bank of Japan

2015 was the third year of Abenomics. That year, the price of resources such as oil fell and the economic growth of emerging Asian developing countries and resource-based countries slowed: the global economy was not booming. The domestic economy of Japan was unstable, and although personal income and employment were improving, there were still deflation and slumping consumer markets. Corporate earnings improved and investment in equipment increased slowly. In this context, the Development Bank of Japan (DBJ) continued to play the role of policy development bank and made an important contribution in investment, financing, crisis response, and promoting sustainable development.

Main Business Data

The total assets of DBJ after consolidation were 15.907 trillion yen in fiscal year 2015 (April 1, 2015—March 2016). DBJ's return on net assets and return on assets were 0.80% and 4.60% respectively in 2015, and the non-performing assets ratio was 0.64%. The total value of securities amounted to 1,803 billion yen, 4.5% less than year 2014; total liabilities amounted to 13.023 trillion yen; loans and borrowed bonds were 7,892.2 and 3,221.9 billion yen respectively; net profit was 129.1 billion yen; investment and financing amounted 3,027.7 billion yen, 19% more than year 2014; and regular profit was 358.6 billion yen. BDJ was rated A1 by Moody's Ratings and A by Standard & Poor's Rating. DBJ's main sources of funding were the government (which invested 65 billion yen in 2015) and bond issuance.

Highlights of the Year

Support Financing and Investment Projects

In terms of financing, DBJ's total financing was 2,861.3 billion yen in 2015. In addition to projects of traditional cooperation with other financial institutions, DBJ increasingly diversified their offerings with products such as non-recourse loans and structured finance to cope with the increasingly diverse financing needs. In terms of investment, DBJ set up "specific investment business" on May 20, 2015 to enhance the competitiveness overseas and promote the regional development. The amount invested was 166. 3 billion yen in 2015. As for consulting business, DBJ provided advisory services to enterprises and other financial institutions, based on their perennially accumulated social network and extensive business experience, earning profits of 10. 1 billion yen in 2015.

The Crisis Response Operations

DBJ began building a crisis response network in the aftermath of the financial crisis and the East Japan earthquake in 2011. According to the Japan Finance Corporation Act, DBJ was one of the financial institutions established to provide credit after natural disasters and other major crises. DBJ helped companies build disaster response strategies to withstand disaster risks and provided emergency funds to deal with disasters in the aspects of business continuity plans, seismic facilities, and IT backup systems. In addition to continuing to aid in the recovery of enterprises damaged by the East Japan earthquake in 2011, DBJ also responded to the following disasters recently: volcanic eruption in Kuchinoerabu-jima, No. 18 typhoon, heavy rain on April 21, and the Kumamoto earthquake in April 2016. In addition, DBJ also provided measures for small- and medium-sized enterprises which suffered car supply chains damages after the earthquake. The financing amount totaled 5,601. 9 billion yen, of which 268. 3 billion yen was used to provide guarantee for damages and 361 billion yen was used to purchase commercial paper.

Enhance the Competitiveness of Japanese Companies Overseas

With the fierce competition brought by the development of emerging countries, globalization, the saturation of the domestic market due to low birth rates, and an aging and sluggish economy, DBJ strove to enhance the competitiveness of Japanese enterprises. More specifically, DBJ focused on promoting the access of Japanese small- and medium-sized enterprises to international markets with the full use of their technique and management experience. Through March 2016, DBJ established a special fund named "Competitiveness Enhancement Fund". The special fund has invested in 12 projects, with a cumulative total of 129 billion yen. The invested companies included new energy companies, new technologies companies, and innovative Japanese companies, including SF Solar Power, Japan Electric Co. , Ltd. , and Maritime Innovation Japan.

Specific Investment Operations

"Specific Investment Operations" was set up specifically to promote local vitality and competitiveness of enterprises from 2015 to 2020, mainly by mobilizing the enthusiasm of capital investment of private financial institutions and guaranteeing those investments. To this end, DBJ set up the "Investment Division" in June 2015 and developed policies such as the Japan Revitalization Strategy (revised in 2015), and established the basic principles for City, Residents and Job Creation (revised in 2015). DBJ also formed a mutual fund with local financial institutions (6 mutual funds were founded in 2015) to fully utilize the knowledge and experience of DBJ and local financial institutions through cooperation. At the same time, in addition to specific investment operations, in order to further promote the rapid development of the emerging capital market, DBJ also developed "growth co-invasive facilities" to provide advice to relevant enterprises. In addition, DBJ provided all aspects of support to local enterprises together with other enterprises, financial institutions, and investors.

Among them, the project to strengthen local vitality was the most important project. Specifically, DBJ established the "Enhancing Local Vigor Program" to provide financial support for outstanding local enterprises, set up the "Local Future University" to train local talents, among which the most noteworthy is the establishment of "Innovation Center" investing in 43 creative projects in 2015, set up "Private Finance Initiative Promotion Corporation" (PFI), and held regular "PPP/PFI classes". In addition, "Local Contribution M&A Project" was set up in order to provide financial and technical support for enterprises in the local economy.

Overall, DBJ basically fulfilled its tasks required by the government in 2015, enhanced the vitality of the local economy, and safeguarded against natural disasters and other crises, which provides a useful demonstration of what DFIs are able to achieve.

Column 4 -3	"DBJ Environmental Rating" System Helps Japanese Companies Sustainable Development

DBJ is a large, state-owned, Japanese, integrated policy financial institution with registered capital of more than $ 10 billion. It falls under the direct control of the Ministry of Finance and is based on the "Development Bank of Japan Law". DBJ's investment and financing directions are determined by the government. The DBJ is a non-profit institution that does not participate in market competition. As an integrated policy financial institution, DBJ mainly provides long-term and stable capital supplies to projects that are beneficial to Japanese economic and social development.

"DBJ Environmental Rating" is DBJ's original rating system, which determines financing priority according to how friendly enterprises are to the environment. In 2004, in order to better promote the development of environmental protection by the enterprises, DBJ introduced this system. The system aims to reduce environmental pressures and promote environmental protection investments among enterprises. Through the environmental management evaluation system developed internally, DBJ rates the environmental performances of enterprises that apply for loans. DBJ then provides special low- interest loans with different levels according to the evaluation grades. DBJ supports the enterprises to increase investment in environmental protection.

The Features of "DBJ Environmental Rating"

1) Grading assessment. The most important characteristic of "DBJ Environmental Rating" financing business is that the borrower and interest rates are determined by the environmental rating results of the enterprises. low- interest loans are provided mainly for the purchase of software and hardware and R&D investment related to environmental protection. DBJ will evaluate the environmental management of the enterprises after receiving the applications of environmental protection special loans and determine the appropriate lending rates according to the rating results.

2) Based on international and domestic environmental trends, a fair and impartial evaluation system was established. Each year, participants in the DBJ Environmental Rating System Volunteer Committee, composed of experts from relevant fields, revise and publish the annual environmental inspection report, in combination with the international and domestic environmental protection trends of the year.

3) Face to face investigation and evaluation with the enterprises.

4) Direct interviews with business managers.

5) Rich experience in evaluation.

6) Customer diversification. Manufacturing and non-manufacturing firms, large enterprises, and regional concentration enterprises are all involved.

7) The use of DBJ's logo. The enterprises that gained the financing service of "DBJ Environmental Ratings" are allowed to use the DBJ logo in official website and public materials to show its environmental protection capability and sustainable development ability.

The measures of "DBJ Environmental Rating"

The evaluation includes 120 quantitative and qualitative evaluation indexes which cover three areas, namely "environmental management system", "enterprise's environmental investment and countermeasures in all fields", and "processing ability of main environmental problems". Each field has a maximum score of 250 points. In order to qualify, firms must receive at least 120 points (at least 110 for medium-sized enterprises points) out of the 250 points. Qualified enterprises are divided into three different grades based on the level of the scores, and DBJ determines the interest rate of low- interest loans according to the grades. The evaluation index of the evaluation system differs across industries, with the existing system able to serve 13 different industries.

The Process of "DBJ Environmental Rating"

The process of "DBJ Environmental Rating" involves: primary screening, a survey with questions involving the enterprises' environmental status, and a second inspection with published results. Primary screening is the inspection based on the statement information and public information of the checked enterprises inside DBJ. During the survey, DBJ collaborates with the executives to confirm the information that firms do not publish. In addition, the executives present the environmental features of their companies. Using this information, the two parties exchange views on the future direction and policies of the enterprises. The second inspection (results published) is done by staff outside DBJ. They release the results of the "DBJ Environmental Rating" of the checked enterprises after reviewing the first two steps of the process, the enterprises' conditions, and holding the internal judgement meeting. DBJ raises money based on the results of the rating and issues the environmental rating report to the enterprises.

All the enterprises that meet the financing requirements of DBJ can be the service recipients of "DBJ Environmental Rating". The same goes for general financing, the principles of funds do not include special interest-bearing policies. Through the end of March 2015, the "DBJ Environmental Rating" system had successfully provided financing services 472 times since its creation, with the flow of funds amounting to roughly 800 billion yen.

Korea Development Bank

In 2015, Korea Development Bank (KDB) acted as a "Global Pioneer" by receiving CNY Qualified Foreign Institutional Investor (RQFII) eligibility for the first time in Korea. Meanwhile, KDB played the role of "Economy Facilitator" by supplying industrial funds totaling an unprecedented amount of KRW 67 trillion. The role of "market leader" was also fulfilled by solidifying Korean Benchmark-issuer status. "Creative Sector Incubator" was KDB's fourth role, for it expanded their reach to ventures and start-ups through "Global Partnership Fund II".

In all, 2015 was a memorable year, with continuous pursuit of the vision to become a "Financial Engine of Korea's Growth, Global KDB". With this vision, KDB has drawn five mid-to long-term strategic tasks: promoting the creative economy; leading advancement in the financial industry; reinforcing market safety net functions; building the foundation for sustainable policy finance; and preparing for reunification of Korea. Since its establishment, KDB has laid the foundations of Korean economic development. Today, it aims to play a more vital role in invigorating the nation's economy.

Main Business Data

As the end of 2015, KDB's assets amounted to KRW 309,492 billion, 11.8% more than in 2014. The increase stemmed mostly from gains in other assets, as Daewoo Shipbuilding, Marine Engineering Co., Ltd., and other entities were newly included as consolidated subsidiaries. Liabilities also rose at a similar rate of 11.6% to KRW 275,549 billion, due mainly to increases in bonds and other liabilities. Equity rose by 14.3% to KRW 33,942 billion as issued capital and retained earnings both increased. Issued capital increased by KRW 2,055 billion through an additional capital injection from the Korean government during 2015 (see Table 4.1).

Table 4. 1 Assets and Liabilities of KDB: 2014—2015 (Units: Billion Wons)

	2015	2014
Total Assets	309,491. 7	276,704. 8
Cash & due from banks	7,894. 7	10,895. 3
Securities	82,107. 2	94,267. 6
Loans	142,440. 2	143,484. 4
Others	77,049. 6	28. 057. 5
Total Liabilities	275,549. 4	247,004. 2
Financial liabilities held for trading	—	394. 0
Deposits	41,431. 5	41,665. 8
Borrowings	33,576. 2	37,814. 4
Bonds	121,617. 0	120,731. 3
Others	78,924. 7	46,398. 8
Equity	33,942. 3	29,700. 6
Issued capital	17,235. 4	15,180. 4
Capital surplus	1,579. 2	1,621. 6
Retained earnings	9,266. 4	7,577. 0
Capital adjustments	225. 5	223. 7
Others	4,763. 8	4,411. 0
Accumulated other comprehensive income	872. 0	686. 9

Total loans grew by 4. 4% to KRW 128,926 billion as a decrease in household loans was nullified by an increase in corporate and public loans. While loans to large enterprises grew by 1. 5%, loans to SMEs increased significantly by 17. 2%, leading to an increase in corporate loans by 4. 5% from 2014 to KRW 124,914 billion.

Deposits and borrowings both decreased by 0. 6% and 11. 2% respectively, while bonds rose by 0. 7%, leading to an increase in the proportion of bonds in overall funding from 60. 3% in 2014 to 61. 9% in 2015.

Considering the expansion of KDB's business, the issuance of Industrial Finance Bonds (KDB Bonds), which is the main source of its funding, consolidated KDB's role in economic growth. The amount of KDB Bonds issued in 2015 stood at KRW

33. 7 trillion. In addition, KDB also issued $ 3. 5 billion worth of bonds denominated in foreign currency. Compared to the end of 2014, the balance increased KRW 47 trillion and $ 4. 4 billion.

Domestically, KDB Bonds ranked third at the end of 2015. Considering the global e-conomic slowdown, Bank of Korea cut policy rates twice in 2015, and the average funding costs of newly issued KDB Bonds dropped by 0. 8% as well. Though KDB Bond's rate is considerably lower than other public institutions' bond rates, its high profile guaranteed its role of key benchmark rates as well.

The expanding of deposit business was accompanied by increased focus on corporate deposits and checking accounts, which reduce funding costs and minimize market frictions.

Highlights of the Year

In the field of corporate banking, KDB prevented financial distress through providing emergency funds of KRW 1. 5 trillion to enterprises facing liquidity constraints SMEs, and credit unions with credit enhancement. In addition, KRW contributed KRW 4. 8 trillion for numerous projects amounting to KRW 15. 6 trillion through the "Corporate Investment Stimulus Program" as future growth engines. To manage risk preemptively, KDB reinforced its regular liquidity checkups and encouraged corporations with liquidity shortages to improve their financial soundness.

Meanwhile, KRW 37. 0 trillion was provided to SMEs and MEs through KDB, which accounted for 54. 7% of supply of total funding. The total amount of Mutual Growth Fund, which aims at fostering SMEs growth, remained above KRW 500. 0 billion for the third consecutive year, reaching approximately KRW 518. 0 billion. In addition, KDB supplied On-lending program, a policy program promoting SMEs and MEs by providing over KRW 6. 4 trillion to 3,846 companies, among which most of them were in unsatisfactory financial situations. Among the KRW 6. 4 trillion, 71% was extended to promote technology financing.

In 2015, KDB also strengthened market safety net functions by restructuring Korean companies. Taking urgent actions to minimize impacts from financial difficulties of large conglomerates, KDB continues to engage in proactive corporate restructuring as the economic slowdown was expected to last through 2016. Meanwhile, preemptive measures, such as voluntary restructuring and improvement, will be encouraged through assistance of accumulated knowledge and experienced professionals.

As the only Korean bank with license to arrange domestic corporate bond issuances,

KDB maintained its leading position in the investment banking business. Super companies like Nomura International Funding from Singapore and Pingan Lease from China all successfully financed through KDB's support. With volumes of derivatives trading reaching KRW 957. 0 trillion and a year-end balance of KRW 475. 0 trillion, KDB was recognized as the "Best Derivatives Provider". In addition, KDB carried out its market maker role in the KRW/CNY direct trading market and ended 2015 with a market share of 8. 6%. A number of M&A services were also completed in 2015. KDB largely provided advisory services to corporate clients undergoing restructuring and in need of suitors. KDB also completed a number of financing transactions for its clients seeking business expansion through M&A.

To promote companies with competitive technologies and to help venture firms and start-ups, KDB has long accumulated expertise and experienced human resources in the technology finance field. In 2015, KDB developed industry-leading IP financing products, built foundations for creative finance, and carried out diversified consulting services. These services have supplied more than KRW 500. 0 billion to companies in need, including KRW 165. 7 billion in 2015, which was 78. 7% more than that of 2014, leading the domestic technology financing market.

In the field of alternative investment, KDB put greater focus on domestic social organizations and municipal development projects. In 2015, KDB arranged 15 social organizations and 49 regional projects with a total worth of KRW 13. 0 trillion, which demonstrated its unchallenged status as a leader. Its 16 private equity funds also ended 2015 with capital commitments totaling KRW 8,154. 3 billion, representing a market share of 13. 9%.

The overseas business of KDB expanded quickly in 2015 as well. In July 2015, KDB became the first bank in Korea to secure RMB Qualified Foreign Institutional Investor (RQFII) eligibility and China Interbank Bond Market (CIBM) qualifications. The opening of a branch in Qingdao, China shored up the business presence in the Chinese market. KDB also established two PF desks in London and Beijing, which specialized in structured financing of ships and aircrafts. Among the total volume of overseas syndicated loans arranged by KDB as a mandated lead arranger in 2015, ship/aircraft financing accounted for 47. 9%, general corporate loans for 39. 0%, and PF for 13. 1%.

To other respects, KDB's pension assets under management (AUM) increased by 19. 7% from 2014, ending 2015 at KRW 4. 1 trillion. Its custody balance ended at KRW 21. 244 trillion, with an increase of 27. 9%. Its expansion and diversification in research studies also facilitated the sustainable development of industries in Korea. By implementing credit models for lenders and identifying potential changes in the macroeconomic and financial environment, KDB can respond with effective countermeasures against potential adversities. Escalating efforts on technical evaluation also present detailed pictures of Korea's major industries, analyzing its competitiveness. This provides information on the latest issues and technological focuses by industry.

2015 was not a smooth year for KDB. The depression in the shipbuilding industry hit their creditors and policy banks hard. Daewoo Shipbuilding & Marine Engineering (DSME), Hyundai Merchant Marine co., ltd (HMM), and Samsung Heavy Industries (SHI) successively experienced crises due to overcapacity and a shrinking of demands. Coping with the problems, KDB encouraged HMM to join THE Alliance, a newly established container shipping alliance and participated in the restructuring of SHI. In June 2016, KDB and Korea Export-Import Bank financed these shipbuilding giants with a fund established by the Korean government and Bank of Korea, worth a total of 9.9 billion dollars.

Column 4 –4	Korea Development Bank's Countermeasures in Structural Adjustment toward the Korean Shipbuilding Industry Crisis in Early 2016

The shipbuilding industry has been one of Korea's most important economic pillars and the nation's policy focus ever since the strategic goal of "prospering the nation through shipbuilding industry and boosting the economy by the improvement of shipbuilding cooperation" was put forward in the 1970s. However, with the shipbuilding industry sluggish in the overall global sphere in recent years, South Korea is also embroiled in this industrial downturn due to the exceptionally bleak maritime market and low demand for new shipbuilding. As such, its profitability continues to deteriorate.

In the face of imminent crisis, the South Korean government, together with Korea Development Bank and the financial sector, put forward a variety of policy schemes and relief programs. Meanwhile, the shipbuilding companies took different self-aid approaches, including layoffs, restructuring, and selling non-core assets, to overcome adversity.

This paper will first briefly depict the current situation of the shipbuilding industry crisis in South Korea, and then analyze KDB's—being the main creditor—countermeasures in structural adjustment and relief programs towards this crisis.

Status Quo of Shipbuilding Industry in South Korea

1) Overall Condition

Evaluated from the three main indicators (completions, new orders, and orders booked) and personnel structure over the past 10 years, South Korea had relatively satisfactory performance. The industry experienced slump and stagnation in varying degrees during the global financial crisis in 2008. However, when South Korea first implemented structural adjustment, the shipbuilding industry quickly restored a high-speed upward momentum from the recapitalization and restructuring of big cooperation by buying out smaller companies.

However, in 2015, the global maritime market shrunk greatly. South Korean shipbuilding corporations suffered heavy losses: the three leading companies Hyundai Merchant Marine, Samsung Heavy Industries, and Daewoo Ship Engineering Company (hereafter referred to as "BIG 3") suffered losses of more than \$ 5 billion. Through the first quarter of 2016, the business losses of the "BIG3" soared to nearly \$ 80 billion. One of the main indicators, namely booked orders, also demonstrates their adversity. In the first quarter, only Hyundai Merchant Marine received two orders of Suez oil tankers. Samsung Heavy Industries and Daewoo Ship Engineering Company received no orders. This meant overall orders booked amounted to only 20 million CGT, which was a 90% drop compared to the performance in the same period in the previous year.

2) Status Quo of "BIG 3"

By of the end of 2015: Daewoo's debt ratio reached up to 4,266% ; Samsung Heavy Industries' debt ratio was 306% , and its outstanding obligation amounted to 13.3 trillion won; Hyundai Merchant Marine's debt ratio was 221% , with outstanding obligations amounting to 34.2 trillion won.

Daewoo Shipbuilding Marine Engineering Co (DSME) was the first to fall into crisis. Due to the sluggishness of the industry, DSME had been suffering heavy losses from the delay and cancellation of marine business orders. As a shareholder, Korea Development Bank and other creditors had credited 4.2 trillion won in cash assistance (\$ 3.7 billion). However, Korean Development Bank stated that as of February 2016, the DSME would no longer receive any cash transfer from creditors.

Hyundai Merchant Maritime (HMM) also suffered heavy losses. In April

2016, following the collapse of DSME, HMM also fell into crisis and applied to become a subsidiary of the KDB to avoid bankruptcy. HMM transferred its share capital to KDB at a 7：1 ratio. Financial regulators of South Korea and creditors of HMM agreed to convert the company's debt into equity in order to maintain its operation until HMM's operation returned to normal.

Samsung Heavy Industries (SHI) tried hard to rescue itself. By the end of May 2016, SHI submitted its "self-rescue plan" to its main creditor KDB, trying to save itself from the shipbuilding industry crisis. Specific measures included: selling the shares of Samsung Hotel and Doosan Engine in return for financing of 220 billion won ($ 180 million); shutting down some of the shipbuilding facilities temporarily; and restructuring the Board. It is reported that SHI has carried out its self-rescue operations since last September, and has sold 100 billion won worth of assets, while cutting 500 employees.

Countermeasures in Structural Adjustment in the Crisis

Due to overcapacity in global and Korean shipbuilding, Korean shipbuilding companies are experiencing structural adjustment by scaling down operations. The Korean government and financial sector share the same expectations about the future shrinkage of the Korean shipbuilding sector in the face of shrinking demand. On this basis, Korea Development Bank made a series of adjustments depending on the condition of different ship companies:

1) Financing the Shipbuilding Companies with a 11 trillion Won Fund ($ 9.9 Billion) Set Up by the Government

On June 9, 2016, the Korean government and the central bank announced a $ 9.9 billion fund for purchasing hybrid bonds issued by two state-owned banks— the Korea Industrial Bank (KDB) and the Korea Export-Import Bank (KEXIM). These bonds will provide funds for struggling shipbuilding and shipping companies. As the two state-owned banks with the highest exposure to the shipbuilding industry, they have $ 47 billion of non-performing loans associated with shipbuilding companies and shipping companies. KDB is a major creditor of the major shipyards and shipping companies being restructured include DSME and HMM. South Korea's three shipbuilding giants are accelerating the consolidation. The government claimed that HMM, Samsung Heavy Industries, and DSME had submitted a financing plan to the creditors, intending to raise 8.41 trillion won (about $ 7.3 billion) by taking measures such as selling assets and cutting staff.

2) Taking Different Strategies toward BIG 3 and Encouraging the Shipping Companies to Explore Pathways of Recovery

In early May 2016, the KDB announced it would continue to provide financial support to the three major shipping companies. The debt repayment period would also be extended for the BIG3 to provide them with extra "reassurance". It is one of the strategies taken by the government to encourage shipping companies explore ways to achieve recovery.

Urged the HMM to join the World Container Shipping Alliance ("THE Alliance"): in early May, six container shipping companies—Hapag-Lloyd, Hanjin Shipping, Yangming Shipping, Merchant Shipping Mitsui, Nippon Yusen, and Kawasaki Kisen—officially announced the formation of THE Alliance. At the same time, the largest shareholder of the HMM (which is ranked 15th in global shipping capacity) —the KDB—urged the HMM to join the THE Alliance. Benefits from joining would include achieving the complementation of the shipping routines and ports, coordinating shipping schedules, mutually hiring shipping space, sharing information, constructing shared terminals and heaps, and sharing inland logistics systems.

Participate in the discussion of Samsung's Self-Rescue Plan: in May, SHI submitted a restructuring plan to its major creditor—the KDB—promising to raise 300 billion won by disposing of its non-core assets, dismissing 500 employees, and halting some of its shipyard businesses. The KDB participated in the discussion of SHI's Self-Rescue Plan and hoped that SHI could promote a series of complete restructuring processes to revive its struggling shipbuilding business. Especially, the KDB hopes that the entire Samsung Group would also get involved in the Self-Rescue Plan of its subsidiary SHI.

Apart from the preceding measures, central and local governments of South Korea have also introduced a large number of other countermeasures including: (a) introducing Corporate vitality law and other supporting laws to promote industrial structure optimization; (b) enhancing supervision from the financial sector on shipbuilding enterprise restructuring to optimize the overall competitiveness of Korean shipbuilding; and (c) increasing technological research and development which could lead the industry's transformation to becoming well-rounded, service-oriented enterprises. Cases including: (a) R&D of a new generation of intelligent merchant marines, energy-saving ships and digital shipyard; (b) the financial support launched by local governments of Gyeongsangnam-Do, including the reduction of local tax rates, extension of tax payment deadlines, and other tax relief measures.

In a nutshell, the global maritime market currently faces a sharp contraction, and shipbuilding enterprises of South Korea suffered heavy losses in the marine industry, especially the "BIG 3". Hence, their common creditor and the leading development financing institution KDB is actively engaged in managing the crisis by providing financial instruments and structural adjustment assistance. The Korean government, society, and enterprises are also actively discussing the way out for the shipbuilding industry.

Chapter 5　National DFIs in Medium-/low-income Countries

Vnesheconombank

2015 was a hard year for the Russian economy. Several factors had negative effects on its development, such as EU and US sanctions against Russia, the consequential restriction of trade and economic relations with foreign countries, a significant drop in carbon prices, and a weakening ruble. As a result, investment in Russia fell sharply by 8.4% in 2015.

In such a challenging environment, Vnesheconombank (VEB) took the responsibility of resisting the crisis. During the year, VEB continued fulfilling its functions as a national development institution by integrating resources, playing an important role in overcoming the crisis, promoting national economic development, and increasing employment. Its priorities include financing long-term investment projects, supporting underlying industries crucial to stable economic development, promoting regional economic development, supporting high-tech and innovative industries, supporting SMEs and exports, and playing the role of agent for the government of the Russian Federation.

Main Business Data

As we can see, the dollar funds declined from $ 17.99 billion to $ 15.79 billion, the euro funds declined from 23.3 billion to 20.4 billion, and ruble funds increased from 374.2 billion to 384.9 billion.

VEB has made up for the reduction of credit funds from other banks mainly by increasing domestic bonds. Despite weak investment activity on the domestic securities market, VEB placed bonds for RUB 15 billion on the domestic market and refinanced bonds for a nominal value of RUB 79 billion. Due to the EU and US sanc-

tions, the Bank did not place any Eurobonds and Eurocommercial Papers. By the reporting date, overall mid- and long-term borrowings raised from banks amounted to
$ 8.8 billion (as calculated at the exchange rate of the Bank of Russia on December
31, 2015). Having analyzed restrictions introduced by the sanctions against VEB,
many European banks indicated their readiness to provide long-term loans against insurance coverage of national export insurance agencies (EIAs) in euros to fund up to
85% of the value of import contracts with European counterparts. In 2015, some European banks made proposals for financing equipment supplies from France, Italy,
Germany, Denmark, and the Czech Republic. VEB and China Development Bank
(CDB) signed a CNY 10 billion facility agreement to fund VEB's projects implemented in Russia together with Chinese companies and projects providing exports to China. For the first time in the Bank's history, a tied facility agreement was denominated in yuan.

Highlights of the Year

Financing of Investment Projects

The Bank continued to fully meet its commitments for investment projects and ad hoc
programs of national importance. VEB provides financial support to investment projects in the form of loans and equity investments by issuing guarantees to secure obligations of stakeholders of third parties. Lending remains the main form of financing.

In 2015, VEB started financing 6 investment projects worth a total of RUB 162.2
billion, with the Bank's commitment standing at RUB 92.9 billion. By year-end, the
Bank had provided RUB 24.1 billion.

In the reporting year, VEB completed 8 investment projects. By year-end 2015,
VEB granted loans to 159 investment projects, for two of which the Bank issued
guarantees. VEB's support to investment projects by the end of 2015 are illustrated
by the following figures:

· RUB 1,359.2 billion loans for investment projects;

· RUB 35.4 billion equity financing to projects (investment in shares/equity
stakes);

· RUB 1.5 billion guarantees;

· RUB 199.6 billion loans granted for investment projects in priority areas of economic modernization. These include projects for improving energy efficiency and saving, developing medical equipment and pharmaceuticals, space-based technologies,

and telecommunications;

· RUB 469. 0 billion loans granted for innovation projects.

Within the period under review, the biggest increase in lending came from metallurgy (43. 3%), chemicals and petrochemicals (38. 1%), and electronics (about 37. 6%).

The projects produced a positive economic and social effect, creating new points of growth through the construction and modernization of the existing facilities, generating new jobs, and increasing tax revenue for all levels of government.

Project Examples:

1) Construction of the Boguchany Aluminum Smelter:

Total project value: RUB 50. 4 billion.

VEB's approved commitment: $ 1. 5 billion.

The Boguchany Aluminum Smelter updated its equipment and reproduced aluminum in August 2015. This increased taxes and other receipts to all level of government by RUB 447. 0 million and created 391 new jobs.

2) Construction of an ammonia, methanol, and carbamide plant:

Total project value: $ 2. 2 billion.

VEB's approved commitment: $ 1. 8 billion (loans) and RUB 1. 5 billion (equity investment).

The complex was put into operation at the end of 2015. Contracts with world leading carbamide traders for 500,000 tons per annum were executed. Taxes and other budget receipts to all levels of government increased by RUB 1. 6 billion and 356 new jobs were created.

3) Development of the Kurumoch international airport:

Total project value: RUB 7. 5 billion.

VEB's approved commitment: RUB 4. 6 billion.

The reconstruction of the airport (including a new 42,000 square meter passenger terminal and a cargo terminal) was completed in 2015. The new airport terminal is the first project built from scratch as part of the preparation of the transport infrastructure for the 2018 World Cup. Tax and other budget receipts to all levels of government increased by RUB 965. 5 million.

Support for Priority Development Regions

By the beginning of the reporting period, VEB had signed cooperation agreements with 58 constituent entities of the Russian Federation. In 2015, the Bank signed a memorandum of cooperation with the authorities of the Saratov region and a memorandum of cooperation with the Russian Federation Ministry of Crimean Affairs.

To work out more efficient approaches to cooperate with regional authorities, VEB has adopted a new format for establishing partnership relations—cooperation with the plenipotentiary representatives of the President of the Russian Federation in the federal districts.

By the end of 2015, the total loans granted by VEB for project financing in North-Caucasian Federal District (NCFD) amounted to RUB 23. 5 billion (to 6 investment projects). VEB's subsidiary—OJSC North Caucasus Development Corporation (NCDC, or the Corporation) —has been actively participating in implementing investment projects in NCFD.

By the end of 2015, NCDC had participated in 6 investment projects in NCFD. Through January 1, 2016, the total funding by the Corporation amounted to RUB 5. 4 billion. By January 1, 2016, VEB had participated in 10 NCFD investment projects, including an interregional project implemented in Far Eastern Federal District (FEFD). By the end of the reporting year, total loans granted to NCFD projects amounted to RUB 50. 6 billion, with equity financing of up to RUB 25. 9 billion.

Far Eastern Federal District and Baikal Region Development Fund (the Fund) are an important element of the government's support to help speed economic development in the region. In 2015, 6 projects were identified as a priority, with overall funding of RUB 74 billion, including the Fund's commitment of RUB 9. 5 billion.

Non-commercial organization Single-industry Town Development Fund (SITD, or the Fund) also started its work in 2015. The Fund was established to consolidate efforts towards economic diversification of single-industry towns, to coordinate actions aimed at building necessary infrastructure, and to launch investment projects in single-industry municipalities.

Total loans extended by VEB to fund projects in single-industry towns reached RUB 237. 3 billion by January 1, 2016. Through the reporting date, VEB took part in the financing of 19 such projects. Overall, RUB 60. 3 billion was extended to projects in single-industry towns in 2015.

Support for Small- and Medium-Enterprises

In 2015, the SME Financial Support Program (the Program), run by JSC Russian Bank for Small and Medium Enterprises Support (SME Bank), provided more accessible loans for SMEs with financial support from VEB. The Program provides SMEs with loans for a longer period with lower prices, which substantially benefit the SMEs. Thanks to the Program, the amount of loans obtained by SMEs has greatly increased.

By January 01, 2016, the funds extended by VEB to fund the Program totaled RUB 56.7 billion. At the end of 2015, funds provided to SMEs by the Program amounted to RUB 105.7 billion. The average weighted interest rate for loans extended to SMEs by partner banks under the Program reached 13.2%. Yet, it is considerably lower than current market rates. The share of loans with maturities of over 3 years in total loans to SMEs exceeded the previous year's figure by nearly 7 percentage points and had reached 83.9% as of January 1, 2016.

Support for Exports

Support for non-commodity exports is one of VEB's key objectives as a bank for development. However, in 2015, the challenge is even larger. On one hand, the sanctions from the EU and the US restricted the development of export. On the other hand, the development outlook of the world economy is not promising. To overcome these bad impacts, VEB enlarged its support for exports. Total loans for support of export trade in 2015 amounted to RUB 32.4 billion, which is 1.6 times larger than the amount in 2014. Through the end of 2015, total loans for support of export trade amounted to RUB 88.6 billion. In the reporting year, the Bank provided 79 guarantees for a total worth of RUB 99.3 billion. Through the end of 2015, guarantees provided by VEB amounted to RUB 397.5 billion.

Despite the negative external and internal economic factors, VEB provided financial support for Russian exports to more than 20 countries. Most of the exported products were high-technology goods. The Bank's export support areas include transport, transport machine building and power engineering, nuclear power, aircraft building, and rocket and space projects.

The Russian Export Centre (the Centre), VEB's specialized subsidiary, was established in the reporting year. Its aim is to provide comprehensive support to Russian exporters as a one-stop-shop service and develop targeted solutions to promote particular export projects.

Agent for the Government of the Russian Federation

Extending and executing state guarantees of the Russian Federation. In the reporting year, the Bank signed 111 state guarantee agreements, with RUB 211.4 billion worth of state guarantees. The state guarantees are funded by the government financial allocation and aim to provide security for investment projects, thereby leveraging more investment funds and promoting the implementation of the project.

Overall, by the end of 2015, VEB kept records of 614 state guarantees of the Russian Federation totaling RUB 3,123.7 billion. In 2015, the Bank verified the financial standing of 115 principals, whose obligations were secured by the state guarantees of the Russian Federation.

Management of pension savings. The Russian residents' pension consists of two parts—the labor pension and the pension savings. The Pension Fund manages the labor pension, and the pension savings is voluntarily chosen by the residents to be managed by the government or a private management company.

Since 2003, VEB has been performing the functions of a state trust management company (STMC) for pension savings of insured citizens of the Russian Federation.

VEB forms two portfolios for the citizens of the Russian Federation, who have not exercised their right to choose a private pension fund (PPF): an extended investment portfolio and an investment portfolio of government securities.

By the end of 2015, the market value of the extended investment portfolio amounted to RUB 1,990.2 billion (at the start of the year, this value was RUB 1,892.3 billion). At year-end, the extended investment portfolio had returns of 13.15% p. a. Over the period under review, the market value of the government securities portfolio more than doubled from RUB 10.5 billion to RUB 22.7 billion. The return on the government securities portfolio was 15.31% p. a. The yields on invested pension savings in the extended investment and government securities portfolios exceeded the annual inflation rate by 0.25% p. a. and 2.41% p. a. respectively.

In 2015, the Russian Federation Pension Fund transferred to VEB RUB 2,166 million worth of payment reserve resources and RUB 321.2 million worth of pension savings of insured citizens entitled to a term allocated pension payment, to be held in trust and to form the respective portfolios.

The pension reserve payment portfolio (at market value) increased in the reporting period from RUB 2,562.5 million to RUB 4,916.1 million. The term allocated pension payment portfolio grew from RUB 247.7 million to RUB 565 million. The major challenges of managing the portfolios in 2015 were to prevent their depreciation and ensure liquidity. At year-end, the returns on the pension reserve payment portfolio and term allocated pension payment portfolios were 11. 59% p. a. and 11. 28% p. a. respectively.

In October 2014, the Bank's Supervisory Board approved VEB's Development Strategy 2015 – 2020 (the Strategy). By the end of 2015, VEB exceeded the Strategy target in many respects:

· VEB's loan portfolio amounted to RUB 2,432. 8 billion, which is above the Strategy target at year-end 2015 (RUB 1,950 – 2,100 billion).

· The export support loan portfolio amounted to RUB 86. 6 billion, which is below the Strategy target at year-end 2015 (RUB 145billion) by 40. 2%.

· By January 1, 2016, the amount of loans extended to SMEs reached RUB 105. 7 billion, thus exceeding the Strategy target (RUB 100 billion) by 5. 7%.

· Total funds raised by VEB amounted to RUB 2,518. 6 billion, which is within the Strategy targets at year-end 2015 (RUB 2,415 – 2,580 billion).

· Funds raised on capital markets reached RUB 1,568. 0 billion, which exceeded the Strategy target by 39. 4% at the end of the reporting period.

· The public funds and the funds of the Bank of Russia raised on favorable terms were considerably lower than the Strategy target by 34. 6%.

Under the sanctions regime and therefore with an inability to borrow on foreign capital markets, VEB successfully raised funds by placing bonds in the domestic market, which shows its strong capacity. Overall, in 2015, VEB has effectively raised funds, financed various projects, promoted the development of infrastructure and innovative industries, and supported SMEs and exports. It has played a unique and important role in overcoming the crisis and promoting national economic development in the Russian Federation.

Column 5 –1 Foundation for Development of Single-industry Cities Promotes Transformation of Russian Industrial Cities

The development dilemma of industrial cities is a global issue that many other developed countries also face. At first, large industrial enterprises are built in a region. After that, people will gradually migrate where the business go. As the enterprises grow, a city can be formed. When the market environment changes or raw materials run out, enterprises can go into crisis, which causes unemployment. Decreasing employment also results from technical progress. Due to the singular industrial structure of the city, it is difficult for the residents to be re-employed. Detroit, the car-manufacturing city in the USA, once the center of the auto industry, has gone bankrupt.

Dilemma and Transformation of Russian Industrial Cities

The issues facing Russian industrial cities are the product of having been a planned economy, which had Russian characteristics. During Soviet times, a great many of the enterprises were built in areas that were sparsely populated by people but rich in raw materials. Due to its vast size and the lack of infrastructure construction such as road building, the industrial cities were closed to the outside. Currently, there are 319 industrial cities in Russia with a total population of 14 million, which accounts for 10% of Russia's population. Only 71 industrial cities' economic situations are relatively normal while the others are experiencing varying challenges associated with economic development. To assist these cities in forming more diversified business, creating more jobs, and attracting investments, Foundation for Development of Single-industry Cities (FDM) was established in 2014 with the support of President Putin. The foundation is one of the Vnesheconombank's subsidiaries. Over the past two years, FDM has been facilitating the development of industrial cities by investing in infrastructure construction, creating large investment projects, and stimulating private investment. The operation of FDM is supported by the Russian government. FDM received RUB 3 billion ($ 46. 95 million) in fiscal subsidies in 2014 and RUB 4. 5 billion ($ 70. 42 million) in 2015. It is projected that FDM will receive RUB 10. 8 billion ($ 0. 169 billion) both in 2016 and in 2017. On June 22, 2016, Prime Minister Medvedev signed Resolution No. 549 resolution to enlarge the FDM's duty range to all 319 cities. Through the end of 2015, FDM had signed 17 comprehensive protocols with various local governments and had conducted validity assessments for investments and infrastructure construction projects in 10 regions. FDM also approved a series of project applications and had started early preparations in 18 cities. FDM planned to invest about RUB 30 billion ($ 0. 47 billion) in the coming 3 − 5 years for the purpose of improving the economy of 30 − 35 industrial cities. It is estimated that this plan will attract private investments of more than $ 1. 486 billion.

The Way FDM Works

The local government and enterprises of an industrial city, who are the most willing to launch transformation projects, lack funds and support from the central government. In addition, weak infrastructure limits their capacity to develop. Under such circumstances, the role of FDM is crucial.

1) Organizing

Based on local features, FDM organizes local governments, Vnesheconombank, foundations, and enterprises to make transformative programs. The program can be activated after approval by the FDM Review Board. Each industrial city has social and environmental monitoring institutions that were approved by federal government, so that central and local governments as well as Vnesheconombank and FDM representatives can receive information about the city. Since 2015, some underdeveloped cities have become "priority development regions" so that their situations will be closely monitored. They are also scheduled to receive preferential tax policies.

2) Financing

FDM promotes transformation in two general ways: improving infrastructure and building agro-industrial parks to attract private investments. It has specific regulations for the application procedures and qualifying conditions of projects:

· The industry of a new project should be unrelated to the original pillar industry of the city. Within the new project, raw materials that are from the original pillar industry should represent no more than 50% of required materials. A new project should also provide the original pillar industry merchandise or services that are no more than 50% of total output. The original pillar industry's share of a new project should not exceed 50% as well.

· A new project should have both economic and social benefits, be devoted to providing new jobs that are independent of the original pillar industry, and absorb investments for the city.

· FDM would invest RUB 0. 1 – 1 billion for each project and this investment should not exceed 40% of the total value of the project. Investment cycle must not be greater than 3 years and loans must be paid off in 8 years.

· The cost to receive FDM funding is an annual interest rate of 5%.

· FDM undertakes the role of project manager.

Looking through the key projects FDM supported, it is clear that new enterprises are mainly small- and medium-sized, or companies in the area of waste recovery, metal processing, or high-tech. It is noteworthy to point out that FDM particularly emphasizes activating the local economy by stimulating small- and medium-enterprises. The assistance for a single small start-up could reach RUB 0. 5 million.

3) Training

Making and implementing transformation plans are quite hard. When local residents are suffering from unemployment and low standards of living, the authority of the government and enterprises is questioned. Strong leadership is required to overcome these questions. To enhance the ability of the leading team members in administrating and programming, FDM additionally set up training programs to help them build systems to improve communication with citizens.

Cases

1) In 2015, FDM launched a transformation project in Naberezhnye Chelny, Tatarstan, where the Russian truck manufacturer "KAMAZ" was located. KAMAZ has always been working on improving competence and profit margins by improving productivity, optimizing their mode of production, and lowering costs. As productivity increased, the company cut a great many employees due to the redundant labor force and cut 4,000 hectares of its plant. FDM launched five projects in this city: "TEMPO", which produced steel bar from waste; "KAMSKY", a sausage producer; "HAIER", an air conditioner company; "MASTER", an united information site that served small- and medium-enterprises, "KARMA crystal", an artificial sapphire producer. In addition, FDM and the Tatarstan government cooperated on infrastructure construction. In 2016, the issue of implementing an urban power grid had been solved, while road infrastructure was still incomplete. FDM had granted more than $ 9.9 million for road construction. Local government also provided $ 3.13 million. During 2015 – 2020, to the project expected to create 3,438 jobs and to absorb $ 0.135 billion of investment.

2) In 2015, FDM invested in Krasnodar's transformation project. It contained infrastructure construction like building pipelines and establishing the "Bogoslovsky industrial park" to attract investors. Plans included building plants in this park for aluminum ware manufacturing, alumina waste reprocessing, drilling equipment manufacturing, decontaminant manufacturing, producing mineral

supplements and inorganic pigment from alumina waste, soil conditioner and adsorbent producing, as well as composite materials producing from polymers and wood waste.

3) In January 2015, FDM signed an agreement with Boris Dubrovsky, state governor of Chelyabinsk Oblast, concerning Asha's development. The agreement planned to build an agro-industrial park which covered 150 hectares and would create 1,500 jobs four years. The project would cost more than RUB 7 billion.

4) In March 2015, FDM had made some progress in building Chegdomyn industrial park in Khabarovsk Krai. Chegdomyn had a population of 12,500. FDM had invested about RUB 0.5 billion, which created 615 jobs. There were five programs in progress and three power enterprises had been completed.

5) In June 2015, FDM planned to invest RUB 0.28 billion to support Belaya Kholunitsa (Kirov Oblast) construct industrial parks and infrastructure. 10 enterprises had come to the park to focus on forestry and the chemical industry.

Such transformative cases are numerous. However, those measures do not take effect immediately. Because industrial city development is a deep-rooted issue, it takes a long time to solve. However, there is no doubt that launching funding projects, combining the power of governments and companies, absorbing investments, and establishing effective supervision frameworks will contribute to turning underdeveloped areas into new sources of economic growth.

Development Bank of Mongolian

The Development Bank of Mongolian (DBM) is a policy financial institution wholly-owned by the Mongolian government aimed at investing and lending funds in the infrastructure sector to assist the government complete its strategic program. During the year of 2015, Mongolia experienced a financial crisis as the price of raw materials fell sharply, China's economy slowed down, and foreign investment declined in Mongolia. In this context, DBM, as a financial institution directly under the Mongolian government's management, made an important contribution to the investment, financing, crisis response, and sustainable development of enterprises.

Main Business Data

As of June 1, 2016, the total assets of DBM were 6. 62 trillion MNT (about $ 2. 698 billion) and total liabilities were 6. 36 trillion MNT (about $ 2. 62 billion). The total equity of DBM are 257 billion MNT (about $ 106 million). Profit for the period are 39. 05 billion MNT (about $ 16. 1 million). Risk weighted capital ratio is 11. 0% and return on assets (ROA) is 0. 61%, rate of return equity is 15%. Standard & Poor's rating agency downgraded the sovereign rating of Mongolia to B- with stable outlook on 19 August, 2016. Moody's rating agency downgraded the sovereign rating of Mongolia to B3 from B2 on August 2016.

In 2015, DBM's total assets reached 6. 07 trillion MNT, an increase of 0. 56 trillion MNT (about $ 229 million) from the previous year. Total liabilities were 5. 78 trillion MNT (about $ 2. 346 billion), representing an increase of 0. 52 trillion MNT compared to the previous year. Total share capital was 0. 29 trillion MNT (about $ 117 million). Total bonds increased by 0. 25 trillion MNT which was a 14. 4% increase from the previous year. Total loans increased by 0. 14 trillion MNT in 2014 compared to the previous year, but net profit decreased by 32. 8%. Among other funds, the receivables from the Ministry of Finance were 8. 448 billion MNT.

The main sources of DBM's funding include domestic and foreign bonds, medium-term notes, and government borrowings. Bank deposits amounted to 15. 3 billion MNT and deposits placed in other banks amounted to 0. 44 trillion MNT. On May 26, 2015, DBM deposited $ 50 million in the Mongolian Trade and Development Bank, and the two sides signed a repurchase contract for the first time, which agreed on a 6. 1% coupon for 125 days and an expiration date of April 4, 2016.

Through December 31, 2015, DBM had issued 0. 15 trillion MNT of bonds to the Domestic Trade Bank at a 4% coupon rate, in order to build or improve accommodations for ASEM representatives. DBM issued a one-year coupon at an annual interest rate of 4%, and financed 170. 595 billion MNT from the Mongolian Trade Development Bank to offer loans to ETT Company for the construction of roads and infrastructure. In February 2014, DBM loaned to the ETT Company 1,705. 95 billion MNT of funds at an annual interest rate of 4. 25%.

Through December 31, 2015, government borrowing amounted to 2. 564 trillion MNT ($ 1. 125 billion), syndicated loan financing amounted to 0. 60 trillion MNT ($ 262 million), loan financing from China Development Bank reached 0. 302 trillion MNT ($ 133 million), loan financing from International Investment

Bank amounted to 42. 364 billion MNT ($ 19 million), loan financing from Ves-checonom Bank (VEB) amounted to 35. 162 billion MNT ($ 0. 15 billion), and loan financing from Commerz Bank reached 23. 733 billion MNT ($ 10. 4 million) (see Figure 5. 1).

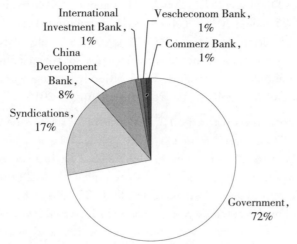

Figure 5. 1   DBM's Borrowings in 2015

Available-for-sale securities refer to DBM's own property in Mongolia Securities Co. , Ltd. (MIK). On December 3, 2015, MIK changed the ownership structure of the company to a joint-stock company, changing its company name to MIK Co. , Ltd. In March 2014, DBM invested 10 billion MNT ($ 4,386,000) in Mongolia Securities Co. , Ltd. and signed a contract to hold 14. 88% stake in the company. MIK announced the dividend information in the third quarter of 2015, in which DBM received $ 23. 64 million worth of dividend profits.

At the end of 2015, MIK traded successfully on the stock exchange at a price of 12,000 MNT per share ($ 5. 26). To maintain a 14. 88% stake in its existing MIK shareholding, DBM proposed to purchase an additional 462. 294 shares at the price indicated above, with a price of 9,000 MNT ($ 3. 95) per share on December 31, 2015. The total investment value was 10. 5 billion MNT ($ 4,655,300).

On October 27, 2015, DBM received "B2-" from Moody's Ratings. On November-ber 3, 2015, DBM received "B / B" from Standard & Poor's Ratings Services.

Highlights of the Year

The DBM assisted the Mongolian economy with its sustainable development, diversified development in many fields, and producing higher value-added products. The DBM maintains the following important programs: the Mongolian government's policy plan for railway transportation; Sai Mountain industrial area project; and roads and energy facility programs that are built through bond financing and will be repaid after completion.

The Mongolian government will build a highly efficient financial institution capable of financing independently in international markets. The goals of creating such an institutions include enhancing Mongolian competitiveness and financing capacity in the international market, and reducing government guarantees and loans repaid by the state budget. DBM will repay the loan of the company with no government guarantee, which was previously repaid from the state budget with the government guarantee. In addition, DBM plans to complete all of the 2018 government guarantees repayment of the funds, and from 2018 to reduce the amount of loans. The government of Mongolia maintained a policy of direct investment in socially efficient programs.

On February 18, 2015, Mongolia passed the Debt Management Act, whereby DBM would be the only bank entitled to 100% government guarantees, while other banks are entitled to 85% government guarantees.

On June 11, 2015, in order to repay 0.17 trillion MNT worth of debt payments loaned in 2014, DBM transferred government bonds ($ 0.55 million and 0.35 billion MNT) to the Central Bank of Mongolia at a price of 0.14 trillion MNT, with the rest paid in cash. On December 27, 2015, DBM used $ 60 million of government bonds as collateral, and signed a sale and repurchase contract with the Mongolian Trade and Development Bank.

DBM provided a loan to ETT, which was expected to pay back. DBM invested $ 200 million in loans to ETT (at the end of 2015, loan funds amounted to 0.40 trillion MNT, about $ 175 million). These loans were adjusted based on the past loans, thus repayment date was postponed to 2017. These loans were guaranteed by the government: if the ETT fails to fulfill its contractual obligations, the corresponding loans will be fully repaid from the state budget (including contingency interest).

DBM issued three loans to the ETT, and the Mongolian government paid 100.27 trillion MNT of the loan interest and loan overdue payments resulting in additional interest. Through this adjustment, DBM received 10 trillion MNT worth of government bonds and received future tax deductions of 90.269 billion MNT.

Bank Pembangunan Malaysia Berhad

Bank Pembangunan Malaysia Berhad (BPMB) is wholly owned by the Malaysian government through the Ministry of Finance. It was incorporated under the Companies Act 1965 on November 28, 1973 with the original objectives of assisting entrepreneurs involved in small- and medium-industries through the provision of various financing facilities, entrepreneurial training, and advisory services. In addition to providing direct financing, BPMB spearheading the growth of Malaysia's strategic economic sectors through its subsidiaries and affiliate companies.

Given a volatile macro-economic environment, the year 2015 was tough for almost every sector in the country, including banking. It was a challenging year for the banking sector amidst volatility and uncertainty over commodity prices, financial markets, as well as global economies, coupled with a highly competitive operating landscape. Margin compression, slower loan growth, higher financing costs, and lackluster capital market activity continued to put a drag on the banking sector's performance in 2015. Despite the prevalent headwinds, BPMB performed relatively well whilst ensuring that they continue to focus on creating long-term value for their stakeholders.

Main Business Data

In 2015, economic uncertainty led to a difficult operating environment for BPMB Group. Across the banking industry, margins remained low with higher capital requirements reducing returns. Amidst these challenges, BPMB Group generated before tax profits of RM 124.8 million in 2015, compared to RM 306.4 million in 2014. The decrease of 59.3% is mainly due to a substantial drop in charter hire income of GMVB, a subsidiary of BPMB, and higher impairment of loans, advances and financing as well as assets, particularly vessels. Subsequently, this high impairment of loans, advances and financing has resulted in Group losses of RM 12.7 million, compared to after tax profits of RM 124.7 million in the previous year.

Unit Profit before Tax: Million Ringgit

Unit Total Assets: Hundred Million Ringgit

BPMB Group's total assets decreased from RM 29.9 billion in the previous year to RM 26.7 billion at the end of 2015, largely from a drop in net loan assets of BPMB. This drop was mainly due to chunky repayment of loans by a single borrower and prepayments by a few borrowers during the year under review. Total liabilities of BPMB Group also dropped to RM 19. 7 billion from RM 22. 4 billion in the previous year, attributed to repayment of borrowings.

Highlights of the Year

In supporting the national development agenda and contributing towards economic growth, BPMB had approved a total of 23 projects amounting to RM 3. 5 billion in 2015. Against a backdrop of slower growth in the banking sector, the approvals decreased by 35. 2% from approvals in the previous year. In 2015, RM 2. 8 billion, or 80. 0% of approvals, was transferred to the infrastructure sector; RM 0. 5 billion, or 14. 3% of approvals, was transferred to the technology sector; the remaining RM 0. 2 billion, or 5. 7% of approvals, going to the maritime sector. There were no approvals for the oil & gas sector in 2015.

BPMB has tightened its loan approval process whereby vessel financing is targeted at borrowers who have strong financial profiles. Additionally, BPMB has been focusing on loans related to government-initiated projects and borrowers with strong history of payment.

Infrastructure

Funding for infrastructure projects continued to be the Bank's forte, accounting for 80% of the Bank's current financing/loan portfolio as of December 31, 2015. For the period under review, the Bank approved financing and loans for 18 infrastructure projects.

In tandem with the government's initiative to further improve the basic infrastructure facilities of the nation, 15. 4% of the infrastructure financing and loans approved were transferred to the road/ highway sub-sector (RM 436. 1 million for five projects), 52. 6% to the area development sub-sector (RM 1,489. 5 million for five projects), and 13. 9% to the tourism sub-sector (RM 394. 0 million for six projects). About 18. 1% (RM 511. 4 million) of the remaining balance was allocated to various projects under the utilities and port sub-sectors (see Figure 5. 2). A total of RM 1, 910. 6 million, (67. 5% of the approved amount of financing and loans) under the infrastructure sector, are for government-backed projects, with two projects under the "Private Finance Initiatives" (PFI) program. PFI is a mechanism introduced by the government to promote private sector involvement in the provision of public services and BPMB has actively participated in this program. As the end of 2015, a total of 33 PFI projects amounting to RM 6. 2 billion were financed by BPMB.

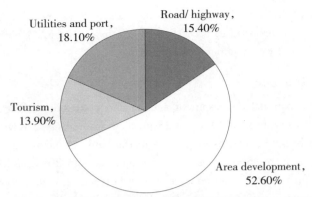

Figure 5. 2   Investment structure of Infrastructure in 2015

Technology

BPMB's appropriations in the technology sector accounted for about RM 500 million of the total appropriations approved. Of the total, 28. 1% was approved for the advanced manufacturing sub-sector, 47. 3% was approved for the ICT sub-sector, and the remaining 24. 6% was approved for the environment conservation sub-sector (see Figure 5. 3).

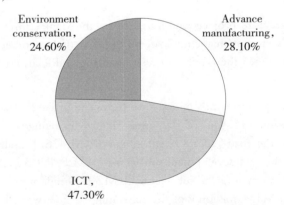

Figure 5. 3   Investment structure of Technology in 2015

Maritime

The supply of shipping vessels remained higher than demand for most shipping services. Slow global economic growth and continued deliveries of new vessels has led to a capacity glut, which limits companies' abilities to raise rates charged for shipping freight, thereby constraining revenue and earnings growth. As a result of the unfavorable environment, there were no vessels being financed by BPMB in 2015. The only project financed by BPMB under the maritime sector was a shipyard with a financing value of RM 200. 0 million.

Oil and Gas

The oil and gas sector has been volatile given the slump in oil prices, slow rollout of domestic developments, downscaled projects, declining marine charter rates, increasing competition from foreign manufacturing firms, and deteriorating regional prospects. Slower project rollouts and delays in new tenders have translated into a cut in earnings for local oil and gas players. Against a landscape of weak market conditions, there were no approvals under BPMB's maritime sector in 2015.

Industrial Development Bank of Turkey

In 2015, which was marked by disappointing global economic growth rates, the pace of economic expansion that had prevailed for a time in emerging markets was interrupted. Advanced economies such as the US, Europe, and Japan entered a period of moderate recovery, while Brazil, Russia, and other commodity-producing countries experienced a deep recession alongside China's economic slowdown. Despite fluctuations in the global economy, Turkey maintained its macroeconomic discipline. In 2015, the Turkish banking industry expanded by 10. 5% . Total loan volume increased by 13. 5% , with local currency loans up by 15% and foreign currency loans up by 9. 9% . The growth rate of non-performing loans (30. 2%) remained subdued relative to previous years.

2015 commenced as a lackluster year due to parliamentary elections. Moreover, the re-elections, in tandem with currency fluctuations, exacerbated economic uncertainties, causing investment appetite to decrease. However, in 2015, Industrial Development Bank of Turkey (TSKB) effectively managed risks through a diversified loan portfolio and created value for its shareholders.

Main Business Data

In 2016, TSKB's total assets reached 24 billion TL ($ 6. 45 billion) with an increase of 15. 8% , while the net profit reached 476. 4 million TL ($ 128 million) with an increase of 17. 1% . The Bank's cash loans grew by 26. 7% to 17. 3 billion TL ($ 4. 65 billion) and the shareholders' equity increased by 17. 7% to 29 billion TL ($ 780 million). The Bank's profitability ratio was 2. 1% at the end of 2016, while the average return on equity was 17. 6% . Besides on an annual basis, the asset quality of TSKB remains healthy with a non-performing loan rate of 0. 3% .

93% of the Bank's loan portfolio was composed of foreign currency loans. The share of US dollar-denominated loans was 57% , whereas the Euro-denominated loans corresponded to 36% of the loan book. The Bank's active role in capital markets and its long-term and sustainable funding structure on the back of close and long-term relationships with supranational organizations are expected to have a persistently positive impact on both the profitability and solvency of the Bank.

Highlights of the Year

TSKB conducts its banking operations with the mission of supporting Turkey's sustainable development. The Bank provides clients with funding obtained from international institutions in a variety of investment areas, including renewable energy, energy and resource efficiency, the environment, sustainable tourism, healthcare, education, and SME financing. In 2015, TSKB secured $ 950 million worth of funding from international markets to support investments undertaken by the private sector. In 2015, TSKB disbursed $ 600 million in project finance cash loans. Energy power plant projects took the lion's share of cash loans, followed by a range of other areas such as electricity distribution, other privatizations, logistics, and real estate.

Support the Development of Low Carbon Emission Manufacturing

The share of loans with a sustainability theme in the TSKB's loan portfolio stood at 50% in 2015. The effective and accurate use of renewable energy resources is extremely important in a period where the authorities are trying to tackle climate change and transition Turkey to be a low carbon economy. Renewable energy resources also have a key role in reducing Turkey's dependence on foreign resources. Over the last six years, TSKB has provided medium- and long-term financing to the Turkish private sector to improve resource efficiency. 103 energy and resource efficiency projects have been financed so far, making up 10% of TSKB's total loan portfolio. The projects cover the tourism, chemistry, automotive, steel, cement and textile, mining, energy, and other sectors.

As the end of 2015, the Bank has extended around $ 500 million in loans and supported more than 100 projects related to manufacturing processes, waste management, and energy and resource efficiency. TSKB has played an instrumental role in combatting climate change and meeting Turkey's ever-increasing demand for energy.

Besides, as Turkey's first carbon-neutral bank, TSKB encourages and motivates those stakeholders in its area of influence to undertake sustainability-related initiatives.

Support the Establishment of Industrial Corporations and the Development of the Private Sector

Over the years, TSKB has played a key role in the establishment of many industrial corporations, which serve as the building blocks of the private sector in the country. As the end of 2015, the share of loans extended to SMEs in the total loan book was 16%.

Throughout the whole year, TSKB signed thematic funding agreements equaling a total of $ 340 million which is composed of $ 150 million from JBIC's Renewable Energy and Energy Efficiency Loan, $ 100 million from EIB's Loan for SMEs and Midcaps, and $ 75 million from IFC's Renewable Energy, Resource, and Energy Efficiency Loan.

Support to Arts & Culture

Conducting its operations in line with the principle of creating value and carrying out successful cooperation in the area, TSKB is an ongoing sponsor of the concerts that are part of the Istanbul Music Festival organized by the Istanbul Foundation for Culture and Arts.

The Bank received widespread praise from concertgoers for its sponsorship of "Dancing Paris", held on June 8, 2015 as one of the major events at the Istanbul Music Festival. In 2014, TSKB started to offset the carbon footprint of the sponsored concerts, which included emissions from musicians and audience members traveling to the concert area. TSKB thus broke new ground by pairing sustainability with arts sponsorship. How TSKB did this is described below.

With a project started two years ago, the Bank sends personalized Gold Standard Voluntary Emission Reduction (VER) certificate to its business partners and clients as a New year's gift. With this certificate, TSKB effectively neutralizes its stakeholders' individual carbon footprints arising from everyday activities such as transportation, heating, and energy for the year. The Gold Standard VER Certificate was developed in line with the rules, methodologies, and guidelines set by the International Gold Standard. It is based on a Voluntary Emission Reduction project approved by independent enterprises that are accredited according to the United Nations Framework Convention on Climate Change.

Agricultural Bank of Turkey

2015 was a year in which Turkey's economy was impacted by global economic developments. Despite suffering from the Fed's long-anticipated interest rate hike, the European Central Bank's expansionist monetary policies, geopolitical risks, and inflation, the Turkish economy still managed to register growth. In 2015, Agricultural Bank of Turkey's total assets reached TL 302. 8 billion in value and increased by 22. 3% compared to the previous year. Focusing on sustainable profitability and productivity, the Bank once again increased its net profit, just as it has done consistently every year.

In 2015, the Bank's net profit grew by 27. 5% to TL 5. 2 billion. In addition to its core business activities of financing agricultural production, agroindustry, and industrial endeavors, trade finance has also emerged recently as one of the business lines in which the Bank was increasing its competition. The support that the Bank provides to real economic activity grew faster than the overall sectoral average in 2015. Cash loan disbursements to corporate customers increased by 44% from the previous year and reached TL 68 billion in value while non-cash credit was also up by 45% and totaled TL 53 billion. Additionally, in 2015, Agricultural Bank of Turkey (TCZB) opened 112 new domestic branches and further expanded its geographical reach in its home market.

Main Business Data

The strategic goals of TCZB in 2015 are described below:

The Bank wanted to focus on cultivating value-creating, sustainable relationships with all of its customers; to increase productivity through business process institutionalization as well as through continuous improvement and development; to increase synergies among its domestic and international subsidiaries, affiliates, and international branches through the expansion of the Agricultural Finance Group; to rapidly adapt to technology and operations that are highly digitalized and centralized; to keep HR management objective and transparent as well as ensure the sustainability of its business model both by improving its current employees' skills and by also being a center of attraction for new talent; to take maximum advantage of the opportunities afforded by technology in order to secure a competitive advantage; to optimize its balance sheet so that its structure can become more customer-focused and also to manage expenditures without hindering revenue growth.

TCZB seeks to strengthen its financial structure through sustainable growth, profitability, and productivity. In 2015, the Bank continued to reinforce its equity-compatible balance sheet structure through the asset and liability management strategies to which it adhered. The Bank remained on course in terms of capital adequacy, profitability, and productivity.

A designated primary dealer in the Turkish government debt market, TCZB continued to successfully maintain that position in 2015. The Bank played an active role not only in the primary market but also in secondary markets, where it traded on behalf of its own customers as well as for national and international financial institutions. Because of such trading last year, the Bank ranked second, as measured by total transaction volume, in the Borsa Istanbul Debt Securities Market, for which performance it was awarded by the exchange. The Bank's FX trading was up by 29% in 2015.

In 2016, the Bank's total assets reached 357. 76 billion TL ($ 98. 5 billion) with an increase of 18. 1% while the net profit reached 6. 58 billion TL ($ 1. 82 billion) with an increase of 27%. In 2016, agricultural loans provided by the Bank increased by 25% to 42 billion TL ($ 11. 6 billion).

Highlights of the Year

€ 100 Million from the French Development Agency

A twelve-year, € 100 million line of credit was obtained from the French Development Agency to provide attractively-priced financing to agricultural-sector SMEs that process animal-source foods. This line of credit is to be used as loans to SMEs engaged in the non-primary (non-animal husbandry) aspects of animal-source food production in order to finance modernization projects that will bring them into compliance with EU hygiene and environment standards. The line of credit will also help SMEs satisfy the requirements of Turkish laws and regulations governing veterinary services, plant health, food, and animal feed.

Council of Europe Development Bank Credit Agreement

In 2014, a seven-year agreement was signed with the Council of Europe Development Bank to provide a total of € 50 million in credit through Ziraat Finansal Kiralama, TCZB's leasing subsidiary. Having been transferred to TCZB in 2015, the first tranches of this credit were then turned over to ZFK. Under the terms of the credit agreement, at least 15% of the total amount must be lent to businesses that are operating in Turkey's priority-development regions. The main goal of this program is to enable micro-, small-, and medium-sized businesses active in many different endeavors such as manufacturing, construction, agroindustry, tourism, trade, and logistics to undertake productive investments and also to meet their working capital requirements for such investments. Other objectives include helping these businesses create new jobs and improving their ability to protect existing ones, creating a positive social impact and supporting the leasing industry.

World Bank Credit for SMEs and Larger-sized Enterprises

Funding received from the World Bank is used to support small businesses (those that employ no more than 250 people) and medium-sized businesses (those that employ no more than 1,500 people) by meeting their needs for investment and working capital, overcoming difficulties in obtaining credit, and helping them to create jobs. Lending under this $ 200 million line of credit, the agreement for which was originally signed in 2010, was successfully completed in the first quarter of 2015.

European Investment Bank Credit Financing for SMEs and Larger-sized Enterprises

In 2015, TCZB began lending from the second € 100 million tranche of a € 200 million line of credit which had obtained under an agreement with the European Investment Bank to finance SMEs and larger-sized enterprises. As per the agreement, this credit is being used both to support borrowers' efforts to pursue growth by increasing output, productivity, and employment, and to provide them with the investment and operating capital they need. Another stated objective is to help reduce interregional disparities in development levels.

Saudi Export Program Credit

In 2013, TCZB secured a $ 50 million line of credit from the Saudi Export Program (SEP) to finance the importation of goods of Saudi Arabian origin into Turkey. Disbursements continued successfully in 2015. Under the SEP, customers who import a wide range of goods other than petroleum from Saudi Arabia are provided with low-cost financing on terms of up to three years to pay for them.

German Development Bank Credit

In 2014, TCZB signed a 10-year agreement with the German Development Bank to supply € 150 million in financing to SMEs that are located in rural areas or are part of the agricultural value-creation chain.

KOSGEB Support Programs

TCZB and the Small and Medium Enterprises Development Organization (KOSGEB) have entered into an agreement to give businesses that apply to agency under its support programs easier access to sources of financing.

Pharmacy Support Package

On March 23 , 2015 , TCZB introduced its " Pharmacy Support Package" and began offering it to pharmacists whose Social Security Corporation collections and payments are made through the Bank. This comprehensive package of advantageous banking and credit products and services is designed both to assist the country's pharmacies and pharmacists , and to support the Bank in its efforts to achieve leadership in this business line.

Women Entrepreneurs Support Package

On December 4 , 2015 , TCZB launched the " Ziraat Women Entrepreneurs Support Package" , which aims to help women entrepreneurs play a bigger role in the national economy by supporting their business activities.

Seven New Mutual Funds Were Launched

In order to diversify the range of collective investment options that are made available to Agricultural Finance Group customers , last year seven new mutual funds were added to the existing lineup. These include a hedge fund , a fund of funds , a real estate investment trust equity fund , a sharia-compliant hedge fund , a sharia-compliant equity fund , a sharia-compliant FX fund , and a sharia-compliant lease certificate participation fund. Of the seven newly-launched funds , the last four were introduced as alternatives for customers who prefer interest-free collective investment schemes.

Syndicated Loans

In 2015 , TCZB conducted its third syndicated loan. 41 banks from 19 countries took part in the syndication when it was undertaken in April. Coordinated by Bank of America Merrill Lynch International Limited , the deal secured for TCZB a total of $ 1. 1 billion in two tranches , one with a 354-day maturity at 6-month LIBOR/EURIBOR + 0. 70% and the other with a 367-day maturity at 6-month LIBOR/EURIBOR + 0. 80%. The Bank will be using this funding in its ongoing efforts to effectively support its customers through the increasingly broader and more diversified range of foreign trade finance products and services that it offers.

Support for the Agricultural Sector

Financing agricultural endeavors is one cornerstone of TCZB's mission. The Bank focuses on providing financial support in line with national agricultural policy. TCZB stands by its customers with sustainable funding models which will enable businesses that are involved in agricultural production to increase their capacity, modernization, profitability, and productivity, which will create added value.

The total volume of credit extended to finance the agricultural sector by TCZB was 35.8 billion TL in 2015. At the end of the year, the Bank had 634,689 agricultural credit customers. In keeping with its mission to support agricultural endeavors, TCZB supplies subsidized credit as specified by government decrees to customers who are engaged in various aspects of agricultural production. The rates charged on such lending typically vary between 0 and 8.25% on an annual basis.

Column 5-2　Factors Affecting Credit Ratings of Turkish Banks

In recent years, the Turkish economy has continued to grow at a stable pace and the banking sector is performing well with a continually growing asset size and net profit. According to data released by Turkish Banking Regulation and Supervision Agency (BDDK), the Turkish banking sector's net profits increased by 63.4% compared to the previous year to $ 8.85 billion in the first 8 months of 2016, whereas total assets stood at $ 835.8 billion. Meanwhile, credit reached $ 529.97 billion, the average capital adequacy ratio was 16.03% for the January–August period, and the core capital adequacy ratio was 13.80%. However, the credit ratings of Turkish banks have changed frequently in 2016. Turkey's development banks such as TCZB and TSKB are operating well and financially sound. Moreover, as the second largest bank of Turkey, TCZB is maintaining sustainable profitability and has a huge network of branches all across the country. Despite doing well, why the ratings of these banks been lowered as well?

2016 was a tough year for Turkey. Turkey's involvement in the conflict in neighboring Syria and the breakdown of the Kurdish peace process appear to have triggered several high-profile terrorist attacks claiming multiple fatalities. An unsuccessful coup attempt in July confirms heightened risks to political stability. Syrian refugees have caused a series of social problems in Turkey and increased the economic burden of Turkey. The negative outlook for Turkey's economic risk has resulted in negative changes to the banks' ratings and put pressure on banks' credit standing. After the unsuccessful coup attempt, Turkey's fiscal risk, security risk, political instability, and worsened geopolitical environment, led credit rating agencies such as Moody's, Fitch Ratings, and Standard & Poor's to downgrade the sovereign ratings of Turkey. Moody's cut Turkey's credit rating to "junk" status. Accordingly, more than a dozen banks' ratings have been affected (see Table 5.1 and Table 5.2).

Table 5.1　The Ratings of Agricultural Bank of Turkey

Credit Rating Agency	Category	October 2015	October 2016
Fitch Ratings	Foreign Currency Long-term IDR	BBB	BBB –
	Outlook	stable	Negative
	Foreign Currency Short-term IDR	F3	F3
	Local Currency Long-term IDR	BBB	BBB –
	Outlook	stable	Negative
	Local Currency Short-term IDR	F3	F3
	National Long-Term Rating	AAA (tur)	AAA (tur)
	Outlook	stable	stable
	Support Rating	2	2
	Support Rating Floor	BBB –	BBB –
	Viability Rating	bbb –	bbb –
Moody's	Outlook	Negative	stable
	Long-term Bank Deposit Foreign Currency	Baa3	Ba2
	Short-term Bank Deposit Foreign Currency	P-3	Not-Prime
	Long-term Bank Deposit Domestic Currency	Baa3	Ba1
	Short-term Bank Deposit Domestic Currency	P-3	Not-Prime
	Baseline Credit Assessment	ba1	ba2
	Adjusted Baseline Credit Assessment	ba1	ba2

Table 5. 2　The Ratings of Industrial Development Bank of Turkey

Credit Rating Agency	Category	October 2015	October 2016
	Foreign Currency		
Fitch Ratings	Long Term	BBB –	BBB – –
	Outlook	Stable	Negative
	Short Term	F3	F3
	Local Currency		
	Long Term	BBB	BBB –
	Outlook	stable	Negative
	Short Term	F3	F3
Fitch Ratings	Other		
	Support Rating	2	2
	Support Rating Floor	BBB-	BBB-
	National Long Term Rating	AAA（tur）	AAA（tur）
	Outlook	Stable	Stable
	Baseline Credit Assessment	ba2	ba2
	Long-term Issuer Rating Foreign Currency	Baa3	Ba1
	Long-term Issuer Rating Domestic Currency	Baa3	Ba1
Moody's	Outlook	Negative	Stable
	Short-term Issuer Rating Foreign Currency	P-3	Not-Prime
	Short-term Issuer Rating Domestic Currency	P-3	Not-Prime

Fiscal Risk

The Turkey's fiscal discipline was basically stable in 2015 despite the holding of two closely contested parliamentary elections. The central government deficit narrowed slightly to 1.2% of GDP, from 1.3% of GDP in 2014. As a result, the general government debt/GDP ratio fell to 32.6% at the end of 2015, compared with a peer median of 42.6% of GDP. The implementation of pre-election spending commitments is expected to worsen the fiscal position in 2016, with the central government deficit expected to widen to 2% of GDP, but the debt/GDP ratio will remain on a downward path. Refugee and security expenses pose expenditure pressures. Rising use of public private partnerships, which are not fully accounted for at the Treasury, are another fiscal risk. Turkey's economy is still nominally growing, but with inflation of 8%, it has actually begun to decline.

In addition, the huge trade deficit accumulated over more than two decades has placed a heavy burden of external debt on Turkey. External vulnerabilities are a key credit weakness. Net external debt is very large compared with peers at an estimated 38.4% of GDP at the end of 2015, compared with the 'BBB' median of 3.4%, reflecting the financing of persistently large current account deficits. Lower oil prices have driven a cyclical decline in the current account deficit, which was halved in nominal terms between 2013 and 2015 and is forecast at a seven-year low of 3.5% of GDP in 2016. There is no evidence of a structural improvement in the external position. Some experts pointed out that as the country with the highest current account deficit among the G20 members, Turkey relies on the inflow of investment funds to finance current account deficits and external debt. Meanwhile, the value of the Turkish lira against other currencies is declining sharply. The USD/TRY rate has soared from 2.8 at the end of 2015 to over 3.5 at present. Affected by the unsuccessful coup attempt and security conditions, the external financing vulnerabilities of Turkey are becoming more and more serious, resulting in a reversal of the declining trend of the debt/GDP ratio and a worsening of external imbalances.

Political Instability

Prolonged and deepened political instability undermines economic performance and threatens the economic policy credibility of Turkey. The attempted coup in Turkey and the authorities' reaction highlight political risks to the country's sovereign credit profile. The media has reported that more than 6,000 people have been arrested, including judges and prosecutors. This could put further strains on institutional integrity amid plans to formally increase the powers of the presidency. The authorities responded to the coup attempt with a purge of the followers of those it blames, with around 70,000 public sector workers suspended by August 19. The government was able to regain control of the situation rapidly after the coup attempt, but the political fallout could refocus attention on Turkey's large external financing requirement if it results in significantly diminished international investor confidence.

Low World Bank governance scores for political stability have long been a feature of Turkey's sovereign credit profile. Domestic shocks also have the power to damage investor perceptions of sovereign creditworthiness. If political instability further exacerbates the investment environment and further increases fiscal pressure, Turkey's economic, fiscal, and debt indicators may be worse than expected and become a destabilizing factor affecting sovereign ratings and financial institution ratings.

Security Risk and the Worsening Geopolitical Scene

Turkey's security risks are increasing as a result of the "Kurdish Problem", neighboring Syria's problems and attacks by ISIS. Terrorist attacks in Istanbul and Ankara have caused multiple fatalities in 2016. Turkey's security conditions have worsened outside of the context of the coup attempt. The removal of a large number of senior military officials may hinder the capacity to address ongoing security challenges. Turkey shot down a Russian air force jet in November 2015 and Moscow retaliated with trade sanctions. Since then the two countries have made significant progress to mend relations with each other, but the impact of the conflict has not completely disappeared.

The attacks are having a material impact on the tourism sector, which is around 3% of GDP and 13% of current external receipts. Revenues from foreign tourist arrivals were down 41% in 2016 compared to the previous year. A diplomatic rapprochement with Russia should provide some support to the sector, but without a significant improvement in security conditions, a broad-based recovery is unlikely.

Elections in November 2014 resulting in another term for the Justice & Development Party (AKP) have eased domestic political uncertainty, but the prospect of constitutional reform in order to strengthen the powers of the presidency means some uncertainties linger.

Impacts on Banks and Institutions

The ratings of the banks are primarily sensitive to a change in Turkey's sovereign ratings. The credit situation of banks in Turkey is closely linked to country risks, access to foreign credit markets, and the lira exchange rate.

It can be said that the attempted military coup was the trigger for many problems which directly resulted in the increase in downside risks for Turkish banks' credit profiles and ratings. The Fitch Ratings continue to view the Turkish banking sector as fundamentally sound, as reflected in the investment-grade ratings of most large lenders, and do not expect any sharp movements in banks' financial metrics in the near term. In addition, there has been little evidence of deposit instability triggered by the attempted coup, and the central bank has indicated its readiness to provide liquidity support to the sector. However, the sharp lira depreciation following the attempted coup highlights the banking sector's exposure to foreign-currency lending risks, with FX-denominated loans making up around a third of the total sector portfolio. Following the significant depreciation of the lira in recent years, banks are likely to suffer some losses on these exposures. Moreover, a further sharp deterioration of the lira would increase risks to banks' asset quality and put pressure on capital ratios as a result of the increase in the lira value of FX loans.

Individual banks' asset quality ratios could also come under renewed pressure from exposure to the troubled tourism sector, which could suffer further from increased political instability. However, on a sector basis, banks' lending to the tourism industry is small (around 3% of loans), while the thawing of relations with Russia could provide some respite in terms of tourist flows.

Rating decisions made by international credit rating agencies are sometimes guided by political motives instead of economic indicators, so credit ratings cannot fully reflect Turkey's environment of trade and investment. However, with the downgrade, Turkey will have difficulty in attracting foreign investment to make up for its current account deficit. Since factors affecting credit ratings of Turkish banks such as political instability, the geopolitical environment, and security risk are uncertain, Turkey's sovereign ratings and financial institutions' ratings also have uncertainty and may even change frequently.

Brazilian Development Bank

In 2015, the growth of the world's macro economy remained slow, and major economies still experienced stagnant economic growth. As a result, there was declining international trade, a record-low business and consumer confidence index, and a depreciation of the Brazilian real relative to the US dollar. These factors further imposed pressures on Brazil's economic development: both S&P and Fitch downgraded Brazil's investment capacity, Brazilian business profitability remains below its historic average, the cost of loans has risen, and risks of stock investments have increased. However, despite the gloomy economic condition and doubts from citizens and regulatory institutions, Brazilian Development Bank (BNDES) makes contributions in promoting Brazilian investments and sustaining domestic economic development.

Main Business Data

In 2015, BNDES held total assets of BRL 930.6 billion. Its net earnings reached BRL 6.2 billion, which was a 5.4% reduction from the previous year's BRL 8.6 billion. BNDES also confirmed that, from 2015 onwards, BRL 36.6 billion worth of instruments eligible as tier one capital will no longer be presented in net equity; instead, this portion is now integrated into liabilities with the National Treasury. In addition, BNDES has invested approximately BRL 135.9 billion in more than 950,000 projects, primarily those in the fields of electricity, transportation and logistics, and green economy. This is a 28% decline from the previous year.

Highlights of the Year

Improve Accountability and Transparency

In order to respond to the demands from society and regulatory agencies, BNDES strove to improve accountability and transparency. Since 2008, public access to operational information has been a featured characteristic of BNDES. In 2015, BNDES built a more transparent website upon the existing information system, allowing easier access to information and adding main financial conditions onto the website. Newly added information includes terms, rates, and financial guarantees.

Undertake Environmental Responsibilities

BNDES sought to satisfy the highest international standards in sustainability and environment, related to both the analysis of investment projects and the practices to be implemented by companies in Brazil. In addition to the formation of Amazon Fund, BNDES provided BRL 20 million for seven projects related to the Atlantic Forest Biome. At the same time, BNDES also funded projects studying extraction of second-generation ethanol from sugarcane waste to help the Brazilian government meet its goal of reducing greenhouse gas emissions by 35% by 2025.

Promote Infrastructure Construction

In 2015, BNDES invested BRL 29. 4 billion in financial projects in the energy and logistics sectors. For example, credit was approved for two highways in important transport areas for Brazilian agribusiness and wholesale trade. Also, the Brasilia, Guarulhos, and Viracopos airport projects are now in the final disbursement phase. For projects related to urban mobility and sanitation, BNDES disbursed BRL 10. 4 billion. Among all relevant operations, the expansion of municipal water supply and sanitation systems in the state of Rio de Janeiro received a contract for BRL 295. 6 million worth of funding from BNDES. Other infrastructure construction included Line 4 Subway for the 2016 Olympic Games, Light Rail Vehicle, and Trasoeste BRT.

Support Innovative Micro-, Small-, and Medium-size Enterprises (MSME)

In 2015, BNDES Innovative MSME Program approved 66 operation projects with BRL 101. 5 million disbursed. Another key program, BNDES ProBK Program, has also invested BRL 230 million in approved and contracted operations. Half of these operations are with MSMEs.

On the other hand, BNDESPAR, an integral subsidiary of BNDES, serves to promote the sustainable development of the Brazilian economy, complementing the financing products offered to the supported projects. In 2015, BNDESPAR funded over 1 ,000 innovative enterprises, especially those based in technological innovation.

Development Bank of Southern African

Established in 1983, the Development Bank of Southern African (DBSA) is a state-owned bank owned by the government of the Republic of South Africa and a leading development finance institution in the Southern African region. DBSA is committed to promoting economic development in South Africa and the whole of Africa, optimizing human resources, and improving institutional capacity. In 2015, DBSA continued to increase financial support for infrastructure projects and assisted the South African government in providing high quality infrastructure services to the population.

Main Business Data

Through the end of 2015, DBSA possessed a development fund of ZAR 63. 1 billion, spanning 13 SADC (the Southern African Development Community) countries, mainly in the energy, road, water, transport, and social infrastructure sectors. DBSA is committed to practicing the values of "high efficiency, shared vision, integrity, innovation and service orientation" and aims to build Southern Africa into a prosperous and harmonious, region free of poverty. DBSA continues to expand its financing for development and is committed to raising People's living standards through social infrastructure, boosting economic growth through investment in economic infrastructure, and supporting regional integration.

DBSA has four main resources, including social capital, financial capital, intellectual capital, and human capital. In terms of social capital, DBSA emphasizes its relationship with customers, partners, and governments, and has business relationships with 13 countries. In terms of intellectual capital, DBSA has 31 years of experience in infrastructure development and has the intellectual support of the government of South Africa. In terms of financial capital, its funds come mainly from issuing debt, net assets, and other financial resources, such as business or investment income. In 2015, DBSA's capital and reserves were ZAR 237 billion; it obtained development funds of ZAR 2. 5 billion from the government and had interest-bearing debt of ZAR 46. 2 billion. In addition, business operations brought a total of ZAR 27 billion. In terms of human capital, its main human capital is comprised of the health, knowledge, and skills of its workers. In 2015, the Bank had 459 employees, 88 of which were dedicated to supporting the construction of infrastructure.

Highlights of the Year

In order to adapt to its own strategic transformation better, DBSA upgraded its strategic objectives. In 2015, DBSA had three strategic objectives. The first was to promote the expansion of business and maximize development results. The second was to provide a complete solution for infrastructure construction in Southern Africa. The third was to achieve financial sustainability, maintain profitability, improve business efficiency, and increase net asset value. In order to achieve these three strategic objectives, DBSA further proposed the following strategic initiatives.

Providing Creative Solutions for Infrastructure in Southern Africa

Infrastructure development was a priority for the DBSA in 2015. In that year, DBSA invested $ 100 million in infrastructure projects in Southern Africa and approved projects totaling ZAR 6. 4 billion. Investment projects under preparation were worth ZAR 260 billion, mostly in the energy and transportation sectors. In 2015, DBSA invested ZAR 13 billion in infrastructure development in total. Among these 113 investment projects, the energy sector received ZAR 7 billion, the water sector received ZAR 2. 1 billion, the transport sector received ZAR 1. 3 billion, and the communications sector received ZAR 350 million. For infrastructure investment, ZAR 5. 4 billion was spent in urban areas. In urban areas, DBSA completed three master plans about infrastructure projects, with a total of 60 completed projects, 27 projects still being planned, and 84 projects being implemented. In non-urban areas, DBSA completed the construction of 15 schools (with 48 more still under construction), 1,128 houses, 60 medical consultation rooms, and 26 health clinics. DBSA has more effectively solved problems concerning market and customer needs through innovation, utilizing product diversification to achieve greater competitive advantage, accelerating infrastructure development, and expanding infrastructure coverage.

Creating and Sustaining an Efficient Culture

To DBSA, human resources are the most valuable resource. DBSA was committed to building a challenging and stimulating work environment to attract, expand, sustain, and reward the outstanding staff, and to enhance cohesion and promote development. In order to coordinate human resources, the Board of DBSA established the HRNSE Commission, which is responsible for implementing its human capital strategy and coordinating management, social, and ethical issues, including the appointment and removal of staff.

Developing and Utilizing the Strategic Cooperative Partnership

DBSA was devoted to the expansion of selected market sectors and penetration into geographical markets by developing strategic cooperative partnerships with other institutions. These strategic cooperative partnerships enabled DBSA to gain more information and project funding, thus expanding its competitive advantage. DBSA developed strategic cooperative partnerships actively with clients and partners to make development plans and promote the implementation of infrastructure projects. For example, in 2015, DBSA actively cooperated with the International Development Financing Club (IDFC) and continued to participate in the World Economic Forum (WEF) positively, accelerating the implementation of infrastructure projects.

Promoting the Progress and Expansion of Business

DBSA devoted itself to building its business operation model, to providing fund for development more efficiently, and improving its project execution. In 2015, DBSA increased investment in education, health care, and sanitation, including building schools, improving school infrastructure, improving housing conditions for residents, establishing clinics and medical consultation rooms, and repairing the facilities in clinics.

Setting up the Green Fund to Support the Growth of the Green Economy in Southern Africa

The Green Fund, established in 2013, aimed to support Southern Africa's economic transformation and lead Southern Africa to a low- carbon green development path. In 2015, the Green Fund approved 15 projects, totaling ZAR 455. 1 million, mainly focused on the fields of renewable energy and waste treatment and recycling.

Establishing Employment Fund to create More Jobs and Employment Opportunities

The Employment Fund, set up in 2012, was committed to providing financial support for job creation-oriented projects. In 2015, the Employment Fund invested ZAR 513. 8 million in total, creating 401,217 permanent jobs and 9,468 temporary jobs. 6,551 workers completed short-term internships and 66,483 received vocational training.

In all, in 2015, DBSA focused on infrastructure development, provided financial support for the development of energy, transport, and water resources in Southern Africa, and boosted the economic growth in the region. For the next three years, DBSA has launched the "three-year development target" to improve People's livelihood further and promote sustainable economic development in Southern Africa.

Development Bank of Kazakhstan

The Development Bank of Kazakhstan (DBK) continues to successfully carry out the strategic tasks assigned to it. Despite certain difficulties experienced by the country's financial sector, DBK finished the year with a net profit of 5. 7 billion tenge.

Under the state program of industrialization, DBK plays the role of the main investment institute of the country, providing financial support to the private sector and to state initiatives (including infrastructure projects) by providing medium- and long- term low- interest loans to non-primary sectors of the economy.

In accordance with the law of the Republic of Kazakhstan "On banks and banking activity in the Republic of Kazakhstan", DBK is not a second-tier bank and has a special legal status. DBK is not subject to prudential regulation by the national regu- lator. A special law of the Republic of Kazakhstan "On Development Bank of Ka- zakhstan" regulates the activity of DBK.

100% of DBK shares are owned by the National Holding "Baiterek" JSC (the sole shareholder) with 100% state participation in the authorized capital. The authorized capital of DBK as of December 31, 2015 was 353,667,511 thousand tenge.

Main Business Data

As of December 31, 2015, DBK assets were 2,128 billion tenge, an increase of 63% compared to the previous year (see Figure 5.4).

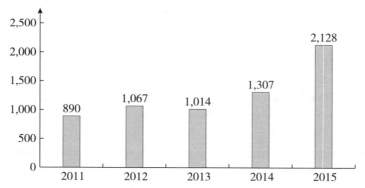

Figure 5.4　Changes of Total Assets of DBK: 2011 – 2015 (Unit: Billion Tenge)

As of December 31, 2015, DBK liabilities were 1,772 billion tenge, an increase of 78% from the beginning of the reporting year (see Figure 5.5).

The amount of equity capital of DBK as of December 31, 2015 was 356 billion tenge, an annual increase of 43 billion tenge.

Taking all of this into account, DBK net profit in 2015 was 5.7 billion tenge, which was 49% lower than in the previous year (11.3 billion tenge in 2014).

Net interest income of DBK was 31 billion tenge, an increase of 5 billion tenge or 18% compared to the previous year.

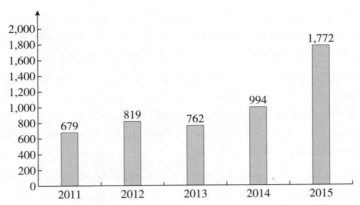

Figure 5.5   Changes of Liabilities of DBK: 2011 – 2015 (Unit: Billion Tenge)

DBK's 2015 credit portfolio amounted to 1,452 billion tenge, an increase of 78% compared to the previous year.

Highlights of the Year

Crediting

DBK significantly increased lending to the economy of Kazakhstan, matching or exceeding their planned targets. The consolidated loan portfolio of DBK increased four-fold. By the end of 2013, the amounted in the loan portfolio was 378 billion tenge; at the end of 2015, that value was about 1.45 trillion tenge. The scope of projects receiving financing expanded. To date, the Bank portfolio is comprised of projects in the sectors of metallurgy, oil refining and petrochemicals, machine building, food, construction, and transport.

In 2015, DBK funded enterprises of non-primary sectors in the amount of 262.3 billion tenge, or 66% of all loans issued by second tier banks in those sectors.

In 2015, for projects in the processing industry, DBK granted 216.5 billion tenge or 83% of all loans issued by second tier banks in those sectors.

At the end of 2015, the volume of DBK's loan portfolio 1,452 billion tenge, or 96% of all loans issued by second tier banks in those sectors.

By the end of 2015, DBK in the long-term crediting of enterprises of manufacturing industry 1,180 billion tenge, or 151% of all loans issued by second tier banks in those sectors.

Project Financing

Since its establishment, DBK has approved 111 investment projects worth 4,897.8 billion tenge. DBK's contributions amounted to 2,469.2 billion tenge and 95 export transactions worth 613.5 billion tenge with DBK contributing 373.9 billion tenge.

For 14 years, with the financial support of DBK, production capacity of 79 investment projects worth 1,648.7 billion tenge was launched with KDB contributing 786.2 billion tenge, of which:

55 projects worth 527.4 billion tenge in the manufacturing industry;

6 projects worth 77.9 billion tenge in the production and distribution of electricity;

11 projects worth 128.9 billion tenge in transport and logistics;

5 projects worth 27.2 billion tenge in communications;

2 projects worth 24.8 billion tenge in tourism infrastructure.

About 20.4 thousand permanent jobs were created in the operation of these newly-built enterprises.

Information on the investment projects approved for financing in 2015 is provided below:

DBK began supporting the construction of a plant for the production of sodium cyanide with a capacity of 15,000 tons in Karata. Taking into account that at the moment sodium cyanide is imported, implementation of this project will contribute to import substitution and export development of domestic products. The plant employs about 500 people.

DBK began supporting the production of petrol of ecological class K5 corresponding to Euro-5 standard. The capacity of motor fuel production in this new plant will be 114,000 tons of petrol AI-92 and 86,000 tons of petrol AI-95 per year. The project will reduce the shortage of motor fuels in the domestic market, eliminate the dependence on imports of motor fuels, and increase the exports of fuels.

Project for construction of plant for production and processing of flat glass in Kyzylorda. The project is one of the most significant projects of the regional program of industrial and innovative development. The plant will cover the need of the domestic market by 100%.

Project for construction of a complex for production of railway wheels in Ekibastuz. The project is being implemented within the second five-year plan of industrialization. New production is scheduled to start in 2017. Production capacity will increase from 75 thousand wheels per year to 200 thousand. As much as 60% of production will be exported.

In terms of the sectoral composition of approved investment projects and export operations, the largest share of projects are in chemicals and petrochemicals (41%) metallurgy (22%), mechanical engineering (16%), and production of building materials (13%).

Funding

In order to ensure the necessary funding base, DBK uses a variety of borrowing tools, both on the domestic and international capital markets – bond issue and placement, attraction of interbank and budget lending, syndicated loans, deposit attraction, and others.

Using these tools, the Bank attracted 12.7 billion tenge worth of funding within intra-group financing of "Baiterek" Holding in 2015.

During the implementation of the "Nurly Zhol" (Light Road) program to support domestic producers and exporters, 85 billion tenge was allocated from the National Fund of the Republic of Kazakhstan for the following areas:

Support of domestic automakers – 30 billion tenge;

Support of production of passenger cars – 5 billion tenge;

Support of exporters – 50 billion tenge.

Also, within the framework of the Resolution of the Government No. 124 for financing large-scale businesses in the manufacturing industry, 50 billion tenge borrowings were allocated from the National Fund of the Republic of Kazakhstan to DBK on March 13, 2015.

On December 18, 2015, DBK redeemed the fifth tranche of those bonds issued as Eurobonds in 2010 for the amount of about $ 285 million, including the principal debt of $ 277 million and the tenth coupon payment for the amount of $ 76 million.

With the official visit of the Prime Minister of the Republic of Kazakhstan to China in March 2015, DBK signed a loan agreement with the China Development Bank in the amount of $ 650 million to finance projects in energy, transport, infrastructure, manufacturing, information technologies, agriculture, and other areas, which will provide mutual benefits to both countries and will contribute to expansion of bilateral

China-Kazakhstan economic and trade cooperation.

In March 2015, a loan agreement with the Bank of Tokyo-Mitsubishi UFJ Ltd was signed for the amount of $ 10 million for pre-export financing of "Kazzinc" LLP.

In June 2015, another application of funds in the amount of € 4. 7 million on credit agreement with HSBC took place, which was signed in 2014 to finance the project of "Aktobe rail and structural steel plant" LLP under the SACE insurance.

At the end of 2015, the amount of debt owed to creditors by DBK was $ 5. 78 billion.

DBK-Leasing

At the end of 2015, "DBK-Leasing" JSC financed 27 leasing transactions totaling 35,708. 7 million tenge.

The funded projects include:

"Azerbaijani Railways" CJSC – financing of export of Kazakhstan locomotives ("LBP" JSC) for "Azerbaijani Railways" CJSC (international leasing transaction);

"Kazakhmys Corporation" LLP – modernization of machine-building production;

"Istkomtrans" LLP – purchase of cars under the leaseback scheme.

The largest industry concentrations in the leasing portfolio are manufacturing (46. 9%) and transportation and warehousing (39. 6%).

"DBK-Leasing" JSC, as part of the state investment policy, takes part in the implementation of such government programs as the "Roadmap 2020" and "Productivity 2020. "

The mission and vision of DBK are defined in the development strategy of "Development Bank of Kazakhstan" JSC for 2014 – 2023, approved by the Board of Directors decision dated July 14, 2014, and have not changed over the past year.

DBK's mission is to promote sustainable development of the national economy by investing in non-primary sectors of the country.

According to the mandate of DBK, the main sectoral priorities are projects in non-primary sectors of the economy: metallurgy, chemistry and petrochemistry, mechanical engineering, processing of agricultural products, and industrial infrastructure (energy, transport, telecommunications, and facilities in the service sector).

In the Bank's vision, it sees itself becoming:

The country's leading operator for evaluating and structuring large infrastructure and industrial projects for the private sector and the government;

A specialized state development institution that provides timely and sufficient funding of projects in the fields of industry and infrastructure;

A financial institution that provides the best financing in local currency;

One of the largest financial institutions in Kazakhstan in terms of assets with recognized competence in international markets;

A main agent to attract long-term and low- cost loans and investments for corporate clients.

The results of 2015 show that the financial performance of DBK is good, the sources of funding are more diversified, and international cooperation is abundant. DBK successfully promotes the sustainable development of Kazakhstan's national economy by financing the real sector, improving the investment climate, and building new production lines.

National Bank of Foreign Economic Activity of the Republic of Uzbekistan

The development strategy of the banking and finance system of Uzbekistan after independence featured state participation so that the country would be prepared for the transition to a free market. This approach was based on the key development principles of the country elaborated by the former President Islam Karimov.

One of the prioritized reformation directions of the Uzbekistan economy was the creation of a favorable business and investment climate to attract foreign investments. Uzbekistan adopted a stable and targeted economic policy that involved in growing investment and FDI. Analysis of the involvement of the Uzbekistan banking system with the formation and development of cottage economy shows that the commercial banks paid special attention to lending just those branches that the country particularly needed to ensure complete economic independence.

Main Business Data

National Bank of Foreign Economic Activity of the Republic of Uzbekistan (NBU) is the leader of the Uzbekistan banking system. According to data from 2015, the Bank's share comprised about 25% of all assets. The Bank's consolidated balance in terms of the equivalent of the national currency Soum (net) made up 16,070 billion

Soum. During the period from 2010 to 2015, it increased by 9,080 billion Soum, or by 2.3 times; in 2015, the consolidated balance grew by 3,152 billion Soum, or 24.4%.

During the period from 2010 to 2015, the Bank's capital in terms of the national currency Soum (considering the subordinated bonds and other subordinated debts) increased by 260% and totaled 2,124 billion Soum.

The authorized capital of the Bank increased by 35 billion Soum in 2015 following the resolution of the President of the Republic of Uzbekistan dated October 26, 2015 No PP-2420 "On Additional Measures of Further Growth of Capitalization of the Banks and Enhancement of Their Investment Assets", and the resolution of the Cabinet of Ministers of the Republic of Uzbekistan No 367 dated December 18, 2015 "On the Introduction of Changes in the Articles of Agreement of the National Bank of Foreign Economic Activity of the Republic of Uzbekistan".

At the end of 2015, the Bank's authorized capital was 160.946 billion Soum (39 billion Soum and $ 400 million), a 28% increase from 2014.

In 2015, with the consideration of new provisions of the Central Bank of the Republic of Uzbekistan, stage-by-stage introductions of the requirements envisaged by the international standards of Basel III, the capital adequacy ratio was 18.9%; tier I capital adequacy was 14.2%; the leverage ratio was 7.0%; and the current liquidity ratio was 101.8%. All of these fall under the minimum regulatory requirements of the Central Bank of the Republic of Uzbekistan – 10%, 7.5%, 6%, 30% correspondingly.

Due to being highly-leveraged, the Bank kept significant reserves for broadening its clientele base. Maintaining reserves permits the Bank to not only timely and fully carry out necessary payments both in internal and external financial markets, but also satisfies the needs of the Bank and its clients in the development of the financial and economic activity.

In 2015, the Bank's profit increased by 23.4% relative to 2014. ROA was 0.6% and ROE was 5.3%.

Efficiency indicators are traditionally not high as the Bank implements directed lending on privileged terms that assists development of the basic branches of the economy, small business, and private entrepreneurship, as well as implementation of social programs and others.

The main task of the asset and liabilities management is controlling the risk imposed by the external environment and changes in the assets/liabilities structure.

The principal aims of the asset/liability management policy implemented by the Bank are: the achievement of stable and effective financial results, growth of capitalization, maintenance of the necessary liquidity level to cover cash flows, ensuring the needs of any client for high quality banking services, the accumulation and optimization of revenues from the placement of funds on terms of admissible risk level, and the achievement of the balanced structure of assets and liabilities of the Bank by maturities.

The share of earning assets was 83% of total assets. Compared with the previous year, earning assets for 2015 grew by 27.6% and total assets grew by 24.4%.

Credit operations accounted for a 61% of total assets of the Bank. The Bank provides all-round credit support of the processes of modernization and technological refurbishment of infrastructure. In addition, the Bank encourages the development of small businesses, private entrepreneurship, the service sector, and household work, as well as provides credit support of social and economic development programs of the regions.

The NBU has an account on the balance sheet of the Central Bank of the Republic of Uzbekistan as reserves to pay possible asset loss. These reserves accounted for 14% of NBU's total assets.

In addition, deposits within the other banks made up 13% of NBU assets. Placements in the investments and securities made up 5%. The share of fixed assets and other property of the Bank in its total assets structure made up 1% (see Figure 5.6).

On the liability side of their balance sheet, 90% is in liabilities while 10% is in capital.

Payable loans made up 50%, which are attracted for future refinancing and related to the role of the Bank as an agent attracting foreign investments for the government of the Republic. The share of clients' deposits makes up 36% of total liabilities. The share of the securities issued by the Bank is 1% and deposits of the banks are 2%. The Bank's capital makes up 10% of total liabilities (see Figure 5.7).

Highlights of the Year

NBU in the International Arena

The banking system must play an important role in promoting international coopera-

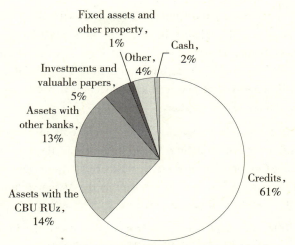

Figure 5. 6   Structure of Bank's Assets (Net)

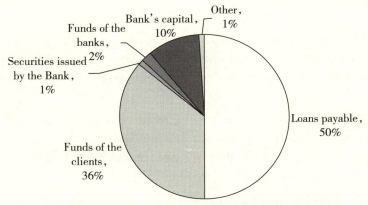

Figure 5. 7   Structure of Bank's Liabilities

tion. Constantly developing foreign relations, the Bank actively assists integration of the Republic of Uzbekistan with the international financial community.

The largest banks of the world are among the NBU's main foreign : German Commerzbank AG and Deutsche Bank AG; American J. P. Morgan Chase, Citibank, and the Bank of New York Mellon; Swiss Credit Suisse; Japanese Sumitomo Mitsui Banking Corporation (SMBC), Bank of Tokyo Mitsubishi UFJ (BTMU), and others.

Among the international financial institutes and development banks, the following are the main partners of the Bank: the Chinese Development Bank (CDB), Export-Import Bank of China (Chexim), Export-Import Bank of Korea (Eximbank of Korea), Korean Development Bank, Islamic Development Bank, Asian Development Bank, Japanese Bank of International Cooperation, International Financial Corporation, and others. Today, NBU's network of partner banks covers nearly 667 banks in 80 countries, including 24 banks of Uzbekistan.

In the course of 2015, the Bank signed bilateral documents on cooperation, such as the Agreement on Cooperation, totaling $ 100 million with the Japanese Bank Sumitomo Mitsui Banking Corporation, the Framework Credit Agreement with the German Commerzbank AG totaling € 250 million, as well as the Memorandum on Mutual Understanding with the Deutsche Bank AG totaling $ 800 million.

Since December 2007, the Bank has actively cooperated with the international rating agency "Moody's Investors Service". Since November 2008, it has also cooperated with the Standard and Poor's Agency. All ratings have the forecast "stable".

Lending

The former President of the Republic of Uzbekistan Islam Karimov always drew People's attention with his statements on the necessity of widening banks' operations to attract investments in large production, small business, and private entrepreneurship.

In 2015, NBU paid special attention to the increase of credit volumes in view of organizing new modern production methods, modernization, and technological refurbishment of enterprises. Credit portfolio volumes reached 9,975 billion Soum, an increase of 24% compared to the same period of 2014.

Foreign currency credit sources are refinancing from foreign banks, the Fund of Reconstruction and Development of the Republic of Uzbekistan, and the Bank's own funds National currency sources include the Bank's own assets, the Central Bank, and the Ministry of Finance of the Republic of Uzbekistan.

As a result of the implementation of such a policy, high technology productions have been created in the Republic, leading to the manufacture of competitive products. Progressive shifts have taken place not only in production methods, but also in export nomenclature. With these shifts, Uzbekistan now exports more final products rather than raw materials. Simultaneously, these measures help the Bank improve the serious unemployment problem.

In 2015, the Bank continued rendering credits aimed at the execution of the Resolution of the President of the Republic of Uzbekistan No PP-1438 dated November 26, 2010 "On Priority Directions of Further Reformation and Raise of Stability of the Financial and Banking System of the Republic for 2011 – 2015 and Achievement of the High International Rating Indicators". As of January 1, 2016, investment credits made up 86% of the total credit portfolio of the Bank.

To execute the Resolution of the President of the Republic of Uzbekistan No PP-2282, the Bank participated in financing the construction of homogeneous, large-scale individual housing in rural areas.

To support small business and private entrepreneurs, the Bank financed projects in the following major areas: acquisition of modern technologies for processing dairy, livestock, and other agricultural products, development of the service sector including tourism, personal land plots for developing livestock and farming entities, female entrepreneurs, and others.

Along with this, in view of improving material living conditions of the population, the Bank carried out consumer credits for the acquisition of domestically produced furniture, electronic goods, and home appliances and provided student loans. 2015 credits were 121% higher than 2014 credits. As of January 1, 2016, credits for "Support in Providing Housing to Young Families" were 35. 3 billion Soum.

In 2015, the Bank contributed to the development of the real sector of the economy by targeting key sectors and lending to small business, private entrepreneurs, and farming entities. The Bank helped the government achieve its economic development goals, improved the employment of the population, and made a great contribution to the social and economic development of the region.

Project Financing

After regaining independence, the leadership of Uzbekistan put a lot of work in law making and creating a favorable business and investment climate. This required modernization of the entire financial system of the country.

In the first days of independence, the NBU provided reliable support to the government in this work. Former President of the country Islam Karimov tasked the Bank with becoming a globally competitive institution able to serve foreign trade operations of the domestic companies, assist growth of export capacity of the country, and attract foreign investments and advanced technologies into the Uzbekistan economy.

Currently, the NBU is the largest investment bank in the country. During the period of its operation, the Bank has actively participated in the implementation of many national and regional programs. The majority of these projects target the fuel and energy, agro-industrial, textile, transportation, communications, and mining sectors. The Bank strives to utilize all opportunities to provide long-term loans to enterprises and organizations for constructing new facilities, introducing new technologies, and manufacturing competitive output.

Credits provided by the Bank aim to develop priority sectors of the economy, finance measures to modernize the operation and introduction of new highly-efficient production methods, support small business, and create and develop new products to become less reliable on imports.

To execute the Resolution of the President of the Republic of Uzbekistan No. PP-2264 "On the Investment Program of the Republic of Uzbekistan for 2015", the Bank has taken part in the implementation of a number of large investment projects, including those attracting foreign credits guaranteed by the government of the Republic of Uzbekistan needed for investments and lending. Thus, within the framework of implementing large investment projects in 2015, financing was organized for the credits totaling $ 185. 51 million. They include the following investment projects:

NHC Uzbekneftegas constructed the Ustyurt gas-chemical complex [amount of the refinanced FRR RUz credit ($ 100. 0 million), guarantee letter of credit ($ 195 million)].

JSC Uzbekiston Temir Yullari constructed the electrified railway road line "Angren-Pap" (the amount of the refinanced credit of CPR Eximbank is $ 350. 0 million).

JSC Uzbekiston Temir Yullari renovated the locomotive depot and acquired 11 electric freight locomotives (the amount of the refinanced credit of CPR Eximbank is $ 42. 17 million).

JSC Uzbekiston Temir Yullari acquired two high speed passenger electric TALGO trains from Spain (the amount of the FRR RUz credit refinanced by the Uzbek National Bank is € 19. 0 million).

The Center of Radio Communications, Radio Broadcasting and Television started the project "Development of the Network of Terrestrial Broadcasting of the Republic of Uzbekistan" (the amount of the refinanced credit of the Japanese Bank of International Cooperation is $ 62. 59 million).

Poitakht Kurilish va Khizmat started the project "On the Measures on the Completion of the Construction of the International Class Hotel in Tashkent" (the amount of the FRR refinanced credit is $ 42. 0 million).

The Ministry of Agriculture and Water Resources of the Republic of Uzbekistan started the project "Reconstruction of the Pumping Station 'Kukumbai' in the Navoi Region" (the amount of the CPR Eximbank credit refinanced by the Uzbek National Bank is $ 3. 78 million).

Support for Small Business and Private Entrepreneurship

Small business development is one of the priorities of the economic reforms implemented in the Republic. To support small businesses, the Bank issued 1. 8 trillion Soum worth of credit. Projects in the following areas were financed: the acquisition of modern technologies for processing dairy, livestock, and other agricultural products, development of the service sector including tourism, personal land plots for developing livestock and farming entities, female entrepreneurs, and others.

NBU, a reliable and sustainable financial institute, is important for the social and economic development of Uzbekistan. It promotes the implementation of policy aiming at further deepening democratic market-oriented reforms and liberalization of the economy, modernization and diversification of activities, and ensuring competitiveness of domestic goods and services in domestic and international markets.

The Bank should sensibly respond to all events happening in the financial and banking system of the country and the world by adopting timely and effective measures. Based on this, the most important priorities of the Bank include improving their own legislative framework, introducing modern bank governance, ensuring competitive advantages, and others.

Chapter 6　China Related DFIs

China Development Bank

In 2015, the international situation remained complicated, and the economic downward pressure increased. China's economy grew by 6. 9% in 2015, showing moderate but stable and sound momentum of development. China Development Bank (CDB) aligned itself with macroeconomic policy and national strategic priorities, facilitated China's stable economic growth, structural optimization and transformation, and improvement of the People's livelihood, played the countercyclical role of development finance. The Bank was actively involved in formulating national strategies and policies, including China's 13th Five-Year Plan, the "Belt and Road (B&R)" initiative, the coordinated development of the Beijing-Tianjin-Hebei Region, and the Yangtze River Economic Zone. CDB was established as a major player in the global financial market.

In March 2015, the State Council approved the CDB Reform Plan, its positioning and regulatory planning roadmap. This plan clearly defined CDB as a development finance institution and reminded the Bank to keep its business activities closely aligned with China's key medium- and long-term economic goals, and to become more effective at delivering development financing to key industries and underdeveloped sectors and during critical periods. The CDB Reform Plan supports not only its own sustainable development, but also overall economic development in China.

Main Business Data

At the end of 2015, CDB had total assets of CNY 12. 62 trillion, a balance of loans of CNY 9. 21 trillion, and a cumulative recovery rate of 98. 78% that continued to lead the industry for the sixteenth consecutive year. The Bank also further enhanced sustainability and risk management, delivering a net profit of CNY 102,788 million, ROA of 0. 90%, ROE of 11. 74%, and capital adequacy of 10. 81% (see Table 6. 1).

Table 6. 1   Financial Highlights   (Billion CNY or %)

	2015	2014	2013	2012	2011
Total assets	12,619. 70	10,317. 00	8,197. 20	7,534. 90	6,252. 30
Loans outstanding, gross	9,206. 90	7,941. 60	7,148. 30	6,417. 60	5,525. 90
Non-performing loan ratio	0. 81%	0. 65%	0. 48%	0. 30%	0. 40%
Allowance for loan losses to total loans	3. 71%	3. 43%	3. 05%	2. 82%	2. 22%
Total liabilities	11,549. 40	9,636. 20	7,627. 80	7,025. 10	5,807. 00
Debt securities outstanding	7,301. 40	6,353. 60	5,840. 60	5,302. 20	4,476. 40
Total shareholders' equity	1,070. 30	680. 8	569. 4	509. 9	445. 3
Capital adequacy ratio	10. 81%	11. 88%	11. 28%	10. 92%	10. 78%
New profit	102. 8	97. 7	80	63. 1	45. 6
Net interest income	158. 4	178. 7	171. 5	154. 4	116. 5
Return on average assets	0. 90%	1. 06%	1. 02%	0. 92%	0. 80%
Return on average equity	11. 74%	15. 63%	14. 82%	13. 21%	10. 76%

Highlights of the Year

Supporting the Real Economy

In 2015, the Bank further optimized its resource allocation to increase support to medium- and long-term financing and investment projects and enable development finance to make solid contributions in boosting the supply of public goods. With new loans of CNY 889. 2 billion, the Bank helped ensure that the funding needs were comfortably met for major projects and key areas in infrastructure, basic and pillar industries, including railways (CNY 121. 6 billion), public highways (CNY 273 billion), electric power (CNY 137.1 billion), water resources (CNY 79.7 billion), petroleum and petrochemical (CNY 278.9 billion), and public infrastructure (CNY 160.6 billion) (see Figure 6.1).

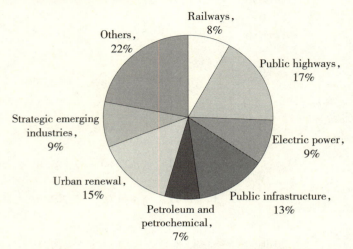

Figure 6.1 Loan Balance of CDB: Breakdown by Industry

Financing Urban Renewal

In 2015, the Bank continued to increase its funding support to urban renewal initiatives, and with a total lending of CNY 750.9 billion which was not only a historical high but 1.84 times the amount of 2014, the Bank made tremendous contribution to build 5.8 million new homes ahead of schedule and ensured that follow-up projects were adequately funded. The balance of urban renewal loans was CNY 1.31 trillion (see Figure 6.2).

By cooperating more closely with the Ministry of Housing and Urban-Rural Construction and local governments, CDB worked to develop synergies with government agencies and to better align lending activities with local renewal plans. CDB also increased its funding in disadvantaged regions, promoting monetized relocation for urban renewal projects. The Bank helped reduce real estate inventory through monetized relocation solutions, and promoted innovative financing methods, including those for government procurement services. It also stepped up our efforts to incorporate public and private funding via combined bonds and loans, as well as through syndication loans and other channels.

CDB derived remarkable results in Urban Renewal including Subsided Mining Cities in Heilongjiang, Jilin City, Kaifeng, etc. The projects hold great promise to the local

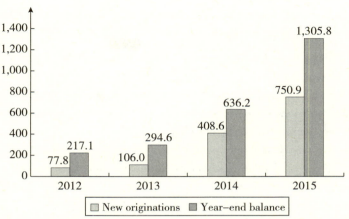

Figure 6. 2   The Origination and Year-end Balance of Urban Renewal Loans
(Unit: **Billion CNY**)

low- income families. The Bank endeavored to maximize the ripple effect of urban renewal projects. By improving the living conditions of run-down areas, the Bank aimed
to promote the comprehensive amelioration in various sectors, including new urbanization, environmental improvement, and sustainable cultural heritage preservation.

Promoting Balanced Regional Development, Industrial Upgrade and Trans-formation

In 2015, the Bank aligned its focus with state's development strategies and increased
its funding supports to national development priorities, including new urbanization,
urban-rural integration, Made in China 2025, Internet + , coordinated development
of Beijing-Tianjin-Hebei Region, and Yangtze River Economic Zone.

In 2015, the Bank increased its funding support to facilitate the accelerated development of central and western China and a new round of economic revival of old industrial bases in northeast China, including new loans of CNY 549. 4 billion to central
and western China, and CNY 77. 4 billion to old industrial bases in northeast China.
New progress was also made in aiding the development in Xinjiang and Tibet, with
new loans of CNY 22. 8 billion to Xinjiang and CNY 16 billion channeled to Tibet
and Tibetan regions in four provinces. Meanwhile, the Bank committed a total lending of CNY 2. 1 trillion to fund relevant initiatives from 2015 to 2017.

The Bank spared no efforts in supporting the people-centered new urbanization initiatives, and established itself as a lead bank in the new urbanization causes, as it continued to explore diversified and sustainable funding sources and make substantial

contributions to sponsor key projects in transportation upgrade, industrial park construction, and urban-rural integration.

In 2015, the Bank made strong efforts to support industrial restructuring and upgrade initiatives and strategic emerging industries, and assisted enterprises in their bid to become higher-end competitors in selected sectors, including integrated circuit, flat panel display, and new energies and materials. As part of its commitment to help promote the development of under-developed sectors, the Bank worked closely with the Ministry of Industry and Information Technology, the National Development and Reform Commission and other government agencies, and participated in policy research in integrated circuit industries. In the year, total lending to strategic emerging industries amounted to CNY 253 billion, and at the end of 2015, the balance of these loans was CNY 795. 7 billion.

The Bank made solid contributions to promote its green services and projects aimed to protect and improve the environment, with priorities on pollution prevention and remediation, soil restoration, cyclic economies, and the development and application of clean and renewable resources. At the end of 2015, the balance of the Bank's green loans was CNY 1. 57 trillion.

Support Poverty Alleviation and Contribute to Bettering People's Livelihood

In 2015, the Bank actively engaged and worked with government agencies and local governments, adopted innovative financing options, and guided private efforts to pool resources in promoting development initiatives aiming at poverty alleviation, agricultural upgrade and new village building, small- and medium-sized enterprises (SMEs), and education, among other livelihood improvement causes. The Bank deepened its cooperation with government agencies, maintained close working relationships with the State Council Leading Group Office of Poverty Alleviation and Development, the Central Office of Rural Affairs, the National Development and Reform Commission, and the Ministry of Transport, and increased its efforts in providing much-needed access to expertise and information. The Bank also explored how balanced urban-rural development initiatives could be leveraged to benefit poverty alleviation efforts, and actively promoted poverty alleviation through relocations, rural infrastructure constructions, education and healthcare, and development of unique industries. The Bank adopted new financing methods and increased medium- and long-term funding to support agricultural and rural development, focused on supporting the development of SMEs as part of its obligations to poverty alleviation and promoting innovations and start-up businesses. It further expanded the coverage of its education loans to 70% of the counties across the state and 100% of the higher education institutions.

In the year, the Bank provided CNY 212. 2 billion loans to most-deprived regions and counties, and raised donations of CNY 11. 4 million for four designated aid-receiving counties and one county for which the Bank assumed major poverty-alleviation responsibility. At the end of 2015, the balance of poverty alleviation loans of the Bank amounted to CNY 962. 3 billion, including CNY 32. 6 billion in loans for agricultural modernization, CNY 262. 5 billion for rural development, CNY 2. 82 trillion for SMEs (CNY 1. 12 trillion to micro and small business), CNY 18. 7 billion for education.

Deepening International Cooperation, Supporting the B & R

CDB serves the national economic and diplomatic strategies, promotes the implementation of high-profile projects; promotes China's "Go Global" with the power of development financing.

In 2015, the Bank made active efforts in deepening the reform of the management system and practices for its international operations and further strengthening its overseas network, with the addition of its London Representative Office. CDB advocates promoting cross-border Renminbi loans and carrying forward Renminbi internationalization.

CDB devoted extensive resources to a series of high-profile projects along the B & R route and extended $ 14. 9 billion of related loans. The Bank actively cooperated with China's high-level reciprocal visits with the B & R countries, signed 70 cooperation documents, involving the amount of financing more than $ 65 billion, covering the areas of energy, mineral resources, transportation infrastructure, production capacity, financial and high-tech cooperation, which promoted deepening of cross-country pragmatic cooperation.

The Bank promoted the bilateral and multilateral cooperation mechanism and a variety of special loans to build dominant platforms for the B & R projects. CDB actively participated in and promoted the China-Kazakhstan bilateral production capacity cooperation, China-Mongolia-Russia economic corridor; promoted business development with the multilateral cooperation mechanism of SCO Interbank Consortium, ASEAN Interbank Consortium, BRICS New Development Bank, Eurasia Economic Forum, etc. ; set up special loans for small and medium enterprises APEC, promoted the establishment of special loans for China—ASEAN infrastructure projects and China—Eastern Europe projects, provided accurate support for the B & R construction. The Bank committed about $ 190 billion related to countries, and at the end of 2015, cumulative drawdowns amounted to $ 155. 6 billion, with a balance of loans of $ 111. 4 billion, accounted for 1/3 of the total international business balance.

Enhancing bond Issuance and Financing Practices, Reinforcing Integrated Financing Capabilities

The Bank promoted CDB bonds in the primary and secondary markets by building a complete product portfolio with benchmark, floating rate, and extra long-term bonds, and by securing issuance channels across the interbank market, bank counters, and exchanges. In 2015, the cumulative annual issuance of Renminbi bonds amounted to CNY 1,136.1 billion, and increased its all-time bond issuance to CNY 11.8 trillion. Meanwhile, the listing of $ 1 billion USD-denominated bonds and € 500 million Euro-denominated bonds on the London Stock Exchange was a breakthrough moment for CDB in terms of multi-currency funding. The Bank fostered greater synergies between itself and its subsidiaries, delivering diversified services to key sectors and projects. CDB scaled up our offerings of securitized products, issuing 11 such products worth CNY 101.3 billion, and we maintained our leading position in the bond underwriting market with a cumulative of CNY 759.65 billion for the year. By offering bonds at an average interest rate 23 basis points lower than the market average, CDB helped lower financing costs in the real economy.

CDB will continue in its mission to strengthening China's competitiveness and improving People's livelihood.

· Supporting supply-side structural reform. CDB will prioritize financing for major national infrastructure projects, including urban renewal, railways, and water projects; promote industrial innovation, transformation and upgrades, aid poverty alleviation; and promote international cooperation by delivering financial services to China's B & R initiative.

· Synergizing business management and operations. By leveraging cross-market and diversified financing capabilities, the Bank will develop synergies between investments and loans, bonds and loans, and leasing and lending activities. CDB will empower the real economy by offering more varied financial services, channeling public and private funds, and encouraging resource pooling with peer financial institutions.

· Boosting asset and liability management. CDB will raise its overall profitability by diversifying financing channels, bolstering budgeting and financial planning, improving internal and external pricing practices, and promoting intermediary services.

· Upholding risk management and internal control. CDB will apply strict criteria to project development; enhance risk-based research, monitoring, forecasting, and early warning systems; promote greater accountability; and maintain our asset quality threshold.

Export-Import Bank of China

Founded in 1994, the Export-Import Bank of China (Chexim) aims mainly at facilitating the export and import of Chinese mechanical and electronic products, completing sets of equipment and new- and high-tech products, assisting Chinese companies with comparative advantages in their offshore project contracting and outbound investment, and promoting international economic cooperation and trade. It is dedicated to fully play its role in pursuing steady growth, conducting structural readjustment, supporting foreign trade and implementing the "going global" strategy, and make due contribution to the sustainable and sound development of the national economy.

Chexim implemented China's overseas development strategy, such as the Belt and Road strategy and the building of railways, highways and regional aviation networks in Africa, signed agreements on and launched a number of important overseas projects. It enhanced mutually beneficial cooperation with China's neighbors, with priority given to connectivity and industrial capacity cooperation projects in support of the building of a community of shared destiny between China and its neighbors. Chexim enhanced practical cooperation with countries in Central and Eastern Europe, Latin America and Oceania in various fields.

Chexim had been promoting China's import and export optimization, gave strong support to exporting competitive Chinese products, including complete sets of equipment, new- and high-tech products and high value added products with proprietary intellectual property and proprietary brands. Priority was placed on exporting complete sets of equipment manufactured in China and related technologies, services and standards. It also facilitated import of more advanced technologies and key equipment to ensure the steady growth of China's foreign trade and improve the trade mix.

Chexim had also been supporting the development of the real economy and facilitating economic structural adjustment, transformation and upgrading. To improve the quality of Chinese made products, it supported Chinese enterprises in carrying out independent innovation and technological upgrading and transformation, using resources efficiently, and enhancing the capacity to manufacture major technical equipment.

Main Business Data

In 2015, the Bank maintained the momentum of steady growth in business scale.

The Bank's approved on-balance-sheet loans totaled CNY 1,101.6 billion, total contracted loans stood at CNY 1,180.9 billion, and total loan disbursement reached CNY 1,077.4 billion. As the end of 2015, the Bank's outstanding on-balance-sheet loans amounted to CNY 2,148.2 billion, its off-balance-sheet on-lending stood at $ 14.6 billion, and its on-balance-sheet and off-balance-sheet assets totaled CNY 2,935.2 billion. The Bank have supported the export of mechanical and electronic equipment, high-tech products, offshore contract projects and outbound investment amounting to $ 391.2 billion in total, and the import of technical equipment and resource products with a total amount of $ 200.5 billion. During 2012 – 2014, annual operating income and expenditure were basically flat. In 2015, as exchange earnings increased by 2,107% compared to 2014, operating revenues increased by 111.8% than 2014. While operating expenses increased by 119.3% owing to 168% increase of loss of impairment of assets or loss of bad debts than 2014. Net profit grew by 27.5% (see Table 6.2 and Figure 6.3). In 2012 – 2015, the Bank assets, liabilities and loans steadily increased (see Table 6.2 and Figure 6.4). At year-end, the outstanding balance of foreign trade loans stood at CNY 891.387 billion, up by CNY 90.094 billion year on year. The outstanding balance of overseas investment loans was CNY 206.349 billion, a year-on-year increase of 22.96%. The outstanding balance of international cooperation loans was CNY 571.919 billion, a year-on-year increase of 22.76%. The outstanding balance of loans for supporting greater openness was CNY 478.522 billion, a year-on-year increase of 31.87% (see Figure 6.5). The Bank's international credit ratings remained the same as China's sovereign ratings.

Table 6.2　The Bank Financial Highlights in 2015 (Unit: CNY 1,000)

Annual	2015
Operating income	48,430,436.94
Operation cost	44,520,715.13
Year-end	**2015**
Total asset	2,833,473,407.60
Total liability	2,524,005,049.37
Total loans	2,052,496,636.02
Net profit	5,142,943.08

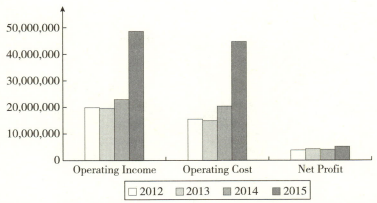

Figure 6. 3　Operating Income, Operation Cost and Net Profit in 2012 – 2015
(Unit: CNY 1,000)

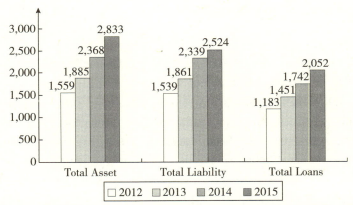

Figure 6. 4　Total Asset, Total Liability and Total Loans in 2012 – 2015
(Unit: CNY 1,000)

Highlights of the Year

Implementing China's Overseas Development Strategy

In 2015, In the course of implementing the Belt and Road Initiative and carrying out international industrial capacity and equipment manufacturing cooperation and other major strategic plans, the Bank signed agreements on and launched a number of important overseas projects. The Bank enhanced mutually beneficial cooperation with China's neighbors, with priority given to connectivity and industrial capacity cooperation projects in support of the building of a community of shared destiny between Chi-

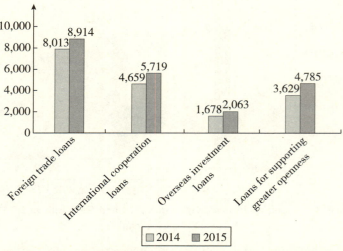

Figure 6. 5   Outstanding Balance of Loans (Unit: CNY 1,000)

na and its neighbors. Chexim actively assisted Chinese enterprises in expanding overseas operation, conducting more overseas M&A transactions and undertaking more business projects.

The Adama Wind Power Project is the first overseas wind power project that a Chinese company serves as a general contractor. The project is great significant for China's wind power standards to be applied overseas as it uses Chinese equipment, design and construction standards. It has helped improve the source structure of power grids, alleviate power shortages, create more jobs, and promote the economic development and social stability in Ethiopia. The Port Qasim Coal-fired Power Project in Pakistan and the Sirajganj 220MW Combined Cycle Power Plant were major projects under the Belt and Road Initiative, which would export Chinese technologies and standards and boost international industrial capacity cooperation.

Belarus is an important juncture from which the Silk Road Economic Belt reaches out to Europe. China's export of high-end intelligent electric locomotives to Belarus and the successful implementation of the Railway Electrification Project will be exemplary because they will not only deepen China-Belarus economic and financial cooperation and trade and enable China's railway equipment and services to explore the European market, but also help increase the transportation capacity of railway networks and create more jobs.

Promoting China's Import and Export Optimization

In 2015, Chemix gave strong support to exporting competitive Chinese products, including complete sets of equipment, new- and high-tech products and high value added products with proprietary intellectual property and proprietary brands. Priority was placed on exporting complete sets of equipment manufactured in China and related technologies, services and standards. Chemix made major efforts to help boost the development of China's shipbuilding and aviation industries. It helped Chinese shipbuilding companies secure overseas orders, stabilize production, overcome market difficulties and explore new ways of business growth through upgrading. The Bank intensified support to Chinese aircraft manufacturers to enhance their capability for making independent innovation, import aviation supplies and technologies, conduct overseas M&A transactions, and export Chinese made aircrafts.

To implement China's large aircraft strategy, the Bank and the Commercial Aircraft Corporation of China Ltd (COMAC) signed a CNY 50 billion Financing Framework Agreement with the aim to satisfy the financing needs of COMAC in its R&D, manufacturing and sale of Chinese made civil aircrafts.

The Hospital Ship built by China Shipbuilding & Offshore International Co., Ltd., was the world's first large hospital ship for civil use, and it was also the first large passenger vessel built with international standards and exported by China. This project had helped Chinese shipyards to adjust their product structure and accumulate expertise and experience for building similar specialty ships and cruise ships, thus playing an important role in enhancing the international reputation and core competitiveness of Chinese shipbuilders.

SMD Company is a world leading manufacturer of deep-sea robot and subsea engineering machinery. Its major products are deep-sea robots and equipment for subsea trenches and cables. This acquisition enables Chinese companies to acquire more advanced technologies and greater market access to marine engineering equipment and expand its core technologies to deep-sea robots and other high-end subsea equipment, filling the vacuum in China's deep-sea equipment industry.

Supporting the Development of the Real Economy

To improve the quality of Chinese made products, Chemix supported Chinese enterprises in carrying out independent innovation and technological upgrading and transformation, using resources efficiently and enhancing the capacity to manufacture major technical equipment. It also provided financial support to boost the development of strategic emerging industries. The Bank increased financing support to the development of green, circular and low- carbon economy, and to the upgrading of industries with high pollution, waste discharge and energy consumption to make them more energy efficient and environment friendly. Chexim also helped promote the use of new and renewable energy.

The successful implementation of Shenyang Blower Works Group's large-scale turbine compressor set manufacturing and testing base project showed that China was leading the world in building key parts of ultra-large air separation units. It also marked another breakthrough in the domestication of major technological equipment in China's high-end equipment manufacturing industry.

The 18,000-TEU Container Vessels built by China State Shipbuilding Corporation (HK) Shipping were the world's largest TEU container vessels. Their R&D, design and construction were all carried out independently in China, breaking the monopoly of foreign shipbuilders in the field. The successful implementation of the project was another example to showcase the Bank's commitment to implementing national policies and supporting China's shipbuilding industry.

International Exchanges

In April 2015, Chexim signed a number of cooperation agreements on connectivity and energy with the Pakistani partners. The implementation of related projects will ease power shortages in Pakistan, improve local infrastructure, promote regional connectivity and advance the building of China-Pakistan Economic Corridor. In May 2015, Chexim signed nine agreements on energy, connectivity and manufacturing, totaling over \$ 1.1 billion. The implementation of related projects will promote local economic development, give strong support to international industrial capacity cooperation, and facilitate the implementation of the Belt and Road Initiative and the aligning of the Initiative with the development strategies of counties along the routes of the Belt and Road. In December 2015, Chexim signed agreements on energy, connectivity and financial cooperation. On the sidelines of the Johannesburg Summit of the Forum on China-Africa Cooperation, the Bank signed several cooperation agreements on infrastructure with government representatives of Kenya, Senegal and Gabon with a total value of CNY 19.68 billion.

In 2015, the Bank continued to deepen cooperation with multilateral financial institutions and international organizations. In June and November, the Bank signed an MOU with the United Nations Industrial Development Organization and with PTA

Bank respectively. In September, the Bank bought 2,529 more C-class shares of the African Export-Import Bank, with the total shares reaching 5,151. During 2015, representatives of the Bank attended the annual meetings of the Inter-American Development Bank, the Asian Development Bank, the African Development Bank, the Eastern and Southern African Trade and Development Bank and other multilateral financial institutions.

Social Responsibility

In 2015, the Bank actively fulfilled its social responsibility by carrying out poverty reduction and public benefit programs. A number of projects were implemented in areas covering energy conservation, environmental protection, agriculture, rural areas, the rural population, poverty alleviation, and small- and micro-businesses, to ensure sustainability not only in economic and social development but also in environmental conservation.

The Bank made great efforts to support green, circular and low- carbon economy. It supported enterprises with high energy consumption and high waste discharge, including steel producers, in carrying out technological transformation to recycle industrial waste and utilize crop straw and treat waste water. The Bank also financed many clean energy projects in wind power, photovoltaic power and new energy automobiles.

The Bank gave priority to modern agricultural projects, including the import and R&D of agricultural science and technology, modern seed industry, farming machinery manufacturing, facility agriculture and fine processing of agricultural products. It also placed priority on other key areas, including the construction of agricultural product export and logistics base and overseas investment cooperation projects in agriculture. By the end of December 2015, the outstanding balance of the Bank's agriculture-related loans was CNY 211. 406 billion, taking up 9. 84% of the Bank's total on-balance-sheet outstanding loans. The outstanding balance of loans for the "going global" agricultural projects reached CNY 136. 94 billion, covering 57 countries and regions worldwide.

The Bank increased cooperation with the State Council Leading Group on Poverty Alleviation. By the end of 2015, the Bank had launched more than 200 financing based cooperation projects on poverty alleviation in 28 provinces and regions and 14 contiguous poverty stricken areas. Among these projects, 143 were key poverty relief projects recommended by the State Council Leading Group on Poverty Alleviation. The Bank approved nearly CNY 13. 4 billion of loans to these projects and the outstanding balance amounted to CNY 8. 3 billion.

Agricultural Development Bank of China

Founded in 1994, Agricultural Development Bank of China (ADBC) is the only agricultural policy oriented bank under the direct leadership of the State Council in
China and is mainly responsible for raising funds based on State credit, undertaking
agricultural policy financial businesses, appropriating fiscal funds for supporting agriculture as an agent and serving agriculture and rural economic development according
to laws, regulations, guidelines and policies of the State.

The year 2015 witnessed major breakthroughs made by ADBC in reform and development. ADBC established six overall development strategies. The Bank has unswerv-
ingly grasped the operation direction of policy banks, took development as the first
priority; strengthened two basic guarantees, i. e. strengthened Party self-discipline
and intensified behavior governance according to laws; stuck to the "three-in-one"
function positioning by executing the state will, serving the needs from agriculture,
farmers and rural areas, and following the banking law; expanded four ways led by
reform, innovation, technology and talent; made all efforts to serve five areas, including national food security, priority poverty alleviation, agricultural modernization,
integrated development of urban and rural areas, and national major strategies; a-
chieved balanced promotion of modernizing governance structure, operating model,
product service, control mechanism, technological support and organization system.

In 2015, ADBC made all efforts to serve purchase and reserve of grain, cotton and
edible oil to underpin economic development and social stability; took the initiative
to support priority poverty alleviation to enhance weak aspects in completing the
building of a moderately prosperous society in an all-round way; gave strong support
to key water conservancy project construction and strengthened public goods supply;
worked innovatively to support new urbanization and promote coordinated development of urban and rural areas; stepped up promotion of funds for key construction
projects to add impetus to economic development, benefited 4,338 projects, which
could result 3 – 5 folds of social investment; promoted the implementation of reform
scheme and achieved phased results.

Main Business Data

At the end of the year, outstanding loans amounted to CNY 3,441. 04 billion, representing an increase of CNY 609. 67 billion from the end of preceding year and a year-on-year increase of CNY 281. 02 billion or 21. 53%. During the year, net input by the Bank in "agriculture, farmers and rural areas" reached CNY 780. 34 billion, 2. 4 times of the reading in 2014, scaling a record high and sending the total assets of the whole Bank into a new stage of CNY 4 trillion. Bonds issued in the year came to CNY 864. 97 billion, and at the end of the year, bond balance was CNY 2,746. 74 billion and deposit balance was CNY 937. 5 billion. In the context of shrinking interest margin, ADBC continuously offered preferential interest rate to agriculture and achieved pre-provision profit of CNY 35. 14 billion by such internal control methods as cost reduction and control. The year-end non-performing loan ratio remained at a low level of 0. 83% (see Table 6. 3).

Table 6. 3 Financial Highlights in 2015 (Unit: CNY 100 million)

Item	2014	2015
Total assets	31,420. 31	41,831. 32
Outstanding loans	28,313. 51	34,410. 37
Total liabilities	30,687. 35	40,844. 96
Borrowings from PBOC	3,220. 00	3,058. 00
Bonds issued	21,188. 56	27,467. 36
Owner's equity	732. 97	986. 36
Paid-in capital	200	570
Book profit	140. 79	207. 84
Pre-provision profit	441. 6	352. 51
Income tax expenses	63. 09	54. 45
Net profit	77. 7	153. 39
Return on assets (%)	1. 53	0. 96
Return on owner's equity (%)	64. 36	40. 88

Highlights of the Year

Credit Business

1) Serve national food security. ADBC strictly performed its function as a policy bank, spared no effort to serve national food security, maintain the stability of the

grain and edible oil market and protect the interests of farmers, and realized sound development of the lending business for grain and edible oil. In 2015, ADBC granted a total of CNY 573. 795 billion loans for purchases and reserve of grain and edible oil. ADBC earnestly carried out the state's policy of cotton purchase and reserve and proactively supported enterprises in purchasing cotton according to market conditions in order to help them realize industrialization. ADBC issued CNY 46. 4 billion loans for 2014 cotton purchase in total.

2) Serve priority poverty alleviation. In 2015, the Bank launched loans for relocating the poor and such loans experienced rapid development, poverty alleviation by policy finance started smoothly. Since its launch in August, ADBC examined and approved 491 loan applications for relocating the poor, which helped relocate 5,770,000 people, including 3,610,000 impoverished people in profile. The year-end loan balance is CNY 80. 8 billion.

3) Serve agricultural modernization. To promote the development of modern agriculture, the Bank earnestly implemented the state's agricultural rural policies, spared no effort to promote loans for land transfer and scale operation, and preferentially supported agent construction of government-invested projects and franchise project financing. During the year, the Bank granted CNY 2. 137 billion of loans for rural land transfer and scale operation. ADBC actively supported the field of agricultural science and technology innovation. To improve the overall agricultural productivity, it focused on supporting the promotion and application of agricultural scientific and technologic achievements in such fields as seed sector, agricultural machinery and water saving irrigation and provided relevant credit funds. During the year, ADBC granted a total of CNY 6. 818 billion loans for agricultural science and technology projects, supporting 196 enterprises.

4) Serve integrated development of urban and rural areas. The Bank promoted balanced distribution of public resources and equal exchange of elements between urban and rural areas to speed up construction of less-developed fields in rural areas and to promote integrated development of urban and rural areas. As the end of the year, the balance of loans to renovation of shack settlements was CNY 49. 814 billion. The Bank accumulatively granted CNY 28. 383 billion of loans to renovate 58. 62 million m^2 floorage, newly construct 53. 02 million m^2 floorage and benefit 390,000 households and 1,360,000 people. As the end of the year, the balance of loans to rural land reclamation was CNY 427. 271 billion, representing an increase of CNY 43. 34 billion or up by 11. 12% over the beginning of the year; the Bank accumulatively

granted CNY 180. 86 billion of loans to reclaim 795,000 mu land, newly cultivate 1, 161,000 mu land, reclaim 888,000 mu land for urban construction and renovate 7, 984 villages, realizing the intensive and economical utilization of land resources.

5) Serve national major strategies. In 2015, ADBC, by providing special bridge loans, supported 49 projects among the state's 172 major water conservancy projects. Specifically, CNY 8. 9 billion of the loans went to the backbone project of continuous auxiliary water-saving transformation for large- and medium-sized irrigation districts; CNY 4. 8 billion went to Phase I of the east and middle routes of South-to-North Water Transfer Project; CNY 3. 8 billion went to the project of leading water from Yangtze to Huaihe River; CNY 2. 9 billion went to the project of river pattern control and channel improvement of the middle and lower reaches of Yangtze River; and CNY 1. 5 billion went to field high-efficiency water saving irrigation project. As the end of the year, ADBC's balance of loans for water conservancy projects was CNY 358. 9 billion, up CNY 104. 7 billion over end-2014, representing an increase of 41. 2%; loans actually granted in 2015 totaling CNY 162. 5 billion, up CNY 89. 2 billion over 2014, representing an increase of 121. 69%. In the year, the loans helped solidify 43 unsafe reservoirs, increase 857 million m^3 of retain water, increase or improve 15,944,000 mu irrigation areas, dredge 6,646 kilometers of river channels, and ensure the water supply for 21,057,000 people.

Investment Business

ADBC gave full play to the counter-cyclical regulation of policy-based finance, established ADBC fund for key construction projects as required by the State Council, made all efforts to promote fund investment and made great progress in intermediary business, investment banking, asset management and equity investment.

1) Fund for key construction projects. During the year, the investment projects cover 34 items of five categories including improvement of People's livelihood, "agriculture, farmers and rural areas", urban infrastructure construction, major infrastructure and transformation and upgrading. The special fund investment, as a new model better supporting strategic financial policies and supply-side structured reform under the new normal, broke the bottleneck in investment growth and played an important role in "promoting investment and stabilize development".

2) Intermediary business. During the year, ADBC's revenue from intermediary business scored CNY 1. 052 billion, up by CNY 93 million from 2014, maintaining a momentum of stable growth on the base of reducing charges and cutting profits.

3) Investment banking. ADBC issued the first phase of Fayuan credit assets backed securities (worth CNY 3. 357 billion) in 2015.

4) Asset management business. In 2015, ADBC launched a total of seven wealth management products involving CNY 1. 48 billion and approved eight provincial branches' application for opening corporate wealth management business. The Bank also obtained the qualification for futures margin depository business and was ready for opening.

5) Equity investment business. As the end of 2015, China Agricultural Industry Development Fund and Modern Seed Industry Development Fund accumulatively invested 32 projects, involving an amount of CNY 3. 7 billion.

Information Construction

ADBC completed compatible renovation of integrated business system, upgrade of credit management system, R&D of futures margin depository business system and other R&D works related to corporate Internet banking system; optimized integrated business, second-generation payment and host-to-host systems and open access platform. ADBC completed the construction of software testing system and formulated CMMI3-rate construction standards to strengthen R&D management and quality control. ADBC carried out scientific and technological innovation researches. ADBC carried out innovation researches including core system construction, IT infrastructure planning, data warehouse construction of agriculture policy banks, construction of benefiting-farmers Internet platform, transfer and adoption of knowledge of credit management system, and computing "resource pool" . The Bank organized innovation researches on data governance and mining application, and clearly put forward its general idea, objectives and major tasks in promoting big data mining and application.

The Asian Infrastructure Investment Bank

Since Chinese President Xi Jinping proposed to build the Asian Infrastructure Investment Bank (AIIB) in October 2013, AIIB has been the focus of international attention. After more than 800 days of intense preparation, AIIB, co-founded by 57 founding members, was formally established on December 25, 2015, and it held a grand opening ceremony and the establishment meeting of the Board and the Board of Directors in Beijing from January 16 to 18, 2016. The 17 founding member states had ratified the Agreement on Infrastructure Investment Banking in Asia and submitted an instrument of ratification. Those 17 countries accounted for 50. 1% of the total share, triggering the agreement into effect. In the ten months after its establishment, AIIB had been widely recognized by the international community for its high standards, high efficiency, and environmental responsibility, attracting more than 30 countries to apply for membership. The first four projects totaling $ 509 million were formally approved on July 12, 2016 and the next two projects totaling $ 320 million were approved by the Board of Directors on September 28, 2016. Achieving the target of providing $ 1. 2 billion worth of loans in 2016 was just around the corner.

In 2016, AIIB focused on infrastructure development and other productive industries, including highways, electricity, shantytown transformation projects, etc. This was a good example of AIIB's commitment to "proving financing support in the development of infrastructure and to promote interconnection in Asia", "efficiency", and "green" development concepts.

The first four projects totaling $ 509 million approved on July 12, 2016 included:

1) The Bangladesh electricity transmission upgrading and loan expansion project, which was worth a total of $ 165 million.

2) The Indonesian National slum upgrading project, which was jointly financed by AIIB and the World Bank (WB), in which AIIB offered loans of $ 216. 5 million.

3) The Pakistani M4 National highway (Saoerot and Ha'nevar) loan project, which was jointly financed by AIIB and the Asian Development Bank. AIIB and AsDB offered loans of $ 100 million respectively. The Department for International Development (DFID) provided $ 34 million for the project (the project was officially commenced on August 13, 2016).

4) The road improvement project between Dushanbe, the capital of Tajikistan, and the border of Uzbekistan was a joint project of AIIB and EBRD. The two banks provided loans of $ 27. 5 million, with a total project amount of $ 55 million.

The next two projects totaling $ 320 million approved on September 28, 2016 included:

1) The expansion of a hydropower station project in Pakistan, with a loan of $ 300 million, was jointly financed by AIIB and the World Bank.

2) The 225MW combined cycle gas turbine power plant project in Myanmar, with a loan amount of $ 200 million, was jointly financed by AIIB and other multilateral development banks and commercial banks.

Some projects submitted to AIIB for loan applications included (incomplete statistics) :

1) In March, India sought a loan from AIIB to support the plan promoted by Prime Minister Modi to increase the installed capacity of a solar plant to 100 GW by 2022.

2) In May, Russia submitted to AIIB sixteen projects in the Far East and suggested that AIIB participate in the seaway development projects in the north, with a total investment amount of $ 80 billion.

3) In August, the Indonesian government applied for a loan of rupiah. 16. 2 trillion (about CNY 8. 239 billion) for the Pekanbaru-Dumai expressway project.

4) In September, Mongolia sought financing support from AIIB for a number of railway projects, including the construction of a 550-kilometer rail between China and Europe.

Thus, AIIB is a real, large-scale, international financial development institution. In addition to learning from each other in sharing knowledge, building capacity, and exchanging personnel, AIIB also carried out substantive cooperation with the Work Bank, the Asian Development Bank, the European Investment Bank, the European Bank for Reconstruction and Development, and other multi-development organizations in the aspect of project financing.

At the same time, commercial institutions such as the Canada Pension Plan Investment Board (CPPIB) and the Hong Kong Infrastructure Financing Facilitation Office (IFFO) expressed their willingness to establish long-term cooperation with AIIB. This would help AIIB to accumulate experience, enhance management capabilities, and reduce operational risks in a short time. This would lay the foundation for enhancing efficiency and the industry perception of AIIB, thereby building confidence in the international arena. These relationships would help guarantee the construction of large infrastructure projects in Asia, facilitating and strengthening investment in infrastructure worldwide.

From the overall performance of AIIB in 2016, AIIB was obviously different from existing multilateral development banks in terms of its mode of governance and operation, with its own distinct characteristics and unique advantages.

AIIB's Governance and Operations were Open and Inclusive

First, the Agreement stipulated that AIIB would undertake global sourcing in its lending programs instead of being limited to procurement in Member States, thereby allowing recipient countries to purchase the products that were best suited to their projects and maximize the benefits.

Second, China, as the sponsor and largest shareholder of AIIB, did not seek long-term veto power in voting. According to the shareholding structure established by the Agreement, as the largest shareholder, the Chinese side held 30. 34% of AIIB shares, which was 6. 94 percentage points higher than the total equity of the second to fifth largest shareholders (23. 4%). In accordance with international practice, the 30. 34% of shares belonging to the Chinese side be roughly equal to the corresponding voting rights, but in order to reflect solidarity, the share of Chinese voting power had been cut modestly (the Chinese side only has 26. 06% to vote).

Third, AIIB welcomed new members from five continents, not restricting itself to only having Asian countries. In September 2016, AIIB initiated the process of reviewing the applications submitted by more than 30 countries such as Greece and Canada. Canada's application, announced on August 31 and the first from a North American country made a real difference in improving relations between China and Canada and promoting the warming of Sino-US relations. These new members are expected to join the AIIB in early 2017, at that time, the total number of AIIB members will exceed 90.

AIIB's Governance and Operations were Efficient and High Quality

First, AIIB had no permanent Executive Board and the Board of Directors directly supervised management, operating efficiently with a clear division of responsibilities. There are only a few offices besides the headquarters in China, and the current number of employees is between 500 and 600, approximately 1/6 and 5% of the sizes of AsDB and the World Bank staffs.

Second, AIIB simplified the approval process of loaning. At the beginning of its existence, AIIB was already deeply aware of the adverse impact of the harsh rules of the existing international financial institutions on long-term development. Therefore, AIIB reformed the approval process of projects, including shortening the approval process and improving approval efficiency, to build an efficient, and sufficient financial institution.

Third, AIIB had a highly-diversified shareholder structure, a three-tier organizational structure formed by the Board of Directors, the Board of Governors, and the management layer. AIIB had also formed a good modern governance model, as the institutional guarantee was consistent with AIIB's adherence to high standards. At present,

AIIB is preparing a consultative group composed of former international dignitaries and well-known scholars to be responsible for providing policy recommendations for AIIB's development strategy and day-to-day operations.

AIIB's Governance and Operations were Pragmatic and Flexible

Since its opening, AIIB has used three investment methods including bank loans, equity investments, and business guarantees. In addition to the traditional sovereign credit guarantee loans, AIIB would also make a direct equity investment to the public and private sector under the Agreement.

This model is highly flexible, more conducive to the PPP model, and could obtain higher returns by taking larger risks in some cases. In addition, AIIB could also act as a guarantor to provide intermediary services to facilitate investment between the demand side and the supply side. The combination of the three investment models could greatly enhance AIIB's adaptability to the market and make greater contributions to regional development financing. By promoting the PPP model, AIIB could integrate market resources to participate in infrastructure construction, could induce others to enter the market via a multiplier effect, and enhance the attractiveness of infrastructure projects for private sector investors.

In general, with the principles of simplicity and green development, AIIB has taken into account the practical needs of developing countries, steadily promoted project financing in the areas of institution-building, business operation, and infrastructure, actively carried out mutually beneficial cooperation with international multilateral development agencies, and won widespread recognition and praise from the international community. Among many multilateral development agencies, AIIB has shown unique advantages and capabilities, with its governance and operations being open and inclusive. In addition, AIIB is highly efficient, pragmatic, flexible, and has high standards. As an emerging financial development institution, its attractiveness and influence are expanding and its status as a global financial institution is becoming more and more consolidated.

Column 6 – 1	Asian Infrastructure Investment Bank has Entered a Period of Intensive International Collaboration

As the global economy slid into recession, infrastructure construction programs along the Belt and Road area have drawn great interest from many countries. Financial institutions including European Investment Bank, European Bank for

Reconstruction and Development, Asian Development Bank (AsDB), and World Bank, and major economies including Russia, India, and EU, were pushing forward with collaboration with AIIB. Several large-scale projects have come to the attention of the global capital market.

International Financial Institutions have a Strong Desire to Collaborate with AIIB

As AIIB established, the following international financial institutions have shown great interest in enhancing cooperation and project matching with AIIB.

EIB is a multilateral institution and its shareholders are the EU member states. It provides lending for sustainable and innovative small- and medium-enterprises in the EU as well as other areas such as Turkey and Africa. Sources revealed that there were a few internal discussions at EIB regarding AIIB, and EIB contacted many Chinese banks and AIIB early on. the President of EIB Hoyer visited Beijing in May 2016 to discuss building a partnership with China in the area of energy and energy saving, especially in extreme climate and pollution treatment issues. The enthusiasm EIB showed was closely related to the Chinese government's claim that it had strong interests in investing in Europe and would like to participate in the "Juncker Plan".

EBRD mainly provides support for central and eastern European countries' economic revival. As these countries transform into market economies, EBRD is extending its target countries to include Middle Eastern, North African and Central Asian countries and Greece, which are in great need of infrastructure. It is to say, EBRD's supporting project is highly related to China's Belt and Road Strategy. In January 2016, China officially joined EBRD, which laid a solid foundation for China-EU cooperation in infrastructure and the advance of Belt and Road Strategy.

NDB and AIIB, two sister organizations, both focus on infrastructure financing projects. They have common interests in Asian regions where developing countries such as China and Russia dominate. However, the two of them do not have conflicting business models or rules. In contrast, both sides actively seek to co-finance projects. In March 2016, the Russian government approved AIIB and NDB to issue securities in Russia. This was to promote development of Russian infrastructure and financial markets. The two banks confirmed the Ruble loan project, which would become one of the most important fields of future development. Meanwhile, both sides planned to absorb more financing in

Russian market. NDB did not directly collaborate with AIIB in the first projects in April, yet the presidents and the bank officials have sent messages about achieving regional complementary cooperation.

AsDB, which is dominated by Japan and the US., also expressed its interest in collaborating with AIIB and mutually contributing to regional development. In March 2016, AsDB President Takehiko Nakao said a financing project, which was pushed forward by AsDB and AIIB's co-financing, was expected to be approved in the second quarter in 2016. A big advantage of AsDB is that it has 29 branches, centered in Asia. This makes it convenient for the local governments and residents to communicate with, so that projects can be carried out smoothly. Since AIIB has no such branches, the two banks may cooperate.

World Bank showed stronger desire for collaboration. WB signed the first co-financing framework agreement with AIIB in mid-April, which paved the way for future cooperation. WB and AIIB are currently discussing nearly one dozen co-financed projects in sectors that include transport, water, and energy in Central Asia, South Asia, and East Asia. Under the agreement, WB will support the co-financed projects in areas like procurement, the environment, and social safeguards. It will also play a leading role in these co-financed projects.

In conclusion, EIB and EBRD are gradually strengthening relationships with AIIB executives, showing their willingness to cooperate. NDB and AIIB are further seeking co-financed projects besides issuing securities jointly. AsDB and WB both are both discussing and signing co-financing framework agreements with AIIB, which promote the establishment of AIIB's governance system, thereby enhancing its operation efficiency and international image. This cooperation will lead to the financing of large-scale infrastructure projects in Asia.

AIIB's First Financing Projects are Materializing

On April 19, 2016, AIIB's first financing projects became the focus of the public. These projects mainly provide financing for building three highways in Central Asia: a highway from Shorkot to Khanewal in Pakistan, which is supported by AIIB, AsDB, and the UK's Department for International Development; a highway from Dushanbe to Tursunzoda in Tajikistan, which is supported by AIIB, AsDB, and EBRD jointly; and a ring road in Almaty, Kazakhstan, supported by AIIB, WB, and EBRD. The highway in Pakistan was already under construction in August, 2016.

In addition, Russia and India both revealed AIIB's financing projects in 2016. AIIB expected to provide India a $ 500 million loan for developing solar energy. The President of Russian Far East Development Fund (FEDF), Alexei Chekunkov, said FEDF would propose to co-finance with AIIB 19 projects in Russia. The total investment of $ 9 billion would be used in resource mining infrastructure, an international transport corridor, and port and airport construction in Siberia and the Far East.

AIIB's Attraction and Inclusiveness

AIIB President Jin Liqun revealed earlier that AIIB was taking new members. The Bank has 57 founding members. In March 2016, Poland officially became a founding member of AIIB, with a share of $ 831. 8 million, or 0. 83% of AIIB's capital. The Harper government in Canada refused to join AIIB so that Canada was not able to be a founding member of AIIB. The current Canadian government has expressed its willingness to join AIIB and was welcomed by President Jin Liqun. Potential new members includes Hong Kong and Taiwan: Hong Kong will join AIIB in 2017; Taiwan refused to join because of application procedure, nonetheless this issue will be solved in the future.

AIIB's first projects have received global attention while greater China-Asia cooperation opportunities were revealed. As more and more countries communicate with AIIB, some western nations that initially questioned the Bank are now reconsidering. It is expected that as the Asian financing projects are launched, a transparent and fair operating mechanism is shown, more and more collaboration will be achieved and AIIB will increase its attraction and inclusiveness greatly.

The BRICS New Development Bank

The BRICS New Development Bank (NDB), established on July 21, 2015, is the first international multilateral development bank in history independently established and led by emerging market countries. Besides, it is a strong complement to existing multilateral and regional financial institutions committed to economic growth and development around the globe. It aims to support infrastructure construction and sustainable development of BRICS countries and other emerging markets and developing countries. At the same time, it aims at easing dependence on the dollar and the euro. In January 2016, the board committee of NDB passed the major policy and charter of bank operation. In February, NDB signed a headquarters agreement with the Chinese government and signed a memorandum of understanding with the Shanghai Municipal People's Government successively. Since then, NDB started its full-scale operation. NDB started its business in 2016, and made brilliant achievements. NDB has made positive progress in two respects at least. First, it has approved seven green renewable energy projects, worth more than $ 1.5 billion. Second, it has successfully issued the first batch of 3 billion CNY green bonds.

The Seven projects Approved by NDB in 2016

NDB approved the first loan projects since its establishment on April 15. The total size of these projects is $ 811 million. These projects are set to support 2,370 MW of renewable energy power generation capacity of member countries, reducing annual emissions of carbon dioxide by 4 million tons. The first four projects are renewable energy power generation projects in Brazil, solar roof power generation projects in Shanghai Lingang Hongbo New Energy Development Co., Ltd. in China, renewable energy power generation projects in India, and transmission network construction projects in South Africa.

In mid-July, NDB decided to finance the hydropower station project in the Republic of Karelia, with a total investment of 11.8 billion rubles (about $ 190 million). Russian Direct Investment Fund and China Energy Engineering Group Co., Ltd. are equity investors in this project. The project was officially launched on October 17, 2016 and is scheduled to be completed in 2019.

On November 22, the board of NDB approved two new projects in China and India: the Putian Pinghai Bay Wind Power Project in Fujian (CNY 2 billion) and the Madhya Pradesh Road Construction Project ($ 350 million). Fujian Putian Pinghai Bay Wind Power Project is expected to generate 873 million kWh of electricity each year, reducing carbon dioxide emissions by 870,000. The roads supported by the Madhya Pradesh Road Construction Project work as transportation hub, connecting central and coastal areas in India, and are helpful to the development and upgrading of neighboring regions.

BRICS countries and some other developing countries are in urgent need of energy restructuring. However, the current development of new energy and other high-tech industries rely on venture capital. Therefore, strong support of development finance is needed. NDB will integrate the financial sector and the energy sector together and leverage capital investment in the energy sector to accelerate the energy restructuring of emerging economies and developing countries. These projects will greatly contribute to BRICS's efforts to improve energy efficiency, tackle climate change and environmental degradation, balance development and environmental concerns, and energy saving and emission reductions. This is in full compliance with NDB's goal of providing financial support for sustainable development. Thus, green finance is not only the development focus of NDB, but also an important frontier area for the global development community as a whole.

The First Batch of CNY Green Bonds Issued by NDB in 2016

On July 18, NDB successfully issued the first batch of CNY 3.0 billion worth of green financial bonds. The maturity of each bond is 5 years, the interest rate is 3.07%, and the subscription ratio is 3.1 times, attracting a wide range of domestic and foreign investors to enthusiastically subscribe. The funds raised will be used specifically for green industrial projects in BRICS countries, other emerging economies, and developing countries. These projects include the first green energy projects approved in April, the Karelia hydroelectric project in Western Russia, the Rand loan to South Africa to deal with the volatility of the dollar, and other projects. The main and debt ratings of the bonds are rated as AAA by domestic ratings.

The bond issuance is NDB's debut in the capital market, but also the first time that a multilateral development bank has been approved to issue CNY green financial bonds in the Chinese inter-bank bond market. The bond issuance reflects both the characteristics of NDB itself, but also the conceptual and practical innovation of international development finance. On the one hand, the CNY-denominated value reflects China's unique advantages as the world's second largest economy and the host country of the BRICS Bank, reflecting the prudence and pragmatism of NDB's management and the confidence of the international financial market in the internationalization of CNY. On the other hand, the green financial bonds highlight the concept of green and sustainable development, filling the business gaps of existing international development financial institutions.

Future focuses

Over the first year of operating, NDB progressed with a highly efficient and stable step. It can be said that the issuance of green bonds to provide member countries with stable, low-cost financing channels reflects the NDB's investment and financing direction by highlighting the concept of green and sustainable development. At the same time, NDB is also facing some difficulties and challenges from not possessing an international rating, from liquidity risk, from BRICS countries conflict in interest, from a non-perfect banking system, and so on. In the face of the challenges and opportunities, NDB will strategically make future plans while taking a long-term perspective. It will not only learn mature experience and practices from existing multilateral development banks, adhere to international, normative, and high standards, and continuously improve operational transparency, but also make appropriate improvements and innovations in the existing policies, institutional systems, and other aspects.

NBD plans to expand new space for cooperation among BRICS countries, and innovate development and financing models. In recent years, the turbulence of international capital markets has caused many difficulties for developing countries to utilize foreign capital. On the one hand, NDB should further develop the currency business to provide stable and cost-effective financing channels for member countries. It is said that NDB has planned to continuously issue local currency bonds in other BRICS countries. On the other hand, NDB should also widely mobilize policy-oriented operating institutions, commercial banks, insurance funds, and the private sector to invest in infrastructure projects. In addition, the use of the public-private partnership models will be useful in helping member countries achieve economic and social development actively and prudently.

NBD plans to build a new pattern of all-round cooperative partnership, and strengthen multilateral development agencies. From a global perspective, NDB, led by emerging economies, should work with the World Bank and other multilateral development banks in areas such as poverty reduction, the maintenance of the world economic order, and infrastructure development. From a regional perspective, NDB should also actively seek cooperation and form all-round cooperative relations based on complementary advantages, such as the vision and planning of China's initiative to implement the Belt and Road.

NBD plans to improve the global economic governing order and improve the decision-making power of emerging economies. NDB has the potential to become the "quasi-central bank" of the BRICS and emerging economies and to complement the "contingency reserve fund" to form a new global financial stability network, providing help to developing countries by stabilizing monetary and financial systems. NDB members are equal, which highlights the new international economic order characterized by democracy and equality, and reflects the general trend of democratization of international relations.

In 2017, NDB will participate in 15 infrastructure projects by lending $ 2. 5 billion. In addition, NDB will also participate in international market ratings in 2017. It may also issues bonds in the international market. In terms of expanding its staff, although the NDB mainly relies on borrowing professionals from five member states, recruitment is currently under way. In the first quarter of 2017, there will be 10 directors in place and a team ranging from 100 to 150 people will be formed in addition to new hiring professionals. In terms of the loan application process, at present, different countries currently apply for loans with different loan procedures. In general, it takes 6 months from the project application to approval. NDB will also be committed to improving efficiency and shortening the project acceptance time. 2018 may introduce the first batch of new members.

Over the past year, NDB has accomplished a number of important tasks in a low-key manner: identifying the management team and operating model of the Bank, approving seven green renewable energy projects, and successfully issuing the first CNY-denominated green bonds (CNY 3 billion). NDB will also face more opportunities and challenges in the process of going forward. We believe that NDB, a multilateral development organization created entirely by emerging economies, will continue to grow with the aim of sustainable development, glowing with unlimited vigor and vitality, and is moving towards professional, efficient, transparent, and green goals.

The Silk Road Fund Corporation

China's Leading Group for Financial and Economic Affairs convened its eighth meeting on November 4, 2014, at which China's President Xi Jinping proposed the concept of "Silk Road Fund". On November 8 of that year, President Xi officially announced that China would invest $ 40 billion to set up the Silk Road Fund, which was welcomed by many countries as one of the three institutions (Silk Road Fund, Asian Infrastructure Investment Bank, and BRICS New Development Bank) that aimed to implement the Belt and Road strategy. Some "heavily indebted poor countries" have low sovereign ratings and high loan costs so that the past sovereign financing model has been unsustainable, while the new model of equity financing with debt and loans would be more reasonable.

The Silk Road Fund Corporation has made substantial efforts in improving corporate governance since 2015. The board of directors, board of supervisors, and top management team have been established and the Fund's daily operations are now on the right track. First, a relatively clear delineation of the Silk Road Fund Corporation's function has formed, namely being a long-term development and investment fund. Second, a scientific and efficient governance structure has formed by the formation of the board of directors, board of supervisors, and top management team. In addition, professional committees like the Strategy Planning Committee, Investment Committee, and Audit Committee, improve certain working mechanisms continuously. Third, a relatively standard and well-organized framework of investment management has formed, namely sticking to the investment principles characterized by "docking, efficiency, cooperation and opening-up". Fourth, management is cultivating a positive corporate culture, adopting a flat management structure and people-oriented management philosophy, and advocating team spirit with regard to, pioneering enterprise, coordination, and efficiency. At the same time, the Silk Road Fund Corporation has done substantial work, and the program investment has made virtual progress.

On April 20, 2015, the Silk Road Fund, the Three Gorges Group, Pakistani Private Power and Infrastructure Board signed the cooperation memorandum and initiated the first foreign investment, which was witnessed by China's President Xi Jinping and Pakistani Prime Minister Nawaz Sharif. On June 5, the Silk Road Fund signed a cooperation agreement with Sinochem Group to jointly invest in Italian Pirelli SPA Company. On August 31, the Silk Road Fund signed a memorandum of cooperation with Kazakhstani Agency for Export and Investment to establish the China-Kazakhstan Capacity Cooperation Fund, witnessed by China's President Xi Jinping and Kazakhstan's President Nazarbayev. On September 3, the Silk Road Fund signed an agreement of partial equity framework with Russian NVTK on purchasing Russia Yamal liquefied natural gas. On December 14, the Silk Road Fund signed framework agreement with Kazakhstani Agency for Export and Investment, on establishing China-Kazakhstan Capacity Cooperation Fund. On December 17, the Silk Road Fund signed a trade agreement with Russian NVTK on purchasing Russia Yamal liquefied natural gas. The Silk Road Fund has successfully initiated five cross-border FDI projects since its establishment. The above projects respectively represent the active attempts of the Silk Road Fund to conduct cooperation in key fields like greenfield development, international mergers, and energy cooperation.

The Silk Road Fund has participated and delivered speeches in international forums. Mr. Jin Qi, the President of the Silk Road Fund, attended "2015 Annual Meeting of China's Overseas Enterprises" on March 20, presented at Asia-Europe Interconnective Industry Dialogue on May 28 and Lujiazui Financial Forum on June 27, and gave speeches at the CICC Entrepreneurs Forum on November 3 and 2015 Financial Summit on December 14. In addition, the Silk Road Fund signed a memorandum of cooperation with Kazakhstani BAITEREK JSC in Beijing on December 14. They agreed to comprehensively take advantage of resources, like finance, information, law, and institutional resources, to conduct cooperation in ways such as equity and debt financing under the framework of the China-Kazakhstan Capacity Cooperation Fund, thereby seeking cooperation opportunities in prioritized areas such as production capacity and information technology. On December 21, President Jin Qi met Mr. Mahesh, the Nepali ambassador to China and former Secretary-General of the Nepali government. On December 10, Wang Yanzhi, the general manager of the Silk Road Fund, met with the minister of Georgia's Ministry of Economy and Sustainable Development.

In terms of financial cooperation, the Silk Road Fund has signed a series of cooperation letters of intent with several financial institutions at home and abroad in 2015. On September 3, the Silk Road Fund signed a memorandum on investment and cooperation in Beijing with Russia's State Development, Foreign Trade Bank, and Russian Foreign Direct Investment Fund, which was witnessed by China's President Xi Jinping and Russia's President Putin. According to the memorandum, the Silk Road Fund would jointly conduct cooperation with the Russian side on projects in the fields of infrastructure, industry, electric power and energy, and others. On December 4, President Jin Qi met with a delegation led by the President of Hong Kong Monetary Authority, and the CLO of Hong Kong Association of Banks, to discuss cooperation affairs. On December 9, the Silk Road Fund signed a framework agreement with China Export & Credit Insurance Corporation on serving the Belt and Road Strategy and supporting enterprises going abroad, illustrating that the two sides have established a long-term, stable strategic partnership in overseas market development, the investment and financing of outbound projects and risk management. It would greatly help bring their advantages into full play and provide more comprehensive investments and financing services for those enterprises going abroad.

Over the past year, the Silk Road Fund has made fruitful explorations. The achievements that the Silk Road Fund has achieved over the past year were closely linked to four principles and three thoughts. The first principle is linking. The investment from the Silk Road Fund must be connected to the development strategies and plans of other countries. The Belt and Road strategy does not set any strict geographical boundaries. The Silk Road Fund would participate in certain projects as long as inter-connection is needed. The second principle is efficiency. All the money from the Silk Road Fund is burdened with CNY debt. Since the Silk Road Fund is not aid-oriented or contributory, the operations must adhere to market principles. Money must be invested in profitable projects so that the rights and interests of shareholders can be safeguarded. The third principle is cooperation. Since the Silk Road Fund is not a multilateral development organization, it shall abide by laws and regulations in China and in other regions or countries and maintain international market practices and financial order. The last one is openness. The Silk Road Fund is willing to conduct investment and financing cooperation with multilateral financial institutions regionally and globally.

Among the three thoughts, the first level is linking, which focuses on the macro level. Resource factors should be allocated and optimized in wider ranges, and the linking among real demands, responsibilities, and interests must be realized. The second level focuses on industry and the formation of industry chains. Under the framework of the Belt and Road, financial institutions should support enterprises transitioning from the old model of merely undertaking contracting projects to "BOT" (building-operation-transfer). The resource integration of the industry and technological upgrading can be driven by exporting Chinese equipment and conducting capacity cooperation, so that our industry can upgrade to a higher level in the value chain in global industry. The third level is centered on financing and forming capital-oriented thinking. To invest abroad would help those enterprises do business abroad. By venture capital financing, the Silk Road Fund can comprehensively take advantage of various financing ways and currency portfolios, such as equity, bond, fund, and domestic and foreign currency, thus providing support of efficient capital portfolios for various projects and speeding up the cycle of capital and improving investment efficiency.

The "go global" strategy of the Silk Road Fund would face particular risks in certain countries: geopolitical risks (the global major geopolitical risks were concentrated in the Middle East, South Asia, East Europe, and Northeast Asia), terrorism, operation risk, market risk, and others, which is caused by lacking operation experience in international projects. Therefore, the Silk Road Fund has set up a well-designed risk control mechanism. First, the Silk Road Fund has established the incentive and constraint mechanism to share risks with enterprises. The governance structure, characterized by clearly identified property rights and responsibilities, can identify the operation and management responsibilities of each investor. Second, the Silk Road Fund has designed reasonable risk mitigation and compensation mechanisms. Risks would be thoroughly teased out in project evaluation and due diligence inspection. Risk-aversion mechanism should also be well designed in an investment plan. Third, the exit mechanism should be properly mapped out. A commercially-strong project can go public and the Fund will exit upon realizing a positive return on investment. The infrastructure project can exit by transferring ownership to local government, going public, or transferring part of the equity to realize proper returns after the project is completed. Fourth, attention should be paid to local culture, laws, and regulations when investing in other countries. A pending project needs to be fully checked to see whether it is consistent with local policing and standards to avoid improper investment risks.

The Silk Road Fund will continue to position itself as a medium- and long-term investment fund. It holds the principles of "opening-up, inclusiveness, and reciprocity", and is devoted to providing financing support for economic cooperation, and bilateral or multilateral inter-connectivity under the framework of the Belt and Road. The Silk Road Fund will work with enterprises and financial institutions at home and abroad to promote common development and prosperity in China and around the world using the Belt and Road strategy.

Chapter 7　Associations of DFIs

Association of Development Financing Institutions in Asia and the Pacific (ADFIAP)

Association Members

Membership shall be open to financial institutions/banks engaged in the financing of development, whether industrial, service, or other productive sectors of the economy.

The Association shall have the following types of membership:

Ordinary: institutions in Asia and the Pacific engaged in the financing of development as a significant activity.

Special: regional or sub-regional financial institutions in Asia and the Pacific; financial institutions outside the Asia-Pacific region with which the Association may decide to establish and maintain a relationship; and other financial institutions within or outside the region given Observer Status by the ADFIAP Board of Directors on a case-to-case basis.

Sponsor / Sustaining: public and private institutions, non-government organizations and individuals that support the purpose and mission of ADFIAP and are willing to pay membership dues or contribution to assist the Association financially.

Associate: institutions with provincial or state-wide operations on the recommendation of a member-institution in that country.

Organizations and other financial institutions: commercial banks with units or departments that cater to development-oriented activities, such as SME banking, microfinance, environmental lending, housing finance, and related undertaking.

Honorary: individuals who have performed outstanding services in the field of development banking, or who have been closely connected with the profession of development banking or have served ADFIAP for many years, may be conferred with Honorary Membership by the General Assembly.

Mission and Vision

The mission of the ADFIAP is to advance sustainable development by strengthening the development finance function and institutions, enhancing capacity of members and its human resources, and advocating development finance innovations.

Through the provision of development finance services by its members, ADFIAP envisions a future of sustainable economic, environmental and social development and growth in the region, with its people as the ultimate beneficiary.

History and Governance

The idea of an association of development bankers had originated in Manila in 1969 at the Fourth Regional Conference of Development Financing Institutions of Asia and the Pacific under the auspices of the Asian Development Bank. Such an idea further gained substance during the UNIDO Banker's Meetings which commenced in 1970 in Paris. At the last UNIDO Meeting in Caracas, it was learned that two regional associations, namely the Latin American (ALIDE) and African (AADFI) regional associations, had been formed.

It was also reported in Caracas that similar institutions were contemplated for the Arab countries and for countries in Eastern Europe. The DFIs from Asian and the Pacific region attending the Caracas meeting agreed then that it would be timely to form an Association of Asia-Pacific DFIs.

At the end of the sixth Regional Conference, October 1, 1976, 31 DFIs attending the Conference in Manila under the auspices of AsDB jointly signed a memorandum of agreement to adopt the constitution of what came to be known as the Association of Development Financing Institutions in Asia and the Pacific or ADFIAP, and affirmed their interest in becoming members of the Association.

The governance structure of the Association is as follows:

General Assembly: the highest body that meets every two years to elect the Board of Directors of the Association and passes upon organizational matters.

Board of Directors: the governing body that passes upon policy matters. It is composed of not more than 30 duly elected voting members of the Association that elect from among them the Chairman, three Vice-Chairman and the Treasurer. The Secretary General is an ex-officio member of the Board.

The Association is managed by a Secretary General assisted by service unit heads that constitute the Secretariat.

The Secretariat has a fully functioning business center and full-time professional staff to carry out its programs, engagements, and assignments. Its main service units are: membership, projects, training & credentialing, information, and finance & administration. The Association's Asia-Pacific Institute for Development Finance conducts regular training courses and manages the credentialing program of the Association.

The Board Process

The ADFIAP Board of Directors sets the future of the Association. It sets its vision and mission and operational goals.

1) The Association shall be managed by a Board of Directors consisting of not more than thirty (30) Ordinary Members. The Board of Directors shall appoint a Chairman, not more than three Vice-Chairmen, and a Treasurer.

2) The Board of Directors shall appoint a maximum of three (3) Advisers from the non-voting members, i. e. Special, Cooperating, and Associate, to sit in the Board of Directors as ex-officio members.

3) The Board Members are personally committed to the mission of the Association, willing to volunteer sufficient time and resources to help achieve its mission and to fulfill their fiduciary responsibilities.

4) The Secretary General shall serve as a voting member of the Board of Directors.

5) To allow for significant deliberation and diversity, the Board is made up of elected member-institutions represented by their Chief Executive Officers and/ or Chairmen, whoever is designated by the member-institution.

6) The Association's Constitution determines the term limits of the Directors.

7) The Board Members do not receive compensation for their service.

8) The Board nomination process is announced to the Association's general membership so that interested members can nominate themselves or others.

Communications

ADFIAP and its partner, the European Organization for Sustainable Development (EOSD) successfully held the 6th Global Sustainable Finance Conference (GCSF 6) in Karlsruhe, Germany on July 14 – 15, 2016. Over 100 delegates from 35 countries around the world attended the event.

The overall objective of the GSFC is to contribute in the sustainability transformation of the financial services industry by providing an international forum for key stakeholders from across the world to share knowledge and experiences and to work together for a strong, fair, safe and resilient financial services industry that works in harmony with the natural environment.

The conference covered a wide range of sustainable finance topics including, among others, innovating banking and finance for a sustainable future, sustainable banking and finance best practice examples from Russia, Pakistan, Nigeria and Malaysia, climate action and financial institutions, the role of financial institutions on the sustainable development goals (SDGs) 2030, and sustainable finance and local government units. The program also included a visit at the Fraunhofer Institute, one of the largest and most renown applied research facility in Germany and meeting with "green" start-ups. The conference was also the occasion for the presentation of the Global Sustainable Finance Awards 2016.

ADFIAP and the Berlin-based Renewables Academy AG (RENAC), with support from the German Federal Ministry for Environment's International Climate Initiative and the German Embassy in Manila, launched its partnership project called, "Green Banking—Capacity Building on Green Energy and Climate Finance" on January 26, 2016 at the New World Hotel in Makati City, Philippines.

The main objective of this 3-year (2015 – 2018) capacity-building program is to support financial institutions in building up new business lines for financing renewable energy and energy efficiency projects and to make use of internationally-provided climate finance instruments. The program is complementary to RENAC's CapREG (Capacity Development on Renewable Energy and Grid Integration) project. The project is scholarship-based and offers different kinds of training (both online and face-to-face courses), study tour programs, networking events and exchange of experiences for professionals in India, Indonesia, Thailand, Vietnam and the Philippines. It also aims to develop a "Green Banking Specialist" degree program.

Association of African Development Finance Institutions

Till October, 2016, Association of African Development Finance Institutions (AADFI) has 79 members, including 59 ordinary members, 14 special members and 6 honorary members.

Association Members

Ordinary Members: Any African national institution, including Banque Algérienne de Développement, Banco de Poupanca E Credit (Angola), Industrial Development and Workers Bank of Egypt and Agricultural Development Bank.

Special members: any African regional and sub-regional institution, including Fonds Africain de Garantie et de Coopération Economique, Southern African Development Community-Development Finance Resource Centre (SADC-DFRC), Banque de Développement des Etats de l'Afrique Centrale, Conseil de l'Entente, African Export and Import Bank, Economic Commission for Africa, PTA Bank, Shelter Afrique Centre, Fonds de Solidarité Africaine, Arab Bank for the Economic Development of Africa, Banque Ouest Africaine de Développement, Groupe de la BIDC/ECOWAS Bank, Banque Africaine de Développement, East African Development Bank.

Honorary members: any African or non-African international institution, including Exim-Bank of India, World Association of Small and Medium Enterprises, Giordano dell'Amore Foundation, Banco Portugues do Investimento, Banque Internationale pour la Reconstruction et le Développement, International Finance Corporation.

Missions

Promote economic and social development in Africa through cooperation between banks and financial institutions. Strengthen cooperation in financing for economic and social development. Establish a systematic mechanism for the exchange of information among member institutions. Accelerate the process of economic integration in Africa. Encourage academic research and consensus on issues of common interest.

History

The very first meeting of Directors of African Development Banks was held in August 1969 in Freetown, Republic of Sierra Leone. The purpose of the meeting, convened by the African Development Bank, was to ascertain their views on ways and means of strengthening cooperation between their institutions and the Bank.

Further meetings were held in Abidjan in May 1970 and were attended by representatives of the Development Banks of 23 African countries and delegates from regional institutions, such as the East African Development Bank and the Union Africaine et

Malgache des Banques de Développement. Representatives of various international banks and other financing institutions also attended the meeting, which discussed a wide range of issues pertaining to organization, management and resource mobilization of the national development banks.

The outcome of a meeting held in Abidjan from 4 to 7 March 1975 was the creation of the Association of African Development Finance Institutions under the auspices of the African Development Bank. The establishment of the Association met the need for a continent-wide coordination and economic solidarity. The inaugural assembly held in Abidjan set up a liaison committee to draw up and finalize the Association's legal instruments. These were adopted by the Association's First General Assembly, which was convened for that purpose in Dakar, Senegal, on 2 and 3 May.

Governance

The Association is composed of a General Assembly, an Executive Committee and a General Secretariat.

The General Assembly is the supreme organ responsible for laying down policies, determining regulations and other necessary provisions. The General Assembly holds its ordinary meetings once a year in one or other of the African countries in which its members are located.

Pursuant to the Association's by laws, Extraordinary Assemblies may also be convened. The General Assembly comprises all the members of the Association.

The Executive Committee is responsible for conducting the Association's activities and supervising the General Secretariat. It comprises the Bureau, composed of the Chairman and two Vice-Chairmen. Five members representing the five sub-regions of the Continent as defined by the UN Economic Commission for Africa or as may be determined from time to time by the General Assembly; and a member elected by the Special and Honorary members.

The General Secretariat is the organ responsible for the implementation and managing the day-to-day activities of the Association. Through protocol services, the General Secretariat assist the business activities in Côte d'Ivoire, especially cooperate with the African Development Bank Group.

Communications

AADFI held its 42nd Ordinary General Assembly Meetings in Lusaka, Republic of Zambia from May 22 to 24, 2016.

The Opening Ceremony, the working sessions and the Closing Ceremony took place at the Mulungushi International Conference Centre in Lusaka, Republic of Zambia, under the Chairmanship of the Mr. Patrick Dlamini, Chairman of AADFI, CEO of Development Bank of Southern Africa (DBSA).

91 delegates from 39 member and partner-institutions observers participated in the 42nd Ordinary General Assembly of AADFI.

The 42nd OGA adopted 13 critical resolutions reflecting the AADFI member-institutions' commitment and eagerness to ensure the sustainability of the Association.

China Association for the Promotion of Development Financing

Founded in 2013, the China Association for the Promotion of Development Financing (CAPDF) mainly consists of enterprises and institutions that are engaged in the development field, experts and scholars who are engaged in the researches of development finance theory, and related research institutes. Serving various market subjects in China's development finance field, CAPDF establishes platforms of communication and cooperation among enterprises in the development field, governments at all levels, related financial institutions and research institutes. The goal of CAPDF is to deepen the financial cooperation of different market subjects, to promote market, credit, and institutional development by using development finance methods, and to make contributions to the simultaneous development of China's industrialization, informatization, urbanization, and agricultural modernization.

In 2016, CAPDF devoted itself to the following work: promoting green development, ecotourism development, and characteristic town construction, as well as promoting green development cooperation in China, Northeast Asia, and around the world; setting up a technical evaluation center to establish the credit basis between technology and finance, as well as supporting technical enterprises by using various forms of finance to strengthen the connection between the real economy and the financial system; actively promoting international communication and economic cooperation in the development finance field; establishing an inclusive development financing service mechanism to support poverty alleviation and create fair financing opportunities for poverty-stricken areas to grow strategic industries and difficult social groups. CAPDF mainly focus on the following aspects.

Promote Green Development and Cultivate the Ecological Economy

At present, what restricts the development of some big cities is not land resources, but the weak ecological carrying capacity caused by rapid expansion of cities. Such an ecological restriction has offset many advantages of urbanization to a certain extent. No matter how high the land value is, traditional basic land prices and various capital relations will be destructively and subversively restructured once the ecological environment deteriorates. Therefore, green development and ecological economy are required. In the 4 + 8 areas in south and north China (Inner Mongolia, Heilongjiang, Jilin, Liaoning, Fujian, Jiangxi, Hunan, Sichuan, Guangdong, Guangxi, Guizhou and Yunan Province), the forest coverage rate is high and water resources are abundant, with no overdevelopment. The value of these areas lies in the high quality and scarce ecological resources. CAPDF is dedicated to transforming the traditional development mode of areas with superior ecological resources to develop ecological finance and green finance, and to turn the ecological advantages into development competitiveness.

In 2016, to promote the construction of 4 + 8 Green Development Platform and project landing, CAPDF held a series of activities including the Green Development Discussion Meeting and the Northeast Asia Green Development (Mohe) Forum with Ganzhou municipal government of Jiangxi Province and local governments in Daxing'anling Prefecture of Heilongjiang Province. CAPDF also organized and participated in a series of conferences and meetings related to green development, including the Annual Summit on Ecological Design and Green Manufacturing for Industrial Products in China 2016, Seminar on the Development of Characteristic Towns in 2016, and China IUR Cooperation and Innovation Conference. Cooperating with local governments, enterprises, and financial institutions, CAPDF established the 4 + 8 Green Development Platform, built the collaboration mechanism among local governments, initiated the China Green Industry Investment Fund and China Characteristic Town Investment Fund, and accelerated the construction of green financial asset trading centers and consumer finance companies.

Promote Innovative Development and Improve Industrial Finance

Technological progress and scientific innovation are the fundamental driving forces for long-term sustainable economic development. However, due to the absence of a social atmosphere encouraging technological progress, attention paid to technology by traditional finance institutions is inadequate, leading to the decrease of technical professionals engaged in economic management, and understanding and financial support for industrial development are insufficient. China's private enterprises are gradually growing as an important force for technological progress. However, with the limited support they can get, the development of technological private enterprises is restrained. In 2016, CAPDF set up a think-tank to evaluate the projects of technological private enterprises, with Shanghai Fareast Credit Rating taking charge of enterprise valuation, so as to support technological enterprises by using various forms of finance.

In August 2016, CAPDF held the First Technology Evaluation and Appraisal Meeting in China to evaluate and appraise four special technologies in the areas of integrated precision forming, environmentally-friendly fire control, "internet plus" community health care, and marine life search & rescue system, and promote related investment and financing for the projects. Moreover, CAPDF actively promoted the construction of think-tanks, online platforms, and project pools. The technology evaluation index system and big data are also in the discussion. In November, in order to promote communication and cooperation among countries along the Belt and Road and to accelerate the transformation and upgrading of China's manufacturing, CAPDF and Xi'an Jiaotong University jointly held "The Belt and Road" High End Forum on November 2016, which covered economic and industrial quality management regulations, intelligent manufacturing, and quality innovation.

Promote International Cooperation of Development Finance

CAFDF was authorized by China's Ministry of Foreign Affairs to be the organizer of financial coordinating country activities of the Conference on Interaction and Confidence-Building Measures in Asia (CICA). CAPDF also cooperates with German Energy Agency (Deutsche Energie-Agentur) in designing the financial model which allows Chinese firms to pay back debts using energy permits, supporting energy saving, emission-reduction, and smog elimination in Hebei Province with the introduction of advanced German technology and production methods, and preparing the Sino-German International Forum on Green Development. CAPDF held a series of international forums, including the Annual Meeting for Chinese Outbound Investment Companies 2016 in March jointly held by the China International Chamber of Commerce for the Private Sector (CICCPS), the first cross-border E-commerce Summit in June 2016, and the first and second Aviatic Silk Road International Forum in January 2016 and January 2017, organizing the members of CAPDF to participate in the construction of the Belt and Road strategy.

Promote the Development and Inclusive Financial Service Mechanism

CAPDF strives to create fair financing opportunities for poverty-stricken areas, growing strategic industries, and vulnerable social groups.

Investigating the basic situation of poverty-stricken areas to promoting ecological poverty alleviation are some of CAPDF's primary goals. CAPDF collected basic information regarding the ecological agriculture and ecotourism of 592 cities or counties in 12 provinces (4 + 8 areas in south and north of China) while experts are organized to research the resource factor endowment, help poverty-stricken areas find their development advantages, and establish their green development resource tank. Cooperating with Chinese Association for Poverty Alleviation & Development (CAPAD) in promoting agricultural poverty alleviation in Qinxian County of Shanxi Province, CAPDF conducted the research project on poverty alleviation and development, which can provide co-intelligence support for poverty alleviation projects.

CAPDF signed the *Cooperation Agreement of Mohe County Ecological Construction and Characteristic Small Town Complex Demonstration Project with Daxing'anling Prefecture of Heilongjiang Province*, so as to explore ways to support forest tourism and ecological economic development through PPPs (public-private partnerships), help build an international city of tourism and leisure, and create financing opportunities for remote areas.

Establish the Development Finance Featured Think-tank

The development finance featured think-tank established by CAPDF is developing rapidly. In 2016, the think-tank published *Global Development Financing Report* and think-tank series, which included *Foreign Development Financing Law* and *Frontier of Silk Road Economy and Culture*. CAPDF also built the development finance information system, releasing the *International Newsletter for Development Finance* and *The Belt and Road Financial Dynamics of Islamic Region and Nations*. With the goal of developing a communication platform of industry experts, CAPDF held the Development Financing Legal & Regulatory International Symposium, establishing direct contact with development financing institutions in Russia, France, Germany, and Japan, jointly held the Industry Development Report Meeting 2016 with the State Information Center of China, and organized the Africa Electricity and Agriculture Investment Symposium.

Part 3　Analysis and Outlook of DFIs

Chapter 8   The Structures and Tendencies of DFIs[*]

We described the details of 30 development financial institutions (Hereafter referred to as DFIs) in Part 2, including 12 multilateral and 18 national DFIs. Among them, 6 of the 18 national DFIs are from high-income countries and 12 are from low- & middle-income countries. The 12 multilateral DFIs include both institutions dominated by high-income countries and low- & middle-income countries. Therefore, we will analyze and summarize the structures and trends of these 30 DFIs from both the national and multilateral dimensions as well as from both the high-income and low- & middle-income country dimensions in the following.

Global Development Financial System Dominated by the United States and Regional Powers

The Influence of low- & Middle-income Countries has Risen Rapidly

If we divide time into three periods, before 1965, 1965 to 2000, and after 2000, then we will find that newly established institutions are mainly from low- & middle-income countries. Before 1965, economically-advantage, high-income countries set up a number of national and multilateral DFIs to support economic development of neighboring countries and regions. Since 1965, especially after 2000, with the economic growth of low- & middle-income countries and the needs of economic development during the transition period, many low- & middle-income countries have set up their own DFIs.

Figure 8.1 shows that 12 DFIs were established before 1965. The number of DFIs established reached 20 by 2000. In the 15 years from 2000 to 2015, 10 DFIs were

---

* Our sample is composed of 30 institutions. The index of total assets, total equity, ROA and ROE include data on 26 institutions. The index of maximum loan term includes data on 22 institutions. Other indices include data on 27 institutions.

set up, of which 8 were from low- & middle-income countries, only 2 were from high-income countries. The proliferation of DFIs in low- & middle-income countries shows that they generally recognized that effective allocation of social resources and economic development cannot be achieved simply by relying on the market system completely, they must rely on DFIs, which can effectively allocate resources and make significant contributions in the economic development of the countries and the regions.

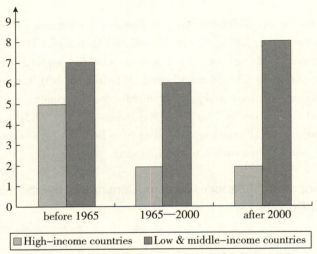

Figure 8.1　Founding Times of DFIs Led by High-income
and low- & Middle-Income Countries

Since 1965, the growth of DFIs dominated by high-income countries has slowed down significantly. Over the past 50 years, there were only four newly established institutions dominated by high-income countries, which were the Asian Development Bank, the European Bank for Reconstruction and Development, the Bank of North-Rhine Westphalia, and the Development Bank of Japan. This also shows that the high-income-country-dominated development financial system has entered a relatively mature stage.

The rapid economic development of China has also greatly improved the overall scale of DFIs in low- & middle-income countries. The scale of DFIs in low- & middle-income countries (except China) is far less than that in high-income countries.

National Development Banks Still Lead the Global Development Financial System

In terms of total assets and total equity (see Figure 8. 2), the size of national DFIs is far larger than that of multilateral DFIs. This shows that the national development financial system mainly supports the economies of individual countries. Among these national DFIs, the CDB has the largest scale, accounting for more than one-third of total assets of global development financial institutions, and it functions by implementing macroeconomic policies, guiding social investment, etc. In addition, KfW, NRW, and CDC are also relatively large. The assets of WB ranked first among multilateral DFIs, leading global loan assistance.

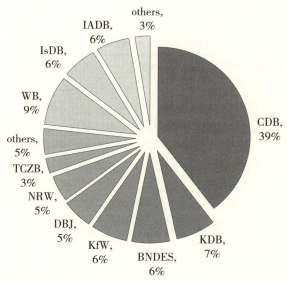

Figure 8. 2   Comparison of National and Multilateral DFIs' Total Equity

National DFIs aim to support economic development within their own country, whereas the main objective of multilateral DFIs is to meet regional or global economic development needs. During recent economic globalization, countries have demanded to strengthen communication and exchanges, promote cooperation, and jointly cope with the risks and challenges of achieving regional economic development. There is no doubt that China has made great efforts to promote mutually beneficial economic cooperation. Of the four multilateral DFIs newly established after 2000, both AIIB Investment Bank and NDB BRICS are closely related to China, which also highlights

China's growing influence in world financial markets.

Of 30 sample institutions, there are eight national DFIs established before 1965, four established from 1965 to 2000, and six established after 2000, while the number of newly established multilateral DFIs was four in all three periods. In each of these periods, the number of newly established national DFIs was greater than or equal to the number of newly established multilateral DFIs. This suggests that DFIs have been more focused on their own country's economic development since establishment.

The Multilateral Institutions are Dominated by the United States and Regional Powers

Listed in Table 8.1 are the structures of equity ownership in multilateral institutions in the sample of 30 institutions.

Table 8.1 Equity Structure of Multilateral Development Finance Institutions

Institution Name	Income Level	Headquarters	Ownership Structure (2015)
WB	high	Washington D.C, the United States	The United States (15.85%), Japan (6.84%), China (4.42%), Germany (4.00%), UK (3.75%), France (3.75%)
EBRD	high	London, England	The United States (10.1%), France (8.6%), Germany (8.6%), Italy (8.6%), Japan (8.6%), UK (8.6%)
IADB	high	Washington D.C, the United States	United States (29.34%), Argentina (10.77%), Brazil (10.77%), Mexico (6.92%), Canada (6.29%)
AsDB	high	Manila, Philippines	Japan (15.67%), United States (15.56%), China (6.47%), India (6.36%), Australia (5.81%)
AIIB	low- & middle	Beijing, China	China (28.7%), India (8.3%), Russia (6.5%), Germany (4.6%), Korea (3.7%)
NDB BRICS	low- & middle	Shanghai, China	China (20%), Russia (20%), Brazil (20%), India (20%), South Africa (20%)

(continued)

Institution Name	Income Level	Headquarters	Ownership Structure (2015)
EDB	low- & middle	Almaty, Kazakhstan	Russia (65. 97%), Kazakhstan (32. 99%), Belarus (0. 99%), Armenia (0. 01%), Tajikistan (0. 03%), Kyrgyz Republic (0. 01%)
AfDB	low- & middle	Abidjan, Côte d'Ivoire	Nigeria (9. 320%), US (6. 6%), Japan (5. 5%), Egypt (5. 4%), South Africa (4. 8%)
Caribbean DB	low- & middle	Barbados, West Indies	Jamaica (18. 62%), Trinidad and Tobago (18. 62%), Canada (10. 02%), the United Kingdom (10. 02%), Germany (6. 00%), China (6. 00%)
IsDB	low- & middle	Jeddah, Saudi Arabia	Saudi Arabia (23. 52%), Libya (9. 43%), Iran (8. 52%), Nigeria (7. 66%), United Arab Emirates (7. 51%)

The United States Holds the Largest Influence among Multilateral Institutions Dominated by High-income Countries

The United States, as the largest shareholder of WB, IADB, EBRD, and the second largest shareholder of AsDB, has a leading voice in multilateral DFIs dominated by high-income countries. Furthermore, both WB and IADB's headquarters are located in Washington. It is obvious that the United States plays a key role in multilateral cooperation as the main leader in these institutions. Japan and Germany, as the second and third largest shareholders after the United States, also have important positions.

In addition, the ownership of multilateral DFIs dominated by high-income countries is dispersed, and control is shared by several large shareholders (mainly high-income countries), retaining the advantages of relatively concentrated equity and an ownership structure with checks and balances. For instance, in the case of EBRD, its major shareholders are the United States (10. 1%), France (8. 6%), Germany (8. 6%), Italy (8. 6%), Japan (8. 6%) and the United Kingdom (8. 6%), which are all the high-income countries with a balanced shareholding. It is not only beneficial for retaining the overall control of high-income countries, but it is also set up to allow for a relationship of interaction between major shareholders to coordinate the interests of all parties.

Regional Powers in low- & Middle-income Countries Regional Multilateral Institutions

AIIB, NDB BRICS, EDB, AfDB, Caribbean DB, and IsDB, are all regional multilateral institutions composed of major members of the region and some countries from other continents. As such, the ownership structures reflect diversification.

Specifically, the founding members of AIIB, the result of Chinese initiative, include 57 countries from Europe, America, Oceania, Africa and other regions, and major shareholders are China (28.7%), India (8.3%), Russia (6.5%), Germany (4.6%), and South Korea (3.7%). IsDB's main members are Middle Eastern countries: Saudi Arabia (23.52%), Libya (9.43%), Iran (8.52%), Nigeria (7.66%), and the United Arab Emirates (7.5%). EDB has a high degree of equity concentration with Russia taking absolute control with a 65.97% stake and Kazakhstan as the second largest shareholder with a 32.99% stake. In general, multilateral DFIs dominated by low- & middle-income countries promote regional cooperation, with regional powers as major shareholders. However, the integration of low- & middle-income countries is weaker than that of high-income countries, and regional interconnections from economic activity such as trade and investment need to be further strengthened.

Business Model: Sovereign Credit Similarities, Capital Operational Differences

Funding Sources are Mainly Based on Borrowing, Issuing Debt, and Government Funding

Compared with traditional commercial banks, DFIs have stronger policy guidance. They rarely take in public deposits, but most of them are able to acquire asset support from the government. In addition, DFIs borrow from other financial institutions and issue debt in domestic and international financial markets as ways of raising funds (see Figure 8.3).

Among the existing 30 DFIs, all institutions have borrowed and issued debt for financing. 20 institutions receive direct government funds (VEB and DB Philippines two institutions have no data available about whether they receive government funds) and

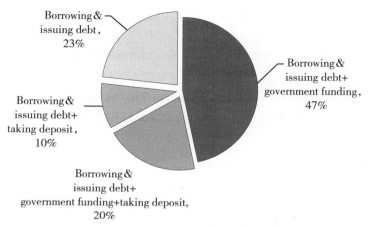

Figure 8.3 DFI's Funding Sources Ratio

only nine take deposits from the public as a source of funding (see Table 8.2). Between these nine DFIs, only three of them—NRW BANK, CDC, and KDB Development Bank—are DFIs in high-income countries, while the other six are all from low- & middle-income countries. At the multilateral and country level, among the 11 multilateral DFIs, four are not directly funded by the government: IADB, EDB, AfDB and IsDB. The remaining seven receive budget transfers from the government. Simultaneously, all multilateral institutions and most high-income countries' DFIs do not absorb deposits from the public. It can be seen that multilateral DFIs and most institutions in high-income countries are less engaged in deposit-taking operations, and a large majority of the multilateral DFIs are financially supported by the government.

Table 8.2 DFI's Funding Source

Borrowing & Issuing Debt	Government Funding	Taking Deposit
All	Except IADB, EDB, AfDB, IsDB, CDC, TSKB, TCZB, BANDES	NRW, CDC, KDB, NBU, IDBI, DB Philippines, IDWB, Ziraat Bankasi, BPMB

Financial Products are Increasingly Diverse

DFIs in High-income Countries and low- & Middle-income Countries

Because of relatively developed and mature financial markets in their countries, DFIs in high-income countries offer a wide range of financial products, while DFIs in low-

& middle-income countries mainly rely on the traditional deposits & loans and cash transfer business. This reliance is due to the fact that financial markets in low- and middle-income countries are underdeveloped and the financial system is not yet perfect.

As shown in Figure 8.4, loans are the most popular financial business, with more than 70% of institutions with loan guarantee business, followed by trust services, deposit accounts, savings accounts. Micro insurance accounts for the lowest proportion of DFI activity.

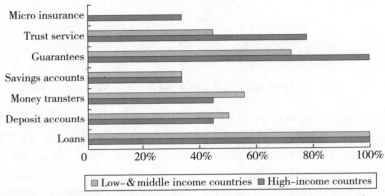

Figure 8. 4   Comparison of the Business Models of DFIs in low- & Middle-income Countries and High-income Countries

Non-traditional banking activities, such as trust services and micro insurance, are more prevalent among DFIs in high-income countries: the share of trust services of DFIs in high-income countries is 34% higher than those in low- & middle-income countries. Micro insurance exists only in DFIs of high-income countries. Deposit accounts and money transfers account for a higher percentage in DFI activity in low- & middle-income countries. It can be seen that financial products in DFIs of high-income countries are more flexible and plentiful, while products of institutions in low- & middle-income countries are relatively traditional and conservative.

Multilateral DFIs' Business Model is Relatively Simple

Multilateral DFIs, which aim to promote development and reduce poverty, focus on providing financial support at the national level to developing countries; therefore the business in multilateral DFIs is more concentrated than the business of national DFIs in that country. Loans and loan guarantees are carried out by more than 80% of multilateral DFIs, whereas only 25% of multilateral DFIs perform trust services and money transfers (see Figure 8. 5).

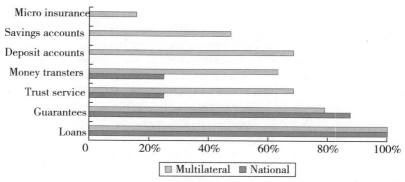

Figure 8. 5   Comparison of Business Model between National and Multilateral DFIs

The multilateral DFIs did not provide other banking services beyond these four, but national DFIs also provided deposit accounts, savings accounts, micro insurance, and other services. Compared with multilateral DFIs, the business scope of national DFIs is more wide reaching. Thus, national DFIs mainly provide more support and convenience for their own country's economic development, so its operating business is more extensive and comprehensive; while the multilateral DFIs' business model is relatively simple and centralized because their direct clients are at the national level.

DFIs Industrial Investment is Relatively Concentrated

Loans of the DFIs cover a wide range of areas, and the capital investment industry is relatively concentrated. The vast majority of DFIs (more than 95%) provides loans to the construction, infrastructure, and energy sectors (see Figure 8. 6 and Figure 8. 7).

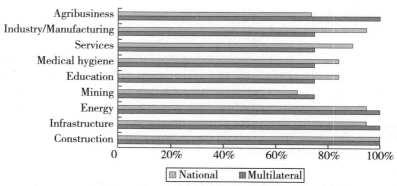

**Figure 8. 6   Comparison of Capital Investment Industries between National
and Multilateral DFIs**

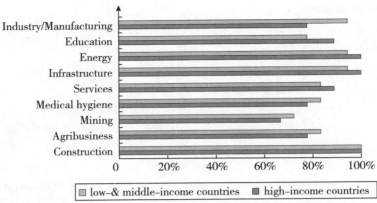

Figure 8.7 Comparison of Capital Investment Industries between DFIs in low- & Middle-income Countries and High-income Countries

Multilateral DFIs are more inclined to invest in large, capital-intensive industries, while national DFIs are more focused on domestic economic and social development projects. It can be seen from Figure 8.6 that there is a greater share of multilateral DFIs investing in agribusiness, mining, infrastructure, and energy than national institutions, mainly because of the long-term investment period, high demand for capital, high yield uncertainty, less market-oriented capital investment, and relatively similar industry attributes in these externally strong industries, so it is easier to get the financial support from multilateral institutions. On the other hand, national institutions are more focused on industries such as industry & manufacturing, services, education, and medical hygiene. As the amount invested in these projects is relatively small and the differences among countries are large, it is unfavorable for the multilateral institutions to carry out the assessment; therefore more investments in these areas are taken by national DFIs.

From the perspective of the national institutions, investments in low- & middle-income countries are more focused on the relevant areas of the country's current development, while high-income countries invest more in value-added industries. Figure 8.7 shows that the proportion of DFIs in low- & middle-income countries is higher in areas such as agribusiness, industry & manufacturing, mining, and medical hygiene than the proportion of DFIs in high-income countries in these areas. These are the areas that need to be improved in developing countries. DFIs in high-income countries are more focused on value-added areas such as education, energy, services, and infrastructure. But in general, all kinds of DFIs investment are targeted towards relatively concentrated areas, such as providing public goods with externalities or overcoming the bottleneck area of a specific stage of economic development.

Targeted Markets

Multilateral DFIs Pay More Attention to Financial Support at the National Level

Most of the DFIs choose micro, small, and medium enterprises and large private corporations as their targeted markets. But the targeted markets of multilateral and national DFIs are quite different. Multilateral DFIs are more concerned on country-level financial support and all eight multilateral institutions available in the sample provide financial support to their member countries at the national level (see Figure 8.8).

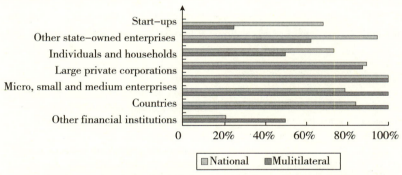

Figure 8.8   National and Multilateral Institutions: Financial Support to Different Market Players

The main objective of multilateral DFIs is to promote the economic development of member countries and the financial support to member states is mainly proved by delivering loans and offering funding. Multilateral DFIs support domestic investments in a wide range of sectors by providing low interest rate credit to member states; meanwhile, they also provide developing countries with grants to support their economic and social development.

National DFIs are More Concerned with State-owned Enterprises, Start-ups, and Individuals & Households

National DFIs support the development of state-owned enterprises, large and medium sized enterprises, while also focusing on start-ups, individuals & households. 95% and 89% of the national institutions provide loans for their state-owned enterprises and large private enterprises, while 68% could meet the financing demand of the venture enterprises and start-ups. At the same time, 74% also give financial support to individuals & households to provide guarantees for the individual's and family's housing, livelihood, and educational expenses (see Figure 8.8).

Lending Products: DFIs in High-income Countries Prefer High-risk Enterprises such as Innovation Companies and Start-ups

DFIs in high-income countries provided more diversified lending products. All DFIs in high-income countries in our sample provided loans for start-up activities, loans for working capital, long-term loans, and syndicated loans to their clients, whereas only 50% of DFIs in low- & middle-income countries provided loans for start-up activities. 56% of DFIs in high-income countries provided unsecured loans which have high risks, while only 33% of DFIs in low- & middle-income countries provided unsecured loans (see Figure 8.9). This shows that DFIs in high-income countries lend more to high-risk enterprises like innovation companies and start-ups while DFIs in low- & middle-income countries mainly provide traditional loans such as long-term loans and short-term loans.

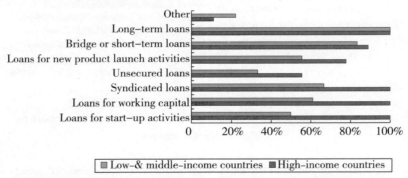

Figure 8.9 Comparison of Lending Products between DFIs in low- & Middle-income Countries and High-income Countries

This shows that DFIs in high-income countries are more supportive of innovation-driven economic development by providing loans for start-up and new product launch activities to support the development of venture business and start-ups. This helps small enterprises in high-income countries gradually develop, promoting the development of weak industry. It benefits economic transition and innovation-driven economic development. This contrasts with the experience of most DFIs in low- & middle-income countries, which provide a smaller variety of lending products such as traditional loans, which indicates that their willingness to take on risk is lower than DFIs in high-income countries.

Loan Term Structure: High-income Countries and Multilateral DFIs have a Longer Average Loan Life

The maximum loan term of DFIs in high-income countries is longer than that for DFIs in low- & middle-income countries. This is mainly because high-income countries are more resilient to risk. The shortest maximum loan term of DFIs in high-income countries is 6 – 10 years and institutions with up to 20 years of loan terms account for 67% of DFIs in those areas. However, DFIs from low- & middle-income countries have relatively short maximum loan maturity, with 75% of institutions providing loans with maturities of less than 20 years. The number of institutions with 11 – 20 year maximum maturities is the largest, accounting for 50% of the total, while only 6% of the institutions provide the longest loan period of more than 30 years.

Multilateral DFIs, because of their stronger risk resilience, have longer maximum loan terms than national DFIs. As can be seen, the maximum loan term of all multilateral DFIs is greater than 10 years. The longest loan durations are for periods of 11 – 20 years, 21 – 30 years, and over 30 years, with each range accounting for about 1/3 of multilateral DFIs. Among national institutions, the share providing 11 – 20 years loan terms represents the largest share, accounting for 47% of institutions. DFIs with the maximum loan term which is less than or equal to 5 years, 6 – 10 years and 21 – 30 years account for 13%, 20%, and 20%.

Profitability: DFIs in low- & Middle-income Countries are in Good Operating Condition

The return on assets (ROA) is an indicator of how profitable a company is relative to its total assets. The return on equity (ROE) measures the rate of return on the shareholders' equity. Both of these indicators reflect the profitability of DFIs. Although profit maximization is not the objective of the DFIs, profitability can reflect their operating condition and their ability to resist risks.

According to Figures 8. 10 through 8. 13, member countries of EDB, which is dominated by Russia, have suffered a severe economic downturn due to continued low international oil prices. Both ROA and ROE are negative for EDB, whereas the ROA and ROE of the remaining 25 institutions are positive, indicating that most DFIs are in good operating condition.

On the other hand, among the top ten DFIs with the highest ROA, only the EBRD and CDC are in high-income countries. The remaining eight institutions are in low-

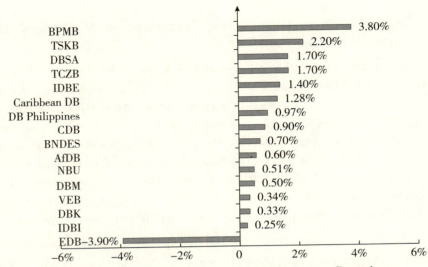

Figure 8. 10   ROA of DFIs in low- & Middle-income Countries

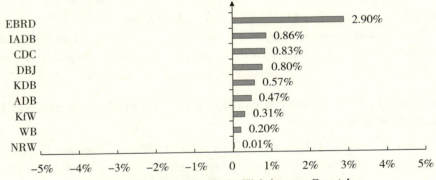

Figure 8. 11   ROA of DFIs in High-income Countries

& middle-income countries. Among the top ten DFIs which have highest ROE, only the EBRD is in high-income countries. This fact shows that DFIs in low- & middle-income countries are more profitable than DFIs in high-income countries.

According to the data analysis of lending products, DFIs in high-income countries lend more to high-risk enterprises like innovation companies and start-ups, which leads to their commitments having higher risks. The total assets of DFIs in high-income countries are much larger than those in low- & middle-income countries (except for CDB), so their ROA and ROE are significantly lower than those in low- & middle-income countries.

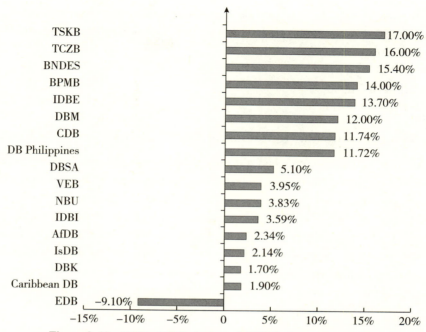

Figure 8. 12   ROE of DFIs in low- & Middle-income Countries

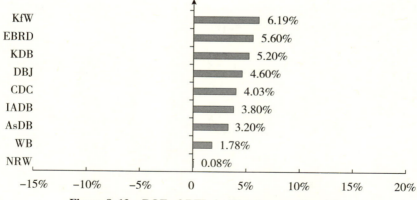

Figure 8. 13   ROE of DFIs in High-income Countries

Because DFIs in low- & middle-income countries are in good operating condition, they can increase their risk-resistance abilities, so they are potentially providing more high-risk supportive loans. DFIs in low- & middle-income countries can develop new financial products and find new profit models through which they can spur innovation and reform. They can provide more financial support to high-risk enterprises such as innovation companies and start-ups, thus promoting the development of an innovation-driven economy.

Development Trend

DFIs Dominated by low- & Middle-income Countries Developed Rapidly

DFIs in high-income countries had a dominant position in the development financial market which resulted from their capital accumulation and pre-emptive moves prior to 1965. Since 2000, they have reached a relatively mature stage, and are now increasing steadily. While low- & middle-income countries developed very fast since 1965, they have gradually set up DFIs to support their own countries' development. The latter is still in the ascendant phase and its overall size has exceeded the DFIs dominated by high-income countries. In particular, 80% of the newly established DFIs after 2000 are dominated by low- & middle-income countries.

Figure 8. 14 and Figure 8. 15 show that from 2006 to 2015, the total assets of DFIs in high-income countries increased from $ 1. 55 trillion to $ 2. 09 trillion, with an average annual growth of 3. 48% ; total equity increased from $ 0. 23 trillion to $ 0. 29 trillion, with an average annual growth of 2. 61%. Overall, individual DFIs in high-income countries are steadily growing.

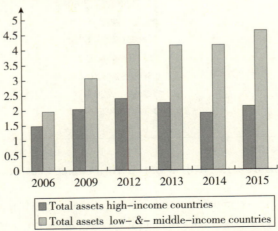

Figure 8. 14   Total Assets of DFIs in High-income and low- & Middle-income Countries
(Unit: Trillion Dollars)

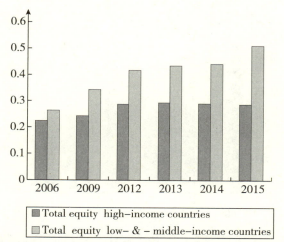

Figure 8. 15   Total Equity of DFIs in High-income and low- & Middle-income Countries
(Unit: Trillion Dollars)

Meanwhile, the total assets of DFIs in low- & middle-income countries increased from $ 2. 03 trillion to $ 4. 60 trillion, with an average annual growth of 12. 66% , and total equity increased from $ 0. 27 trillion to $ 0. 51 trillion, with an average annual growth of 8. 89%. DFIs in low- & middle-income countries developed rapidly, a result of the rapid expansion of the CDB. In addition, we can find that since 2012, for both DFIs in low- & middle-income countries and in high-income countries, their assets had the phenomenon of decreasing first and then rising. We think the main reason for this phenomenon is the debt crisis in Europe. After 2014, the crisis gradually subsided and the total size of global DFIs began to rise again.

The Overall Profitability of the DFIs is on the Decline

In the ten years from 2006 to 2015, the profitability of DFIs declined. The simple mathematical average of return on assets declined from 2. 01% in 2006 to 0. 82% in 2015 and the simple mathematical average of return on equity declined from 9. 25% in 2006 to 6. 69% in 2012, recovering to 8. 13% in 2015 (see Figure 8. 16 and Figure 8. 17).

The financial crisis caused the global economic downturn and the recovery has been slow, leading to the decline in profits. The decline in the profitability of DFIs in high-income countries is even more remarkable. Because of the global financial crisis in 2008, the return on assets of DFIs in high-income countries was only – 0. 16% in 2009. Compared to 2009, the operation of DFIs in high-income countries in recent years has improved and in 2015 the return on assets was 0. 81% , the highest ROA since 2009, but the ROA and ROE of DFIs in high-income countries are still lower

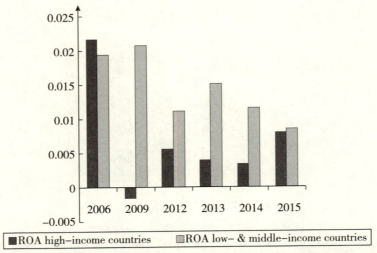

**Figure 8. 16   ROA Comparison between DFIs in low- & middle-income and
High-income Countries**

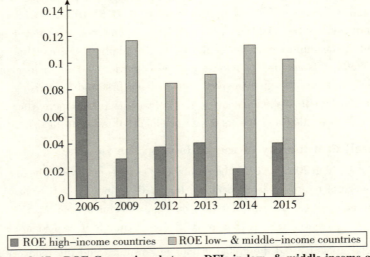

**Figure 8. 17   ROE Comparison between DFIs in low- & middle-income and
High-income Countries**

than those in low- & middle-income countries. It indicates that the profitability and
operating conditions of DFIs in low- & middle-income countries are relatively better
than those of DFIs in high-income countries.

In addition to the impact of the financial crisis and the global economic downturn, DFIs in high-income countries lend more to high-risk enterprises like innovation companies and start-ups, which leads to their commitments having higher risks. DFIs in low- & middle-income countries are in good operating condition and can increase their risk-resistance abilities. As a result, they could potentially provide more high-risk supportive loans. In the future, DFIs in low- & middle-income countries can provide more financial supports to high-risk enterprises such as innovation companies and start-ups, better serving the development of an innovation-driven economy.

Conclusions

· The global development financial system dominated by high-income countries is relatively mature, with overall assets and equity growing steadily; meanwhile, the influence of DFIs from low- & middle-income countries is rising rapidly, with the overall assets and equity of institutions in these countries booming; finally, the reginal powers are leading the DFIs.

· The main sources of funding for DFIs are borrowing from other financial institutions, issuing debt, and receiving budget transfers from the government. Taking deposits from the public has been a supplementary source.

· DFIs have diversified capital flows. Institutions from high-income countries provide a wide range of financial products, including insurance, trust, and other non-bank financial business; while institutions from low- & middle-income countries are still mainly focused on traditional bank deposits, loans, and cash transactions. Compared to national institutions, the business model of multilateral institutions is more simple and focused.

· DFIs provide financial support to a wide range of industries. Multilateral institutions are more inclined to invest in large, capital-intensive industries; institutions from low- & middle-income countries are more focused on the relevant areas concerning their current development, while institutions from high-income countries invest more in value-added industries.

· Multilateral institutions pay more attention to financial support at the national level; national institutions are more concerned with state-owned enterprises, start-ups, individuals, and households. Institutions in high-income countries prefer high-risk enterprises such as innovation companies and start-ups.

· The maximum loan term of DFIs is proportional to their risk tolerance; the maximum loan term of DFIs in high-income countries and multilateral institutions is longer than DFIs in low- & middle-income countries and national institutions.

· The overall profitability of DFIs is on the decline. The operating conditions of institutions in low- & middle-income countries are relatively better than institutions in high-income countries.

Chapter 9   Global DFIs' Investment and Cooperation in 2016

This chapter generally describes the investment of global DFIs and their cooperation with one another. On the one hand, we intend to conduct deep analysis on the distribution of DFIs' investment among different regions and fields; on the other hand, it is also worth considering how and to what extent DFIs develop their cooperation with others.

All the data we use in this chapter is based on the *Financial Newsletter of Global DFIs* published fortnightly by CAPDF. The *Newsletter* contains over 100 pieces of information per issue, covering the performance of nearly 50 DFIs in international communication, financial cooperation, regional development, key projects, and other areas. We have extracted crucial information on a variety of variables (e. g. involved institutions, the amount of investment, project type, etc.) and recoded them to form a simple database, which laid the foundation of our data analysis.

It should be noted that the analysis here is based off of information from 20 issues of the *Financial Newsletter of Global DFIs* but does not necessarily reflect the investment and cooperation behavior for all DFIs in all fields at all times. The following conclusions are drawn from this sample.

Investment of Global DFIs

Investment Distribution among Different Fields[①]

The Investment in Different Fields Tends to be a Roughly Three Ladder-like Distribution

According to Figure 9. 1, the total investment by DFIs among different fields is a

---

① The classification of fields is aligned with the *Financial Newsletter of Global DFIs*.

long-tailed distribution, which indicates that several fields have absorbed the vast majority of investment, while the rest has been dispersed among the other fields. This is illustrated by the fact that the sum of investment in the four leading fields accounts for about 55% of the total.

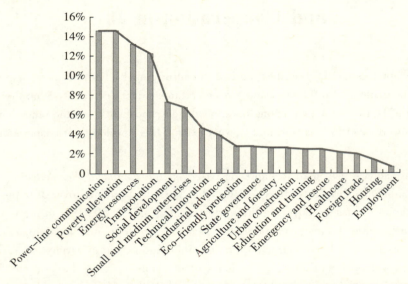

Figure 9. 1   Percentage of Total Investment in Different Fields by DFIs in 2016

Specifically, the first group of fields consists of power-line communication (14. 77%), poverty alleviation (14. 77%), energy resources (13. 36%) and transportation (12. 38%). They are the most important investment fields for DFIs both currently and traditionally. The second group is composed of social development (7. 38%), small and medium enterprises (6. 81%), technical innovation (4. 69%) and industrial advances (3. 95%) and attracts increasing attention of DFIs nowadays. The third group comprises eco-friendly protection (2. 79%), state governance (2. 75%), agriculture & forestry (2. 64%), urban construction (2. 59%), and the remaining fields.

Different Kinds of DFIs Focus on Different Fields

Generally speaking, multilateral DFIs appear more inclined to engage in industrial advancement, poverty alleviation, healthcare, and housing projects. As for national DFIs, they pay more attention to employment, emergency & rescue, and urban construction. There seems to be no significant differences in the investment in agriculture & forestry, social development, and transportation (see Figure 9.2).

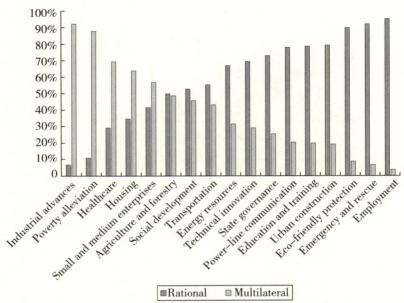

Figure 9. 2   Investment Distribution among Fields of Multilateral and National DFIs in 2016

Furthermore, things also get different when it comes to national DFIs when they are divided into two groups by income. DFIs in medium- and low- countries attach more importance to fields like poverty alleviation, social development, healthcare, and agriculture. By striking contrast, DFIs in high countries spend more on eco-friendly protection, education & training, industrial advances, and urban construction (see Figure 9.3). The difference makes sense considering these two kinds of countries may be at different stages of development and face different socio-economic problems.

Multilateral DFIs Invest in more Fields, but Several National DFIs still have Diversified Investment

Generally we would expect that multilateral DFIs invest in more fields, while national DFIs may stay more focused in certain several areas as they mainly serve their own countries. Data in our sample basically supports the argument. Multilateral DFIs invest in about three fields more on average compared to national DFIs and all of the

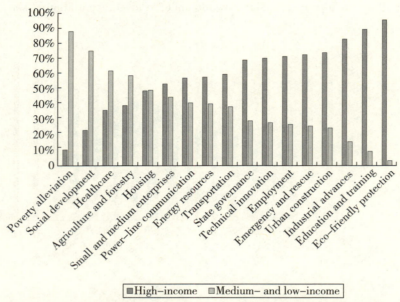

Figure 9. 3   Investment Distribution among Fields of DFIs in High-income and Medium- and low- income Countries in 2016

top six DFIs in terms of the number fields invested in are multilateral. But we also cannot neglect that some national DFIs, such as KfW, CDB and JBIC, have diversified their investment.

Investment Distribution among Regions

Investment Varies a lot in Different Regions and Some Hot Regions of Investment have Emerged

According to our data, DFIs invested in 128 different countries in 2016, covering the majority of all the countries and regions in the world today. Particularly, the concentration ratio of investment varies from region to region. For instance, the capital layout of DFIs tends to be highly dispersed among the whole of Africa, northern Europe, and the Caribbean. However, we also see DFIs investing in key countries around Asia, Latin America, and parts of Western Europe.

As for countries, generally, China, Russia, Egypt, Indonesia, Philippines, India, Kazakhstan, and Brazil have become the hottest spots. In spite of the dis-

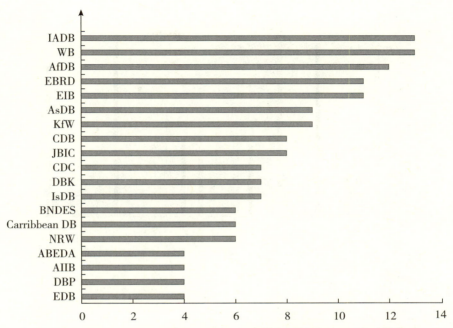

Figure 9. 4   The Number of Fields in which DFIs Invested in 2016

persed investment in Africa, this continent also holds a large volume of investment.

DFIs Focus on Different Fields in Different Regions

In total, the investment distribution in different regions is apparently heterogenous (see Figure 9. 4 and Figure 9. 5). The investment scatters around the several main fields to a similar extent in Western Europe, Eastern Europe, and Latin America. But in all the other regions, we see at least one hot investment area, like energy resources in Central Asia, power-line communication in Southeast Asia and Africa, and SMEs in Southern Europe. We could partly attribute this phenomenon to the resource endowment distribution: for instance, Central Asia indeed has abundant energy storage. Additionally, economic development matters a lot. As we can see, compared to Latin America and Africa, DFIs invest much more in technical innovation but relatively less on transportation in Western Europe, which makes sense from a perspective of economic and social circumstances.

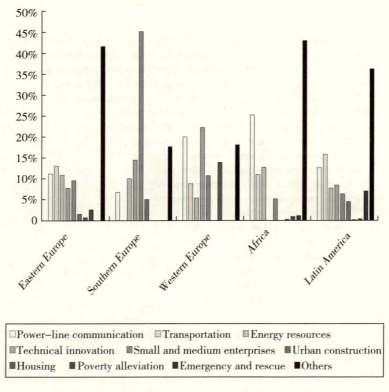

Figure 9.5   The Investment Distribution among Fields in

Different Regions① in 2016 (1ˢᵗ part)

Global DFI Cooperation in 2016

In the global financial system, different types of institutions have their own accumulated resources and areas of expertise. One strategic challenge facing DFIs is figu-
ring out how to strengthen multilateral cooperation among each other, non-developmental
mental financial institutions, non-financial enterprises, governments, and international organizations. Once this cooperation is in place, these different types of actors will specialize in their comparative advantage, achieving a more effective inte-

---

①   The figure does not show the investment distribution in Northern Europe and Northern A-
merica where investment by DFIs was too limited.

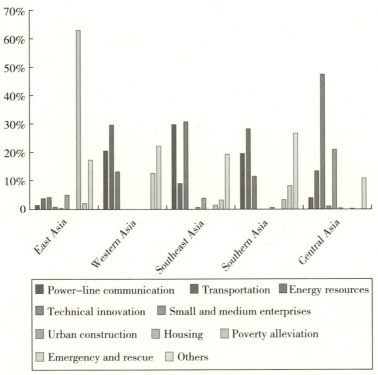

Figure 9. 6　The Investment Distribution among Fields in Different Regions in 2016（2ⁿᵈ part）

gration of resources. Based on the data collected from the *Financial Newsletter of Global DFIs*, there were 207 events referring to cooperation related to DFIs in 2016.

Generally, a DFI could have 5 kinds of cooperative partners according to the data collected: ① other DFIs; ② non-developmental financial institutions like commercial banks, insurance companies, investment banks, and so on; ③ non-financial enterprises, especially industrial corporations in all fields; ④ government (sector), international organizations (both multilateral and regional); and ⑤ non-profit public organizations like educational institutions and industry associations and foundations. Figure 9. 7 shows the amount and the corresponding proportion of cooperation events between DFIs with each kind of cooperative partner.

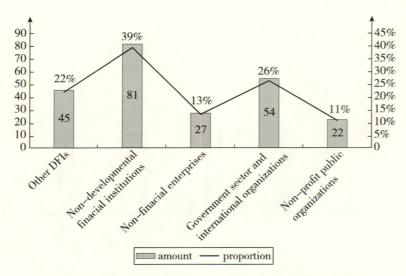

Figure 9. 7   Cooperation Events Related to DFIs in 2016[①]

Most Cooperation has Taken Place between DFIs and Other Non-developmental Financial Institutions

As shown in Figure 9. 7, DFIs obviously have more cooperation with non-developmental financial institutions than with any other type of cooperative partner. The amount of cooperation between DFIs and non-developmental financial institutions appears to be nearly twice the amount of cooperation events among DFIs. Undoubtedly, non-developmental financial institutions are the most important cooperative partners of DFIs at present. Moreover, one DFI also tends to have more cooperation with the government and international organizations than other DFIs.

DFIs shoulder a great mission to facilitate the implementation of public policy and the achievement of national development goals. As such, they take great efforts to guide financial capital from other institutions like commercial banks to the provision of fundamental public goods such as infrastructure. So it might not be surprising to see the great gap between cooperation among DFIs and DFIs' cooperation with non-developmental financial institutions. However, there still exists huge space for further advancing the mutual trust and multilateral cooperation among DFIs.

----

① The total sum of all kinds of cooperation events is more than 207, because some events involved more than 2 types of cooperative partners.

Different DFIs have Different Main Cooperative Partners and Cooperative Preferences

Multilateral DFIs Spend More on Cooperation and Seem to be More Inclined to Cooperate with Other DFIs

Although multilateral DFIs are obviously fewer than national ones around the world, they have more of every type of cooperation event than national DFIs, which illustrates a stronger cooperative preference of multilateral DFIs. Besides, multilateral DFIs have closer ties with non-developmental financial institutions and other DFIs. Their cooperation with non-financial enterprises is relatively much less, while national DFIs attach more importance to the relationship with the latter (see Figure 9.8). Another difference is that national DFIs are more closely linked with the government sector and international organizations.

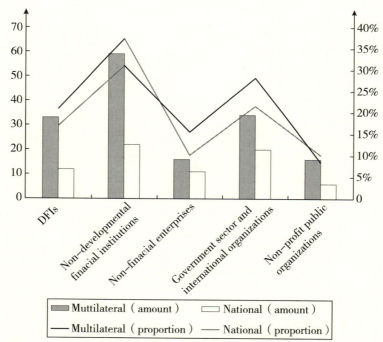

Figure 9.8   The Amount of Cooperation Events with Different Partners and
Corresponding Proportion for Multilateral and National DFIs in 2016

DFIs from High Income Countries have Much Closer Cooperation with Non-developmental Financial Institutions, while DFIs from low- and Medium-income Countries Prefer to Cooperate with the Government Sector and International Organizations

In our sample, DFIs from high-income countries pay more attention to cooperation and their principal partners are non-developmental financial institutions. As for DFIs from low- or medium-income countries, they mainly cooperate with the government and international organizations (see Figure 9.9). Additionally, DFIs from high-income countries have more cooperation with other DFIs than DFIs from low- or medium-income countries in terms of the amount of cooperation. However, DFIs from low- or medium-income countries seem to depend more on other DFIs, for they cooperate more with other DFIs than the other four kinds of cooperative partners.

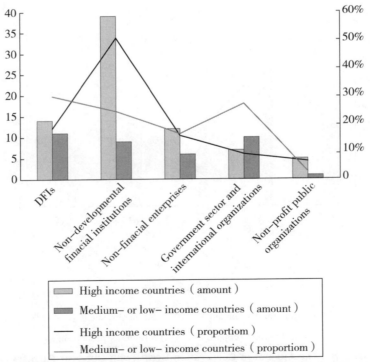

Figure 9.9   The Amount of Cooperation Events with Different Partners and Corresponding Proportion for DFIs from Different Countries by Income in 2016

The Cooperation between DFIs and Other Institutions (not Including Other DFIs) Covers Diversified Business

Combined investment is the main form of cooperation between DFIs and non-developmental financial institutions. This capital is put into a variety of business contexts such as setting up a fund, launching a company, sharing risk, digital management consulting, and so on. For example:

· KfW and Helaba jointly invested nearly $ 160 million in ENERCON for the building of Peralta I-II in Uruguay.

· DBJ and Mitsubishi UFJ jointly established the largest special fund for healthcare in Japan.

· IFC, EIB, and Ecobank signed an agreement for risk sharing and the latter two banks would participate in the risk management carried out by IFC now.

DFIs and non-financial enterprises mainly cooperate in comprehensive business services and combined investment. For example:

· IDB signed an agreement with Maersk and Sealand pledging to provide SMEs with more opportunities for financing and training based on the platform of Connect Americans.

· Silk Road Fund signed a tripartite collaborative agreement to bring advanced techniques and experience of solid waste management from Europe to China.

· CDC, Roquette, and another electric power company in France jointly invested to establish the first power station using deep geothermal energy around the world.

Cooperation between DFIs and the government or international organizations covers quite a few areas, including both financial (such as loans and combined investment) and non-financial (such as R&D). For example:

· EIB, EU, and French Development Agency jointly offer € 106 million for a project in Kabbalah to meet the demand of water in Bamako.

· IDB, OECD Development Center, and ECLAC published Latin American Economic Outlook.

DFIs and non-profit public organizations mainly cooperate in talent support and training as well as a few financial items. For example:

· CAF set up the 1st CAF Management and Leadership Training Program co-sponsored by Del Rosario University and ICESI university.

· EBRD and Croatian Employer's Association jointly started a program supporting the growth of youth in private enterprises.

· IDB held a creative product contest with a research institute to search for entrepreneurial talents with innovative abilities in science and technology.

In our sample, cooperation events involving at least three different kinds of institutions comprise about 10% of the total, which is not a considerable proportion. However, such multilateral cooperation itself is usually a breakthrough in the conventional pattern of cooperation. It allows for interactions between state and social capital and the full use of each participating member's comparative advantage, such as a firm using its accumulated experience and technology, inspiring and reinforcing future DFI cooperation. A good example is the cooperation among CDC, CNP Assurances, Natixis, and OCTO, in which they teamed up to develop an experimental stage for non-cash collateral management of securities lending by block chain. The stage is used to push the automation of contract implementation forward and has proven to be a beneficial exploration for improving regulatory efficiency of process. As the general trend indicates, the enhancement of closer cooperation between DFIs and other institutions is inevitable, which presents a challenge for all the participants to avoid miscalculations and build broader strategic trust. The promotion of institutional encouragement and guarantee in all levels is also urgently called for.

The Cooperation among DFIs Themselves Seems to be "Narrow"

According to our data, the amount of cooperation events among DFIs is limited and these cooperation events only cover few areas. Furthermore, as many as 44% of the 45 cooperation events just refer to the signing of a memorandum of understanding or framework agreement. But whether or not it has been carried out or it is still on paper, combined investment turns out to be the main form of cooperation. Most of the combined investment is put into infrastructure construction and sustainable development of energy use, like the joint investment to build highways in Pakistan by AsDB and AIIB and to the extension of hydroelectric power in South Asia by WB and AIIB. A small amount of the combined investment is put into non-financial enterprises, like the endeavor of debt restructuring to solve the DSME debt crisis by KDB and Chexim.

Although the cooperation among DFIs still seems to be "narrow", more and more positive signs are emerging. We can see several DFIs have taken some steps to look for the possibilities of deeper cooperation in different dimensions. In financial business, a few DFIs including KfW teamed up with European Investment Fund to support ENSI, a cooperation and risk sharing platform to encourage SME lending via the capital markets. In non-financial areas, actions to promote resource sharing of information like INFRALATAM Database jointly established by IADB and CAF are also of great significance. In the future, we believe extending the fields of cooperation should be considered an important path for DFIs to set up mutually-constructive partnerships and promote positive-sum exchanges.

The DFIs' Cooperative Network Tends to Be Sparse and Dispersed, while a Few DFIs Begin to Play an Increasingly Active Role in the Communication of the Global DFI System

Based on the 45 cooperation events, we have drawn the DFIs' cooperative network as below (see Figure 9. 10).

There are three characteristics of the cooperation among DFIs:

1) The cooperative network tends to be sparse. Generally speaking, the connectivity of the whole network is fairly low—most of the DFIs only establish cooperative partnership with 1 or 2 other DFIs. According to our calculation, the intensity of the cooperative network is only 0. 11, which means that the chances for two DFIs to have any cooperative tie are only 11%.

2) The cooperative network tends to be dispersed. Very few DFIs share long-term cooperative relationships in different events. Frequent cooperation can only be observed within a few DFIs like AsDB and EDB. In short, cooperative clustering has not yet emerged, either from a global or regional perspective.

3) A few DFIs, represented by the big nodes in the network, begin to shift more emphasis to the cooperation and play an increasingly important role in the communication of the network. Among those big nodes, most of them are multilateral DFIs such as WB, AIIB, EIB and IADB, while some national DFIs like CDB and JBIC also contribute a lot to the global financial system.

Nowadays, the cooperation among DFIs has aroused more and more attention from various organizations. Forming a network of combined global infrastructure requires a level of financial support and market building that no single DFI can handle on its own due to the sheer amount of money required and the number of projects involved.

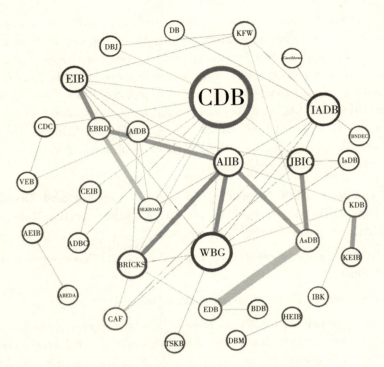

Figure 9. 10   DFIs' Cooperative Network in 2016

Note: In the network graph above, every node represents a DFI. The size of a node stands for a DFI's level of activeness. The larger its size is, the more cooperation it has participated in during 2016. Besides, the line linking two nodes only exists when the two DFIs have cooperation and the wider the line is, the more cooperation events there are taking place between the two DFIs.

We see dramatic potential for DFIs to build a more connected and integrated cooperative network to achieve agglomeration. How to make those crucial nodes become the real bridges in a connected global DFI system and how to further involve institutions on the margins of the network are important issues that DFIs need to consider.

References

Annual Reports

AsDB, AsDB Annual Report 2015, 2016.

ADBC, Agricultural Development Bank of China Annual Report 2015, 2016.

AfDB, AfDB Annual Report 2015, 2016.

ABEDA, Arab Bank for Economic Development in Africa Annual Report 2015, 2016.

Bank Pembangunan, Bank Pembangunan Annual Report 2015, 2016.

BNDES, BNDES Annual Report 2015, 2016.

CAF, CAF Annual Report 2015, 2016.

Caribbean DB, Caribbean DB Annual Report 2015, 2016.

CDB, CDB Annual Report 2015, 2016.

CDC, CDC Development Report 2015, 2016.

Chexim, Export-Import Bank of China Annual Report 2015, 2016.

DBJ, Securities Report of Development Bank of Japan, 2016.

DBK, Development Bank of Kazakhstan Annual Report 2015, 2016.

DBSA, DBSA Annual Report 2015, 2016.

EBRD, EBRD Annual Report 2015, 2016.

EDB, EDB Annual Report 2015, 2016.

EIB, EIB Annual Report 2015, 2016.

IADB, IADB Annual Report 2015, 2016.

IsDB, IsDB Annual Report 1437H, 2016.

JBIC, JBIC Annual Report 2015, 2016.

KDB, KDB Annual Report 2015, 2016.

KfW, Financial Report 2015, 2016.

NBU, Report on the Activity of NBU in 2015, 2016.

NRW, NRW. Bank Financial Report 2015, 2016.

NRW, NRW. Bank Housing Market Report 2015, 2016.

Oekom-Research, Oekom Corporate Responsibility Review 2016, 2016.

TSKB, TSKB Annual Report 2015, 2016.

VEB, VEB Annual Report 2015, 2016.

World Bank, World Bank Annual Report 2015, 2016.

TCZB, Agricultural Bank of the Republic of Turkey Annual Report 2015, 2016.

Articles and Books

CAPDF, Global Development Financing Communication, 2015 – 2016.

Bai Qinxian, Li Jun. Research on the Legislation and Related Issues of China's Policy Financing [J]. Shanghai Finance, 2005 (11): 4 – 7.

Bai Qinxian, Wang Wei. An Overview of Policy Financing [M]. Beijing: China Finance Press, 2013: 203 – 205.

Bai Qinxian, Wang Wei. A Comparative Study on Policy Financing Legislation Between China and Foreign Countries [J]. Financial Theory and Practice, 2005 (12): 3 – 6.

Bai Qinxian, Wang Wei. A Comparative Study on the System of Policy Financing and Development Financing on Overseas [M]. Beijing: China Finance Press, 2005: 169 – 174.

CAPDF, Islamic Banking and Finance in OBOR Countries: New Developments, 2015 – 2016.

Development Bank of Japan, Start with Kumamoto earthquake, revitalize Kyushu tourist industry: "3 volunteering" and "characteristic repair", 2016.

EIB, InnovFin Advisory Flysheet, 2016.

Foundation for Development of Russian Single-industry Cities (FDM), Foundation for Development of Single-industry Cities, Regulations of FDM participating in and/or promoting Russian federal industry cities' new investment projects, 2016.

Guofeng Sun. Theory of Development Financing Institutions. [J]. Tsinghua Financing Review, 2014 (7): 73 – 77.

Hu Yuxin, Why Moody's Downgraded Turkey's Credit Rating. [J]. China Financialyst, 2016 (10): 115 – 116.

IsDB, A Clean Secure Future Reshaping Turkeys Energy Sector, 2016.

Jian Wang. International Comparison among Development Financing Institutions. [J]. Financial Development Review, 2014 (8): 129 – 135.

Li Zhihui, Li Weibin. China's Development Financing: Theory, Policy and Practice [M]. Beijing: China Finance Press, 2010: 362 – 365.

Li Zhihui, Wu Yue. Research on the Construction of Regulation System of Development Financing Institutions [J]. Modern Finance and Economics, 2007 (2): 20 – 27.

Liu Xiaohong. A Study on the Transformation of China's Policy Banks [M]. Changsha: Hunan People's Press, 2010: 180 – 181.

Mingming Lai, Li Ma. On Development Financial Governance Models and Innovation in China. [J]. Journal of Liaoning University (Philosophy and Social Sciences), 2007 (4): 119 – 124.

Ministry of Commerce of the PRC official website, Juncker Plan will Establish the "European Strategic Investment Fund", 2016.

Oekom-Research, 2015: A Milestone For Sustainability, An Opportunity For Sustainable Investment, 2016.

Panizza U. , Eduardo L. , Alejandro M. . Should the Government Be in the Banking Business? The Role of State-owned and Development Banks. [J]. Inter-American Development Bank Working Paper, 2004: 15.

Xing Huiqiang. China's Policy Banks to the Transformation of Development Financing Institution and its Legislation [J]. Journal of Law, 2007 (1): 65 – 68.

Yi Yan. The History of Development Financing Institutions and the Challenges. [J]. Review of Financial Development (in Chinese), 2016 (7): 20 – 28.

Abbreviations

Abbreviation	Full name
Multilateral DFIs	
WBG	World Bank Group
AsDB	The Asian Development Bank
IADB	Inter-American Development Bank
EDB	Eurasian Development Bank
AfDB	The African Development Bank
EBRD	European Bank for Reconstruction and Development
Caribbean DB	Caribbean Development Bank
IsDB	The Islamic Development Bank
ABEDA	Arab Bank for Economic Development in Africa
CAF	Corporación Andina de Fomento/ Development Bank of Latin America
National DFIs	
KfW	Kreditanstalt für Wiederaufbau/ Reconstruction Credit Institute
CDC	Caisse des Dépôts et Consignations
DBJ	Development Bank of Japan
KDB	Korea Development Bank
DBM	Development Bank of Mongolia
BPMB	Bank Pembangunan Malaysia Berhad
VEB	Vnesheconombank/ Bank for Development and Foreign Economic Affairs
DBK	Development Bank of Kazakhstan

(continued)

Abbreviation	Full name
NBU	National Bank for Foreign Economic Activity of the Republic of Uzbekistan/ National Bank of Uzbekistan
TSKB	Turkiye Sinai Kalkinma Bankasi/ Industrial Development Bank of Turkey
TCZB	Türkiye Cumhuriyeti Ziraat Bankasl/ Agricultural Bank of Turkey
BNDES	Banco Nacional de Desenvolvimento Econômico e Social / Brazilian Development Bank
DBSA	Development Bank of Southern Africa
China related DFIs	
CDB	China Development Bank
Chexim	The Export-Import Bank of China
ADBC	The Agricultural Development Bank of China
AIIB	Asian Infrastructure Investment Bank
NDB BRICS	New Development Bank BRICS
Associations of DFIs	
ADFIAP	Association of Development Financing Institutions in Asia and the Pacific
AADFI	African Association of Development Finance Institutions
CAPDF	China Association for the Promotion of Development Financing

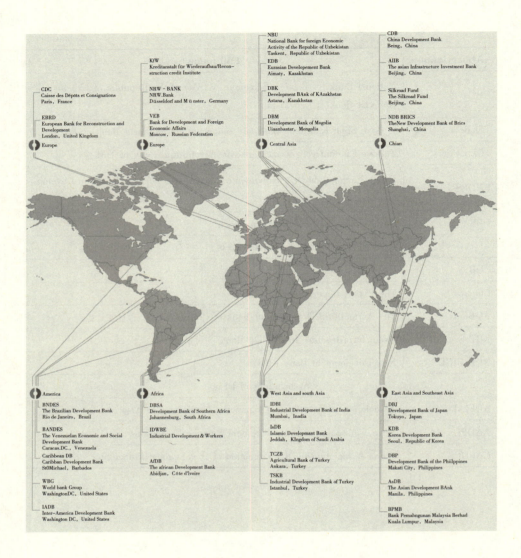

CDC
Caisse des Dépôts et Consignations
Paris, France

EBRD
European Bank for Reconstruction and
Development
London, United Kingdom

Europe

KfW
Kreditanstalt für Wiederaufbau/Recon-
struction credit Institute

NRW · BANK
NRW.Bank
Düsseldorf and M ü nster, Germany

VEB
Bank for Development and Foreign
Economic Affairs
Moscow, Russian Federation

Europe

NBU
National Bank for foreign Economic
Activity of the Republic of Uzbekistan
Taskent, Republic of Uzbekistan

EDB
Eurasian Developement Bank
Aimaty, Kazakhstan

DBK
Development BAnk of KAzakhstan
Astana, Kazakhstan

DBM
Development Bank of Mogolia
Uiaanbastar, Mongolia

Central Asia

CDB
China Development Bank
Being, China

AIIB
The asian Infrastructure Investment Bank
Beijing, China

Silkroad Fund
The Silkroad Fund
Beijing, China

NDB BRICS
TheNew Development Bank of Brics
Shanghai, China

Chian

America

BNDES
The Brazilian Development Bank
Rio de Janeiro, Brazil

BANDES
The Venezuelan Economic and Social
Development Bank
Caracas.DC., Venezuela

Caribbean DB
Caribban Development Bank
St0Michael, Barbados

WBG
World bank Group
WashingtonDC, United States

IADB
Inter-America Development Bank
Washington DC, United States

Africa

DBSA
Development Bank of Southern Africa
Johannesburg, South Africa

IDWBE
Industrial Development & Workers

AfDB
The african Development Bank
Abidjan, Côte d'Ivoire

West Asia and south Asia

IDBI
Industrial Development Bank of India
Mumbai, Inaida

IsDB
Islamic Developmant Bank
Jeddah, KIngdom of Saudi Arabia

TCZB
Agricultural Bank of Turkey
Ankara, Turkey

TSKB
Industrial Development Bank of Turkey
Istanbul, Turkey

East Asia and Southeast Asia

DBJ
Development Bank of Japan
Tokuyo, Japan

KDB
Korea Development Bank
Seoul, Republic of Korea

DBP
Development Bank of the Phiilppines
Makati City, Philippines

AsDB
The Asian Development BAnk
Manila, Philippines

BPMB
Bank Pemabngunan Malaysia Berhad
Kuala Lumpur, Malaysia

Acknowledgement

The report is prepared by China Association for the Promotion of Development Financing. In the process of writing, the students of School of Foreign Languages, Peking University, Peking University Law School and Beijing Foreign Languages University undertook the task of collecting basic data and information of various development financing institutions. They are An Mengqi, Chen Xi, Wang Shimin, Hasigaowa, Li Lin, Li Qianqian, Song Gao, Tang Chen, Tang Shan, Wang Zi, Yang Ting, Zhang Hanlu, Zhao Yingying, Liu Xiran, Qi Hanbo, Kong Jinlei, Sun Lingling, Sha Fan, Wang Cong, Jiang Wanru, Zhao Yuehui, Chen Zhuang, Deng Haimo. Dong Weijia, Xu Qiyuan, Zhu Dandan from CASS wrote the first chapter and the eighth chapter, Dr. Li Zhen of Peking University wrote the second chapter, Luo Yi wrote the ninth chapter.

Zhang Jucheng and Xue Tianyi of China Association for the Promotion of Development Financing proofread the work. During the review period, important suggestions were made for perfecting the report.

The report is the collective wisdom of a team, integrating the creativity and solid work of all the above-mentioned people. We thank them for their professional spirit and teamwork, and thank them for their courage to meet the challenges of this pioneering work. We also thank for their faith in international cooperation in development financing and all their efforts to this end.